GOVERNORS STATE UNIVERSITY

3 1611 00021 4673

W9-BEP-366

34

ASSESSMENT OF LEARNERS
WITH SPECIAL NEEDS

UNIVERSITY LIBRARY
GOVERNORS STATE UNIVERSITY
UNIVERSITY PARK, IL. 60466

Richard L. Luftig

MIAMI UNIVERSITY

ASSESSMENT OF LEARNERS WITH SPECIAL NEEDS

ALLYN AND BACON

Boston   London   Sydney   Toronto

GOVERNORS STATE UNIVERSITY
UNIVERSITY PARK
IL 60466

*To my mother, Estelle Bloom, who has given me her love
along with a desire for knowledge that has been with me my
entire life; and to my in-laws, Anton and Constance Ruffo,
whose love and support in me have never wavered—this
book is dedicated to you. I love you all.*

LC 4031 .L84 1989

Luftig, Richard L., 1949-

Assessment of learners with
special needs

233936

Copyright © 1989 by Allyn and Bacon

A Division of Simon & Schuster
160 Gould Street
Needham Heights, Massachusetts 02194–2310

All rights reserved. No part of the material protected by this
copyright notice may be reproduced or utilized in any form or by
any means, electronic or mechanical, including photocopying,
recording, or by any information storage and retrieval system, without
written permission from the copyright owner.

Developmental editor: Elizabeth Brooks
Composition buyer: Linda Cox
Cover administrator: Linda K. Dickinson
Editorial-production service: Grace Sheldrick, Wordsworth Associates
Manufacturing buyer: Bill Alberti
Cover designer: Christy Rosso

Library of Congress Cataloging-in-Publication Data

Luftig, Richard L., 1949–
  Assessment of learners with special needs.
  Bibliography: p.
  Includes index.
  1. Handicapped children—Education—United States.
2. Handicapped children—United States—Psychological
testing. 3. Educational test and measurements
—United States. 4. Examinations—United States
—Interpretation. 5. Disability evaluation—United
States. I. Title.
LC4031.L84 1988   379.9′0973   88–16819
ISBN 0–205–11733–3

Printed in the United States of America
10 9 8 7 6 5 4 3 2 1 88 89 90 91 92 93

BRIEF CONTENTS

CONTENTS

PREFACE

My goal in writing *Assessment of Learners with Special Needs* is to help readers understand and use tests appropriately in the education of special needs students. When used properly, tests can be invaluable tools for diagnosing learning and other problems and for identifying performance strengths. Tests can also provide information about specific curricular areas in need of remediation. In fact, some tests even yield information and recommendations about educational activities designed to remediate measured learning problems. For these reasons, expert knowledge of tests and testing is vital for educators to serve students effectively.

Assessment of Learners with Special Needs is the result of a decade of teaching assessment and diagnosis courses, both at the pre-service (undergraduate) and graduate levels. Over the years, I have noticed that many students possess an approach–avoidance relationship with assessment and testing instruments. Both pre-service and in-service special educators must deal with tests daily. In-service teachers test their students (or have someone test them), interpret results, and then make instructional decisions based on the information yielded. Likewise, college students are tested throughout their educational careers. They have grown accustomed to being tested with both formal and informal assessment instruments and to receiving rewards and punishments (in the form of grades) in response to test results.

Nevertheless, most of these individuals are uncomfortable with assessment, and many distrust or even fear the assessment process.

Some of this uneasiness may emanate from a fear of the statistics involved in understanding the assessment process. Such anxiety, although mild, is often widespread among students. Thus, in teaching assessment, I feel that students' aversions to the topic must be overcome first.

This general aversion to assessment and statistics is unfortunate. Because of it, a number of test users have become largely uninformed test consumers. For example, a significant number of educational professionals cannot judge the comparative merits of tests or choose tests appropriate to their educational needs. These people do not typically (although undoubtedly they *could*) read and understand technical test manuals to judge the adequacy of critical variables, such as reliability, validity, and standardization. Likewise, many teachers do not adequately assess the quality of the test items they write for their own informal tests. Finally, a proportion of practicing educators do not interpret the results of tests appropriately or use that information in ways that can help their students.

The central goal of *Assessment of Learners with Special Needs* is to develop informed test consumers. The testing field is a multimillion dollar industry with thousands of commercially available tests. However, no government agency analogous to the Food and Drug Administration protects test consumers from poorly designed or inappropriate tests. We thus must help the population become informed test consumers who heed the credo Caveat Emptor—Let the Buyer Beware.

A second goal of this book is to explain necessary statistical concepts in a way that reduces anxiety while giving readers a conceptual understanding of how a test's technical quality is assessed. The operational definition of this goal is simple: Help the readers to understand the technical sections of a test manual and to critique statistically their own tests and test items.

A third goal is to help the reader become an assessment *clinician* rather than simply a *technician*. The latter administers and scores tests proficiently; the former uses tests to diagnose students' problems and to design remediational instruction activities and materials. The aim is to help the reader gain an overview of available tests and choose the one needed to make the necessary and appropriate clinical judgments.

Key areas in assessment are informal testing and curriculum-based assessment. Chapters 11 and 12 are devoted to these important topics. These chapters can help teachers develop their own informal tests and assess student performance in terms of criterion-referenced goals linked to the student's individual curriculum.

A fourth goal of this text is to help the reader understand the processes that underlie assessment in the core academic areas. For example, a teacher cannot assess reading without first understanding the reading process. This holds for the other key academic areas taught in school. Thus, the introductory section of each subject-area chapter (Chapters 16–19) contains an overview of how that process develops and operates. Additionally, assessment in nontraditional areas is included in Chapters 20–22.

These three chapters deal with important areas often overlooked in traditional assessment, including career education (Chapter 20), perceptual–motor–sensory assessment (Chapter 21), and the assessment of children's social skills (Chapter 22). This third topic is one of the fastest growing areas in the testing field, with affective, social skills, and self-concept assessment becoming an integral part of student programming.

Finally, because it is vitally important that informed test consumers *use* the information gathered, the last chapter (Chapter 23) is devoted to the application of assessment data in making educational decisions. This chapter also includes an important discussion on writing a test report that is useful to practitioners and parents. The essential link between writing a useful test report and creating sound, remediational programming based on report information is stressed in this final chapter.

I believe that a text written in a nonthreatening, sequential manner, which presents assessment information within the framework of informed consumerism, can help to create a generation of professionals who choose and use tests wisely. If this book contributes to that endeavor, then it will fulfill my expectations.

Acknowledgments

There are many people who deserve thanks for help in the conceptualization and preparation of this book. First and foremost, I would like to thank Elizabeth Brooks of Allyn and Bacon. Through all of the editorial changes, trials, and tribulations that accompanied this book, Beth was the one constant. She was my sounding board, my advisor, and most of all, my friend. My thanks also to Grace Sheldrick, Wordsworth Associates, for her editorial-production assistance.

I would also like to thank Carolyn Muncy and Mary Ann Van Patten for their help in typing and preparing the manuscript. Without their aid, this book would have been impossible.

Finally, I would like to thank the following reviewers for their helpful comments and suggestions during the development of this book: Brian Cobb, University of Vermont; Jeff Messerer, Northeastern Illinois University; Lamoine Miller, Northeast Louisiana University; and Michael Wiebe, Texas Woman's University.

ASSESSMENT OF LEARNERS
WITH SPECIAL NEEDS

CHAPTER 1

Educational Assessment and the Informed Test Consumer

Introduction

Everyone who has attended school, applied for a job, or served in the armed forces during the last thirty years has been administered some type of educational or psychological test. Nevertheless, many people still remain uncomfortable or uninformed about tests and their uses. While we acknowledge the need for testing, many of us have doubts about the accuracy of the information yielded by tests as well as about how that information is interpreted and used.

Such feelings are neither surprising nor completely unfounded. We have all heard stories about people denied jobs or admission to schools based on poor test performances, but who nevertheless went on to become highly successful. Most people have, at one time, taken a test convinced that they have done well only to receive a poor grade. And many people have received poor test marks convinced that they knew the information but that the test asked the "wrong" questions. People who have negative experiences with tests often come to see them as roadblocks to be hurdled or circumvented in order to gain what they want in life.

The Assessment Dilemma in Education

Educators sometimes experience problems resolving their feelings about tests and testing. On one hand, educators have been tested throughout their school years and may be anxious or misinformed about tests and their uses. On the other hand, educators have closer daily contact with tests and the testing process than do virtually any other professionals because a large part of their duties involves the evaluation of students. Thus the educator's dilemma: how to deal with tests

1

and testing on a daily basis while resolving personal feelings of anxiety about the testing process.

Knowledge: The Key to Understanding about Tests

It is human nature to be most concerned and anxious about things we do not fully understand. This is also true for tests and the testing process. When tests and their appropriate uses and methods for proper interpretation are understood, testing becomes more manageable and useful for educators and students. Such understanding makes tests another important tool the informed educator can use to understand and serve students.

Tests and the Testing Industry

The last thirty years have seen dramatic growth in the creation and marketing of tests as an extension of the publishing industry. *Tests in Print* (Mitchell 1983) and the ninth edition of the *Mental Measurements Yearbook* list and review more than three thousand separate, commercially available tests. These tests are divided into fourteen main categories with numerous subclassifications (see Table 1-1). Taking into account teacher-made tests commonly used but not commercially available, tests written in foreign languages, and tests not reviewed in the above-mentioned anthologies, the number of tests being used in schools today is quite large!

It has been estimated that 250 million standardized (we'll discuss this term shortly), commercially available tests are administered to students each academic year. In addition, the testing field has given rise to a large support industry, including books and anthologies that review tests, journals and magazines devoted to testing and measurement, test scoring and interpretation services, and education courses which train individuals in testing and test interpretation. Thus, information about

Table 1-1   Major Classifications of Tests and the Percentage of the Classifications of All Tests Published (1985)

Type of Test	Percentage of Test Market
Personality	25
Vocational/Occupational	21
Miscellaneous	10
Language	10
Intellectual/Aptitude	7
Reading	4
Developmental	4
Achievement	3
Mathematics	3
Speech/Hearing	2
Motor	2
Neuropsychological	1
Social Studies	> 1

Source: Adapted from L. R. Aiken (1988). *Psychological Testing and Measurement*, 6th ed. (Boston: Allyn and Bacon).

the tests available to educators and other professionals is more important than ever.

Caveat Emptor

Caveat emptor is Latin for "let the buyer beware." This statement is as true for the testing industry as for any other area of purchase.

This is not to suggest that the testing industry is dishonest or fraudulent. However, tests come in many forms and sizes. They yield different types of information and can be used for certain purposes but not others. They differ in reliability (see Chapter 8), in their usefulness in measuring what the educator wants to measure, and in the amount of error they contain.

Although consumers are protected from many harmful products by government agencies like the Food and Drug Administration, no comparable agency oversees the production and marketing of tests. Nor is there a clearinghouse to classify or rate commercial tests to ensure that educators and school district personnel buy the correct tests for their needs. For test purchasers and users, *caveat emptor* is the operative term. It is the educators' responsibility to be knowledgeable about the tests they buy and use.

The Test User as Consumer

Test users must become sophisticated and informed consumers and must learn certain skills to help them choose and use appropriate testing instruments. Figure 1-1 lists the skills needed by informed test consumers.

As shown in Figure 1-1, informed test consumers know what they want from tests and whether the test being considered fills those needs. They know the strengths and weaknesses of individual tests and how those tests can help them make educational and programmatic decisions. Such consumers understand the error inherent in each test (as shown in Chapter 8, all tests contain error) and the effect of such error on educational decisions. They comprehend the relationship between appropriate test administration, scoring, and interpretation, and they can score tests and appropriately interpret the results. Finally, and perhaps most important, informed test consumers can adequately judge the closeness of fit between the students to-be-tested and the types of students for whom the authors designed and standardized their test.

Informed test consumers do not purchase an inappropriately constructed test or adopt a test because an acquaintance uses it or because it is popular. Realizing that every test contains error, informed test consumers understand that tests cannot make decisions for professionals. They know what tests can and cannot realistically do for their users (see Figure 1-2) and are confident and knowledgeable in their interaction with testing instruments. The goal of this text is to help teachers become informed test consumers.

Figure 1-1 Skills Required of the Informed Test Consumer

1. Knowing the type of test.
2. Knowing precisely what the test does and does not measure.
3. Knowing the type/age of the pupils for whom the test has been designed.
4. Understanding the degree of "match" between the type of student for whom the test has been designed and the current test taker.
5. Knowing the competitive tests in the field and the attributes of those tests.
6. Understanding the types of scores and information that the test yields.
7. Understanding the rules for administration, scoring, and interpretation.
8. Understanding the technical aspects of the test, such as standardization procedures, reliability, and validity.
9. Understanding the relationship between the degree of error in the test and the correct interpretation of the test's scores.
10. Having foresight about how test information will be used and applied in the test taker's educational programming.

Figure 1-2 What Tests Can Do and Cannot Do

What Tests Can Do:
1. Yield information difficult to obtain otherwise.
2. Yield information in controlled settings.
3. Compare test-taker results with those from a controlled, scientifically selected peer group.
4. Compare test taker results with a set of objective criteria.
5. Test information in an objective, nonemotional manner.

What Tests Cannot Do:
1. Make decisions.
2. Predict the future.
3. Choose educational programming.
4. Remediate student deficiencies.
5. Give foolproof information.

The Assessment Process

The purpose of educational and psychological tests is *assessment*. Assessment is the process of gathering information using appropriate tests, instruments, and techniques (Hargrove and Poteet 1984). This information is gathered (1) to identify problems in student learning and behavior and (2) to make programmatic, curricular, and instructional decisions about students.

The two components of assessment are *measurement* and *evaluation*. Measurement consists of the administration and scoring of tests. Basically, it involves number gathering. Evaluation refers to the subsequent interpretation of the test results (see Figure 1-3). It is making sense out of the numbers and scores that have been gathered during measurement.

Measurement is inappropriate and fruitless without adequate evaluation. It is simply "bean counting" without any interpretation of the meaning of the numbers. However, evaluation based on inappropriate or sloppy test administration and data collection is not only useless but also potentially harmful to the test taker. Such evaluation means that educational decisions will be based on inaccurate information. Figure 1-4 contains the assumptions made regarding measurement and evaluation and, hence, appropriate assessment.

Figure 1-3 Measurement versus Evaluation

Measurement involves:
1. Test administration
2. Test data collection
3. Test scoring

Evaluation involves:
1. Interpretation of test scores
2. Combining and interpreting information from more than one source or test
3. Synthesis of various measurements
4. Diagnosis and/or subjective interpretation

Figure 1-4 Assumptions Made in Test Measurement and Evaluation

1. Test taker speaks/uses the language in which the test is written.
2. Test taker is not experiencing a temporary or permanent condition that would jeopardize test-taking ability.
3. Test is appropriate for test taker.
4. Test giver is knowledgeable in test administration, scoring, and interpretation and will follow all specified testing procedures.
5. Test giver is knowledgeable in test taker's language.
6. The test is culture- and language-fair for the test taker.
7. Test information has been fairly and objectively obtained, scored, and interpreted.
8. The test yields a reliable and accurate picture of the test taker's abilities and behavior.
9. All tests contain error, and the error in the present test and test situation has been taken into account.

The Strategies of Assessment

Assessment is more than just administering, scoring, and interpreting tests. Tests are *tools* knowledgeable educators and clinicians use to answer questions about the educational and psychological functioning of students. Tests are information-gathering instruments, similar to our eyes and ears. However, they cannot make decisions for us; that process is reserved for people.

The educational professional and clinician incorporate assessment instruments in three assessment strategies (Choate et al. 1987; Hargrove and Poteet 1984). These strategies are *diagnostic looking, diagnostic asking,* and *diagnostic listening.*

Diagnostic Looking

Diagnostic looking involves the systematic observation of student behavior in order to understand or detect a pattern to that behavior. It is observing behavior while attempting to explain why that behavior occurs. For example, a teacher can systematically analyze a student's math worksheet by trying to detect a pattern of errors that occurs regularly in the child's arithmetic functioning. In doing this, the teacher moves from simply identifying arithmetic answers as right or wrong to understanding why the child's correct and incorrect responses occur. The strategy of diagnostic looking can be used with any student product or set of behaviors that can be observed and analyzed.

Diagnostic Asking

A good clinician knows that learning about a client or student often depends on asking the right questions. For example, if you ask a child what he or she did in school today, the answer might be "Nothing." However, if you pointedly ask what activities the child engaged in during reading class, or what story was read during silent reading time and what is remembered from it, you will likely receive a different (and more detailed) answer.

Diagnostic asking entails asking students the types of questions that will yield insight as to why they behave as they do and/or commit the errors they are exhibiting. An example of diagnostic asking is to have a child orally tell you exactly what he or she did (and why) in solving a given arithmetic problem. Another common example, used by virtually every classroom teacher, is asking comprehension questions during oral reading. Of course, the usefulness of the diagnostic asking strategy depends on both the quality of the diagnostic questions asked and the insight of students into their behavior.

Diagnostic Listening

Perhaps you have heard the saying, "He hears but he does not listen." We often hear what people are telling us without really listening to both the overt (surface) as well as covert (underlying) messages they are relaying.

Diagnostic listening is listening rather than simply hearing. More specifically, it is carefully attending to and analyzing a student's oral responses in order to understand what the individual is implying. For example, suppose you ask two classmates how things are going. Susan answers with a cheery, upbeat "Okay!" whereas Steven answers "Okay" with a low, mournful sigh, sounding as if he has just lost his best friend. Both have given you the same answer. However, even a relatively unsophisticated level of diagnostic listening discloses that Susan is feeling good and Steven is depressed. Similarly, by actively listening to a student's or client's overt and covert messages, teachers and clinicians can gain insight into how the individual is really acting and feeling.

Purposes of Educational Assessment

Generally, educational assessment seeks to answer five main questions (Compton 1984):

1. What is the student's current functioning level in the basic academic skill areas?
2. What, if any, are the student's *specific* skill deficiencies in each basic academic skill area?
3. What are the student's strengths in these areas?
4. What and how shall the student be taught?
5. How well is the student progressing toward his or her educational goals?

These questions are answered in terms of five types of educational processes: *screening, classification decisions, diagnostic testing, program planning,* and *progress evaluation.* Although these processes are discussed in greater detail in subsequent chapters, a brief definition of each in terms of its influence on assessment decisions is appropriate.

Screening

The first phase of the assessment process is screening. During this phase, all children are given a cursory or preliminary examination or test to identify students who *might* have a problem. Students identified during the screening as perhaps having a learning problem are then given a more in-depth assessment to ascertain whether initial suspicions were correct. Screening examples include tests children receive before entering kindergarten and the vision and hearing acuity tests throughout the school years.

Students who do not indicate a possible problem by screening receive no further evaluation. Thus, it is important that screening procedures not overlook students who perform as if they have no potential problem when, in fact, such a problem does exist. Such students have fallen through the cracks in the screening process and have lost the opportunity for further testing and remediation. This is the most serious error that can occur during the screening procedure.

Classification Decisions

Under federal law and the statutes of most states, students cannot receive special education services unless they are classified as eligible to receive those services. There are a variety of categories under which students may be classified in order to receive such compensatory services. These categories include such differential diagnoses as demonstrating mental retardation (this category has various subclassifications), learning disabilities, sensory impairment, physical handicaps, and behavioral disorders.

Typically, each state has its own classification system as well as eligibility requirements. To classify children as *handicapped* (some states use the terms *exceptional* or *disabled*), assessment instruments are administered to children thought to possess such exceptionalities. Children meeting the eligibility requirements specified by the state in which they reside can then be given compensatory special education services at taxpayer expense. Fur-

ther discussions on law, eligibility requirements, and special education classification are included in Chapter 2.

Diagnostic Testing

In contrast to screening, diagnostic testing is usually a lengthy, involved process. The goals of diagnostic testing are to ascertain and identify the child's specific weaknesses and strengths in academic or behavioral functioning. Typically, a battery of tests is administered to the student. Such tests include assessment in perceptual functioning, language, academic skills, memory, and other areas. The interpreted results form the basis of a lengthy report and diagnostic profile, which educational professionals can use to identify the academic and behavioral areas needing remediation.

Program Planning

Following classification/placement and diagnostic testing comes program planning. It is not enough to administer and interpret test scores; test results must be used to create instructional activities and materials that will remediate student weaknesses. Effective program planning incorporates a child's strengths to increase the probability of learning while creating instructional procedures designed to remediate weaknesses. This emphasis on using assessment results to remediate student educational and behavioral deficiencies is why the entire process is often called *diagnostic prescriptive* teaching.

Progress Evaluation

After program planning has taken place and the student's educational program has been implemented, two important questions arise: (1) Have the student's problems been remediated? (2) To what extent has the program played a part in such remediation? Monitoring student progress involves pretesting a student before implementing the educational program and then posttesting the same pupil after the remediation program has been completed. To the extent that the posttesting shows definitive improvement, the student is said to have made progress.

Program evaluation questions the relative success of a number of students receiving the same program or set of instructional materials. Thus, for example, a given reading series or set of language materials can be evaluated for its effectiveness in improving the academic functioning of a number of students.

Assessment Tools and Techniques

To answer the five assessment questions stated earlier, a variety of assessment tools and techniques are commonly used. These include *formal tests, informal tests, criterion-referenced tests, rating scales, interviews,* and *observations* (Choate et al. 1987; Hargrove and Poteet 1984). Although these tools and techniques are discussed in detail in later chapters, they are briefly defined here.

Formal Tests

Formal tests are commercially available, *standardized* instruments; the term *standardized* means that they possess specific directions and rules for administration, scoring, and interpretation. These procedures must be followed exactly to obtain valid and meaningful results.

Additionally, standardized tests have been administered to a representative group or sample of individuals; this sample becomes the comparison group against which the individual test taker is compared. The average of the children in the comparison group becomes the basis for the test *norms*. Norms are the standards or averages against which individual test takers are measured. For this reason, such instruments are also called *norm-referenced* tests.

Formal tests can be designed to be administered to groups of persons or to people individually. Individually administered tests are usually more flexible in terms of administration and the questions and responses that test takers can ask and make. Most formal tests designed specifically for special education students are individually administered.

Informal Tests

Informal tests have not been standardized. These include most teacher-made tests. Informal tests are designed to be easy and quick to administer and score and do not require extensively trained test givers. They are also usually less expensive to create than are formal tests. Teacher-made tests also have the added advantage of being directly related to the content being taught in the individual classroom. On the negative side, most informal tests lack the technical quality of formal tests.

Criterion-Referenced Tests

Recall that in formal, norm-referenced tests, a student's score is compared against that of a comparison norm group. Thus, these tests make *interperson* comparisons. In criterion-referenced tests, the individual student's test results are compared against a given benchmark or criterion rather than against the results of other students. For example, imagine that all children's test scores are compared against each other with the top 10 percent receiving *A*s, the next 20 percent receiving *B*s, and so on. This would be a norm-referenced test. On the other hand, if all children who correctly mastered 90 percent of the math problems received an *A,* no matter how many *A*s were given out, this would be a criterion-referenced test. Thus, in a criterion-referenced test, children compete with themselves (*intraperson* comparison) rather than against other test takers.

Whereas norm-referenced tests are often used to ascertain relative rank order within a group of test takers, criterion-referenced tests are very useful in diagnosing specific areas of strength and weakness for an individual student. More discussion on criterion- and norm-referenced tests is included in Chapters 11 and 12.

Rating Scales

On a *rating scale,* there is no correct or incorrect answer. Rather, the respondent chooses from a variety of alternatives, such as always, sometimes, and never. The possible responses lie along a continuum from which the student chooses one. Another type of rating scale contains only two choices, yes and no, and constitutes a *checklist.* Rating scales are useful in assessing clinical and behavioral attributes of students.

Interviews

The interview is a direct, face-to-face conversation. Interviews are particularly useful when the professional wants to discuss a person's behavior with parents, caregivers, siblings, teachers, and other concerned individuals. Interviews yield information about the individual in situations that the teacher may not be able to observe, such as behavior in the home or in social situations outside of school.

Interviews can be structured or unstructured. Structured interviews contain guidelines for conducting the interview or specific questions for the professional to ask. An example of a commercially available, structured interview is the Vineland Social Maturity Scale – Interview Edition (Sparrow, Balla, and Ciccheti 1984), which measures adaptive behavior of severely handicapped clients by having the professional interview persons familiar with the behavior of the client.

Observations

In this technique, the student is observed directly by the professional, and a specific or *target* behavior is observed and recorded. Additionally, the conditions under which the target behavior occurs are carefully recorded so the relationship between occurrence and/or frequency of behavior and environmental conditions can be systematically analyzed. Observational recording is particularly useful in observing and later modifying unacceptable client behaviors, such as aggression or off-task behavior.

The Abuse and Misuse of Assessment Instruments

Uninformed test consumers often inappropriately choose tests based on poor reasoning or lack of knowledge. They also often misuse and misinterpret the tests they purchase. Once tests have been purchased and administered, uninformed test consumers may commit one or more of five common errors (Anastasiow 1973; Compton 1984; Wallace and Larsen 1978).

1. Generalizing the interpretation of test scores to groups of test takers not represented in the norm sample or to groups for which the test has not been designed.

2. Overinterpreting scores by creating significant differences between two test scores where, in fact, the differences between the scores are insignificant.

3. Teaching "to the test." That is, teaching students the answers to questions likely to be on the test or that they know *will* be on the test.

4. Violating the administration and scoring rules of the test. For example, giving the students more time than allocated to finish the test or giving them points because they were "onto the right answer."

5. Putting too much stock in a single test and classifying or making decisions about a child based on only one test.

An uninformed test consumer can make a host of other errors that can cause administration, scoring, and interpretation errors. To the extent that such errors are kept to a minimum, assessment and assessment procedures will help rather than harm students and will be a positive rather than negative influence on their lives.

The Goal of This Text

We all make mistakes, and professionals who administer, score, and interpret educational tests are no different. However, uninformed test consumers are more likely than their informed counterparts to choose the wrong tests for a given situation or to choose tests of poor technical quality. Likewise, uninformed test consumers are likely to administer tests incorrectly and make errors in scoring and interpretation that lead to inappropriate educational programming for students.

This text can help you become an informed test consumer. As such, you will be able to critique the merits of tests and make informed choices about which tests are appropriate for your use. As an informed test consumer you will be able to assess the technical quality of tests and fully understand the scope and limits of the information yielded by tests. You will also understand the processes that underlie the abilities being tested (e.g., reading, spelling, arithmetic) and be able to choose tests that adequately measure the aspects of those abilities. The informed test consumer will have a working knowledge of the tests available so that choices can be made from the full range of tests on the market. Finally, you will learn what to *do* with the testing information that you score and interpret, that is, how to transform test information into educational programming for special needs learners.

Informed test consumers must have a working knowledge of basic statistics to be able to assess the technical quality of tests as well as understand the types of tests available and how they differ. They must be able to read a test's technical manual and discern what the author is saying about the test. These skills are explained in this text.

Being an informed test consumer is not easy, but it is vitally important. Tests are diagnostic tools; they are not, as some believe, the magical answer to every educational problem. When used correctly as part of a well-planned assessment program by competent and informed educators, tests can provide essential information about a student. But tests chosen on the basis of poor criteria, incorrectly administered and scored, or inappropriately interpreted are worse than useless. They are counterproductive and can prove harmful in the education of students who become the victims of inept test consumers. This text is dedicated to preventing such damage to students.

SUMMARY

Most individuals have been tested at one time or another. Testing is an integral part of the educational environment as well as the workplace. Nevertheless, many people feel uneasy about tests due to a lack of information regarding what tests and the testing process can and cannot accomplish. This unease probably applies to teachers and other educational professionals as well.

The testing industry is one of the fastest growth areas of the publishing business, with several thousand commercial tests presently available to the consumer. Unfortunately, no protection agency currently exists to screen and select tests for potential users. It thus is important that educational professionals become informed test consumers who can choose tests on their merits and use them appropriately.

The purpose of testing is assessment. Assessment is the process of gathering information and using appropriate tests, instruments, and techniques to make programmatic, curricular, and instructional decisions about students. Assessment contains two components—measurement and evaluation. Measurement is the administration and scoring of tests; evaluation involves the subsequent interpretation of test results.

The three main assessment strategies are diagnostic looking, diagnostic asking, and diagnostic listening. Diagnostic looking involves the systematic observation of student behavior for the purpose of understanding behavior patterns. Diagnostic asking entails asking questions that yield insight into students and their performance. Finally, diagnostic listening involves actively listening to student responses in order to understand the underlying implications and meanings of what is being said.

Educational assessment seeks to answer five main questions in terms of the following educational assessment processes: screening, classification, diagnostic testing, program planning, and progress evaluation. Screening is administered to all students to identify those who may have possible problems and those who exhibit no problems in the areas screened. Students who demonstrate possible problems are then tested in depth. Classification decisions are made to qualify students for compensatory educational services under state or federal law. Diagnostic testing is the in-depth testing administered to students who demonstrated possible problems during the screening phase. Diagnostic testing indicates specific student strengths and weaknesses in the areas assessed. Program planning, which follows diagnostic evaluation, is the creation of programs to remediate student weaknesses. Finally, progress evaluation assesses the curricular program as a means of remediating the student's weaknesses as well as similar weaknesses demonstrated by other pupils.

A number of different types of assessment tools are available, including formal tests, informal tests, criterion-referenced tests, rating scales, interviews, and observations. These tools are described in detail in subsequent chapters.

STUDY QUESTIONS

1. What is test consumerism? What are its defining attributes? Why is it important?

2. What can tests legitimately do and not do for test consumers? What is the meaning of the statement "A test can make educational decisions for professionals"? Is this a legitimate use of tests? Why or why not?

3. What are the components of assessment? What is the difference between measurement and evaluation? Can you have one without the other? Why or why not?

4. What are the main questions assessment seeks to answer? How do these questions differ from one another, and why is each question important?

5. What are the three main strategies of assessment? What does each strategy entail? Why is each important?

6. What are the main types of educational assessment processes? How do they differ? What are their uses, and what types of information does each yield?

7. What are the major types of assessment tools? How do they differ? What are their defining attributes? In what types of situations would each assessment tool be educationally useful?

CHAPTER 2

The Historical and Current State of Assessment in Special Education

KEY CONCEPTS

- A history of assessment
- Assessment and special education
- Public Law (PL) 94-142 and educational assessment
- Screening and identification
- Due process
- Quality of assessment
- Educational placements and options
- Construction of individualized educational plans (IEPs)

The tempting traps of inexperience are to examine where we are and to forget where we have been. Such might be the case for professionals relatively new to the field of assessment (particularly assessment in special education), who began working in education after 1975, a year unparalleled in significance.

Today we see a system of schooling that not only guarantees appropriate educational experiences for all handicapped children but also mandates fair and unbiased assessment designed to provide an *appropriate* education for each child. Included in this mandate is a demand for assessment that acknowledges the cultural diversity of children and that uses culturally fair and unbiased tests. However, this has not always been the case. In fact, this so-called age of enlightenment in assessment and special education has a brief history. However, to see how far we have traveled, we must explore the historical relationship between assessment and education.

Assessment in the Historical Perspective

Many histories begin the story of assessment at the turn of the twentieth century. However, although the majority of assessment history takes place during this time, it is important to realize that the roots of testing began centuries earlier, as far back as 2200 B.C.

The System of Chinese Civil Service Testing

The use of tests designed to make inferences about a person's skills and competencies dates back at least to 2200 B.C. (DuBois 1970; Wardrop 1976). The Chinese emperor at that time decided to institute a testing system for appointed officials that would test each official on his competency every three years. After three such examinations (nine years in office), officials either had to be promoted or dismissed. This practice continued, becoming formalized into a sort of civil service system in which the competency and skills of appointed government officials were regularly assessed. The practice ended in 1905 because of changes in the Chinese political and social systems.

As European contact with the Chinese developed, this form of civil service testing spread to France and Great Britain, and from there to the United States. Today the system of skill and competency testing is an accepted form of assessment that permeates American life, and it has contributed to a general acceptance of educational assessment (DuBois 1970; Wardrop 1976). (See Table 2.1.)

Table 2-1   A Chronology of Assessment History

2200 B.C.	Mandarins set up civil-service testing program in China.
1219 A.D.	First formal oral examinations in law held at University of Bologna.
1575	J. Huarte publishes book, *Examen de Ingenios,* concerned with individual differences in mental abilities.
1636	Oral examinations for degree certification used at Oxford University.
1795	Astronomer Maskelyne of Greenwich Observatory fires his assistant Kinnebrook when their observations of transit time of Venus disagree.
1860s	Beginning of use of written examinations in schools and governmental organizations in Great Britain, continental Europe, and the U.S.
1869	Scientific study of individual differences begins with publication of Galton's "Classification of Men According to Their Natural Gifts."
1879	Founding of first psychological laboratory in the world by Wilhelm Wundt at Leipzig, Germany.
1884	F. Galton opens Anthropometric Laboratory in London for International Health Exhibition.
1887	G. Fechner formulates the first psychological law.
1888	J. M. Cattell opens testing laboratory at the University of Pennsylvania.
1893	J. Jastrow displays sensorimotor tests at Columbian Exhibition in Chicago.
1897	J. Rice publishes research findings on spelling abilities of U.S. schoolchildren.
1904	C. Spearman describes his two-factor theory of mental abilities.
1905	First Binet-Simon Intelligence Scale published. C. Jung uses word-association test for analysis of mental complexes.
1908	Revision of Binet-Simon Intelligence Scale and C. Stone's Arithmetic Tests published.
1908–14	E. L. Thorndike develops standardized tests of arithmetic, handwriting, language, and spelling.
1916	Stanford-Binet Intelligence Scale published by L. Terman.
1917	Army Alpha and Army Beta, first group intelligence tests, constructed and administered to U.S. army recruits; R. Woodworth's Personal Data Sheet, the first standardized personality inventory, used in military selection.

1919	L. Thurstone's Psychological Examination for College Freshmen published.
1920	National Intelligence Scale published. H. Rorschach's Inkblot Test first published.
1921	Psychological Corporation, first major test publishing company, founded by Cattell, Thorndike, and Woodworth.
1923	First achievement test battery, Stanford Achievement Tests, published.
1924	T. L. Kelley's *Statistical Method* published.
1925–50	Spread of standardized testing, development of methodology and technology of testing.
1927	First edition of Strong Vocational Interest Blank for Men published.
1936	Soviet Union bans psychological tests. First volume of *Psychometrika* published.
1937	Revision of Stanford-Binet Intelligence Scale published.
1938	H. Murray publishes *Explorations in Personality;* O. K. Buros publishes first *Mental Measurements Yearbook.*
1939	Wechsler-Bellevue Intelligence Scale published.
1942	Minnesota Multiphasic Personality Inventory published.
1949	Wechsler Intelligence Scale for Children published.
1960	Form L–M of Stanford-Binet Intelligence Scale published.
1969	A. Jensen's paper on racial inheritance of IQ published in *Harvard Educational Review.*
1970–	Increasing use of computers in designing, administering, scoring, analyzing, and interpreting tests.
1971	Federal court decision requiring tests used in personnel selection to be job relevant (*Griggs* v. *Duke Power*).
1974	Wechsler Intelligence Scale for Children–Revised published.
1975–	Growth of behavioral assessment techniques.
1981	Wechsler Adult Intelligence Scale–Revised published.
1985	*Ninth Mental Measurements Yearbook* published. *Standards for Educational and Psychological Testing* published.

Source: L. R. Aiken (1988). *Psychological Testing and Assessment,* 6th ed. (Boston: Allyn and Bacon). Used by permission.

University Examination System

University exams are another root of educational assessment. The testing of university students for educational competencies dates back to thirteenth-century France where oral examinations were used at the Sorbonne and later at Louvain University. In the sixteenth century a system of written examinations was used for students at Jesuit universities for the dual purposes of testing learning and educational placement. Such examinations were used at Oxford University in 1636 for degree certification; written questions were adopted at Cambridge in 1828. By the middle of the 1800s, virtually every university in Europe, the United States, and Canada used some form of written examination to certify competency in the professions.

The Psychology of Individual Differences

As the infant stages of psychology began to grow in the late nineteenth and early twentieth century, psychologists became increasingly interested in assessment for the purpose of measuring psychological differences between individuals. It had been evident for years that people differed in both physical and mental characteristics. Psychologists were interested in the extent to which people differed and in how these differences could be measured precisely and systematically.

Sir Frances Galton, a scientist interested in human heredity, opened a laboratory in London in 1884. He studied individual differences, such as height, weight, color discrimination, breath rate, hand steadiness, and a variety of other characteristics. Eventually, Galton compiled data on almost ten thousand persons.

Much of Galton's work was carried on by James McKeen Cattell. After working with Galton in England, Cattell established a laboratory at Columbia University in New York. He devoted himself to studying such variables as perception and sensory acuteness, "sense of effort," "mental time," and "mental intensity." Cattell was convinced that these variables were correlated with mental capacity and academic success. Although he was unable to show such a relationship, Cattell did contribute significantly to the area of assessment by developing one of the first psychological test batteries.

Cattell also contributed indirectly to the fields of psychology and assessment through the graduate students he attracted to his laboratory to study with him. These students included E. L. Thorndike, E. L. Strong, Jr., and R. S. Woodworth, all of whom had a major influence on psychological assessment.

Binet and the Testing of Intelligence

A key point in the history of psychological assessment occurred with Alfred Binet's work in the testing of intelligence. Binet began his work at the laboratory at the Sorbonne in Paris in 1892 and later became its director. He was interested in the study of individual differences in intellectual functioning. As he continued his work, Binet became convinced that the best way to assess intellectual functioning was to develop a battery of diverse tests to measure the various aspects of thought, memory, and perception. In 1902, Binet published the results of a study in which he administered twenty different tests designed to measure individual differences in intellectual functioning.

In 1904, the French minister of public instruction in Paris appointed a special commission of professionals to recommend how academic instruction could benefit mentally retarded individuals. This was a time in France, the goal of which was the blossoming of individuals to their full potential. It was believed that a humane goal of education was to help mentally retarded and intellectually deficient children reach their potential through public instruction. The problem, however, was how to identify and distinguish these children from the unmotivated or mentally ill. Binet was appointed to the commission.

Binet, in collaboration with Theodore Simon, devised thirty tests that could be objectively scored and used to differentiate mentally retarded from nonretarded students. These tests required pupils to carry out simple verbal commands, coordinate movements, recognize and use common objects, define words, and complete sentences.

Binet and Simon tested large groups of children at various chronological ages (CA) and collected data as to the average age at which a task could be successfully performed. Each item was placed at the age level at which 60 to 90 percent of the students in that age group passed the item. This average age was designated as the mental age (MA) for performing the task. If a child could successfully perform a task earlier than the average child, his or her level of intellectual functioning was average or higher than average. However, if the child could not successfully perform the task until he or she was older than the average child, mental functioning was considered below normal and at least some level of retardation was indicated.

In 1916, Lewis Terman developed the concept of the intelligence quotient (IQ) based on the work of Binet and Simon. The IQ is a ratio (fraction) that compares a child's mental age to chronological age. A child of a given

CA who can perform items of average children of the same CA possesses an IQ of unity (CA = MA; MA/CA = 1). However, a child who can successfully perform only items that average younger children can pass has an IQ below unity (MA < CA; MA/CA < 1). A younger child who can perform tasks ordinarily passed only by older counterparts possesses an IQ greater than unity. Later, this ratio score was multiplied by 100 to eliminate decimals and/or fractions. More discussion of IQ testing appears in Chapters 13 and 14.

Educational Assessment in the United States

Assessment and World War I

In 1917, the United States was involved in World War I. As men rushed to enter the armed services, military professionals realized that they needed some way to classify recruits on a variety of attributes, including educational and intellectual functioning. It would be wasteful to place potential officers in the front lines and disastrous to promote intellectually incapable individuals to positions of command. A system was needed to classify recruits quickly into the military roles for which they were best suited.

Enter A. S. Otis, a student of Lewis Terman (who developed the Stanford–Binet intelligence test in the United States). Otis had developed but not published a group intelligence test that could easily be administered to a large group of individuals at one time and scored with a minimum of difficulty. Otis's test, which became known as Army Alpha, was adopted by the military and administered to over a million army inductees during World War I.

Note how the concept of assessment had changed from the time of Binet to that of Otis. Test administration moved from individuals to groups, from the probing of individual abilities to that of mass classification. In France, Binet had used his tests to identify special needs learners, whereas the Army Alpha was designed to place people into categories for which they were believed best suited. Assessment had come a long way in America, but many people thought it had moved in the wrong direction.

Cultural Superiority and Racism

As the results from the Army Alpha tests were analyzed, psychologists and other social scientists were shocked. The mental age of army recruits, considered the pride of American manhood, was unbelievably low, the average mental age being about thirteen. The IQs of blacks tested were usually significantly lower than those of their white counterparts, and recruits from the South tended to score lower than recruits from the North. Many social scientists interpreted these results to mean that the collective IQ of Americans was dropping due to the influx of immigrants and the genetic "inbreeding" of persons considered "socially inferior." This supposed trend was labeled by some as the "threat of the feeble-minded" (Karier 1972). This purported threat led to the formation of a number of social policy committees, including The Committee on the Heredity of the Feeble Minded whose board of directors included various prominent psychologists (Wardrop 1976).

This perceived threat led to a number of repressive measures in the United States that continued well into the 1950s. Such measures included strong laws and quotas against immigrants, especially those from Eastern and Southern Europe. Also included was the forced sterilization of more than 8,500 people considered genetically inferior and the passage of sterilization laws for mentally deficient persons. In addition, laws were passed prohibiting racially mixed marriages. Some of these laws remained on the books of many states until the middle of this century. Questions on such IQ tests as the Stanford–Binet were thought to be biased to reflect a social class and occupational hierarchy; they were clearly biased against non–English-speaking, non-Nordic, or non-Anglophile groups.

Assessment from World War II to the Present

From World War II to the present, assessment has changed in four major ways: the sophistication of designed instruments, the application of technology, the institutionalization of testing into the fabric of American life, and the philosophy of assessment.

Regarding the sophistication of developed assessment instruments, the development of the discipline of psychometrics has aided in creating sound, objective assessment instruments that possess a strong reliability and validity. A detailed discussion of these variables appears in Chapters 8 and 9 of this text.

Another aspect of modern assessment is the use of technology. After World War II, punch cards were developed to speed the encoding of data while sorting machines were used to score tests. The next advancement was machines able to read graphite (pencil marks) on specialized scoring sheets. Such scoring sheets are still used with many tests today.

The age of computers has continued to revolutionize assessment. Many tests are now available on computer. Others can be administered by computer with test-taker responses made on a microcomputer, and the test scored immediately by the same program. As computers continue to evolve and become more powerful, the capabilities of assessment instruments to handle the increasingly sophisticated technology will also grow.

A third change in assessment is the acceptance of testing into the mainstream of American life. Virtually everyone in the United States has been tested in school, on the job, in the military, or in some other capacity. Rather than be offended by this intrusion of testing, most people have accepted it as part of life in a technological society. Many employers and in-

stitutions, including schools, hospitals, and the government, base key decisions on tests and test information.

Perhaps most important are the relatively recent changes in assessment philosophy. Until recently, the purpose of tests, especially in school, was to categorize and label individuals. Children took educational and psychological tests early in their school careers and were tracked in school, some to academic, college-bound programs, others toward blue-collar positions. Children were labeled mentally retarded or nonretarded solely on the results of IQ tests. The fact that these tests might be culturally unfair or biased or that they might contain error and lack validity was given very little attention. Tests were given, and decisions about people's lives were made.

This philosophy has begun to change. Tests legally cannot have as much impact as they once did in categorizing and labeling people. Rather, the purpose of assessment is largely *diagnostic,* designed to assess a person's strengths and weaknesses in order to suggest ways to remediate the weaknesses and build on the strengths. Thus, and not a moment too soon, the purpose of assessment has come full circle to what Binet and his associates wanted—to help people use their potential and to contribute to the meaning and dignity of their lives.

Special Education and the Field of Assessment

There have always been exceptional children, but through the years they have been treated with varying degrees of concern. Before the 1800s, most services provided for exceptional individuals were protective and custodial (e.g., asylums and institutions); not until the seventeenth century were educational services for handicapped children provided (Hallahan and Kauffman 1982; Kauffman 1981).

Most of the early pioneers of special education were European physicians, such as Jean Marc Gaspard Itard (1775–1838), Philippe Pinel (1745–1826), Edouard Seguin (1812–1889), and Maria Montessori (1870–1952). These names (except for Montessori) illustrate the French influence on the Age of Humanism, the same philosophy of helping people reach their full potential that motivated the minister of education in Paris to hire Binet and Simon to identify and aid mentally retarded students in the schools. In general, these physicians stressed the following approaches in helping exceptional children. Many of these five approaches still form the educational underpinnings of contemporary special education (Hallahan and Kauffman 1982).

1. The belief that every child can be helped to reach his or her full potential.
2. Individualized instruction: using the child's special characteristics, *not* a prescribed curriculum, as the basis for instruction.
3. A carefully sequenced curriculum.
4. Systematic arrangement of the child's physical and psychological learning environment.
5. Immediate reward (positive reinforcement) for correct performance and behavior.

During the 1800s, Americans became increasingly aware of special education for handicapped children. Among the professionals involved in creating humanistic educational services for exceptional children were Samuel Gridley Howe (1801–1876), who started one of the first schools for the blind and another for the mentally retarded in the United States, and Thomas Hopkins Gallaudet (1787–1851), who founded the first American residential school for the deaf. However, just as the philosophical goals of the assessment movement changed during and after World War I, prevailing attitudes toward the handicapped also changed.

The Decline of Special Education in America

During the years between the two world wars, attitudes toward and services for exceptional children took a turn for the worse. Earlier goals of humane educational services for handicapped persons evolved into institutionalization, sterilization, and forced eugenics. Many of these changes were due to the fears of many people that America was breeding a generation of feebleminded individuals who would continue to reproduce, thus significantly lowering the collective intelligence of the country. Other reasons included beliefs in racial and cultural superiority that espoused theories of hereditary mental inferiority among certain cultural and racial groups. The reasoning was that educational services for such inferior groups would be a waste of money. Unfortunately, this attitude prevailed in America until well after World War II.

Special Education: 1950–1975

Although the treatment of handicapped individuals became somewhat less repressive after World War II, it still left much to be desired. A real-life example can best illustrate this point. While teaching moderately to severely mentally retarded students in a public school, the author met the mother of a nineteen-year-old Down's Syndrome person. The mother related what life had been like for her and her daughter during the 1950s and 1960s. The difficulties had begun when Sarah was born. The hospital refused to place the Down's Syndrome child in the nursery with the other infants. Instead, the baby was kept in isolation. A counselor at the hospital informed the mother that for everyone's sake she ought to have the baby institutionalized—something the mother refused to do. Finally, in utter thoughtlessness, a hospital representative trying to find the mother's bed in the public ward called out loudly, "Where's the mother of that idiot baby!"

The mother decided to keep Sarah despite the protestations and dire warnings of every professional who interacted with her. When

Sarah reached school age, her mother naïvely went to enroll her. She was haughtily informed by a school official that no services existed in the school system for her daughter and furthermore that the system was under no obligation ever to provide services. They suggested again that Sarah be institutionalized.

For *five years* this mother pleaded with school officials to provide some services, at least part time, for Sarah. The school system continued to refuse. Finally, when Sarah was ten years old, the mother, aided by a sympathetic kindergarten teacher, persuaded the school system to relent a bit. School system officials informed Sarah's mother that the child could attend school two hours a day *if* she drove Sarah to and from school, stayed in school with her at all times, and agreed that the teacher could ask Sarah and her mother to leave the classroom at any time. Sarah's mother gratefully accepted all of the conditions. So much for the good old days of special education!

Assessment and Special Education in the Modern Age: Litigation Leading to Public Law 94-142

Background

The types of experiences that Sarah and her mother encountered were common during the 1950s and 1960s. In fact, these things were happening so frequently to parents and their handicapped children that parents began to band together. At first, these groups functioned as support organizations; parents came together once or twice a month to share the loneliness and anxiety of having a mentally retarded child. However, in 1950, certain groups merged into the National Society for Retarded Children (now known as the National Association for Retarded Citizens, or NARC). From a membership of 125 chapters and 13,000 members in 1950, NARC has grown to more than 1600 chap-

ters and 250,000 members. As the association has grown, it has evolved from a support group to a political advocate group fighting for the rights of mentally retarded citizens (Hallahan and Kauffman 1982).

Litigation in Special Education and Assessment

As NARC grew so did its political impact. During the late 1960s and early 1970s, NARC as well as other advocate groups began to use the judicial system to force communities and school systems to provide humane educational services and appropriate assessment for special needs learners. This led to a series of landmark test cases regarding special education and assessment. These cases included those discussed next.

Hansen v. *Hobson* (1967): This case took place in Washington, D.C., on behalf of black students who claimed that blacks were assigned in disproportionate numbers to lower-ability school groups (tracks). The chief issue was whether the assessment instruments (standardized achievement tests) were fair in assessing the abilities of these students. The judge ruled against the fairness of the tests on the basis that they were relevant for and biased toward white, middle-class students. Thus, students could not be labeled or "categorized" on the basis of "white," culturally unfair tests. *Hansen* v. *Hobson* set a precedent for the issue of cultural fairness in testing.

Mills v. *Board of Education* (1972): In this case, the court found that handicapped students had a right to a free and appropriate education and that it was unconstitutional for a school to exclude a handicapped student from such an appropriate education on the basis of the person's handicap. In addition, the court held that a handicapped student had the right to a "constructive education," which might include any specialized curriculum and instruction needed to make that education construc- tive. The case established the groundwork for due process hearings before any exclusion from school, termination, or classification into a special program took place. *Mills* v. *Board of Education* was clearly a landmark decision for the educational rights of the handicapped.

Diana v. *State Board of Education* (1970) and *Covarrubias* v. *San Diego Unified School District* (1971): Two landmark cases addressed the is- sues of inappropriate assessment leading to misclassification of students as handicapped or special needs. Both were settled out of court. In the first case the California Depart- ment of Education agreed to test all children whose native language was not English in *both* English and their primary language. It also agreed to reevaluate all Mexican–Ameri- can and Chinese students currently enrolled in classes for the "educable mentally re- tarded" using nonverbal items and testing them in their primary language. Finally, it agreed to eliminate culturally unfair items from its assessment tests and to develop IQ tests culturally fair to Mexican–American stu- dents and standardized on a Mexican–Ameri- can population. The Covarrubias case ex- tended the Diana decision by allowing plain- tiffs monetary damages as a result of being misclassified as mentally retarded.

Pennsylvania Association for Retarded Citizens v. *Commonwealth of Pennsylvania* (1971): This case was one of the most far-reaching deci- sions. Up until this time, any child in Pennsyl- vania judged by school district personnel to be "unable to profit from school attendance" could be excluded from school. In 1971, the Pennsylvania Association for Retarded Citi- zens (PARC) filed suit charging that exclusion of mentally retarded children from school was unconstitutional. After much negotiation, the parties settled out of court, with Pennsylva- nia's agreeing to do the following:

1. Locate and identify all handicapped pupils of school age.
2. Provide medical and psychological assess- ment and evaluation for all children excluded from school to determine best educational placement.
3. Provide a free public education for all handi- capped children residing in the state.
4. Reassess and evaluate all handicapped stu- dents currently enrolled in segregated educa- tional facilities.
5. Submit a plan of educational programs so that all handicapped children could be placed in appropriate programs.

A key aspect in *PARC* v. *Pennsylvania* (as well as in *Frederick, L.* v. *Thomas* (1976, 1977) was that the school was responsible for actively and appropriately screening and as- sessing students in order to identify and serve handicapped students.

The parents of handicapped children in Pennsylvania had won a landmark victory. But what about children in the other forty- nine states? The national legislation needed to protect their rights was not long in coming.

The Creation of Public Law 94-142

Background

In 1975, Congress passed Public Law 94-142. This comprehensive legislation provides full educational opportunity for more than eight million handicapped children, many of whom had previously been denied basic educational services. For the first time, the law provided the following rights to handicapped children of school age.

1. Appropriate screening and identification as- sessment.
2. Due process regarding classification, place- ment, and programming. This due process applied both to parents or guardians and to handicapped children.
3. Protection against discriminatory assess- ment.
4. Placement in the least restrictive educational environment (LRE).
5. An individualized educational program (IEP) for each handicapped child.

Many of us have heard so much about PL 94-142 and have grown so accustomed to its implementation that perhaps we have lost sight of its meanings and implications. However, each of the five provisions listed previously possessed implications for exceptional children that were earthshaking. To understand these implications, we must examine each provision.

Screening and Identification

PL 94-142 mandates that state departments of education are responsible for locating, assessing, and identifying all handicapped students in their states. In practice, however, states have usually assigned this task to local public school districts.

The identification of handicapped children involves *screening*. This means that children in a given school system must be adequately assessed in order to ascertain whether they *might* possess a handicap. Children who appear possibly to possess a handicap are referred for in-depth testing. Screened students determined not to possess a handicapping condition receive no further assessment.

Schools are responsible for developing a screening plan. Usually this plan entails a variety of formal and informal assessment procedures that are conducted by teachers and other school personnel. Such procedures may include quickly administered formal tests as well as checklists, observation forms, and interviews with people close to the child.

Due Process

Students thought to possess a handicap are referred for further assessment and come under the auspices of the due process procedures of PL 94-142. Due process refers to the concepts that a person's rights (in this case, the rights of both child and the parents) are procedurally protected and that the school system can take no action without the informed consent of all parties. In short, it provides protection for the student and the family. Following is a discussion of due process procedure under PL 94-142.

1. Notice of Referral. If the screening assessment indicates that the child may possess a handicapping condition, the child is then referred for further, in-depth assessment. At this time, parents must be informed in writing that the student has been so referred. The parents must also be informed if such assessment is contemplated for the purpose of possibly changing the child's educational program. Figure 2-1 is a notice of referral.

2. Information about Rights. Parents must be notified of their rights at the same time that they are informed that the school district wishes to assess their child. Parents have the right to refuse permission for assessment. They also have the right to participate in the assessment and to have input in any educational decisions made for their child. Parents have the right to request an independent evaluation from someone not employed by the school district, to inspect all of the child's records and test results, and to request a due process hearing if they disagree with the educational plan proposed for their child.

3. Permission to Assess. Parents must consent in writing to have their child assessed before any such assessment can take place. The permission form must be written in the parents' primary language and must possess clear, unambiguous language. It must contain an explanation of the procedures to be used, the safeguards undertaken to protect the child's rights, and the purposes for which the assessment information is being sought. The parents must also be told that they may refuse consent if they wish. Figure 2-2 contains a copy of a permission form used by a typical school district.

4. Independent Evaluation. If parents wish an independent evaluation, the school system must provide information as to where one can be obtained. This independent evaluation is to be free to the parents *if* they disagree with the school's evaluation *and* if the school system cannot prove that its evaluation was appropriate. Otherwise, an independent evaluation must be paid for by the parents. Regardless of who pays, the school system must consider the results of the independent evaluation in any educational decisions made for the child.

5. Access to School Records and Confidentiality of Assessment Results. Parents have the right

Figure 2-1   Notice of Referral

_____
(Date)

Dear Parent(s):

As was recently discussed with you, _____ has been
                                                    (Child's name)

referred for an individual evaluation to assist us in planning a better program for your child.

Enclosed are two copies of the Parent Permission for Evaluation form which describes the
reasons for the requested evaluation, and who will provide the evaluations.

PLEASE SIGN AND RETURN ONE COPY OF THE PARENT PERMISSION FORM IN THE
ENCLOSED ADDRESSED, STAMPED ENVELOPE.

Enclosed is a copy of the Information for Parents brochure which outlines YOUR RIGHTS AS A
PARENT. It also describes the next steps if you give permission for your child to be evaluated,
how the results will be used, and how the school will protect the confidentiality of the
information about your child. We are also enclosing a Special Education Eligibility Criteria
and Program/Services Description brochure.

Thank you for your cooperation. If you have any questions, or need additional information,
please contact _____, at _____.
                                                                         (Telephone)

                                                           Sincerely,

                                                           _____
                                                           (Name)   (Position)

Enclosures: Information for Parents brochure
                    Special Education Criteria/Programs brochure
                    Parent Permission Form (2 copies)

Copies: Central file, parent, building

Source: Hamilton City School System, Hamilton, Ohio. Used by permission.

Figure 2-2 Parent Consent Form

PARENT PERMISSION FOR EVALUATION

Name of Student _____ Birthdate _____

Building _____ Date _____

As part of our concern with the progress of every pupil in school, an evaluation has been proposed in order to gather information about the best learning situation for your child. This evaluation may include observations of your child, examination of school records, consultation with school staff, and administration of various educational and/or psychological tests. Please read the Information for Parents brochure which outlines in greater detail the evaluation procedures and your rights and responsibilities as a parent.

The following relates to your child's proposed evaluation:

1. Concise description of suspected problem.

   _____

   _____

2. Reason evaluation has been requested.

   _____

   _____

3. Persons who may conduct the evaluation.

   NAME   TITLE

   _____   _____

   _____   _____

This is to certify that I have received information concerning the proposed evaluation procedures, my rights as a parent, and the special education eligibility criteria and program services. I understand that the results of the evaluation will be shared with teachers, principal and other appropriate school personnel.

Check one and sign:

☐ I Hereby APPROVE of _____ being evaluated by
   designated school personnel.   (Name of child)

☐ I Hereby REFUSE permission to evaluate _____
   by designated school personnel.   (Name of child)

   _____   _____
              Date

                                        _____
                                        Signature(s)   (Parent, guardian)

If parent permission is refused, it would be helpful to school personnel if the reason(s) for not giving permission to evaluate could be provided.

_____

Source: Hamilton City School System, Hamilton, Ohio. Used by permission.

to see any school records concerning their child, and they must be advised of this right. If the parents disagree with any statements in the child's records they can request that the records be amended. The school must consider this request within a reasonable amount of time and respond. If this request is refused, the school system must advise the parents of their right to a hearing on this matter. All assessment records are considered strictly confidential. A child's records cannot be divulged to anyone except the parents without parental permission. A record must be kept of all people who view the child's assessment records.

6. Assessment Results. Parents must receive the results of the assessment regardless of whether the child is found to possess a handicapping condition. These results must be explained in a meeting of the parents, the professionals who participated in the assessment, and the student (if that is appropriate). Such a meeting must be held at a time convenient for the parents. Parents must be told in clear, easy-to-understand terms the results of the assessment, whether or not the child possesses a handicapping condition, and what educational services are contemplated. If special educational services are contemplated, an Individualized Education Plan (described later in this chapter) must be clearly outlined. Parents have the right to bring an adviser or legal counsel to the meeting.

7. Right of Approval or Disapproval. Parents have the right to approve or disapprove of the proposed educational program suggested by the school district. They must decide whether they agree or disagree with the classification the child has received, as well as whether they agree with the type of placement being offered (e.g., self-contained class, mainstreamed class, tutor, etc.). If the parents disagree with either the assessment results or the proposed program, they may request an impartial due process hearing. Likewise, if the parents refuse to approve the plan, the school district may request such a hearing.

If the parents approve the program, they must sign a permission form allowing the child to be placed in the agreed program and receive the agreed services. Figure 2-3 contains a sample of such an acceptance form.

The Due Process Hearing

When the parents and the school system cannot agree on the assessment procedure, results, or suggested educational placement, either side may request a due process hearing. Such a hearing involves a decision rendered by an impartial, qualified hearing officer who listens to both sides present their case.

Parents must be informed about free or low-cost legal representation before the hearing. At the hearing, both sides present evidence and both are allowed to cross-examine and call witnesses. All evidence to be presented must be disclosed to both parties at least five days before the hearing.

Following the decision of the hearing officer, either side may file an appeal with the State Department of Education. In such cases, the State Department of Education reviews the case and renders a decision. If either side is still dissatisfied with the outcome, civil action may be taken. During the due process procedures the child's educational program may not be changed.

Although these due process regulations may appear overly tedious and exacting, they do serve their intended purpose—the protection of the person's rights. For too long, school systems were able to act capriciously in rejecting educational services for any child they wished. Likewise, as we have seen in such court cases as *Hansen* v. *Hobson* and *Diana* v. *Board of Education,* schools often incorrectly classified students as handicapped and made decisions about their educational futures based on inappropriate assessments.

With the advent of due process procedures, this has changed. Now parents *must* be advised, at every step of the process, what is happening to their child, what might happen in the future, and of their rights under the law. After all, their child is being affected, and they deserve a say in their child's educational future. Due process assures that right.

Quality of the Assessment Procedure

A child's schooling is greatly affected by information revealed by the educational assessment. In fact, even the decision to refer the child for in-depth assessment is based on an initial screening assessment. Therefore, the

Figure 2-3   Parent Acceptance/Rejection of the Proposed Educational Program

XI.   IEP Conference Date _____

   Conference Participants:

_____
(Chairperson)   Name   Title

_____
   Name   Title

_____
   Name   Title

_____
   Name   Title

_____
   Name   Title

   ☐   I have reviewed the IEP and <u>accept</u> the Program and Placement recommendation.

   ☐   I <u>do not accept</u> the program and placement recommendation.

   ☐   I agree to waive my right to notification of placement by certified mail.

_____   _____
      Date   Signature of Parent

                                     _____

Current laws mandate that handicapped children be re-evaluated by an assessment team at least once every three years. This is to notify you that your child will be re-evaluated during the school year _____.

Source: Hamilton City School System, Hamilton, Ohio. Used by permission.

educational assessment should be of high quality and contain a minimum amount of error
(what constitutes error is discussed in the next
chapter).

Quality of assessment means that the assessment should be fair, objective, and nondiscriminatory. It must not discriminate against
the child on the basis of race, culture, language, or ethnic background. In other words,
it cannot penalize the child because of the
environment in which the child operates.

The last two decades have seen a growing
awareness among educators and psychologists
that certain assessment instruments have been
unfair to culturally diverse children. This
means that it has been found that some tests
ask questions solely within the life experience
of white, middle-class children and discriminate against the knowledge and experiences of
minority children. In such cases, when minority children do not perform well on a test, we
might infer that their intellectual functioning is
suspect rather than conclude that the test itself
may have been unfair.

To understand how difficult it is to succeed
on tests based on information that is unknown
to you because of your cultural background,
try answering the test items in Table 2-2, which
is based on knowledge an inner-city youth
might possess. How would you do on these
items? What if you were told that based on
your poor results you had been diagnosed as
mentally retarded and would be assigned to a
special education class? How would you feel?

Probably you would protest that the test
was unfair—that it asked you questions you
had no way of knowing. And you would be
absolutely right. But that was (and often is)
precisely the problem with some assessment
instruments administered to culturally diverse
students. These students are penalized for
what they cannot possible know, given their
cultural background.

To insure against misdiagnosis based on an
unfair assessment, PL 94-142 specifies the following eight assessment guidelines:

Table 2-2 Examples of Items from a
Culturally Different Intelligence Test

1. "Showing your colors" refers to: (a) demonstrating racial pride, (b) demonstrating cow-
   ardice, (c) demonstrating bravery, (d) wear-
   ing your gang jacket.
2. "Doing a line" refers to: (a) using cocaine,
   (b) performing a dance, (c) standing in a po-
   lice line-up, (d) waiting for your unemploy-
   ment check.
3. "Deuce-and-a-quarter" refers to: (a) twenty-
   seven cents, (b) a game of craps, (c) fifty
   cents, (d) an Oldsmobile Electra 225.
4. "Mother's Day" refers to (a) the second Sunday in May, (b) the day after Christmas, (c)
   the first and fifteenth of each month, (d) the
   third Sunday in August.
5. A man's "blood" refers to (a) the liquid in his
   veins and arteries, (b) a black brother, (c) a
   true friend, (d) a street fight.

Answers: 1(d), 2(a), 3(d), 4(c), 5(b).

1. That the assessment instruments selected be
   chosen and administered in such a way as to
   be culturally fair and nondiscriminatory.
2. That the test be administered in the child's
   native language.
3. That the test giver be specifically trained to
   administer the test as well as be familiar with
   the child's cultural background.
4. That the test be valid for the specific purposes for which it is being used.
5. That the assessment instruments be tailored
   to assess specific needs rather than test a single (global) type of intellectual functioning
   (e.g., IQ).
6. That no *single* test be used as the sole criterion for determining educational placement.
7. That the evaluation be made by a miltidisci-
   plinary team, including at least one teacher
   who possesses detailed knowledge of the suspected disability.
8. That the child be assessed in all areas relative to the suspected disability, including
   health, perception, social status, emotional
   health, general intelligence, academic performance, communication, and motor abilities.

In summary, PL 94-142 mandates that the
assessment be fair. It cannot penalize a child
on the basis of language or culture, nor can a

child be diagnosed as possessing a disability on the basis of one (possibly unfair) test administered by one person. If we are going to base so much of a child's educational programming on the assessment being performed, that assessment must be sound. Nothing less can be tolerated.

Least Restrictive Setting

PL 94-142 mandates that children with special needs be placed in educational programs most closely approximating those of their nonhandicapped peers. That is, whenever possible, exceptional students should be placed in educational settings that maximize their integrated contact with nonhandicapped pupils. Additionally, children with special needs should be placed in the *least restrictive environment* (LRE). This involves placing students in a learning situation that offers the most latitude and freedom to experience, interact, and learn.

The concept of LRE has caused much confusion regarding the most appropriate placement for exceptional children. Contrary to some opinion, LRE does *not* always mean mainstreaming, that is, placing every child in a regular class with nonhandicapped peers. Rather, LRE involves taking into account the unique cognitive, social, and emotional characteristics of each child and placing students in an educational environment that can best facilitate their educational needs. For some individuals, LRE might mean a self-contained class in an integrated public school. For others, it might necessitate a self-contained day school (rather than a residential facility). For these individuals, a fully mainstreamed placement might not be appropriate.

Individual Education Programs

PL 94-142 mandates that an Individualized Educational Program (IEP) be developed for each exceptional learner. This IEP must possess the following six components:

1. A statement of the child's level of educational performance.
2. A statement of annual goals stated in behavioral terms.
3. These annual goals translated into short-term instructional objectives.
4. A statement of the specific educational services to be provided for the child.
5. The projected date of initiation and the duration of these services.
6. The specific criteria and evaluation procedures for determining that these goals are being achieved.

Current Level of Educational Performance: An assessment of a child's current level of educational performance is usually accomplished by in-depth achievement testing in which a student's academic performance is compared to that of peers. By making such comparisons (usually in the form of age- or grade-level performance), we can readily ascertain the areas of a student's academic achievement deficiencies.

Figure 2-4 shows the levels of current educational performance indicated by a student's IEP. This IEP section lists the achievement tests that were used as well as summary information regarding the child's performance on the tests. It also includes the dates of test administration.

A Statement of Annual Goals: The statement of annual goals reflects the educational levels at which the child will be operating at the end of the school year (or the next IEP evaluation period, whichever comes first). These goals represent the relatively few, long-range, summary behaviors that we predict the student will accomplish. They represent observable behaviors the student will accomplish at the end of the IEP's life span.

Short-Term Objectives: Short-term objectives explain how the annual goals will be reached. They are the means-to-the-end, se-

Figure 2-4 Current Levels of Educational Functioning Taken from an IEP

INDIVIDUALIZED EDUCATION PROGRAM

School Year   1988 (Fall)

Name Robbie _____   Birthdate August 5, 1978 Age 10 _____   Date May 10, 1988 _____

Parents _____   Address _____   Phone _____

District of Residence   Lincoln _____   County Butler _____   Building   Hayes Hall _____

I. Evelutions Completed/
   Information Gathered

II. Present Levels of Performance in the following areas:

1) Intelligence, 2) Academic Performance, 3) Social/Emotional Status, 4) Adaptive Behavior, 5) Learning Modality, 6) Communicative Status, 7) Other.

Math:
   Wide Range Achievement Test
   (date: Nov. 30)
   Key Math
   (date: Nov. 30)
   Peabody Individual Achievement Test (date: Dec. 2)

Reading:
   Wide Range Achievement Test
   (date: Nov. 30)
   Peabody Individual Achievement Test (date: Dec. 2)
   Woodcock Reading Mastery
   (date: Dec. 2)

Spelling:
   Wide Range Achievement Test
   (date: Nov. 30)
   Peabody Individual Achievement Test (date: Dec. 2)
   Test of Written Spelling
   (date: Dec. 2)

1. The student has demonstrated the following grade placement scores on the listed tests. Math: WRAT (3.5), Key Math (3.6), PIAT (2.5). Reading: WRAT (3.2), PIAT (1.8 reading recognition; 2.8 reading comprehension), Woodcock (2.3). Spelling: WRAT (2.7), PIAT (2.9), TWS (1.9 total, 2.0 predictable, less than 2.4 unpredictable).

2. Academic Performance: On Robbie's last report card (Oct. 1988), he received "B's" in spelling and math and "C's" in reading and science. He is in the middle reading group in his class. It is his second year in the second grade and his grades are improving dramatically.

3. Social/Emotional Status: No problem.

4. Adaptive Behavior: No problem.

5. Learning Modality: Robbie is in the regular classroom and he is in the LD tutor room for 45 minutes two times/week, plus is tutored for 90 minutes two times/week at the University.

6. Communicative Status: Robbie has no speech problems, although he does not speak in class often.

---

quenced objectives that culminate in the accomplishment of each annual goal. Examples of annual goals and short-term, sequenced objectives leading to the achievement of those goals are shown in the reading section of a sample IEP in Figure 2-5.

Statement of Specified Educational Services: The IEP must specify in detail the educational services the child will receive in order to reach the annual goals. Such services include class placement as well as special services such as speech and language training, adaptive physi-

Figure 2-5 Annual Goals and Short-Term Objectives of a Child's IEP

Annual Goals	Short-Term Instructional Objectives	Evaluation Procedures and Criteria
1. Robbie completes multiplication problems up to and including the three times table.	1a. Given concrete objects and verbal prompts, Robbie will orally compute multiplication problems in the three times table with 90% accuracy.	90% accuracy on daily teacher-made activities.
	1b. Given multiplication problems in the three times table, Robbie will write the answer of each problem in 5 sec. or less with 90% accuracy.	90% accuracy with 5 sec./problem as observed by teacher.
Reading: 1. Robbie increases speed of reading at second grade level, reading fluently and accurately.	1a. Given a 2.2 passage, Robbie will repeatedly read the passage until he reads 175 words/minute with three trials daily and less than 2 errors/minute.	Precision teaching chart.
	1b. Given a 2.8 passage, Robbie will repeatedly read the passage until he reads 175 words/minute with three trials daily and no more than 2 errors/minute.	Precision teaching chart after 1a is met.
2. Robbie reads regular words phonetically, orally.	2a. Given lists of phonetically regular words, Robbie will read the words orally by breaking them into syllables, with 95% accuracy.	Daily teacher-made activities.
	2b. Given lists of phonetically regular words with blends, Robbie will read the words with 90% accuracy.	Daily made activities and teacher observation.
3. Robbie comprehends silently read passages at the second grade level.	3a. Given passages from a 2.2 reader and instructed to read silently, Robbie will answer specific and general comprehension questions pertaining to the passage with 90% accuracy.	Daily teacher-made observation.
4. Robbie listens to and comprehends orally read stories.	4a. After being read a story by the teacher, Robbie will answer comprehension questions about the story with 100% accuracy.	Teacher observation.

cal therapy, and occupational therapy. The description of the services provided becomes the basis for the child's academic program, with the professionals providing these services joining the child's educational team. The team ap-proach to providing special education services is discussed in detail in Chapter 4.

Projected Dates of Initiation and Duration of Services: The IEP must list the initiation date for the services as well as the duration of these services. These dates effectively define the life span of the current IEP and give all parties a clear understanding as to when reevaluation of the IEP will occur.

The IEP initiation and duration dates serve several purposes. By clearly specifying when reevaluation will occur, they make the issue of program review and reevaluation relatively automatic. These dates also provide team members a reasonable time in which to reach the long-term goals. The parties involved realize that these goals will not be achieved tomorrow, but they will take time. Finally, initiation and duration dates strongly demonstrate that the IEP is temporary. That is, devising an IEP for a learner and providing certain educational services does not condemn the student to a lifetime of receiving these services. Rather, educators adopt a wait-and-see attitude indicating that the educational program for the student will be modified as learning and other variables warrant.

The Purpose behind IEPs: The key word underlying the concept of the IEP is *accountability*. Accountability is not blame or finger pointing when the student does not reach stated goals. Rather, it involves making educators responsible for creating meaningful, relevant, and attainable curricula for children with special needs and for implementing these programs in educationally sound ways. Educational programs for exceptional children can no longer be confused with baby-sitting services. As one parent of a mentally retarded child said, "Schools can't issue a life's supply of crayons when the child enters school and collect them again when he graduates." Rather, PL 94-142 mandates that professionals state unequivocally what they expect exceptional students to accomplish while they attend school.

IEPs challenge educators to devise meaningful, valid curriculum programs and to teach them. Educators are asked to use their expertise to predict what the student should and will learn and are held accountable for those judgments. If students do not achieve those goals, educators are asked (not accused) what went wrong and how instruction can be modified in order to reach those goals. Thus, the onus of responsibility is taken away from the students; they cannot be blamed for poor learning because they are handicapped. Rather, the responsibility for their appropriate learning is laid squarely where it belongs, on the professional's doorstep.

SUMMARY

Although the first incidence of assessment dates back to almost 2200 B.C. and continued through European history, assessment really developed at the close of the nineteenth century, when Binet was hired to develop tests to identify mentally retarded students in the Paris schools. Binet developed the first intelligence test and devised the IQ based on the average child's mental and chronological ages.

In the United States, the concept of assessment changed from individual to large-scale (group) testing. During World War I, Otis developed the Army Alpha, a group intelligence test. The results of the Army Alpha test shocked many people. Based on the results, repressive legislation was passed regarding restrictive immigration, forced sterilization, and prohibitions against interracial marriages.

From World War II to the present, tests have continually become more sophisticated in terms of the quality of the instruments and the technology that the tests and their support systems use. Additionally, the last quarter-century has seen great acceptance of tests by the general population, with testing becoming institutionalized into the fabric of American life. The specialization of testing has developed into the field of psychometrics while the technology of assessment has also advanced. Assessment has been accepted by most Americans as a fact of life, with virtually every individual being assessed educationally and psychologically at some time.

The field of special education has experienced peaks and valleys. Humane services for handicapped persons can be traced to seventeenth-century Europe, in general, and particularly to France where such physicians as Itard, Pinel, and Seguin attempted to assess and humanistically educate handicapped children. During the 1800s, Americans became increasingly aware of special education and developed specialized schools for educating exceptional individuals. During the years between World Wars I and II, however, the treatment of handicapped individuals became more repressive, with public educational services being denied many handicapped persons. Not until parents formed political advocacy groups for the handicapped did the educational climate for exceptional learners begin to change.

During the 1960s and early 1970s, advocacy groups and parents litigated to improve the lives of and educational services for handicapped persons. It was generally found that handicapped children were entitled to an appropriate public education as well as nondiscriminatory assessment. However, until 1975, there was no national legislation covering the assessment and education of handicapped students.

PL 94-142, passed in 1975, constituted the first national legislation. It requires full educational opportunity for handicapped children, many of whom had previously been denied educational services. PL 94-142 provides for (1) appropriate screening and identification; (2) due process in regard to assessment, placement, and programming; (3) protection against discriminatory assessment; (4) placement in the least restrictive environment; and (5) an individualized educational program.

Screening and identification require the state to identify all handicapped children in need of special educational services. This job is usually left to school districts and involves screening procedures with referral of individuals who indicate a possible handicapping condition.

Due process refers to the rights exceptional children and their parents or guardians possess in the referral, assessment, placement, and programming procedures. These rights include notice of referral, information about rights, permission for assessment, independent evaluation, parental access to school records, confidentiality of assessment results, access to assessment results, and approval or disapproval of educational placement.

PL 94-142 mandates quality assessment procedures. This means that the assessment must be administered and evaluated in a fair, nondiscriminatory way that does not penalize the child regarding handicaps or cultural background. To accomplish these goals, a number of guidelines must be followed.

The education of exceptional students must take place in the least restrictive environment (LRE), one that offers the most latitude and freedom to experience, interact with peers, and learn. LRE represents the educational setting in which children can operate to the best of their potential. A variety of educational placements are open to special needs learners.

Individualized education programs (IEPs) are mandated for exceptional learners. Each IEP contains a statement of the child's current educational levels, a statement of annual goals and short-term objectives, a listing of the specific educational services to be provided, the projected dates of initiation and duration of service, and specific criteria and evaluation procedures for determining whether goals have been reached. IEPs infer accountability, not blame. They represent best-guess estimates as to where the student will be educationally after a given period of instruction. If these goals are not reached, the curriculum, instructional methods, and materials may have to be modified accordingly.

STUDY QUESTIONS

1. Outline the history of educational assessment. When did educational assessment really come into its own? Why?

2. Describe in your own words Binet's concept for identifying intellectually deficient children. What is the relationship between chronological and mental age? How is mental age determined?

3. Outline the historical changes in assessment philosophy and practice in the United States. How did this change in philosophy reflect American ideals and beliefs? Were they democratic or undemocratic? Defend your answer.

4. Outline the history of special education during the last 150 years. How does this history relate to the history of assessment during this same period?

5. Describe the major components of PL 94-142. How do they operate? What safeguards are built into the law to protect each of the following: students, parents, school system, professionals?

6. A school wishes to refer a student for in-depth assessment. What procedures and rules must the school system follow? If the parents refuse permission, what recourse does the school have?

7. Describe an IEP meeting in terms of who should be there, what should be discussed, and what programmatic changes should take place. What happens if the parties cannot agree on these changes? Describe the process for resolving such conflicts.

8. Describe an IEP. What should it contain? In what form? Give examples of sound annual goals and short-term objectives designed to reach those goals.

9. Take an annual goal and task analyze it. Is your task analysis adequate? Defend your answer.

10. Imagine you are an attorney bringing suit against the school system, arguing that minorities are disproportionately represented in special education programs. What evidence would you use? What would your arguments be regarding educational assessment?

11. Assume you are the defense attorney in this case. What would your arguments be for the defendants? Be as specific as possible.

CHAPTER 3

Types of Tests and Their Uses

Robert, an eighth grader, came to the university reading clinic during the summer months. Robert's junior high school status was unusual because most students who came to the clinic were in elementary school. Nevertheless, Robert was at the clinic and in need of remediation.

Robert's reading behavior was also unusual. When he was administered a battery of diagnostic reading tests, he performed *four years* below grade level. Most students enrolled at the clinic were reading one or two years below grade level; a student reading four years below grade level was astonishing. At first, it was suspected that the clinic's test results were in error, but when the battery was repeated, the results were the same.

Robert's cumulative school record was requested, and what the record contained was shocking. Almost from the first grade, Robert's report card grades were consistently poor. Nearly all of his grades in language arts subjects ranged from *C* minus to *D* plus. Only twice in six years had he received a grade in language arts as high as *B* minus. Yet Robert had never repeated a grade, nor had he ever repeated a language arts unit of instruction. He was passed on to each subsequent language arts unit without remotely mastering the previous material.

How could this happen? If the learning of subsequent material depends on the mastery of earlier information, why had he never been "sent back" to master the earlier material?

Robert's case is not unique. Considering the way many school systems use tests, test results, and grades, Robert's case, although severe, is very common.

Two Purposes of Evaluation: Summative and Formative

Robert's plight stemmed from the way that tests and grades were used to evaluate his school performance. Basically, there are two methods of evaluation—*summative* and *formative*.

Summative Evaluation

Summative evaluation is a way of summing up or giving a final summary of learning (Howell, Kaplan, and O'Connell 1979a; Scriven 1967). It occurs after a unit of instruction has been completed, usually for the purpose of giving a grade or deciding the percentage of material learned. An example of a summative system is a school grading or marking period. Usually this period lasts anywhere from six to ten weeks. At the end of this period, a summary grade for each subject is entered on the student's report card. This grade reflects how much the student has learned during this time period.

In a summative system, evaluation is used to create a grade distribution for students. However, after the summary grades are given, all students move on to the next unit of instruction. This is what happened to Robert during his eight years of school. With summative evaluation, test results typically are not used in any diagnostic or remediational manner. Such evaluation merely sums up learning as the student moves to the next learning level. The summative evaluation model is depicted in Figure 3-1.

Formative Evaluation

In formative evaluation, testing is frequent and intermittent, occurring after each brief period of instruction. Formative evaluation ascertains whether the student has mastered a small unit of instruction before allowing the learner to enter the next small instructional sequence (Howell et al. 1979a; Scriven 1967). Students who have not mastered a unit of learning are *not* allowed to advance to the next unit. Rather, the failed unit is retaught or modified to optimize learning. Thus, formative evaluation is ongoing, occurring often at the end of every lesson or class period. When formative evaluation indicates lack of learning, remedial instructional procedures are immediately instituted. A formative evaluation model is shown in Figure 3-1.

Types of Assessment Instruments

Assessment information can be used in various ways that have real-world implications for the education of students. Thus, choosing the right types of assessment instruments and using them appropriately are crucially important issues for test consumers.

Informed test consumerism initially may appear difficult or even impossible. There are hundreds of different assessment instruments on the market, each purporting to be the perfect instrument. The variety is enough to cause confusion and even resignation for teachers wishing to choose and use tests wisely.

However, understanding assessment can be simplified somewhat if the myriad of assessment instruments are placed within a 2 × 2 framework, with *referencing* as one factor and *specificity of information* as the other. This model, as well as examples of tests that might fall into each cell, is shown in Table 3-1.

Referencing

It was time for the first open school night of the school year. Mrs. Jackson, a second-grade

Figure 3-1 Summative and Formative Evaluation Models

Summative Evaluation

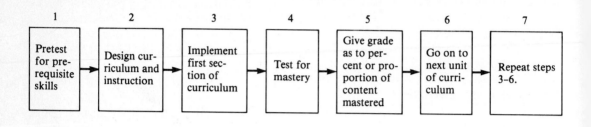

Formative Evaluation

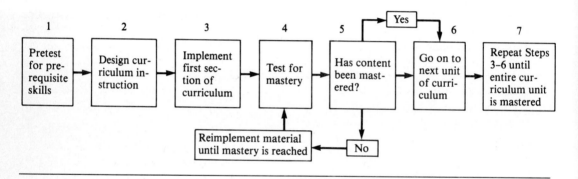

Table 3-1 The 2 × 2 Factorial Model of Test Referencing and Specificity

	Global Tests	Diagnostic Tests
Norm-Referenced	Peabody Picture Vocabulary Test Wide-Range Achievement Test California Achievement Tests	Woodcock Reading Mastery Tests–Revised Stanford Diagnostic Reading test Stanford Diagnostic Arithmetic Test KeyMath Diagnostic Arithmetic Test
Criterion-Referenced	None	Stanford Diagnostic Reading Test Stanford Diagnostic Arithmetic Test SRA Math Probes Diagnosis: An Instructional Aid, Reading

teacher, carefully laid out each student's work in packets on the child's desk for parents to inspect. She was sure that as parents inspected their child's work and noted the progress they would be proud of and satisfied with that child's performance.

However, most of the parents were unhappy. After inspecting their child's work, almost every parent approached Mrs. Jackson with the same question. Although they were glad to see their child making progress, they wanted to know how their child was doing relative to the other children in the class. Was their child above or below "normal" for the class?

Mrs. Jackson and the parents were communicating on different wavelengths. Mrs. Jackson wanted to discuss each child's progress and show how each one was mastering subject matter skills. Parents, on the other hand, wanted to know how their child was doing in comparison to other children. Their satisfaction with their child's educational progress seemed dependent on the progress of the other children in the class. To them, the information that Mrs. Jackson was giving was incomplete. What was she trying to hide?

The issue between Mrs. Jackson and the parents was one of *referencing*. Referencing is the comparison of a child's score to other scores. Without such comparisons, interpretation of results is extremely difficult (Clift and Imrie 1981; Worthen and Sanders 1973).

Norm-Referenced Tests: There are two types of referencing, *norm-referencing* and *criterion-referencing*. In norm-referenced testing, an individual's score is compared against test results of peers. This peer group can be the other children in the class or some distant norm or sample group, whose scores are contained in the test manual. In either case, the individual's score is compared to the test scores of peers and placed in a distribution or continuum. For this reason, norm-referenced tests are considered "between people" assessments (Clift and Imrie 1981; Shepard 1979).

Norm-referenced tests yield a variety of information and are legitimate for certain purposes. Typically, they help answer whether a child's performance is so different from that of peers that further assessment is warranted, and they aid in curriculum planning decisions. Table 3-2 (A) lists the advantages and disadvantages of norm-referenced tests.

Table 3-2 Advantages and Disadvantages of Norm-Referenced and Criterion-Referenced Tests

A. *Norm-Referenced Tests*
  Advantages
  1. Aid in classifying students.
  2. Select students for fixed quota requirements.
  3. Reveal how much a student has achieved compared to others.

  Disadvantages
  1. Do not indicate general mastery; only mastery *relative* to the mastery of others is revealed.
  2. Because grades do not signify a definite amount of knowledge, interpretation regarding standards is difficult.
  3. Tend to diminish motivation, especially for students accustomed to suffer when compared with peers.

B. *Criterion-Referenced Tests*
  Advantages
  1. Individualize evaluation of students.
  2. Diagnose student difficulties.
  3. Indicate mastery of material.
  4. Certify competency.
  5. Do not establish fixed quotas.

  Disadvantages
  1. Tell us what the student knows but not in relation to peers.
  2. Unrealistic for teachers to expect mastery by all students.
  3. Sometimes difficult to interpret test results succinctly.
  4. Difficult to devise a grading system using these tests.

Criterion-Referenced Tests: Criterion-referenced tests measure the child's learning against some objective criterion or standard, not against the achievement of others (Kaplan and Saccuzzo 1982; Lin 1980). Whereas norm-referenced tests measure how John does in relation to Sally (and everyone else in the class), criterion-referenced tests assess the extent to which John has mastered material and the improvement he has made based on the defined criterion.

Criterion-referenced tests are particularly appropriate in helping teachers plan learning programs for individual children. They tell precisely where the child is operating and suggest areas that need remediation. Items on criterion-referenced tests are often linked to specific instructional objectives. Such linkage allows the teacher to diagnose each student's learning problems. Because criterion-referenced tests treat each student as an individual, these tests measure "within person" learning. Table 3-2 (B) indicates how criterion-referenced tests satisfy various assessment concerns.

Validating the Criterion of Criterion-Referenced Tests: Suppose there was a test entitled the Zippy Test of Functional Mathematics that measured the daily, functional arithmetic skills people need every day. Now suppose that each item on the test dealt with calculus (not an everyday, functional math skill for most people). Would the criteria for this criterion-referenced test be appropriate? Probably not.

On the other hand, suppose that the objectives for this test actually dealt with functional math but were not constructed in acceptable behavioral form (e.g., the child will know how to add). Again, the criteria for this criterion-referenced test would be inadequate.

These two examples illustrate that a criterion-referenced test is only as strong as the criteria and objectives on which it is based. A criterion-referenced test that possesses criteria that are not useful, practical, or valid cannot yield meaningful information on what the child can and cannot do. Likewise, tests containing objectives that are poorly designed or contain nonprecise language cannot offer information as to whether the child has reached that objective. For these reasons, the informed test consumer should check both the appropriateness and the preciseness of criteria and objectives before adopting any criterion-referenced test.

Setting Acceptable Performance Levels in Criterion-Referenced Tests: Creating criterion-referenced tests requires that an acceptable level of learning (criteria) be established *before* students take the test (Brown 1983; Lin 1980). This raises the question of how high (or low) acceptable levels of performance should be.

Proponents of the mastery learning concept (Block and Burns 1976; Bloom 1976) have asserted that levels of acceptable learning performance should be extremely high or at mastery. In fact, many educational professionals believe that acceptable levels of learning and performance should be at a *minimum* of 85 percent. Their argument holds that no one wants a doctor who mastered only 75 percent of medicine or an airplane pilot who received a flying score of only 80 percent. Likewise, educators argue that "passing" a student on to subtraction who has mastered only 70 percent of the material on addition ensures future academic failure (as in the case of Robert described earlier in this chapter). Thus, criterion-referenced testing must be formative in nature and possess mastery levels of acceptable performance. Figure 3-2 shows how criterion-referenced and norm-referenced academic performance can be reported.

Specificity of Test Information

The other variable in our 2×2 model of assessment instruments is specificity of test informa-

Figure 3-2 A Sample Norm-Referenced and Criterion-Referenced Report Card

Norm-Referenced

Name: Maria Cervantes	Grade 6	Quarter	Year
		1 2 3 4	*1988–89*

Subject	Achievement Level	Effort
Language Arts	1	1
Social Studies	1	1
Arithmetic	2	2
Reading	1	1
P.E.	P	2
Music	P	1
Art	P	1

Code		Effort	
1 =	Above grade level	1 =	Above average
2 =	At grade level	2 =	Average
3 =	Below grade level	3 =	Below average
P =	Pass		
F =	Fail		

Criterion-Referenced

Arithmetic Skill	Date Mastered *(85% level)*

Concepts
A. Community property of addition — 9/24
B. Place value — 10/1

Computational Skills
A. Addition
  Adds two-digit numbers — 10/5
  Knows number facts 10–19 — 10/5
  Adds two-digit numbers while carrying — 10/15
B. Measurement
  Reads clock (analog and digital) — 10/1
  Understands dollar value — 10/7

tion. This refers to the depth and amount of specific information contained in test score information. Tests are usually either *global* or *diagnostic* in nature. Global tests yield unitary, general information about the test taker that is represented by one or two general scores (e.g., a child's overall reading score or grade level). Diagnostic tests, on the other hand, yield a great deal of specific information about a child's performance in a given area. For example, a diagnostic reading test would contain not only information about the child's general reading ability (e.g., grade level) but also infor-

mation about performance in specific reading areas (e.g., word attack, sight words, different types of comprehension). In general, diagnostic tests are more useful in identifying student strengths and weaknesses than are their global counterparts, and they yield more useful programming and remediation information than do global tests.

Formal versus Informal Tests

Formal tests are standardized, commercially available assessment instruments. At the opposite end of the spectrum are informal or teacher-made tests. Informal tests are common in education and are used at virtually every grade level from kindergarten through college (Fleming and Chambers 1983; Gage and Berliner 1984; Hammill and Bartel 1982).

Both types of tests have advantages and disadvantages. By using a commercially available test, the teacher (if he or she is an informed test consumer and test manual reader) is assured that the test has been well constructed, that it has a demonstrated reliability and validity, and that items have been properly constructed and standardized. These tests also usually have adequate and appropriate norms against which to compare a child's score.

However, because a formal, commercially available test is constructed for a large (usually national) market, quite probably it will not precisely mirror the content that the teacher covered in class. Likewise, the group on which the formal test was standardized must differ in some ways from the individual students who take the test.

Informal tests have the advantage of being specific to the content and the children in the individual classroom (Lazar-Morrison, Polin, Moy, and Burry 1980; Yeh 1980). After all, who knows more about the content that is covered and the students in the classroom than the person teaching the children each day? The major disadvantage of teacher-made tests is that they usually have not been standardized, normed, and pilot tested to the extent of formal tests; the burden of such responsibility falls on the classroom teacher. If teachers are using informal, teacher-made tests to a great extent (thus greatly affecting the educational lives of their students), shouldn't these tests be as well constructed and sound as their formal counterparts (Fleming and Chambers 1983; Quinto and McKenna 1977)? The construction of good teacher-made tests is discussed in Chapters 11 and 12.

Other Dimensions on Which Tests Differ

Aptitude versus Achievement Tests

Aptitude tests are tests of psychological function or ability. They measure innate abilities or potentials rather than what the student has learned (Gage and Berliner 1984). Two examples of aptitude are intelligence and artistic ability because these two variables are thought to be innate rather than learned. Achievement tests measure performance that is a result of learning. Thus, measuring school learning would be an example of an achievement test.

Sometimes the distinction between achievement and aptitude becomes inexact (Anastasi 1980a; Ebel 1980; Green 1974). For example, even though most intelligence tests purport to be aptitude tests, an inspection of many of the test items indicates that they really measure past learning (achievement). Some psychologists have used the distinction that aptitude tests predict future behavior whereas achievement tests measure the results of previous training (Becker 1974; Carroll 1974). However, this distinction still begs the question because it is possible for predictive tests to contain items that require the learning of previously presented information.

Some psychologists have suggested using the term *developed abilities* rather than distinguishing between tests of aptitude and achievement (Anastasi 1980a; Cronbach 1970). This term represents a continuum with tests that place maximum emphasis on direct training (subject matter proficiency) at one end and tests that reflect maximum innate or untrained abilities (e.g., perception or analytical reasoning) at the other. However, it is important to remember that in any aptitude test under discussion, to some extent, past learning is being measured. Likewise, in any achievement test, the ability (aptitude) to learn is also being indirectly assessed.

Group versus Individual Tests

The category of group versus individual tests refers to the number of people who take the test at any one time. A group test involves more than one test taker at a time (in fact, the group may be quite large). With an individual test, the ratio of test taker to test administrator must be one to one. In a group test, the test taker reads or is read the instructions, with subsequently little opportunity for clarification. During an individually administered test, instructions can be rephrased or clarified to the extent that the test administration procedures allow.

The choice between using an individual or a group test is often determined by the characteristics of the test taker. For example, group tests require strong reading or listening skills. They also require the test taker to follow directions and work well independently—skills in which special needs learners often are deficient. Thus, group-testing procedures often penalize special needs students, and the subsequent interpretation of these students' test scores can be difficult because a poor score may indicate either a lack of subject-matter knowledge or poor test-taking ability.

Individual tests allow the test examiner to probe student skills in ways that are not possible with group tests. With individual tests, cues and prompts can be supplied by the tester (as much as test administration procedures allow). Additionally, individual tests usually supply more diagnostic information than group tests do, and this information can be translated into educational programming for special needs learners. For these reasons, individual tests are usually preferable to group tests when working with exceptional children.

Speed versus Power Tests

Have you ever walked away from a test frustrated that you knew the material but did not have adequate time to finish the exam? If so, then you have experienced the problems of a *speed* test, a test having a limited time period in which to finish. Some tests are highly speeded, that is, the test items are relatively easy but the time allowed to finish the test is severely constrained (e.g., twenty minutes to complete eighty multiple-choice questions), and there is a strong penalty for incorrect answers.

On the other hand, the author once took a statistics test and was given three hours to finish. However, it did not matter—the test was so difficult that the students could have spent five hours and they still would not have answered the questions correctly. This was a severe *power* test, a test that allows students enough time to finish but that has test items of moderate to extreme difficulty.

Most tests are at least partially speeded, having a time limit by which the test must be completed. However, strongly speeded tests should be avoided for exceptional learners. To be successful on a speeded test, the test taker must be a good and a fast reader. Additionally, severely speeded tests force the test taker to think quickly, accurately, and unemotionally—traits in which many special needs learners experience difficulties. Thus, if a special needs learner does poorly on a severely speeded test we cannot be sure whether the test taker did not know the test material or the speeded nature of the test caused the problem. For these reasons, exceptional learners should be given adequate time to finish any tests they take.

What Tests Can and Cannot Tell Us

Achievement, Diagnostic, and Predictive Tests

Tests have three basic functions. First, they can tell us in a general (global) sense where the child is currently operating, that is, how the child is doing overall. Second, tests provide an in-depth understanding of how the child is operating in any given area. A test can not only tell us that the child is experiencing academic difficulties but can also describe precisely in what subareas the child is experiencing those difficulties. Finally, tests can make predictions (best guesses) as to what the academic future might hold for the child if remediation, or at least a change in educational program, is not imminent.

Different types of tests achieve these three functions. An achievement test can describe a child's overall, global functioning. Examples of such tests are the Wide-Range Achievement Test, the Metropolitan Achievement Test, and some informal, teacher-made achievement tests. To give us an in-depth knowledge of the child's strengths and weaknesses, there are diagnostic tests, such as the KeyMath Arithmetic Test and the Woodcock Reading Mastery Tests. Finally, predictive tests give us a best guess estimate of how someone will do in the future if things remain unchanged. For example, the Scholastic Aptitude Test (SAT) purports to predict how high school students will do in college.

What Tests Cannot Do

With this functions in mind, it is possible to say what tests can do. But there are things that tests cannot legitimately do, including:

1. Predict the future.
2. Tell us what decisions should be made.
3. Weigh efficiency versus humane allocation of resources in decision making.
4. Tell us what should be done with test results.

Tests can only give us information. What we do with that information will always be a distinctly human decision.

Basic Assumptions of Tests

Like statistics, tests can usually be used and interpreted in many ways. As mentioned in Chapter 2, tests historically have been used to make humane decisions about children's education as well as to restrict immigration of certain cultural groups. They have also been used to exclude children from programs and as a basis of racism. In short, tests are only as sound as the person(s) using them.

Certain assumptions underlie all tests. To the extent that these assumptions are understood and met by test givers, test interpretation will be sound. If these assumptions are violated, test results may be worthless or even injurious to the test taker. Let us examine some basic assumptions.

The Person Giving the Test Is Skilled and Well Trained

Certain tests require so much specialized training to administer that only certified, licensed personnel (e.g., school psychologists or clinical psychologists) can administer them. Other tests require moderate or even minimal training. However, regardless of the test being administered, it is assumed that the test giver is trained and familiar with that test's administration, scoring, and interpretation procedures. A single mistake during any one of these phases can invalidate the test and render the results virtually useless.

The implications of this discussion should be clear. *When you administer a test, know what you are doing.* The test administrator should read the test manual carefully before giving the test and should be acquainted with procedures and rules. It is also advisable to practice with someone before administering the test to the target child. This dry run can reveal possible pitfalls or mistakes that can then be avoided in the actual test-giving situation. In summary, preparation and training *before* test administration is the best way to prevent mistakes. Improvising while giving the test must be avoided.

The Test Is Given in Compliance with the Rules

Every test contains administration proce-dures. These procedures contain the rules and conditions under which the test must be administered. In order for test results to be interpretable and meaningful, the test proce-dures regarding administration, scoring, and interpretation must be followed.

Sometimes teachers think they are being kind in stretching the test rules for a particu-lar test taker. Actually, all they are doing is invalidating the test. The teacher who gives a student additional time to finish a speed test makes the testing situation invalid. The same applies to the teacher who scores a test liber-ally because he or she knows what the student "meant" to write. In all matters of test admin-istration, scoring, and interpretation, the pro-cedures outlined in the test manual *must* be strictly followed.

The Standardization Group and the Child Taking the Test Are Comparable

Tests are designed for certain types of chil-dren. Even when a test has been designed for "all" children, inspection of the standardiza-tion or norm group will often indicate that pre-dominantly one race, culture, or economic group dominated the pilot test group. For ex-ample, the original version (prior to the 1980 version) of the Peabody Picture Vocabulary Test (PPVT) was standardized on a white, middle-class population living in Nashville, Tennessee, and attending parochial school (the test has since been revised). Would this test be appropriate for a poor, native Ameri-can child living in rural North Dakota? Would this child's test results be in any way compara-ble with those of the children on which the PPVT had been normed?

Even with criterion-referenced tests, the child must have the cultural experiences and background on which the test questions are based. If you asked a child in rural upper Michigan to name the four seasons, and he answered bear, rabbit, trout, and deer, would he be right or wrong? Cultural fairness in test-ing is discussed in Chapter 14. For now, it is crucial for the reader to realize that compati-bility of culture and standardization group is a central assumption of tests.

Behavior Has Been Adequately Sampled

Suppose a teacher wanted to assess whether a child could add. A test consisting of one addition problem was administered, and the child answered the problem incorrectly. Can the teacher make a valid assumption that the child cannot add? Obviously not. The child might be able to add quite well, but some-thing in this one problem could have contrib-uted to computational error. Perhaps the child committed a careless mistake. The point is that to conclude that the child can or cannot add, considerably more than one addi-tion problem must be administered.

To make conclusions and interpretation possible, tests must adequately sample mate-rial. Besides asking enough questions to draw meaningful conclusions, tests must ask ques-tions from a *cross section* of content. This lat-ter point can be demonstrated again using the addition test. What if the teacher had asked twenty addition problems, but they all dealt with single-digit numbers? Could we draw any conclusions about the child's ability to add two- and three-digit numbers, regroup, and add decimals and fractions? Clearly not, because all of the subject matter had not been adequately sampled. To the extent that all components of a given subject matter area are adequately sampled, decisions regarding the child's abilities in those areas will be reason-ably accurate. If such areas are inadequately sampled, the child's behavior will be incor-rectly interpreted.

All Tests Contain Error

Every test contains error (Graham and Lilly 1984; Lyman 1978; Nunnally 1978). *Error* is defined simply as everything in the test or the testing environment (including the test taker) that is not controlled. The more error there is in the test and testing situation, the more difficult it is to interpret test scores accurately. The less error, the more reliable the test and its information.

Lyman (1978) has identified five sources of error in test scores: the person taking the test, the examiner/scorer, the test content, time, and situation-induced error. Person error is caused by all of the motivations, knowledge, and affects that impact the test taker on the day of the test. Have you ever taken a test suffering from a headache or a cold? How did that affect your test performance? "If I had felt better, I would have scored a lot higher," you probably told yourself after receiving the test results. How a child feels and what a child is experiencing in the outside world affect that child's test results. For example, the author knows of a child who had to take a test on the day his parents were in a divorce court arguing his custody. Surely, this affected his test-taking performance and contributed to error.

A second source of error is the examiner who makes mistakes in administration or scoring. Data have also indicated that in some cases the child's being culturally different from the examiner made a difference in test scores, even when the test examiner did everything else correctly (Lefley 1975). For these reasons, the examiner as a source of error must be taken into account.

Test content represents a third type of error. All tests contain a finite number of items. If another set of items had been used or if items had been worded differently, a child's score might have been different. To the extent that this is true, test content error exists.

A fourth source of error is time. This is represented by the consistency of a person's test answers over time. If a child took the exam and then retook the test a short time later, would the answers be similar or different? To the extent that they are different, the test contains time error. As we discuss in Chapter 8, one reliability measure is a gauge of time error in a test.

The last source of error is situation-induced error, which applies to all aspects of the test situation not included in the previous four error types. For example, the physical conditions of the test site can cause situation-induced error. The author once gave the same exam to two sections of a college class. One section took the exam in a quiet classroom. The other section took the same exam in the same classroom but during a rainstorm with the roof leaking. When a trash can was placed under the leak the water bounced and echoed in the metal container like gunshots sounding in a deep cave. Which group do you think did better on the exam? This situation-induced error had to be taken into account when the tests were graded and evaluated.

How Error Affects a Test

Chapter 8 describes how error affects the confidence that can be placed both in the test and in an individual's test score. For now, consider a test that possesses a large degree of time error. In such a case, a respondent's answers would differ greatly over a short period of time if the test were taken on more than one occasion. This concept is known as test–retest reliability. If a person's answers were quite divergent, the problem would be which answers to believe. If we believed the first set of answers and the second were actually true, we would be in error, and our ability to interpret this person's test-taking behavior would not be very reliable.

Likewise, consider a test-taking situation that contained a large degree of test-taker and situation-induced error. In the first case, the person might not feel well or might rather be somewhere else. In this case, we could not be sure that we were obtaining a true measure of that student's abilities, nor could we place much confidence in the scores obtained. On one occasion the author was forced to test a student in a room next to the school cafeteria shortly before the lunch hour. The student was obviously hungry, and the aromas wafting into the testing room did not help the child's attention span. Under these circumstances could anyone be sure that the child had tried his best on the test or had even been attending to task? Clearly, the large degree of error involved contributed to a lack of confidence in the test results.

The implications are clear for the test giver and test taker. To increase the reliability, usefulness, and interpretability of a test and test scores, decrease the amount of error. Such efforts will represent time well spent.

SUMMARY

Students are often promoted from one academic unit to the next and from grade to grade even though they receive low grades. This is because most schools use a system of summative evaluation in which students receive a grade at the end of a unit of instruction or at the end of a designated marking period. Summative evaluation represents a percentage or proportion of material learned. After summative evaluation has occurred, the learner moves on to the next unit of instruction.

Formative evaluation, the opposite of summative evaluation, is an ongoing, frequent assessment that occurs after a brief unit of instruction. Students who have not mastered the day's material or the lesson have the material retaught or rephrased until it is learned at a high level of criterion. The purpose of formative evaluation is to remediate learning deficiencies rather than to give a summative grade.

Assessment instruments can be conceptualized in a 2 × 2 framework with referencing as one factor and specificity of test information as the other. Referencing refers to the comparison of test scores. In norm-referencing, the learner's test scores are compared with the scores of peers. These peers can be persons in the child's environment or a standardization group created when the test was developed and pilot tested. Criterion-referenced testing compares the child's test scores against his or her own performance and some objective, predetermined criteria.

An issue in criterion-referenced testing is the setting of levels of acceptable performance. Many professionals advocate a mastery level of at least 85 percent, which the learner would have to attain before the criteria would be considered to be reached. This is known as mastery learning.

Specificity of test information refers to the depth and amount of information a test yields. Tests are either global or diagnostic in scope. Global tests yield unitary, general information about a given subject matter, whereas diagnostic tests yield specific, detailed, and in-depth information about the subject. Diagnostic tests are preferable for diagnosing and planning remediation of children's learning deficiencies.

Tests can be formal or informal. Formal tests are standardized, commercially available tests; informal tests are usually teacher made. Formal tests have the advantage of being product tested and standardized; however, informal tests can sample content directly covered by the specific classroom teacher. Teachers creating informal tests must carefully assess the reliability, validity, and appropriateness of their tests.

Aptitude tests purport to measure innate abilities or potentials, whereas achievement tests purport to measure learned behavior. In reality, the distinction between them is difficult because most aptitude tests measure at least some past learning and achievement tests measure some innate abilities. Some psychologists have suggested that the aptitude–achievement distinction be replaced by a continuum of developed abilities.

A test is either a group or an individual assessment instrument. Group tests are given to more than one person at a time; individual tests must be given in a test taker–test examiner ratio of one to one. Because group tests depend so heavily on reading and sophisticated test-taker behaviors, individual tests are recommended for special needs learners.

Tests differ regarding their speed and power properties. A highly speeded test imposes severe limitations on the time test takers have to respond. Power tests give test takers ample time to make their responses. Most tests are speeded (timed) to at least some degree, but highly speeded tests should be avoided with special needs learners.

Achievement tests indicate in a general sense where the learner is currently operating; diagnostic tests give in-depth information as to the learner's strengths and weaknesses. Predictive tests give best-guess estimates of where the learner will be operating in the future if conditions do not significantly change. Although tests can do many things, they cannot tell the future, make decisions, or weigh the humanity versus cost efficiency of making a given decision.

Tests possess some basic assumptions including: (1) the person giving the test is skilled and trained; (2) the test is being given in compliance with its rules; (3) the child and the test standardization group are comparable in acculturation; and (4) all tests and testing situations contain error.

Error is defined as everything in the test situation and test that cannot be controlled. The five basic errors involve the test taker, the test examiner, the test content, time error, and situation-induced error. As error increases, confidence in the test and the test results decreases. The wise test consumer is responsible for reducing error as much as possible.

STUDY QUESTIONS

1. Describe typical classroom situations in which summative and formative evaluation procedures might take place. What procedures would be used? For what purposes and how would information from these procedures be used?

2. Describe the variables in the 2 × 2 design of tests. What kinds of tests would appear in each cell? Under what conditions would you want information from each cell in the design? How would you use this information?

3. Assume you are Mrs. Jackson during open school night. What would you tell parents who wanted to compare their children's work with that of the other children in the classroom? How would you explain norm- and criterion-referenced assessment to them? How could you help them accept your method of assessing students?

4. Mr. Jones has adopted criterion-referenced assessment and has decided to advance students to the next unit of instruction when they learn 70 percent of the material. Is this appropriate? Why or why not? How does Mr. Jones's plan relate to that of mastery learning?

5. The Canasota School District has decided to adopt a system of group assessment because it is more cost effective. Do you think this is wise? For which type of students would group assessment be appropriate? For which groups would it be inappropriate? Defend your answers.

6. Are there any testing conditions in which a severely speeded test would be appropriate? What would these conditions be? Why are more speed tests given than power tests? What is the relationship between ease of test questions and speed and power tests?

7. What is the relationship between predictive tests and chronological time? Are there any situations that justify predictive tests? Give some examples.

8. Give two real-life examples of each of the five types of error. How should the test examiner deal with each error type?

CHAPTER 4

The Transdisciplinary Team Approach in Assessment

KEY CONCEPTS

- The transdisciplinary team approach
- Using a multifactored assessment
- Characteristics of the transdisciplinary approach
- The three functions of the assessment team
- Team members and their roles
- Team decision-making processes
- Three types of decisions made by the team
- Key activities used by the transdisciplinary team
- Ethical standards used by the team in assessing children

The decision regarding who will or will not be designated as handicapped has far-reaching implications that affect the lives of students (Ryberg and Sebastian 1981; Zigmond and Silverman 1984). A child's educational career as well as potential employment avenues are determined in part by the educational services provided. For these reasons, a professional's responsibility for appropriate and fair assessment is enormous. Nevertheless, the history of special educational assessment before the enactment of PL 94-142 is less than exemplary regarding learners with special needs (Fewell 1984; *Larry P.* v. *Riles* 1979; Reschly 1980). In fact, unfair assessment and diagnosis resulting in inappropriate educational services was a major impetus for the passage of PL 94-142 (Golin and Ducanis 1981; Semmel 1984).

The Single-Person Approach to Assessment

Perhaps one of the biggest obstacles to fair and nondiscriminatory assessments, before the implementation of PL 94-142, was that assessments were usually carried out by one individual. After the assessment was completed, this same person would typically be responsible for deciding the child's educational placement (Kabler, Carlton, and Sherwood 1981; Magliocca and Rinaldi 1982). Usually, this individual was the school psychologist.

School psychologists did not intend to be unfair in their assessments of students with special needs. Rather, such assessments were often carried out with unfair instruments and based on discriminatory assumptions. Many psychologists were not knowledgeable about developmental differences between children (Fewell 1984), nor were they particularly adept at adapting tests to the child's capabilities. Furthermore, many psychologists were inexperienced in assessing such important features of the child's environment as parent–child and child–environment interactions.

Because most of the psychologists were Anglo-Saxon whites, they did not possess a critical understanding of the culturally diverse child's life-style and culture necessary to assess these children fairly (Kabler and Carlton 1982; Strum 1985). The English-speaking psychologists and English-language tests put the culturally different test takers at a severe disadvantage (Magliocca and Rinaldi 1982). For these reasons, a major assumption of PL 94-142 was that many assessment instruments and much of the information obtained from students suspected of possessing a learning handicap were invalid due to biases of race, language, and culture.

The Transdisciplinary/Multifactor Approach: A System of Checks and Balances

The need for fair and nondiscriminatory assessment led directly to the concept of *multifactored* assessment. Multifactored assessment is the inclusion of a number of factors in the assessment, evaluation, and services provided for students with special needs (Magliocca and Rinaldi 1982; Tucker 1981). Such factors include, but are not restricted to, developmental and cognitive variables, adaptive behavior, intelligence, medical considerations, and consideration of the child's larger environment, such as parents, the home, culture, and language.

Multifactored assessment permits a system of checks and balances. It assures that the largest possible number of factors will be considered in assessing and diagnosing learning problems. By considering a large number of factors, the variable of intelligence, although important, does not become the sole reason for educational decision making. The multifactored approach makes assessment and evaluation more meaningful and valid. Table 4-1 is a list of variables that should be considered in a multifactored assessment.

Multifactored assessment has identified more special needs learners and resulted in more diverse and integrated services. For example, Table 4-2 contains a profile of special education services provided for handicapped students in the Baltimore City School System in the years immediately before and after the implementation of multifactored assessment procedures (Magliocca and Rinaldi 1982). The table shows that multifactored assessment resulted in doubling the number of students identified and served. Additionally, such assessment resulted in a dramatic decrease in the number of students being assigned to self-contained classes for the handicapped, with more students mainstreamed or placed in resource rooms. Finally, when multifactored assessment was used, the number of children diagnosed as *mildly mentally retarded* (developmentally handicapped) dropped by more than 50 percent. Students diagnosed as mentally retarded on the basis of a unitary factor assessment were no longer diagnosed as such when multiple factors were used.

The Transdisciplinary Team Approach to Multifactored Assessment

Multifactored assessment for students suspected of needing special education services is mandated by PL 94-142. The next step is to determine who will carry out such multifactored assessment.

Table 4-1   Factors to Be Considered in a Multifactored Assessment

1. General Health	Physical or Organic Contraindication, Hearing Acuity, Visual Acuity, Specific Psychiatric Disorders	Standard Medical Procedures, Audiometry, Ophthalmological, Otolaryngological, and Optometric Procedures
2. Motor	Gross Motor Skills, Fine Motor Skills, Balance and Coordination, Writing	Frostig Test of Motor Perception and Abilities, Ayres Handwriting Scale, other measures of motor perception and motor skills
3. Language	Auditory Discrimination, Receptive and Expressive Language, Auditory Memory, Speech	WISC Verbal Scale, Illinois Test of Psycholinguistic Abilities, Templin-Darley Articulation Test, other verbal and language measures
4. Visual Motor	Visual Discrimination, Receptive and Output Visuo-motor and Visual Memory	WISC Performance Scale, Bender Gestalt Visual Motor Test, Bender Visual Memory Tests, other visual motor and visual perception measures
5. Behavior	Attending Behavior, Impulse Control, Frustration, Distractibility, Thought Processes	School and Home History, Social/Psychological Observation, Anecdotal Observation
6. Social/Emotional Development	Family Relationships, Authority Relationships (School and Home), Peer Relationships, Reality Orientation, Special Life Events	Social Maturity Scales, School and Home History, Social/Psychological Observation, Anecdotal Observation
7. Academic Achievement	Reading, Spelling and Mathematics, Proficiency, Writing, and Overall Academic Achievement	Iowa Tests of Basic Skills, Wide Range Achievement Test, other formal and informal instructional assessment

Source: L. A. Magliocca and R. T. Rinaldi (1982). Multifactored assessment for the handicapped, *Theory into Practice* 21, 109. Used with permission.

Rarely is one person expert enough in such diverse areas as intelligence testing, adaptive behavior, cognitive and physical development, sociology, medicine, and education to carry out a multifactored assessment alone. And that rare individual might still bring to the assessment situation a set of biases and cultural assumptions that the multifactored assessment concept seeks to eliminate (Fenton, Yoshida, Maxwell, and Kaufman 1979). Therefore, the multifactored assessment should be administered by a *team* of professionals. This team approach helps to guarantee expertise in all of the factor areas and to eliminate bias by a single professional in assessing and evaluating the student.

The Transdisciplinary Team

In response to this need, PL 94-142 mandated the use of the multidisciplinary or *transdisciplinary* team to assess and evaluate students (Golin and Ducanis 1981; Kabler and Carlton 1982). In this approach, professionals from various disciplines work together to assess, evaluate, and make educational programming

Table 4-2 Children Served and Types of Services Provided Prior to and after Implementation of Mandated Multifactored Assessment in the Baltimore City Schools

	School Year	
Service Provided	**1973–74**	**1977–78**
Percent of total school population served	8%	16%
Total number of handicapped students served	14,500	21,500
Handicapped students in special schools	2,500	3,000
Handicapped students in self-contained classes	11,000	6,000
Handicapped students in mainstreamed environments	0	9,500
Handicapped students classified as:		
Learning disabled	200	4,000
Language disabled	20	5,000
Educable mentally retarded	13,000	5,500
Trainable mentally retarded	1,000	1,000

Source: L. A. Magliocca and R. T. Rinaldi (1982). Multifactored assessment for the handicapped, *Theory into Practice* 21, 106–113. Used with permission.

Figure 4-1 Characteristics of the Transdisciplinary Team

1. The team consists of various professionals with different types of expertise.
2. The area of functioning that may be addressed by each team member is *not* rigidly defined. All team members have input into all team decision areas.
3. Joint evaluations are permissible.
4. The team meets prior to, during, and following evaluation.
5. The entire team formulates program recommendations.
6. The team maintains responsibility for seeing that the child's program is implemented.
7. The team remains accountable for the program and must design and institute follow-up procedures.

The Three Functions of the Transdisciplinary Team

The three main functions of the transdisciplinary team are identifying the problem, exploring alternatives, and selecting a solution (Kabler et al. 1981; Kabler and Carlton 1982). Each function is vitally important for the student's proper placement and educational programming and must be properly carried out so that appropriate programming can occur. (See the flow chart summary on p. 56.)

Identifying the Problem

At this stage, the function of the transdisciplinary team is twofold. Team members must identify whether the child possesses a learning problem and they must specify the precise nature of that problem. During this phase, each team member performs the following tasks:

1. Problem assumption: Team members are given the opportunity to assess the child and specify what they believe is the child's specific, primary problem.
2. Past intervention: The team outlines the complete history of all of the intervention strate-

recommendations for a learner. Team members are responsible for assessment in their area of expertise, for reporting findings, and for making recommendations to the team. Team members have input into all aspects of the child's diagnosis and educational programming (Andrews 1974; Kabler et al. 1981; Thurlow and Ysseldyke 1979). Figure 4-1 shows the basic attributes and functions of the transdisciplinary team as they assess, evaluate, and recommend placement and programming for special needs learners (Kabler and Carlton 1982; Renne 1977).

gies that have already been tried to remediate the child's problems.

3. Intervention effectiveness: In addition to listing past intervention strategies, the effectiveness of each strategy in remediating the child's problems must be recorded. The team evaluates not only the child's behavior but also the efficiency of past educational programming used with that child.

Exploring Alernatives

In this phase, the team explores possible remediational options. This phase represents a brainstorming approach to problem solving—each team member is encouraged to suggest remediational alternatives. More specifically, the team's tasks are as follows:

1. Identify student needs: The student's specific needs as perceived by each team member are identified and recorded.
2. Hypothesize alternatives: A set of hypothesized alternatives designed to remediate the problem are generated.
3. Alternative evaluation: Each hypothesized alternative is evaluated by the team in terms of feasibility and probability of success in remediating the problem.

Selecting a Solution

In this very important stage, an alternative for remediating the problem is chosen based on its probability for success. Additionally, a detailed educational plan for implementing the solution is mapped out. More specifically, the team performs the following:

1. Alternative selection: An educational choice is made from the set of hypothesized alternatives. This alternative is selected based on its feasibility as well as its probability of remediating the problem.
2. Alternative implementation: The chosen alternative is converted into a detailed educational plan to be implemented for the child.
3. Designation of team assignments: Each team member is assigned responsibilities for implementing the plan.

4. Timetable for implementation: A timetable is developed for implementing the plan.
5. Follow-up: A plan is developed for reevaluating the effectiveness of the plan after a determined length of time.

Transdisciplinary Team Membership

The transdisciplinary team is responsible for identifying a student's problem, generating a detailed programming alternative designed to remediate the problem, and then reevaluating both the student's progress and the effectiveness of the educational program. Many professionals believe that the team approach to assessment, program design, and evaluation is one of the most important developments in fair and appropriate educational placement of and programming for special needs learners (Hasazi, Rice, and York 1979; Kabler and Carlton 1982). However, a team is only as good as its members. Thus, the composition of the transdisciplinary team is a vital element in successfully helping children with special needs.

A brief outline of transdisciplinary team membership and members' roles appears in the chart on p. 56 (Fig. 4-4). The basic transdisciplinary team consists generally of thirteen individuals, with some members acting as *core* members and others holding *adjunct* membership. A person's type of membership varies as a function of the nature of the child's specific problem(s). For example, whereas a physician and a physical therapist might hold adjunct membership when dealing with the problems of a mildly mentally retarded (developmentally handicapped) child, they might hold core membership when dealing with a physically disabled child. Membership type thus depends largely on the perception and identification of a child's problem.

Note that the transdisciplinary team concept includes a team chairperson. That person's job is to oversee the activities of the entire team, set in motion fact-finding activities, monitor the implementation of suggested programs, and make sure that follow-up activities are instituted. The chairperson's role is delineated in more detail in Figure 4-2.

In general, the members of the transdisciplinary team can be categorized into six categories: school professionals, parents/guardians and student, school support personnel, medical personnel, psychomotor development personnel, and psycho/social/emotional personnel.

School Professionals

School professionals include teachers and administrators. Teachers can be categorized into classroom teachers (either regular or special) who deal with the child on a day-to-day basis and resource room teachers who see the child on a limited basis during the school day. School administrators can be classified as building principals, school district directors of special education, and other supervisors such as the assistant superintendent of schools.

The role of classroom teachers is to inform team members as to how the child is achieving and behaving in the regular school environment. They can also offer key information regarding the child's social skills in both structured classroom activities and unstructured activities, such as lunch and recess. In terms of assessment, regular teachers would usually administer and evaluate achievement tests to gauge a student's performance compared to age- and grade-related peers. Such information is influential in team decisions regarding the least restrictive environment for the student.

Special education teachers (both classroom and resource room) provide information obtained under more specialized and individualized conditions. The assessment instruments administered and evaluated by these professionals include in-depth, diagnostic tests designed to identify a student's specific strengths and weaknesses. With this information, the team can make specific programmatic recommendations regarding the specialized curriculum, instruction, and materials the student needs in order to learn effectively.

School administrators also play an important role. They possess detailed information regarding placement options available in the school district. Building principals can modify the physical facilities (i.e., the school) and professional staff assignments to implement the program selected by the team. Finally, because of their experience in supervision and decision making, school administrators are logical choices to chair the team, unless there are strong reasons to the contrary (Fenton et al. 1977a; Sherr 1977).

Parents/Guardians and Student

For two main reasons, it is essential that parents/guardians and the student be part of the transdisciplinary team. First, PL 94-142 states specifically that parents/guardians and students are to serve and have input on the team. Second, and perhaps more important, who knows the situation better than the parent/guardian and the child?

Parents/guardians can contribute essential information about the child's behavior outside the school environment. Children are in school only about six hours a day for about 180 days each year. The rest of the time, they are usually in the care of parents/guardians. Parents and/or guardians can supply much needed information about home behaviors, emotional and psychological development in the community, and relationships with siblings and peers.

It is also essential, whenever possible, that the student be involved with the team. After all, the student is the one most affected by the team's decisions and should have input into these major educational changes. In addition, the student can give additional insights in explaining behaviors and describing attitudes, likes, and dislikes.

Figure 4-2   Roles of Transdisciplinary Team Members

Chairperson

Puts information-gathering activities in motion.

Establishes timetable for completing evaluation.

Makes sure assessment procedures are implemented.

Makes team assignments.

Acts as clearinghouse for assessments carried out by team members.

Establishes dates and sets up preliminary conferences.

Prepares written evaluation of team members.

Schedules and conducts IEP meetings.

Consults with teacher and parents one month after placement.

Schedules and monitors periodic review and follow-up.

Schedules reevaluation within three years.

Teachers

Help identify problems.

Consult with other educational professionals.

Discuss case with building principal.

Provide review of child's educational program, history, and achievement status.

Assess and evaluate current levels of academic performance.

Attend team meetings; present and interpret academic information.

Submit assessment reports to team chairperson.

Attend IEP conference.

Sign IEP.

Implement IEP and participate in follow-up evaluations.

Educational Specialists and Resource Teachers

Consult with teacher on request.

Review student's current educational records.

Meet with team.

Conduct and evaluate in-depth, diagnostic educational assessment.

Help assess other areas of child's functioning.

Present and interpret information for the team.

Submit assessment summaries to chairperson.

Attend IEP conference.

Participate and consult with classroom teacher as needed and specified.

Medical Personnel

Coordinate medical history and pertinent information.

Consult with teacher on request.

Review available medical records.

Conduct medical assessment as needed.

Assist in other assessments as needed.

Attend team meetings.

Present and interpret medical information.

Submit summary information to chairperson.

Attend IEP meeting.

School Psychologist

Consults with teacher on request.

Assists in determining whether referral is warranted.

Assesses cognitive and intellectual functioning of child.

Assists in assessing adaptive, social, and psychological functioning.

Attends team meetings.

Presents and interprets information for the team.

Submits summary information to chairperson.

Attends IEP meeting.

Provides follow-up evaluation as specified and needed.

School Administrators

Consult with teacher on request.

Review current educational program.

Assist in referral process.

Possibly chair team.

Attend team meetings.

Resolve team conflicts.

Report on available services in district and other districts.

Attend IEP meeting.

Help implement staffing and materials environment required by IEP.

Sign IEP.

Notify superintendent of team decisions.

Students should be allowed team membership with accompanying input rights when they are old enough to understand the committee's role and its goals. Some authors have suggested that student team membership should be automatic in all cases of mild handicap if the child is of junior high school age or older (Sherr 1977). As team members, students are invited to attend all team sessions and to contribute to team decisions.

School Support Personnel

School support personnel include psychologists, speech–language professionals, and other teachers in the child's program, such as the art instructor and music teacher. The school psychologist, although no longer in total control of the evaluative and programmatic decisions regarding students, is still an important team member. Psychologists are usually responsible for administering and evaluating assessment instruments that require specialized training and licensure. Such tests include most intelligence tests and other specialized measures of intellectual–cognitive functioning. In addition, the psychologist aids the team by presenting detailed psychological reports that evaluate the student's levels of aptitude and ability, as well as predicting future behavior based on such test results. At team meetings, the psychologist helps set realistic goals for the student based on the pupil's aptitude, ability, and expectancy levels.

The speech–language professional is also a key team member. This person assesses and evaluates the student's communication skills and identifies areas of language disability. The speech–language clinician helps the team administer and evaluate both formal and informal language instruments and suggest remediational language programming for the child. If the child does not engage in oral (speech) communication, the language professional also functions as the reference person in designing and implementing alternative and augmenta-

tive communication measures, such as manual sign or visual symbol systems.

Medical Personnel

The medical personnel are the student's physician(s) and the school nurse. The school nurse's role is to perform any medical screening mandated by the team, while the physician's responsibility is to administer and evaluate any in-depth medical tests conducted with the student. Participating physicians can include a family doctor, ophthalmologist and hearing specialist, orthopedic surgeon, and any other medical specialist needed by the student. After medical assessment has taken place, the physician(s) reports to the team any medical limitations that should be considered when the child's instructional program is created. The nurse then becomes responsible for ensuring that medical restrictions and specifications are followed.

Psychomotor Development Personnel

Psychomotor personnel are concerned with the child's physical and motor development. Such professionals include the physical therapist, the school nurse, the adaptive physical education teacher, and any other staff involved with the child's physical development. Their input is of secondary importance when working with children who possess mild handicaps, such as mild mental retardation and learning disabilities. However, their roles take on primary importance when dealing with children who possess serious handicaps or physical disabilities.

The adaptive physical education teacher becomes a key team member when the student possesses motor disabilities. Responsible for the motor and physical fitness of the child, the teacher also helps the student develop successful motor patterns and skills. This professional is responsible for administering and evaluating motor assessments, as well as designing and implementing the motor development portion of the student's program.

The physical therapist can also play an important role on the team. This professional is concerned with the student's motor development and can be involved in developing or restoring lost motor function. Physical therapists work closely with parents, teachers, and the adaptive physical education teacher to make sure that the motor programs designed for the student are carried out and implemented at home and at school.

Social and Emotional Personnel

These professionals, responsible for the social, emotional, and psychological well-being of the child, include the school social worker, psychologist, and family counselors. The social worker contributes to the team by making home visits, interviewing parents and the child in an environment away from school, and giving the team input into the child's cultural and environmental background. The social worker also helps design goals to be carried out at home and helps parents implement those goals.

The psychologist is responsible for the child's psychological well-being. This job includes administering and evaluating psychological instruments, diagnosing mental illness, and suggesting therapeutic alternatives when they are warranted. In some cases, the clinical psychologist outlines programs to be carried out by counselors and psychiatric social workers.

Team Decision Making

Nonspecialized, Democratic Team Decision Making

The ultimate responsibility of the transdisciplinary team is decision making. But how should those educational decisions be made? One argument is that each team specialist should make the decisions regarding that particular discipline. In this framework, for example, the school psychologist would be responsible for assessment and evaluation decisions in the intellectual–cognitive area. Likewise, medical personnel (i.e., the student's doctors and the school nurse) would assume total responsibility for programmatic decisions regarding the student in medical areas.

The alternative to this specialized approach is an undifferentiated, democratic decision-making process. With this approach, the experts assess and evaluate the student in their own areas of expertise, but decisions are made by the *entire* team. Thus, each area expert reports back to the entire team and makes recommendations. Final decisions rest with the entire team, with each expert having a single vote.

Many experts assert that the nondifferentiated, democratic decision-making approach is best when making programmatic decisions for learners with special needs (Fenton et al. 1979; Fenton et al. 1977a, b; Kabler and Carlton 1982). On the other hand, the specialized approach appears to work best in the following four situations (Fenton et al. 1979; Fenton et al. 1977a, b):

1. The problem is single faceted rather than multifaceted.
2. One solution is clearly correct or better than all others.
3. The leader has the proven skill to synthesize all members' opinions into a single, unified opinion.
4. General acceptance of decisions by individual group members is not very important.

Clearly, these criteria do not apply in most of the decisions that need to be made by the transdisciplinary team. In most cases, the problem is not single faceted. Rather, the programming decisions that must be made for learners with special needs are complex. Second, there is seldom one correct answer regarding the child's programming. Instead, there are usually various programmatic decisions that can be made, and the team's task is to choose the *best* solution. Finally, it is crucially important that all team members support the programmatic decisions made for the student. Members must work together for the educational good of the pupil. The best way to get people to support a decision is to make them feel they have had input into the decision-making process.

For these reasons, it appears that the non-differentiated, democratic decision process is best. Such a process helps assure that all team members actively participate in decision making and eventually support what is decided. Likewise, the nondifferentiated approach helps guard against too much weight being attached to a team member's possibly biased decision. This safeguards the rights of the student and guarantees a fair, nondiscriminatory assessment.

Types of Decisions Made by the Team

The transdisciplinary team makes many decisions for each pupil it serves. These decisions can be better understood when placed in a three-tiered framework of *diagnosis, placement,* and *programming.*

Decisions of Diagnosis

The first set of decisions the transdisciplinary team makes concerns diagnosis. Diagnosis entails detailing specifically how and at what levels the student is operating and behaving. The information includes specific weaknesses or deficiencies that the student possesses as well as how this individual is operating relative to age- and grade-related peers. The information-gathering tools are achievement and in-depth diagnostic tests as well as assessments of cognitive and intellectual development, physical development, neurological and psychomotor functioning, and social and adaptive maturity. After gathering all the information in these areas, a set of diagnostic decisions are usually reached. The team's ac-

Figure 4-3   Team Decisions of Diagnosis, Placement, and Programming

A. *Team Activities during the Diagnosis Phase*
  1. Gather information relevant to the student and his or her environment.
  2. Assess and evaluate the student's strengths and weaknesses.
  3. Summarize information relevant to the case.
  4. Interpret information relevant to the case.

B. *Team Activities during the Placement Phase*
  1. Use student needs as guidelines for judging possible placement alternatives.
  2. Evaluate each placement alternative as a function of the school system's effectiveness in delivering the alternative.
  3. Evaluate each alternative in terms of relative probability of the student's success in interacting in such an environment.
  4. Consider the restrictive status of each alternative placement.
  5. Choose the placement with the highest probability of success based on items B2 through B4.

C. *Team Activities during the Programmatic Phase*
  1. Suggest the student's subject matter needs.
  2. Suggest possible instructional methods for the student.
  3. Suggest possible instructional materials for the student.
  4. Set evaluative criteria for judging the instructional program in terms of improvement in the student's functioning.
  5. Set a date for review and follow-up assessment of the student and the program

tivities relating to diagnostic decisions are shown in Figure 4-3 (A).

Placement Decisions

Once the proper set of diagnoses have been made, the team must decide the appropriate

Figure 4-4   Steps Taken by the Transdisciplinary Team

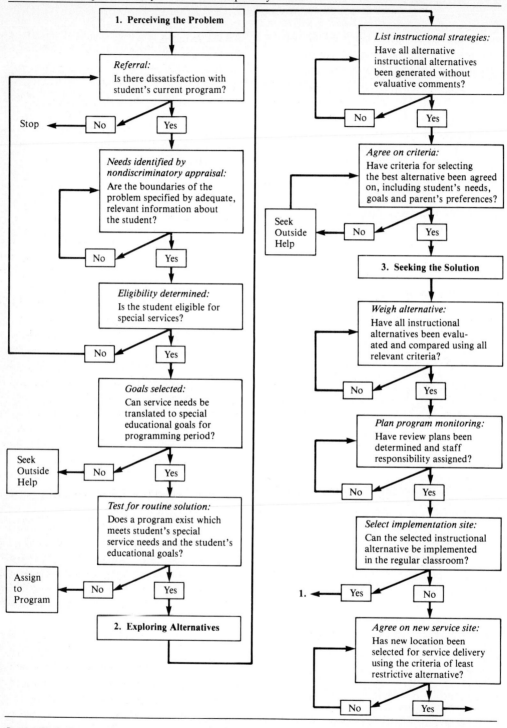

Source: K. S. Fenton, R. K. Yoshida, J. P. Maxwell, and M. J. Kaufman (1977). *A Decision Model for Special Education Programming Teams* (Connecticut State Department of Education). Used by permission.

educational placement for the student. As we have discussed, a variety of special educational placements are available for special needs learners, ranging from a mainstreamed placement through self-contained classes and self-contained schools. Each choice differs in its degree of restrictiveness to students, that is, in the degree to which it allows learners to function in a nonrestrictive, integrative environment. PL 94-142 mandates that the student be placed in the least restrictive educational environment. The team's primary responsibility is to identify that environment.

In deciding the best (and least restrictive) placement for the student, the team must consider a number of factors. These factors include the student's operational strengths and weaknesses (indicated by the diagnostic phase), as well as the individual's instructional needs in relation to available educational alternatives. These considerations are shown in Figure 4-3 (B, C). Figure 4-4 is a flow chart of the steps taken by a team when making a placement decision for a student.

Instructional Programming Decisions

In the instructional decision-making phase, the team's responsibilities include creating educational programming designed to remediate the student's specific weaknesses. Specifically, the team's task is to design in-school and at-home activities that will help to remediate the student's problem areas and help the student reach his or her learning potential.

The instructional programming process consists of five distinct stages (Affleck, Lowenbraun, and Archer 1980; Anderson 1982).

1. Establishing long-term and short-term goals.
2. Selecting instructional activities and materials designed to reach these goals.
3. Selecting a data-recording system to chart educational progress.
4. Implementing instruction.
5. Modifying the instructional plan as required.

To a large extent, the responsibility for each process falls to the classroom and resource room teachers as they design and implement remediational programming with the goal of improving the student's learning and other behaviors. However, if the team is using the undifferentiated, democratic format, every team member should have input on the instructional decisions.

Ethical Standards

The professional and ethical conduct of the transdisciplinary team must be above question. To that end, a number of organizations have issued publications that deal with the ethical and professional conduct required of team members during assessment, evaluation, and diagnosis. These publications include the *Casebook for Providers of Psychological Services* (American Psychological Association 1981), *Responsibility of Users of Standardized Tests* (American Personnel and Guidance Association 1980), and *Standards for Providers of Psychological Services* (American Psychological Association 1977). Each of these publications should be read by any professional aspiring to become a member of a transdisciplinary team.

There are a number of requisites for team members. These include a high degree of expertise in assessment and diagnosis; a strong, up-to-date knowledge of curricula, materials, and methods needed to teach exceptional learners; and knowledge about and empathy for culturally diverse parents and children. Additionally, team members must be able to work cooperatively with other specialists. Finally, team members must be able to write clear and concise reports. If a report cannot be easily read and understood by teachers, parents, and other interested parties, then the team has not fulfilled its responsibility.

A number of authors have outlined the ethical responsibilities and behaviors that team

Figure 4-5   Ethical Considerations for Transdisciplinary Team Members

1. Before any testing takes place, permission is sought and received.
2. As much as possible is learned about the child *before* assessment takes place to ensure an appropriate assessment battery.
3. Persons administering the assessment give only those tests they are qualified to give.
4. Assessment instruments are used and read only by qualified personnel.
5. Assessment instruments are chosen and selected for a reasonable purpose.
6. Diagnosis and placement decisions are *not* made on the basis of one test, one test technique, or one assessment session.
7. Predictions about young children based on assessments are discouraged.
8. Results of assessments are stated in clear, easy-to-understand language that nonprofessionals such as parents can readily understand.
9. Emotionally loaded words and professional jargon are avoided in test reports.
10. In addition to weaknesses, student strengths are also outlined.
11. Test results must report any environmental variables (noise, distractiveness, etc.) that took place in the testing environment.
12. Test results must report whether the child is on medication or suffering from a significant handicapping condition that would have interfered with test results. If such conditions do exist it is the tester's responsibility to explain how these variables were compensated for in the testing situation.
13. Parents must be informed of all need for further assessment.
14. All procedures are explained to parents, and permission is obtained if further assessment is needed.
15. Test information is only disseminated to qualified personnel directly involved in the child's case. All information must be treated as strictly confidential by all parties.

members must demonstrate in the areas of assessment, evaluation, and diagnosis (Fallen 1981; Stellern, Vasa, and Little 1976). Figure 4-5 summarizes these ethical considerations.

To guarantee fair and appropriate assessment, diagnosis, placement, and educational programming, it is vital that these ethical behaviors be rigorously followed.

SUMMARY

A fair and appropriate assessment is crucial for proper diagnosis, educational placement, and remediation of learning problems. However, special needs learners have not always been assessed fairly. For one reason, bias has often occurred when assessments have been administered by an individual. Such single-person assessments are subject to error due to language and cultural biases on the part of the test examiner. Thus, multifactored assessment, which measures variables in addition to intellectual functioning, is mandated by PL 94-142. These factors include intellectual functioning, development, cognitive functioning, language, adaptive and social behavior, and the child's environment outside of school.

Multifactored assessment is carried out by the transdisciplinary team. In this approach, professionals from various disciplines make diagnosis, placement, and programming decisions for the student. The various disciplines include, but are not restricted to, the teaching staff, related school staff (e.g., school psychologists and speech/language clinicians), school administrators, medical personnel, social/psychological/emotional personnel, and physical development staff. The student's parents/guardians are always included on the transdisciplinary team, and the student should be included whenever feasible.

The transdisciplinary team makes many decisions. These decisions can be separated into three main areas: identifying the problem, exploring alternatives, and selecting a solution. Identifying the problem includes problem assumption, exploring the history of past intervention, and judging that intervention's effectiveness. Exploring alternatives involves identifying the student's needs, hypothesizing alternatives, and exploring the feasibility of each alternative solution. Finally, selecting a solution includes selecting one of the alternatives and implementing that alternative.

Each team member has an important function. The chairperson coordinates all functions of the team, and the regular teacher informs the team of the student's behavior in the regular classroom and conducts norm-referenced achievement testing. The special education teacher conducts in-depth diagnostic testing and summarizes the student's specific strengths and weaknesses. School administrators function as chairpersons and provide information regarding school district policy and positions and available educational placements. The parents/guardians and the student inform the team of the student's behavior outside the school environment as well as of their placement wishes. The school psychologist assesses the child's intellectual functioning, and the speech/language clinician makes language assessments and designs language intervention programs. Medical personnel assess the student's medical history and provide input on any medical restrictions that must be placed on the student's program. The job of the psychomotor personnel is to assess and remediate any psychomotor or gross motor difficulties the student may be encountering. Finally, the social/psychological personnel

deal with any psychological or emotional problems the student may be exhibiting.

Teams should use the nonspecialized, democratic decision-making model. In this model, every team member has input into all team decisions instead of decisions being made by isolated members. The nonspecialized, democratic model ensures against a team member's bias and psychologically commits team members to the final decisions.

The transdisciplinary team makes the basic decisions of diagnosis, placement, and intervention. Diagnosis decisions specifically detail how and at what level of expertise the student is operating. Such information includes outlining specific student weaknesses. Placement decisions involve placing the student in the least restrictive educational environment in which the student can successfully operate. Finally, instructional programming decisions involve creating educational programs to remediate the student's educational and behavioral weaknesses. Any instructional programming must contain periodic follow-up and review of the success of the placement and program in remediating student weaknesses.

Each team member must operate under a strict code of ethics. Such ethics have been delineated in numerous publications of professional organizations. The responsibilities of team members include working for the best interests of the student, conducting unbiased assessments, displaying a high degree of skill in their areas of expertise, working cooperatively with other team members, and writing clear, concise assessment reports. It is also vitally important that each team member regard the parents and the student as valuable members of the transdisciplinary team.

STUDY QUESTIONS

1. What are the potential dangers of a single-factored assessment? Are there any advantages to such an assessment? Traditionally, who was responsible for single-factor assessment? What were this person's responsibilities in making the assessment?

2. Describe the checks and balances inherent in multifactored assessment. Why would they help ensure fair and unbiased assessment?

3. Describe the transdisciplinary team approach to assessment. Who are the basic team members? What are their roles?

4. What are the three functions of the transdisciplinary team? How are these functions implemented by team members?

5. How are decisions made by the team? Describe the advantages and disadvantages of the specified and undifferentiated approaches to team decision making. Under what circumstances would each type of decision making be appropriate?

6. Describe the code of ethics and conduct that team members are expected to follow. Why is this code important for fair and unbiased assessment?

CHAPTER 5

Skills Needed
in Assessment
and Diagnosis

KEY CONCEPTS

- The concepts of measurement, evaluation, and diagnosis
- The case for misdiagnoses
- Necessary skills for good assessment and diagnosis: Psychological, psychometric, and psychosocial skills
- Techniques of assessment, application, and synthesis
- Analysis of product
- Application skills
- The atomistic versus holistic assessment approach
- Synthesis of assessment information
- The PAGE technique for problem solving and diagnosis
- Considerations for sound assessment and diagnosis
- Prior considerations: The testing environment and the child

Regardless of the age, grade level, educational placement of students, or subject matter taught, teachers working with exceptional students inevitably engage in assessment activities. It is estimated that 250 million standardized tests are given to students each year. As this figure represents only formal, standardized tests and not teacher-made, informal instruments, the number of estimated yearly assessments is clearly conservative.

How valid are these assessments? The ultimate success of any assessment depends on the skill and competence of those persons involved in the process. How a test is administered and what is done with the data collected separate valid from invalid assessments and lead to appropriate or inappropriate educational decisions.

In recent years, professionals have become increasingly aware of the importance of defining the skills needed to carry out valid assessments and of training educators to acquire those skills (Cegelka 1978; Daniels and Altekruse 1982; Division for Children with Learning Disabilities 1978; McNutt and Mandelbaum 1980). Likewise, teacher-training programs have identified assessment competencies that prospective educators must acquire to design appropriate educational programs for exceptional students. This chapter identifies and discusses the skills needed to carry out valid assessment and diagnosis.

Assessment versus Measurement

Although almost anyone can administer a test, hopefully that person is a skilled *technician* in test administration and scoring. However, in order for appropriate assessment and diagnosis to occur, the professional must also be a skilled *clinician*. A clinician possesses not only the technical skills to administer tests but also the skill and expertise to interpret, synthesize, and apply assessment information. In addition, the clinician makes decisions and predictions based both on test data and from other available sources. To accomplish this goal, the clinician brings to the assessment situation a knowledge of tests and testing procedures, as well as skills in interviewing, observation, behavioral analysis, and informal assessment.

A sound clinician possesses sound technical skills, that is, an understanding of the principles of testing and the ability to administer appropriate educational and psychological tests fairly and accurately. One can be an assessment technician without being a clinician. In fact, many educators are precisely that. They administer and score tests adequately but do not make competent decisions and diagnoses about the child. In short, being a sound technician is a requisite skill for a clinician, but one can be a sound technician and still not possess clinical skill and expertise (Arter and Jenkins 1979; Brown 1983; McNutt and Mandelbaum 1980).

For the purpose of this discussion, the term *measurement* is used synonymously with the technical skills needed to collect information from test administrations. Measurement skills include the ability to administer a test and collect data and to understand the statistical and mathematical components of standardized tests. The term *evaluation* refers to the ability to interpret or make sense out of collected data in meaningful and appropriate ways (Brown 1983; Kaplan and Saccuzzo 1982). Finally, the term *diagnosis* refers to the clinical skills needed to synthesize and apply measurement and evaluative information in order to make predictive statements regarding a student's learning problems. Diagnosis also entails suggesting educational programming to remediate learning problems (Bransford 1979; Lerner 1981; Van Etten and Adamson 1973). In the process of diagnosis, the clinician uses insight and draws on background and experience to evaluate and interpret the data collected (Brown and French 1979; Painting 1979).

The Importance of Diagnostic and Clinical Skills

Many profesionals believe a crisis of misdiagnosis and inappropriate educational placement exists for many exceptional students (Gerber and Semmel 1984). The main reason for misdiagnosis and misplacement appears to be a lack of clinical and diagnostic skills on the part of educational professionals (M. Smith 1982; Ysseldyke, Algozzine, and Thurlow 1980).

Examples of problems of misdiagnosis and a lack of clinical skills have been empirically demonstrated. For example, in a study in which the behavior of nonreferred students was assessed for potential learning disabilities, the *false positive* rate (the rate of students wrongly identified as possessing a disability) was as high as 75 percent. On the other hand, about 25 percent of the students actually in classes for the learning disabled were *not* diagnosed as learning disabled (Ysseldyke et al.

1980; Ysseldyke, Algozzine, and Epps 1982). In other studies, when experienced assessment professionals were given profiles of students' test scores, they were only able to distinguish mildly handicapped from nonhandicapped children at chance levels (Epps, Ysseldyke, and McGue, in press). Such misdiagnosis and inappropriate clinical judgments were demonstrated both in situations in which professionals studied students' profiles singly or in teams (Gerber and Semmel 1984; M. Smith 1982; Ysseldyke, Algozzine, and Thurlow 1980).

Other researchers have found significant variance in diagnosis and placement of handicapped children based on such factors as state and school system of residence (Gerber and Semmel 1984; Nelson 1982); test and examiner cultural bias (Sherman and Robinson 1982; Strum 1985; Strum and Ribner 1984); sex bias (Clarizio and Phillips 1986); prior familiarity with the student (Fuchs and Fuchs 1984; Fuchs, Featherstone, Garwick, and Fuchs 1983; Fuchs, Fuchs, Garwick, and Featherstone 1984); familiarity with the student's language (Lefley 1975); and examiner sensitivity and accuracy during testing and scoring (Einhorn and Hogarth 1978; Fuchs and Fuchs 1984). Thus, there are a number of factors that mitigate against fair, appropriate assessment and diagnosis being carried out for exceptional students. Students who do not need services are often diagnosed as handicapped whereas students in need of services are missed. And each mistake in diagnosis affects a child's life profoundly and perhaps irreversibly.

The Teacher as Clinician and Diagnostician

One way to reduce the number and magnitude of diagnostic and clinical errors in assessment is to improve teachers' clinical skills. Teachers are in a unique position to observe, analyze, and diagnose the learning behavior of students. Psychologists and other professionals interact with the student only occasion-

ally, but teachers observe student behaviors daily. Such behaviors are observed over a wide range of situations; formal tests sample only a small number of student behaviors (Gerber and Semmel 1984). Thus, teachers can act as sound diagnostic instruments for diagnosing the learning problems of exceptional students (Brown and Saks 1983; Gerber and Semmel 1984).

However, if teachers are viewed as assessment and diagnostic instruments, their judgments must be subjected to the same criteria of reliability and validity applied to formal tests. Put another way, just as the goal of test makers is to limit (or eliminate) the degree of error in a test, the goal of teachers/clinicians should be to reduce or eliminate the amount of error in their diagnostic judgments (Gerber and Semmel 1984). Unfortunately, an existing body of research questions the reliability and validity of teachers' clinical and diagnostic judgments (Brown and Saks 1983; Kornblau 1982; Shavelson and Stern 1981). For this reason, teachers must strive to acquire and refine their assessment and diagnostic skills in order to reduce error (Gerber and Semmel 1984; Shavelson and Stern 1981). The more skilled teachers are in making clinical judgments, the more the error in their assessments and diagnoses will be reduced.

Three Skill Areas for Assessment and Diagnosis

The skills and attributes teachers need to carry out sound assessment and diagnosis have their roots in three types of competencies (Daniels and Altekruse 1982; Shertzer and Linden 1979). These competencies involve *psychological*, *psychometric*, and *psychosocial* skills.

Psychological Skills

It is important that teachers understand (and use) the basic tenets of educational and psychological theories. Such theories are helpful in understanding and interpreting student behaviors and in making qualified and appropriate educational diagnoses (Cegelka 1978; Daniels and Altekruse 1982; Hunter 1981). Teachers should be knowledgeable in the areas of child and adolescent development; characteristics of exceptional children; theories of learning, development, cognition, and personality; behavioral management theory; and curriculum development and planning (Cegelka 1978; Hunter 1981). Whenever possible, teachers should also possess broad experience in these areas gleaned from working in public school programs, community diagnostic clinics, sheltered workshops, and other related programs.

The belief is that a strong base of psychological theory and expertise will enable the teacher/clinician to accomplish the following five goals (Daniels and Altekruse 1982; Remer 1981):

1. Demonstrate competency in critically analyzing educational–remediational suggestions.
2. Organize and interpret assessment information.
3. Demonstrate sound observational and other behavioral techniques.
4. Design behavioral remediation programs.
5. Meet ethical and moral responsibilities in assessment and diagnosis.

Psychometric Skills

Teachers must be skilled in choosing, administering, and scoring appropriate assessment instruments. They must also understand the concept of intelligence as well as the developmental "milestones" at which children's behaviors typically occur and that typify developmentally delayed children.

In selecting, administering, and scoring standardized tests, teachers should possess the following six subcompetencies:

1. Ability to judge the reliability, validity, and appropriateness of the assessment procedure being considered.
2. Ability to interpret test scores correctly and give accurate information about scores.

3. Ability to discern false claims and misrepresentations of tests and test scores.
4. Knowledge that assessment procedures demand different levels of competence in administration, scoring, and interpretation. Teachers should recognize the limits of their competency prior to assessing students and should perform only assessments for which they are prepared.
5. Ability to administer assessments under conditions comparable to the standardized conditions.
6. Sufficient technical training to interpret test results.

Psychosocial Skills

To interpret and use test results, teachers must have knowledge of the social, environmental, and cultural background of the test taker. Whereas children come from all types of socioeconomic and cultural backgrounds, teachers and clinicians tend to come from white, middle-class environments (Alley and Foster 1978; Mercer 1974). There is nothing *wrong* with either cultural background. The problem arises with tests and test interpretations that are Anglocentric and discriminate against other cultural groups (Leonard and Weiss 1983; Taylor and Payne 1983).

For example, what are the answers to these questions?

1. When should you say "please"?
2. When is Washington's birthday?

You probably answered "when you want something" and February 22, answers that are correct as judged by most tests. But what if a child answered "when you do not understand what someone said" (some Midwest and/or Appalachian cultures) and April 5 (Booker T. Washington's birthday)? If the clinician was insensitive to the child's cultural background, those answers might be scored as incorrect even though they were entirely appropriate in terms of the child's background.

It is vitally important that the clinician understand and empathize with the child's cultural and environmental background. Additionally, the clinician should be able to understand the child's language or dialect and converse with the child in that language. When the clinician does not possess these requisite skills the child is at a severe disadvantage, and the probability of error in the assessment increases dramatically.

Necessary Assessment and Clinical Competencies: Techniques, Applications, and Synthesis

This section discusses specific competencies that the teacher/clinician must possess to carry out appropriate assessment and diagnosis. Each of these competencies represents key skills needed by teachers to collect and interpret assessment information as well as to diagnose children's learning problems. These competencies include more than administering and scoring tests; they include key clinical skills that, although informal and nonstandardized, are nevertheless important in the assessment and diagnosis process.

The key competencies in assessment and diagnosis can be grouped into three main categories: *techniques, applications,* and *synthesis* (McNutt and Mandelbaum 1980). Technique involves collecting the factual information (data gathering) needed for application and synthesis to occur. Application includes the decisions, in advance of data collection, as to what information should be collected and why, what the proper collection techniques are, and how the data should be used. Finally, synthesis uses the collected data in meaningful ways to make valid and appropriate diagnoses.

Techniques

All assessment data can be obtained and organized through one or more of three basic techniques: *analysis of product, interviewing,* and *observation.* Each technique can be used in various ways and contributes to the total collection of assessment information. Although there is some degree of overlap in the manner and purpose for which the various procedures are used, certain procedures work best for collecting certain types of assessment information. Analysis of product is discussed here. Interviewing and observation are discussed in depth in Chapter 11.

Analysis of Product: Analysis of product occurs when a teacher examines a student's work, for example, scoring a test, grading an essay, or checking homework assignments. Products can be classified along two main dimensions—types of tests and knowledge areas (Gronlund 1985; McNutt and Mandelbaum 1980; Wallace and Larsen 1979). The test dimension includes norm-referenced, criterion-referenced, and informal tests. The knowledge dimension reflects teacher expertise in test selection, construction, administration, and interpretation.

As discussed in Chapter 3, norm-referenced tests allow a student's results to be compared with some known group's performance (i.e., the norming sample). They are used for comparisons *between* students. Criterion-referenced tests compare the student's performance with a specified skill domain or set of competencies. These competencies act as benchmarks against which student mastery is compared. Informal tests are usually teacher made and/or student specific. Constructed for a particular student (or students), they are geared to the subject matter and educational curriculum that these students are experiencing. Chapter 11 deals with the construction of good informal tests.

Test Selection: Teachers must be knowledgeable in test selection, that is, in determining which type of test is most appropriate. Tests should be selected in terms of test purpose, the match between test and test taker, and the test quality. The first questions to be an-

swered are Why is this test being given? and
What do we hope to find out about the child
by administering this test? Initial questions of
purpose focus on whether the teacher is seeking norm-referenced or criterion-referenced
information. Once this is determined, the
teacher then questions the area of functioning
to be assessed and the degree of specificity
needed in data collection. For example, if the
teacher wants to gain information as to the
student's general functioning in a subject matter area, a global achievement test is sufficient. However, if the teacher wants to collect
in-depth, diagnostic information about functioning in a specific skill area (e.g., specific
skills in reading), then an in-depth diagnostic
test is required.

It is important that the teacher ensure that
the selected test is appropriate for the test
taker. For example, suppose a teacher wants
to give a norm-referenced test, which was standardized on an urban, white, middle-class
population, to a poor, rural, southern black
child. This child's test results might be inferior
to those of the test's norm group. Someone
could interpret these test results to mean that
this child was educationally deficient and in
need of special services. But would this necessarily be a valid conclusion? This child might
have performed poorly because the norm
group (and hence the test) was inappropriate
for this particular test taker. In such a case,
designating the child as handicapped would be
inappropriate and erroneous.

Inappropriate matches between test and
test taker are not restricted to norm-referenced tests. Teachers using criterion-referenced tests must make sure that the test taker
has had an apportunity to learn the material
covered by the test. Clearly, there is little usefulness in giving a test of sixth-grade arithmetic material to a student in the fourth grade.
The student would show complete nonmastery of these arithmetic concepts. But that
would only prove that the student had not yet
learned the material. Criterion-referenced

tests require compatibility between the content and the test taker.

The final issue in test selection is to assess
the quality of the proposed test. A plethora of
tests are on the market, many measuring the
same concepts or subject areas. Not surprisingly, all of these claim to be good. Virtually
all test authors and publishers make strong
claims in their test manuals and advertising
materials as to why the prospective test buyer
should purchase their test.

The clinician must be an informed test consumer and choose a test based on quality. In
addition, knowledge of the content area is
needed to ensure that the test adequately covers the content it claims to be assessing. Figure
5-1 contains some key questions the teacher
should ask when assessing the quality of a test.

Test Construction: A knowledge of adequate test construction is very important in
creating criterion-referenced, teacher-made
tests. In addition, although most teachers are
not involved with constructing norm-
referenced tests, knowing how such tests are
constructed can be useful when evaluating the
quality of norm-referenced instruments.

Test construction skills center around is-

Figure 5-1   Key Questions in Assessing Test
Quality

1. What area(s) does this instrument assess?
2. Does it cover the areas and yield the type of
   information I need to help my students?
3. Is the test culturally and racially fair?
4. What are the characteristics of the standardization (norm) group (if one was used)?
5. How were test items developed?
6. Is the information yielded global or
   diagnostic?
7. What is the reliability of the test? How was it
   ascertained?
8. What is the validity of the test?
9. What is the degree of error in the test?
10. What is the reputation of the test? What do
    experts say about its quality?

sues of creating test items. This entails constructing a pool of sound test items while eliminating inadequate questions. This topic is discussed at length in Chapter 11.

Competency in Test Administration: The test examiner must be competent in test administration or the test and its results will be invalid. It is the professional's job to determine objectively that tests have been administered in strict accordance with accepted procedures and to view any interpretation of tests otherwise given as misleading and inaccurate.

Competency in test administration includes the consideration of factors that occur before and during administration. These include such factors as the pupil's life circumstances, the testing environment, the rapport with the student, and the student's level of attention, motivation, and fatigue.

Proficiency in Interpreting Test Results: Proficiency in interpreting test results must be one of the clinician's skills. The interpretation of standardized tests requires the ability to make sense statistically out of scores, to interpret test behavior in meaningful ways, and to choose scores that offer the most meaningful interpretation of the child's behavior.

The competent examiner also tries to interpret the student's overall test behavior. The clinician is interested in how the student approached and handled certain aspects of the test. Any relevant comments the student makes during the test-taking situation (e.g., This is too hard or I'm not good at this) are also of use. Specifically, when interpreting a student's behavior, the teacher might ask the following questions:

1. What was the student's response style to different aspects of the test? Did the student show eagerness to complete the test or demonstrate avoidance?
2. What was the student's approach to the test? Did he or she appear confident? Did the student seem to be guessing?
3. What comments did the student make? How did the comments relate to the test content and the test results?
4. Did the student show consistent test behavior or did test-taking behaviors change from situation to situation?
5. What was the test taker's behavior on parts of the test that indicated strong functioning areas? What was the behavior on weak functioning areas?
6. Were the test results consistent with the student's behavior in the classroom? How were they different? Should such differences be viewed as significant? Why or why not?

Finally, the clinician must choose *which* scores to accept and interpret. This is true with both norm-referenced and criterion-referenced tests. Two major criteria for choosing to use a test score are *usefulness of information* and *specificity*. Usefulness of information represents the degree of value a given score possesses in making clinical–diagnostic judgments about a student. Usefulness is an indication of how good the information is in helping make educational and instructional decisions. The degree of usefulness of a given test score depends largely on the purpose for which the test was given. For example, if the teacher suspected that the pupil was not operating at the expected grade level, a norm-referenced test that indicated a grade equivalent score comparing the level functioning of the student to that of the norm group would be appropriate. However, a grade equivalent score would not be very useful if the teacher wished to understand in greater detail the student's specific areas of weakness. In this case, more diagnostic tests and test scores would be needed.

Specificity refers to the degree of detail the clinician wishes to extract from the assessment of the student. The greater the desired detail of the student's strengths and weaknesses, the greater the need for specificity of information yielded by the test. Generally, criterion-referenced and diagnostic tests yield more specific information than do norm-referenced, global tests. Thus, the type of test given and the test score used and interpreted depend on the purpose of the information (usefulness of score) and the required degree of specificity.

Application Skills

Before determining which basic technique to use in gathering assessment information, the clinician must decide what is to be measured, why it is being measured, and what is to be done with the information gathered. These decisions are very important because they influence both the choice of test and testing techniques and how that collected information will impact on the education of the student.

What Area Is to Be Assessed? The area to be assessed should be specifically identified from the following four areas of information: *academic, behavioral, physical–sensory,* and *vocational.* Academic information is gathered from all of the core content areas (language, reading, arithmetic, spelling, writing, and written expression) and from other academic subject areas that are usually part of the student's curriculum (social studies, science, health, etc.). Behavioral information is drawn from, but not limited to, appropriate and inappropriate classroom behaviors, adaptive behavior, problem-solving skills, emotional/mental health functioning (e.g., self-concept), and social interaction skills. Areas in the physical–sensory domain include fine motor and gross motor psychomotor functioning, the dexterity needed to perform daily

functions adequately, and perceptual acuity. Finally, vocational assessment includes such areas as job interests and aptitudes, specific job skills, and work habits. Academic assessment is discussed in greater detail in Chapters 16 through 19, behavioral assessment in Chapter 22, physical–sensory assessment in Chapter 21, and vocational assessment in Chapter 20.

When defining the area to be assessed, it is not enough simply to define a general or generic core area (e.g., reading). Rather, the core area usually needs to be broken down into subcomponent skills or life situations. Figure 5-2 demonstrates this process for the area of reading using an *atomistic* educational approach (McNutt and Mandelbaum 1980). In this atomistic approach, reading has been broken down into a number of subskills (e.g., phonics, sound blending, inferential comprehension). Although the atomistic approach is generally used in diagnostic assessment, in some cases, especially with older students whose skills may be better developed, the clinician may use a *holistic* approach (see also Figure 5-2). Holistically, reading would be measured in a variety of situations (e.g., newspapers, textbooks, recipes). Whether the atomistic or holistic approach is used, the clinician must know what area is to be assessed and how the subcomponents of the major skills will be broken down *before the assessment is carried out and data collected.*

Figure 5-2 Atomistic and Holistic Approaches to Reading Assessment

A. *Atomistic: Subcomponents of Decoding and Comprehension Skills*

1. Auditory-visual discrimination
2. Phonics
3. Sight word recognition
4. Structural analysis
5. Comprehension
6. Study skills

B. *Holistic: Can student adequately read the following:*

1. Newspaper
2. Recipe
3. Instructional manual
4. School materials
5. Materials for enjoyment

Why Are Data Being Collected? Why data are being collected translates into a more operational question for the clinician, What types of information are needed? Figure 5-3 shows four purposes of data gathering: *screening, classification, instructional planning,* and *evaluating pupil progress.*

Screening assessment is gathering information regarding the probability that a student possesses a learning, behavioral, or physical deficiency or difficulty. The clinician uses screening procedures to test quickly and efficiently a large number of individuals and identify accurately those who might possess problems. Based on the results of screening, more in-depth assessment might be carried out.

Assessment for classification purposes attempts to qualify a student as eligible for special educational services. To qualify for government funded educational aid, states must show that students receiving special services meet eligibility requirements. Each state has its own eligibility requirements that students must meet in order to qualify for special educational services. Classification assessment is usually norm-referenced and global in nature.

Assessment for planning decisions is used to help teachers design and implement educational programs to remediate the learning problems of exceptional children. Assessment in this area is almost always in-depth and diagnostic and usually individual rather than group oriented. Assessment for planning decisions can be both formal and informal.

Finally, assessment can measure student progress in a given program. Such assessment also usually measures program success in remediating the student's learning weaknesses. Although the most traditional measure of student progress is global (e.g., grades), newer measures tend to be more criterion-referenced. These measures typically match student learning to a set of in-depth objectives that are individualized in scope.

Figure 5-3 Purposes of Assessment Data Collection

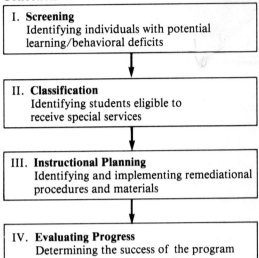

How Will Information Be Used? Determining the use of assessment information is a key step. Assessment data recorded and entered in a child's cumulative folder and then forgotten are useless and a waste of time. Likewise, assessment data used to stereotype and stigmatize a student can damage the individual. Assessment data must be used positively to help students reach their potential.

To a large extent, what is done with assessment data depends on why the data were collected. Data can be used to verify the need for services, to help plan a sound educational program, or to evaluate progress after a period of remediational instruction. In all cases, procedures mandated by PL 94-142 must be followed, with confidentiality respected and parents permitted full access to assessment data and interpretations.

Application of Assessment Information: There are six basic ways to use assessment data (Cone 1978; Stengel 1985). These are for purposes of *characterization, comparison,* and *rating–ranking* and for deciding *accident–intention, occasional–frequent,* and *mechan-*

ical-insight dimensions (Stengel 1985). Characterization is the use of assessment information to describe the student at some particular time. The purpose of characterization is to show where the student currently is operating without making any judgments or educational diagnoses about the appropriateness of those operating levels. Characterization is most useful in initial, global assessment, which takes place after initial referral and screening.

Using assessment information for comparisons is an essential characteristic of assessment. Comparisons are made either against relative or absolute criteria or against other people (usually a norm group or the student's peers). Comparisons are made in one or more of the following ways:

1. Against goals or ideas. In this case, the question is Where is the student operating in respect to the defined criteria or desired state? This is a criterion-referenced assessment comparison.
2. Against stages of development. Here the comparison question becomes How does the student compare within the scope of childhood development?
3. Against the average student. The question is How does the student compare against the typical student in the class or norm group? This is a norm-referenced comparison.
4. Against the presence or absence of characteristics. How the student operates within a given situation or environment is compared to how the student operates within another environment or situation.

Rating–ranking performance is used either to compare the student to an ideal or standard (rating) or to make a relative comparison against other students (ranking). As such, rating is criterion-referenced assessment, whereas ranking is norm-referenced assessment. An example of rating would be judging athletes at a baseball tryout camp on the basis of athletic ability. Athletes who showed outstanding athletic ability (as judged by a baseball talent scout) would be given professional contracts whereas the majority of those applicants who did not show

outstanding ability would be rejected. An example of ranking would be to compare the athletes against each other with such designations as most talented, second most talented, and least talented. Ratings and rankings are used most often in informal assessment. They are discussed in greater detail in Chapter 11.

Merely noting characteristics or using ratings and rankings does not establish any information about the accident–intention dimension of gathered data. Student performance, for example, could be the result of some accidental condition (e.g., the student correctly guessed at a set of test questions or accidentally dropped a pile of dishes). Performance could also be based on intent, skill, or deliberate behavior (e.g., the student actually knew the test material or threw the dishes in anger). Assessment information should be subjected to questions of accident versus intention.

The accident–intention dimension is hard to measure behaviorally because it is difficult to determine a student's intent. Therefore, the occasional–frequent dimension is often used to identify skilled or accidental happenings. Basically, the more often a behavior occurs, the greater the assumption that it is based on intent or skill. For example, an unskilled student could score high on a test once by chance. However, if a student consistently scored high on tests, we would assume that the person was skilled in that area. Likewise, if dishes are dropped once, it could be an accident. However, a student who consistently breaks dishes is either doing it on purpose or is very uncoordinated. In either case, it would be best to assign such a student to another job.

Finally, assessment information can be used to shed light on the mechanical–insight dimension. Even though a given behavior occurs frequently, the student may not possess much insight into or understanding of that behavior. Such performance could be the result of rote behavior or the student's plugging in some formula to solve the problem. The clinician must assess that the student truly understands the behavior in terms of process and is not simply operating by rote. This mechanical–insight dimension is particularly important in core academic areas, such as arithmetic and reading comprehension.

Synthesis

Synthesis, the most important of the three assessment areas discussed in this chapter, is often omitted from assessment courses and texts. Synthesis is the process of combining all the pieces of discrete and separate data collected during the assessment phase to form coherent conclusions. These conclusions then become the basis for diagnosis, resulting in instructional programming designed to remediate the child's educational weaknesses (McNutt and Mandelbaum 1980).

The various steps in the synthesis process include:

1. Separating information that appears to be accurate from information that may need verification. Information collected from secondary sources (e.g., interviews) or inferred behavior (e.g., paper and pencil tests) is subject to error. Even direct observation may contain error due to problems of interpretation or behavioral change caused by the clinician's intrusiveness. Thus, the clinician must determine which information is accurate and which requires further verification. Generally, the greater the number of independent sources that verify a piece of information, the more likely the information is accurate.

2. Determining if conflicting assessment information is present. If conflicting information does occur, the clinician must decide which information should be considered more accurate. In such situations the clinician must find out why such discrepancies exist.

3. Eliminating information that is redundant or not useful for diagnosis and instructional planning. Some information collected will be irrelevant to the diagnosis and planning process whereas other information will be crucial. The clinician must use only information that is relevant, keeping in mind that information can be accurate but still irrelevant.

4. Comparing and interpreting the information in useful ways to draw conclusions important to diagnosis and future remediational planning. This is the final step in diagnosis, the reason that information gathering, application, and synthesis have taken place. It *is* diagnosis.

A Diagnosis Model: The PAGE Technique

The PAGE technique was created to aid the clinician in diagnosing student learning problems (Hargrove and Poteet 1984). PAGE is an acronym for *perceive, ask, generate,* and *evaluate.* PAGE helps the clinician identify the areas of student difficulty and inquire into why such difficulties are taking place. Finally, PAGE allows the professional to evaluate the validity of such diagnoses.

The Four Stages of PAGE

In the perception stage of PAGE the clinician uses assessment information to verify that a learning problem exists. Such information typically comes after referral and screening and validates the referral or positive identification from the screening test.

Once the problem has been verified, the clinician's role is to ask why the problem is taking place. At this stage the clinician identifies the universe of reasons possibly causing the problem (e.g., poor motivation, learning disability, cognitive variables, environmental variables, etc.). From these possible alternatives, the clinician chooses the most probable explanation and uses this explanation as the working hypothesis. Finally, the clinician tests this hypothesis, verifying it or finding it false. If the hypothesis is verified, it forms the basis of the clinician's diagnosis of the learning problem. If the hypothesis is false, a new hypothesis is formulated and tested.

The PAGE technique helps the clinician interpret assessment data in terms of a working hypothesis to test whether that hypothesis can become the basis of the diagnosis of learning difficulties. Once a hypothesis is verified, the clinician/teacher can then become involved in creating educational programming designed to remediate these weaknesses. As such, the PAGE technique is extremely useful in preventing teachers from designing inappropriate educational programming based on faulty educational and diagnostic hypotheses.

SUMMARY

At some time during their teaching careers teachers engage in assessment activities. It is estimated that more than 250 million standardized tests are administered each school year, along with at least as many informal, teacher-made tests.

How these assessment data are interpreted and used is a vital part of the educational process. The ultimate success of educational programming for exceptional children depends on the skill and competencies of the professionals giving and interpreting the tests. The goal of assessment is to design remediational educational programming.

It is crucial that the teacher using assessment instruments be a skilled clinician. The professional should possess not only the technical skills needed to administer tests appropriately but also the skills to interpret, apply, and synthesize assessment information. The clinician makes predictions and decisions about learners with special needs based on test data and other informational sources.

The clinician must possess sound measurement, evaluation, and diagnosis skills. Measurement skills, those needed to collect information adequately from test administrations, include the ability to collect data and to understand the statistical and mathematical components of tests. Evaluation skills entail interpreting tests and making sense out of test data in meaningful ways. Finally, diagnosis refers to the clinical skills needed to apply and synthesize measurement and evaluative information.

Some educational researchers believe that a crisis of misdiagnosis exists in special education due to the lack of clinical and diagnostic skills of educational professionals. One way to reduce the number and magnitude of clinical and diagnostic errors is to teach professionals these needed skills. Teachers are in a unique position to observe, analyze, and diagnose student behavior, but they must be well trained to do so. Teachers can function as diagnostic tests, but to do so successfully they must be submitted to the same tests of reliability, validity, and error reduction as are standardized tests.

The skills teachers need to carry out sound assessments and diagnoses are rooted in three types of competencies: psychological, psychometric, and psychosocial. Psychological competencies require that teachers possess and use the basic tenets of educational and psychological theory. Teachers should understand child and adolescent development; characteristics of exceptional children; theories of learning, development, cognition, and personality; behavior assessment; and curriculum development and planning.

Teachers must also possess the strong psychometric skills needed to administer and interpret tests. These skills include understanding reliability and validity, interpreting test scores, discerning false claims of tests and test scores, and administering and scoring tests fairly and appropriately.

Psychosocial skills include understanding the social, environmental, linguistic, and cultural background of the test taker in order to interpret test scores more appropriately. Teachers and test examiners must not be Anglocentric in their outlook toward culturally different children. Taking cultural and environmental factors into account reduces the errors in test score interpretation.

The key competencies of assessment and diagnosis fall into the areas of techniques, application, and synthesis. Techniques involve collecting factual information; application deals with deciding, prior to assessment, how data will be collected and used. Synthesis consists of using collected data in meaningful ways to make valid and appropriate diagnoses.

Assessment data can be obtained through the techniques of analysis of products, interviewing, and observation. Analysis of a product occurs when the teacher examines a student's work. Products can be classified along the dimensions of test types and knowledge areas. Tests are norm-referenced, criterion-referenced, and informal. Knowledge areas involve teacher expertise in test selection, construction, administration, and scoring. Norm-referenced tests compare students against other test takers or a peer group. Criterion-referenced tests compare students against a set of objective criteria. Informal tests are teacher-made and can be norm- or criterion-referenced.

Test construction is an important issue in assessment. Skills in test construction center around issues of item construction. Test items should be valid and appropriate for the test takers. Finally, teachers must be competent test administrators and make sure that the test is given according to the testing procedures.

Proficiency in test interpretation is a key clinical skill. This skill includes understanding the statistical basis of norm-referenced tests and interpreting not only the score but also the child's overall test-taking behavior. Finally, the clinician must know which scores to use from a given test. Two major criteria for choosing one test score over another are usefulness and specificity of information.

Application skills involve deciding, before assessment information is gathered, what should be measured, why the information is being gathered, and what should be done with the data. Four main sources of assessment information are academic (cognitive), behavioral, physical/sensory, and vocational. During assessment, the area to be tested is usually broken down into subcomponent skills. Such assessment may be atomistic or holistic in scope, and the philosophy adopted by the clinician will determine how the subcomponents are defined.

The four main purposes for data collection are screening, classification, instructional planning, and evaluating pupil progress. Defining the purpose of the assessment will determine largely how the assessment is carried out, what types of data are collected, and how information is evaluated and interpreted.

The six basic ways to use assessment data are: characterization, comparison, and rating–ranking, as well as deciding accident–intention, occasional–frequent, and mechanical–insight dimensions. Each method of using data is extremely important in the application process. Decisions regarding the purposes for and use of assessment information should be made prior to the assessment.

Synthesis is a key assessment area that consists of taking all the information and data that have been collected and combining them to form coherent conclusions. These conclusions then become the basis for diagnosis. The various steps in synthesis include separating accurate information from information that must be verified, determining when conflicting information is present and reconciling such discrepancies, eliminating redundant and irrelevant information, and interpreting information in educationally useful ways.

The PAGE model is a technique for diagnosing learning problems. PAGE stands for perceive, ask, generate, and evaluate. This technique helps the clinician form and test working hypotheses in order to diagnose and remediate students' learning problems.

STUDY QUESTIONS

1. What is the difference between an assessment technician and a clinician? Can a person be one without being the other? If so, how?

2. Why are clinical and diagnostic skills important? What is the relationship between possessing these skills and reducing error in diagnoses?

3. What are the three skill areas of assessment and diagnosis? What are the basis skills of each area? How would they apply to assessment of special needs learners?

4. Define clinical techniques, applications, and synthesis. What are their roles in assessment?

5. What is analysis of product? How is it used during the assessment process?

6. What are the variables that effect good test selection? How does selection of good tests reduce assessment error?

7. Define two techniques of informal assessment described in the chapter. How do the techniques differ from one another? How do they differ from formal tests?

8. Define and describe the major application skills of assessment. Why are they important?

9. Describe the six basic ways in which data information is used. Define each process. Why are they important?

10. What is the difference between atomistic and holistic assessment? Under what conditions would each type of assessment be used?

11. What is synthesis in the assessment process? Why is it vitally important? What happens to assessment if synthesis is not used?

12. What is the PAGE technique and how is it used in assessment? Why is it important?

CHAPTER 6

Distributions and Statistics: The Key to Understanding Norm-Referenced Tests

Something about the word *statistics* can make some adults nervous and cause a few prospective teachers to change majors. For some people, facing an entire chapter dealing with statistics invokes all of the enthusiasm of having a tooth pulled.

It doesn't have to be that way. Although statistics may not be fun for most people, they need not be incomprehensible or intimidating. Anxiety over statistics may be a major reason for the lack of informed consumerism in test choice, use, and interpretation. Given such anxiety, some teachers and other professionals abdicate this field of knowledge to test authors, publishing companies, and salespersons—people with a vested interest in selling you their test. The seller's job is made even easier when the prospective buyer does not possess the requisite statistical background to discern good tests from poor. Although a little knowledge can sometimes be dangerous, a little knowledge of statistics will help the prospective teacher become a wise test consumer.

This chapter introduces the statistical information needed to understand tests—especially norm-referenced tests. To understand the material presented in this chapter, the reader needs only basic mathematical skills and the ability to square a number and find a square root. If necessary, all of these operations can be performed with a small calculator. With knowledge of basic statistics, the test consumer will be able to judge appropriately the technical adequacy of the tests they use.

The Function of Statistics

What are statistics, and why are they needed? In general, statistics are numbers that summarize and condense information. As such, statistics are numbers that summarize a body of other numbers.

This summarizing function of statistics is important. For example, suppose we were interested in whether the height of professional basketball players had increased over the years. The obvious way to investigate would be to examine the height of each professional basketball player (approximately 300 players) for each of the last ten seasons. But such an examination would yield 3,000 separate numbers (heights). This huge array of numbers would be unwieldy and uninterpretable. Somehow these 3,000 numbers must be condensed or summarized.

This is precisely what statistics can do for us. We could, for example, find the average height of professional basketball players for each of the last ten years. This calculation would yield 10 numbers instead of 3,000.

Then by examining this relatively small field of numbers, we could readily see whether a trend of increased height existed.

The Misuse of Statistics

Some people say that statistics lie. Whereas such a statement may reinforce people's distrust and fear of statistics, it is nevertheless untrue. Statistics do not lie, but they can be interpreted in inappropriate ways that lead to inappropriate conclusions.

For example, take the often quoted statistic that the majority of automobile accidents occur within twenty-five miles of home. One could conclude from this statistic that it is safer to take a long trip than a short trip. But such an interpretation would be inappropriate. Long trips are not safer than short ones. Rather, because more short trips are taken than long journeys, more accidents related to short trips will occur. Thus, a salesperson who wants to sell you a long trip, and who claims that taking such a trip is safer than staying around town, is using statistics inappropriately (Hooke 1983).

Unscrupulous or uninformed individuals often use statistics to win people to their way of thinking or to convince them to purchase tests and other educational products that are inappropriate or poorly constructed. The best way to counter such statistical claims is to be an informed statistical consumer who understands the purposes for which statistics can and cannot be used. One must be able to judge whether the statistics used to describe a given set of data are appropriate and whether the statistics, once obtained, are being interpreted correctly.

The First Step in Statistics: Understanding Scales of Measurement

Types of Scales

A measurement *scale* is a method or way of comparing numbers or scores. It is the particular system or mode in which such numbers are compared. Whenever measurement of an event occurs, it is important to know what type of scale was used in obtaining the observation. Distinctions between scales are important because certain types of statistical procedures are appropriate for some scales but not for others. The following discussion deals with four types of scales: *nominal, ordinal, equal, interval,* and *ratio scales.*

Nominal Scales: The word *nominal* means "naming things." Nominal measurement therefore involves taking measurements on a scale that simply names or catalogs observations.

For example, suppose you decided to take a census of the occupations of parents of the students in your class. You could assign salespeople the category 1, doctors 2, auto mechanics 3, and so forth. With each occupation assigned a category, you would be using a nominal scale.

Note that in this example no weight or significance is attached to the numerals (categories). No qualitative significance is attached to higher or lower numerals. The numerals merely indicate the category of a person's occupation. Thus, nominal scales measure only qualitative distinctions and make no attempt to measure size or magnitude.

Ordinal Scales: Ordinal scales rank observations in terms of size or magnitude. Categories used in ordinal scales can be expressed in everyday language (e.g., first to least, best to worst, shortest to tallest) or can be numerical (e.g., 1 to 10). Suppose, for example, you wished to rank five students on their ability to spell this week's list of spelling words. You could give the list of words to the students, grade the correctness of their responses, and rank order the students' performance from highest to lowest. Such ranking would represent use of an ordinal scale.

Note, however, that ordinal data do not reveal *how much* better one person's score is

from that of another. An unwary interpreter of ordinal scale data might falsely interpret the results to mean that the students were equidistant from one another in their performance. The inability of ordinal scales to distinguish the magnitude of differences between respondents is a major limitation.

Equal Interval Scales: With equal interval scales, the difference (known as the interval) between responses or numbers is reflected as a difference in magnitude. However, ratios of magnitude (e.g., twice as much, half as much) cannot be expressed in equal interval scales because such scales do not possess a meaningful (absolute) zero.

The concept of absolute zero is best explained by an example. Suppose that on Tuesday the temperature in a given city was 25°F. On Wednesday, however, a heat wave moved in and the temperature soared to 50°F. We can say that Wednesday was hotter than Tuesday (an ordinal measurement) and that, furthermore, it was twenty-five degrees warmer on Wednesday than on Tuesday (an equal interval measurement). However, we cannot say that it was *twice* as warm on Wednesday as it was on Tuesday (a ratio statement).

To make meaningful ratio statements, we must have an absolute zero, a point under which the property we are measuring ceases to exist. But Fahrenheit temperature does not contain a zero point (we can have temperatures lower than 0°F). Therefore, ratio statements about the temperature's being twice as hot on Wednesday cannot be made.

Most educational measurement falls into the equal interval measurement category. For example, consider the concept of IQ. Does a child with an IQ of 100 possess twice as much of the construct as a child with an IQ of 50? The answer is no because there is no absolute zero in IQ, the point at which IQ is nonexistent in a human being. Thus, ratio judgments in IQ testing are meaningless (although uninformed people still engage in the practice).

Even though ratio judgments cannot be made with equal interval scales, such scales are very useful in educational practice. It is useful, for example, to know that Sally is two grade levels ahead of the rest of her class in reading or that Jacob has jumped two units in arithmetic functioning in five weeks, even if we cannot make meaningful comments about the ratios of Sally's and Jacob's progress. Likewise, we can make meaningful judgments about children who possess IQs of 100 and 50, respectively, even if we cannot make statements about one IQ's being twice as great as the other.

Ratio Scales: Ratio scales reflect the magnitude of differences between numbers (observations). However, the ratios of those numbers are also meaningful because ratio scales possess absolute zero points. For example, suppose Juan and Peter are weight lifters. Juan can lift 150 pounds over his head whereas Peter can lift 300 pounds (an equal interval measurement). It is also appropriate to say that Peter can lift twice as much weight as Juan because there is a point of zero weight being lifted (no pounds). Thus, weight has an absolute zero.

Ratio scales are used primarily in the physical sciences for measurements of weight, length, and time. Ratio scales, however, are relatively rare in the educational and social sciences, where equal interval scales predominate.

Discrete versus Continuous Variables

Variables are the things being measured or investigated. For example, if you are measuring children's reading level on a given test, reading level (as measured by that test) is the variable under investigation.

Discrete Variables

Suppose you want to investigate the gender of children enrolled in special education classes for the mildly mentally retarded (developmentally handicapped). In this case, all your observations will fall into one of two classes—male or female. There can be no in-between scores. Thus, sex is a *discrete* or *noncontinuous* variable. Examples of other discrete variables are birth dates, eye color, and blood type.

Continuous Variables

On the other hand, suppose you want to measure the weights of adults living in a certain town. In this case, there would be a great range of weights (approximately 100 to 400 pounds), especially if you measured in fractions of pounds. The weights would fall along a range of scores instead of into discrete classes or categories. Thus, weight is a *continuous* variable.

Most variables in educational assessment are continuous. For example, a child's IQ score falls along a range of scores from approximately 20 or 25 to 200, or above. Likewise, scores on a teacher-made math test would also fall along a range of possible scores from 0 to 100 percent. These test scores would be examples of continuous variables.

Frequency Distributions

Suppose you are gathering information on the IQs of 110 children enrolled in the fifth grade at Morgan Elementary School. You administer a standardized test of intelligence and obtain an IQ for each student (Table 6-1).

Study the data contained at the top of Table 6-1. Do the data make sense or are they simply a jumbled mass of 110 numbers?

It should be obvious that something needs to be done with these IQ scores to make sense out of them. One basic step is to count the number of times each score appears. We can then gain a sense of whether some scores are more common than others. Counting the frequency of given scores is known as a *fre-*

Table 6-1 Frequency Table for IQs of 110 Students at Morgan Elementary School

IQ Scores Collected for 110 Students

154	131	122	100	113	119	121	128	112	93
133	119	115	117	110	104	125	85	120	135
116	103	103	121	109	147	103	113	107	98
128	93	90	105	118	134	89	143	108	142
85	108	108	136	115	117	110	80	111	127
100	100	114	123	126	119	122	102	100	106
105	111	127	108	106	91	123	132	97	110
150	130	87	89	108	137	124	96	111	101
118	104	127	94	115	101	125	129	131	110
97	135	108	139	133	107	115	83	109	116
110	113	112	82	114	112	113	142	145	123

Frequency Table for the 110 IQ Scores

X	f	X	f	X	f	X	f
154	|	135	||	116	||	97	||
153		134	|	115	||||	96	|
152		133	||	114	||	95	
151		132	|	113	||||	94	|
150	|	131	||	112	|||	93	||
149		130	|	111	|||	92	
148		129		110	|||||	91	|
147	|	128	||	109	||	90	|
146		127	|||	108	||||||	89	||
145	|	126	|	107	||	88	
144		125	||	106	||	87	|
143	|	124	|	105	||	86	
142	||	123	|||	104	||	85	||
141		122	||	103	|||	84	
140		121	||	102	|	83	|
139	|	120	|	101	||	82	|
138		119	|||	100	||||	81	
137	|	118	||	99		80	|
136	|	117	||	98	|		

quency distribution. The frequency distribution for the IQ scores of the 110 fifth graders at Morgan Elementary School appears in the lower portion of Table 6-1.

Frequency Polygons

Although Table 6-1 is helpful, these frequency data could be made even clearer if it was converted into pictorial form.

Figure 6-1 contains a frequency polygon or curve for the IQ score data presented in Table 6-1. On the X axis are the IQ scores of the children; on the Y axis is the frequency with which each score appeared.

A Note of Caution

It must be emphasized that frequency distributions and curves are appropriate only for con-

Figure 6-1   A Frequency Polygon for the IQ Scores of 110 Students at Morgan Elementary School

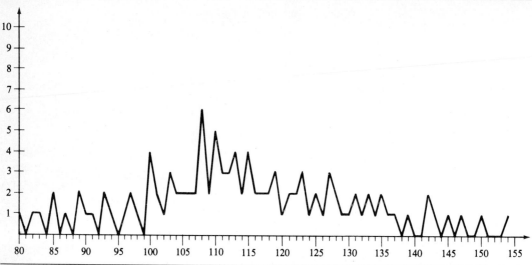

tinuous variables, that is, for variables in which a range of scores is possible. A frequency curve is inappropriate for discrete variables, such as sex and blood type. A *histo-* *gram*, which measures the number of times a score falls into a discrete category, is the appropriate pictorial tool for discrete variables. An example of a histogram is shown in Figure 6-2.

Figure 6-2   A Histogram

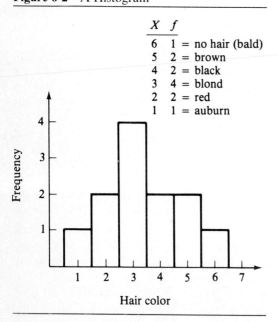

X	f	
6	1	= no hair (bald)
5	2	= brown
4	2	= black
3	4	= blond
2	2	= red
1	1	= auburn

Shapes of Frequency Distributions

Rather than draw a frequency distribution for each measured variable, professionals have described basic *types* of distributions. Each type of distribution is defined by certain characteristics and attributes. Two distributions of the same category will possess many of the same characteristics. In this way, the professional can understand the attributes of a given distribution without necessarily having to draw it.

Basically, a distribution is described by three characteristics: *shape, central tendency,* and *variability*. Central tendency and variability are described later in this chapter. Basically, central tendency measures the location of the center of the distribution and variability describes how the scores are spread throughout the distribution. This section deals with the shape of distributions.

Figure 6-3   Normal and Skewed Distributions

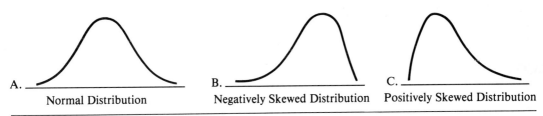

A.   B.   C.

Normal Distribution   Negatively Skewed Distribution   Positively Skewed Distribution

Normal or Symmetrical Distributions

Normal distributions are symmetrical and bell shaped (see Figure 6-3[A]). In a normal distribution, a vertical line can be drawn through the middle of the curve so that one side of the distribution is a mirror image of the other.

Distributions that are not symmetrical and normal are *skewed*. If a distribution has more higher scores than lower scores, the peak of the curve is skewed to the right, and the curve is said to be negatively skewed. If the curve possesses more lower scores than higher scores, the peak of the distribution is skewed to the left, and the curve is said to be positively skewed. Figure 6-3 (B, C) shows negatively and positively skewed distributions.

The Central Limits Theorem and Normal Distributions

Normal distributions are often desirable because they indicate an appropriate range and frequency of scores. They also possess some unique properties. One method of assuring that a given frequency distribution approaches normal shape, without actually drawing the distribution, is through the central limits theorem.

The central limits theorem states that the more scores or observations collected and figured into the frequency distribution, the more that distribution will approach the shape of a normal curve. The central limits theorem can be demonstrated by an example. Suppose you want to enter into a frequency distribution children's test scores that could range from 0 to 100. For some reason you only give the test to 5 children in a school of 1,000 pupils. How can you assume that these five scores are representative of all the children in the school? In fact, you may have a set of very unrepresentative scores.

Now you decide to give the test to 500 students instead of 5. In such a case, scores become more representative and an unrepresentative score counts for only $\frac{1}{500}$ of the distribution. Thus, as the number of observations increases, so does the manner in which the frequency distribution takes on the shape of a normal curve.

Measures of Central Tendency

As mentioned at the beginning of this chapter, statistics summarize data. The better (and more accurately) a given statistic summarizes a body of data, the more useful the particular statistic.

Measures of central tendency are statistics that summarize data and identify the single most representative score for an entire distribution. As such, measures of central tendency offer statistics useful for summarizing or capsuling an entire frequency distribution.

However, a useful statistic must do two things well: summarize data and summarize them accurately. Measures of central tendency, although easy to understand, suffer from a degree of inexactness that can lead uninformed consumers to errors of interpreta-

Figure 6-4   The Mode: The Most Frequent Score in a Distribution

A. Single Mode
Scores

86
80
75
75
75   mode = 75
74
73
72
72
70

B. Bimodal Distribution

86
84
82
82
82   modes = 82, 75
80
75
75
75
74

C. An Example of Interpretation Problems Using the Mode
Mr. Johnson's Class Scores

90
75
75
60
40
42   mode = 75   (Range of scores is wide. Mode is at high end of distribu-
35   tion.)
31
26
20
15

Mr. Taylor's Class Scores

90
86
85
84
82
80   mode = 75   (Range of scores is relatively narrow. Mode is at low end of
75   distribution.)
75
74
73
70

tion. The limitations of each measure of central tendency must be clearly understood by the test consumer in order to avoid shoddy statistical interpretation.

The Mode

The mode is the most common score that appears in a distribution. Example A in Figure 6-4 shows the test scores received by ten students. Because more students received a score of 75 than any other score, 75 is the mode.

There can be more than one mode in a distribution. In example B in Figure 6-4, the scores of both 75 and 82 were achieved the most number of times by students. Thus, this distribution is *bimodal*, the two modes being 75 and 82.

Although the mode is easy to understand, it is not especially accurate in summarizing data. For example, examine the scores in Mr. Johnson's and Mr. Taylor's classes on the same test (example C in Figure 6-4). The mode for each class is the same, but the distribution of scores is radically different. The scores in Mr. Taylor's class are at about the mode, but the scores in Mr. Johnson's class are far below the mode. Thus, to infer from the mode that the distributions in the two classes were about the same would be blatantly inaccurate.

The Median

The median is the score that divides a distribution in half. That is, one-half of the scores in the distribution fall below the median and one-half of the scores fall above the median.

To find the median of a distribution, first rank order the scores from highest to lowest. Next, find the score that half the scores fall above and half fall below. In the case of an even number of scores in a distribution, the number between the two median scores is the

Figure 6-5   Finding the Median of a Distribution

A. Original scores.

22
15
10
29
21

B. Arrange scores from highest to lowest.

29
22
21
15
10

C. For odd-numbered distribution, find the midpoint in distribution.

29
22   2 scores
21 ◄
15
10   2 scores

D. For even-numbered distribution, find two midpoint scores and interpolate halfway between the two scores.

29
22
24 ⎫
21 ⎭   middle 2 scores
15
10

$$24 - 21 = 3$$
$$\frac{3}{2} = 1.5$$
$$21 + 1.5 = 22.5$$
$$(24 - 1.5 = 22.5)$$
$$\text{median} = 22.5$$

true median. Figure 6-5 shows how to determine the median for an odd and also an even number of scores in a distribution.

The goal of the median is to describe the exact midpoint of a distribution. In this way, it is more accurate than the mode in summarizing distribution data. However, keep in mind that the median is not concerned with the magnitude of differences between scores in a distribution. Rather, it is only concerned with the midpoint score.

The insensitivity of the median to the magnitude of scores can be seen in the two score distributions shown in Figure 6-6. Even though the medians of the distributions are the same, distribution A has many scores at the extremes. The median simply is not designed to reflect the magnitude between scores in distributions.

The Mean

The mean is the arithmetic average of scores in a distribution. It is calculated by totaling the scores and dividing by the number of scores in the distribution (see Figure 6-7).

Unlike the median, the mean does reflect the magnitude of differences between scores. This is apparent in Figure 6-7, where the extreme scores of distribution A caused the mean to be much lower than the mean for distribution B. However, the mean's reflections of the magnitude of differences in scores can be a blessing or a curse. For example, examine the distributions in Figure 6-7. Since the first distribution contains only five scores, the two extreme scores represent 40 percent

Figure 6-6 The Median Does Not Reflect the Magnitude of Scores

Distribution A

$$
\begin{array}{l}
30 \\
25 \\
\textcircled{21} \qquad \text{Median} = 21 \qquad \text{Mean} = \dfrac{94}{5} = 18.8 \\
10 \\
\underline{8} \\
94
\end{array}
$$

Distribution B

$$
\begin{array}{l}
1000 \\
25 \\
\textcircled{21} \qquad \text{Median} = 21 \qquad \text{Mean} = \dfrac{1064}{5} = 212.8 \\
10 \\
8
\end{array}
$$

Figure 6-7 The Mean

A. Calculating the mean
Scores (x)

$$
\begin{array}{l}
5 \\
15 \\
20 \\
5 \\
25
\end{array}
$$

$$\text{mean } (\overline{X}) = \frac{\Sigma(\text{sum}) \text{ of } X}{n}$$

Where:

X = each raw score of the distribution

$$\Sigma X = 5 + 15 + 20 + 5 + 25 = 70$$
$$n = 5$$
$$\frac{70}{5} = 14 = \overline{X}$$

B. The weight of magnitude on the mean when the distribution contains few and many observations

Distribution A	Distribution B
Scores	Scores
100	100
20	20
10	20
10	10
5	10
$\dfrac{145}{5} = 29$	10
	15
	15
	15
	10
	20
	5
	5
	25
	25
	15
	10
	10
	20
	25
	$\dfrac{385}{20} = 19.25$

of the total scores of the distribution and heavily pull down the mean. The second distribution has the same extreme scores. However, because this distribution contains twenty scores instead of five, the extreme scores have much less effect on the mean of the entire distribution.

Figure 6-7 also demonstrates the relationship between the mean and the central limits theory. As the number of scores in a distribution increases, the mean increases in its accuracy for describing a distribution. Likewise, if the number of scores in a distribution are relatively few, the median is probably the better statistic to use. When given the median or mean of a distribution, the informed consumer of statistics should first determine the number of scores in that distribution before accepting those statistics as valid.

Measures of Central Tendency and the Normal Distribution

If a person is informed about the shape of a distribution (i.e., whether it is normal, or positively or negatively skewed), that person possesses precise information about the relationship between the mean, median, and mode of that distribution. As shown in Figure 6-8, for example, the three measures of central tendency are precisely the same for a normal distribution. Because the mode is the most frequent score, it occurs at the height of the distribution. But the highest point of the distribution is also the precise midpoint of a normal distribution (the median). Finally, the average (mean) score is the arithmetic average that, in a normal curve, falls precisely at the middle of the distribution. Thus, with a normal distribution,

if you know one measure of central tendency, you know them all.

The relationship between the three measures of central tendency and skewed distributions is also shown in Figure 6-8. In a positively skewed distribution, more scores exist at the lower end of the distribution than at the higher end. Therefore, the mode will be a relatively low score, the median higher, and the mean highest. The opposite holds for a negatively skewed distribution, where there are more high scores than low scores. In this case, the mode is a relatively high score, the median lower, and the mean lowest.

Statistics of Dispersion

Two of the three characteristics of distributions, shape and central tendency, have been discussed. We now turn to measures of dispersion (variability).

Dispersion or *variability* (the terms are often used synonymously) refers to the way scores either cluster together or spread across a distribution. A distribution with clustered scores tells us that a significant proportion of the people scored about the same on a given measure; a wide range of scores indicates that people were quite diverse in how they scored on the given test or variable.

Sometimes a wide range of variability is

Figure 6-8 Measures of Central Tendency for Normal and Skewed Distributions

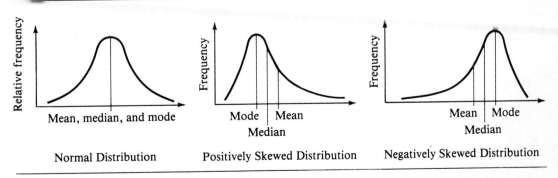

Normal Distribution Positively Skewed Distribution Negatively Skewed Distribution

desirable; at other times it is not. Preference for wide variability will depend on the purpose of the test and what the test examiner hopes to find. For example, Figure 6-9 (A) shows the scores for a spelling test. The scores are clustered on the high end of the distribution. A teacher might be happy with this distribution if it means that a high percentage of the students have mastered the academic content (it could also mean the content was very easy). However, suppose a college admissions officer, faced with the prospect of accepting only 10 percent of applicants, received a distribution of SAT scores similar to those in Figure 6-9 (B). These scores also are clustered, but the officer has a problem. Where should the cutoff for acceptance be made? Simply accepting the top 10 percent of the applicants

Figure 6-9 Low Variability on Two Distributions

A. *Teacher's Spelling Test—Low Variability Desired (narrow distribution with many high scores indicates spelling mastery)*

Scores	Frequency
92	3
89	2
88	3
85	5
83	2
80	3
70	1
65	1
60	2

B. *College Admissions Test (only top 10 percent of scores admitted)*

Scores	Frequency
98	10
97	12
96	8
95	10
93	8
91	12
90	15
88	6

might mean rejecting students who missed the cutoff by only one point! Thus, in cases in which are tests are given to spread people apart and show differences among scores, high variability is desired. If tests are designed to indicate mastery of content, low variability (with many high scores) is preferable.

Kurtosis and Dispersion in Distributions

Although the term *kurtosis* sounds like a tropical disease, it refers to the way scores are pictorially spread out in a distribution. Different types of kurtosis in distributions are shown in Figure 6-10. In the first example, the peak of the curve is narrow. This means that many scores are clustered together. Such high clustering produces a *leptokurtic* curve. The second curve shows a moderate clustering pattern, which appears most often in normal curves. This is a *mesokurtic* clustering pattern. Finally, scores that possess a great deal of variability and do not cluster result in *platykurtic* curves (the last example).

By knowing the general kurtosis of a distribution, the statistical consumer can view in a glance the clustering pattern of scores. In so doing, some cursory conclusions can be drawn about whether the test performed as desired, either separating test scores or indicating homogeneity of scores.

Other Measures of Dispersion

The Range

The range is the simplest measure of dispersion, but it is also the least accurate. The range represents the distance from the highest score in the distribution to the lowest score. The formula for finding the range is $(H - L) + 1$, where H is the highest score in the distribution and L represents the lowest score.

Although the range reveals the largest pos-

Figure 6-10 Kurtosis in Distributions

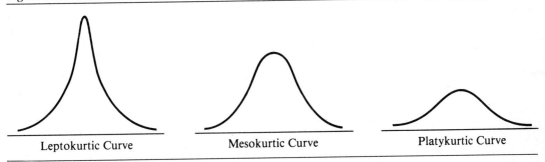

Leptokurtic Curve   Mesokurtic Curve   Platykurtic Curve

sible spread of scores, it takes into account only the extreme scores and ignores the scores in the middle. Consider, for example, two distributions:

- Distribution 1: 1, 5, 7, 9, 13
- Distribution 2: 1, 5, 7, 9, 90

These distributions are identical except for the last score. However, whereas the range for Distribution 1 is 13, the range for Distribution 2 is 90. An uninformed consumer given these ranges of distribution might be led to make inappropriate statistical and educational inferences.

The Standard Deviation and Variance

Perhaps a better way of measuring dispersion, rather than finding the distance between the extreme scores, is to note how scores are dispersed around the mean of the distribution. Because the mean is at or near the midpoint of the distribution (especially for normal distributions), such measures of dispersion would exhibit less extreme fluctuations than would range distributions.

The *standard deviation* represents the average distance or deviation of scores from the mean. This means that the standard deviation divides the distribution into markers or segments that reflect whether scores cluster around the mean or whether they are dispersed more widely throughout the distribution.

To find the standard deviation, there are some intermediary statistical steps that include finding statistics called the *sum of squares* (*SS*) and the *variance* (s^2). As long as we keep our goal in mind—finding the average deviation of scores from the mean—understanding these statistical manipulations is not difficult.

To find the standard deviation, we must first find the deviation (distance) of each score from the mean. Examine the distribution of scores shown at the top of Figure 6-11. Since we are looking for the distance of scores from the mean, we must first find the mean of the distribution. As can be seen from Figure 6-11(A), the mean, or arithmetic average for this distribution, is 30/5 = 6.

Now since we wish to find the deviation or difference of each score from the mean, we must subtract the mean from each raw score (see Figure 6-11[B]).

Sum of squares (*SS*) represents the *sum* of the deviation scores. This means that we need to add up the deviation scores. However, if you do this, you will find that the sum equals zero (see Figure 6-11[B]). In fact, the sum of deviation scores *always* equals zero because positive and negative deviation scores in a distribution always cancel each other out. Thus, before we can sum deviation scores we need

Figure 6-11   Finding the Standard Deviation

A. Distribution Mean

5
6
8                    $\overline{X} = \dfrac{30}{5} = 6$
4
7
‾‾‾
30

B. Finding the Sum of Squares (SS)

Score $\overline{X} = 6$	Deviation Score	Deviation Score^2
5	$5 - 6 = -1$	$-1^2 = 1$
6	$6 - 6 = 0$	$0^2 = 0$
8	$8 - 6 = 2$	$2^2 = 4$
4	$4 - 6 = -2$	$-2^2 = 4$
7	$7 - 6 = 1$	$1^2 = 1$
	0	10

C. Finding the Variance (s^2)

$s^2 = \dfrac{SS}{n}$ $SS = 10$ $n = 5$

$\dfrac{10}{5} = 2 = s^2$

D. Finding the Standard Deviation (s)

$s = \sqrt{s^2} = \sqrt{2} = 1.41$

to square them (hence, Sum of Squares) in order to remove the sign from the deviation scores. Figure 6-11(B) shows the Sum of Squares (10) for this distribution.

Now that we have the Sum of Squares, we want to find the *average* deviation from the mean. To obtain the average, divide the sum by the number of scores (5). Dividing the Sum of Squares (*SS*) by the number of scores (*n*) produces the variance (s^2), defined as the average squared deviation of scores from the mean (see Figure 6-11[C]).

There is one more calculation to determine the standard deviation. What we have is the average, squared deviation from the mean. What we wish to find is the average deviation from the mean. We must eliminate the square. By taking the square root of the variance (see Figure 6-11[D]), we obtain the standard deviation (*s*), defined as the average deviation from the mean.

What Shape, Central Tendency, and Dispersion Tell Us about Distributions

Once we know the shape, central tendency (particularly the mean), and dispersion (especially the standard deviation) for a distribution, we know virtually everything that is necessary. For example, the shape of the distribution tells us whether the distribution is normal or skewed and if skewed, in which direction. As discussed shortly, there are some distinct advantages in having a normal distribution, particularly as it relates to gleaning additional information about the distribution. Also, by knowing the shape of the distribution, we know how the mean, median, and mode lie in relation to one another.

The mean of the distribution provides information about the average or prototypical score. It tells us where the average score lies and gives us some introductory summarization of the data.

Finally, the standard deviation yields some precise information about the spread of scores around the mean. The larger the standard deviation, the more dispersed the scores. Likewise, a small standard deviation denotes scores clustered more tightly around the mean. Depending on the conclusions to be drawn from the data, a small standard deviation may be favorable or unfavorable.

The Mean, Standard Deviation, and Normal Distribution

A normal distribution has some special statistical properties that make it useful in analyzing data. For example, because the normal distribution is symmetrical, precisely as many scores lie above the mean as below. The same holds for the standard deviation. As many standard deviation units (three) fall below the mean as fall above (see Figure 6-12).

A normal distribution also provides information as to the percentage of scores that fall

Figure 6-12   Standard Deviation

A. Percentage of Cases Falling within Standard
   Deviation Units of the Normal Curve

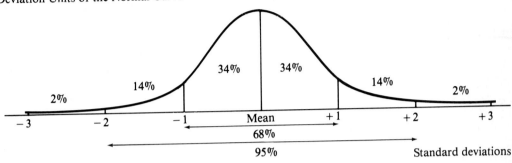

B. Distribution of IQ's in the General Population
   as Predicted by the Normal Curve

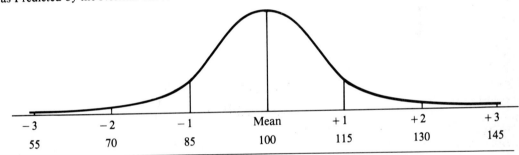

within standard deviation units. We already know that 50 percent of all cases in a normal distribution fall below the mean and 50 percent place above the mean. As shown in Figure 6-12, it is also known that approximately 34 percent of scores fall between the mean and one standard deviation below and approximately 34 percent fall between the mean and one standard deviation above (34% + 34% = 68%). Thus, more than two-thirds of all scores fall −1 to +1 standard deviation unit from the mean. Likewise, we expect approximately 14 percent of all scores to fall between −1 and −2 standard deviation units below the mean and approximately 14 percent to fall between +1 and +2 standard deviations above the mean. Thus, we can expect

68 percent plus 28 percent (96 percent) of all cases to fall ± 2 standard deviations from the mean. Finally, we can expect virtually all of the remaining cases to fall between −2 and −3 and +2 and +3 standard deviation units from the mean. Thus, in a normal curve we know that the distribution is symmetrical and also where percentages of cases in that distribution will fall.

The usefulness of information regarding the normal curve is apparent when considering the distribution of a variable such as intelligence (IQ) in the population. We know a number of things about intelligence as measured by standardized intelligence tests. First, we know that intelligence is normally distributed. Second, the Wechsler Intelligence Test for Children (WISC), one of the most popular intelligence tests, possesses a mean IQ of 100 and a standard deviation of 15. Thus, we can draw a normal distribution for IQ and readily see what proportion of the population we expect to possess various IQs (Figure 6-12[B]). As shown in Figure 6-12(B), we would expect approximately 2 percent of the population to possess measured IQs lower than 70 (often a cutoff score for mental deficiency). In fact, the finding that as many as 10 to 25 percent of certain cultural groups were being placed in classes for the mentally retarded prompted Jane Mercer's famous study in which she charged that cultural bias in intelligence tests resulted in a higher incidence of diagnosis of mental retardation for culturally different individuals. Finally, Figure 6-12(B) shows that less than 1 percent of the population would possess IQs higher than 145 (extremely gifted). Rare are the geniuses like Wolfgang Mozart and John Stuart Mill, who historians and psychologists estimate had IQs in the 180 to 200 range.

The Concept of Correlation

The final concept discussed in this chapter is *correlation*. Correlations refer to *relatedness*, that is, to the relationship between two objects or events. For example, in education, a relationship might exist between reading achievement and the number of books parents read to a child at home. By and large, children who were read many books when they were young grow up to be good readers. This is an example of a positive correlation.

Correlations can also be negative. An example of negative correlation is that between the amount of positive reinforcement and inappropriate behavior. That is, as positive reinforcement for appropriate behavior increases, the amount of inappropriate behavior decreases.

It should be understood that correlation is

not causation. The fact that two events are related does not mean that one event caused the other. Again, consider the relationship between being read to at home as a child and reading achievement. There is no degree of certainty that being read books as a child caused the person to demonstrate high reading achievement. Many other factors probably affected reading achievement, including intelligence, motivation, and school reading curricula. We can say that being read to as a child and reading achievement are connected or related in some way—that a relationship exists between the two variables. Confusing correlation for causation is a mistake commonly made by people unfamiliar with statistics. Such an error often contributes to inappropriate conclusions regarding educational tests, programs, and teaching methods.

Correlation Coefficients

Correlation coefficients are the numerical indication of the strength of the relationship (correlation) between two events or variables. Consider again the example of being read to as a child and reading achievement. Few people would argue that this relationship holds for every child. Rather, this relationship probably is stronger for some children and weaker for others. Some children who were read hundreds of books grew up to be terrible readers.

The most common way of expressing correlation coefficients is with the *Pearson Product-Moment* coefficient (expressed as r).

Correlation coefficients indicate the degree in which the correlational relationship holds for the people or the events measured. Correlation coefficients can range from $r = 0.00$ (no correlation) to $r = \pm 1.00$ (perfect correlation). The higher the correlation, the greater the r coefficient.

Subsequent chapters demonstrate the usefulness of Pearson Product-Moment coefficients in understanding the usefulness, predictability, reliability, and error in tests. Thus, understanding the general concept of correlation, and Pearson coefficients in particular, will help test consumers understand the technical aspects of tests and make informed choices.

SUMMARY

Statistics are numbers that summarize information. They help make sense out of data by condensing large bodies of information into manageable size. Unfortunately, statistics are often accused of lying. Statistics cannot lie; they can only be used and interpreted in appropriate or inappropriate ways by consumers.

Measurement is obtained by using one of four scales: nominal, ordinal, equal interval, or ratio. Nominal scales simply name or catalog observations. Ordinal scales rank order observations from top to bottom on some dimension. However, ordinal scales do not reveal the magnitude of the differences between ranked data. Equal interval scales reveal the magnitude of differences between observations but not the ratio of those differences. This is because equal interval scales do not possess an absolute zero. Ratio scales can reflect the ratio of differences between observations because the scales possess a true zero.

Variables are discrete or continuous. Discrete variables fall into a limited number of discrete classes or categories. Continuous variables contain a range or continuum of possible scores.

Frequency distributions are a way of analyzing and interpreting data. In frequency distributions, the frequency of occurrence of scores or observations is recorded.

Frequency data can be depicted in pictorial form as polygons or frequency curves. However, frequency curves (distributions) are only appropriate for continuous variables. Discrete variables can be depicted as histograms.

Frequency distributions are either symmetrical (normal) or skewed. Skewed distributions are either positive or negative.

The central limits theorem states that the greater the number of observations collected, the more the resulting frequency distribution will approximate a normal curve. The central limits theorem is useful for predicting a frequency's shape based on the number of observations collected.

Measures of central tendency are statistics that identify the single most representative score for an entire distribution. However, measures of central tendency are often inexact, which can lead to errors of interpretation.

The three measures of central tendency are the mode, median, and mean. The mode is the most frequently occurring score in a distribution. The median is the score that divides the distribution exactly in half. The mean is the arithmetic average of the distribution. The median is not affected by the magnitude of scores in the distribution; the mean is affected by such scores. In a normal distribution, the mean, median, and mode have the same value. However, in skewed distributions the three values are different, depending on the size and nature of the skew.

Dispersion or variability refers to the way scores cluster together or are spread throughout a distribution. Dispersion can be pictorially represented by kurtosis. Distributions with scores that cluster are leptokurtic; distributions with scores spread throughout are platykurtic. Normal distributions are said to be mesokurtic.

The simplest measure of dispersion is the range, which is defined as the difference between the highest and lowest scores in a distribution. However, the range can be a highly inaccurate and misleading statistic.

The standard deviation measures the dispersion of scores around the mean. It is the average deviation from the mean. To find the standard deviation we must first find the mean, sum of squares, and variance. The greater the standard deviation, the more scores are spread throughout the distribution (and the less they cluster around the mean).

In a normal distribution, the same percentage of scores and number of standard deviation units fall above and below the mean. In addition, predictions can be made as to the number of cases in the distribution that will fall between standard deviation units. This information is useful in education and psychology when comparing predicted results with actual data collected in the population at large.

Correlation refers to the degree of relatedness between variables. Variables can be positively or negatively correlated, or they can be uncorrelated. Correlation, however, is not causation. Because two variables are correlated, it does not mean that one is responsible for causing the other to occur.

Correlation coefficients indicate the strength of correlations. Coefficients range from 0.00 to ± 1.00. The most commonly used correlation coefficient is the Pearson Product-Moment Coefficient (represented by r).

STUDY QUESTIONS

1. What are statistics? How should they be used? What are appropriate uses of statistics?

2. What are the four types of scales? Give examples of how each type of scale would be used in an educational or psychological setting.

3. Delineate between discrete and continuous variables. Give educational or psychological examples of each.

4. Create a frequency polygon for the following scores:

Scores	Frequency
100	1
98	1
95	2
91	1
89	4
84	3
81	4
79	2
75	6
71	5
68	2
64	5
60	2
59	2
55	1

5. Define the three main characteristics that describe distributions. Why are these variables important in defining and understanding distributions?

6. Find the mean, median, and mode for the distribution supplied in question 5.

7. What is the central limits theorem? Why is it important? What are the implications of the theorem in pilot-testing tests and/or creating standardization–norm groups?

8. What are the attributes of a normal curve in terms of shape and measures of central tendency?

9. Describe the advantages and disadvantages in the three measures of central tendency. For what types of situations would each measure be appropriate?

10. What is dispersion? Define the two main statistics of dispersion described in this chapter.

11. For the distribution given in question 5, find the standard deviation.

12. What is correlation? How does it differ from causation? Give an example of correlation without causation.

13. How is correlation expressed? Give an example of positive and negative correlational relationships in the real world.

CHAPTER 7

Scoring and Interpreting Test Scores

Congratulations! You have made it through the chapter on statistics! Perhaps you are now thinking that with the last chapter behind you, you will not have to deal with the subject of statistics for the rest of this text. Unfortu-nately, this is not the case. Even though you will not have to learn any more statistics, you will need to apply the statistics you have learned in many ways. For example, in this chapter, you use your statistical knowledge in scoring, converting, and interpreting test scores. In addition, Chapters 8, 9, and 10 on reliability, validity, and test norms require the application of statistics. Finally, to judge the appropriateness of tests as a whole and to gauge the effectiveness of individual test items, you need your statistical skills. If you use these skills wisely, you will be well on your way to becoming an informed and pru-dent test consumer.

What Follows Test Administration?

Suppose that you have chosen and adminis-tered a commercially available standardized test. You made sure that the test was appropri-ate for the child in terms of background and culture and you administered the test in strict accordance with the test procedures outlined in the test manual. The question now is, What should be done next?

The next three steps in the process after test administration are *scoring, conversion,* and *interpretation* of results. These steps are crucial if the test results are to be meaningful and used in relevant ways by the educational professional. Tests that have improperly scored items are worse than useless—they yield incorrect information. The conversion process involves converting test scores to other measures in order to make interpretation meaningful. Finally, an understanding of these converted scores and the type of information they yield is vital to proper interpretation of test scores. If any of these processes breaks down, then the time, expense, and effort that went into selecting and administering the test have been wasted.

The Necessary Question of Accuracy

Just as there can be errors of test selection and administration, there can also be errors in test scoring and interpretation. The person scoring the test must be sure that the items have been scored correctly. This entails ensuring that the arithmetic computations in test scoring have been followed properly and that the scoring is free from errors. This is especially true for tests scored by hand. In such cases, the scorer must be sure that the correct scoring key is followed, that the key corresponds to the items being scored, and that the arithmetic is performed correctly.

Perhaps the primary cause of scoring error with hand-scored tests is scorer fatigue. It is a tedious job to hand score a large number of test papers. To offset errors of fatigue, the scorer should take frequent breaks from scoring and avoid scoring tests in distracting or noisy environments. Finally, it is advisable to score all papers twice to ensure scoring accuracy. A second scoring can be done either by the original scorer at a later date or by a colleague who double-checks the scorer's accuracy.

In many cases, standardized tests allow for machine or computer scoring using a scanner form. However, the use of machine-scoring forms does not release the teacher from the responsibility of ensuring that the tests have been scored correctly.

Computer scanner forms contain their own type of error, error generated by the test taker. These forms pick up any stray marks made on the page, and these marks may be interpreted as answers by the computer and scored as incorrect responses. Likewise, answers inadequately eradicated will also be interpreted as answers. Thus, when using computer-scanning sheets, the teacher or exam proctor should scan each sheet as it is handed in by the student to make sure that no stray marks appear on the answer sheet.

Computer-scanning sheets are also prone to another type of test-taker error. Because the student must transfer the answer from the test to the answer sheet, the question number must correspond to the item number on the scanning sheet. For example, if a student answering item 4 places the answer next to item 5 on the scanning sheet, the answer might be scored as incorrect. Again, the teacher or proctor must make sure *at the time that students hand in their papers* that item numbers on the test and the scanner sheet agree. Such errors made by students during test taking will significantly increase resultant errors during test score interpretation.

Scoring Norm-Referenced Tests

Chronological Age: The First Step in Scoring Norm-Referenced Tests

Virtually every norm-referenced test requires the child's chronological age (CA). Some tests require only the child's age in years and months; other tests require the CA in portions of months (days). Such CA information is used by the test scorer–interpreter when using the test tables in the manual to convert and interpret the child's test score.

Finding the child's chronological age is accomplished by simple subtraction (see Figure 7-1). As shown in Example 1, the current date in terms of year, month, and day is placed on the first line; the child's birthday is placed on the second line. Years, months, and days are then subtracted to yield the child's exact chronological age.

Sometimes borrowing or regrouping has to be carried out (see Example 2). In such cases, the average month is calculated as containing thirty days (ignoring the fact that some months differ).

When the child's chronological age has been calculated in terms of years, months, and days, it is standard procedure to round off the days to the nearest month. If the number of days is 15 or greater, round off to the next month; if the number is lower than 15, round to the preceding month.

The CA is typically expressed as hyphens or decimals on norm-referenced tests. In the hyphenated system, the age of a child who is 10 years and 4 months would be represented as 10-4. The decimal system, however, is a little trickier. Decimals represent tenths whereas years are represented by twelve months. Always be aware that a CA ex-pressed as a decimal represents tenths of a year, not number of months. Thus, the CA 10.5 is not ten years and five months but rather ten and one-half years, or ten years and six months.

Raw Scores

Raw scores are the test items that are scored. Test items are scored as either correct or incorrect, with each correct score assigned a point value. Usually, the point value for each item answered correctly is one, but point values may vary, with certain items worth two or more points. The raw score is calculated by adding up the total number of points earned over all the test items.

The procedure for calculating raw scores is:

1. Score each item as either correct or incorrect.
2. Assign the appropriate point value to each item. Incorrect items are scored as zero.
3. Add the number of points earned. This is the student's raw test score.

Correction for Guessing Scores

Some tests, particularly multiple-choice tests, contain a correction for guessing. This correction is a formula that takes into account not only the number of items the student an-

---

Figure 7-1 Calculating Chronological Age

Example 1

	Year	Month	Day
Current Date	1988	10	27
Child's Birthday	−1979	2	22
Chronological Age	9	8	5

Example 2

	Year	Month	Day
Current Date	1987	12 + 5 = 17	30 + 4 = 34
Child's Birthday	−1979	8	14
Chronological Age	8	9	20

Figure 7-2   How Test-Taking Strategy Affects Test Results

Test = 100 items (multiple choice)
5 alternatives per test item
Chance Levels = 100/5 = 20 items correct

Test Results (Both Students Possess *No* Knowledge of Subject Matter)

	Kareem	Sarah
Items attempted	0	100
Items guessed at	0	100
Items answered correctly		
by guessing	0	20
Score on test	0	20

swered correctly, but also the number of items answered incorrectly.

A correction for guessing is used to compensate for different test-taking styles and strategies among students. Such differences are demonstrated in Figure 7-2, which contains two test scores taken from a 100-item, five-choice multiple-choice test. Imagine that both Kareem and Sarah know nothing about the subject matter on which they are being tested. That is, they both contain an equal knowledge base (zero). However, Kareem and Sarah possess different test-taking strategies. Kareem's strategy is to answer only

questions for which he knows the answer. If he does not know the answer, he leaves the question blank. Sarah, however, is a guesser. If she does not know the answer to a question, she ventures a guess, hoping that she is correct.

Remember, neither student knows anything about the subject matter. As shown in Figure 7-2, chance levels on the test would equal twenty (100 items ÷ 5 choices/item = 20). Thus, although Sarah knows nothing about the subject matter and guesses at every item, she should receive a score of twenty "by chance." However, Kareem does not guess at test items. Because he leaves all items blank for which he does not know the answers, Kareem's score is zero.

As shown in this example, the large difference between Kareem's and Sarah's test scores has resulted from their test-taking strategies rather than from differences in subject matter knowledge. To compensate for such differences in test-taking strategies, some tests have adopted a correction for guessing strategy.

The use of the correction-for-guessing formula appears in Figure 7-3. Such correction is obtained by subtracting the number of incorrectly answered questions from the number of

Figure 7-3   Calculating the Correction for Guessing

Formula

$$\text{Correction} = R - \frac{W}{K-1}$$

Where: R = Number of items answered correctly

   W = Number of items answered incorrectly (blank answers do not count)

   K = Number of alternatives per test item

	José	Bill
Items answered correctly	65	65
Items answered incorrectly	35	20
Items left blank	0	20
Alternatives/Item	4	4
Corrected score	$65 - \dfrac{35}{3} = 65 - 11.6 = 53.4$	$65 - \dfrac{20}{3} = 65 - 6.66 = 58.34$

correct answers and dividing by the number of alternatives per item minus one.

Converting Raw Scores

Raw scores are numbers without meaning. To interpret raw scores and determine their meanings, they must be converted into other scores using statistical procedures.

Note, however, that converted scores are only as good as the person interpreting them. Each type of converted score possesses unique information. The test consumer must know precisely what information each type of converted score does and does not yield in order to guard against faulty or inappropriate interpretation of students' test scores.

Types of Converted Scores

Developmental Scores

Developmental scores refer to the fact that children at different ages and levels of cognitive and physical development function differently. For example, we would not normally expect a three-year-old child to be able to do trigonometry. Such behavior is typically learned by much older children. Likewise, by the time a person is fifteen, we would expect a knowledge of how to speak. A fifteen-year-old who could not speak would be considered severely handicapped or disabled. Thus, development scores reflect the expectation that children at certain ages will typically be able to do certain things.

If a child does things before expected, given the child's age, we say that the child is developmentally advanced. Likewise, a child is considered developmentally delayed if unable to do the things that other children in that age bracket can accomplish. Thus, developmental scores give us an approximate benchmark as to when children typically perform given behaviors.

Age Scores: The simplest type of developmental score is the *age score* (sometimes called age equivalents). Age scores convert raw scores into the average chronological age at which children typically engage in a behavior. For example, suppose Jacques, age five, achieves a raw score of twenty-eight on the Peabody Individual Achievement Test (PIAT). This score is then located in the test manual to see at what age a child would typically receive such a score. This age then becomes Jacques's grade equivalent score. Age scores are typically recorded in years and months of chronological age.

Grade Scores: Another type of developmental score is the grade score or grade equivalent. Grade scores, rather than reporting the typical age at which a child engages in a certain behavior, report the typical school grade in which such behavior usually occurs. Jacques's corresponding grade score on the PIAT (raw score = 28) would be grade 2.6.

A Consumer's Tip: What Developmental Scores Do and Do Not Tell Us

Developmental scores yield information about the typical age or grade at which most children acquire a behavior and compare the test-taker's behavior to that of a "typical" child. However, it is important to know that there is a wide range of ages or grades at which a behavior might typically occur. For example, consider the age at which children typically learn to speak. Although the typical child might acquire language at about eighteen months, the onset of speech anywhere from twelve to twenty-four months would be considered average or normal. Additionally, the difficulties of making conclusions about the typical age of onset of speech are compounded by the phenomenon of children who are slow to speak, but who speak in sentences rather than single words when they do begin talking. Keep in mind that what is typical or average actually represents a range of typicalness among students.

The problem becomes even greater when grade equivalent scores are considered. In norm-referenced, educational assessment, grade equivalent scores are probably used to report test performance more frequently than any other form of converted score. Parents want to know at what grade level their children are operating, and teachers apparently feel comfortable using grade equivalent scores. But what do these scores really mean? They refer to the typical grade at which a child acquires a given skill, but what constitutes a typical grade? We know that there are differences between localities, states, and sections of the country regarding the curriculum typically experienced by students in each grade. Thus, it is difficult to identify typical grades at which different skills are obtained. For this reason, grade equivalent scores must be interpreted with great care. Although we discuss them as if we have a precise knowledge of what they entail, in reality there is a significant degree of confusion in determining what grade scores actually mean.

Other Types of Converted Scores

Percentiles: A percentile (sometimes referred to as the percentile rank) indicates the percentage of students in a norm group who received the same raw score or a lower raw score than the test taker. For example, on the Peabody Picture Vocabulary Test (PPVT), a student with a CA of ten years, four months achieved a score of 110. With reference to the norms of the test, this raw score placed the student in the fifty-fifth percentile. This means that 55 percent of the norm group who were the student's age scored at or below the student's score.

Using Percentiles Appropriately: Keep in mind when using percentiles that they are not percentages. That is, a student in the sixtieth percentile did not achieve a raw score of 60 percent correct on the test. Rather, that student scored as well as or higher than 60 percent of the students in the norm group who took the test. Interpreting percentiles as percentages represents a major error in interpretation.

In addition, percentiles represent how the test taker did in comparison to the test's norm group. A test taker could score low on the test in comparison with classmates but still score in a high percentile in comparison with the test norm group. This could happen particularly if the student's class or peers possessed different demographic characteristics than the norm group.

Finally, percentiles are almost always provided for different chronological ages or educational grades of students. The test consumer should be aware that percentiles containing data collected on children whose ages or grades differ from those of the test taker are inappropriate. For example, what would it prove to compare the score of a six-year-old child with the percentile table of ten-year-old children? It would be no surprise if the younger child scored in the lowest percentile ranks with such a comparison. Students must be compared to the appropriate percentile group if comparisons are to be relevant and meaningful.

Standard Scores

Standard scores are among the most useful and meaningful of all converted scores. A standard score uses the most meaningful measure of central tendency (the mean) and measure of dispersion (the standard deviation) of the raw score distribution to convert raw scores. These converted scores are then combined to form a new *standardized* distribution that possesses some special characteristics (discussed later in this chapter).

Standard scores and distributions are particularly useful in making *different test distributions comparable*. This important property of standard scores is best demonstrated by an example. Suppose a student received a raw score of seventy on an arithmetic exam. The next day, the student received a score of sixty on an English exam. The question is, On which test did the student do better?

Looking at the raw scores, an uninformed test consumer might say that the arithmetic score was better than the English score. But such an interpretation could be erroneous.

One way to judge the student's performance on each test is to compare the scores with those of other students. For example, the mean on the arithmetic exam was sixty; the mean on the English test was fifty-six. Thus, we could say that because the student scored ten points higher than the mean on the arithmetic test but only four points higher than the mean on the English test, the performance was better in arithmetic than English. However, because the arithmetic score and English score came from *different* distributions, we still cannot conclude that the student did better in arithmetic. In fact, any comparison of the two distributions of raw scores would be like comparing apples and oranges.

To determine with statistical certainty which test performance was better, we must *standardize* the distribution of each test distribution to make the comparison meaningful. This is accomplished by making statistical adjustments to each distribution. These statistical adjustments are made in the form of standard scores and distributions, and they are the reason that standard scores are so useful in aiding test score interpretation.

What Is a Standard Score?

A standard score is a conversion of a raw score. Standard scores make the different distributions of raw scores comparable by using the mean and the standard deviation of each raw score distribution. These standard scores

are then converted to a new standardized distribution, which possesses special, common characteristics.

z-**Scores:** A *z*-score is the most basic standard score. The *z*-score standardizes the distance between a raw score and the mean of the raw score distribution by using the standard deviation to measure that distance.

A *z*-score possesses a sign and a numerical value. The sign indicates whether the *z*-score falls above or below the mean of the distribution. A negative *z*-score falls below the mean, a positive *z*-score above the mean. The numerical value of the *z*-score indicates distance from the mean. The greater the numerical value, the farther the *z*-score is from the mean of the distribution.

Deriving the *z*-Score: To derive a *z*-score, we must first find the mean and the standard deviation of the raw score distribution. As described in Chapter 6, the mean is the arithmetic average of the distribution. To determine the standard deviation it is necessary to find the Sum of Squares (SS), defined as the sum of the squared deviation of scores from the mean, and the variance (s^2), which is the average of the squared summed scores (SS/n). The standard deviation is the average deviation of scores from the mean, defined operationally as the square root of the variance. For a review on finding the standard deviation of distributions refer to Chapter 6.

The derivation of *z*-scores and the *z*-score distribution is illustrated in Figure 7-4. As shown, the mean of the test score distribution is 77, and the standard deviation is 14.8.

With these values we can find each student's *z*-score. The formula for deriving the *z*-score is:

$$\frac{X - \overline{X}}{s}$$

where X represents the raw score, $\overline{X}$ is the mean of the raw score distribution, and s is

Figure 7-4   *z*-Score Derivation

Student	Raw Score (*X*)
Azrah	70
Maria	100
Marisha	85
David	90
Amy	85
LeRoy	50
Ito	60
Hee Yun	75
François	90
Monica	65

$$770/10 = 77 = \overline{X}$$

A. Derivation of Sum of Squares and Standard Deviation

	$(X - \overline{X})$	$(X - \overline{X})^2$
Azrah	$70 - 77 = -7$	49
Maria	$100 - 77 = 23$	529
Marisha	$85 - 77 = 8$	64
David	$90 - 77 = 13$	169
Amy	$85 - 77 = 8$	64
LeRoy	$50 - 77 = -27$	729
Ito	$60 - 77 = -17$	289
Hee Yun	$75 - 77 = -2$	4
François	$90 - 77 = 13$	169
Monica	$65 - 77 = -12$	144
	0	2210 = *SS*

$$s^2 = \frac{SS}{N} = \frac{2210}{10} = 221$$

$$s = \sqrt{221} = 14.8$$

B. Derivation of z-Scores

	Raw Score	Derivation	z-Score
Azrah	70	$(70 - 77)/14.8$	-0.47
Maria	100	$(100 - 77)/14.8$	1.55
Marisha	85	$(85 - 77)/14.8$	0.54
David	90	$(90 - 77)/14.8$	0.88
Amy	85	$(85 - 77)/14.8$	0.54
LeRoy	50	$(50 - 77)/14.8$	-1.82
Ito	60	$(60 - 77)/14.8$	-1.15
Hee Yun	75	$(75 - 77)/14.8$	-0.14
François	90	$(90 - 77)/14.8$	0.88
Monica	65	$(65 - 77)/14.8$	-0.81

$$z = \frac{X - \overline{X}}{s}$$

the standard deviation of the raw score distribution.

We can use arithmetic to compute each student's *z*-score from his or her corresponding raw score (Figure 7-4 [B]). Thus, we see from Figure 7-4 (B) that Azrah's *z*-score, which corresponds to her raw score of 70, is

$$(70-77)/14.8 = -0.47$$

Likewise, the raw scores of the other nine students can be similarly converted to *z*-scores.

Let us inspect Azrah's *z*-score (-0.47) and see what it tells us. First, the negative sign indicates that it falls below the mean of the class distribution. But how far below? Exactly 0.47 units. But how *much* is 0.47 of a *z*-score unit? To answer this question and interpret Azrah's test results more fully we must know the characteristics of a *z*-score distribution.

Characteristics of the *z*-Score Distribution: Because *z*-scores are standard scores, all *z*-score distributions possess the same characteristics. This attribute allows us to compare different test distributions after converting raw scores to standard scores. The characteristics of *z*-score distributions are:

1. *Shape:* The *z*-score distribution will have the same shape as the original distribution of raw scores. If the raw score distribution is normal, the *z*-score distribution will be normal. Likewise, if the raw score distribution is skewed, the *z*-score distribution will be skewed.

2. *Mean:* The mean of any *z*-score distribution will always be zero. This can be demonstrated by summing the $(X - \overline{X})$ scores in the raw-score distribution and dividing by the standard deviation. In Figure 7-4, for example, the sum of the $(X - \overline{X})$ scores is $0/14.8 = 0$.

3. *Standard deviation:* The standard deviation of a *z*-score distribution will always equal 1.00. Referring to Figure 7-4, the raw score standard deviation of 14.8 = 1 *z*-score standard deviation.

Using these characteristics of the *z*-score distribution, the student *z*-score shown in Figure 7-4 can be drawn as a *z*-score distribution

Figure 7-5 Distribution of z-Scores

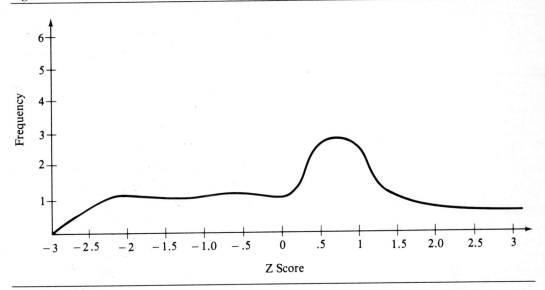

to see how each student did on the test (Figure 7-5).

By inspecting the students' z-scores, we can see how each one performed relative to the other students who took the exam. Take, for example, Azrah's z-score of −0.47. Not only was Azrah below the mean, she was approximately one-half standard deviation below. Furthermore, *if* the class distribution was normal (which it is not), we could expect approximately 34 percent of all the test scores to fall between the mean and −1 standard deviation. Armed with this information, we probably should not be alarmed with Azrah's score of −0.47.

Other Standard Scores

The T-Score: Z-scores are relatively cumbersome to work with because of their sign and their decimal form. To alleviate these problems, some tests use the T-score, a derivation of the z-score that eradicates both negative signs and decimals. The formula for T-scores is:

$$T = 10z + 50$$

In cases where z-scores are carried out to the hundredths place, the hundredths must be rounded off to the nearest tenths place to eradicate the z-score decimal when the corresponding T-score is calculated.

Figure 7-6 (p. 102) shows how T-scores would be derived for each z-score shown in Table 7-1. In this example, Azrah's z-score of

Table 7-1 Derivation of T-Scores ($T = 10z + 50$)

Student	z-Score	Sample Computations	T-Score
Azrah	−0.47	(−.5 × 10 + 50)	45
Maria	1.55	(1.5 × 10 + 50)	66
Marisha	0.54	(.5 × 10 + 50)	55
David	0.88		59
Amy	0.54		55
LeRoy	−1.82		32
Ito	−1.15		38
Hee Yun	−0.14		49
François	0.88		59
Monica	−0.81		41

−0.47 is rounded to −0.5. It is then multiplied by 10, yielding a score of −5.0. Finally, 50 is added to this score to obtain a *T*-score of 45. This *T*-score of 45 is exactly equivalent to Azrah's *z*-score of −0.47.

Characteristics of the *T*-Score Distribution: Like the *z*-score distribution, the *T*-score distribution possesses certain characteristics:

1. *Shape:* The shape of a *T*-score distribution is the same as the *z*-score distribution from which it is derived. Skewed *z*-score distributions are represented by identically skewed *T*-score distributions. The same applies to normal distributions.

2. *Mean:* The mean of any *T*-score distribution is 50. Because the mean of a *z*-score distribution is zero, the *T*-score formula ($T = 10z + 50$), yields a mean of 50 ($10[0] + 50 = 50$).

3. *Standard deviation:* The standard deviation of any *T*-score distribution is 10. This is derived by multiplying the standard deviation of any *z*-score (1) by 10.

Tips on Using *T*-Scores: Many tests express their standard scores in terms of *T*-scores

because they eradicate both the sign of *z*-scores as well as decimals. The test consumer, however, must always keep in mind that *T*-scores are not percentages or number of items correct. That is, a *T*-score of 50 is neither a score of 50 items answered correctly nor is it 50 percent of the total items with correct answers. Rather, a *T*-score of 50 indicates the mean of the *T*-score distribution, and every 10 *T*-score units represents one standard deviation from the mean. Finally, because *T*-scores are derived from *z*-scores, the factors that contribute to appropriate interpretation of *z*-scores also hold for *T*-scores.

Stanines: The last standard score discussed here is *stanines* (standard nines). Stanines divide the normal distribution into nine equal areas. Whereas a normal distribution contains six standard deviation units, stanines divide the distribution into smaller segments than standard deviation units. An increasing num-

Figure 7-6   *z*-Scores, *T*-Scores, and Stanines in the Normal Curve

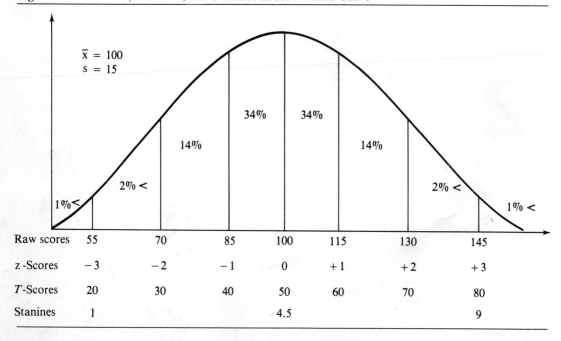

Raw scores	55	70	85	100	115	130	145
z -Scores	− 3	− 2	− 1	0	+ 1	+ 2	+ 3
T-Scores	20	30	40	50	60	70	80
Stanines	1			4.5			9

$\bar{x} = 100$
$s = 15$

34%   34%
14%   14%
2% <   2% <
1% <   1% <

ber of test authors report their standard scores in stanine form because stanines are somewhat easier to conceptualize and understand than are *z*-scores and *T*-scores.

A Final Word on Standard Scores

Raw scores, *z*-scores, *T*-scores, and stanines can be confusing. To help eliminate some of this confusion Figure 7-6 shows how a normal distribution of raw scores (e.g., IQ scores), *z*-scores, *T*-scores, and stanines would look superimposed on a hypothetical normal distribution. It is apparent that information expressed in raw scores, *z*-scores, *T*-scores, and stanines is related—all of the converted, standard scores are derived from raw scores. Nevertheless, standard scores allow for greater interpretive power than do raw scores because the mean and standard deviation of converted scores have been standardized to allow for comparisons. However, the informed test consumer must not grant too much interpretive power to converted scores. They provide information between students, usually between the test takers and some norm group. To the extent that the characteristics of the test taker and the norm group are similar, such comparisons may be valid. However, to the extent that the test taker and the norm group are different, interpretations may become invalid or even dangerous.

SUMMARY

Three processes take place after a test has been administered: item scoring, raw score conversion, and score interpretation. All three processes must be appropriately carried out for relevant and meaningful assessment.

Scoring error can lead to errors of test interpretation. All items must be checked for scoring accuracy. Fatigue is perhaps the greatest contributor to error in hand-scored tests. For this reason, tests should be scored in quiet environments with frequent breaks for the test scorer.

Tests scored by machine (computer) use scanner sheets. However, these scanner sheets are also subject to scoring error due to stray or inappropriate marks made on the scanning sheet by the test taker. To reduce error with computer-scored tests, the teacher or test proctor should quickly check the student's scanner sheet before the student leaves the examination room.

The calculation of chronological age (CA) is usually the first step in scoring norm-referenced tests. CA is usually determined in years and months. Care must be taken in interpreting CA, espcially when fractions of years (months) are expressed in decimals.

The raw score represents the scored test items. A point value is assigned to the total number of correctly answered items; this value represents the raw score. A correction for guessing can be applied to a raw score. A correction for guessing is a formula in which incorrectly answered items are subtracted from the raw score point value received for answering items correctly. The correction for guessing is used to compensate for differences in test-taking styles among people.

Raw scores in themselves are meaningless. They must be transformed into converted scores and interpreted in order to have meaning.

There are many types of converted scores. Developmental scores are among the most popular used by test authors. Developmental scores compare the test-taker's performance to the age or developmental level at which the behavior was exhibited by a norm group. Three typical types of developmental scores are age and grade scores and developmental quotients. Extreme caution must be used when interpreting developmental scores.

Percentiles represent the percentage of students in the norm group who received the same or a lower score than the one achieved by the test taker. The fiftieth percentile represents the median for the distribution. In interpreting percentiles, the consumer should not confuse percentile with percentage of correct responses.

Standard scores are among the most useful of all converted scores. A standard score uses the raw score distribution's mean and standard deviation to convert raw scores into something more meaningful. Standard scores allow for comparability of distribution data.

The z-score is the most basic standard score. It represents the distance between a raw score and the mean of the raw score distri-bution, using the standard deviation to measure that distance. The z-score distribution possesses a mean of 0 and a standard deviation of 1.

Z-scores possess a sign as well as decimal values. To eradicate these burdensome properties, the T-score was developed. The T-score is a transformation of the z-score; it has a mean of 50 and a standard deviation of 10. Care must be taken in interpreting z- and T-scores.

Stanines (standard nines) are standard scores that divide a distribution into nine equal parts. As such, stanines are smaller than standard deviation units that divide the distribution into six equal parts.

STUDY QUESTIONS

1. How is chronological age (CA) calculated? Calculate the CA of a child born March 27, 1977. Express this age both in hyphenated and in decimal form.

2. On a seventy-item, five-choice multiple-choice test, Hank answered fifty-five items correctly and fifteen items incorrectly. Mary, on the other hand, answered forty items correctly, twenty items incorrectly, and left ten items blank. Using the correction-for-guessing formula, calculate Hank's and Mary's adjusted scores.

3. What are the major types of developmental scores? Why are they popular with parents and educators? What are the major disadvantages of these types of scores?

4. What is a percentile? How does it differ from a percentage? What would it mean if we said that Larry was in the eightieth percentile on a norm-referenced test? What do we call the fiftieth percentile?

5. What is a standard score? Why is it useful? What are the major standard scores usually reported in tests?

6. Consider the following distribution:

Student	Score
Mike	92
Demetra	67
Bob	81
Amy	89
Lee	85
Reiko	88
Lloyd	75
Bwan	72
David	91
Carol	61

Find the corresponding z-scores and T-scores for each student's raw score.

7. Define stanines. How do they differ from standard deviations? How many stanines are there in a normal curve?

CHAPTER 8

Assessing the Reliability and Error in Tests

In some ways, physical scientists have it easier than psychologists, educators, and other social scientists because they can make measurements that are relatively easy to obtain and calibrate. Suppose, for example, that a physical scientist wants to measure the length or width of this textbook. The person would only need to take a ruler, make the measurements, and record them, secure in the knowledge that neither the ruler nor the book would change in its attributes the next day.

In psychology, however, measurements are not that easy. For example, suppose we want to measure a child's spelling ability using a given test. We administer the test and record the test's "measurement." But if given the test again tomorrow or next week, would the child's score be exactly the same? Probably not. The child might have learned the spelling words in the interim between the two tests, or perhaps the student did not feel well the day of the test. We can be relatively certain that the two scores would be somewhat different. Measurements on people change over time.

There is also the question of the measuring instrument. A ruler does not change from day to day. But what about psychological and educational tests? How much *measuring error* is in a given test, and how can we precisely measure that error? Rather than using precise instruments, psychologists and educators are forced to use "rubber yardsticks" that may over- or underestimate a person's psychological or educational abilities (Nunnally 1978).

The topics of reliability and error measurement deal with the preciseness of psychological and educational tests. Measuring test reliability and error represents an attempt to deal with these "rubber yardsticks," to measure both their preciseness and their variance (degree of elasticity). In short, a knowledge of test reliability and measuring error gives the test consumer information on the precision of the assessment instrument being used.

It is crucial that informed test consumers know the degree of error contained in the educational tests they use. Millions of important decisions about schoolchildren are made every day based on the results of formal and teacher-made (informal) educational tests. Yet, *every one* of these decisions is based, at least in part, on an educational test that contains at least some error. As we see later in this chapter, many tests contain small or moderate levels of inexactness, but others contain relatively large amounts of error in the preciseness of their measurements. Thus, it is possible, even probable, that many faulty decisions about children's futures are made by uninformed clinicians based on relatively inexact tests!

Unfortunately, imprecise educational and psychological tests are not required to carry warning labels like other harmful products. Rather, it is up to the informed test consumer to know the preciseness of the testing instrument being used and to temper educational and clinical decisions accordingly. Test consumers who do not know the degree of inexactness and error in a test abrogate their rights as clinicians. Unfortunately, in such a case it is the child who suffers.

The Concept of Error in Testing and Tests

Defining error is simple; dealing with it is difficult. Basically, error is everything in the test and the test situation that cannot be controlled and that might influence a test score. For example, a student's poor performance on a test because of a headache represents error. The test results infer that the student does not know the material, and that is what we might erroneously assume if we did not know about the headache. Likewise, two clinicians observing the same pupil at the same time may come away with two different sets of observations. This also represents error. After all, they were both observing the same pupil and should have come away with the same set of observed behaviors. In short, anything that can lead to faulty conclusions about a person's test results constitutes error.

Unfortunately, error is everywhere, and we have a tendency to overlook it. When we do this, however, we commit a serious mistake. When we forget about a student's headache, or a room temperature that reached ninety degrees as the pupil struggled to complete the exam, or errors that were made in scoring an exam, we conclude that individuals performed poorly because they were deficient in the information that the test measured. Consequently, we make invalid assumptions about students.

Error can also be contained *within* tests. For example, some poorly constructed tests have items that possess two correct answers (or no correct answer). Other tests seem to have absolutely nothing to do with the material covered in class. Such tests contain a great deal of error. In fact, on some tests, the less you actually know about the subject matter the better your chance of answering the test items correctly! When clinicians and educational professionals forget about error or take it for granted, their erroneous decisions about students can be dangerous.

Types of Error

Errors of Administration

Several years ago, the author was teaching university summer school in an old, windowless building in which the air conditioning periodically broke down. During these periods, when the classroom became unbearably hot, the instructor noticed that student attention waned significantly. Eyes drooped, students concentrated on the sticky, humid conditions in the room instead of on the lecture, and everyone, including the instructor, actively eyed their watches.

Unfortunately, the air conditioning broke down during the final exam. Students began fanning themselves, desperately trying to cool off while concentrating on their finals.

Not surprisingly, the final exam grade of every one of the twenty students was lower than their grades for the rest of the semester. In fact, the final exam score of every student had dropped at least one-half letter grade! What was the instructor to do? Clearly, he could come to one or both of two conclusions: either the students did not know the material, or the extreme conditions had affected student performance.

Of these two possible conclusions, only the first hypothesis, that the students' lack of knowledge accounted for poor test scores, would have led to a fair assessment. The other conclusion would have been caused by errors of test administration that had little or nothing to do with the students' knowledge of the material.

In attempting to identify the correct conclusion, the instructor asked himself what the probability was that every student's final exam grade would be lower than his or her grade for the rest of the course. Such an occurrence, that each student did not know the material, seemed highly unlikely. The probability that the extremely uncomfortable test conditions had contributed to testing error seemed more plausible. Thus, the author disregarded these test results, created a new exam, and asked the students to retake the test under more favorable conditions. Offered the opportunity to have the low scores eradicated from the calculation of their grades, the students readily agreed. Perhaps this was not the best solution to the problem, but it was an attempt to help compensate for an obvious error of administration.

The testing environment may contain variables that cannot be controlled, and by definition, such variables contribute to test error. It is the test administrator's responsibility to make sure that variations in the test environment are controlled as much as possible.

Test-Taker Error

Donita, a first-grade student, was frightened. Throughout the week Donita's teacher, Mrs. Morris, had been talking about the Iowa Achievement Tests that the children would be taking. She kept telling the children *not* to worry about the tests, but to make sure that they got plenty of rest during the week of the tests because the tests were very important. She also sent a note home to parents explaining the testing procedure.

The more Mrs. Morris told the class not to worry, the more Donita worried. She began to believe that if she did not do well on the tests she would be kicked out of school. By the time test day came, Donita was anxious, had a headache, and felt sick to her stomach.

Donita scored in the lowest third of test takers when compared to the norm group. Can we infer from her score that Donita is not achieving well in school? Of course not. Donita's test anxiety, her psychological state, and her psychosomatic symptoms all contributed to error in her test performance. These sources of error had detracted from Donita's ability to achieve a valid test score.

Children bring their outside environment into test-taking situations. Physical illness, psychological stress, anxiety about home situations, and tensions contribute to error in students' test-taking behaviors and test results. Common sense tells us that clinicians and educators should be aware of environmental problems in test-taking situations, especially with young or less experienced test takers. If necessary, and in extreme situations, students may need to be excused from a test with the test administered another time when outside factors can be better controlled and test-taker error reduced.

Domain and Item Error

Suppose we want to test your ability in the domain of American history from 1865 to the present. You are given a test that asks only questions from 1900 to 1914. You answer all of these questions incorrectly. Based on your test results, is it fair to infer that you do not know American history from 1865 to the present?

On the other hand, suppose the test does ask about history from 1865 to the present, but it asks only one question from each historical period. You answer the majority of these questions incorrectly. Again, is it fair to assume that you do not know American history?

In both examples, the answer would be no. In the first scenario, questions of a limited period (1900–1914) were used, even though the test was supposed to sample history from 1865 to the present. In the second example, although the range of American history was sampled, a severely limited number of questions (i.e., one) was asked from each era. You might have answered that one item incorrectly by chance or because the item was poorly constructed. In each sample, your test score and the inferences regarding that score would contain a great degree of error.

Parallel or Equivalent Test Forms: Test makers help to control domain and item error by creating parallel or equivalent test forms. Each test form covers the same content in the same domain (e.g., American history from 1865 to the present). The central assumption of the parallel form technique is that if the two forms were given to the same student, one right after the other, the student would score about the same on each test. To the extent that the student scored radically differently on the two test forms, the test would contain a large degree of domain and item error. This is the procedure followed when a test maker develops and tests alternate forms of an assessment instrument.

Test Length: Another form of domain and item error occurs when not enough questions are asked on each topic in the domain. For example, if our American history test asked only one question on World War II, that question might be answered correctly or incorrectly by chance. However, it is doubtful that twenty questions on World War II could all be answered correctly or incorrectly on the basis of chance.

In general, the more items a test contains on a given topic or subject, the less domain and item error that test will possess. Longer tests (tests that contain more items testing each domain) generally contain less error and are more reliable than are shorter tests. Of course, there are limits to which error can be reduced by adding items. For example, a test of seven hundred items might actually *increase* error due to fatigue and boredom. Common sense should be used when determining how much to lengthen tests to decrease domain and item error.

Errors of Agreement

Mr. Wagner was disturbed over James's poor class participation. He decided to institute a program in which James would receive points toward earning a prize when he participated in class and would not receive points when he did not participate. To free himself from watching James and tracking his participation, Mr. Wagner enlisted the help of both the aide and student teacher. They were to keep track of James's participation record.

At the end of the day, Mr. Wagner asked the two observers how many points James had earned toward his prize. To his amazement, he found that the two observers disagreed on the number of times James had participated as well as on the total amount of class time that James had engaged in active classroom participation. Mr. Wagner found himself in a dilemma. Which observer should he believe? And how many points had James really earned toward his prize?

The lack of agreement between observers is a source of error. Known as *interrater* agreement (or interrater reliability), such agreement often becomes an issue in behavioral observational assessment. In cases in which the observers do not agree on what happened or how much of a given behavior was exhibited, the usefulness of the observations is seriously diminished and the results are subject to errors of interpretation.

Reducing Errors of Agreement: Often when two observers cannot agree, the observations of a third person are accepted. However, this is begging the issue. The differing observations of three people may actually contain more error than those of two, even when the observations of the third person are accepted as true.

Errors of agreement can be reduced by using two strategies. The first involves precisely and behaviorally defining the behaviors to be observed. For example, instead of recording "participation," the observers could have been instructed to record the frequency and duration of verbal utterances that James made directly to the teacher in response to the teacher's question or statement. Such precise behavioral definitions restrict subjective interpretation by observers and reduce error stemming from interrater disagreement.

The second strategy in reducing errors of agreement is rigorous and specific observer–rater training. Persons should not be allowed to make observations without first receiving in-depth instruction and training on how to make those observations. Training should include practice in making observations in controlled, simulated situations. Training sessions may take only an hour or two or may take days, depending on the nature and specificity of the observations and on the subtlety of the behaviors being observed. Despite the initial time-consuming nature, observer training will go far in reducing errors of agreement, thus making observations of student behavior more meaningful and useful.

Errors of Stability and Time Sampling

Suppose a child scored 82 percent on an arithmetic test. Suppose also that we have reason to doubt that grade and we give the student the same test four hours later. The child's score on the second administration of this test is 60 percent. Which test do we accept as the correct score? Which test is in error?

Errors of stability arise to the extent that a person's scores are different on two administrations of the same test. Of course, the longer the period of time between tests, the longer the child would have to study the material or to mature. Likewise, it is also possible that on some measures, such as psychomotor tasks, the child could benefit from practice between test administrations. However, all things being equal, a person's scores on two tests should be stable. The more stable the scores, the less error there is in interpreting the scores as real or true. The less stable the scores, the greater the degree of error there is in interpretation. When a student's scores on the same test are discrepant, we cannot know which score to believe.

The Concept of Reliability

Test Consistency

The goal of constructing sound tests is to eliminate as much error as possible. One way of operationally defining *test error* is in terms of test *consistency*. Test consistency refers to a general belief among professionals that what a test measures and how that information is assessed should not fluctuate from time to time and situation to situation. Rather, information yielded by the test over time and situations should be stable and relatively unchanging (Brown 1983; Bush and Waugh 1982).

As mentioned earlier, educational and psychological tests contain more error than measurement in the physical sciences. Educational and psychological tests are subject to errors of administration, test-taker variables, domain and item content, and observer agreement. For these reasons, tests can differ drastically in their consistency. The differential degrees of consistency in various tests must be an important topic of interest to the informed test consumer.

Test Reliability

The generic term given to the measurement of test consistency is *reliability* (Bush and Waugh 1982; Gronlund 1985). Reliability data yield information about a test's consistency and stability in measuring the test-taker's domain abilities.

Reliability is concerned with a basic set of questions that center around the issue of whether scores from a given assessment instrument are consistent (Brown, 1983). More specifically, reliability is concerned with the following:

1. What is the relationship between scores obtained under different testing conditions?
2. How much would a person's score change if the test were taken a second time?
3. How close is the obtained score to the person's true score?

4. Is the test consistent enough so that it can be used with confidence and the results applied in a practical manner?

Reliability allows us to assess a degree of confidence in accepting and generalizing test results. There are different types of reliability, such as *test-retest, internal consistency, alternate form*, and *interrater* reliability. These types of reliability and how they are ascertained are discussed in greater detail later in this chapter.

Mathematically Defining the Concept of Reliability

Observed versus True Scores

One fundamental concept of reliability can be explained by introducing the idea of the *true score*. A person's true score is the score he or she *would* have obtained on a given test if not for error. That is, the true score represents the accurate measure of a person's knowledge, abilities, and skills on a given domain if that person could be tested with an error-free instrument in an error-free environment.

But as we have seen, error always exists in tests and test situations in numerous forms. Error can influence test results by artificially inflating a test score (e.g., the student correctly guessing at items) or by lowering a score (e.g., the test containing misleading items). In either case, the relationship of test scores and error can be mathematically represented by the expression:

$$X = T + E$$

Where:

X = the test score that was obtained

T = the hypothetical true score

E = error

Note that this equation is for the test score of one individual. However, because reliability is a property of tests rather than of people, we need to devise an analogous equation for groups taking a test. This parallel equation can be expressed as:

$$s_X^2 = s_T^2 + s_E^2$$

Where:

s_X^2 = the observed variance for a distribution of test scores

s_T^2 = the hypothetical true variance for that distribution of test scores

s_E^2 = the error variance for that distribution of test scores

Relationship between Reliability, True Score, and Obtained Score

As we have seen, there is a relationship between true scores, error, and obtained scores. The greater the degree of error (defined as the variance contained in a distribution of obtained scores), the greater the discrepancy between true and obtained scores. The smaller the degree of error, the smaller the difference between true and obtained scores.

Reliability can be mathematically defined as the ratio of true variance in a set of scores to the total, obtained variance. Algebraically, this relationship can be expressed as:

$$r_{xx} = \frac{s_t^2}{s_o^2}$$

Where:

r_{xx} = the reliability of a test

s_t^2 = variance of a distribution of true test scores

s_o^2 = variance of the obtained scores of a test distribution

The relationship between reliability and the variance of true and obtained scores can be seen mathematically in Figure 8-1. Again, note that reliability involves a set or distribution of test scores, not a single score from one person.

Figure 8-1 Relationship between the Variances of Obtained and True Scores in the Reliability Relationship

$$r_{xx} = r_{t/o} = \frac{s_t^2}{s_o^2}$$

such that:

r_{xx} = the reliability of a test

$r_{t/o}$ = reliability of "true" scores to obtained scores

s_t^2 = variance of a distribution of true scores

s_o^2 = variance of a distribution of obtained scores

If $s_t^2 = 5$ and $s_o^2 = 6$, $r_{xx} = 5/6 = .83$

If $s_t^2 = 5$ and $s_o^2 = 12$, $r_{xx} = 5/12 = .42$

s_o^2 = error; as s_o^2 increases, r_{xx} decreases.

How Do We Find True Scores?

If there is always test error, how can we ever know a person's true score? And if we cannot find the true score, how can we identify the degree of discrepancy between true and observed scores?

The answer is that because all tests contain error, the best we can ever hope to do is estimate true scores and true score variances. Thus, reliability is an estimate of the degree of error in a test, and as an estimate, it is itself subject to error.

Estimating Reliability

To understand how to estimate reliability, we must introduce the equation that defines test variances.

$$s_o^2 = s_t^2 + s_e^2$$

where

s_o^2 = variance of a distribution of obtained scores

s_t^2 = variance of a distribution of true scores

s_e^2 = error variance in a distribution of scores

This equation shows that the variance of a set of obtained scores equals the true variance of that distribution plus the error variance of that distribution.

Algebraically, it is possible to divide each side of an equation by the same number without altering the equation. Thus, we can divide each side of this equation by s_o^2, getting:

$$\frac{s_o^2}{s_o^2} = \frac{s_t^2}{s_o^2} + \frac{s_e^2}{s_o^2} =$$

$$1.00 = \frac{s_t^2}{s_o^2} + \frac{s_e^2}{s_o^2}$$

Recall, however, that the equation for reliability is:

$$r_{xx} = \frac{s_t^2}{s_o^2}$$

Hence, we can substitute:

$$1.00 = \frac{s_t^2}{s_o^2} + \frac{s_e^2}{s_o^2} \quad \text{with:}$$

$$1.00 = r_{xx} + \frac{s_e^2}{s_o^2}$$

Our next goal is to isolate r_{xx} on one side of the equation. Using elementary algebra, we can accomplish this as follows:

$$1.00 - \frac{s_e^2}{s_o^2} = r_{xx} + \left(\frac{s_e^2}{s_o^2} - \frac{s_e^2}{s_o^2} \right) =$$

$$1.00 - \frac{s_e^2}{s_o^2} = r_{xx}$$

Substituting once more, we find that:

$$1.00 - \frac{s_e^2}{s_o^2} = r_{xx}$$

$$\frac{s_o^2}{s_o^2} - \frac{s_e^2}{s_o^2} = r_{xx} =$$

$$\frac{s_o^2 - s_e^2}{s_o^2} = r_{xx}$$

Now we have a way of estimating reliability while bypassing the problem of not being able to obtain true error-free scores. The reliability of a test can be algebraically expressed as the test error variance subtracted from the obtained test variance divided by the obtained test variance. As we see shortly, all of these measures can be readily obtained from a distribution of test scores.

The variance of obtained scores (s_e^2) represents the degree of error in a given test and test situation. From the reliability equation, we can see that as this error increases, the numerator of the ratio decreases, making the fraction and resultant reliability smaller. Likewise, as the degree of error in a test decreases, the numerator increases, making the fraction and resulting reliability larger. Figure 8-2 demonstrates this relationship.

How Reliability Coefficients Are Expressed

As shown in Figure 8-2, reliability coefficients represent the ratio between the error variance and the variance of obtained scores. As such, reliability ratios are usually expressed as coefficients ranging from 0.00 (no reliability) to 1.00 (perfect reliability). The higher the reliability coefficient, the less error there is in the test and the more confidence we can place in an individual's test score. Conversely, the lower the reliability coefficient, the more error in the test and the less confidence we can place in a given test score.

Figure 8-2   Relationship between Error Variance and Reliability

As s_e^2 increases, reliability decreases.

If

$s_o^2 = 4$ and

$s_e^2 = 3$

then

$$r_{xx} = \frac{s_o^2 - s_e^2}{s_o^2} = \frac{4 - 3}{4} = \frac{1}{4} = .25$$

However, if s_e^2 decreases to 2, then

$$r_{xx} = \frac{s_o^2 - s_e^2}{s_o^2} = \frac{4 - 2}{4} = \frac{2}{4} = .50.$$

How Much Error Is in a Test?

A technique for calculating the approximate percentage of error in a test score is to square the reliability (r_{xx}^2) and then subtract this figure from 1.00 (perfect reliability and no error). This lets you roughly gauge the approximate percentage of error that would be contained in a given test score.

For example, suppose the reliability coefficient of r_{xx} = .70 was obtained for a given test. To ascertain the degree of true variance in the test, first square this reliability statistic (.49). This means that approximately 49 percent of a person's test score would be his or her true score and approximately 51 percent of the score ($1 - r_{xx}^2$) is due to error in the test.

How Much Reliability Is Enough?

Inspect the reliability coefficients and the resultant r_{xx}^2 in Table 8-1. As shown, a r_{xx} of .50 would yield a r_{xx}^2 of .25 (true score) and error of .75 ($1 - r_{xx}^2$).

Obviously, this high degree of error is quite unacceptable in a test. Yet there are professionals and school district personnel who are making educational decisions affecting students' lives based on tests that contain 75 percent error. This is an unacceptable practice that would cease if all test consumers understood more fully the concept of test reliability and error.

What, then, are acceptable levels of reliability and test error? As shown in Table 8-1, a reliability of .70 yields a r_{xx}^2 of .49 and a ($1 - r_{xx}^2$) of .51—virtually a toss-up between true score and error. Thus, a test should probably possess a minimum reliability of .70 before it is used by the informed test consumer. However, this represents only a *minimum* level of acceptance. Whenever possible, tests with reliabilities higher than .70 should be used. Tests with reliabilities below .70 probably

Table 8-1 Percentages of True Score and Error in Tests of Varying Reliabilities

r Reliability	r^2 True Score	$(1 - r^2)$ Error
.90	.81	.19
.80	.64	.36
.70	.49	.51
.60	.36	.64
.50	.25	.75
.40	.16	.84

should be rejected outright by the informed test consumer.

A Word to the Informed Test Consumer Regarding Test Reliability Information

Information about the reliability of a given test should always be made available to consumers in the test manual. If a test manual does not contain reliability information, the informed test consumer should *not* assume that the test author simply forgot to include this information. Rather, such an omission is a warning. Either the reliability for the test was never obtained or it was so poor that the author decided to omit the information, hoping that a naive test consumer would use the test anyway.

Likewise, reliability information should be reported in language that a reasonably educated test consumer (without an advanced degree in statistics) can understand. If the information is written in highly technical or difficult language, or if the author clouds the reliability issue, the consumer should be skeptical and should seek further information and interpretation of the reliability information. Do not be fooled about a test's reliability simply because the author sounds impressive. The informed test consumer should reserve the right to interpret the appropriateness of a test's reliability and make an appropriate assessment decision on the test's adoption and use.

Types of Reliability

As mentioned earlier in this chapter, reliability is a measure of the degree of consistency in a test. It allows us to answer questions regarding how much a person's test score would change if the test were administered a second time as well as the degree of confidence we can place in a test score. It is assumed that a person's scoring difference on two administrations of the same test would be caused by error, defined as everything in the test and test situation (including the test taker) that was not controlled.

Three types of reliability are discussed in this section: *stability, equivalence,* and *internal consistency.* Each type of reliability carries its own procedure for finding the reliability coefficient statistic. Table 8-2 summarizes the basic types of reliability and how they are assessed from test distributions.

Stability

Stability is a measure of consistency. Estimates of stability reliability yield information as to how stable a test score is over time.

Typically, in measuring the stability of a test, a person would be given the same test twice, the interval of time between testing ranging anywhere from a few minutes to several years. However, most intervals between testing are hours or days. This method is known as *test-retest* reliability.

The assumption behind test-retest reliability is that the same person taking the test twice should score about the same. Differences in the same person's scores on administrations of the same test are attributable to error.

Equivalence

Professionals often need to construct parallel forms of a test for a variety of reasons. For example, if a student is to be tested on the same material a number of times, different test forms containing different questions must be used so the student will not expect or study for specific items. Likewise, a teacher might use alternative forms of a test to discourage cheating in a large test-taking setting.

When parallel forms of a test are used, however, the tester is faced with a difficult

Table 8-2 Types of Reliability and How They Are Assessed

Type of Reliability	Method of Testing	Procedure
Stability	Test-Retest	Give the same test twice to the same group. Test interval varies; can be minutes, days, or months.
Equivalence	Equivalent Forms	Give parallel forms of the test to the same group in close succession.
Stability/Equivalence		Test-retest with equivalent forms.
Internal Consistency	Split-Half	Give test once. Divide test into odd and even items. Compare reliability of the two halves as if they were two separate tests.
Kuder-Richardson Formula		Multiple comparisons of internal consistency.

question: Are the two forms equivalent? That is, would a test taker score about the same regardless of which form was administered? To the extent that administration of both forms to the same person does not yield the same score, the test contains error. Thus, assessing equivalent reliability is a priority for the informed test consumer when more than one form of a test is used.

Internal Consistency

Suppose we split a test in half (odd vs. even items). If these test halves were treated as two separate exams, would they be equivalent? Would both halves be equally difficult? Would a student's scores on the two halves be the same?

The answer to each of these questions should be yes. To the extent that the halves of a split test are not equal in difficulty or do not yield the same score, that test lacks internal consistency. Internal consistency is assessed by two methods: split-half reliability and the Kuder–Richardson (KR-20) formula. Both methods are discussed in this chapter.

Methods for Testing the Reliability of Tests

The Test-Retest Method

In the test-retest method of assessing reliability, students actually take the test twice, usually using alternate forms of the test (although theoretically the same test can be given twice to students). In using the alternate form format, half the students receive Form X followed by Form Y whereas the remaining students receive Form Y followed by Form X. The scores on the two test administrations are then correlated. To the extent that the correlation is high, individual students are scoring about the same on each test form (i.e., they are performing like themselves) and reliability is high. To the extent that the correlation

between individual test scores on the two test forms is low, students are not performing like themselves and reliability is low.

The test-retest method of assessing reliability is critically dependent on the time interval between test and retest. Short intervals (minutes or a few hours) will inflate reliability estimates, whereas longer intervals (weeks or months) will deflate estimates of reliability. Choosing the correct time interval depends on the stated purpose of the test. It is therefore critical that the test consumer understand the test-retest interval used and why that interval was chosen by the test author.

Calculating Test-Retest Reliability: Test-retest reliability can be assessed using the formula:

$$ r = \frac{N\Sigma XY - (\Sigma X)(\Sigma Y)}{\sqrt{N\Sigma X^2 - (\Sigma X)^2} \sqrt{N\Sigma Y^2 - (\Sigma Y)^2}} $$

Where:

X = scores on the A form of the test

Y = scores on the B form of the test

N = number of people who took the test

Σ = sum of numbers

An example of how test-retest reliability is calculated is shown in Figure 8-3. In Figure 8-3, X and Y represent alternate forms of the same test. Each student has taken both forms of the test in order to calculate test-retest reliability. To calculate ΣXY (known as the sum of products), we must multiply each person's score on the X and Y forms and sum those products (shown in the fifth column in Figure 8-3). This summed figure is then multiplied by the number of people who took the test (10). Likewise, the scores on each alternate form are summed and multiplied together (the third column in Figure 8-3).

Calculation of the test-retest reliability numerator and denominator is shown in Figure 8-3. Here, *each* score in the X and Y forms is squared, summed, and multiplied by the number of people who took the test. Likewise, the summed total of scores for each test form is

Figure 8-3   Calculating Test-Retest Reliability

Student	Test Score on Form X	Test Score on Form Y	X^2	Y^2	XY	$(10)(XY)$
Jorgé	40	40	1,600	1,600	1,600	16,000
Sue	31	27	961	729	837	8,370
Amy	50	53	2,500	2,809	2,650	26,500
David	50	47	2,500	2,209	2,350	23,500
Bridget	47	52	2,209	2,704	2,444	24,440
Willis	47	47	2,209	2,209	2,209	22,090
Luís	39	36	1,521	1,296	1,404	14,040
Diane	50	56	2,500	3,136	2,800	28,000
Ricardo	25	30	625	900	750	7,500
Ann	42	40	1,764	1,600	1,680	16,800
$N = 10$	$\Sigma X = 421$	$\Sigma Y = 428$	$\Sigma X^2 = 18,389$	$\Sigma Y^2 = 19,192$	$\Sigma XY = 18,724$	$\Sigma(10)(XY) - 187,240$

$$r = \frac{N(\Sigma XY) - (\Sigma X)(\Sigma Y)}{\sqrt{N\Sigma X^2 - (\Sigma X)^2}\sqrt{N\Sigma Y^2 - (\Sigma Y)^2}}$$

Numerator

$$N(\Sigma XY) - (\Sigma X)(\Sigma Y) = (10)(18,724) - 180,188 = 187,240 - 180,188 = 7,052$$

Denominator

$$\sqrt{N\Sigma X^2 - (\Sigma X)^2}\sqrt{N\Sigma Y^2 - (\Sigma Y)^2}$$

$N\Sigma X^2 = (10)(18,389) = 183,890$
$N\Sigma Y^2 = (10)(19,192) = 191,920$
$(\Sigma X)^2 = 177,241$
$(\Sigma Y)^2 = 183,184$

$N\Sigma X^2 - (\Sigma X)^2 = 183,890 - 177,241 = 6,649$ $N\Sigma Y^2 - (\Sigma Y)^2 = 191,920 - 183,184 = 8,736$
$\sqrt{6649} = 81.54$ $\sqrt{8,736} = 93.46$

$(81.54) \times (93.46) = 7,620.7$

Calculation of reliability (r)

$$r = \frac{7052}{7620.7} = .925 \text{ or } .93$$

also squared, with the appropriate arithmetic functions carried out to reach the denominator. Finally, Figure 8-3 shows the final calculation used to compute the test-retest reliability of this test. As shown, the test-retest reliability calculates to $r = .93$, a very high reliability coefficient.

The Split-Half Method

In split-half reliability, a test is given and then divided into halves that are scored like two separate tests. A special formula is then applied that treats the two halves as if each were the length of the whole test. The central assumption of the split-half method is that each person's scores on the two test halves should be quite similar. That is, a person's scores on each half of the test should be highly correlated. To the extent that the scores on each half are highly correlated, the test is considered reliable. To the extent that a person's scores on each test half are different, the test is considered unreliable.

Split-half reliability is calculated using a formula known as *coefficient alpha*. (See Figure 8-4.) This formula looks at the degree of variation in each half of the test as opposed to the degree of variation in the entire test. The higher the variation in either (or both) of the two test halves, the lower the split-half reliability. To the degree that variation in the test halves is low, split-half reliability for the test is high.

Calculating Split-Half Reliability: Split-half reliability is calculated using the formula:

$$R = \frac{2[s_T^2 - (s_{odd}^2 + s_{even}^2)]}{s_T^2}$$

Where:

R = split-half reliability

s_T^2 = variance of scores on the whole test

s_{odd}^2 = variance of scores for odd-numbered items of the test

s_{even}^2 = variance of scores for even-numbered items of the test.

Figure 8-4 shows the calculations for split-half reliability. First, the means ($\overline{X}$) are found for the total test and for the odd- and even-numbered items of the test. Next, the sums of squares (SS) are found for the total test and for each test half. Finally, the variance for the total test is found and applied to the split-half reliability formula.

The split-half reliability shown in Figure 8-4 for this test is only moderately high (split-half reliability estimates usually yield the highest estimates of all the reliability formulas). This is not surprising considering the total test scores and each person's scores on the test halves. First, there is a wide spread among people's total test scores. Second, scores on the split-halves of the test are relatively discrepant for most of the test takers. For example, although we would expect James to score about the same on each half of the test, he scored one-third higher on odd-numbered items than he did on even-numbered items.

Not knowing the reason for this discrepancy contributes to error and hence to low reliability. Such discrepancies between scores on odd-numbered and even-numbered items of the test are also apparent for other test takers in Figure 8-4.

The Kuder–Richardson 20 Formula

In addition to the test-retest and split-half methods, there is another technique for measuring test reliability. This method, the Kuder–Richardson 20 formula (Kuder and Richardson 1937), is popular because it eliminates the extra work of splitting a test into two halves or creating alternate forms. The Kuder–Richardson 20 formula allows the simultaneous consideration of all possible ways of splitting a test and making comparisons and performs all these comparisons with one fomula. Therefore, it is frequently used to measure test reliability.

Using the KR-20 Formula: The KR-20 formula is:

$$\text{KR-20} = R = \frac{N}{N-1} \times \frac{(s_{test}^2 - \Sigma_{pq})}{s_{test}^2}$$

Where:

R = estimate of the reliability using KR - 20

s_{test}^2 = variance of the test

N = number of items in the test

p = the proportion of people getting each item correct

q = the proportion of people getting each item incorrect (for each item, $q = 1 - p$)

Σ_{pq} = the sum of the products of $p \times q$ for each test item

Calculation of a test's reliability using the KR-20 formula is shown in Figure 8-5. The first section of the figure shows how five students performed on each item of a ten-item test. Each correct answer was given one point, and each incorrect answer was given a score of 0. The test score for each student was then calcu-

Figure 8-4 Calculating Split-Half Reliability

Student	Total Score (X_T)	$(X_r - \bar{X}_T)$	$(X_R - \bar{X}_T)^2$	X_{odd}	$(X_{odd} - \bar{X}_{odd})$	$(X_{odd} - \bar{X}_{odd})^2$	X_{even}	$(X_{even} - \bar{X}_{even})$	$(X_{even} - \bar{X}_{even})^2$
James	15	−5.9	34.81	9	−1.7	2.89	6	−4	16
María	17	−3.9	15.21	9	−1.7	2.89	8	−2	4
Le Chan	22	1.1	1.21	11	.3	.09	11	1	1
Melba	20	−.9	.81	11	.3	.09	11	1	1
Sandra	24	3.1	9.61	11	.3	.09	9	−2	4
Juan	24	3.1	9.61	12	1.3	1.69	13	3	9
Jeanette	26	5.1	26.01	12	1.3	1.69	12	2	4
Leah	18	−2.9	8.41	10	−.7	.49	14	4	16
Anna	18	−2.9	8.41	9	−.7	2.39	8	−2	4
Stefan	25	4.1	16.81	13	2.3	5.29	8	−2	4

$\Sigma(X_T) = 209$ 0 $SS_T = 130.9$ $\Sigma X_{odd} = 107$ 0 $SS_{odd} = 18.1$ $\Sigma_{even} = 100$ 0 $SS_{even} = 63$

$N = 10$ $\qquad s_T^2 = \dfrac{SS_T}{N} =$ $\qquad \bar{X}_{odd} = \dfrac{107}{10} = 10.7$ $s_{odd}^2 = \dfrac{SS_{odd}}{10} =$ $\bar{X}_{even} = \dfrac{100}{10} = 10$ $s_{even}^2 = \dfrac{SS_{even}}{N} =$

$\bar{X}_T = \dfrac{209}{10} = 20.9$ $\qquad \dfrac{130.9}{10} = 13.09$ $\qquad \dfrac{18.1}{10} = 1.81$ $\dfrac{63}{10} = 6.3$

$$R = \frac{2[s_T^2 - (s_{odd}^2 + s_{even}^2)]}{s_T^2} = \frac{2[13.09 - (1.81 + 6.3)]}{13.09} = \frac{2[13.09 - 8.11]}{13.09} = \frac{2(4.98)}{13.09} = \frac{9.96}{13.09} = .76$$

lated, and the variance of the test was determined by calculating the mean and the sum of squares (SS), as done in past examples.

The calculation of the proportion of people answering each item correctly and incorrectly and the sum of products appears next in Figure 8-5. For example, four of the five people (4/5 = .80) answered item 1 correctly; hence, p_1 = .80. Conversely, one of five (1/5 = .20) answered item 1 incorrectly, hence q_1 = .20. This process is repeated for all items in the test. Next, pq is calculated for each test item (e.g., .80 × .20 = .16). The ten pq products are then summed (Σpq = 1.92). Finally, the appropriate numbers are substituted in the KR-20 formula as shown in Figure 8-5.

Interpreting the Reliability from Test Manuals

Perhaps one of the most intimidating jobs facing an informed test consumer is interpreting

Figure 8-5 Calculating Reliability Using the KR-20 Formula

					Item Score						
Student	1	2	3	4	5	6	7	8	9	10	**Total Score**
Miguel	+	−	+	+	+	+	−	−	+	+	7
Steve	+	+	+	+	+	+	+	+	+	+	10
Rahaaf	+	+	+	+	+	−	−	−	−	−	5
Sarah	−	+	−	+	−	+	−	+	−	−	4
Amy	+	+	+	+	−	−	+	−	+	−	6
N = 5											32

Key: + = item answered correctly = 1
− = item answered incorrectly = 0

$$\overline{X} = \frac{32}{5} = 6.4$$
$$SS = 21.2$$
$$s^2 = 4.24$$

	1	2	3	4	Item 5	6	7	8	9	10
p	.80	.80	.80	1.00	.60	.60	.40	.40	.60	.40
q	.20	.20	.20	0.00	.40	.40	.60	.60	.40	.60

p = percentage of students who answered each item correctly

q = percentage of students who answered each item incorrectly

| pq | .16 | .16 | .16 | 0 | .24 | .24 | .24 | .24 | .24 | .24 |

Σpq = 1.92

$$KR\text{-}20 = \frac{N}{N-1} \times \frac{(S^2_{test} - \Sigma pq)}{S^2_{test}}$$

$$KR\text{-}20 = \frac{5}{4} \times \frac{(4.24 - 1.92)}{4.24}$$

$$KR\text{-}20 = \frac{5}{4}(.55) = .69$$

reliability information from the test manuals of commercially available tests. Often, manual pages are filled with a confusing array of statistical information that makes no sense to the reader.

In reading and interpreting reliability information from test manuals, the test consumer should gather the following information.

Type of Reliability Used: What type of reliability has been assessed by the test author? Was it test-retest (alternate form) or split-half? Or was reliability assessed using one of the available formulas (e.g., one of the KR formulas or a variation of the coefficient alpha)? Nunnally (1978) has advocated a hierarchy of choice for estimating test reliability. According to Nunnally, the first choice is a test-retest/alternate form method with approximately a two-week testing interval. The second choice in the hierarchy is the split-half method, and the third choice is one of the KR or coefficient alpha formulas.

Reliability Coefficient of the Entire Test: Often, authors spend much effort describing the reliability of subtests or the reliability of individual items. Before examining this information, the test consumer should find the reliability of the entire test. If it is low, the other reliability information is irrelevant. Low reliability for the entire test is sufficient reason not to use the test.

The Reliability of Subtests: Again, you may not wish to use individual subtests with low reliabilities. You must at least treat results obtained on such subtests with caution.

Never doubt your abilities as an informed test consumer. If the test author does not provide readily understandable reliability information in the test manual, be suspicious. If in doubt, seek help in interpreting the reliability information. Do not assume that the test reliability is appropriate because the information is complex. Again, let the consumer beware!

What If Reliability of My Teacher-Made Test Is Low?

If you are considering a commercially available test with low reliability, do not use it. Considerations of how to improve low test reliability should have been made by the test author. You cannot improve the reliability of commercially available, standardized tests.

However, when dealing with a teacher-made test with relatively low reliability there may be ways to improve the reliability. These procedures are discussed here.

Test Length

In most cases, increasing the length of a test will make it more reliable due to increased domain and item reliability. How much the reliability is increased depends on the reliability of the original test.

A formula exists for estimating the extent to which the reliability of a test will be increased by doubling the number of items in the original instrument. The formula for assessing this is:

$$r_{new\ test} = \frac{2r_{old\ test}}{1 + r}$$

As shown in Figure 8-6, a test with an original reliability of $r = .70$ increases to a reliability of .82 when the number of test items is doubled.

However, if the original test already contains a larger number of items (e.g., 100 or

Figure 8-6 Calculating Reliability Increase When Doubling the Number of Test Items

Old test $- r = .70$

$$r_{new\ test} = \frac{2r_{old\ test}}{1 + r_{old\ test}} =$$

$$\frac{2\,(.70)}{1 + .70} = \frac{1.40}{1.70} = .82$$

more), doubling the number of items may actually increase error by adding factors of fatigue and boredom. Thus, teachers must be careful when increasing the number of test items not to actually decrease reliability.

Using a Correction for Guessing

A student guessing at the answer to an item increases error and decreases test reliability. Although it appears the individual knows the material, actually the student only guessed correctly. Additionally, when some students guess and others do not, reliability is decreased even further.

For these reasons, the formula to correct for guessing (outlined in Chapter 7) should be used. In fairness, however, students should be informed that they will be penalized for incorrect responses and that they should answer only those questions to which they know answers.

Variance within the Test Situation

As mentioned earlier in this chapter, everything should be done to standardize the test-taking environment. For example, students in one section cannot be given more time to finish an exam than are students in a second section. Likewise, such variables as noise and temperature should be standardized as much as possible. Whenever feasible, all students should be tested in the same room, at the same time, and under the same conditions to eliminate such variables as stimulation, fatigue, and test-taking motivation.

The Standard Error of Measurement

You will recall that there is a strong relationship between the degree of error in a test and the discrepancy between a person's true and obtained scores. Basically, the greater the degree of error in the test, the greater the difference between the true and obtained scores.

We have already determined that obtained scores can be inflated or deflated in respect to true scores due to test error. Suppose an individual takes the same test an infinite number of times. This person's obtained score would, at times, exceed the true score, would sometimes be lower than the true score, and on a small number of occasions equal the true score (this would occur by chance). That is, over a large number of administrations, the obtained score would overestimate, underestimate, or equal the true score.

We could place all of these infinite administrations of the same test on the same person into a distribution and compute an average (mean) and a standard deviation of the difference between the student's true and obtained scores. This information would give us the average discrepancy between true and obtained scores, thus yielding an index of the degree of error in the test. However, this procedure would not be feasible in terms of time, money, and the student's willingness to take the same test an infinite number of times.

Fortunately, there is a statistic for estimating the degree of error in a test without having to administer the test many times to the same person. This statistic is the *standard error of measurement*.

The standard error of measurement (SEM) uses the reliability and standard deviation of a test distribution to estimate the degree of error in a test. The formula for finding the standard error of measurement is:

$$\text{SEM} = s\sqrt{1 - r_{test}}$$

Where:

SEM = standard error of measurement

s = the standard deviation of the test distribution

r = the reliability of the test

Calculation of the SEM is shown in Figure 8-7 using the distribution of scores from Figure 8-3. In Figure 8-3 the calculation of the reliability coefficient was $r = .93$. From the

Figure 8-7   Calculating the Standard Error of Measurement (SEM)

Student	Score	$(X - \bar{X})$	$(X - \bar{X})^2$
Jorgé	40	−2.1	4.41
Sue	31	−11.1	123.21
Amy	50	7.9	62.41
David	50	7.9	62.41
Bridget	47	4.9	24.01
Willis	47	4.9	24.01
Luis	39	−3.1	9.61
Diane	50	7.9	62.41
Ricardo	25	−17.1	292.41
Ann	42	−0.1	.01
	421	0.00	664.90

$r = .93$ (see Figure 8-3)

$$SS = 664.90$$

$$s^2 = \frac{SS}{N} = \frac{664.90}{10} = 66.49$$

$$\bar{X} = \frac{421}{10} = 42.1$$

$$s = \sqrt{s^2} = \sqrt{66.49} = 8.15$$

$$SEM = s\sqrt{1 - r}$$
$$SEM = 8.15\sqrt{1 - .93}$$
$$SEM = 8.15(.26) = 2.15$$

distribution reproduced in Figure 8-7, we see that the standard deviation for the first administration of the test (the one typically used in calculating the SEM) is 8.15. Using the reliability and standard deviation values in the standard error of measurement formula, we arrive at a SEM of 2.15.

Using Confidence Intervals

Although the SEM gives us information about the amount of error in a distribution of test scores, we still need information about how much error there is in a person's individual score. Given a person's single test score, how do we know the extent that this score represents the true score and how much error there is in the score?

The aptly named statistic that deals with the degree of error in an individual score is the *confidence interval*. The confidence inter-

val allows us to place intervals or brackets around a score. Such intervals give us information about the probability that the scores within this bracket are the person's true scores. For example, if a 95 percent confidence interval of 5 points is found for a given test, and if a student scores 80 on that test, then we can be 95 percent confident that the true score falls ± 5 points from the achieved test score. Thus, the true score ranges from 75 to 85.

We can have varying degrees of confidence (50 percent, 75 percent, etc.) that a given interval of scores represents a person's true score. The greater the desired degree of confidence, the wider the interval must be. As shown in Figure 8-8, the necessary bracket or interval around a score is relatively small to achieve 50 percent confidence, but that interval becomes systematically larger as we approach 95 percent, the usual acceptable level of confidence.

Figure 8-8 Confidence Intervals Widen as the Degree of Needed Confidence Increases

For this example, SEM = 5

Needed Confidence	Confidence Interval Bracketed around a Test Score
50%	± 3.35
68%	± 5.00
90%	± 8.20
95%	± 9.80
99%	± 12.85

Areas of Normal Curve Falling within Commonly used z-Scores

Percentage of Area between Mean and z	Percentage of Area beyond z	z-Score
95	5	1.65
99	1	2.32
90	10	1.40
85	15	1.04
80	20	0.84
75	25	0.68

SEM = 3

Amy's test score = 90

Desired confidence interval = 95%

Area under normal curve = confidence interval = 95%

z-score corresponding to $\frac{1}{2}$ area = 47.5% = 1.96

Upper limit = $x + z$ (SEM) = 90 + 1.96(3) = 95.88 ≈ 96

Lower limit = $x - z$ (SEM) = 90 − 1.96(3) = 84.12 ≈ 84

Calculating the Confidence Interval

To calculate the confidence interval, we use both the SEM and the percentage of the normal curve that falls + an arbitrarily designated z-score (for a review of z-scores, see Chapter 7). With a normal curve, we statistically expect a certain area to fall within given z-score units. The area falling within given z-scores of the normal curve can be found in the appendix of virtually any statistics text. For purposes of our discussion the areas falling within commonly used z-scores are shown in Figure 8-8.

The formulas for finding confidence intervals are:

Lower limit of interval =
$$X - (z\text{-score area}) \text{ (SEM)}$$

Upper limit of interval =
$$X + (z\text{-score area}) \text{ (SEM)}$$

Where:

X = student's obtained score on test

z-score area = area falling within ± z-scores on the normal distribution as revealed by z-score area table

SEM = standard error of measurement for the test distribution

Figure 8-8 shows how a confidence interval is calculated for a given score. As shown,

Amy received a score of 90 on her arithmetic test. The SEM for the arithmetic test is 3. To find the confidence interval to place around Amy's score at the 95 percent confidence interval, we need to look up the z-score that covers 95 percent of the area in the normal curve $\pm$ that z-score. Figure 8-8 shows this figure is 1.96. We then substitute for the confidence interval formula and find that the upper limit of the 95 percent interval is 90 (Amy's score) + 1.96 $\times$ 3 (SEM) or 95.88 (rounded to 96) with the lower limit 90 $-$ 1.96 $\times$ 3 = 84.12, or 84. Thus we can say with 95 percent confidence that Amy's "true score" on the arithmetic test ranged from 84 to 96.

The Relationship between Reliability, Error, SEM, and Confidence Intervals

Looking at Figure 8-8, we see that there must be a relatively wide range of scores in the interval for us to be 95 percent confident of Amy's arithmetic score. Consider that many instructors place a score of 85 in the $B+$ range; a score of 95 usually earns a grade of A or $A+$. Because of the size of the confidence interval, Amy's true score can be anywhere from a $B+$ to an $A+$, a range of one full letter grade. Why did this relatively wide spread occur?

Again, consider the relationship between reliability, error, SEM, and confidence interval. As reliability decreases, both error and SEM increase, with the result that the confidence interval widens. Likewise, as reliability increases, error decreases and the confidence interval narrows. A relatively narrow band or bracket around scores is desir-

able. Narrow confidence intervals are easier to interpret, whereas wide intervals lead to the problem we have with Amy's arithmetic test score. We simply do not know her true operating level on this test.

A Final Note on Reliablity, Error, and Confidence Intervals

Certain people, some of them test authors, believe that issues of reliability, test error, and confidence apply only to norm-referenced tests that make comparisons between people. This is not true. Teachers who use criterion-referenced or curriculum-based tests (these are reviewed in Chapter 11) must also be concerned with the degree of error in such tests. Although criterion-referenced tests do not make comparisons between people, such tests must be as free of error as possible and possess proven reliability if we are to have confidence in them. Faulty decisions can be made with error-filled criterion-referenced tests just as easily as with norm-referenced instruments. And the decisions can be just as costly to students.

Some people believe that the issues of test reliability, error, and confidence are the test author's responsibility, not the responsibility of the test consumer. Again, this is untrue. When consumers give up their right to assess the quality of given tests, they can be sold unreliable tests that contain a high degree of error. No consumer agency protects test users; the best defense against poor tests is vigilant test consumerism. More important, informed test consumers must protect students against the use and abuse of poor tests.

SUMMARY

Making accurate measurements in such social sciences as education and psychology is difficult due to the concept of error. Error represents all of the variables that are not con-

trolled either in the test or in the test situation. Types of errors include errors of administration, test-taker errors, domain and item errors, and errors of agreement.

Test reliability data yield information about the degree of confidence we can place in a test. Reliability data inform us about the test's stability and consistency in measuring the test-taker's abilities. The logic of the concept of reliability is that a person's scores (within-person variation) on multiple administrations of a test (or a split-half version) should be relatively stable compared to differences between people's test scores (between-people variation).

Reliability is expressed as a reliability coefficient (r). This coefficient is defined as the correlation between obtained scores on a test and true scores. This correlation is found by determining the degree of variability (expressed by the variance) between true and obtained scores. Reliability coefficients are expressed as decimals ranging from 0.00 to 1.00. The higher the decimal, the greater the test reliability.

The inverse of reliability yields an indication of the degree of error in a test. To obtain the degree of truth in a test, reliability must be squared (r^2). Conversely, $(1 - r^2)$ yields an indication of the percentage of error in a given test or test score. A minimum reliability of $r = .70$ should be achieved before a test is considered for adoption. Such reliability would yield an r^2 (true score) percentage of 49 percent and an error percentage of 51 percent.

The various methods for assessing the reliability of tests include test-retest, alternate forms, the split-half method, and the use of formula coefficients such as the Kuder–Richardson 20 (KR-20) formula. In the test-retest method, students actually take the test twice using alternate forms of the test. A correlation is found between the scores of the two administrations. To the extent that such a correlation is high, individual students are performing about the same on each test form and reliability is high. To the extent that the correlation is relatively low, students are not performing consistently and reliability is low.

In the split-half method, a test is given and then divided into halves, with each half scored as a separate test. We expect that people would score consistently on each half of the test. To the extent that this occurs, the test is considered reliable. To the extent that people's scores on the two halves are uncorrelated, there is error that cannot be accounted for, and the test is considered unreliable.

The third method of calculating reliability is to use a coefficient formula such as the KR-20. The KR-20 formula is popular because it eliminates the extra task of splitting a test in half or creating alternate forms of a test. The KR-20 formula allows simultaneous consideration of all possible ways of splitting and comparing scores and performs these comparisons in one formula.

Teachers should assess the reliability of their informal tests. Nunnally has created a hierarchy of choices regarding methods of assessing reliability. In this hierarchy, test-retest using alternative forms is considered most appropriate, followed by split-half and the KR-20 formula, respectively.

Educators must become proficient in reading and interpreting reliability information given in the technical manuals of standardized, commercially available tests. Informed test consumers should be able to derive information from these manuals regarding the overall reliability of the test. They should understand how overall test reliability was assessed as well as the reliability of any subtests. Reliability information should be written in language a reasonably informed test consumer can understand. When reliability information is in doubt or cannot be readily understood, aid in interpreting that reliability information should be solicited before the test is adopted.

Standardized, commercially available tests with low reliability should be rejected. However, some things can be done to raise the reliability of teacher-made, informal tests. These procedures include doubling the length of the test (within reason), using a correction for guessing, and standardizing test administration procedures and environments. Questions of test-taking fatigue and motivation should also be taken into account.

The standard error of measurement (SEM) is a statistic that uses the reliability and the standard deviation of a test to measure more precisely the degree of error in a test. The relationship between reliability and SEM is inverse. As reliability decreases, error and SEM increase. Conversely, as reliability increases, error and SEM decrease.

Confidence intervals allow us to place intervals or brackets around a score. Such intervals yield information about the probability that the scores within that bracket reflect the person's true score. Thus, a 95 percent confidence interval of 5 points means that we can be sure with 95 percent confidence that if a student's achieved score is 90 on an exam, the true score will be anywhere from 85 to 95.

Confidence intervals are calculated using the area between positive and negative z-scores in the normal curve. As the degree of confidence increases, so does the size of the interval. A 95 percent confidence interval is the minimum accepted confidence bracket that is usually placed around scores.

STUDY QUESTIONS

1. What is error in testing? Why is it crucial to take error into account when interpreting test scores?

2. What are the different types of error? Give examples of how each type of error is found in actual testing situations.

3. How can one reduce errors of agreement? Give specific suggestions for educational professionals interested in this issue.

4. Define the concepts of consistency and reliability. How are the two concepts related?

5. What is the mathematic relationship between true scores, obtained scores, and error? What does this relationship mean in real-life terms?

6. Is it ever possible to find true scores? Why or why not?

7. How is reliability expressed? What is the relationship in reliability between true and obtained scores?

8. What is the operational formula for reliability? How was it mathematically derived?

9. A test has a reliability of .60. What is the percentage of true score in that test? What is the percentage of error?

10. What are the major types of reliability? What does each type represent? How is each type calculated?

11. Using the test scores listed below, calculate the reliability for this teacher-made test.

Student	Test Administration 1	Test Administration 2
Mike	90	84
Sarah	78	81
Toby	82	83
Leah	98	90
Sarkis	77	70

12. How can teachers increase the reliability of their tests? What are the advantages and disadvantages of each of these methods?

13. Calculate the standard error of measurement for the data set in question 11. Now find the confidence interval at the 95 percent level for each score in the set for Test 1, and place each score of this test in the confidence interval.

CHAPTER 9

Assessing and Judging Test Validity

In the late 1960s Willie Griggs, a black employee of the Duke Power Company in Draper, North Carolina, had a problem. Griggs was classified as a laborer by the power company. His primary job responsibilities were sweeping and cleaning. He felt he had the skills and experience needed to be promoted to the next higher job classification, that of coal handler. However, to qualify for this position, the power company required applicants to pass a general intelligence test. Griggs took the test, and was informed by the company that his test score was not high enough to merit promotion.

Griggs and his black coworkers were not willing to accept the company's decision. They investigated and found that of the ninety-five employees at the Draper station, fourteen (approximately 15 percent) were black. Of the fourteen, thirteen were assigned to the laborer classification, and the majority of these individuals had been told that their intelligence test scores were not high enough for promotion.

Griggs and his coworkers sued the company for engaging in discriminatory employment practices. Griggs argued that the intelligence test was being used to keep black workers from gaining better jobs in the company. The company argued that the test was needed to improve the quality of the work force and ensure safety on a hazardous job (coal handler).

During the trial, the court requested that the company prove that the intelligence test possessed relevancy for predicting success on particular jobs. After hearing the company's arguments, the court ruled that the intelligence test had no significant relationship with success on the job of coal handler. It ruled that the test had become an irrelevant obstacle to minority groups seeking upward job mobility and was thus a discriminatory practice.

As a result of *Griggs* v. *Duke Power,* employers must now show that tests used in employment or promotion practices are directly related to success on the job that is to be performed. The Supreme Court of the United States made a clear statement on the necessary *validity* of educational and psychological tests.

What Is Validity?

Validity is relatively easy to define but difficult to put into practice. Validity refers to whether a test measures what it purports to measure. It also defines the usefulness of that test for making predictions and decisions about individuals.

The test consumer must keep this two-part definition of validity in mind when deciding whether or not to use a given test. First, a test must measure what it says it is measuring. What good is an arithmetic test that actually measures reading skills? Second, a test must be of value when making decisions about individuals. That is, the test must be appropriate for making inferences about the population being tested. This was the central issue in *Griggs* v. *Duke Power.* How good is an intelligence test in predicting who will or will not be a good coal handler? Likewise, if an entrance examination like the Scholastic Aptitude Test (SAT) is used as a guideline for accepting or rejecting college applicants, it had better possess value in helping to decide whether test takers will or will not succeed in college.

The Relationship between Validity and Test Reliability

As noted in Chapter 8, it is an absolute requisite of tests that they be reliable. Unreliable tests possess a high degree of error. One role of valid tests is to support sound inferences about individuals, but they cannot do so if they contain a high degree of error. Thus, valid tests must be reliable.

However, a test can be reliable and still be invalid. Consider, for example, a test that purports to be an arithmetic test but really is a measure of a child's reading ability. Such a test may be highly reliable—the child may score about the same after retesting because reading ability did not change over the two test administrations. But the test is not valid because it did not measure what it purported to measure. Thus all valid tests are reliable, but not all reliable tests are valid. Put another way, reliability is a necessary but not a sufficient condition for validity.

Expressing Validity

Like reliability, validity is often expressed as a coefficient (r^2_{xy}). Statistically, validity (r^2_{xy}) is often expressed as the proportion of relevant variance between people on a test (relevancy defined as the purpose for which the test is being given). For example, the validity of a test designed to measure arithmetic functioning would depend on its proficiency in identifying students operating well in arithmetic from those who were operating poorly. This predictive power is expressed by r^2_{xy}, which varies from 0.00 (zero validity) to 1.00 (perfect validity).

Remember that the validity coefficient is a proportion. It represents the proportion of true or valid variance between people's test scores to the error variance (everything that is not valid variance). Thus, the validity coefficient is expressed as:

$$r_{xy}^2 = \frac{s_v^2}{s_e^2}$$

Where:

r_{xy}^2 = the validity coefficient

s_v^2 = the valid variance between people on a test

s_e^2 = error variance

Just as some tests possess a variety of reliability coefficients, they can also possess different validity coefficients. This is because test validity can change depending on what variables (criteria) are being used. Nevertheless, there are some guidelines for understanding the validity information contained in test manuals. These are:

1. The higher the validity coefficient, the greater the test's validity. Coefficients approaching 1.00 indicate relatively high validity.

2. Validity coefficients should usually approach at least .70 before a test is considered sufficiently valid for making inferences and predictions about students.

3. Validity coefficients should be available for both the entire test and for subtests. They should be read and interpreted separately by the test consumer.

4. If validity information is not included in the test manual, do not assume that the author simply forgot to include it. It probably is missing because the validity is quite low or it was never assessed. Such tests should be used with extreme caution or not at all.

Not all tests express validity in coefficient form. Some tests describe validity in prose form. In this case, the test consumer should read the validity section very carefully to assess whether the test is valid enough to be used for the desired purposes.

Types of Validity

The five types of validity commonly used in educational and psychological measurement are *face, content, predictive, concurrent,* and *construct* validity. Many professionals classify predictive and concurrent validity under the heading of *criterion-related* validity; this practice is adopted in this text. Table 9-1 contains the major types of validity and the general procedures for their assessment.

Face Validity

We often accept things at face value, that is, things appear appropriate or acceptable at least on the surface. *Face validity* is a similar concept; a test should at least appear to measure what it purports to measure.

Face validity, although the least important type of validity, holds some importance due to its motivational value for test takers. People easily become discouraged or unmotivated if test questions do not at least appear to have something to do with what they have been told the test is supposed to measure.

At times, however, a test may be purposefully devised to lack face validity. This is the case with certain personality or trait-disorder tests in which respondents might not be completely truthful or might prejudice answers if they knew the true purpose of the test. However, whenever possible or expedient, tests should possess face validity to ensure test-taker motivation.

It must be pointed out that a test possessing face validity is not necessarily valid. A test may appear to measure what it purports to measure but actually contain crucial flaws that seriously diminish its validity and usefulness as a decision-making tool. For this reason, face validity alone should not determine that usage. Rather, the test must be examined for possession of other, more important types of validity before it is adopted.

Content Validity

Harvey was very unhappy. While studying for his important American history test (1860 to the present), he repeatedly asked Mr. Jones,

Table 9-1 Types of Validity and Their Measurement

Type	Definition	Measurement
Face Validity	The appearance that the test measures what it purports to measure.	Ask the test taker for an assessment of the test's face validity.
Content Validity	How well the test assesses subject matter content in terms of representativeness and adequacy of sampling.	Compare content of test items to the universe of content of the subject matter.
Criterion-Related Validity		
A. Predictive Validity	How well a person's test performance predicts future real-life performance.	Compare test performance with real-life performance that occurs at a later date.
B. Concurrent Validity	How well test performance compares with a current level of performance.	A. Give test to expert and nonexpert in the test content area. The two should score differently on the test.
		B. Assess the degree of correlation between the new test and a test possessing a known high degree of concurrent validity.
Construct Validity	Defining a hypothetical but nonobservable educational or psychological trait or variable.	Assess the degree to which a person who possesses those attributes in real life scores high on the construct-identifying test.

his teacher, what he should study. "Study everything," was the usual reply. "You are responsible for all of American history from the Civil War to the present."

Harvey took Mr. Jones at his word. He studied and restudied all of the book chapters and his notes from the entire course and did not spend too much time on any one segment of American history. However, when Harvey took the exam, he was shocked to see that all of the questions were about the Civil War. Harvey felt betrayed. He had studied American history from 1860 to the present, but his exam had queried only one brief episode in that period.

Harvey had reason to be upset. Mr. Jones's test lacked *content validity*. Content validity refers to how adequately test items sample the domain of the subject the test is supposed to measure. Content validity is a comparison between what could be sampled by the test and what actually is sampled.

To a certain extent an assessment of the content validity of a given test is a qualitative judgment. This is because no precise formula exists to measure a test's content validity. However, in judging content validity the test consumer can use four main criteria or benchmark questions:

1. What is the completeness of the sample? Are all the main areas of the subject domain sampled?
2. How thoroughly are the topics of the subject sampled?

3. Are the test items appropriate? Do they test knowledge at a variety of complexity levels?
4. At what level of mastery is content assessed?

Completeness of Sample: The first criterion for judging content validity refers to the completeness or representativeness of the subject matter assessed. Harvey became upset because although the subject matter (or domain) that was supposed to be assessed was American history (1860 to the present), the test dealt only with questions pertaining to the Civil War. From this test, Mr. Jones made inferences about Harvey's knowledge of American history. However, the inferences were incorrect because the test did not sample the entire domain. A major component of content validity is a representative sampling of the entire domain or subject matter, not just a portion of the subject.

Thoroughness of the Topics Being Sampled: The second criterion for judging content validity is the thoroughness of item sampling. Suppose Mr. Jones's test did ask questions about a variety of periods of American history from 1860 to the present, but only asked one question on each period (e.g., one multiple-choice question on the Civil War). Could Mr. Jones infer from that one question that Harvey did or did not possess adequate knowledge on the Civil War? He could not. Perhaps the question was very easy (or very difficult), or perhaps Harvey guessed and got the answer correct by chance. Because the periods of American history were not adequately sampled, the test lacked content validity.

In assessing the content validity of a test, the informed test consumer should make sure that topics or subject matter areas are adequately sampled. This can usually be ascertained by reading the item analysis section of the test manual to see how many questions are asked on each subtopic. A test that samples all subtopics of a domain but that does not ask enough (usually at least three to five questions on each area) lacks content validity.

Levels of Complexity of Test Items: The third criterion for content validity is that questions must assess learning or knowledge at various levels of complexity. For example, it is one thing simply to memorize a fact (e.g., that Columbus is the capital of Ohio) and recite that fact when asked. Applying knowledge and facts (e.g., using a map to get from Columbus to Cincinnati, Ohio) requires more cognitive complexity and use of the subject matter learned.

Perhaps the best way to judge test items for representativeness of complexity is to use the taxonomy of cognitive educational objectives devised by Benjamin Bloom and his associates (Bloom 1956; Bloom, Hastings, and Madaus 1971). Bloom outlined six levels of complexity of educational objectives and/or test items, ranging from the recitation of memorized facts (knowledge) to judging or critiquing finished products (evaluation). Definitions and examples of test items using Bloom's taxonomy of cognitive objectives are shown in Figure 9-1.

It is important that a test sample a student's learning not only at the most basic levels of learning (knowledge and comprehension), but also at the higher levels (analysis, synthesis, and evaluation). Investigators have reported that most test items focus overwhelmingly on the knowledge–comprehension levels of learning (Metfessel, Michael, and Kirsner 1969; Trachtenberg 1974). For example, of more than 61,000 test items assessed for their cognitive taxonomic level, 95 percent were found to be at the knowledge and comprehension levels (Trachtenberg 1974). It is imperative that the test author devise or use items that assess student learning at higher levels of cognitive complexity. Otherwise, teachers risk educating students who can do little more than recite facts or recognize information in multiple-choice form.

Figure 9-1 Definitions and Examples of Test Items Using Bloom's Taxonomy of Cognitive Educational Objectives

Definitions

1. Knowledge. The simplest level of complexity. Requires the student to recall facts or remember previously learned material.
2. Comprehension. The lowest level of understanding. Involves translating material from one form to another by paraphrasing or stating it in the student's own words.
3. Application. Requires the ability to use learned material in new and concrete situations. Involves generalization of learned material.
4. Analysis. Requires the ability to break down materials into component parts. Student understands the relationship between the component parts.
5. Synthesis. Requires the ability to put parts together to form a new whole that is something unique.
6. Evaluation. Requires the ability to make judgments about products or materials based on sound external criteria.

Examples

1. Knowledge
   a. List the names of the fifty states of the United States and their capitals.
   b. What is the product of 5×4?
2. Comprehension
   a. Order the following numbers from lowest to highest.
   b. Match the chemical elements with their symbols.
3. Application
   a. Solve the following arithmetic problem using the communitive property law.
   b. Precisely follow the enclosed recipe.
4. Analysis
   a. Contrast and compare two characters in *Hamlet*.
   b. Point out the pros and cons of nuclear disarmament.
5. Synthesis
   a. Complete a story using the props provided.
   b. Design a one-week nutritious menu.
6. Evaluation
   a. Evaluate the appropriateness of the enclosed menu in terms of nutrition and economy.
   b. Critique another student's paper on the basis of its clarity and organization.

Mastery of Content: The final criterion of content validity is the mastery level required to infer learning. In many ways, requisite mastery is defined both by the teacher and by the importance of the learning task required. For example, consider the jobs of airline pilot and surgeon. Would any of us feel comfortable certifying for these jobs people who scored only 65 percent on their pilot tests or medical boards? Rather, we expect people in these positions to possess perfect or nearly perfect mastery of the skills needed for certification. Likewise, it can be argued that the requisite skills for reading, arithmetic, and other key academic subjects should require high levels of mastery before students are certified as knowledgeable in these areas. Tests with strong content validity should assure that students possess mastery of basic skills in each subject matter area before they are allowed to progress to higher-level skills. This is especially crucial for special needs learners who often do not or cannot acquire basic skills but fall increasingly farther behind as the complexity of the subject matter increases.

In summary, it is essential that educational tests possess strong content validity. Tests that lack the four criteria of content validity just described should probably be rejected as assessment tools by the informed test consumer. Such tests are questionable decision-making tools.

Criterion-Related Validity

Astrologers and fortune tellers earn a living trying to predict the future. However, most of us try to use more accurate and scientific instruments to predict the probability of success in future actions. For example, the stock market investor who reads market trends and listens to a broker's advice is trying to make probability statements regarding investment profits.

Predictions are only as good as the criteria on which they are based. Tests make predictions about the future. For example, a test might predict that a person will perform well on a certain job or succeed in college. Tests also predict that given the current state of a child's functioning in reading or arithmetic, this child will experience difficulties in the future if remediation is not forthcoming. However, like other predictors of the future, tests are only as useful as the criteria on which such predictions are based.

The judging of a test's predictive value is known as *criterion-related validity*. To the extent that we can adequately predict real-life performance from a test, criterion-related validity is high. However, to the extent that real-life performance is independent of test results, criterion-related validity is low.

Criterion-related validity is extremely important. We administer tests for a reason; that reason is frequently the need to make predictions of real-life behavior from a person's test performance. If there is no connection between the two, there is no reason to give the test.

The two types of criterion-related validity are *predictive* and *concurrent* validity. Predictive validity refers to how accurately a current test score can predict future real-life performance. Concurrent validity refers to how well a current test score can predict current real-life performance.

Predictive Validity: Predictive validity involves predicting how a person will do on some future real-life task based on current test performance. Suppose, for example, a group of persons applied for a job. It would be useful if the personnel manager could predict with a certain degree of confidence which applicant would be most likely to succeed in the job. Such predictions are the precise purpose of entrance examinations, such as the Scholastic Aptitude Test (SAT) and the Graduate Record Examination (GRE). They predict with a certain degree of certainty

which students taking the exam are likely to succeed in college and graduate training.

Predictive validity is only as good as the criteria used to make the predictions. This was precisely the issue brought before the Supreme Court in *Griggs* v. *Duke Power*. How good is a general intelligence test in predicting who will be a good coal handler? In educational terms, how good are academic and aptitude tests for predicting who will experience future difficulty in school, who is gifted, or who will or will not succeed in college? Thus, it is crucial that before the predictive validity of a test is accepted, the test author(s) assess the predictive validity against the criteria being assessed.

The predictive validity of a test is assessed in a relatively straightforward manner. Suppose a personnel manager wished to test the predictive validity of a test being used to screen job applicants. This person would administer the test to applicants and score the results. However, the results of these tests would not be interpreted. Rather, the personnel manager would give all the applicants a job or randomly employ a sample of the applicants. At a later time (e.g., six months or a year), the personnel manager would review these employees' test scores and compare their test results to their actual job performance. If there was a strong correlation between what the test predicted for each applicant and the actual job performance, the test would possess strong predictive validity. On the other hand, if the correlation between test scores and actual job performance was weak, predictive validity of the test would also be weak.

Although the practice of giving a test and not interpreting results may seem strange at first, it represents the best way to test predictive validity. However, once the predictive validity of the test has been established, the test consumer can base decisions on test results.

Concurrent Validity: Concurrent validity refers to a test's accurately describing or predicting current rather than future real-life performance. Such validity is important in educational assessment. Suppose a teacher gives a reading test to a child, and the child's performance indicates a significant reading deficiency. In real life, however, the child is reading reasonably well, performing at or about grade level. Such a test would possess extremely weak concurrent validity and probably should not be used. We expect a test to possess concurrent validity, to describe adequately how the test taker is currently operating in the real world. If it cannot do that, it fails a major test of validity.

Like predictive validity, the concurrent validity of a test is relatively straightforward to assess. One method of assessing concurrent validity is to administer the test to a someone recognized as expert in that skill. If the test possesses concurrent validity, it should distinguish between an expert and a nonexpert. For example, a French test could be administered to a student known to be fluent in French. If that student does not score high on the test, the test lacks concurrent validity. Likewise, an academic grade-level test (e.g., a third-grade arithmetic test) could be given to a fifth-grade child known to possess third-grade arithmetic skills. Such a child should score high on the test. If not, something is wrong with either the test or the assignment of grade level for the child.

Concurrent validity can also be tested by the reverse process of administering a test to a student who possesses a known deficiency in the subject area. A reading-disabled student should not score high on a reading test for which we are trying to assess concurrent validity. Such performance would place the concurrent validity of that test in serious question. In short, for concurrent validity to be high, test scores should be consistent with real-life performance in that area.

A third method for assessing concurrent validity is a little more abstract than the others and is based on inference. Suppose a test (Test A) already possesses a proven concurrent validity. A test author then creates a new test (Test B) that has not yet had its concurrent validity assessed. The author of Test B can try to measure the degree of correlation between Test B and Test A. To the extent that Test B correlates with Test A, the two instruments overlap, and Test B also possesses concurrent validity.

Construct Validity

Construct validity refers to the extent that a given test measures a theoretical trait, attribute, or *construct*. Psychological constructs represent entities that professionals have hypothesized exist in individuals but that are not directly observable. For example, the notion of intelligence is a construct. We hypothesize that it exists but we cannot directly observe intelligence in the brain. Rather, we infer intelligence from behavior. Other theoretical entities, such as personality disorders, the need for achievement, self-esteem, and ability levels, are also educational and psychological constructs. Although construct validity is not generally a factor in most educational achievement tests, it is important in many psychological tests that assess personality and intelligence.

The construct validity of tests is evaluated much the same way as concurrent validity. A test hypothesized to measure a construct is administered to a person known to possess that trait. For example, a new test designed to identify obsessive–compulsive individuals would be administered to patients known to be obsessive and compulsive. To the extent that such individuals score high on this trait on the new test, the test would be considered to possess strong construct validity. Conversely, if such individuals did not score high on this test, the test would be considered low in construct validity.

Measuring Validity

Validity can be measured by using the statistic $\hat{Y}$. This statistic refers to the power of the test to predict a person's real-life behavior from his or her test score. The equation for measuring the validity of a test is:

$$\hat{Y} = r_{xy} \left(\frac{s_y}{s_x} \right) (X - \bar{X}) + \bar{Y}$$

Where:

$\hat{Y}$ = validity

r_{xy} = correlation between a test and real-life criteria performance

s_y = standard deviation of the criteria

s_x = standard deviation of the test

X = individual's test score

$\bar{X}$ = test mean

$\bar{Y}$ = actual success of the person on the real-life criteria performance

Figure 9-2 Calculating Predictive Validity ($\hat{Y}$) for College GPA by the Scholastic Aptitude Test (SAT)

$\hat{Y} = r_{xy} \left(\dfrac{s_y}{s_x} \right) (X - \bar{X}) + \bar{Y}$

GPA (average) = $\bar{Y}$ = 2.67

X = student's SAT score

SAT-V (average) = $\bar{X}$ = 580

Standard deviation GPA = s_y = .25

Standard deviation SAT-V = s_x = 80

Correlation between SAT-V and GPA = r_{xy} = .45

$\hat{Y} = .45 \left(\dfrac{.25}{80} \right) (X - 580) + 2.67$

$\hat{Y} = .45 \, (.003) \, (X - 580) + 2.67$

$\hat{Y} = .0014 \, (X - 580) + 2.67$

$\hat{Y} = .0014 \, X - .812 + 2.67$

$\hat{Y} = .0014 \, X + 1.86$

Figure 9-2 shows how predictions ($\hat{Y}$) are calculated. In this example we want to predict a student's college success by using her high school grade point average (GPA) and score (X) on the Scholastic Aptitude Test (SAT). First, we know that the mean GPA ($\bar{Y}$) for pupils in the college to which this student is applying is 2.67. Second, we know that the mean score of the SAT-Verbal test for students in this college is 580 out of a possible 800. Additionally, we know that for this college, SAT scores correlate r=.45 with GPA. Finally, we know that the standard deviation of GPAs at this college (s_y) is .25, and the standard deviation for the SAT-V (s_x) is 80 points. With this information we can calculate an equation for predicting a student's GPA from her SAT scores.

Using $\hat{Y}$ Information

How we can use the $\hat{Y}$ information is shown in Table 9-2. As illustrated, we can make differential predictions about different students' probable success or failure in this particular university given their SAT-V scores. For example, a SAT-V score of 450 would predict a GPA of 2.50 (C+ average) whereas a SAT-V

Table 9-2 Differential Predictions of GPA Based on SAT-V Scores Using the $\hat{Y}$ Equation

SAT-V Score	Predicted GPA
300	2.28
350	2.35
400	2.42
450	2.49
465	2.51
480	2.53
500	2.56
580	2.67
600	2.70
650	2.80
700	2.84
800	2.98

score of 650 would predict a 2.80 GPA (approximately a *B* average). Such information would theoretically be helpful to the admissions director of this university in making admissions decisions.

Notice that the predicted increase in GPA from SAT-V scores ranging from 400 (a relatively low score) to 700 (a very high score) is only about .50, or one-half of a letter grade. In fact, even if the prospective student had achieved a perfect SAT-V score of 800, the predicted GPA would still be only 2.98 (*B*). This phenomenon occurs because r_{xy} (the correlation between the test and the real-life criteria) is only .45, far less than perfect. As any college student can tell you, there are other factors, such as motivation and perseverance, that contribute to college success besides the ability to score well on the SAT-V test. Any college admissions officer who relies too heavily on the predictive value of the SAT-V test in predicting college success is making a mistake. For this reason, the informed test consumer would understand the predictive validity equation as well as the r_{xy} correlation of a given test before making decisions based on test results.

Attaching Confidence to Predictions

As noted in Chapter 8, a confidence interval can be placed around any test score. This interval represents the range of scores a person can actually achieve, given error in the test and testing situation. Likewise, a confidence interval can be placed around the $\hat{Y}$ prediction. To do this, we must find a statistic called the *Standard Error of the Estimate* (SEE). The formula for the SEE is:

$$S_{y|x} = s_y \sqrt{1 - (r_{xy})^2}$$

Where:

$S_{y|x}$ = standard error of the estimate

s_y = standard deviation of the real-life criterion

(r_{xy}) = predictive validity defined as the percentage of variance between the reliabilities of the test and the real-life performance criterion

This formula may strike you as resembling the one for the standard error of measurement, the statistic used in the previous chapter to place confidence intervals around test scores. In fact, we use the SEE exactly as we used the SEM—to place a confidence interval around $\hat{Y}$. The procedure is shown in Figure 9-3. Recall from the example of predicting GPA from SAT-V scores that the standard deviation of the criterion measure (the GPAs at this particular university) was .25, while the correlation (predictive validity power) between the test (SAT-V) and student's GPA was .45. Using these values, we can calculate the standard error of estimate as $S_{y|x}$ = .22.

Now we can place a confidence interval around the predicted GPA for our hypothetical student. To do this, we follow the procedure for finding confidence intervals using the area of scores expected under a normal curve (just as we did in Chapter 8). This is carried out at the 95 percent confidence level in Figure 9-4. As shown in this figure, the *z*-score at which 95 percent of the cases fall within the normal curve is 1.65. Thus, using the 95 percent *z*-score and the standard error of the estimate, we find that the upper limit

---

Figure 9-3 Calculating the Standard Error of Estimate (SEE)

$S_{y|x} = s_y \sqrt{1 \quad (r_{xy})^2}$

s_y = standard deviation of GPA = .25

r_{xy} = correlation between SAT-V and GPA = .45

$S_{y|x} = .25 \sqrt{1 - (.45)^2}$

$S_{y|x} = .25 \sqrt{1 - .20}$

$S_{y|x} = .25 \sqrt{.80}$

$S_{y|x} = .25 \, (.89)$

$S_{y|x} = .22$

---

for 95 percent confidence in a given student's GPA is $+.36$ and the 95 percent confidence level for the lower limit is $-.36$. Thus, as Figure 9-4 shows, a student's GPA as predicted from the SAT-V test can actually vary from 2.14 to 2.86 if we take error into account, a difference of nearly three-fourths of a grade. Again, this indicates that the admissions officer needs to be very careful not to attach too much importance or predictive power to the SAT-V test when making decisions about who will be admitted to the college.

What Does All This Mean?

It is time to review what you know about test validity and using tests to make educational decisions You know that test reliability is not enough—that a test must also be valid. This means that the test must measure what it pur-

Figure 9-4 Placing a Confidence Interval around a Predicted Score

SAT-V Score	Predicted GPA*	
465	2.50	$= \hat{Y}$

z-score of 95 percent of cases falling within the normal curve** $z = \pm 1.65$

$$
\begin{aligned}
\text{Upper Confidence Interval} &= 1.65\,(S_{y/x}) + \hat{Y} &= \\
&= 1.65\,(.22) + \hat{Y} &= \\
&= .36 + 250 &= \\
&= 2.86
\end{aligned}
$$

$$
\begin{aligned}
\text{Lower Confidence Interval} &= -1.65\,(S_{y/x}) + \hat{Y} &= \\
&= -1.65\,(.22) + \hat{Y} &= \\
&= -.36 + 2.50 &= \\
&= 2.14
\end{aligned}
$$

$$
\text{Confidence Bracket}
\begin{bmatrix}
\text{Lower} & \hat{Y} & \text{Upper} \\
2.14 & 2.50 & 2.86
\end{bmatrix}
$$

95 percent Confidence

From Table 9-2
**From z-score—area of Normal Curve Table*

ports to measure and that it must actually possess relevancy for the decisions to be made. You also know about content validity and that a test must pass four criteria of content validity before it is relevant for use in educational decision making. Additionally, you know about predictive validity and judging the power of a test in helping to make educational decisions. You know how to calculate a test's predictive power; but you also know the limitations of a test's power regarding the soundness of the real-life criteria used, the relationship between the test and the criteria, and the degree of error and confidence that can be safely placed in predictions.

This is crucial information for making informed test choices and for making and tempering educational decisions about students based on test scores. Having learned this information, you have progressed greatly toward becoming an informed test consumer and educational decision maker. You know how to ascertain the power and error of your decision-making process before such decisions are made.

Other Factors Affecting Test Validity

A test may not possess strong validity for a variety of reasons. Knowing some of the factors that influence test validity can aid both the test consumer and author in understanding the variables that are important in contributing to test validity.

Reliability

As we have seen, tests are concerned with two types of variance: true variance, which occurs between people as a consequence of individual differences between test takers on the criteria, and error variance, which represents irrelevant differences between test takers that have nothing to do with the criteria being tested. As error increases (and reliability decreases), the true variance that is based on the test-taker's performance on the criteria will decrease. Stated another way, as reliability decreases, so does validity.

Homogeneity of Groups

Suppose you are an admissions officer for one of the best medical schools in the country. In looking over the applications of your applicants you see that their average GPA is 3.88/4.00 with equally strong scores on their medical entrance exams. In fact, the lowest GPA of your applicant pool is 3.15. You must make your choices on some very fine distinctions as applied to student GPA and entrance examination scores.

This group of candidates applying for your medical school would be extremely alike or homogeneous in nature. In such a case, a low GPA (i.e., 3.15) would not be a very good predictor of who would or would not succeed in medical school.

In general, the more homogeneous the group being tested, the more limited the criterion validity of that test. This is because there is less to distinguish the test takers and thus less opportunity to differentiate on the basis of test scores. In such cases, it becomes very difficult to make differential predictions because our prediction equation would virtually predict the same thing for such student or candidate.

Group homogeneity often becomes a factor in educational testing. Some years ago a local school system decided to begin a class for gifted students. They endeavored to allow students into the program on the basis of IQ and school grades. However, virtually every candidate had an IQ over 130 and was a high achiever in school. Due to the homogeneity of the group, the school system had to make predictions and choices about students on the basis of extremely fine distinctions of IQ and grades. In the end, the entire process became invalid and caused hard feelings within the

district. Had these school officials been wiser test consumers they would have realized the difficulty in making valid predictions about criterion performance when the group being tested is extremely homogeneous.

Item Selection

As noted, a test must contain content validity. Content validity is determined largely by the items selected for inclusion on the test. Test items must adequately sample the content at different levels of cognitive complexity. Additionally, they must ask questions in ways that are not confusing to students and that are culturally fair. Finally, items must discriminate well enough between individuals to make the decision-making process valid. Items that are too easy or too difficult do not discriminate between people. Such items invalidate a test and make the decision-making process more difficult.

Norms

In Chapter 10 we discuss norms. Norms must be representative of the person taking the test to make comparisons meaningful. To the extent that such norms are not comparable, decisions will be faulty and the decision-making process will be invalidated.

Validity and the Decision-Making Process

Decisions about individuals cannot be made in a vacuum. Rather, educational decisions about students possess implications—implications for the student, the teacher, and the program. Some of these implications are costly considering the anguish and anxiety caused by wrong decisions; others can improve the quality of a child's education. All of the implications are important in the decision-making process. Some factors that influence the validity of the decision-making process are discussed here.

Availability of Other Data

Even if a given test is valid and useful, the validity of the decision-making process can be improved significantly if other independent tests or tools are also used. For example, suppose a test indicates strong deficiencies in a student's reading achievement. The validity of this assessment can be increased by soliciting independent information about the child's reading behavior from the child's teachers and parents. To the extent that independent assessments agree, the overall validity of the assessment is increased.

The Cost of Making Faulty Decisions

Figure 9-5 contains two decision matrices for a hypothetical jury. The figure shows that there is a 50 percent chance of the jury's arriving at the wrong verdict (this is a very high error probability—in real life we would want to reduce this chance of error significantly). However, in the first court case, the cost of

Figure 9-5 Two Decision Matrices

Type of Decision	Cost of Decision	
	$1.00 Fine	**No Fine**
Correct	No error	No error
Incorrect	Error	Error

Cost of Incorrect Decision—minimal

Type of Decision	Life Imprisonment	Freedom
Correct	No error	No error
Incorrect	Error	Error

Cost of Incorrect Decision—maximal

making a faulty decision is a $1.00 fine; in the second decision matrix, the cost of a faulty decision is a life sentence for an innocent person. Obviously, the cost of making a faulty decision is much more severe in one set of circumstances than in the other.

In the field of education, incorrect decisions can be costly in terms of frustration, anxiety, provision of improper services for students, wasted educational opportunities, and educational costs. These costs must be a factor in the decision-making process. The greater the cost, the more certain the test consumer must be that the decisions being made for students are valid, appropriate, and based on sound criteria.

The Selection Ratio

If you are deciding which students will be included in or excluded from a given program or curriculum, you need to consider your selection ratio. The selection ratio refers to how many applicants you can accept into the program as opposed to how many candidates are applying for entry. For example, if you have 10 openings in the program and 100 applicants, your selection ratio is 10 percent.

Generally, the smaller the ratio of openings in the program to applications received, the more discriminating your decision procedures must be. Suppose only 20 candidates apply for 40 positions. In such a situation, everyone could be admitted into the program (but at what cost?). However, if there are 5 more applicants than there are available positions, some choices have to be made. In such a situation, though, the decision criteria would not have to be severe. If, however, the number of applicants increases so that 100 candidates are applying for only 20 slots (a common occurrence in some medical schools), the selection criteria would have to be relatively severe, and many applicants would be turned away.

Will the Decision Improve the Probability of Success?

This question asks, What is the probability of success if we do not do *anything?* After testing, a decision may be made to make programmatic educational changes for a child. Such action should be taken on the basis that making changes will improve the probability that students will now succeed although they have been failing. If programmatic changes do not increase the probability of student success, then something is wrong with our program or with the validity of our decision-making process. In either case, programmatic changes that hold no hope for increased student success should not be made.

SUMMARY

Validity refers to whether or not a test measures what it purports to measure and to the usefulness of the test in helping to make predictions and decisions about individuals. For a test to be valid, it must accomplish two main objectives: it must adequately describe or represent the person taking the test and adequately make inferences about the test taker.

To be useful, tests must be reliable. Unreliable tests possess a great deal of error. Valid tests are, by definition, reliable. However, a test can be reliable and still be invalid. Reliability is a necessary, but not sufficient, requisite for validity.

Validity can be expressed by a coefficient (r_{xy}^2). It is the proportion of relevant variance between people, which is attributable to true differences on the criteria being measured, to the error variance. A test may possess a variety of validity coefficients depending on the criteria used to define that validity. Subtests of assessment instruments contain their own validity.

Not all tests express validity in coefficient form; some describe validity in prose form. It is the test consumer's responsibility adequately to understand and judge the appropriateness of the degree and type of validity contained in tests.

There are various types of validity. Face validity refers to the concept that a test appears to measure what it purports to measure. Face validity has an important motivational value for test takers. However, at times a test author will intentionally disguise a test's face validity.

Content validity refers to how adequately test items sample the domain of the subject matter the test is supposed to measure. Four criteria for assessing content validity are:

1. All main subtopics of the subject matter should be sampled.
2. Subtopics should be thoroughly sampled.
3. Test items should query information at a variety of cognitive complexity levels.
4. Information should be learned and tested at mastery levels.

Criterion-related validity refers to a test's predictive power. It is present to the extent that a person's real-life performance on a set of criteria can be estimated from the test score. There are two types of criterion-related validity—predictive and concurrent. Predictive validity refers to how accurately a current test can predict future real-life performance. Concurrent validity refers to how well a test can predict current real-life performance. Both types of criterion-related validity are extremely useful in educational assessment.

Construct validity refers to the extent that a test measures a theoretical trait or construct. Constructs represent entities that professionals have hypothesized exist in individuals but that are not directly observable. Examples of constructs are intelligence and personality traits. Validity is measured by the $\hat{Y}$ statistic.

Such equations allow for performance to be predicted from test scores and for differential predictions to be made about a student's probable success or failure on criterion measures. However, $\hat{Y}$ equations are only as strong as the correlation between the test and the real-life criterion performance that they predict. When such correlations are low, the predictive power of $\hat{Y}$ equations is also low.

Confidence intervals can be placed around $\hat{Y}$ predictions. The width of confidence intervals of $\hat{Y}$ depends on the standard error of the estimate (SEE). The larger the SEE, the wider the confidence interval.

Various factors influence test validity. These factors include the test's reliability, the homogeneity of the group being tested, the test items, and the test norms. Various factors also influence the decision-making process. These variables include the availability of other independent data, the cost of making faulty decisions, the selection ratio used, and whether implementing the decision will improve the probability of success for the individual. All of these variables will affect the choice to accept or reject the decision suggested by valid tests.

STUDY QUESTIONS

1. Define validity. Why is it important? What is the relationship between validity and relevance?

2. What is the relationship in tests between reliability and validity? Can unreliable tests be valid? Why or why not?

3. What are the two types of error in tests? How do they differ? What is the relationship between reliability, validity, and the two types of error?

4. How is validity expressed? What do these expressions mean?

5. What are the major types of validity? Define each type. Why is each type important?

6. Identify a topic to be taught and a major subtopic. Design ten to twenty test items for that topic at various taxonomic levels. Create a table of specifications for these items.

7. Devise a plan for assessing the predictive value of a test. Do you think that college entrance exams are predictive of future college success at your university? Why or why not?

8. Identify five educational constructs. How are they assessed?

9. What is $\hat{Y}$? Why is it important? What does it tell us about a person's predicted future performance?

10. What is the Standard Error of Estimate (SEE)? What does it represent? How is it expressed?

11. What are confidence intervals? What is the relationship between confidence intervals, test scores, and $\hat{Y}$?

12. What is true variance? What is the relationship between reliability, error variance, and true variance?

13. What is the effect of group homogeneity, $\hat{Y}$, and error? Why does this relationship occur?

14. Identify the factors of decision making. How do these factors affect the severity of decisions made?

CHAPTER 10

Test Norms and Standardization Groups

KEY CONCEPTS

- The concept of norm-referenced testing and the norm group
- Test norms
- Defining the norm group
- The three Rs of test norms
- Requirements of norm groups
- Random and stratified random samples
- Norm groups and the central limits theorem
- Defining the sampling procedure
- Types of norms
- Methods of representing norms
- What test manuals should tell about norms
- A warning about test norms

A single test score in isolation tells very little about the test taker. For that test score to take on meaning, it must be compared to something. That something can be a set of mastery criteria against which the test-taker's knowledge or skill is measured (criterion-referenced testing), or it can be a comparison between the test taker and similar people who have taken the same test. This is known as norm-referenced testing.

However, comparing a person's score against the scores of others who have taken the same test creates its own set of problems. Against whom should we measure the test score? Obviously it would be impractical, perhaps even impossible, to measure the individual's score against everyone who ever took the particular test. We must somehow choose a group of test scores against which to measure the test-taker's score. Then the person's score will become meaningful.

A Problem of Comparison

Mrs. Rodriguez, a third-grade teacher in a poor rural area, gave a test to her pupil, Billy. Being an informed test consumer, Mrs. Rodriguez realized that Billy's test score meant nothing in isolation—it had to be compared to something to give it meaning. Mrs. Rodriguez decided to compare Billy's test score to the scores of the other children in her class who took the test. Against this comparison group,

Billy scored above average, and Mrs. Rodriguez was satisfied that Billy was operating at about grade level.

A few weeks later, Billy moved to a middle-class, urban area of the state. When Mrs. Rodriguez checked on Billy's progress at his new school, she was shocked to learn that he was far behind the other members of his new class in his third-grade learning. What had happened? Had Billy suddenly become less smart? Had he forgotten material? Was Mrs. Rodriguez a bad teacher? Mrs. Rodriguez did not know how to interpret this information.

The Concept of the Norm Group

One of Mrs. Rodriguez's problems was that not having a large sample of test takers' scores to compare Billy's test score against, she compared it against the only group she had—Billy's classmates. This procedure was perfectly acceptable if all Mrs. Rodriguez wanted to see was how Billy was doing in comparison to his classmates; but these peers were all operating in the same rural, relatively impoverished environment. When Billy was compared against other children from a different set of environmental circumstances (a middle-class, urban environment), the original comparison was not very useful.

Psychologists and test authors, realizing the difficulty many teachers have in making sound, realistic, representative comparisons between test scores, have devised the concept of the *norm* or *standardization group* (the terms are often used interchangeably). Norms are benchmarks to which individuals who take a test are compared. The norm group is a reference group. By making such comparisons the teacher can learn how a student performed relative to others who took the same test at an earlier time.

The norm group of any given test is composed of people who share certain characteristics. For norm group comparisons to be meaningful, the characteristics of people in the norm group should be shared by the individual taking the test. This requisite of shared characteristics between test taker and norm group emphasizes that the interpretation of test scores in norm-referenced testing is relative rather than absolute. That is, we are comparing the test-taker's skills and knowledge against those of similar people, not against a set of absolute criteria (criterion-referenced testing).

The Three R's of Norms

The test results of people in the norm group are represented in the test manual as *norms*. Norms represent the set or distribution of scores of a particular norm group. This distribution of scores becomes the basis for interpreting individual scores.

As we saw in the case of Mrs. Rodriguez and Billy, norms must be appropriate to be meaningful. For norms to be useful and appropriate, they must conform to the three R's: they must be *representative, relevant,* and *recent*. If any of these requisite characteristics is missing or deficient, the test norms are virtually useless, and the test should not be used for comparison purposes.

Representativeness of Norms

As mentioned earlier in this chapter, it would be impossible to include everyone who ever took the test as a member of the norm group. Such a data collection task would be extremely time consuming, costly, and impossible to complete. Therefore, norm groups consist of a *sample* of the total universe of individuals who could have taken the test. Representativeness refers to how adequately this sample approximates the total population of potential test takers.

Two sets of variables influence the repre-

Figure 10-1 Variables That Influence the Representativeness of Norms

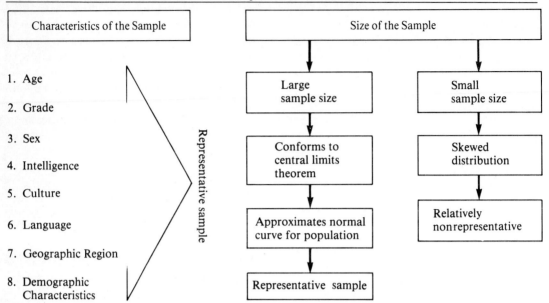

sentativeness of norms: the characteristics of the sample and the size of the sample. The individual variables included in the two sets of characteristics are shown in Figure 10-1.

Types of Samples

There are two types of samples, *random* and *representative* samples. A random sample is one in which people are selected for the norm group at completely chance or random levels. Everyone in the population has exactly the same chance of being selected for inclusion in the norm group.

Representative samples are those in which people are selected for the norm group in a way that obtains a proportional representation in terms of important or salient characteristics. Such salient characteristics are defined by the test author. For example, if it was found that approximately 10 percent of the population was black, and the test author believed that race was a salient variable or char-

acteristic for the norm group, the test author would ensure that 10 percent of the test's norm group was black. However, if the sample was purely random, more or less than 10 percent of the norm group might be black.

Variables in Representative Samples

Age: Perhaps the most important variable to consider in a norm group is chronological age. It is obvious to anyone who studies children that a five-year-old child usually cannot accomplish what a ten- or fifteen-year-old child can do. Thus, it is inappropriate to compare the test scores of one age group with norms obtained from children of a significantly different age group.

Most tests include norms for children at three- to six-month chronological age intervals. Some tests even contain norms at intervals as small as one or two months. Tests that do not account for the ages of students in the norm groups or that possess age categories in their norms that are too wide should probably be avoided.

Sex: There is overwhelmingly strong evidence that boys and girls perform differently on a variety of variables, including verbal ability (e.g., Nash 1979; Sherman 1978), quantitative ability (Fennema 1973, 1982), spatial ability (Sherman 1978; Fennema 1981), problem-solving ability (Garai and Scheinfeld 1968; Lynn 1972), and a host of other traits, abilities, and measures. For these reasons, it is appropriate for norms to possess a representative sample for both boys and girls.

Tests often contain separate norms for males and females rather than grouping them together in the same norm group pool. Depending on the trait being measured by the test, such gender splitting of the norm group can be valuable and render comparisons between the test taker and the appropriate norm group more meaningful.

Grade: Norms should also contain a representative sample of children in terms of school grade. Children in grade one do not study the same curriculum or possess the same skills as children in grade five. Comparing a first-grade test taker to a norm group of fifth graders (or vice versa) would be worse than meaningless. For tests that cover school-related material, grade norms are perhaps even more important than age norms.

Intelligence: Suppose a mentally retarded child took a norm-referenced achievement test and scored in the lowest percentile. This would certainly be discouraging for the child, the teacher, and the parents. But suppose that the norm group against which the mentally retarded child was compared contained no mentally retarded children—in fact, they were all above average in intelligence. Suddenly this child's test results would be neither surprising nor discouraging.

This situation is not as ridiculous as it ap-

pears. Children possessing low intelligence are often administered tests in which the norm group does not contain a representative sample of people with levels of intelligence that range from low to high. Rather, many mentally retarded students are measured against norm groups containing no mentally retarded pupils, with resulting conclusions drawn that they are far behind. However, in reality, the children in the norm group are not their intellectual peers at all.

Because language, achievement, and intelligence have been shown to be correlated (Brody and Brody 1976; Minton and Schneider 1980), a norm-referenced achievement test administered to low intellectually functioning children should possess a norm group with similar intellectual capabilities. Norms made representative for intellectual functioning will help ensure that the low functioning child is truly compared to a norm group of peers.

Race: The issue of tests and race has become and remained controversial over the last decades. Whereas some professionals have argued that achievement and intellectual tests are relatively color blind in predicting success on the performance criterion (Breland 1979; Jensen 1980), others have lashed out at what they perceive as the inherent unfairness of standardized tests against certain racial groups (Mercer 1979; Williams 1974).

Some facts, however, are relatively clear. First, it appears that blacks do score lower than whites on norm-referenced tests of achievement and intelligence (Oakland 1980; Oakland and Laosa 1977). Second, it is quite clear that blacks and other racial minorities, at least in the past, were underrepresented in and even excluded from the norm groups of many norm-referenced tests (Cole 1981; Gordon and Terrell 1981; Hunter and Schmidt 1976). What is less clear is whether the two phenomena are connected, that is, whether blacks historically scored lower on these tests because they were underrepresented on test norms. Luckily, more recent tests do deal with the issue of representativeness of norms for minority children, and such representativeness of norms has increased for these groups (Alley and Foster 1978; Gonzales 1982). However, it does seem crucial that blacks be better represented on norms for tests that black children regularly take. To the extent that blacks and other minorities are underrepresented or excluded on test norms, the validity of such tests for use with minority children is in serous question.

Culture and Language: Culture and language are strong factors in test performance (Alley and Foster 1978; Oakland and Laosa 1977). Evidence suggests that children from different cultural backgrounds interpret test items differently, bring to the test situation a different set of expectancies and knowledge, and generally do not score as high as their Anglo counterparts on standardized tests (Frame, Clarizio, and Porter 1984; Kagan 1971; Lefley 1975; Mercer 1974, 1979). For these reasons it is crucial that culturally diverse children be adequately represented in test norms. Test norms should represent children of all social classes in order to be valid and meaningful.

Geographic and Demographic Variables: The geographic regions of the United States differ in language patterns, belief systems, and values. A phrase or word in the deep South may mean something completely different in New England. A test representative for all children should include children from all the geographic areas of the country in the norm group.

Finally, the test author may wish to take additional demographic variables into account in creating the representativeness of the norm group. For example, a test measuring achievement motivation may need to include in the sample children differing in birth order, whereas a test of values toward employment may need to take into account parents' occupations. A good rule is to include any variable in the representativeness of the norm group that you suspect might be significant. The more variables taken into account, the less error the norm group representativeness will contain and the more valid the test will be for a large cross section of children.

Size of the Sample

Norm group representativeness requires the norm group to be based on an adequate sample size (N). What constitutes an adequate sample size is difficult to define precisely, but recall the central limits theorem from Chapter 6. This theorem states that the larger the sample size (or number of cases), the more the sample will approximate a normal distribution. Because a representative, normal sample is what the test author is seeking in creating the norm group, large sample sizes are more desirable than small samples.

Tests vary in the size of their norm groups. Some test authors construct test norm groups on the basis of very small samples (100 or fewer). On the other hand, the Stanford Diagnostic Arithmetic Test sets an example for large sample size of norm groups with more than 35,000 pupils in grades two through twelve included in the norm group, using both representative and random samples. Generally, the smaller the sample size used in creating a test's norm group, the greater caution the test consumer should use in applying those norms to individual students.

Relevancy of Norms

Relevancy of norms refers to the extent that the norm group(s) of a given test interface or agree with the characteristics of the individual student taking the test. In other words, the test taker whose score is being compared against the test norms should be similar to the norm group in terms of key characteristics and traits. To the extent that the traits and characteristics of the test taker and the norm group agree, the test norms are relevant for the test taker. To the extent that the characteristics of the two do not interface, the test norms are irrelevant for that particular student.

It is important for the test consumer to understand that the relevancy of test norms is relative rather than absolute. That is, while the norms may be completely appropriate and relevant for comparison with one test taker, they may nevertheless be irrelevant and inappropriate for another test taker. Test norms do not change and therefore do not determine relevancy. Rather, the characteristics and traits of the test taker determine the relevancy of norms.

The test user is responsible for determining whether the norms of a particular test are relevant for a particular child. This is accomplished by comparing the characteristics of the test taker with the characteristics of the norm group. If the two are not in agreement in terms of characteristics and traits, the test probably should not be used. If the test is used, comparisons between the test taker and the test norms should not be made.

Recency of Norms

People are not quite the same as they were twenty or more years ago. People's language, beliefs, and knowledge change. For these reasons, norms should be relatively up to date. When norms become outdated (norms more than twenty years old probably can be considered out of date), they should be revised and updated.

The test consumer must make sure that the norms of the test being used are relatively recent and updated. Outdated norms place the usefulness and validity of the test in serious jeopardy.

Types of Norms

A variety of test norms are available to test users. These include national norms, specific group norms, local norms, and school–class norms. The type of norm selected depends on the intended use of the test-taker's score.

National Norms

Most standardized, norm-referenced tests contain national norms. This means that the norm group for these tests was obtained from a representative, nationwide sample of individuals. National norms imply that the test is applicable for any person in the country in which the test was designed who matches the characteristics and traits of the students in the norm group.

A word of caution about national norms is in order. Even though a test proclaims to be appropriate for a national audience (and by implication contains national norms), its norm group may not have been drawn from a national sample. For example, the first edition of a nationally used test (since revised) claimed to be appropriate for use by all children residing in the United States, but its norm group was drawn only from children attending parochial schools in one southern city of the United States! It is not enough that a test claim to have national applicability. To be appropriate for use by children across the country, its norms must be national in scope.

Special Group Norms

Some tests are appropriate for use with all children; other tests are designed for use with a specific population. For example, the AAMD Adaptive Behavior Scale is a test specifically designed to assess the adaptive behavior of mentally retarded individuals. Other tests, such as the Blind Learning Aptitude Test (BLAT), are specifically designed for use with visually impaired or blind individuals. If these and other population-specific tests are to be appropriate for such specialized populations, they have to be normed on such restricted populations. Thus, the AAMD scale was normed on 400 mentally retarded pupils, and the BLAT was normed on 961 blind students.

Even though tests for special populations are normed on a narrow group of specialized students, the students in the norm group should still be representative of the population from which they are being sampled. For example, the BLAT was normed totally on blind students, but those students were nevertheless stratified on the basis of geographic region, age, sex, and socioeconomic status. The same rules that apply for choosing a representative norm sample from a general population apply for choosing a norm group of specialized individuals.

The test consumer who uses specialized norms should not be surprised to find the norm group somewhat smaller than those of general population tests. This is because the population of specialized individuals (e.g., blind persons) is smaller and geographically more diverse than that of the general population. It is more time consuming and expensive to test and include norms for a group of specialized individuals. Nevertheless, test authors should include as large a sample size as possible in specialized tests to conform to the tenets of the central limits theorem.

Local Norms

Sometimes, a test user may find that the national norms of a test do not fit the characteristics of the particular students being tested. Moreover, the test user may wish to use norms that are more indicative of the geographical area or socioeconomic conditions under which the test taker resides. In such cases, the test consumer may wish to use local norms.

Local norms are developed for a particular geographic region, such as a state or city.

Some states, for example, administer their own statewide achievement tests every year to assess the academic achievement of students from various school systems within that state. Likewise, many cities and municipalities give citywide tests for various purposes.

Local norms are obtained in much the same way as national norms (Brown 1983; Ricks 1971). A representative sample of students from the local population is carefully selected and tested; norms are then derived from this population for students taking the test in the future.

The main advantage of local norms is that they allow for direct comparisons between the test taker and those people living in the immediate geographic environment. Such norms eliminate many regional differences that need to be accounted for in national norms. However, the advantage of local norms is also the biggest weakness. Because the norm group is formed from a restricted geographic population, comparisons on a larger scope (e.g., national comparisons) cannot be made. This was precisely the problem Mrs. Rodriguez encountered in the example presented at the beginning of this chapter. She attempted to make sense of Billy's test score after he moved to a different part of the state. When broader educational decisions must be made, national norms are probably more useful than their local counterparts.

School and Class Norms

Sometimes teachers want to compare test takers with their immediate schoolmates. In such cases, school or class norms are appropriate. The procedure for obtaining school- or class-specific norms is the same as that for obtaining local norms. Likewise, the advantages and disadvantages of school–class norms are the same as for local norms. Although class norms may be useful in directly comparing a test taker with immediate peers, such norms hold little or no applicability for broader comparisons between the test taker and children outside the test taker's immediate environment.

What Test Manuals Should Report about Norms

A test manual should be as specific about the norms and norm group as possible. There is no such thing as reporting too much information about the norm group. In reality, many manuals do exactly the opposite; they report too little data for the test user to make informed decisions about the adequacy of the norm group.

At the very least, the test manual should report the following information about the norm group:

1. How representative are the norms? On what basis was the norm group chosen?
2. What are the specific characteristics of the norm group in terms of age, sex, race, intelligence, culture, and other characteristics described in this chapter?
3. What is the sample size? Why was this sample size chosen? What is the proportion of the sample size to the total population?
4. How old are the norms? When were they last revised?
5. For what types of comparisons are the norms useful?

Be careful not to take anything about norms on faith. If the test manual does not report certain information about the norm group, do not assume that the test author merely forgot to report it in the manual. Be

skeptical. Assume that the author did not take the missing factors or variables into account, or that the factors were attended to so poorly that the author decided not to report them. In either case, when the information about norms and norm groups is inadequate, assume that the norms are badly flawed and use another test.

A Final Word on Norms

Norms are comparisons; they are not standards. We use norms to find out how a given test taker is doing in relation to the sample population on which the norms are based. This comparison may or may not be appropriate depending on the degree of interface the test taker has with the norm group.

However, test norms do not tell us how a child *should* perform. They are not judgmental. Nor are they standards that the test taker should measure up to. Rather, decisions on where the child should or should not be performing are left to teachers and other educational professionals. In the end, decisions about where a child ought to be performing need to be made not on the basis of comparing the test taker to peers but on the basis of the requisite skills needed for success in the child's culture and society. These skills were measured by criterion-referenced tests and curriculum-based assessment. Both of these assessments are discussed at length in the next chapter.

SUMMARY

A single, isolated test score tells us nothing about the test taker. For a test to take on meaning, the score must be compared to something. In norm-referenced testing, scores are compared to the scores of a norm group.

Norms are the benchmarks to which individuals who take a test are compared. The norm group is a reference group that allows

the teacher to compare a test-taker's score against similar students who took the same test at an earlier time.

Norm groups are people who share similar characteristics. For comparisons to be meaningful, the characteristics of the norm group and the test taker must be similar.

Useful norms conform to the three Rs—

they are representative, relevant, and recent. Representativeness refers to the fact that the sample of students making up the norm group is representative or characteristic of the total population who could have taken the test. Two sets of variables influence the representativeness of norms: the characteristics of the sample and the sample size.

Samples are random or representative. A random sample is one in which people are selected from the population at completely random or chance levels. Representative samples select people for inclusion in the norm group in such a way as to obtain a proportional representation in terms of important or salient characteristics. Variables to consider in creating representative samples include (but are not restricted to) age, grade, sex, intelligence level, race, culture, and geographic and demographic factors. The more variables taken into account by the test author in creating a representative sample, the more valid that sample.

Sample size is also important in creating the norm group. The larger the sample, the more valid the norm group. The tenet of the central limits theorem applies to norm group sample size.

Norms must be relevant, that is, the characteristics of the norm group must interface with those of the test taker. Norm relevancy is relative; norms may be appropriate for one test taker but not for another. It is the responsibility of the test user to ensure relevancy of norms for particular test takers.

Norms should also be recent and up to date. Norms older than twenty years probably should be revised, and the validity of tests with outdated norms is in serious jeopardy.

There are various types of norms, including national, population-specific, local, and school–class norms. National norms are obtained on a representative, nationwide sample of students. National norms imply that the test is appropriate for use with any child in the United States (or in the country in which the test has been devised) who matches the characteristics of the norm group. It is the test-user's responsibility to ascertain that any test claiming to be national in scope actually contains national norms.

Population-specific norms are used in tests designed for a specific group of students, such as the mentally retarded, blind, or deaf. Although population-specific norms are obtained on a specialized population, they should still be representative of the entire population of those specialized individuals.

Local norms are developed for a particular geographical region, state, or municipality. Local norms possess the advantage of allowing direct comparisons between the test taker and peers living in a close geographical region. However, local norms do not allow for the broader comparisons permitted by using national norms.

School and class norms allow for direct comparisons between the test taker and immediate schoolmates. School–class norms possess the same advantages and disadvantages as local norms.

Test manuals should contain specific and detailed information about norm groups, including: (1) the representativeness of norm groups, (2) the specific characteristics of the norm group, (3) the sample size, (4) the age of the norms, and (5) the types of comparisons the norms allow. The test consumer must be extremely critical of norm group information in test manuals and should reject the test if the information is inadequate.

Norms are comparisons, not standards. As such, norms do not tell where the students ought to be functioning. Such decisions must be made by teachers and other educational professionals.

S T U D Y   Q U E S T I O N S

1. In what two ways can scores be compared? Which method uses norm-referenced evaluation? Which uses criterion-referenced evaluation?

2. What is a norm group? What information does it yield in helping to interpret an individual's test score?

3. What are the three Rs of testing? Why is each one important?

4. What are the two types of samples? How do they differ in their logic and construction?

5. What are the major variables to consider in norm construction? Why is each important?

6. How is norm relevancy defined? Is the concept set by the test or by the test taker? Explain your answer.

7. Why should norms be up to date? Give an example in which this would be most important.

8. What are the different types of norms often used in standardized tests? What are the advantages and disadvantages to each type of norm?

CHAPTER 11

Informal Assessment

When people think of educational assessment they often envision commercially available paper and pencil tests that are administered and scored under strict, supervised conditions. Such tests are usually purchased by a school or school system and graded by hand, using a standardized scoring key, or scored and graded by computer. Student responses are then submitted to strict statistical evaluation with scores expressed in an appropriate standardized form.

There is nothing wrong with such a conceptualization of educational assessment. A large proportion of educational assessment consists of administration, scoring, and interpretation of standardized tests. However, anyone familiar with classroom and educational practices knows that teachers also assess students daily in a variety of less structured but equally important ways. For example, a teacher listening to a child's oral reading asks the child a few comprehension questions to ascertain that the child understands what has been read. Another teacher systematically observes when and under what conditions a child drifts off task. A third teacher analyzes the mistakes on a child's arithmetic paper to gauge areas of weakness or miscomprehension. These are all examples of informal assessment, another commonly used type of educational testing.

Formal versus Informal Assessment

Assessment is either *formal* or *informal.* Formal assessment uses specific and standardized procedures for administration, scoring, and interpretation of tests. Formal tests are norm- or criterion-referenced. Norm-referenced tests compare a student's performance to that of peers or a norm group. Criterion-referenced tests measure the child against a set of stated skills or objectives often tied to the school curriculum. For this reason, criterion-referenced tests are often referred to as *curriculum-based* assessment. Such assessment is discussed in Chapter 12. Informal tests usually lack rigid or standardized procedures dictating administration, scoring and interpretation. Informal tests, however, can yield extremely valuable information to the teacher. Table 11-1 contains the major advantages and disadvantages of formal and informal tests.

Formal and informal assessments differ along a number of dimensions. These dimensions include *setting, type of reference, technical quality, activities, statistics,* and *reporting format* (Guerin and Maier 1983).

Setting refers to the conditions under which the assessment is conducted. Typically, formal assessment is conducted in a relatively structured, well-defined setting. As noted in Chapter 10, standardization of test setting is an important variable in formal assessment to ensure that the assessment is relatively free from this type of error. Informal assessment, on the other hand, is usually conducted in more naturalistic, less structured settings. Such settings include, but are not restricted to, the child's classroom, home, or even the playground and recreation areas when appropriate. Although such settings are less controlled, formal, and standardized than those used in formal assessment, they do allow observation of the child's behavior in a more natural, less contrived environment.

Type of referencing refers to comparisons of the child's test behavior. As we have seen, tests are either norm-referenced or criterion-referenced. Norm-referenced tests compare

Table 11-1   Advantages and Disadvantages of Formal and Informal Assessment

Formal Assessment	
Advantages	**Disadvantages**
Standardized tests	Compares students against each other
Usually commercially available	Not curriculum based
Usually possess proven reliability and validity	Usually yields little diagnostic information
Structured and easy-to-follow administration and scoring	Does not indicate mastery of material
	Too highly structured
Useful test manual	Occasional inappropriateness of norm group

Informal Assessment	
Advantages	**Disadvantages**
Diagnostic	Usually not commercially available
Compares student against curriculum or criterion	Time consuming to create
	Time consuming to administer
Mastery-level test	Unproven reliability and validity
Allows teacher latitude in administration and scoring	Difficulty in interpreting results
	Usually no test manual
Designed for the specific student	

the child's score to those of peers or a norm group. Criterion-referenced tests compare the child's test behavior with some level of performance of the curriculum. Whereas virtually all norm-referenced instruments are formal in nature, criterion-referenced tests can be formal or informal.

Technical quality indicates the extent that the test has dealt with issues of test norms, standardization, item sampling and pilot testing, reliability, and validity. All tests should be technically sound in terms of sampling, reliability, and validity, but some tests deal with these issues more adequately than do others. Generally, informal assessment measures possess less (and sometimes no) information about reliability and validity. This does not mean that the reliability and validity of informal assessment tests are poor; it means that such information is unknown. Nevertheless, lack of technical adequacy is often a weakness of many informal assessment tests and procedures.

Activities are the set of operations or activities contained in the assessment. Activities represent what is actually done during the assessment. Formal assessment activities are ordered and sequenced. They occur in a specified order and are carried out in a specific manner to adhere to the mandates of the formal test. Informal assessment activities are more flexible and open. They can be changed or modified as the teacher sees fit, and new activities can be created if they seem more appropriate. Although strict standardization of activities is lost in informal assessment, spontaneity is gained.

Statistics are the means of reporting the data. With formal assessment, statistical reporting is highly standardized. For example, measures of central tendency, dispersion, and standard scores are generally used in reporting norm-referenced data; statistics indicating percentage of mastery are often used with criterion-referenced procedures. With informal tests, reporting of test information is less

formalized and more idiosyncratic. Teachers can report test information in ways they consider most meaningful and relevant. Statistical analysis is not used to a great extent in the reporting of informal assessment information.

The reporting format is the form or manner in which test information is reported for the test. Formats can be largely statistical or in prose form (e.g., descriptively reporting behavioral objectives passed). Informal tests usually are more descriptive in reporting information than are formal, norm-referenced tests.

Types of Informal Assessment

There are numerous types of informal assessment, and at first this array of procedures might be confusing. However, the assortment of informal assessment procedures can be brought into focus by placing them in a 2×2 factorial design, with *directness* on one axis and *obtrusiveness* on the other (see Table 11-2). Directness refers to the degree that the teacher gains a firsthand view of the child's behavior, as opposed to finding out about it at second hand. For example, a teacher's direct observance of a child's performance or behavior constitutes a firsthand observance. However, if the teacher learns about the child's behavior from interviewing a parent, that constitutes a secondhand collection of data. Both direct (firsthand) and indirect (secondhand) informal assessment carry risks of error. Generally, however, informal assessment information collected through indirect methods is more suspect due to problems of validity and reliability associated with the people doing the reporting.

Obtrusiveness refers to the degree that the assessment enters into or intrudes on the learning environment. For example, a teacher may decide to record a child's naturally occurring behavior silently and covertly during the school day. This represents a relatively unob-

Table 11-2 A 2 × 2 Factorial Design for Informal Assessment Directness of Obtaining Information

	Direct (Firsthand)	Indirect (Secondhand)
Obtrusive	Students are observed directly by teacher. Students know they are being observed. They may act differently than they otherwise would.	Teachers cannot observe the behavior directly. Students know they are being assessed. The interview technique is an example of this type of assessment.
Unobtrusive	Students are observed by teacher without their knowledge. An example of this is naturalistic observation. Students would probably act "naturally" in this type of assessment.	Relying on someone's observations or recollections for data about a student. This is data collection "once removed."

trusive behavior assessment. However, if the teacher stops the natural events of the day and gives the child a pencil and paper test to complete, this represents a highly obtrusive method of assessment. Generally, less obtrusive methods of data collection during informal assessment are desirable.

The major methods of informal assessment fall into eight main forms or categories:

1. *Observation*
2. *Checklists*
3. *Rating scales*
4. *Questionnaires*
5. *Interviews*
6. *Inventories*
7. *Teacher-made tests*

Each method is discussed in this chapter.

Observation

The Need for Systematic Observation

Teachers are natural observers. A large part of a teacher's job is to watch students, observe their performance and behavior, and then respond to or act on the child's observed behavior. Thus, the teacher who listens to Stefan's oral reading and corrects a mispronounced word is responding to an observation. Likewise, the teacher who corrects Martha's inap-

propriate class behavior is responding to an observation.

The problem with most people's observations, however, is that they are not *systematic*. That is, observations tend to be relatively random or haphazard, and they take place when the person's behavior catches the observer's attention. For example, consider two children in the same class. Irina hardly ever misbehaves, almost always stays in her seat, and attends to her school work. Larry, on the other hand, is frequently off task and seems to attend to everyone's business but his own. A teacher who has grown accustomed to Larry's behavior may not take notice (observe) when he is off task. However, if Irina is out of her seat, the teacher might immediately observe such a novel occurrence and respond. Thus, the phenomenon of the teacher's nonsystematic observance of the behavior is often more a function of the novelty of the children's behavior than of the behavior itself.

For observation to be useful it must be systematic. Systematic observation is a planned, nonrandom method of observing behavior that uses specialized techniques of specifying, counting, and recording behavior (Cooper 1981; Wielkiewicz 1986). Systematic observation helps ensure that the conclusions drawn from the behavioral sample will be relatively unbiased and free from error.

Systematic observation is perhaps the most direct form of informal assessment and the least obtrusive. It is the most direct because the teacher does not have to rely on a third party for secondhand information; nor does the teacher need to depend on a pencil and paper test that infers behavior without having the child demonstrate the actual skill. Rather, systematic observation allows the teacher to observe the child's behavior and make a direct judgment as to whether the child possesses the skill being measured. Systematic observation is unobtrusive because the teacher does not interfere with or intrude into the educational environment. Rather, the teacher watches as the child performs naturally in that environment.

This does not mean that systematic observation has no problems. A teacher may miss important behavior during observations. Two or more observers may not be able to agree whether or to what degree a given behavior has taken place. However, procedures have been developed to make systematic observation more exact and error-free. These procedures are discussed later in this chapter.

Continuous Observation

During the initial stages of behavior assessment, a teacher may wish to get an overall view of a student's behavior. That is, the teacher may wish to observe all of a child's behavior over a given period of time to gain a picture of the variables and interactions that influence those behaviors. This *continuous observation* requires the teacher to record all of the child's behavior over a brief period of time (Hartmann and Wood 1982; Hawkins 1986). Continuous observation provides a global view of the child's behavior and allows the teacher to pinpoint specific areas of behavior that may need further observation and modification.

Figure 11-1   Instances of Kevin's Aggressive Behavior during Recess

Date: *April 16*

Time of Observation: *10 – 10:30 AM*

Interval	Number of Instances	Total
10:00 – 10:05	*I I*	*2*
10:05 – 10:10	*O*	*O*
10:10 – 10:15	*I I I I*	*4*
10:15 – 10:20	*I I I*	*3*
10:20 – 10:25	*卅*	*5*
10:25 – 10:30	*I*	*I*
30 minutes		*15*

Figure 11-1 shows a teacher's record of continuous observation for Kevin on the playground during recess. The teacher divided the thirty-minute recess period into six equal segments. In each segment, the teacher observed and recorded Kevin's behavior. As shown in this record, Kevin spent much of the recess engaging in aggressive behavior against other children.

Sequential Observation

A second form of observation is *sequential observation,* sometimes called *sequential analysis* (Alberto and Troutman 1982; Hayes and Nelson 1986). Sequential analysis is similar to continuous observation in that both record all of a child's behavior for a certain period of time. However, sequential analysis also attempts to identify the events that occurred directly before (antecedents) and after (consequences) the child's behavior. In this way, sequential analysis attempts to identify the environmental variables that are interacting with the child's behavior.

Figure 11-2 shows a sequential analysis for

Figure 11-2 Sequential Analysis of Kevin's Behavior during Recess

Date: *April 21*

Time of Observation: *1:30 – 2 PM*

Interval	Instances	Antecedent	Consequence
1:30 – 1:35	*II*	*Robert grabbed bat from Kevin.* *Steven taunts Kevin.*	*Robert strikes Kevin in retaliation.* *Steven runs away.*
1:35 – 1:40	*I*	*Kevin is not chosen for game.*	*Children taunt Kevin for aggressive outburst.*
1:40 – 1:45	*O*	*O*	
1:45 – 1:50	*II*	*Kevin pushed off swing by Ralph.* *Kevin calls Ralph a baby.*	*Ralph strikes Kevin in retaliation.* *Ralph pushes Kevin off swing.*
1:50 – 1:55	*I*	*Kevin taunted by two boys.*	*Boys push Kevin in retaliation.*
1:55 – 2:00	*I*	*Children told to line up to come inside.*	*Children complain to teacher that Kevin cut in line.*
	7		

the behavior demonstrated by Kevin as recorded in Figure 11-1. Here, the teacher has identified the events that occurred directly before and after Kevin's outbursts. The events occurring directly prior to Kevin's aggressive behavior show other children engaged in aggressive behavior with him. Thus, the teacher may need to work with both Kevin and the other children on social skills in the play environment.

After Continuous Recording: Systematic Observation

Continuous and sequential observation allow the teacher to gain insight into the child's general behavior patterns as well as the environmental antecedents and consequences linked to that behavior. Once the teacher has an idea of the child's general behavior, it is possible to focus on a specific set of behaviors with the goal of modifying these target behaviors. Gaining insight about specific behaviors with the goal of behavioral change is accomplished through systematic observation.

Systematic observation consists of three different procedures and processes. These include

1. Precisely describing the behavior to be observed.
2. Selecting the appropriate measuring system.
3. Outlining data collection procedures.

Describing the Behavior to Be Observed

Suppose a teacher decided to observe and record all instances of Martin's off-task behavior. Dutifully, the teacher sits with pencil and paper, ready to record all instances where Martin is not on task. While completing his arithmetic work paper, Martin looks up and stares out the window, pencil to lips; he seems to be calculating an answer in his mind. He then writes the answer to a problem. Did Martin's looking out the window qualify as off-task behavior?

This example shows that even behaviors we think we understand (like off-task behavior) can cause observational confusion due to impreciseness of definition. To eliminate confusion, the behavior to be observed must be precisely and behaviorally defined. Verbs like *undertand*, *know*, and *like* are unacceptable for behavioral observation; words like *write*, *point*, and *say* are more behaviorally precise. Only behavioral verbs should be used to describe behavior to be observed.

Selecting a Behavioral Observation Recording System

After the behavior to be observed has been carefully defined and outlined, an appropriate observation system must be selected. This system should be selected on the basis of the nature of the behavior to be observed and the desired type of behavioral change.

There are two basic observational recording systems—event and interval recording (Alberto and Troutman 1982; Barrett, Johnston, and Pennypacker 1986). Event recording monitors the number of times an event takes place. Teachers who use event recording are interested in learning whether a given behavior takes place and, if so, how frequently it occurs. Interval recording systems are concerned with the length of time a student engages in a given behavior or the length of time it takes the student to begin the behavior.

The various recording systems that fall under the headings of event and interval recordings include *rate*, *frequency*, *topography*, *force*, and *locus* under event recording, and *rate*, *duration*, and *latency* under interval recording (Barrett et al. 1986; Hawkins 1986).

1. Frequency. How many times did the behavior occur? The greater the number of occurrences of the behavior, the greater the frequency.

2. Rate. Frequency data expressed in a ratio of time. For example, Steven's hitting another child four times constitutes a frequency recording; his hitting a child four times in a ten-minute period constitutes rate recording. Rate recording is both an event and interval method of observational recording.

3. Topography. What is the "shape" of the behavior? What does it look like? For example, a description of a child reversing letters on the chalkboard constitutes topography. Likewise, a vivid, visual description of a child's temper tantrum is a form of topography recording.

4. Force. A description of the magnitude of behavior. How strong, loud, forceful, etc. is a given behavior?

5. Locus. A description of where the behavior occurred.

6. Duration. How long did a given behavior last?

7. Latency. How long did it take for the child to begin the behavior? For example, the time it took the child to begin work on a math paper after direction by the teacher to "get to work" constitutes a latency recording.

When should event or interval recording be used? Event recording is most useful in measuring *discrete* behaviors that have an obvious beginning and ending. Examples of discrete behaviors include spelling a word, reading a paragraph, or typing a page. The frequency of occurrence of discrete behaviors is easily determined.

Continuous behaviors are those in which the beginning and ending points are difficult to measure. Behaviors are relatively continuous either because they occur at a high frequency (making it difficult to obtain an accurate frequency count) or because they extend over a lengthy period of time. Interval recording is the preferred method for observational recording of continuous behaviors.

Time Sampling

In observing and recording continuous behaviors, it is suggested that the teacher use *time sampling* procedures (Barlow, Hayes, and Nelson 1984; Hayes and Nelson 1986). In time sampling, the observer selects a discrete period of time in which to observe the child and then divides that time period into equal intervals. If the behavior occurs at least once during the time interval, the interval is scored as positive. If the behavior does not occur during the interval, the interval is scored as negative.

Time sampling is similar to duration recording except that whereas the intervals in duration recording are relatively short (sometimes only seconds), the intervals in time sampling

procedures are longer (usually several minutes). An example of time sampling recording is shown in Figure 11-3. As shown, Lester, although he was supposed to be working on his arithmetic paper, engaged in leaving his seat at least once during four of the six time intervals. Thus, it may be concluded that this behavior needs to be modified.

What are some limitations of time sampling observation? Figure 11-3 points out one of the major problems with time sampling procedures. We see from the first recording that Lester engaged in out-of-seat behavior at least once during four of the six time intervals. However, we do not know how many times Lester left his seat—it could have been once per interval or a dozen times. This problem can be solved by simply enumerating the number of times per interval in which Lester left his seat.

Figure 11-3   An Example of Time Sampling

Behavior: Lester being out of his seat during the 30 minutes (11:30 – 12) allotted for class to work on arithmetic paper.

	11:30 – 11:35	11:35 – 11:40	11:40 – 11:45	11:45 – 11:50	11:50 – 11:55	11:55 – 12:00
Occurrences of behavior	+	–	+	+	–	+

Lester's versus Peter's out-of-seat behavior:
Which one is more serious?

Lester	11:30 – 11:35	11:35 – 11:40	11:40 – 11:45	11:45 – 11:50	11:50 – 11:55	11:55 – 12:00
Occurrences of behavior	+ + + 3	0	+ + 2	0	+ + + + + 5	+ + + 3

Peter	11:30 – 11:35	11:35 – 11:40	11:40 – 11:45	11:45 – 11:50	11:50 – 11:55	11:55 – 12:00
Occurrences of behavior	+ 1	+ 1	0	+ 1	+ 1	0

However, suppose Lester's enumerated seat-leaving behavior is compared with Peter's as shown in Figure 11-3. From this recording we could conclude that Lester's seat-leaving behavior was more serious than Peter's because he left his seat more times. But is this really the case? What if Peter left his seat only once per interval, but he left it for the entire interval? On the other hand, what if Lester left his seat five times per interval, but only for ten seconds each time? Given this information, we would readily see that Peter was actually out of his seat significantly longer than Lester. Thus, data collected using time sampling and duration recording can sometimes lead to erroneous results, and the teacher must interpret time-sampled data appropriately.

Outlining Data Collection Procedures

Once the behavior to be observed has been precisely defined and the observation system chosen, the teacher must then identify the data collection procedures. In doing so the following five questions must be answered:

1. When and where will the observations occur?
2. How many observation periods will take place?
3. Who will be the observers?
4. How will data be recorded?
5. How will observer reliability be assessed?

When and Where Will the Observations Take Place? The answers to this question depend, largely, on the behavior being observed. For example, if the teacher wanted to observe and measure aggressive behavior on the playground, the time and place of observation would naturally be restricted to the playground during recess periods. Likewise, observation of the child's oral reading would be restricted to times during the school day when the child was engaged in sustained oral reading in the classroom.

How Many Observation Periods Will Take Place? In answering this question, the teacher-

observer should realize that once is not enough. It is virtually impossible to make sound, valid conclusions based on only one observational episode. A child may be experiencing a bad day while under observation or may be behaving in an atypical manner. To gain insight into observed behavior, more than one observational episode must be used.

How many sessions are enough? Probably, a child should be observed on at least three to five separate occasions to assure the validity of the observations. If the child acts in a consistent manner during these observational sessions, the teacher may safely infer that the observed behavior is typical and representative.

Who Will Be the Observers? Observations should be carried out only by expert individuals trained in observational techniques. Such experts include, but are not restricted to, teachers, other educational professionals, trained behavioral technicians, and psychologists. However, when these persons are not available, parents, volunteers, college students, student teachers, and others can make systematic observations.

Whoever makes the observations must be well trained. Training should include instruction in the general procedures of observation as well as specific instruction in observing the particular behavior to be measured. This is where precisely defining the behavior to be observed in behavioral, measurable terms is vitally important. The less behaviorally precise and more general the definition of the behavior to be observed, the more subjective the observations of that behavior will be. Thus, the observer must be well trained in recognizing the precise target behaviors specified. Otherwise, the observations will be virtually useless.

Finally, whenever possible, there should be more than one observer per observation session. As was pointed out earlier, the agreement of two independent observers that a behavior has or has not taken place is a key issue in the usefulness of recorded observations.

How Will Data Be Recorded? It is imperative that behaviors be recorded *at the time of observation*. Such recording is usually done with paper and pencil, but in some cases observations can be made using a tape recorder. Whatever the recording mode, do not leave observations to memory, convinced that you will be able to reconstruct and record them later. Record observations as they occur or they will lose much of their validity and usefulness.

The recording system used should include as much information as possible. Excessive information can be disregarded at data analysis time, but too little observational data cannot be reconstructed at a later date. However, a compromise must be reached when recording data. If observers try to write down everything that occurs in an observational session, they may miss important behavior that occurs while they are recording. Observers should try to record enough data for the observational session to be useful but not so much as to overload their processing and observational capabilities.

Observer Reliability: A key issue in making sound observations is observer reliability. This refers to the fact that two people, independently recording the same target behavior in the same session, should make identical observations. To the extent that their observations differ, the observations lack reliability and hence validity.

The professional can do several things to increase observational reliability (Guerin and Maier 1983; Romanczyk, Kent, Diament, and O'Leary 1973). First, the target behavior should be defined as precisely as possible in observable, behavioral terms. Such terms as *social cooperation, on-task behavior,* and *neatness* lead to observational confusion, subjectivity, and lowered reliability.

Second, observers must be adequately trained. Simply describing for them the behavior to watch is not enough. Rather, observers must be trained in observation and recording of specific behaviors. During training, observers should communicate with each other as to what they are watching for and how they are recording data. Agreement between observers before the observational sessions is required. Once the actual observations begin, however, observers must remain independent. They should not compare notes or communicate with each other about what they are observing.

Throughout observation sessions, reliability checks should be made by the professional in charge of the program. If the reliability of observers begins to drop, retraining or renewed communication sessions may be necessary.

Calculating Observational Reliability: A simple method for calculating observer reliability uses this formula:

$$r = \frac{\text{Agreements}}{\text{Agreements} + \text{Disagreements}}$$

In Figure 11-4 there were twenty agreements and five disagreements between two observers. Calculation of the degree of agreement in this case is ⅘, or .80.

Reliability coefficients should also be calculated separately for event and interval (duration or latency) observations. For event observations the formula for calculating reliability is:

$$r = \frac{\text{Smaller number of occurrences}}{\text{Larger number of occurrences}}$$

In this formula the smaller number represents the lesser number of occurrences observed by a particular observer and the large number represents the greater number of occurrences observed during the same session by a different observer. An example of the calculation for the observational reliability for event recording is shown in Figure 11-4.

Figure 11-4   Calculating Observer Reliability

Calculating Degree of Agreements

Agreements = 20

$$r = \frac{20}{20 + 5} = \frac{20}{25} = .80$$

Disagreements = 5

Total Observations = 25

Event Recording

Observer A–8 observations of target behavior

Observer B–12 observations of target behavior

$$r = \frac{8}{12} = \frac{2}{3} = .66$$

Interval Recording

Observer A–Behavior lasted .50 minutes (30 seconds)

Observer B–Behavior lasted .75 minutes (45 seconds)

$$r = \frac{.50 \text{ minutes}}{.75 \text{ minutes}} = .66$$

Finally, the formula for calculating observational reliability for interval recording is:

$$r = \frac{\text{Shorter number of minutes}}{\text{Longer number of minutes}}$$

The shorter number of minutes represents the shorter length of time that a behavior lasted as measured by one observer; the longer number of minutes represents a longer period of duration of the same behavior as measured by another observer. Calculation of duration observational reliability is shown in Figure 11-4.

In general, observational reliability should be at least .80 before the reliability of observers is accepted. However, in most cases, a reliability of .90 or higher should be expected and required (Alberto and Troutman 1982; Hawkins 1986).

Interviews and Questionnaires

A mentioned earlier in this chapter, there are two methods of obtaining information about students: direct and indirect assessment. Observational techniques obtain information directly from students (the behavior of students can be directly observed). This section discusses methods of indirect informal assessment.

Four main forms are used to obtain information indirectly: *interviews, questionnaires, rating scales,* and *paper and pencil measures.* These methods are considered indirect because the behavior in question is inferred from what the informant chooses to tell us.

Interviews are methods of direct contact with informants (usually face-to-face conversations); questionnaires and rating scales require the informant to complete a pencil and paper instrument that is analyzed at a later time. Because the information giver is present at the time of the interview, the interviewer can clarify information or ask in-depth questions. However, with questionnaires, rating scales, and pencil and paper measures, no opportunity for follow-up questions exists. Thus, information from these sources is only as good as the instruments themselves.

Interviews, questionnaires, rating scales, and pencil and paper measures use informants to provide information. These informants may be the target student, parents, teachers, or other professionals involved in the child's life. The teacher should remember that the nature of these indirect instruments increases *error of reporting* and *obtrusiveness.*

Error of reporting occurs because the child is not being directly observed. Instead, information is gathered by listening to or reading about what the student says or what others say about the student. A major drawback of interviews, questionnaires, and rating scales is that they are based on *subjective information.* People usually want to depict themselves or those close to them in a certain manner, or their information is tainted by memory lapses or modifications of reality that have occurred over time. The information gatherer must always recognize the subjective nature of information provided by informants and must interpret their information with a grain of salt. A good rule to follow is that information should be verified by at least two independent sources before it is accepted as valid.

Interviews, questionnaires, rating scales, and paper and pencil reasures are also obtrusive. When people know that their behavior is being assessed they may act differently than when they are unaware of observation. Thus, the responses and behavior of people being interviewed or questioned may not be entirely natural. This must also be kept in mind by the information gatherer.

With these limitations in mind, however, interviews, questionnaires, rating scales, and paper and pencil measures can be useful informal assessment tools. They can provide information about situations and environments in which direct observation is difficult or impossible. In such cases, they may be the only sources of information professionals have. Additionally, in many situations, they may involve less time and be more cost efficient than direct observation.

Interviews

The interview is a conversation in which the information gatherer (interviewer) seeks to elicit specific information. Interviews are *purposeful* conversations structured and guided by the interviewer. Successful interviews contain a variety of components and activities (Guerin and Maier 1983) including the introduction, the interview focus, information gathering, queries, elaborations, and summarization. Figure 11-5 contains the major components and subcomponents of the clinical interview.

Figure 11-5   Components of the Interview

I.   *The Introduction*
   A. Estabish rapport
   B. Set interview environment
   C. Put informant at ease
   D. Provide transition to focus stage

II.   *The Interview Focus*
   A. Set the tone of the interview
   B. Set goals and general theme of interview

III.   *Information Gathering, Queries, and Elaborations*
   A. Structured questions
   B. Queries for unacceptable or unclear answers
   C. Requests for further information

IV.   *Summarization*
   A. Paraphrasing the information given
   B. Reaching consensus on information given
   C. Conversation closing

The Introduction: The key process in the introductory phase of the interview is establishing *rapport*. The interviewer's job is to make the person being interviewed feel comfortable. The interviewer must establish a relaxed atmosphere that assures the informant that the interview is not a cross-examination or inquisition but rather a conversation between two intelligent people. During this stage, it is acceptable for the interviewer to chat with the informant or talk in general terms about things that interest the informant. After rapport has been achieved, the interviewer is then responsible for providing a *transition* to focus the conversation on the primary subject.

The Interview Focus: The interview focus sets the tone of the interview. It clarifies for both interviewer and informant the subject of the interview, the goal of the interview, and the information being sought (Guerin and Maier 1983). This focusing stage is very impor-

tant because interviewer and informant sometimes possess quite different perceptions of
the purposes of the interview. For example,
whereas the interviewer may wish to discuss a
child's reading and study habits at home, the
frustrated parent may wish to talk about all of
the child's misbehaviors around the house.
Any differences in purposes, focus, or scope
of the interview need to be discussed before
in-depth information is gathered.

**Information Gathering, Queries, and Elabora-
tions:** This stage is the heart of the interview
process. It involves gathering the information
that is sought by the interviewer. Through the
interviewer's structured questions, the informant provides data the professional needs to
conduct an informal assessment. This information is obtained through the question and answer format.

Sometimes, however, the informant will
not answer a question to the interviewer's satisfaction or will answer it in a way that creates
confusion, ambiguity, or a need for additional
information. At these times, the interviewer
must use the techniques of query and elaboration (see Figure 11-6).

As shown in Figure 11-6, the first step in
the query–elaboration process is to acknowledge the informant's answer and encourage
expansion or elaboration. This can be accomplished by asking a follow-up question on the
same subject or by requesting further clarification. The elaborated response of the informant is then recorded and acknowledged.
If the elaboration has answered the question
sufficiently, the interviewer moves on to the
next area of the interview. If the elaboration
was insufficient, the interviewer decides
whether to pursue the matter further or accept the incomplete information the informant provided.

Summarization: Summarization is the summing up or paraphrasing of the informant's

Figure 11-6   The Query–Elaboration Process
in Interviewing

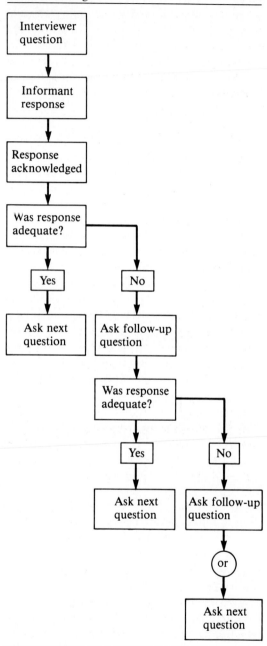

comments into a few sentences. The interviewer and informant then either agree or disagree that this was the essence of the information provided. If agreement is reached, the interview is concluded. However, if consensus between interviewer and informant is not reached, refocus and further elaboration are necessary.

Questionnaires

A questionnaire is an interview in written form. Questionnaires permit an informant to write answers using paper and pencil. This information is later coded and analyzed by the professional.

Types of questionnaires include *checklists* and *rating scales*. Each of these questionnaire types is described below.

Checklists: Checklists are probably the quickest and easiest type of questionnaire for respondents to complete. Checklists offer the informant a number of different descriptions of behaviors; the informant checks off the behavior(s) that are most applicable. A checklist is shown in Figure 11-7.

Checklists allow quick recording and help prevent the observer from overlooking relevant target behaviors. Behaviors can be clustered into major categories and those categories objectively observed and recorded. Checklists aid in controlling errors of observer agreement because observers know precisely the target behavior they are seeking. Additionally, the professional using a checklist can view the totality of a task by checking for all the major component skills that make up that task.

Checklists can be useful assessment tools in observing a variety of behaviors including social skills, academic performance, behavior in need of modification, and psychomotor skills. They are particularly useful in providing a detailed analysis of a pupil's strengths and weaknesses so that remedial activities can be designed to improve learning. Checklists also serve to remind parents and teachers of the goals of the child's program in the area of assessment.

Although checklists are easy to administer and use, they do have problems. One problem is keeping the list of behaviors to be observed at a reasonable, working number. However, when the number of behaviors to be observed is condensed, the scorer may observe a behavior that is not included in the instrument. Another problem is that behaviors can be interpreted idiosyncratically by different scorers. For example, one scorer may interpret *misbehaving* as acting impolitely; another scorer may regard it as being destructive or aggressive. In order to safeguard against ambiguous interpretation of behaviors by raters, checklists should be as precise and explicit as possible.

Rating Scales: Rating scales allow the rater to assign a numerical value to responses instead of simply indicating whether a behavior did or did not occur. With a rating scale, the respondent is given a statement, behavior, or term and then asked to rate it quantitatively in terms of agreement or disagreement, frequency of occurrence, magnitude, or some other variable. Figure 11-8 contains sample questions from a rating scale for assessing childrens' perceived ability to make friends easily.

Four main types of rating scales can be used: *category ratings, numerical ratings, graphic ratings,* and *forced-choice ratings.* Category ratings allow respondents to choose the answer that best answers the question or describes themselves. A multiple-choice question is a form of category rating. Numerical ratings are those in which answers are represented as numbers along a continuum. Respondents choose the number that best describes their answer. Graphic ratings are linear representations along a continuum.

Figure 11-7   A Checklist of Questions for Handwriting

	O.K.	Needs Review
1. Performance observation.		
a. pen or pencil is held properly	☐	☐
b. paper is positioned at a "normal" slant	☐	☐
c. writing posture is acceptable	☐	☐
d. writing speed is acceptable	☐	☐
2. Correct letter formation.		
a. closed letters are closed	☐	☐
b. looped letters are looped	☐	☐
c. stick letters are not loops	☐	☐
d. *i*'s and *j*'s are dotted directly above	☐	☐
e. *x*'s and *t*'s are crossed accurately	☐	☐
f. m's and n's have the correct number of humps	☐	☐
g. all lowercase letters begin on the line (unless they follow *b, o, v,* or *w*)	☐	☐
h. *b, o, v,* and *w* end above the line	☐	☐
i. all lowercase letters end on the line	☐	☐
j. *v*'s and *u*'s are clearly differentiated	☐	☐
k. connecting strokes of *v* and *y* are clearly not *ry* and *ry*	☐	☐
l. uppercase letters are correctly or acceptably formed	☐	☐
m. numbers are correctly formed	☐	☐
3. Fluency.		
a. writing is smooth, not choppy	☐	☐
b. pencil pressure appears even	☐	☐
c. words appear to be written as complete units	☐	☐
d. letter connection is smooth	☐	☐
4. Letter size, slant, and spacing.		
a. lowercase letters are uniform size	☐	☐
b. uppercase letters are clearly larger than lowercase letters	☐	☐
c. uppercase letters are uniform in size	☐	☐
d. tail lengths are consistent and do not interfere with letters on the line below	☐	☐
e. tall letters are a consistent height and are clearly taller than other letters	☐	☐
f. writing is not too small or too large	☐	☐
g. slant of letters is acceptable	☐	☐
h. slant of letters is consistent	☐	☐
i. spacing of letters and words is consistent	☐	☐
5. Student attitude toward writing.		
a. student's opinion of his writing skills	☐	☐
b. "writing is hard"	☐	☐
c. writes too slowly	☐	☐
d. feels good about writing	☐	☐

Source: D. D. Hammill (1986). Correcting handwriting deficiencies. In *Teaching Students with Learning and Behavior Problems,* 4th ed., eds. D. D. Hammill and N. R. Bartel (Boston: Allyn and Bacon). Used by permission.

Figure 11-8   A Self-Rating Scale for Perceived Ease of Making Friends

Instructions: For each statement, circle the box for the answer that is most true for you. There is no right or wrong answer—only the way you feel. Remember to answer each *statement by circling one of the five responses. Make only* one *answer for each statement. Try the first four sample questions on this page first. Wait for instructions to begin.*

1. *It's easy for me to make new friends at school.*

That's always true about me.	That's true about me most of the time.	That's sometimes true about me.	That's hardly ever true about me.	That's not true at all about me.

2. *I'm good at working with other kids.*

That's always true about me.	That's true about me most of the time.	That's sometimes true about me.	That's hardly ever true about me.	That's not true at all about me.

3. *It's hard for me to make friends.*

That's always true about me.	That's true about me most of the time.	That's sometimes true about me.	That's hardly ever true about me.	That's not true at all about me.

4. *It's hard to get other kids to like me.*

That's always true about me.	That's true about me most of the time.	That's sometimes true about me.	That's hardly ever true about me.	That's not true at all about me.

5. *I can find a friend when I need one.*

That's always true about me.	That's true about me most of the time.	That's sometimes true about me.	That's hardly ever true about me.	That's not true at all about me.

The choices along that continuum represent equal intervals. Finally, forced-choice ratings require respondents to select from a set of equally attractive or unpleasant or otherwise similar choices. Figure 11-9 illustrates each type of rating.

In constructing a rating scale, it is important to avoid having too few or too many points on the scale. For example, a yes-no, forced-choice scale is really a checklist since it allows for only two responses. On the other hand, a fifteen-point scale allows a great deal of choice; it also requires extremely fine discriminations by the scorer. In most cases, a five-point scale offers a reasonable compromise. Whenever possible, rating scales should possess an odd number of points. This allows for a scale midpoint. Midpoints can be represented as points indicating neutrality or no opinion or as zero points between positive and negative ratings.

Teacher-Made Tests

Teachers probably administer more teacher-made tests than any other type of informal assessment. Therefore, teachers must ensure that the instruments they administer are well constructed and technically adequate. This can be accomplished by learning the rules of good test item writing.

Considerations in Test Item Construction

There are some general factors or considerations to keep in mind when constructing

Figure 11-9   Examples of the Four Main Types of Rating Scales

Category Ratings

Pick the answer (or answers) that best describes your interactions with strangers.

1. Withdrawn — do not interact.
2. Shy, but will speak when spoken to.
3. Like to participate. Will mingle.
4. An initiator of dialogue. A catalyst for social interaction.

Graphic Ratings

Rate the student on attentiveness in class (4 is high).

```
1          2          3          4
```

Numerical Ratings

How would you rate your child's attitude toward school?

1	2	3	4	5
Hates school	Poor attitude	About average	Very good	Loves school

Forced-Choice Ratings

Check one and only one description of yourself.

1. Shy
2. Withdrawn
3. Happy to mingle
4. An initiator of conversation

---

sound test items (Hopkins and Antes 1978). Adherence to the following considerations will help ensure that teacher-made test items are fair and technically appropriate.

1. A close correspondence should exist between test items and the set of educational objectives being used by the teacher. To accomplish this goal the teacher should make sure that a representative number of test items assesses each instructional objective (see Chapter 9).

2. Base items on important information. Trivial or insignificant material should not be tested.

3. Write items so that correct answers represent knowledge that occurred through specialized learn-

ing of course content. Avoid items that can be answered correctly using general or global knowledge.

4. State items as straightforwardly as possible. Ambiguous or tricky language or complicated grammatical constructions should be avoided. Use simple, precise language and good language expression.

6. Use your own language. Avoid using language taken directly from a textbook or study guide.

7. Avoid clues or suggestions in test items.

8. Recruit colleagues to edit or make suggestions about your test items before you administer them to students.

The three basic types of test item are *selection, supply,* and *problem*.

Selection Test Items

Selection items are those in which the correct answers to questions have been provided. The student's task is to recognize and identify the correct answer. Types of selection items include multiple-choice, true–false, and matching items.

Multiple-Choice: In the multiple-choice format, the student's task is to select the correct answer from a list of alternatives. Multiple-choice items are particularly useful for measuring factual knowledge and information. Multiple-choice items are used perhaps more than any other format on teacher-made tests. For this reason, teachers must construct sound items of this type that contain as little error as possible. A list of suggestions for writing sound multiple-choice items appears in Figure 11-10.

True–False: True–false items are a type of multiple-choice question—one that offers the student only two alternatives to identify the correct answer. Therefore, students have a 50 percent chance of answering a true–false question correctly. This is a major criticism of true–false questions. Other criticisms are that

Figure 11-10 Guidelines for Writing Sound Multiple-Choice Items

1. The stem of the question should convey to the student exactly what information is being sought. The stem cannot be ambiguous or confusing to the student.
2. If possible, the stem of the item should be posed as a question.
3. As much of the wording of the item as possible should be placed in the stem. This avoids the problem of wordy alternatives.
4. Alternatives should agree grammatically with the item stem.
5. There should be enough alternatives to make the item difficult for students who do not know the material. Too many alternatives, however, will confuse or tax the information-processing capabilities of students.
6. Avoid the use of negative wording in the stem and alternatives. When negative wording must be used, it should be underlined.
7. Eliminate all clues and hints from the items.
8. Make all distractors plausible. Distractors should be chosen about equally by unknowledgeable students.
9. Avoid trick questions. Questions should be fair and easy to comprehend.
10. Write items at the students' reading level.
11. The alternative, none of the above, should be used only when there is no one, absolutely correct answer to the question.
12. Vary the placement of correct alternatives in items. Over the course of the test, the correct alternative should appear about equally across all the alternative numbers.

Figure 11-11 Guidelines for Writing Sound True–False Questions

1. Base the item on a central, important idea or concept. Each item should deal with only one concept.
2. Avoid testing trivial content.
3. Avoid specific determiners or clauses. Words like *all, none, always,* and *never* should be avoided.
4. False items should be written so that they sound plausible. Common misconceptions make good true–false items.
5. True–false items should contain positive statements. Avoid using negative terms, but if they must be used, they should be underlined.
6. All true–false items in a test should be about the same length. Many times, true items are longer than false ones because of qualifying phrases. Avoid giving this clue.
7. Include about the same number of both true and false statements.

they test trivial or insignificant information and that they are often ambiguous (Hopkins and Antes 1975).

However, nontrivial true–false items can be developed that adequately measure understanding and comprehension as well as the memorization of information. Items can also be constructed to eliminate much of the error found in many true–false questions. Figure 11-11 contains a set of suggested guidelines for constructing sound true–false items.

Matching: Matching items contain two lists of possible responses and a set of directions instructing students to make a connection between pairs of elements in each set. Each *match* of two responses represents an appropriate connection between the two variables.

Matching items are probably most appropriate for testing basic knowledge concepts. Figure 11-12 contains a set of guidelines for writing sound matching items.

Supply Test Items

Supply items are those in which the correct response must be supplied by the test taker. The three major types of supply items are *completion, short-answer,* and *essay.* Each type differs regarding the extent of the response required and the freedom and latitude the respondent has in making responses.

Completion: Completion items require the least amount of writing by the respondent. However, of the three types of supply items, they allow the least amount of freedom. With completion items, the student is asked to complete (supply) the remainder of an unfinished

Figure 11-12 Guidelines for Writing Sound Matching Test Items

1. The two lists used must be as homogeneous as possible. One list should contain one category of items and the other list should contain a separate category of choices. A given list should not contain a mixture of category items.
2. Keep the lists relatively short. Lists containing more than ten items cause the test taker to search for matching items. This could cause information and memory overload.
3. Include in the list of responses items that do not match any of the premises. Thus, the response list will contain more items than the premise list. If the number of items in the premise and response lists is the same, students will be able to get the last item correct by deduction (if the others have all been answered correctly).
4. Indicate in the instructions whether a response can be used more than once.
5. Present both lists in their entirety on the same page. Students should not have to flip pages back and forth to match responses with premise items.
6. Premise and response items should be single words if possible. If phrases must be used, keep them as short as possible.
7. Labels at the top of the premise and response lists will help in categorizing the lists.

Figure 11-13 Guidelines for Writing Sound Completion Items

1. There should be only one correct answer for each blank. Otherwise, the scorer should be prepared to give students credit for a variety of correct answers.
2. Word the phrases so that all students will possess the same frame of reference. Consider the item:

    Cleveland is on _____ .

    Here, the student could fill in a number of correct answers, including *a lake, Eastern time,* or some other correct response. Instead, use a more precise statement, such as:

    Cleveland is on Lake _____ .

    In this case, the only correct answer is *Erie.*

3. Blanks should be placed at the end or near the end of the statement. This allows for only one reading of the item by the student.
4. Write the item so it contains only one blank or a related series of blanks. Too many blanks cause reading comprehension difficulties.
5. Omit only important words that are related to the field of study.
6. Make all blanks about the same size. Clues about the answer should not be offered by the length of the blank.
7. Make sure that the item is grammatically correct. Make sure that the desired word agrees in sense and number with the rest of the item.
8. Avoid using *a* before a blank. This tells the test taker that the blank word begins with a consonant. Likewise, the word *an* before the blank informs a wise test taker that the answer begins with a vowel.

phrase or sentence. Completion items are most useful in testing basic knowledge skills.

It is important that the incomplete phrase or sentence not be ambiguous. Ambiguous items enable the student to supply a number of appropriate answers. Also, because the item must stand alone without explanatory information, the item must explain its frame of reference and context so it can be answered appropriately by the student. Figure 11-13 contains guidelines for writing well-constructed completion items.

Short-Answer: Short-answer items are a compromise between completion and essay questions. The short-answer item presents the student with a question that can be answered in one sentence or less. The student's task is to answer the question within the framework of a grammatically correct phrase or sentence.

Short-answer questions are useful for testing information at the knowledge and comprehension levels. Because the length of student responses is somewhat limited, it is difficult for short-answer questions to assess learning at higher taxonomic levels. Additionally, the requirement of answering the question with a grammatically correct written product (although a limited written product) can be difficult for certain special needs learners.

The short-answer question must be specific enough so that the student understands what information must be supplied but not so inclusive that the answer is apparent.

The teacher must also be sure that the answer being sought can be given in a single phrase or sentence. Finally, the teacher must make sure that students' responses to short-answer questions reflect their knowledge of subject matter rather than their general difficulties handling the complexities of written expression.

Essay Items: Essay items allow the most freedom and latitude in student responses. Essay items present the student with a narrative question and require an in-depth, written reply. This reply must be in grammatically correct, paragraph form and presented in a logical, sequenced manner. (See Fig. 11-4.)

There is good and bad news about essay questions. The good news is that they allow a great deal of freedom of response and they are probably the best mechanism for measuring higher-order levels of learning. There are, however, negative aspects to essay questions. First, they are highly correlated with writing ability. If a student did not score well on an essay, was it because the student did not know the material in the question or because the student was deficient in the area of written expression? For this reason, essay questions should probably be avoided with students who possess known written expression difficulties.

Another problem with essay tests is that the very freedom of response that makes them attractive can also lead to answers that digress from the questions. Perhaps you have written or scored an essay that differed from the question. Students may do this for two reasons; either they do not adequately understand the question or they do not possess the knowledge to answer the question and decide to change the item to one they can adequately answer. Teachers must be alert to essay responses that differ from the question asked and score these responses accordingly.

A final drawback to essay questions is that they are difficult and time consuming to

Figure 11-14   Guidelines for Writing Sound Essay Items

1. Use essay items for one or more of these student behaviors: explanation, comparison, contrast and comparison, analysis, synthesis, and evaluation. The essay item can also be used to ask students to give opinions and defend those opinions.
2. Essay questions are not appropriate for testing information at the knowledge and comprehension levels.
3. Write the item so that what is expected of students is clear, explicit, and unambiguous. Students should not have to guess what is expected of them.
4. The essay items should be new to students. If they have seen the question before, it will not challenge them to think beyond the rote information they possess.
5. Inform students what the limits of their responses should be. This can be in the form of a word or page count. An estimation of the lower and upper limits of pages students can write is helpful to test takers.
6. Give the relative weights or points that are assigned to sections of the essay. When possible, split the essay into sections so students can answer each section in turn.
7. Items should not require common or world information. Rather, items should assess the specific information that was studied and learned.
8. Instructions in essay questions should use verbs that describe to students what is expected. For example, the words *compare and contrast* or *explain the differences* give students a precise idea of what is expected; phrases like *tell me all you know* or *discuss* are too ambiguous.
9. All students should write on the same items. The practice of allowing students to choose the essays they wish to answer gives no basis for comparisons. Exceptions to this rule are those instances when students have studied different material.

score. Scoring an essay is a subjective task, considerably more subjective than scoring a multiple-choice test. Also, any teacher will tell you that scoring a batch of class essays takes a great deal of time and effort. Fatigue becomes a factor in scoring essays, and the teacher must guard against scoring them quickly so as to be done with the task.

Teachers can use certain procedures to reduce the disadvantages of using essay questions. These guidelines are shown in Figure 11-14. These guidelines will make essay questions easier to use and reduce the error inherent in this type of item.

Problem Test Items

Problem questions are used primarily in mathematics and in technical–scientific areas. Problem questions give students a problem or situation to read and answer. To answer correctly students must apply a given mathematical concept or algorithm. Students then either supply the answer or select it using a multiple-choice format.

Problem items are discussed in greater detail in Chapter 19 on assessing arithmetic ability. Be aware, however, that one disadvantage of this type of test item is that it is highly correlated with reading and reading comprehension ability. For example, if a student did not answer a problem question correctly, was

it due to inappropriate knowledge of the subject matter or to reading–comprehension deficiencies? For this reason, problem items should probably be avoided with students who possess known reading deficiencies.

Using Test Information: Summative versus Formative Evaluation

A test is worthless if the information is not used. As previously noted, teachers can use test results as summative or formative evaluation. Summative evaluation uses test information to give summary grades. It is the traditional use of test information, categorizing children into different scores and deciding who will receive an *A,* a *B,* and so forth. Formative evaluation is an ongoing evaluation in which the student's strengths and weaknesses are repeatedly assessed to provide remediational programming designed to decrease weaknesses.

Formative evaluation is a relatively new process, and it is reflected in the areas of curriculum-based and criterion-referenced assessment. This assessment uses the skills of the student's curriculum as benchmarks against which the student is measured and also seeks to remediate the pupil's deficiencies in areas of the curriculum. Chapter 12 deals with this new and exciting type of assessment.

SUMMARY

The types of assessment are formal and informal. Formal assessment contains specific and standardized procedures for administration, scoring, and interpretation. Informal assessment lacks rigid or standardized procedures. Formal and informal assessment differ along a number of dimensions, including setting, technical quality, activities, statistics, and reporting format.

Generally, the types of informal assess-

ment can be placed in a 2 × 2 factorial design with directness on one axis and obtrusiveness on the other. Directness refers to the degree (firsthand, secondhand) with which the teacher gains a view of the child's behavior. Obtrusiveness refers to the degree that the assessment enters or intrudes into the learning environment. The main types of informal assessment that fall into this 2 × 2 factorial design are observation, checklists, rating scales, questionnaires, interviews, and teacher-made tests.

One useful type of informal assessment is systematic observation. Systematic observation entails the planned, nonrandom observation of behavior and uses specialized techniques of specifying, counting, and recording behavior. Types of systematic observation include continual observation and systematic analysis, which is used to obtain an entire slice of a child's observation.

After continuous observation or sequential analysis has taken place, the behavior to be observed is specified in behavioral, observable terms. Following this, an observational recording system is selected. Recording systems can be event or interval types. Event recording systems include rate, frequency, topography, force, and locus systems. Interval recording systems include rate, duration, and latency systems.

Behaviors are either discrete or continuous. Discrete behaviors have a measurable onset and offset. Continuous behaviors are those in which behavioral onset and termination points are difficult to measure. In recording continuous behaviors time sampling recording systems are useful.

In systematically collecting observation data, the following questions must be answered appropriately. When will the observation take place? How many observations will take place? Who will be the observers? How will data be recorded? How will rater reliability be assessed? If all of these questions are not answered appropriately, the observation data collected will be invalid.

Questionnaires and interviews are useful informal assessment tools. Whereas interviews allow face-to-face contact with respondents, questionnaires usually involve paper and pencil responses to questions. Both interviews and questionnaires use a format that is indirect and obtrusive, and thus they possess certain disadvantages. Interviews contain a number of components, including the introduction, the interview focus, information gathering, the query and elaboration stage, and the summarization stage.

Rating scales allow the informant to give numerical values to their responses. Informants are given statements and asked to indicate numerically the degree of their agreement or disagreement. Four main types of rating scales are category ratings, numerical ratings, graphic ratings, and forced-choice ratings. Rating scales are most useful when they supply specific information given to the respondent.

Teachers probably administer more informal pencil and paper tests than any other type of informal assessment. Teachers can use a variety of different items on their tests. These items include selection, supply, and problem items. Selection items simply require the student to recognize or identify the correct answer from a set of alternatives. Selection items include multiple-choice, true–false, and matching questions.

Supply items require the student to supply the correct answer instead of simply choosing it from a set of alternatives. Supply items differ in the degree of freedom or latitude allowed in student responses. Types of supply items include completion, short-answer, and essay items. Although these supply items offer advantages, they also have the disadvantage of being correlated with written expression ability. In particular, essay questions should probably be avoided with students who possess known written expression difficulties.

Problem items usually assess mathematical or technical knowledge. They are written in prose form. The student's task is to apply a mathematical or technical concept to answer the question correctly. Problem items are highly correlated with reading and comprehension ability and thus should probably be avoided with students possessing difficulties in these areas.

The two applications of test information are summative and formative evaluation. Summative evaluation uses test information to assign grades or summary labels to students. Formative evaluation is the ongoing use of test information to provide feedback on student weaknesses for the purposes of remediation. Formative evaluation is tied to the notion of curriculum-based and criterion-referenced assessment (discussed in Chapter 12).

STUDY QUESTIONS

1. Define formal and informal assessment. How do they differ?

2. What are the advantages and disadvantages of formal and informal assessment? With what conditions or situations should a given form of assessment be used?

3. Define directness and obtrusiveness. What types of informal assessment are obtrusive? Unobtrusive? What forms are direct? Indirect?

4. What is systematic observation? Define continuous and sequential observation. When should each be used?

5. What are the key procedures in systematic observation? Why are they important?

6. What are interviews? What are their advantages and disadvantages? Under what conditions are interviews helpful?

7. What are the components of a good interview? Define each component.

8. What are checklists? When are they useful? What are the advantages and disadvantages of using checklists?

9. What are rating scales? What are the different types of rating scales? What are the components in composing a valid rating scale?

10. When are teacher-made pencil and paper tests appropriate? What are their advantages and disadvantages compared to formal pencil and paper tests?

11. Name and define the different categories of test items. What are the major question types within each category? What kinds of information can each question type assess?

12. What is the difference between summative and formative evaluation? What are the major uses of each evaluation? What types of information does each evaluation yield?

CHAPTER 12

Curriculum-Based and Criterion-Referenced Assessment

Mr. and Mrs. Washington recently attended a school conference regarding their eight-year-old son, William. They had not been pleased with the quality of the work papers he was bringing home. Words were misspelled, letters sometimes reversed, handwriting was frequently sloppy or even illegible, and math papers were incorrect. They wanted to learn what was happening regarding their son's education.

Mrs. Greenberg, William's teacher, tried to alleviate the parents' fears. She reported that William was performing about average compared with the other children in the class. She admitted that some children could spell better than William but others could not. In his other language arts work and mathematics, William was also performing at about the middle of the class.

Mrs. Washington left the conference much relieved. William was like the other boys in the class. He was performing at about average

175

with his classmates, and this satisfied her. Mr. Washington, on the other hand, left the conference with more questions than when he entered. The teacher had not told them what William was expected to learn during this school year and whether or not he was successfully learning that material. What good was it, he thought, to know how William was doing compared to the other children in the class? William needed to acquire a set of skills to be successful in school. Was he learning those skills?

The different reactions of Mr. and Mrs. Washington to the teacher's report on William's performance were based on the way each parent made comparisons. Mrs. Washington and Mrs. Greenberg compared William's work against the work of other children in the class. Compared to these students. William was performing about average or near the fiftieth percentile. Mrs. Washington was satisfied with the knowledge that her son was performing similarly to other children in his class.

Mr. Washington, however, made his comparisons against another benchmark. He rejected the notion that William was doing well in school because he was performing about the same as his classmates. Rather, Mr. Washington was aware that a set of knowledge and skills existed that William needed to acquire to continue achieving in school. He wanted to know how his son was progressing in mastering this content.

Both parents were making comparisons. As we have seen, a child's performance must be compared against something to be meaningful. The difference in this case was how the comparisons were being made.

Norm-Referenced versus Criterion-Referenced Assessment

Norm-Referenced Tests

The traditional method of assessment in the schools has involved comparisons *between* students. Within this format, student performances are compared against one another, and a score is assigned to each pupil depending on the pupil's place in the distribution of people assessed.

This type of assessment is usually translated into grades (Bigge 1988; Howell and Morehead 1986). Students are assigned a grade based on their place in the distribution of test scores. An extreme example of this type of assessment is the student who achieves the highest test score in the class and receives a grade of *A,* even if the test score is relatively low. The grade of *A* is assigned simply because the pupil scored highest on the test compared to classmates.

This type of interperson comparison is implicit in norm-referenced testing. It yields information as to how a given student is performing compared against peers. Norm-referenced testing is *summative* rather than *formative* evaluation, and it is *global* rather than *diagnostic* in scope (Hatfield 1975; Schloss and Sedlak 1986). Summative testing yields a summary or final score about a student that is usually expressed as a grade. It is global because norm-referenced tests usually do not offer diagnostic information about student strengths and weaknesses; rather, they tell in very general terms what the child has achieved relative to peers.

Criterion-Referenced Assessment

Recall that Mr. Washington was not particularly interested in how William was performing in relation to classmates (norm-referenced assessment). Rather, Mr. Washington wanted to know the extent to which William was acquiring skills needed for success in school and necessary for him to move on to more complex academic material. Mr. Washington was requesting criterion-referenced assessment information from the teacher.

Criterion-referenced assessment is intraperson evaluation (Bigge, 1988; Howell and Morehead 1986). It is a detailed description of what the student can and cannot do, not a behavior description related to the performance of others. Criterion-referenced tests describe specific behaviors; they do not summarize behavior and compare it to the performance of peers.

Criterion-referenced tests are both formative and diagnostic. Formative tests give ongoing information on the progress that students are making in learning instructional material. Criterion-referenced scores are diagnostic because they offer detailed information about the child's strengths and weaknesses and provide information about instructional areas in need of remediation.

Attributes of Criterion-Referenced Assessment: The four main attributes to criterion-referenced tests are *curriculum-based* and *behaviorally defined.* They measure *well-defined behavioral domains* and *minimum levels of proficiency* (Alkin 1984; Nitko 1984). Because criterion-referenced tests are curriculum-based, the items contained in these instruments assess key content contained in the child's educational curriculum (Fuchs and Fuchs 1986; Howell 1986). This entails more than just identifying subject matter and subdividing content into a few major subtopics. Rather, curriculum-based assessment requires the analysis of curriculum tasks into small, discrete units of knowledge or performance that are described in precise and specific terms.

Criterion-referenced assessment is behaviorally defined. This means that each skill or task identified in such a test is keyed to a specific instructional objective. Missing a test item indicates that the student has failed a specific instructional objective in the task acquisition chain, and that objective must be remediated. Previous chapters have shown that effective instructional objectives must contain three central elements. First, they must state precisely under what conditions the behavior is to occur. Second, they must define behaviorally what is to occur. This is

accomplished using unambiguous behavioral verbs, not the ambiguous, "fuzzy" verbs sometimes used in defining what students should be learning. Finally, instructional objectives must state the passing criteria of performance for the behavior to be learned.

Soundly constructed criterion-referenced tests possess well-defined behavioral domains. They sample a set of skills or behaviors that the student might be expected to perform as part of the everyday school curriculum. For example, if a child is learning (or has learned) two-digit addition with carrying as part of the school curriculum, then that set of skills should be assessed by any criterion-referenced mathematics test administered to that student. The behavior domain assessed by a criterion-referenced instrument can be as fine and narrow as the teacher desires, but it should not be broadly defined. To illustrate, consider the process of addition. Broad testing of addition skills would give the student a number of different addition problems to solve. This is too broad an approach for a criterion-referenced test and actually approximates a global assessment measure. However, the addition process can be broken down as finely and precisely as the teacher wishes, and each subcomponent of addition assessed by the criterion-referenced instrument. The only qualification for this process is that the assessed areas be those the student is currently experiencing (or has experienced) in the school curriculum.

Finally, criterion-referenced tests describe a minimum level of proficiency. The professional constructing the test needs to define the minimum levels of performance at which it is assumed that the student has mastered the material in the test. Reaching this level of performance indicates that the student is ready to move on to new, related, and more complex material. (This is unlike summative evaluation, in which students receive various scores but still move on to the next set of curriculum materials.) With criterion-referenced tests, minimum performance standards imply that a level of proficiency is required to succeed on the next unit of instruction. This proficiency level must be attained by the student before new material is introduced. For this reason, a minimum level of performance is sometimes called *mastery criterion*.

The Concept of Curriculum

Criterion-referenced tests assess objectives of a child's school program, and the program objectives must be behaviorally defined, with minimum performance levels specified for passing. But where do these instructional objectives come from and how are they formed? To answer these questions, we must define and discuss the concept of *curriculum*.

A curriculum is a *structured* and *sequenced* set of learning tasks or outcomes (Hargis 1987; Howell and Morehead 1986). A curriculum is structured because it is formally defined or outlined. That is, any interested party can inspect a student's curriculum for a given time period (usually a year) and recognize the content the student will receive. A curriculum is sequenced because it is task-analyzed and organized into a set of sequential instructional objectives.

For special needs learners, curricula must be *individualized*. Each special needs student receives a different set of educational experiences depending on needs, learning style, and current levels of operation (Hargis 1987; Schloss and Sedlak 1986). In fact, the Individualized Education Plan (IEP) represents an individualized curriculum for each special needs learner.

A Developmental versus a Functional Curriculum

A curriculum can be *developmental* or *functional* (Schloss and Sedlak 1986). A developmental curriculum is sequenced by the student's chronological age or developmental level. A developmental curriculum takes into consideration what skills a student needs to acquire at a given age or developmental period of life. That material is then taught during the appropriate chronological or developmental time. For example, teaching a person to ride a bicycle or drive an automobile would probably occur during a distinct chronological or developmental period. It would be foolish to teach a ten-year-old to drive an automobile; licenses are issued to teenagers. On the other hand, a sixteen-year-old would probably be more interested in obtaining a driver's license than in learning to ride a bicycle. Thus, these two sets of skills would be taught in some type of developmentally determined curriculum.

A functional curriculum is used when a set of crucial skills or behaviors must be obtained by the individual. Functional curriculum skills are not tied to a developmental sequence. At times, such skills should already have been learned and the opportunity to obtain them is declining. This situation often arises with older students in secondary school programs or with moderate to severe special needs learners. In the first instance, there is limited instructional time left before leaving school to learn the necessary skills needed for life success. These skills need to be acquired before the student graduates and the opportunity for school learning terminates. In the case of moderately to severely handicapped students, there is a set of functional skills that must be acquired for independent, normalized adult living. Because such students are usually delayed in their learning, they probably did not acquire these skills during the appropriate developmental period, and they must be taught at the present time.

The transdisciplinary educational team must decide whether to institute a developmental or functional curriculum. Although a developmental curriculum possesses the advantage of allowing students to learn the same types of material as age-related peers, it is nevertheless true that many special needs learners are developmentally delayed compared to their peers. In such cases, there may be a set of functional behaviors or skills that the team believes is crucial for life success and that students must acquire before leaving school. These cases warrant a functional curriculum. Figure 12-1 contains a checklist teachers can use when choosing a developmental or functional curriculum (Schloss and Sedlak 1986).

Components of a Curriculum

People often use the term *curriculum* in a generic sense, for example, a social studies curriculum in elementary school or a chemistry curriculum in high school. This use of the term in this manner is inexact and means different things to different people. To create a curriculum that determines the content as-

Figure 12-1 Choosing a Functional or Developmental Curriculum

A functional curriculum should be adopted if:

The learner has significant difficulty learning new skills.
The student has not kept pace with his or her peers in the total number of skills acquired.
The student is actually engaged in instructional activities for a very small portion of the day.
The student is approaching graduation.

A developmental curriculum should be adopted if:

The student acquires new skills fairly efficiently.
The student has kept pace or is only slightly behind the level of his or her peers.
The student spends a substantial part of the school day engaged in instruction.
The student will receive a number of years of instruction before graduation.

Source: P. J. Schloss and R. A. Sedlak (1986). *Instructional Methods for Students with Learning and Behavior Problems* (Boston: Allyn and Bacon). Used by permission.

sessed in criterion-referenced tests, we need to define precisely the components that make up that curriculum.

Currently, the components of a curriculum are viewed in two ways, the traditional view and a more recent outlook (Luftig 1987). In the traditional viewpoint, curriculum includes the sum total of everything offered in the student's school program. That is, curriculum is considered to be the overall set of experiences given a child, encompassing everything that goes on in the classroom. Under this definition, objectives, materials, and instructional methods all are components of the curriculum.

The more modern viewpoint regards curriculum as *what* is taught; instructional methods encompass *how* the curriculum is to be implemented (Luftig 1987). Within this framework, curriculum contains the tasks or content to be learned by students, as well as the strategies or algorithms that they use in applying that content.

Tasks: Tasks represent the content to be learned. These tasks, as we have seen, are described as a set of instructional objectives that define in precise, behavioral form (1) the conditions under which performance is to take place, (2) the exact behavior to be demonstrated, and (3) the levels of acceptable performance.

Tasks are usually divided into subtasks. Subtasks represent the manner in which the overall task is broken down into smaller component behaviors. Subtasks can be even further broken down into single responses, and these responses learned and substantially rechained to learn and perform the overall task or behavior. Known as task analysis, this process is discussed later in this chapter.

Strategies: Strategies are the rules, procedures, or algorithms that must be followed to succeed on a task (Howell and Morehead

1986; Luftig 1987). Put another way, strategies are the specific and sequential ways that information is used to achieve the overall objective.

The appropriateness of strategies is task-specific. Strategies themselves are neither good nor bad. Rather, they are appropriate or inappropriate for solving a specific problem. For example, a child may possess a given strategy for subtraction (see Figure 12-2). While this strategy is appropriate for solving the first problem presented in Figure 12-2, it is inappropriate for solving the second problem. The fact that this strategy was appropriate for only the first problem illustrates two points. Students must learn a set of different strategies and also learn to apply the correct strategy in the appropriate situation to reach a given objective.

The appropriate use of strategies involves two processes, *generalization* and *discrimination*. Generalization is a person's ability to transfer or apply strategies appropriate for one situation to another, similar situation. For example, a person who can drive a Ford with an automatic transmission can probably drive a Chevrolet with an automatic transmission. The person generalizes knowledge

Figure 12-2   Strategies for Solving a Subtraction Problem

Strategy—Subtract the smaller number (in units) from the larger number (in units).

Appropriate strategy use

$$
\begin{array}{r}
19 \\
-5 \\
\hline
14
\end{array}
= \begin{array}{l}
9 - 5 = 4 \\
1 - 0 = 1 \\
19 - 5 = 14
\end{array}
$$

Inappropriate strategy use

$$
\begin{array}{r}
22 \\
-6 \\
\hline
24
\end{array}
= \begin{array}{l}
6 - 2 = 4 \\
2 - 0 = 2 \\
22 - 6 = 24
\end{array}
$$

about driving one automobile with automatic transmission (the Ford) to another automobile (the Chevrolet). To accomplish this successfully, however, the person needs to recognize that the two situations are similar and that the strategies for successfully driving the Ford apply to driving the Chevrolet.

Discrimination is the opposite of generalization. In discrimination learning, the person must realize that two situations are dissimilar and call for different strategies. Using the automobile example again, discrimination occurs when the person realizes that driving an automobile with a standard transmission calls for a different set of responses than driving a car with an automatic transmission. Using the same set of responses to drive both types of cars would be disastrous. Overgeneralization of the same strategy in dissimilar situations is known as *perseveration*.

The Need for Content and Strategies in a Curriculum: Both content, defined as tasks and objectives, and strategies are necessary components of a curriculum. Tasks and objectives are virtually useless if a person does not possess strategies and plans on how to use them. In fact, a major weakness in the learning of special needs learners is an inability to be strategic in applying what they have learned (Flavell and Wellman 1977; Luftig 1987). Likewise, one cannot appropriately use strategies without possessing a knowledge base of information to be applied. For example, a student who knows how to subtract and can apply this strategy at the appropriate times would still get subtraction problems wrong if he or she did not know the subtraction facts (content). Hence both content and strategies are requisite components of any school curriculum.

Curriculum-Based Assessment

As noted, a student's curriculum is based on what the individual is expected to learn (content, tasks, and objectives) and on the strategies, plans, and algorithms the pupil is expected to possess in applying learned skills and knowledge. The curriculum can also become the basis for evaluation and assessment. That is, the tasks and objectives of the curriculum become the basis for what is assessed by criterion-referenced instruments. This process is known as *curriculum-based assessment.*

Curriculum-based assessment holds that a student's needs are best met by assessing performance in the context of the child's individual educational program (Gickling and Thompson 1985; Hargis 1987; Tucker 1985). Curriculum-based assessment helps decrease the distance between curriculum (what is taught) and instruction (how content is taught) by making student assessment more dependent on the child's mastering the curriculum than on comparing the pupil to a norm group of peers (Deno 1985; Howell and Morehead 1986). To achieve these goals, the child's classroom curriculum must be precisely defined in terms of overall tasks, component subtasks, and specific instructional objectives (Hargis 1987; Tucker 1985). This implies that curriculum-based assessment depends largely on successfully carrying out the procedure of task analysis. This is our topic of discussion.

Task Analysis and Curriculum-Based Assessment

Task analysis is the process of isolating, sequencing, and describing the key components of a set of behaviors needed to demonstrate the acquisition of a skill or knowledge (Howell and Morehead 1986; Mank and Horner 1988). When all the components of a task have been mastered, the student should be able to perform the target behavior appropriately. Task components are often referred to as *subtasks.* When the essential or key subtasks are learned and chained together, the

entire task has been acquired. Figure 12-3 contains a task analysis for identifying and writing the United States state capitals.

In considering task analysis, two key phrases need to be emphasized: *essential subtasks* and *rechaining.* In creating a task analysis, it is imperative to separate essential from nonessential subtasks. For example, consider the subtasks contained in riding a city bus. Some subtasks are essential (recognizing the name or the number of the bus, giving the driver the correct change, knowing at which stop to get off), but there are also some nonessential subtasks (opening the bus window or reading the advertising on buses). The teacher must separate essential from nonessential subtasks and teach only essential task components.

The second key to successful task analysis is rechaining. Subtasks can be taught in isolation, but eventually they need to be rechained together for the entire task to be completed successfully. For example, it is not enough to be able to recognize the name or number of the bus, give the driver correct change, and exit the bus correctly in isolation. The student must successfully carry out all of these behaviors in the proper sequence to ride a city bus. Rechaining is essential.

Types of Task Analysis

The three main types of task analysis are *temporal, difficulty level,* and *developmental* analysis. Each type is described here briefly.

Temporal Analysis. Temporal analysis is probably the most popular form of task analysis. In this form, the step-by-step sequence of the task is taught in the order that the task is performed in real life. Using a typical temporal analysis, the teacher instructs the student to first do this, then do this, and so forth until the entire task is completed. Examples of temporal tasks include hand washing, certain motor skills, and dressing.

Figure 12-3   Task Analysis for Identifying and Writing the State Capitals

Task: identify in writing the capital city for each of the 50 states

Terminal Objective: Given a ditto with the 50 states listed in alphabetical order, the learner will correctly write the name of the corresponding capital city next to each state. Task will be completed in 30 minutes without reference aids and with 100% accuracy. A response will be considered correct if it is easily distinguishable as the name of the capital city of the state it is written next to.

Subtask 1: able to name (i.e., say) a capital city for each state

Objective 1: Given the name of the state, the learner will say the correct name of the capital city for that state within 5 minutes and with 100% accuracy for all 50 states.

Subtask 2: able to spell the names of the 50 capital cities

Objective 2: Given the names of each of the 50 capital cities verbally, the learner will correctly spell each within 15 seconds. To be correct, each response when written by the examinee should be distinguishable by a third party as the name of the city it represents.

Subtask 3: able to read the names of the 50 states

Objective 3: Given the name of each of the 50 states on a flashcard, the learner will correctly pronounce each within 5 seconds and with 100% accuracy.

Subtask 4: able to write the names of the 50 capital cities in the correct places

Objective 4: Given the task described in the terminal objective (see p. 81) and told the correct answer for each item, the learner will write the answer in the correct place for each of the 50 items, taking no more than 15 seconds per item.

Subtask 5: able to write the names of the 50 capital cities

Objective 5: Given the name of each of the 50 capital cities on a card, the learner will accurately copy each onto a piece of paper, taking no more than 15 seconds per card and with 100% accuracy. Responses will be considered accurate if they are legible enough to be accurately decoded by a third party.

Source: K. Howell, J. Kaplan, and C. O'Connell (1979). *Evaluating Exceptional Children* (Columbus, OH: Charles E. Merrill). Used by permission.

Difficulty Level Analysis: In difficulty level analysis, the subcomponents of a task are analyzed and rank ordered in terms of their difficulty. Easier components are then taught before the more difficult components. In this way, children can build confidence in their ability to learn the task while the learning of more difficult components is postponed until later. Examples of difficulty level analysis include learning to read and spell simple words before more difficult words are attempted.

Developmental Analysis: In developmental analysis, skills are built on each other so that each skill learned is directly related to the preceding one learned. In some ways, developmental analysis is similar to difficulty level analysis in that easier skills are learned before harder ones. However, in developmental analysis not only is the relative ease or difficulty of components assessed but also the relatedness between subtasks. An example of developmental task analysis is learning addition before multiple addition (multiplication) and the inverse operation (subtraction) are learned.

Guidelines for Creating a Task Analysis

A teacher can take a number of steps to ensure a successful task analysis (Guerin and Maier 1983; Howell and Morehead 1986). These steps include the following:

1. Precisely and behaviorally identify the specific task to be learned.

2. Identify the acceptable level of performance for learning the task.
3. Precisely and behaviorally identify the subcomponents or subtasks for the task.
4. Separate essential from nonessential subcomponents in learning the task.
5. Determine the skill level needed for each subcomponent.
6. Determine appropriate alternate, compensatory, or adaptive methods for learning each subcomponent.
7. Assess current student expertise for each subcomponent.
8. Identify whether temporal, difficulty level, or developmental task analysis will be used.
9. Begin instruction for subcomponents where students do not hold requisite skill.

Step 6, identifying alternative or compensatory methods for learning each component, needs explanation. There is more than one way to learn a given subcomponent. For example, one only has to observe children (and adults) tying their shoelaces to realize that people use a myriad of different techniques and steps in tying laces. Components of tasks can be learned in various ways, with no one way being right. Prior to task analysis, the teacher should be aware of alternative methods for learning component skills in case the primary method of learning is blocked for the child. If a teacher possesses alternate methods for acquiring competence in requisite components, the probability increases that the entire task will be appropriately learned.

Carrying Out a Task Analysis

In carrying out a successful task analysis, three distinct stages should be considered: *creating objectives, assessing prerequisite skills,* and *designing scope and sequence.* Creating objectives involves stating in precise, behavioral form each subcomponent of each subtask. Each objective must contain one and only one behavior. If a component skill con-

tains two or more behaviors, the skill should be broken down into a set of specific, one-behavior objectives and then rechained to form the total component task. The more finely and precisely each subskill is defined and broken down, the better it is for programming and learning.

Prerequisite skills are the minimum set of behaviors a student needs in order to learn component skills and, ultimately, the overall task. These skills should be defined in such a way that possessing them greatly increases the probability that the task will be learned by the student; not possessing these prerequisite skills virtually ensures task failure. Students lacking prerequisite skills should be given instruction in acquiring those behaviors before formal instruction in the larger task is undertaken.

Scope and sequence refer to the sequence of subtasks presented to the student once formal instruction in the task has begun. Scope and sequence are based on one of the three types of task analysis—temporal, difficulty level, or developmental. Task analysis requires that no higher or complex step in the scope and sequence be presented until the student has mastered each lower-level skill.

Types of Curriculum-Based Assessment

Four types of curriculum-based assessment are discussed in this chapter: *inventories, work samples* with resultant *error analysis, criterion-referenced tests,* and *diagnostic probes.* These types of assessment are hierarchical, each yields a more detailed level of information than the one preceding it. Each succeeding level involves a greater expense of time to complete as well as a higher level of administrator expertise. However, each leads to greater detail and specificity of diagnostic information.

Inventories

Inventories are screening instruments that assess the child's general skill level on a set of curriculum tasks. As such, inventories usually do not measure whether the child has obtained mastery. Rather, they yield relatively general information about where a child might be experiencing difficulty and where more in-depth assessment is needed.

Keep in mind that inventories usually do not specify whether a child passes or fails a given curriculum task, nor do they assign a level of functioning to the child's performance. Such in-depth assessment is usually accomplished using error analysis, criterion-referenced tests, or diagnostic probes.

Work Samples and Error Analysis

A work sample represents a permanent product of student behavior or performance that can be reviewed and analyzed. A primary example is a student's work sheet in an academic area such as arithmetic. Work samples can also be collected by audio taping students' oral reading or by analyzing job performance skills.

Work samples are quite useful because they can be subjected to the procedure of error analysis. Error analysis is the detailed inspection of a student's incorrect responses on a work sample to ascertain if a pattern of errors exists that is contributing to the wrong answers (Howell and Morehead 1986; Siegler 1983). Three central assumptions underlie error analysis. The first assumption is that errors are not merely the opposite of correct answers. Second, it is assumed that errors do not occur at random or by accident but are due to a set of identifiable reasons. The final assumption is that errors occur in recognizable and correctable patterns (Howell and Kaplan 1980; Howell and Morehead 1986).

Before error analysis developed, students' incorrect responses were merely scored as wrong, subtracted from the total test score, and ignored. Today, there is a growing realization that errors are not just the opposite of correct responses and that attention should be given to the pattern of those errors and the diagnostically useful information they can yield.

Many different types of errors can be made on the same problem. For example, in the arithmetic problem 19 + 7, the correct answer is 26. However, a number of incorrect answers are possible depending on what the child does (see Figure 12-4). The child could add 7 several times instead of once (multiplication, in the first example), complete the inverse operation (subtraction, shown next), or perform the carrying operation incorrectly (final example). All of these incorrect answers differ from one another and from the correct answer. The type of error the child makes yields insight into remediation of arithmetic weaknesses.

Errors do not occur at random or by accident. A student's answers to an arithmetic

Figure 12-4 Types of Errors That Might Be Made on an Addition Problem

7 Added Seven Times	Inverse Operation—Subtraction	Inappropriate Carrying
19 +7 26 +7 33 +7 40 +7 47 +7 54 +7 61 +7 68	19 +7 12	19 +7 116

problem (or any other subject matter response) occur due to the child's belief and knowledge about the subject matter. For example, if the child answered 6 when asked to add 5 + 3, this answer did not come about by chance. Rather, the answer was based on the child's mathematical calculations, memory, and strategies. Something caused the child to answer 6, and it is the teacher's job in error analysis to identify the causal agent.

Most errors occur in recognizable and correctable form, not randomly. Each time the child uses the erroneous concepts that caused the answer 6 to the problem of 5 + 3, the same response will occur. In error analysis the teacher must identify the pattern of children's mistakes and remediate the basic conceptual framework that is causing those mistakes to occur continually (Engelhardt 1977; Howell and Kaplan 1980).

Conducting an Error Analysis

Error analysis entails a number of different processes, including the following (Ashlock 1982; Howell and Morehead 1986):

1. Create an academic environment in which children feel comfortable and nonthreatened and in which errors might occur naturally.
2. Recognize errors when they occur.
3. Thoroughly analyze children's errors.
4. Look for patterns of responses.

Create a Comfortable Environment: One of the most important things a teacher can do is create a nonthreatening educational environment in which children are not afraid to make errors. After all, to have error analysis, you must have errors to analyze. Thus, the teacher must be accepting and noncritical of students so that students will respond freely (Ashlock 1982; Siegler 1983). Additionally, the teacher should *not* instruct during this phase of assessment but should let students respond without giving feedback or reinforcement for answers. Such feedback will occur in

the prescriptive teaching phase, not during the collection of student errors for analysis. During this phase, the teacher must obtain an adequate sample of the student's written work. If errors are going to occur, they should occur during this phase.

Recognize Errors When They Occur: During the error analysis phase, the teacher must provide students with opportunities to make errors. To accomplish this, the teacher administers numerous student work samples and gives students work that is challenging and beyond their mastery level. This is the time to give students numerous work pages so that written work samples can be collected and errors analyzed. Although mundane drill and dittos are not encouraged, it is true that the teacher needs to collect as many work samples as possible to conduct an appropriate error analysis.

Students also need to be given challenging material that has not been been mastered while work samples are being collected. Mastered material is unlikely to contain errors that can be analyzed. The material given to students should be difficult without being frustrating. Such material will be challenging enough to elicit errors that can be analyzed.

Finally, during error collection the teacher must be thorough and systematic. It is easier to recognize patterns of errors when a large number of student responses have been collected. It is important to give students a large number of items to complete that represent the curriculum content. Additionally, anecdotal notes about how students respond during work paper completion can be useful to the teacher performing error analysis. Again, the more information the teacher possesses in terms of quantity and quality of student work samples, the easier it will be to recognize patterns of errors.

Error Types: To analyze patterns of errors, the teacher should be aware of the types of errors that are possible and common in each subject area. Lists and examples of errors are available in a variety of core academic areas including: arithmetic (Howell, Zucker, and Morehead 1985; Reisman 1978); spelling (Greenbaum 1987; Partoll 1976); handwriting (Guerin and Maier 1983); and reading (Ekwall 1976; Johnson and Baumann 1984; Wallace and Larsen 1978). These lists help the teacher group children's academic responses into error patterns. An example of an error pattern list for oral reading is shown in Figure 12-5.

In summary, a teacher can conduct a valid error analysis in helping to diagnose student learning difficulties if four standard procedures are followed (Howell and Morehead 1986; Swezey 1981). These four procedures are:

1. Collect an adequate sample of behavior. This includes collecting data on a large number of problems of the same type. Also keep an anecdotal record of student responses.
2. Encourage student responses. Create an environment conducive to responding. However, do nothing to influence the responses that students make.

Figure 12-5   An Error Pattern List for Oral Reading

Type of Error	Rule for Marking	Examples
1. Omissions	Encircle the omissions.	She did (not) like the cake.
2. Substitutions and mispronunciations	Write in the substituted or mispronounced word.	Everyone ~~went~~ [go] to the movies on ~~Sunday~~ night. [Saturday]
3. Insertions	Write in the insertions.	Please ^[go] help me ^[with] carry the table.
4. Repetitions	Draw a wavy line beneath the repeated word(s).	He came to the back door.
5. Words aided or unknown	Underline the word(s).	The new car was brown and white.
6. Inverted word order	Draw an elongated line between the inverted words.	Sam was not very nice.
7. Words self-corrected	Make a check above the word.	The forest (was) close to the house.

Example of a Coded Passage

Kruger Park is a (wild) animal ~~preserve~~ [present]. The fence (around) the park will (keep) the animals [fender] in and (unlicensed) ^hunters out. The fence is one of the (steps) being taken to protect ~~wild~~ [wet] life in (African) countries. [bad] [fender]

Source: G. Wallace and S. Larsen (1979). *Educational Assessment of Learning Problems* (Boston: Allyn and Bacon). Used by permission.

3. Be thorough and systematic in collecting responses.
4. Seek patterns of responses by students.

Criterion-Referenced Tests

Criterion-referenced tests compare a person's test performance to a curriculum standard rather than to the performance of a norm group. These standards are obtained from the objectives of the curriculum, and answering criterion-referenced test items correctly implies mastery of given subtasks. Criterion-referenced tests help the teacher determine whether the student has acquired a set of skills, knowledge, or behavior.

Criterion-referenced tests are usually more detailed than either informal inventories or task analysis. Whereas inventories often are of a screening nature and error analysis may yield information as to the pattern of error contained in limited work samples, criterion-referenced tests offer detailed information about the precise curriculum subareas in which a child is experiencing difficulties. Rather than yielding a score or grade, items and objectives on criterion-referenced tests are usually scored as pass–fail, a passing designation indicating mastery of content.

Advantages and Disadvantages of Criterion-Referenced Tests

Although there has been a strong movement (sometimes approaching a stampede) toward criterion-referenced tests in recent years, the informed test consumer should realize that these tests, like almost everything else in assessment, possess both advantages and disadvantages. One advantage is that a criterion-referenced test represents *dynamic* rather than *static* assessment (Howell, Kaplan, and O'Connell 1979). Unlike norm-referenced tests, which are given at a certain time and against a definite norm group (static), criterion-referenced tests can be given many times over different chronological periods. This process demonstrates the educational growth and movement of the student.

Criterion-referenced tests also allow meaningful comparisons between the student and the curriculum rather than between students. They represent intraperson rather than interperson comparisons. In most cases, comparisons between persons offer minimal information as to how to help each child who took the test. Well-constructed, criterion-referenced tests yield directly applicable information as to the areas of academic weakness each child possesses. This information can lead to diagnostic instructional strategies designed to remediate those weaknesses.

However, criterion-referenced tests have certain disadvantages. First, some criterion-referenced tests possess inadequately described reliability and validity. This does not mean that the reliability and validity of criterion-referenced tests are low. Often, this technical information is simply inadequately described by the test author. Nevertheless, the informed test user should not assume that reliability and validity are high when such information is not made available by the test author. Rather, if the required technical information regarding reliability and validity is missing from the manual, the test should be used with extreme caution.

Second, a criterion-referenced test only tells us where the child is currently operating, not where the child is expected to operate in the future. Because criterion-referenced tests are not normed, they cannot tell us how the child is operating in relation to peers. Thus, they yield no information as to whether the child is progressing at an acceptable *rate*. Such information is often useful to parents and professionals when making educational decisions.

Third, criterion-referenced tests usually take a great deal of time to administer and score. For example, criterion-referenced tests are generally administered to individuals rather than to groups. This one-at-a-time testing is time consuming if a large number of students need to be assessed. Additionally, some criterion-referenced tests can take a week or more to administer, with the test being administered in short daily sessions. Collected test information must be recorded, coded, and keyed to specific curriculum objectives; it is then scored and interpreted. Although this process yields extremely useful information, it can be time consuming. It may even prove impossible for a teacher to test a large number of students on a criterion-referenced measure without the help of a teacher's aide.

Finally, criterion-referenced test items must be sequenced to follow the steps of learning, and each level of learning must be identified and mastered. This requires a strong component of task analysis as well as the precise construction of many behavioral objectives to describe each learning component. This is not necessarily a bad process (some professionals argue that it is needed for meaningful learning to take place). However, it can be extremely time consuming. Some teachers argue that the time-consuming nature of criterion-referenced tests actually interferes with the instructional process by shifting much needed instructional time from the child to the test.

In summary, both norm-referenced and criterion-referenced tests possess advantages and disadvantages. The advantages of criterion-referenced tests are many and lead to meaningful assessment and diagnostic–prescriptive teaching. Nevertheless, the use of criterion-referenced tests involves costs for both educator and student, and these costs should be recognized by the informed test consumer.

Creating Teacher-Made, Criterion-Referenced Tests

Teachers often find they need to create their own criterion-referenced tests. This is due to a lack of sound, commercially available, criterion-referenced instruments. Moreover, the criterion-referenced tests that are commercially available may not be appropriate to the curriculum being used in a particular school or classroom.

The teacher should take some general considerations into account when creating a criterion-referenced test (Guerin and Maier 1983; Howell, Kaplan, and O'Connell 1979). These nine considerations include:

1. Each instructional goal should be task-analyzed into a set of behavioral objectives.
2. Items should be constructed that correspond to and measure skills directly related to the steps of each behavioral objective.
3. Test only important matters. Avoid testing noncrucial or trivial information.
4. Write items that, when correctly answered by students, reflect knowledge attained through special study of the material, not general knowledge.
5. Establish criterion levels for passing. These levels should be at mastery level, usually at 80 to 85 percent.
6. Include enough items for each behavioral objective to indicate clearly that the student has answered the items through knowledge or performance expertise, not chance.
7. Each item should be presented as straightforwardly as possible. Answering items correctly should not be based on reading ability (except for reading tests) or on ability to answer trick questions.
8. Create a pool of items taken from a variety of sources.
9. Constantly evaluate and redesign items as necessary.

Diagnostic Probes

Diagnostic probes measure a sample of student behavior with a relatively high degree of specificity (Howell and Morehead 1986; White 1986). Such behavior samples, collected during a relatively short period of time, give the teacher an indication of precisely where a child is experiencing weakness. Such probes often occur in the core academic areas and use a *probe sheet* in which the teacher diagnoses a given weakness or set of weaknesses.

Many criterion-referenced tests use diagnostic probes. In one such test (Diagnosis: An Instructional Aid, Shub, Carlin, Friedman, Kaplan, and Katien 1973), the teacher gives a survey test that indicates which one of thirty-four reading probes should be administered to the child. Each probe is further subdivided into specific skills related to reading, with these subskills described as behavioral objectives. By using the probes contained in this test, the teacher can obtain specific information as to where the child is experiencing difficulties in learning to read.

Teachers often need to construct their own diagnostic probe sheets. To do this, follow these four procedures:

1. List the skill or skills to be tested by the probe sheet in precise, behavioral objective form.
2. Task-analyze the overall skill and then list the subcomponent skills in instructional objective form.
3. Create an adequate number of probe questions to ascertain that the student does or does not possess the subcomponent skill.
4. Use a question or problem that assesses only one subcomponent skill.

Diagnostic probes are useful in indicating information about areas of students' weaknesses. Once weak areas of subcomponent skills are identified, those skills need to be task-analyzed and assessed in depth. These subcomponent skills must be listed in behavioral objective form so that remediational instruction can be designed to alleviate weaknesses.

After Curriculum-Based Assessment: Prescriptive Teaching

One of the principal advantages of curriculum-based assessment is the usefulness of the material it yields. Curriculum-based assessment permits ongoing, systematic testing of the child's skills and deficiencies in a program in which component skills are tied to the child's curriculum and expressed in behavioral, measurable terms. Useful as this information is, however, it is of little value unless the teacher uses it meaningfully. Such assessment information must be translated into appropriate instructional strategies designed to help remediate the child's weaknesses.

Diagnostic (prescriptive) teaching seeks to help remediate the child's learning difficulties by identifying the cause of those difficulties (assessment) and designing instructional strategies and materials specifically geared to remediate these deficiencies (Forness and Kavale 1983; Lakin 1983). More specifically, prescriptive teaching considers the following three variables of the child and the learning environment before formulating instructional activities (Dunn and Dunn 1978; Mann, Suiter, and McClung 1987)

1. The task level and task components being assessed.
2. The child's learning style and skill levels.
3. The learning situation and environment.

Based on this information, prescriptive activities are formulated, taking into account available instructional materials and equipment, the instructional situation, the teacher's instructional style, and the instructional environment.

The following five procedures will help you formulate successful prescriptive teaching strategies (Bennett 1982; Lerner 1981):

1. The transdisciplinary (multidisciplinary) team should participate in translating assessment information into prescriptive activities.
2. A variety of assessment instruments, both formal and informal, should be used to diagnose the child's learning difficulties. These instruments should include commercially available tests, rating scales and interviews, systematic observation, and curriculum-based tests.
3. Error analysis techniques should be used to determine the reasons for correct and incorrect performance.
4. Environmental conditions in which the child performs best should be identified.
5. Instructional procedures should be formulated keeping the child's learning characteristics and environment in mind.

By following these guidelines, it is highly probable that relevant, meaningful, and useful instructional activities can be designed to remediate the child's academic weaknesses. However, if such guidelines are not followed, informal assessment is likely to result in little more than a collection of data that is placed in the child's cumulative folder and never translated into meaningful instruction. This is educational mismanagement of the worst magnitude that should be avoided at all costs.

SUMMARY

Tests can be norm-referenced or criterion-referenced. Norm-referenced tests make interperson comparisons and are summative and global in nature. Criterion-referenced tests make intraperson comparisons and are summative and diagnostic in scope. Criterion-referenced tests are curriculum-based and behaviorally defined; they measure well-defined behavioral domains and minimum levels of proficiency.

A curriculum is a structured and sequenced set of learning tasks or outcomes. A curriculum is formally defined and outlined and then sequenced and organized into a set of instructional objectives. A curriculum can be organized either developmentally or functionally. How the curriculum is organized and sequenced depends on what is to be taught and on the learning attributes of the student.

Curricula contain what is going to be taught as well as the strategies needed to apply what has been learned. The appropriate use of strategies requires the processes of generalization and discrimination. These processes depend on the student's recognizing similarities or differences in situations requiring the application of content and strategies.

When the curriculum is the basis for student testing, the testing is curriculum-based assessment. Curriculum-based assessment holds that a student's needs are best met by assessing performance in the context of the child's individual educational program. Curriculum-based assessment implies that tasks have been broken down into subcomponents using task analysis.

Task analysis is the procedure of isolating, sequencing, and describing key components of a task. When all the components have been mastered, the student should be able to perform the overall target task appropriately. Task analysis involves identifying essential subtasks and rechaining those subtasks. Both processes must be carried out successfully to learn the target task. The three types of task analysis are temporal, difficulty level, and developmental analysis.

Inventories, work samples with resultant error analysis, criterion-referenced tests, and diagnostic probes are the four main types of curriculum-based assessment. These assessments are hierarchical in that each yields a more detailed level of information than the one preceding it.

Inventories are screening instruments that usually do not specify whether a child has passed or failed a given task. Generally, they yield information about whether a child is experiencing an academic problem.

Error analysis is used in conjunction with work samples. In error analysis, student errors are diagnosed for possible patterns that could indicate areas of learning weaknesses. Error analysis holds that student errors do not occur at random but are purposeful, and that they are useful in understanding underlying strategies that students use to solve problems.

Criterion-referenced tests are useful in diagnostic assessment. Rather than yielding a summary grade, criterion-referenced tests are keyed to specific instructional objectives and scored pass–fail. Passing a given test item implies mastery of that instructional objective.

Teachers often construct their own criterion-referenced tests. A number of considerations for sound test construction are included in this chapter. Teachers should give particular attention to areas of content and criterion-related validity as well as test-retest reliability in constructing criterion-referenced tests.

Diagnostic probes are used to measure a sample of student learning with a high degree of specificity. Such information gives the teacher a precise indication of where in the curriculum the child is experiencing difficulty. Many criterion-referenced tests use diagnostic probes.

One principal advantage of curriculum-based assessment is the usefulness of the information disclosed. Curriculum-based assessment yields ongoing, systematic, and diagnostic information that gives the teacher insights into remediational programming for students. Suggestions are made in this chapter for applying curriculum-based assessment information to students' remediational programming.

STUDY QUESTIONS

1. Under what conditions is norm-referenced assessment more appropriate than criterion-referenced assessment? What advantages do criterion-referenced tests have over norm-referenced tests in terms of diagnostic and instructional use?

2. Suppose you were the teacher conducting the conference with William Washington's parents. What information would you give to the parents? What part of your information would be norm-referenced and what part would be criterion-referenced test information? Defend your answers.

3. What is a curriculum? How is it defined? What would a typical curriculum for a child include?

4. Describe the conditions under which you would devise a developmental curriculum for a student. Do the same for a functional curriculum. How would the two curricula differ?

5. What are the differences between tasks and strategies? Describe some common academic strategies children must use in school.

6. Describe situations in which one of the strategies you describe in question 5 would be properly applied in terms of generalization. Now describe two strategies in which appropriate discrimination processes must be used.

7. What is curriculum-based assessment? How does it differ from traditional assessment? Why is it important in the assessment of students?

8. Define the processes of task analysis. Choose a task and apply task-analysis procedures. Comment on the appropriateness of your finished task analysis.

9. Describe the different types of curriculum-based assessment. How do they differ in terms of specificity of information?

10. What is error analysis? How is it conducted? If possible, collect a work sample from a student or friend and conduct an error analysis.

11. What are some of the issues in creating sound, teacher-made, criterion-referenced tests? What are the issues of reliability and validity in criterion-referenced testing?

12. What are diagnostic probes? How are they used in assessment? What information do they yield, and how is this information applied in educational programming for students?

CHAPTER 13

Intelligence and Learning Aptitude Tests

KEY CONCEPTS

- Intelligence
- Binet and the notion of intelligence
- Mental age, basal age, and ceiling age
- The nature and structure of intelligence
- Age differentiation
- Factor theories of intelligence
- Spearman's *g* and *s* factors
- Thurston's primary mental abilities
- Vernon's hierarchical model
- Guilford's structure of intellect
- Fluid and crystallized intelligence
- Sternberg's component model
- The Stanford–Binet Intelligence Test
- The WISC series
- Verbal, performance, and full scale IQ
- The Kaufman Assessment Battery for Children
- The Woodcock–Johnson Psycho-Educational Battery
- Group intelligence tests

What makes a person intelligent? What constitutes intelligent behavior? If you asked fifty people at random to define intelligence and intelligent behavior you would likely receive many different answers. To some people, intelligent behavior is the ability to solve problems quickly and efficiently. To others, it entails being creative or seeing a situation in a novel or unique way. To still others, it means adapting well to new situations or living harmoniously rather than at odds with oneself and the environment.

If defining intelligent behavior is difficult, defining and constructing items for an intelligence test is even more problematic. How should we measure intelligence? Does the ability to complete pencil and paper items constitute intelligence? What about people who possess specialized spatial and/or mechanical abilities? Is this a type of intelligent behavior and, if so, how should it be assessed? Finally, what about creative, artistic, and performance behaviors? Should these traits be assessed by an intelligence test?

These are not just academic questions. Millions of intelligence tests are administered to schoolchildren each year, and to a great extent, the educational fate of children depends on their performance on these tests. Scores on intelligence tests often determine who will be included in classes for the gifted, who will be considered for college preparatory classes, and even who will become officers or line soldiers in the military. The intelligence testing field is a multimillion dollar industry; its best-selling authors earn incomes comparable to those in the popular publishing market. With so much depending on the proper purchase, use, and interpretation of intelligence tests, it is imperative that the informed test consumer understand the uses and abuses of intelligence and aptitude tests.

Intelligence and Intelligence Testing

The Concept of Intelligence

Intelligence is a word that we use in our everyday conversation. People act intelligently, possess intelligence, and behave in an intelligent manner. This term conjures up a variety of images and definitions. Thus, before we discuss intelligence testing, we should try to understand the meaning of intelligence.

The term *intelligence* is used so casually today that it is difficult to realize that the word was virtually absent from popular speech barely a century ago. During the last part of the nineteenth century, the philosopher Herbert Spencer and scientist Sir Francis Galton reintroduced the word *intelligence* in reference to individual mental ability. These men, influenced by the work of Darwin, hypothesized that natural selection influenced the way intelligence was distributed among the human

species just as it affected the distribution of physical traits.

Galton set out to prove the hereditary basis of development. Along with such scientists as Clark Wissler and J. McKeen Cattell, Galton attempted to devise a series of sensory development and reaction time tests that they hoped would measure intelligence. However, these studies clearly failed to discriminate between individuals of high and low intelligence. It was left to an obscure French psychologist, Alfred Binet, to change and redefine the definition of intelligence for decades to come.

Binet and the Nature of Intelligence

Alfred Binet, a psychologist interested in intelligence, lived in Paris around the turn of the century. Binet (1890a, b) had decided that intelligence was more complex than as measured by Galton and others. Binet defined intelligence as "the capacity to judge well, to reason well, and to comprehend well" (Binet and Simon 1916, p. 192). The problem for Binet was to devise a set of tasks that would measure such complex behaviors.

In 1904, Binet got his chance. The French minister of public instruction decided to create a procedure for identifying intellectually limited schoolchildren so they could be removed from the regular classroom in which they were failing. These students would then be placed in special, remedial educational environments. The task of identifying intellectually deficient children was given to Binet.

Binet's Concept of Intelligence

Binet felt that people engaged in a variety of behaviors that were intelligent. For example, Binet considered the ability to remember and use information and the ability to use language intelligent behavior. If all these behaviors could be included under the heading of intelligent behavior, what would be the nature of intelligence?

To define intelligence, Binet hypothesized a general, overall measure that he termed *g* (representing general mental ability). According to Binet, *g* was the factor underlying intelligent behavior. Such behavior was defined by Binet as the ability to (1) find and maintain a definite direction or purpose, (2) adjust one's behavior to reach that purpose, and (3) evaluate and adjust the appropriateness of the strategy as needed (Terman 1916). According to Binet, general mental ability was a person's ability to solve problems and adapt to the environment.

Creating the First Intelligence Test

Binet, along with his collaborator, Théodore Simon, set out to measure intelligence. Because he was working with Paris schoolchildren, it was not surprising that many of the tasks he chose to measure intelligence were school related. In creating his intelligence test, Binet was guided by what is now referred to as the principle of *age differentiation* (Kaplan and Saccuzzo 1982). Age differentiation refers to the phenomenon that older children can perform and succeed at more complex tasks than younger children. For example, although we expect an eight-year-old child to read and write, we would be amazed if a two-year-old engaged in similar behavior. Binet searched for tasks that could be completed by approximately two-thirds to three-fourths of all children in a particular age range, by a larger proportion of older children, and by a smaller proportion of younger children. Thus, Binet created a set of age-related tasks and identified the chronological ages at which most children could successfully complete each task (Binet and Simon 1916). Table 13-1 contains examples of tasks that most children

typically were able to complete successfully at a given chronological age.

Mental Age

From Binet and Simon's work on identifying the ages at which most children could successfully complete given tasks came Binet's important notion of *mental age*. According to Binet's 1908 scale, a child's mental age was calculated by comparing his or her performance to the average performance of peers in the child's chronological age group. For example, if a child could successfully perform the tasks that an average eight-year-old could perform, that child's mental age was eight years. However, if the child could only successfully perform tasks that an average six-year-old could perform, the child's mental age would be six.

According to Binet, the calculation of the child's mental age was derived from figuring the child's *basal* and *ceiling* ages. Basal age refers to the highest chronological age at which the child passes every group of tasks. Thus, if a child passes all tasks at the five-year-old level but passes only six of twelve tasks at the six-year-old level, the child's basal age is five years.

In calculating the child's ceiling age, testing continues until the child misses every group of tasks for that given year. For the year in which the child passes some tasks but fails others, the individual receives designated credit in months toward the calculation of mental age.

The Concept of the IQ

By 1916, the potential of Binet's conceptualization of intelligence was becoming known throughout the world. Soon, three English translations and adaptations of his work appeared. The most important of these adaptations was published by Lewis Terman at Stan-

Table 13-1 Samples of Tasks That Children Typically Can Pass at Given Chronological Ages (Binet 1911)

Age 3

Points to nose, eyes, and mouth.
Repeats two digits.
Enumerates objects in a picture.
Gives family name.
Repeats a sentence of six syllables.

Age 4

Gives own sex.
Names key, knife, and penny.
Repeats three digits.
Compares two lines.

Age 5

Compares two weights.
Copies a square.
Repeats a sentence of ten syllables.
Counts four pennies.
Unites the halves of a divided rectangle.

Age 6

Distinguishes between morning and afternoon.
Defines familiar words in terms of use.
Copies a diamond.
Counts thirteen pennies.
Distinguishes pictures of ugly and pretty faces.

Age 7

Shows right hand and left ear.
Describes a picture.
Executes three commands given simultaneously.
Counts the value of six sous, three of which are double.
Names four cardinal colors.

Age 8

Compares two objects from memory.
Counts from zero to twenty.
Notes omissions from pictures.
Gives day and date.
Repeats five digits.

Age 9

Gives change from twenty sous.
Defines familiar words in terms superior to use.
Recognizes all the (nine) pieces of money.
Names the months of the year in order.
Answers or comprehends "easy questions."

Age 10

Arranges five blocks in order of weight.
Copies two drawings from memory.
Criticizes absurd statements.
Answers or comprehends "difficult questions."
Uses three given words in not more than two sentences.

Age 12

Resists suggestion as to length of lines.
Composes one sentence containing three given words.
Names sixty words in three minutes.
Defines three abstract words.
Discovers the sense of a disarranged sentence.

Age 15

Repeats seven digits.
Finds three rhymes for a given word in one minute.
Repeats a sentence of twenty-six syllables.
Interprets pictures.
Interprets given facts.

Adult

Solves the paper-cutting test.
Rearranges a triangle in imagination.
Gives difference between a pair of abstract terms.
Gives three differences between a president and a king.
Gives the main thought of a selection he has read.

Source: L. R. Aiken (1988). *Psychological Testing and Assessment,* 6th ed. (Boston: Allyn and Bacon). Used by permission.

ford University in Caifornia in 1916. This became the first Stanford–Binet Intelligence Test.

Terman's 1916 test contained significant improvements and modifications of Binet's 1908 and 1911 works. For example, the age range was increased to include children from three to fourteen years as well as average and superior adults. Many items were adjusted, and the standardization group was modified and enlarged to include American children (unfortunately, the 1916 Stanford–Binet was standardized completely on a white, native-born population residing in California, thus invalidating the test for all other children). However, probably the largest and most important modification made by Terman was the creation of the concept of the *intelligence quotient* (IQ).

The IQ used both the child's chronological age (CA) and mental age (MA) to create a proportion or ratio in which the two could be statistically compared. To derive the IQ, the child's MA and CA were compared as:

$$IQ = \frac{MA}{CA} \times 100$$

The figure 100 was used to remove decimals or fractions.

The logic of the IQ was such that a child was considered of average intelligence when mental age was in unity with chronological age ($MA \div CA = 1 \times 100 = 100$). In such cases, the child would be performing at the level of chronologically aged peers and the IQ would be 100. If the IQ were less than unity, the child would be operating at a mental age somewhat lower than chronologically aged peers; mentally superior children would be operating mentally at a higher level than their chronologically aged counterparts. Figure 13-1 shows how the IQ might be derived for an intellectually average, deficient, or superior child.

Figure 13-1   Deriving IQ

Intellectually Average Child

Chronological Age = 6 years
Mental Age = 6 years
$$IQ = \frac{MA}{CA} = \frac{6}{6} = 1 \times 100 = 100$$

Intellectually Deficient Child

Chronological Age = 6 years
Mental Age = 4 years
$$IQ = \frac{MA}{CA} = \frac{4}{6} = .66 \times 100 = 66$$

Intellectually Superior Child

Chronological Age = 6 years
Mental Age = 8 years
$$IQ = \frac{MA}{CA} = \frac{8}{6} = 1.33 \times 100 = 133$$

The Deviation IQ: Despite its innovativeness, the concept of the IQ contained problems. For one thing, because the standard deviations for different age groups were different, IQs for different age groups on the Stanford–Binet were not comparable. Second, because MA was thought to peak at about age twenty, it appeared that MA would cease to increase as maturity was reached. For example, in Figure 13-2, it appears that this adult was growing less intelligent as he grew older. However, there was

Figure 13-2   IQ Derivation for a Male at Age Twenty and Ten Years Later: Is He Less Intelligent?

Twenty-Year-Old

CA = 20
MA = 20
IQ = $\frac{20}{20} \times 100 = 100$

Ten Years Later

CA = 30
MA = 20 (Ceiling of MA on test)
IQ = $\frac{20}{30} = .66 \times 100 = 66$

no evidence to support this notion of decreased intelligence as a function of age.

To deal with these problems, the concept of the *deviation* IQ was devised in the 1960 version of the Stanford–Binet. The deviation IQ is a standard score that possesses a mean of 100 and a standard deviation of 16. This means that the average IQ on the Stanford–Binet is 100 and that every 16 IQ points represent one standard deviation. The average score of 100 was devised by considering the concept of unity as the average IQ (MA ÷ CA = 1) and multiplying by 100. The standard deviation of 16 was ascertained by evaluating the standard deviation of the mental ages of each CA level of children in the representative norm group for the test. Using the deviation IQ, scores on the Stanford–Binet can be compared across CA groups. These scores can thus be interpreted in terms of standard deviation, percentages of scores falling within standard deviation groups, and percentiles within the normal curve.

Theories of Intelligence

Every intelligence test examined in this chapter and the next was based on a theory of intelligence that guided the construction of that particular instrument. For this reason, the test consumer must understand the theories of intelligence that influenced test construction. Table 13-2 lists the major theories of intelligence and their proponents discussed in this chapter.

Binet's General Mental Ability

As already noted, Binet believed that intelligent behavior could be described by an underlying general mental ability that he labeled *g*. According to Binet, *g* was the amount of intelligence a person possessed, that is, intelligent persons possessed a great deal of *g*, whereas those less intelligent were deficient in general mental ability. For Binet, mental ability was a unitary and singular construct. As we shall

Table 13-2   Major Theories of Intelligence

Author (Theory Date)	Description	Components
Alfred Binet (1909) Lewis Terman (1921)	Ability to think abstractly and solve problems	g = general mental ability
Charles Spearman (1927)	General factor and specific factors as per specific tasks	g, s_1, s_2, s_3, etc.
Louis Thurstone (1938)	Primary mental abilities	Number, verbal meaning, inductive reasoning, perceptual spatial relations, verbal fluency
Phillip Vernon (1960)	Verbal and mechanical/spatial abilities	Various components, including creativity
J. P. Guilford (1967)	Operations, products, and contents	120 abilities
Raymond Cattell	Crystallized and fluid intelligence	g and f (fluid intelligence)
Robert Sternberg	Triarchic theory of intelligence	Metacomponents; performance, knowledge-acquisition, retention, and transfer components

see, virtually every theory of intelligence conceived after Binet's has been influenced by the concept of general mental ability.

Spearman's Two-Factor Theory

In 1927, Charles Spearman, then a graduate student, formulated a two-factor theory of intelligence (Spearman 1927). According to Spearman, performance on any cognitive task depends on both general mental ability (g) and one or more specific factors or abilities unique to the task being performed. Spearman labeled these specific abilities s and identified the specific tasks needed to complete the cognitive task successfully as s_1, s_2, s_3, and so forth.

At first glance, Spearman's theory may sound simplistic. After all, apparently all Spearman did was add another letter (s) to the intelligence formula without delineating the specific factors. However, it must be understood that Spearman's conceptualization of specific factors or abilities contributing to intelligence was a major breakthrough in psychology. For the first time, intelligence was separated into abilities (plural) and no longer viewed as a monolithic entity underlying mental functioning. Spearman's revolutionary concept of intelligence became the basis for the construction of specific intelligence tests, such as the Raven Progressive Matrices (Raven 1938, 1977) and the Culture-Fair Intelligence Test (Cattell and Cattell 1949, 1957). It also paved the way for future multifactor theories of intelligence and affected virtually every intelligence test constructed thereafter.

Thurstone's Primary Mental Abilities

L. L. Thurstone was a psychologist interested in the factors or abilities that affected intelligence. He identified what he considered to be the seven most important factors or abilities affecting intelligence. These seven factors, la-beled *primary mental abilities*, are shown in the first part of Figure 13-3.

Thurstone's theory of primary mental abilities represented a major achievement in intelligence theory and testing for a variety of reasons. First, it attempted to identify the specific s factors hypothesized by Spearman. Second, it paved the way for future, more detailed theories of intelligence that sought to identify additional factors or abilities influencing intelligence. Finally, it was the principal theory underlying the creation of the Army Alpha and Beta Intelligence Tests and the Otis–Lennon Mental Abilities Tests (Otis and Lennon 1979), perhaps the most popular group intelligence tests used today.

Vernon's Hierarchical Model

Although much of the work on intelligence theory and testing has been performed in the United States, a major theory of intelligence was devised by Phillip Vernon, a British psychologist (Vernon 1960, 1985). Vernon has created a three-tiered model of intelligence (see the second part of Figure 13-3). In this model, there are two major groups of factors that Vernon has identified as verbal–educational (v:ed) and practical–mechanical–spatial (k:m). These major factors are further broken down into groups of abilities as shown by the branching tree model in Figure 13-3. Specific v:ed factors in Vernon's theory are verbal fluency, number reasoning, number ability, and creativity. Areas in the k:m include mechanical comprehension, spatial ability, psychomotor ability, and others.

Vernon's theory contains two very important implications that have influenced the creation of intelligence and ability tests. First, Vernon's model broke new ground in identifying the influence of mechanical–spatial abilities on intelligence. It is now commonly accepted that the ability to diagnose and solve spatial and mechanical problems is a form of intelligent behavior. Vernon's work influ-

Figure 13-3   Theories of Intelligence

Thurstone's Primary Mental Abilities

Verbal meaning (V)—Understanding ideas and word meanings, as measured by vocabulary tests.

Number (N)—Speed and accuracy in performing arithmetical computations.

Space (S)—Ability to visualize form relationships in three dimensions, as in recognizing figures in different orientations.

Perceptual speed (P)—Ability to distinguish visual details and the similarities and differences between pictured objects quickly.

Word fluency (W)—Speed in thinking of words, as in making rhymes or in solving anagrams.

Memory (*M*)—Ability to memorize words, numbers, letters, etc., by rote.

Inductive reasoning (*I*)—Ability to derive a rule from given information, as in determining the rule for a number series from only a part of the series.

Vernon's Hierarchical Model

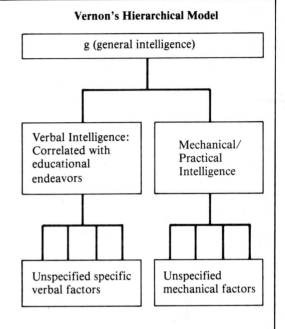

Guilford's Structure of Intellect

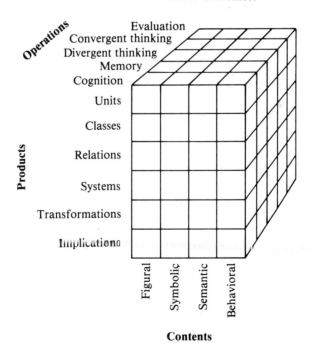

Source: The structure of intellect cube, J. P. Guilford (1967). *The Nature of Human Intelligence* (New York: McGraw-Hill Book Company). Reproduced with permission.

enced the creation of such mechanical–spatial tests as the Minnesota Spatial Relations Test (Trabue 1979) and the Revised Minnesota Paper Formboard Test (Likert and Quasha 1985), as well as nonverbal intelligence tests, such as the Raven Progressive Matrices (Raven 1977) and the Goodenough–Harris Drawing Test (Goodenough and Harris 1963). Second, Vernon's model was one of the first to consider creativity as a form of intelligence. This does not mean, as some argue, that one must be intelligent (as measured by most IQ tests) to be creative; rather, creativity is one form of intelligence. Models that have included creativity as a factor in intelligence have influenced such creativity tests as the Structures of Intellect Abilities (Guilford 1967, 1980) and the Torrance Tests of Creative Thinking (Torrance 1966).

Guilford's Structure-of-Intellect Model

Holding the record for the number of specific abilities contributing to intelligence is the structure-of-intellect model proposed by J. P. Guilford (1967). Guilford has created a model of intelligence that posits 120 possible factors comprising intellect. In Guilford's model, intellect is comprised of five types of *operations,* four *contents,* and six *products.* As such, intelligence is based on a $5 \times 4 \times 6$ factorial model that creates 120 factors of intellect. Guilford's 120 factors can be envisioned by a cube-type model of intellect, as shown in the third part of Figure 13-3.

Guilford's model is perhaps most useful in considering how far we have come in describing the nature of intelligence. Binet's theory held that intelligence consisted of a general mental ability (singular) rather than a set of mental abilities. The next development was the rudimentary (but also revolutionary) model of Spearman, which outlined a set of specific but hazy *s* factors. Guilford's model splintered Binet's *g* factor into as many as 120 specific abilities that contribute to intelli-

gence. By advancing such a theory, Guilford is arguing that to be intelligent or act intelligently, a large variety of skills or abilities must come into play. There is not one overriding general ability that influences how much intelligence a person possesses.

Fluid and Crystallized Intelligence

The theory of fluid and crystallized intelligence has been advanced by R. B. Cattell and his associates (Cattell and Cattell 1963; Horn and Cattell 1966). According to Cattell, *fluid* intelligence is a general type of intelligence applicable to all fields, whereas *crystallized* intelligence is specific to certain areas, such as school learning. Fluid intelligence is used by the individual in tasks that require adaptation to new situations, whereas crystallized intelligence is used in tasks where the person's learning and habits have already become fixed (crystallized).

Cattell views fluid intelligence as more dependent on heredity and crystallized intelligence as more dependent on environmental factors. Therefore, to measure fluid intelligence adequately, the testing instruments should be free of cultural or environmental effects. Crystallized intelligence tests can be influenced by prior learning. The concept of fluid intelligence has influenced the creation of culture-free tests, such as the Culture-Fair Intelligence Test (Cattell and Cattell 1957); the concept of crystallized intelligence has affected the newest versions of the Stanford–Binet Intelligence Scale.

Sternberg's Component Processes

The last and most recent model of intelligence discussed here is that of Robert Sternberg, a psychologist at Yale University. Sternberg has been working on a theory, which he has labeled the *triarchic* theory, that attempts to identify intelligence in terms of the processes involved in problem solving (Sternberg 1984,

1985). According to Sternberg, intelligence consists of a set of developed learning and thinking skills used to solve academic and everyday problems. Sternberg has identified five classes of components that he believes operate in problem solving and that constitute intelligent behavior. Sternberg's model uses an information-processing analogy in which intelligent behavior includes taking in data to define a problem, collecting and organizing data to interpret the problem, devising a purposeful plan to solve the problem, solving it, and evaluating outcomes. Although an in-depth discussion of Sternberg's triarchic theory is outside the scope of this text, the theory does hold promise for redefining how we think of intelligence and intelligent behavior.

Individual Intelligence Tests

The Stanford–Binet Intelligence Scale

Binet's conceptualization of intelligence and IQ has already been outlined in this chapter. Now we can examine in detail one of the most popular and best-selling tests ever developed, the Stanford–Binet Intelligence Scale. This test was first developed by Terman and his associates at Stanford University in 1916; subsequent revisions appeared in 1937, 1960, 1973, and 1986 (Thorndike, Hagen, and Sattler 1986). The newest (1986) version of the test is described here.

Brief Overview of the Scale: The 1986 version of the Stanford–Binet Intelligence Scale retains much of the 1937 and 1960 editions. In 1937, two parallel forms of the scale (L and M) were developed, with the scale devised to measure the general mental ability of persons at half-year intervals from the age of one and one-half to adulthood. As originally conceptualized by Binet, items in the 1937 version were included if they passed three criteria: (1) each item had to possess a test of validity for measuring intelligent behavior; (2) the per-

centage of children passing a given item had to increase as a function of chronological age; and (3) children who passed the item had to possess a higher mental age than children who failed the item. Basal and ceiling ages were computed, and the child's mental age was computed by adding to the basal age the number of months of credit received for passing each subtest up to the ceiling age. An IQ was then computed using the MA ÷ CA × 100 formula.

In 1960, the scale was significantly revised. Items of the 1937 L–M scales were updated and revised and a kit of materials that included various toys and other objects for testing younger children was incorporated. A major change in the 1960 revision was the use of the deviation IQ explained earlier in this chapter. For the 1960 version of the scale, a mean of 100 and a standard deviation of 16 was accepted for all individuals, regardless of chronological age. In 1973, the manual was revised but the test remained virtually the same.

Like the 1960 L–M scale, the 1986 version uses the concept of the deviation IQ. In addition, as many valid and reliable L–M items as possible have been retained. However, a number of new items in the areas of quantitative reasoning, abstract–visual reasoning, and short-term memory have been added.

The items in the 1986 revision also underwent a fairness review to guard against cultural or ethnic bias. All items in the test were examined by a panel of experts on various subcultures, minorities, and ethnic groups in the United States to screen for cultural bias. Items were then field-tested among culturally diverse children to screen items further.

Perhaps most important, the 1986 revision, although not abandoning the concept of general mental ability (g), has conceded the possibility of the existence of specific abilities in the form of fluid and crystallized intelligence. Figure 13-4 illustrates this. General mental ability is still envisioned as the driving force behind all intelligent behavior, but the three

Figure 13-4   General, Fluid, and Crystallized Intellectual Functioning as Used in the 1986 Stanford-Binet Intelligence Scale

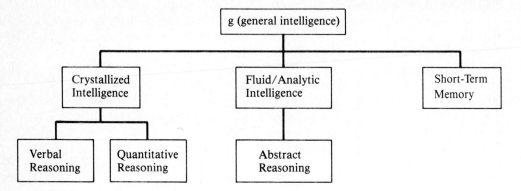

broad factors of fluid intelligence, crystallized intelligence, and short-term memory are shown flowing directly from *g*. Finally, these three second-tier abilities lead to specific abilities, such as verbal reasoning, quantitative reasoning, and abstract–visual reasoning.

Standardization Group Characteristics: The 1916 version of the Stanford–Binet scale was standardized on only 1,000 adults and 400 children, all of whom were white, native-born, and California residents. Subsequent revisions of the scale have endeavored to make the standardization groups more representative.

The 1986 version of the test was standardized on 5,013 persons in nine age groups. The number of people in any given chronological age standardization group ranged from a low of 194 (18–0 to 23–11 years group) to 460 (5–0 to 5–11 years). Attempts were made to obtain a cross sample of persons in the standardization group in terms of geographic region, community size, ethnic group, race, gender, socioeconomic status (SES), and parental occupation and education. The test authors concede, however, that the standardization group was overrepresented for the professional–managerial category of parental occupation and for the college and beyond category of parental education. The higher categories of SES are also overrepresented.

Reliability and Validity: Reliability for the 1986 version was calculated for the different subtests for each age group. Two types of reliability calculation were used: test-retest and the Kuder–Richardson–20 (KR–20) (see Chapter 8 for review). The test-retest method was used only with a preschool and elementary school population.

Using the KR–20 method (reliabilities tend to be relatively higher when this method of calculating reliability is used), reliabilities range from .73 (memory for objects) to .94 (paper folding and cutting). The overall reliability for the entire test using the KR–20 formula was approximately .94. Using the test-retest method (a more conservative technique), reliabilities ranged from .51 (quantitative reasoning—age eight) to .88 (verbal reasoning—age five). Test-retest reliability for the entire test was approximately .90.

The 1986 version of the scale attempted to establish validity by (1) examining the internal structure of the test, (2) attempting to establish a high correlation with other tests measuring intelligence, and (3) seeking a correlation between high and low performance on the test and high and low intelligent behavior in real life.

The test appears to have established its claims of strong validity. For example, it correlates highly with other tests of intelligence and it successfully identifies mentally retarded, gifted, and learning-disabled children previously identified as possessing these attributes. Thus, to the extent that intelligence tests adequately measure what really is intelligence, the Stanford–Binet Scale appears to substantiate its claims of validity.

Summary of the Stanford–Binet for the Test Consumer: The Stanford–Binet remains one of the most popular intelligence tests on the market. Nevertheless, the test consumer should be aware of several of its limitations. First, it is a difficult test to give and score—it can be administered and interpreted only by a licensed school psychologist. Second, it yields severely limited types of information. Basically, it gives the professional a single IQ score—the higher the score, the higher the person's intelligence level. The limitations of such a score harken back to Binet's conceptualization of general mental ability (g). The concept of g and its resulting IQ tells the professional little about what a child can and cannot do. Likewise, it offers little diagnostic information about a child's specific areas of deficiency. Rather, it yields an IQ score that is compared against peer scores in the norm group.

The Stanford–Binet is almost useless for moderately–severely mentally retarded persons. With such severe cases of mental retardation, it is generally unreliable and its construction prohibits adequate measurement of the IQ. Another test of intellectual functioning needs to be used with these individuals.

Finally, it should be pointed out that the 1986 version possesses problems in the areas of standardization groups and reliability. For example, although the scale was normed on approximately 5,000 individuals, this population was spread out among nine age groups. When such factors as geographic region, sex, community size, and ethnic group are factored, very few people appear in each cell of individuals tested. Likewise, the test-retest reliabilities of certain subtests on the scale are quite low. For example, on the qualitative subtest of the quantitative reasoning area, the test-retest reliability for eight-year-old children is only .28, and that for copying on the abstract–visual reasoning test is only .46. Thus, subtest reliability needs to be examined closely for the appropriate age group of the test taker, and interpretation can be tenuous in cases of low or moderate subtest reliability.

The Wechsler Intelligence Scales

David Wechsler (1896–1981) was one of the best known psychologists involved in intelligence testing. In 1939, Wechsler was a psychologist on the staff of Bellevue Hospital in New York City. Wechsler, who was treating adult patients with psychological disorders, wanted an intelligence test that would be valid and useful for this population. He became dissatisfied with the subtests of the 1937 Stanford–Binet scale designed to measure adult intelligence. Consequently, in 1939, Wechsler designed a test intended to measure adult intelligence more adequately. Wechsler called this test the Wechsler-Bellevue Scale Form 1.

Based on this early scale, Wechsler added a second form in 1947. A full revision of the test, titled the Wechsler Adult Intelligence Scale (WAIS), was published in 1955. This scale became an extremely popular intelligence scale for adults; it was revised again in 1981 and renamed the Wechsler Adult Intelligence Scale–Revised (WAIS–R). The WAIS–R is designed to measure adult intelligence from the ages of sixteen to seventy-four.

Other Wechsler Scales

Although the original Wechsler scale was designed for adults, Wechsler soon became convinced that analogous intelligence testing scales were needed for children. Consequently, in 1949 he published an intelligence scale for children entitled the Wechsler Intelligence Scale for Children (WISC). It was revised and updated in 1974 and titled the Wechsler Intelligence Scale for Children–Revised (WISC–R). Today, the WISC–R, designed for children aged six to sixteen, is one of the most popular and best-selling tests in the history of the field.

Wechsler added a third test to the family of intelligence tests in 1967. The Wechsler Preschool and Primary Scale of Intelligence (WPPSI) was designed for children between the ages of four and six and one-half years. All of the Wechsler tests (WAIS–R, WISC–R, WPPSI) contain subtests that are administered to persons in a predetermined order by a trained, certified school psychologist. Table

13-3 shows the subtests and their presentation order for each Wechsler scale.

The Key to the Wechsler Scales: Point and Performance Scales

The Stanford–Binet scales group items by age levels. That is, items in each age level are selected so that two-thirds to three-fourths of children in the assigned chronological age group can pass the items. This arrangement implies two things. First, various types of test content are scattered throughout the scale at different age levels. For example, the eight-year-old level contains some number reasoning, verbal material, and memory items; the ten-year-old level contains different items from these same content areas. Second, and perhaps more important, the subject must pass approximately three-fourths of the items to be considered as operating at that age level. Anything lower than three-fourths and the person fails.

Table 13-3   Subtests of the Wechsler Scales

Wechsler Adult Intelligence Scale– Revised (WAIS–R) (ages 16–74 years)	Wechsler Intelligence Scale for Children– Revised (WISC–R) (ages 6–16 years)	Wechsler Preschool and Primary Scale of Intelligence (WPPSI) (ages 4–6½ years)
Information (V)[a]	Information (V)	Information (V)
Picture Completion (P)[b]	Picture Completion (P)	Animal House (P)
Digit Span (V)	Similarities (V)	[Animal House Retest] (P)
Picture Arrangement (P)	Picture Arrangement (P)	Vocabulary (V)
Vocabulary (V)	Arithmetic (A)	Picture Completion (P)
Block Design (P)	Block Design (P)	Arithmetic (V)
Arithmetic (V)	Vocabulary (V)	Mazes (P)
Object Assembly (P)	Object Assembly (P)	Geometric Design (P)
Comprehension (V)	Comprehension (V)	Similarities (V)
Digit Symbol (P)	Coding (P)	Block Design (P)
Similarities (V)	[Digit Span] (V)[c]	Comprehension (V)
	[Mazes] (P)	[Sentences] (V)

[a]"V" denotes subtests on the Verbal Scale.
[b]"P" denotes subtests on the Performance Scale.
[c]Supplementary subtests on the WISC–R and WPPSI are given in brackets.
Source: L. R. Aiken (1988). *Psychological Testing and Assessment,* 6th ed. (Boston: Allyn and Bacon). Used by permission.

Wechsler was unhappy with this aspect and wanted his tests to use a *point scale* format. In a point scale, credits or points are assigned to each item. When an item is answered correctly, the test taker receives a designated number of points. By using a point scale, all items of a given content area (e.g., number reasoning) can be grouped together and presented in order of ascending difficulty. Likewise, the point scale eliminates the problem of age-level items by designating a number of points for items answered correctly. Finally, Wechsler's conceptualization of the point scale allows not only an overall measure of intelligence but also performance scores for different content areas, such as language and numerical reasoning.

The Binet scales have also been criticized for what many people consider an overemphasis on verbal–language skills. Wechsler agreed with this criticism. He incorporated into his scales the concept of the *performance scale,* in addition to items that measured verbal (language) intelligence. Performance items measure nonverbal intelligence and require the subject to perform (often in the psychomotor domain) rather than simply answer questions. Wechsler and others believed that performance scale items overcame, at least to some extent, the language, cultural, and educational bias found in many verbal–language items purporting to measure intelligence.

The WAIS–R

Overview: The WAIS–R, published in 1981, is based on the original WAIS published in 1955. It consists of eleven tests grouped by content areas assessed. Six areas are assessed in the verbal scale, and five are assessed in the performance scale (see Table 13-4). Items in each test are arranged with items becoming increasingly difficult. Whereas only the arithmetic test in the verbal scale is timed, all of the performance scale tests are timed.

Administration and Scoring: Like the Stanford–Binet, the Wechsler scales can be administered only by a trained, licensed examiner, usually a school psychologist. Detailed direc-

Table 13-4   Subtests of the WAIS–R

1. *Information.* Thirty-three general information questions to be answered in a few words or numbers. Questions are arranged in easy-to-difficult order. Testing begins with item 5; items 1–4 are administered if examinee fails either item 5 or 6. Testing is discontinued when examinee fails seven items in a row. Responses are scored 0 or 1. Responses are affected by familial and cultural background.

2. *Picture Completion.* Twenty-seven pictures on cards, each having a part missing. Examinee is given 20 seconds per picture to indicate what is missing. Testing begins with item 1 and is discontinued when examinee fails seven consecutive items. Responses are scored 0 or 1. The test was designed to measure visual alertness, memory, and attention to details.

3. *Digit Span.* Seven series of digits to be recited forward and seven series to be recited backward. Testing on "digits forward" starts with three digits read aloud (one digit per second) by examiner. Examinee is directed to repeat each series right after examiner has finished. Two trials are given on each series length (two different sets of digits). Testing on "digits forward" continues until the examinee fails both trials of a series or succeeds on nine digits forward. On "digits backward" the examinee is directed to say the digits backward after the examiner has finished saying them forward. Testing begins at two digits backward and continues until the examinee has failed both trials of a series or succeeded on eight digits backward. Score on each set of "digits forward" or "digits backward" is 0, 1, or 2; total score is the sum of part scores on "digits forward" and "digits backward." The test was designed to measure immediate rote memory, but scores are affected by attention span and comprehension.

Table 13-4   *(cont.)*

4. *Picture Arrangement.* Ten sets of cards, each card containing a small picture. Examinee is directed to arrange the pictures in each set of cards into a sensible story. Time limits are 60 seconds on sets 1–4, 90 seconds on sets 5–8, and 120 seconds on sets 9 and 10. Testing is discontinued when the examinee fails five consecutive sets. Responses are scored 0, 1, or 2, depending on accuracy. The test measures ordering or sequencing ability, as well as social planning, humor, and ability to anticipate.

5. *Vocabulary.* Thirty-seven words to be defined, in order of ascending difficulty. Testing starts with item 1 for examinees having poor verbal ability, otherwise with item 4. Testing is discontinued when the examinee fails six words in a row. Responses to each word are scored 0, 1, or 2, depending on the degree of understanding of the word expressed. The test was designed to measure knowledge of words, a skill that is highly related to general mental ability.

6. *Block Design.* Ten red and white geometric designs are presented on cards, the examinee being instructed to duplicate each design with four or nine blocks. Two attempts are permitted on the first two designs, and one attempt on each succeeding design. Testing is discontinued when four designs in a row are failed. Base scoring is 0, 1, or 2 points on designs 1 and 2 and 0 or 2 points on designs 3–10, with bonus points being added for rapid, perfect performance. The test was designed to measure the ability to perceive and analyze a visual pattern into its component parts. In terms of its correlations with total scores on the Performance Scale and scores on the test as a whole, "Block Design" is considered to be one of the best performance tests.

7. *Arithmetic.* Fifteen arithmetic problems in order of increasing difficulty. Testing begins with item 3 and is discontinued after five consecutive failures; items 1 and 2 are given if items 3 and 4 are failed. Fifteen seconds are allowed on problems 1–4, 30 seconds on problems 5–10, 60 seconds on problems 11–14, and 120 seconds on problem 15. Re-

sponses are scored 0 or 1, in addition to bonus points for quick, perfect performance on certain problems. The test measures elementary knowledge of arithmetic, together with the ability to concentrate and reason quantitatively.

8. *Object Assembly.* Four cardboard picture puzzles presented to the examinee in a prearranged format, with directions to put the pieces together to make something. All four puzzles are presented, time limits being 120 seconds on puzzles 1 and 2 and 180 seconds on puzzles 3 and 4. The score for each puzzle is determined by the number of "cuts" correctly joined; bonus points are given for quick, perfect performance. The test was designed to measure thinking, work habits, attention, persistence, and the ability to visualize a final form from its parts.

9. *Comprehension.* Eighteen questions in order of ascending difficulty, requiring detailed answers. Questions are presented until examinee fails six consecutive items. Responses are scored 0, 1, or 2, depending on quality and degree of understanding expressed. The test measures practical knowledge, social judgment, and the ability to organize information.

10. *Digit Symbol.* Examinee is directed to fill in each of ninety-three boxes with the appropriate coded symbol for the number appearing above the box. Testing begins with a practice series, after which the examinee is given 90 seconds to fill in the ninety-three blank boxes with the correct symbols copied from a key listed above. The score range is 0–93 points. The test was designed to measure attentiveness and persistence in a simple perceptual-motor task.

11. *Similarities.* Fourteen items of the type "In what way are 'A' and 'B' alike?" Items are presented in order of ascending difficulty until examinee fails five in a row. Responses are scored 0, 1, or 2, depending on quality and degree of understanding expressed. This test is designed to measure logical or abstract thinking—the ability to categorize and generalize.

Source: L. R. Aiken (1988). *Psychological Testing and Assessment,* 6th ed. (Boston: Allyn and Bacon). Used by permission.

tions for administering and scoring are given in the manual, but additional rigorous training is also needed. Scoring rules are extremely precise, and little latitude is given the scorer. Designated points are given for correctly answered items in each subtest. For the verbal tests, testing ends when a specified number of consecutive items are answered incorrectly. Performance items are timed, with designated points awarded and subtest conclusion specified in the manual.

After all of the subtests have been administered, raw scores are converted to scaled (standard) scores. For each subtest, the mean of the test is 10 and the standard deviation is 3. Scaled scores are obtained from a single table in the test manual and, unlike the Stanford–Binet, these scales are independent of the subject's chronological age. The scaled scores for the verbal, performance, and total subtests are then combined and transformed to yield a verbal, performance, and full-scale, standard score IQ. This score contains a mean of 100 and a standard deviation of 15.

Norms and Standardization Group: The WAIS–R was standardized on 1,880 adults, stratified and representative for age, sex, ethnic and racial makeup, occupation, education, and community size and type. Representativeness was assured by comparing the sample to that of the 1970 census. The WAIS–R asserts that it contains norms representative of the U.S. population.

Reliability: Reliability of the WAIS–R was reported for each subtest, for verbal IQ, performance IQ, and full-scale IQ and was assessed for nine age groups of adults. The split-half procedure for assessing reliability was used. Figure 13-5 shows the reliability ranges of reliability coefficients by age groups for the subtests and different IQs. As shown in the figure, most reliabilities for the subtests and IQ measures are in the range of .90; however,

Figure 13-5   Reliability Coefficients of WAIS–R (Test–Retest Method)

Tests	Range of Reliability by Age Group Tested
Verbal Tests	
Information	.67–.90
Comprehension	.69–.87
Similarities	.74–.87
Arithmetic	(NA)
Vocabulary	.69–.81
Digit Span	.70–.92
Sentences	(NA)
Verbal IQ	.91–.96
Performance Tests	
Picture Completion	.68–.85
Picture Arrangement	.69–.78
Block Design	.80–.90
Object Assembly	.63–.76
Coding	.63–.80
Images	.62–.82
Geometric Design	(NA)
Performance IQ	.89–.91
Full-Scale IQ	.95–.96

some of the reliabilities for certain subtests, such as picture completion, are relatively low.

Validity: The test manual for the WAIS–R presents virtually no validity information. Instead, the manual argues that the validity information presented in the 1939 W–B Scale and the 1955 version of the WAIS is still relevant because the WAIS–R measures the same abilities and there is much overlap between the tests.

The accuracy of this argument is questionable. Although there have been numerous independent studies and articles discussing the WAIS–R (actually more than 1,300 articles and books), the burden of proof regarding the validity of the WAIS–R must fall on the publishers of the test. Until satisfactory proof is provided, the validity of the WAIS–R will continue to be a topic of debate.

Summary of the WAIS–R for the Test Consumer: The WAIS–R possesses a number of advantages over the Stanford–Binet scale. For example, the point scales permit grouping of similar items into subtests and eliminate the need for age scores. Likewise, the performance scale allows for verbal, performance, and full-scale IQ scores.

On the negative side, the reliability of some of the subtests is relatively low, and the validity of the entire test has not been demonstrated by the test author. Perhaps the most glaring weakness of the test is its inability to handle extreme (high and low) IQ scores (a weakness it shares with the Stanford–Binet scale). For example, the lowest score one can receive on the WAIS–R is 41. This score is attained if all items on the test are missed save one, the colors of the American flag. Surely, knowing the colors of the flag should not be worth 41 IQ points. Thus, the WAIS–R may seriously overestimate the IQs of moderately or mildly mentally retarded adults. This test shortcoming must be taken into account when measuring the mentally retarded adult.

The WISC–R

Overview: In 1949, Wechsler published a scale for children, analogous to the WAIS, which he called the Wechsler Intelligence Scale for Children (WISC). In 1974, this scale was revised and became the WISC–R. The WISC–R is designed for children six to sixteen years of age. It is perhaps the most widely used intelligence test today, administered to both normal and exceptional children.

Like the WAIS–R, the WISC–R measures verbal, performance, and full-scale IQ. It contains twelve subtests (the WAIS–R contains eleven), two of which are supplementary. The twelve subtests, along with a brief description of one, appear in Table 13-5.

Administration and Scoring: Similar to the WAIS–R, only a trained, licensed examiner

Table 13-5 Subtests of the WISC–R and WPPSI

WISC–R

Verbal Scale
1. Information: 30 questions
2. Similarities: 17 pairs of words
3. Arithmetic: 18 items
4. Vocabulary: 32 words to be defined
5. Comprehension: 17 questions of situational comprehension
6. Digit Span (Supplementary Verbal Test)

Performance Scale
1. Picture Comprehension: 26 incomplete pictures
2. Picture Arrangement: 13 sets of cards. Arrange sets of 3–5 in proper sequence.
3. Block Design: 11 designs to be constructed
4. Object Assembly: Put puzzles together
5. Coding: Geometric codes
6. Mazes (Supplementary Performance Test)

Subtests of the WPPSI Not Included in WISC–R

1. Sentences: Replaces WISC–R Digit Span Test. Sentences read to child who must repeat them.
2. Animal House: Performance Scale Test. Similar to coding test of WISC–R.
3. Geometric Design: Performance Test. Child draws geometric designs shown to him or her.

may administer the WISC–R. Additionally, because it is designed for children, the examiner must take special care to establish rapport with the test taker. Specified procedures for administration and scoring are outlined in the test manual.

A specified order of test presentation is suggested, with verbal and performance subtests presented alternately. If used, the two supplementary subtests are usually administered last.

The WISC–R differs from the WAIS–R in that the starting point of the test depends on the test taker's age. That is, children of different ages begin at different points on given subtests so that the children do not tire before reaching challenging items. If the child fails the first item, the correct answer is given to make sure the child understood the task.

As with the WAIS–R, a point scale is used for scoring, with different items possessing different point values. Raw scores for each subtest are converted to scaled (standard) scores possessing a mean of 10 and a standard deviation of 3. The scaled subtest scores are then summed to yield verbal, performance, and full-scale IQ, as is done with the WAIS–R. Full-scale IQs can range from 40 to 160.

Norms and Standardization Group: The original WISC was standardized entirely on 2,200 white male and female children chosen as representative of the 1940 census. The WISC–R group improved the quality of the standardization group greatly since both white and nonwhite children were used according to the 1970 census. The group is representative in terms of gender, race and ethnic background, geographic location, education of parents, and father's occupation.

Reliability: Reliability coefficients for the WISC–R and the WAIS–R were both obtained using the split-half procedure. Reliability was assessed for three age groups of students: 7½, 10½, and 13½ years of age. Reliabilities were relatively low for many of the subtests (e.g., .67 verbal information, .68 picture completion) but higher for verbal and performance IQ (approximately .91). Reliability for the full-scale IQ was approximately .96.

Validity: As with the WAIS–R, validity claims for the WISC–R are unsubstantiated. The test does correlate with other IQ measures and with tests of academic criteria, but more substantial evidence of test validity is not provided.

Summary of the WISC–R for the Test Consumer: The WISC–R is probably the most popular intelligence scale used in the schools today. It shares the advantages of the WAIS–R point and performance scales, but it also shares the drawbacks of low subtest reliability, dubious validity, and an inability to measure IQs below 40. Therefore, it should be used and interpreted with caution, and educational decisions based on this scale should also be based on other testing instruments.

The Wechsler Preschool and Primary Scale of Intelligence (WPPSI)

The WPPSI parallels the WAIS–R and WISC–R in its theoretical underpinnings, makeup, administration, and scoring. It consists of eleven subtests; ten are used to compute the IQ and one is supplementary. It contains three new tests not used on the WAIS–R and WISC–R, which are summarized in Table 13-5. Like the WAIS–R and WISC–R, the WPPSI yields a verbal, a performance, and a full-scale IQ.

The WPPSI is appropriate for use with children from four to six and one-half years of age. Establishing rapport with the child taking the test is crucially important, and the manual includes procedures for establishing such rapport.

The reliability and validity of the WPPSI are comparable to the WAIS–R and WISC–R. As with the two other tests, the proven validity of the WPPSI still needs to be more strongly demonstrated.

Other Individual Intelligence Tests

The Kaufman Assessment Battery

Overview: The Kaufman Assessment Battery (K–ABC) (Kaufman and Kaufman 1983) is one of the newer entries into the intelligence test market. The K–ABC is a test battery that assesses children from ages two and one-half through twelve and one-half years of age. The test battery assesses individual intelligence, defined as learning potential and preferred learning style, as well as children's academic achievement. The authors claim that in addition to measuring intelligence, the test battery can be used for clinical psychological assessment, assessment of handicapped children (especially learning disabled children), educational placement and planning, assessment of minority children, preschool assessment, and neuropsychological assessment.

The K–ABC consists of sixteen subtests (see Table 13-6 for a listing and brief description). Intelligence is assessed on three of the scales: simultaneous processing, sequential processing, and the optional nonverbal scale. Scores are reported in the four global areas of sequential processing, simultaneous processing, mental processing composite, and achievement.

Administration and Scoring: The K–ABC can be given by any reasonably well trained educational professional, including the special education teacher. For preschool children, the battery usually takes thirty to fifty minutes to administer. For older children, testing time usually takes fifty to eighty minutes. Materials consist of three easel kits of test items, a manual, scoring forms, and manipulative materials for four of the subtests.

In scoring the K–ABC, a variety of transformed and standard scores are used. Scaled scores with a mean of 10 and a standard deviation of 3 are used by chronological age for the mental processing subtests. These subtests are then combined into sequential processing, simultaneous processing, and composite and nonverbal scales, each possessing a mean of 100 and a standard deviation of 15. Percentile ranks are available for each subtest and for the entire scale. Age equivalents are also available for the mental processing subtests, and grade equivalents can be used for the achievement subtests.

Norms and Standardization Group: The K–ABC contains two sets of norms—one for a

Table 13-6   The Sixteen Subtests of the Kaufman Assessment Battery for Children (K–ABC)

I. *Mental Processing Composite*

   A. Sequential Processing Scale

   1. Hand movements: Ability to perform a series of hand movements in the same sequence as those produced by the examiner.
   2. Number recall: Individual repeats a series of digits in the same order as given by the test examiner.
   3. Word order: Test taker touches a series of pictures in the same order as named by the test examiner.

   B. Simultaneous Processing Scale

   4. Magic window: Individual identifies picture that is exposed slowly from behind a narrow opening or "window."
   5. Face recognition: Child selects from an array of photographs faces that he or she has previously seen.
   6. Gestalt closure: Individual names a partially completed pictured object.
   7. Triangles: Student arranges several triangles in the same pattern as presented in a model.
   8. Matrix analogies: Student selects a picture or geometric form that appropriately completes a visual analogy.
   9. Spatial memory: Individual recalls the placement of pictures on a page after brief exposure to that page.
   10. Photo series: Individual places photographs of an event in chronological order.

II. *Achievement Composite*

   11. Expressive vocabulary: Individual names pictured objects.
   12. Faces and places: Individual names a well-known person, fictional character, or place.
   13. Arithmetic: Individual performs tasks in counting, number operations and concepts, and computations.
   14. Riddles: Individual infers the name of a concept from a list of characteristics given in riddle form.
   15. Reading/decoding: Identifying letters and words in print.
   16. Reading/comprehension: Following written commands presented in sentences.

national comparison and another that allows for socioeconomically atypical children. The national norms were created by examining 2,000 children, 100 at each half-year age interval between two years and six months and twelve years and five months. This group was representative and stratified for sex, parental education, race and ethnic group, geographic region, and community size. The sociocultural norms were based on an additional sample of 496 black and 119 low-SES children who were added to the national norms.

Reliability: Both split-half and test-retest reliability were assessed for the K–ABC. Split-half reliability coefficients ranged from .62 (Gestalt closure) to .92 (triangles) on the mental subtests. For the entire mental processing scale, including the nonverbal scale, reliability ranged from .84 (simultaneous processing) to .95 (on several scales).

Test-retest reliabilities were also obtained for 246 children after a two- to four-week interval. Test-retest reliability on sequential processing subtests ranged from .59 (hand movements) to .86 (Gestalt closure). On the mental processing scale, test-retest reliability ranged from .77 (sequential processing and simultaneous processing) to .93 (composite scale).

Validity: The manual of the K–ABC takes great pains to prove its validity, and these efforts set a standard that other test authors should attempt to follow. The K–ABC demonstrates strong construct, concurrent, and predictive validity. It correlates highly with a number of other tests, including the WISC–R, the McCarthy Scales, and the Cognitive Abilities Test. It also does a good job of predicting future school achievement.

However, the K–ABC is less thorough in demonstrating its usefulness for identifying preferred learning styles and making educational diagnoses and placements. Nor does it support its use as a clinical psychological measure and a tool for diagnosing neurological impairments in children. Its major validity claims are in the more traditional area of intellectual assessment.

Summary of the K–ABC for the Test Consumer: A relatively new entry into the intelligence test market, the K–ABC is provocative in its claim and professed uses. It claims to be an intelligence *and* achievement test; it also claims to be a diagnostic test for educational placement and evaluation, a clinical psychological tool, a culturally fair test, and a test for diagnosing neurological impairments. It is doubtful that any one test can do all this satisfactorily; the K–ABC is no exception.

On the positive side, the K–ABC does attempt to combine intellectual and achievement assessment. It appears, however, that it does a somewhat better job with the former than with the latter. It can be used with exceptional populations, such as handicapped students, and the standardization group attempts to represent both exceptional children and minority and culturally different students. Other positive features are the test's nonverbal intelligence scale and the test manual, which offers reliability and validity information that sets the reporting standard for other tests.

However, the K–ABC simply does not do everything it claims to do. In particular, its value as a clinical psychological tool, as an instrument for assessing neurological impairment, and as a test for educational diagnosis and planning needs further proof. The test consumer should not be deluded into thinking this is an all-purpose tool that can perform every kind of assessment needed. That instrument has not yet been and may never be developed.

The Woodcock–Johnson Psycho-Educational Battery

Overview of the Test: The Woodcock–Johnson Psycho–Educational Battery (WJPB) (Woodcock 1978) is a comprehensive, individually administered set of standardized tests designed to measure cognitive ability, scholastic aptitude, academic achievement, scholastic and nonscholastic interests, and independent functioning. The battery is appropriate for individuals ranging in chronological age from three to eighty and can be used with both handicapped and nonhandicapped populations. According to the test authors (Woodcock 1978), the battery is appropriate for "individual assessment, selection and placement, individual program planning, guidance, appraising gains or growth, program evaluation, and research" (p. 4). The authors envision the battery as both a norm- and criterion-referenced instrument.

There are four parts to the battery consisting of forty-one subtests and a variety of clusters or scales. Part I contains tests of cognitive ability. The twelve subtests and eleven scales in this section measure cognitive ability (Area 1), cognitive factors (Area 2), and scholastic aptitude (Area 3). Part II, which tests academic achievement, contains ten subtests in five cluster areas. Part II assesses student interests in both scholastic and nonscholastic areas, and Part IV assesses independent behavior in four main cluster areas. The areas measuring cognitive abilities and aptitudes are shown in Figure 13-6.

Administration and Scoring: The test materials include two easels that make administration relatively simple and straightforward. The test can be administered by any professional reasonably knowledgeable about testing and measurement. Additionally, test materials include a set of specific training exercises for administration, and these exercises are strongly recommended for test users. Administration time for the entire battery is approximately three hours; Part I requires about one hour, Part II about fifty minutes, Part III about fifteen minutes, and Part IV about forty-five to sixty minutes. Although the test may be administered in four different sessions, the test author recommends that administration of the total battery span no more than a two-day period.

Scoring of the WJPB is complex, and the tester must be careful to avoid scoring errors. Raw scores for each subtest are converted to part scores, which are then summed to produce cluster scores. After a grade score, age score, and instructional grade range are obtained from norm tables for each cluster score, an expected cluster score for the age or grade of the student is entered. A difference is then calculated between each expected and obtained cluster score. Percentile ranks for cluster (difference) scores are then obtained. A zero difference is defined as the fiftieth percentile. Finally, a student summary sheet is created that includes confidence bands placed around scores based on the standard error of measurement. Other scores yielded by the WJPB include a relative "performance index," deviation IQ scores, T-scores, and stanines. However, these scores are not usually entered into the student profile.

A microcomputer scoring package, entitled COMPUSCORE (Hauger 1984), is available for both the Apple II computer and the IBM-PC. This program provides convenient scoring from raw scores of the twenty-seven subtests and reduces both scoring time and scoring error.

Interpretation of test scores is objective rather than subjective. Various norms are provided in the manual. Additionally, a variety of criterion-referenced information is provided. However, before attempting to interpret scores from the battery, test users should possess competency in elementary statistics and testing and measurement theory.

Norms and Standardization Group: The WJPB was standardized on 4,732 individuals who resided in 49 communities. Of these 4732 persons, 3,900 were students enrolled in public school; the remaining 832 were either preschool children or adults. The sample was stratified and made representative for sex,

Figure 13-6   Part I: Tests of Cognitive Abilities Measured on the Woodcock–Johnson Psycho–Educational Battery

Areas	Cluster Scales	Subtests											
		Picture Vocabulary	Spatial Relations	Memory for Sentences	Visual-Auditory Learning	Blending	Quantitative Concepts	Visual Matching	Antonyms-Synonyms	Analysis-Synthesis	Numbers Reversed	Concept Formation	Analogies
I. Broad Cognitive Abilities	Full	X	X	X	X	X	X	X	X	X	X	X	X
	Preschool	X	X	X	X	X	X						
	Brief							X		X			
II. Cognitive Factors	Verbal Ability	X							X	X			
	Reasoning Ability								X	X		X	X
	Perceptual Speed		X					X					
	Memory			X							X		
III. Scholastic Aptitude	Reading Aptitude				X	X			X				X
	Mathematics Aptitude								X	X	X	X	
	Written Language							X	X	X		X	
	Knowledge Aptitude			X				X		X			X

Source: Test Critiques: Volume IV, ed. Daniel J. Keyser and Richard C. Sweetland. Copyright © 1986 by Test Corporation of America, a subsidiary of Westport Publishers, Inc., 330 W. 47th Street, Suite 205, Kansas City, Missouri 64112. Reproduced by permission of the publisher. All rights reserved.

race, occupational status, geographic region, and type of community (urban or nonurban). However, the sample was overrepresented for individuals from the north–central United States and underrepresented for nonurban, southern communities, according to the 1970 U.S. census.

Reliability: The reliability of the WJPB is generally quite acceptable. The reliability of Parts I, II, and III was obtained using the split-half procedure; test-retest procedures were used for only two timed subtests. For Part IV, test-retest procedures were reported for two groups of elementary school children.

The median reliability for the Broad Cognitive Scale (Part I) is .97, with a range of .96–.98 across all age levels tested. The reliability of Part II is in the .90 range, and median reliability for Part III is .83 for scholastic interest and .88 for nonscholastic interest. Reliability coefficients for preschool children are somewhat lower on Parts I, I, and III, but this is to be expected in testing young children.

Validity: Extensive validity information is reported in the test manual, and the validity information offered can serve as an example for other tests of cognitive ability. The results of ten different validity studies are reported, and the battery shows strong criterion-related validity for nonhandicapped and handicapped children and adults. The test also correlates highly with the WISC–R.

Summary of the Woodcock–Johnson for the Test Consumer: In general, the WJPB is a very good tool that contains strong technical quality, reliability, and validity. It offers a great deal of information to the professional. Based on the strength of the battery, its technical soundness, and the quality of the information that it yields, the Woodcock–Johnson is a useful and important tool for intellectual assessment of students.

Group Tests of Intelligence

Group intelligence tests are administered to more than one person at a time. Group tests are characterized by their speed and time efficiency. Rather than taking an hour or more to test one child, many individuals can be tested quickly in a group setting.

However, group tests contain some assumptions and limitations. If these assumptions are violated, considerable error in interpretation will result and faulty conclusions may be reached. Figure 13-7 contains the characteristics and assumptions of group tests.

Most group intelligence tests use the multiple-choice format. Test takers, therefore, must have a sophisticated degree of reading ability. Individuals with poor reading and comprehension skills should not be administered group intelligence tests. If they perform poorly (and they almost inevitably do), we cannot be sure whether their performance

Figure 13-7   Characteristics and Assumptions of Group Intelligence Tests

1. Examiner need not be as highly trained as for individual tests
2. Costs less to administer than individual tests
3. More time efficient than individual tests
4. Usually speeded (timed) administrations
5. Standardization samples usually larger than for individual tests
6. Paper and pencil variety
7. Scoring of the objective variety
8. All items administered to all examinees
9. Reliability usually high
10. Mostly multiple-choice items
11. Usually requires reading ability
12. Usually requires strong test-taking skills

was due to intellectual deficits or poor reading skills.

Group intelligence tests are usually paper and pencil tests. Such tests lack performance-type items, and the persons taking such tests must possess good test-taking and fine-motor skills. People who fill in the wrong boxes or who inadvertently skip items on their answer sheets will get all these answers wrong. Again, we must not confuse poor test-taking or eye-hand skills with mental deficiency. Group intelligence tests also require the test taker to sit still and stay on task for relatively long periods of time—behaviors that many test takers do not possess.

Persons taking group intelligence tests must also have adequate visual acuity. They must be able to see well enough to read the materials accurately. People with uncorrected vision problems that affect reading will not do well on group intelligence tests.

Group tests do not allow for follow-up or in-depth exploration of a test taker's answers. Answers must be brief and objective enough to be scored by machine or stencil. This does not allow test takers to make in-depth responses. Because of this, qualitative interpretation of group intelligence tests is difficult.

Despite their limiting characteristics, group

Figure 13-8   Commonly Used Group Intelligence Tests

Test	Author	Grade	Reported Results	Levels of Test
Otis–Lennon School Ability Test	Otis and Lennon (1982)	1–12	A school ability index; percentile ranks, stanines.	5
Cognitive Abilities Tests	Thorndike and Hagen (1982)	1–12	Standard scores, percentiles, and stanines. Tests contain a verbal, quantitative, and nonverbal index of intelligence.	10
Henmon–Nelson Tests of Mental Ability	Lamke and Nelson (1973) Nelson and French (1974)	K–12	A deviation IQ, percentile ranks, and stanine score.	4
Kuhlmann–Anderson Tests	Kulhmann and Anderson (1981)	K–12	A cognitive skills quotient of a verbal, nonverbal, and the full test batteries. Also includes standard scores, percentile ranks, and stanines.	7

intelligence tests are somewhat useful in assessing the intellectual functioning of large groups of individuals. Additionally, because of their inherent time and cost effectiveness, they are universally used and quite popular with educational professionals. Figure 13-8 contains a listing and brief description of the most popular group intelligence tests.

Because of the assumptions and limitations of group intelligence tests, however, such instruments are probably not appropriate for use with most special education and special needs students. Such students are usually experiencing difficulty in reading and written expression areas; they may also be experiencing deficits in visual acuity, fine-motor, and test-taking skills. For these reasons, when group intelligence tests are used with special needs students, they should be regarded as screening measures that disclose areas requiring more in-depth intellectual assessment.

SUMMARY

Intelligence is defined in many ways. The first attempts to define and measure intelligence were made by philosophers and scientists interested in social Darwinism. However, the pioneer of intelligence and intelligence testing was Alfred Binet.

Binet designed the first intelligence test based on the concept of mental age. Mental age is calculated from the identified basal and ceiling ages of a child. The concept of the IQ, as devised by Terman in 1916, was calculated by comparing the child's mental age and chronological age.

The deviation IQ was designed to allow comparison of children's IQs at different age levels. The deviation IQ possesses a mean of 100 and a standard deviation of 16.

To some extent, the history of intelligence theories has been driven by attempts to redefine intelligence from Binet's conceptualization of general mental abilities to specific abilities and factors leading to intelligent behavior. Such theories include Spearman's two-factor theory, Thurstone's primary mental abilities, Vernon's hierarchical model, Guilford's structure-of-intellect model, Cattell's fluid and crystallized intelligence, and Sternberg's triarchic theory of intelligence.

A variety of individual intelligence tests are used today with children and adults. The oldest is the Stanford-Binet, the most recent revision of which was published in 1986. Perhaps the most popular scales used are the Wechsler scales, including the WAIS–R, WISC–R, and WPPSI. Wechsler scales provide a verbal, performance, and full-scale IQ. Other tests commonly used in the schools include the Kaufman Assessment Battery for Children and the Woodcock–Johnson Psycho–Educational Battery.

Group intelligence tests are administered to more than one individual at a time. These tests are popular because of their time and cost efficiency. Nevertheless, it is assumed that individuals who are administered group intelligence tests are good readers and that they posses good test-taking skills, fine-motor perception, visual acuity, and strong verbal abilities. Because many handicapped individuals are deficient in these areas, group intelligence tests generally should not be used for the majority of special needs learners.

STUDY QUESTIONS

1. What is the difference between aptitude and achievement? Name three standardized aptitude tests and three standardized achievement tests. Is it possible to have a "pure" aptitude test? Why or why not?

2. Identify the major theories of intelligence. Which standardized IQ tests are driven by these major theories?

3. Define g. Why is it difficult to conceptualize and work with regarding remedial curriculum planning for children?

4. Outline the attempts to redefine intelligence into specific abilities. Who are the major theorists, and how have they redefined intelligence? Do you believe that there is one intelligence or many? Defend your answer.

5. What are the major strengths and weaknesses of the Stanford–Binet Intelligence Scale? Do you think that it is useful for handicapped students? Defend your answer.

6. In what ways do the Wechsler scales and Stanford–Binet Scale differ? Which one do you advocate for use with handicapped children? Defend your answer.

7. Outline the major strengths and weaknesses of the WISC–R. Is its popularity justified in your opinion? Why or why not?

8. What are the major strengths of the Kaufman Assessment Battery for Children? Is it appropriate for use with handicapped children? Do you feel the information it provides is educationally useful? Defend your answer.

9. Outline the areas measured by the Woodcock–Johnson Psycho–Educational Battery. Is this an aptitude or an achievement test? Does it offer information useful for children's educational programming? Would you advocate using it with handicapped children? Why or why not?

CHAPTER 14

Intelligence and Aptitude Testing of Special Populations

KEY CONCEPTS

- Identifying special populations
- Problems in intelligence testing of special population students
- The issue of cultural fairness in testing
- Tests for persons with sensory and motor impairments
- Pictorial tests of intelligence
- Culture-fair tests
- Tests of adaptive behavior
- The system of multicultural pluralistic assessment (SOMPA)

Each category of special needs learner is unique in terms of both the major characteristics that help define each group and the ways that such persons should be assessed. The intelligence and aptitude of special education learners can be assessed using many of the standard, individual instruments described in Chapter 13. However, exceptional individuals possess a variety of test-taking and information-processing characteristics that increase errors of test administration and interpretation when standard tests are used.

The test-taking and information-processing skills that special education persons display on intelligence and aptitude measures take various forms. For example, sensory impaired individuals experience difficulty reading or hearing instructions and items on commonly used intelligence tests. Likewise, physically or motorically impaired individuals have difficulty making appropriate responses to certain items on such tests as the Stanford–Binet and the Wechsler scales. Although less obvious, students possessing receptive language difficulties and persons from culturally diverse backgrounds may find it difficult to perform up to their capabilities on commonly used intelligence and aptitude tests.

When the special test-taking and information-processing characteristics of exceptional individuals are not taken into account by educational professionals, test administration and interpretation may be invalidated. The result would be faulty and erroneous conclusions based on invalid test scores. Avoiding such test invalidation and increased error in the testing of special eduation students should be the goal of every professional involved in the education of and programming for exceptional individuals.

Who Are the Special Populations?

The Sensory Impaired

The visually and hearing impaired were the first group that professionals realized needed special consideration in intelligence testing. It was obvious that visually impaired and blind persons would not be able to read test instructions, nor would they be able to perform adequately many of the performance-type items contained in intelligence tests. Visually impaired persons would thus score lower and appear less intelligent than their sighted counterparts on the basis of their sight impairment, not their intellectual ability.

Likewise, hearing impaired and deaf persons would suffer from a bias inherent in many intelligence tests. They would not be able to hear special directions or questions from test givers and would be penalized if they possessed inadequate lip-reading skills. Many hearing impaired persons who suffer from verbal skills deficits (both receptive and expressive) would also be penalized by the verbal nature of many intelligence tests. Such test bias would, of course, contribute to administration and interpretation errors.

Physically Handicapped and Motor and Speech Impaired Persons

Persons who experience difficulty in speaking, writing, or pointing experience difficulty in taking intelligence tests. These individuals may not be able to ask questions about procedures or give answers in understandable terms. Additionally, they may not be able to write adequate answers or may not possess the fine-motor control needed to fill out answer sheets. Motorically impaired persons (e.g., those with cerebral palsy) may find it difficult to complete many performance-type items, particularly items that are severely speeded (timed). Testers must take into account the special response difficulties of physically handicapped and speech impaired persons.

Persons with Learning Disabilities

One definition of learning disability is that although the person possessing such a disability is *not* intellectually impaired (mentally retarded), nevertheless the student is not achieving in school. Using this definition, we must effectively delineate mental retardation from learning disabilities and processing deficits, as indicated by intelligence and aptitude tests.

Learning disabled children, despite possessing normal intelligence, often experience difficulty on group intelligence tests (Bryan and Bryan 1986; Ross 1980). Possible reasons for this difficulty include:

1. The child has a modality bias against spoken and/or written instructions.
2. The child may have difficulty attaching meaning to words.
3. The child may not understand consecutive speech.

For these reasons, intelligence testing with learning disabled children should proceed very carefully. The tester should take into account the special learning and processing characteristics or deficits of the learning disabled test taker. Great care must be taken so that the learning disabled child is not misdiagnosed as mentally retarded.

Developmental Disabilities

Traditional intelligence testing of persons possessing developmental disabilities (mental retardation) can often be difficult and contain error. Such persons, especially children, do not adequately understand the tasks expected of them, nor do they possess the requisite language and processing skills needed to complete items appropriately. Additionally, developmentally delayed individuals usually are not adequately represented in the standardization groups on which commonly used intelligence norm samples are based. This contributes to making these tests untenable for use with developmentally delayed persons. Finally, because many developmentally delayed individuals come from culturally diverse environments, some intelligence tests risk being culturally biased against them.

For these reasons, some professionals advocate using the concept of *adaptive behavior* to assess the intelligence and aptitude of developmentally delayed persons (Grossman 1983; Patton and Payne 1986). Adaptive behavior refers to whether the person meets the standards required for normalized, independent behavior in personal terms and in an occupational context (Haring and McCormick 1986). This behavior is assessed in terms of the person's age and cultural surroundings. Measuring the adaptive behavior of persons possessing developmental disabilities is particularly important. The possession of skills needed for independent living is a central thrust in the educational programming of these students. Figure 14-1 contains major developmental components of adaptive behavior at particular developmental levels. Major adaptive behavior assessment instruments are discussed later in this chapter.

Culturally Diverse Individuals

Culturally diverse individuals represent a special population for consideration in intelligence and aptitude testing. Although not a handicapped population, culturally diverse children may become disadvantaged if tests are biased against them on the basis of their culture.

The issue of cultural fairness in tests has

Figure 14-1 Developmental Aspects of Adaptive Behavior

I.   *Infancy and Early Childhood*
   A.   Sensory-motor skills
   B.   Development of adequate communication skills
   C.   Self-help and self-care skills
   D.   Development of social skills

II.   *Childhood and Early Adolescence*
   A.   Basic academic skills
   B.   Using reasoning and judgment in dealing with the environment
   C.   Continued development of social skills (same sex and opposite sex)

III. *Late Adolescence and Adulthood*
   A.   Development of vocation
   B.   Development of family
   C.   Social responsibilities

been addressed both legislatively and judicially. PL 94-142 mandates that assessment instruments for the diagnosis and educational placement of students must be culturally fair. In addition, the courts have ruled in various cases that culturally biased tests cannot be used in job placement or in predicting job success. Such judicial and legislative mandates have resulted in attempts to create culturally and linguistically nonbiased intelligence and assessment instruments. A number of these tests are discussed in this chapter.

Testing Persons with Sensory and Motor Impairments

A limited number of intelligence tests can be used with sensory impaired persons. These include the Haptic Intelligence Scale for Adult Blind, the Blind Learning Aptitude Test, and the Hiskey–Nebraska Test of Learning Aptitude. In addition, the verbal and performance scales of the WISC–R have been appropriately modified for sensory impaired individuals.

The Haptic Intelligence Scale for Adult Blind

Overview: The Haptic Intelligence Scale for Adult Blind (HIS) (Shurrager and Shurrager 1964) is a nonverbal scale similar to the performance tests of the WAIS. Four of the HIS tests are modifications of the WAIS performance tests: Block Design, Digit Symbol, Object Assembly, and Object Completion. Additionally, two tests, Bead Arithmetic and Pattern Board, are specifically designed for blind adults. The HIS tests require that test takers possess tactile discrimination and good finger manipulation skills.

Administration and Scoring: Administration and scoring are accomplished using procedures similar to the WAIS (see Chapter 13).

Norms and Standardization Group: The subjects in the standardization group were from four designated geographic regions in the United States. For this group, visual acuity did not exceed 5/200 with correction in the better eye. Both whites and blacks were included in the sample, based on the 1950 census.

Reliability: The test-retest procedure was used over a six-month interval with 136 subjects. Test-retest reliability for the entire scale varies from .70 to .81, depending on the age of the subject. The total HIS shows a split-half (internal consistency) reliability of .95.

Validity: Very little is known about the predictive or concurrent validity of the HIS. However, the verbal IQ of the WAIS is a better predictor of intelligence of blind persons than is the HIS (WAIS, $r = .79$; HIS, $r = .57$). This casts some doubt on the usefulness of the HIS for measuring intelligence of blind individuals.

Summary of the HIS for the Test Consumer: The HIS is a nonverbal test patterned after the WAIS. It is unfortunate that the test authors chose *performance* rather than verbal items to test the intelligence of blind adults. It would seem that performance items are precisely those tasks that are difficult for blind individuals to carry out. Thus, the HIS might artificially underestimate the intelligence of blind individuals, penalizing them for a lack of skill on performance items. Put another way, would a blind person score low on the HIS due to defective intelligence, or due to lack of skill on performance tasks because of blindness? This point is reinforced by the test's requirement of tactile performance skill and the finding that the WAIS verbal tests are better predictors of intelligence than is the HIS.

The Wechsler Scales

With some modifications, the Wechsler scales are sometimes used to test the intelligence of visually and auditorily impaired persons. The verbal scale subtests of the Wechsler tests are used for visually impaired persons; performance scale subtests are used to a greater extent for hearing impaired individuals. It was found that the test performance of blind or visually impaired test takers does not suffer when Braille and large print versions of the Wechsler scales are used (Jordan and Felty 1968; Vander Kolk 1977). On the other hand, available information indicates that deaf children often score lower on the WISC–R than their hearing counterparts. It is not known, however, whether these differences are real or artificially induced by test bias and test conditions (Levine 1974; Sisco and Anderson 1978). Unfortunately, few data exist on the validity of the WISC–R for deaf children.

Blind Learning Aptitude Test

Overview: The Blind Learning Aptitude Test (BLAT) (Newland 1969) is designed for intelligence testing of blind children between the ages of six and twelve. Its author, believing that other available intelligence tests give a biased (and negative) picture of the learning potential of blind individuals, devised the BLAT so that:

1. Items are in bas-relief form of dots and lines.
2. The spatial discrimination needed to decipher these dots and lines is greater than that needed for reading Braille.
3. Only the instructions are verbal.
4. Verbalization by the test taker is kept to a minimum.
5. A variety of test-element patterns have been developed.

The BLAT samples a number of distinct types of behavior including discrimination, generalization and transfer, sequencing, analogies, and pattern and matrix completion.

Administration and Scoring: The BLAT uses a series of training questions and items for the test taker before the actual test is undertaken. This allows the examiner to ensure that the test taker understands the behavior required. The BLAT yields two types of scores: a learning–aptitude test age and a learning–aptitude quotient that is similar to an IQ. The learning test age is defined as the midpoint of an age range earned as a result of performance on the BLAT. The learning quotient is a deviation score with a mean of 100 and a standard deviation of 15 (not 16 as in the deviation IQ of the Stanford–Binet).

Norms and Standardization Group: The BLAT was standardized on 961 blind students who attended either day or residential schools for the blind. The sample was stratified by geographic region, age, racial and ethnic background, sex, and SES, in accordance with the 1960 United States census.

Reliability: The BLAT reports consistency (split-half) and test-retest reliability. Seven months after the original test was administered, retesting was performed for 93 children, aged ten to sixteen (a group older than that for which the test was designed). Test-

retest reliability ranges from .87 to .93. Split-half reliability, reported for 961 children in the norm sample, is .93.

Validity: The validity of the BLAT is only estimated in the test manual; the author asserts that it correlates highly with other tests of intelligence. However, the predictive and concurrent validity of the BLAT must be further assessed and confirmed.

Summary of the BLAT for the Test Consumer: The BLAT is one of the few intelligence tests available for younger blind individuals (ages six to twelve). It is relatively well standardized and constructed. The feature of training students to perform tasks prior to the actual test may be a good idea. On the other hand, it may lead to artificially higher scores due to a practice effect. The test possesses strong reliability, but the test-retest reliability was demonstrated on children somewhat older than those for whom the test was designed. The validity needs further demonstration. Nevertheless, the BLAT is a relatively sound test for measuring the learning aptitude of young blind children.

Hiskey–Nebraska Test of Learning Aptitude

Overview: The Hiskey–Nebraska Test of Learning Aptitude (HNTLA) (Hiskey 1966) is a standardized, individually administered aptitude–intelligence test developed and sampled on both a deaf and a hearing population. It was originally created in 1941, and the current HNTLA is a revision of that earlier test. One of the few available tests that provides norms for deaf children, it is appropriate for use with persons between three and sixteen years of age.

The HNTLA consists of twelve subtests (see Table 14-1) that are basically power, performance tests. Test-taker responses are nonverbal (made by pointing).

Table 14-1 Subtests of the Hiskey–Nebraska Test of Learning Aptitude

1. Bead Patterns (ages 3–10 only): Student copies bead patterns by stringing beads from memory.
2. Memory for Color (ages 3–10 only): Student recalls visually presented series of colors after a short delay period.
3. Picture Identification (ages 3–10 only): Student matches identical pictures.
4. Picture Association (ages 3–10 only): Student matches pictures to other picture pairs based on conceptual relationships.
5. Paper Folding (age 3–10 only): Student folds pieces of paper to reproduce those created by the test giver.
6. Visual Attention Span (all ages): Measures ability to remember the sequence of pictures after a short delay period.
7. Completion of Drawings (all ages): Student isolates the missing parts of drawings and sketches in the missing parts.
8. Memory for Digits (age 11 and above): Student reproduces sequences of visually presented numbers.
9. Puzzle Blocks (age 11 and above): Student assembles disassembled cube into a whole. Timed.
10. Picture Analogies (age 11 and above): Student solves visually presented analogies.
11. Spatial Reasoning (age 11 and above): Student assembles disassembled parts to create whole objects.
12. Block Patterns (all ages): Student builds block patterns from pictorial representations.

Administration and Scoring: Deaf children receive instructions in pantomime; hearing children receive verbal instructions. If verbal instructions are given, norms for hearing children are used. Only examiners familiar with deaf children and well trained in using the HNTLA should administer and score the test. The manual gives specific instructions for establishing rapport with deaf test takers.

A variety of scores are available with the HNTLA. When pantomime instructions are given, norms for the deaf are used. These norms yield a learning age (LA) and learning quotient (LQ) for deaf subjects, based on the median age scores of the subtests. For hearing subjects, a mental age (MA) and IQ are available. The author points out that LQs and IQs are not equivalent and comparable. Furthermore, in assessing the learning aptitude of deaf children, he suggests considering only the LQ.

Norms and Standardization Group: The revised HNTLA was administered in ten states to 1,107 deaf children and 1,101 hearing children, ages two years, six months to seventeen years, five months. The deaf children were enrolled primarily in state schools for the deaf instead of in more mainstreamed settings. No other information is given on the deaf population that made up the norm group. The hearing children were chosen on the basis of parent's occupation and corresponded closely to the 1960 United States census. No further information is given regarding the hearing children.

Reliability: Only split-half reliability (internal consistency) is reported for the HNTLA. These reliabilities are reported for a wide range of chronological ages in the categories of three to ten years and eleven to seventeen years. Split-half reliability for the three-to-ten-year range is .95 for deaf subjects and .93 for hearing subjects. In the eleven-to-seventeen-year range, split-half reliability is .92 for the deaf group and .90 for the hearing students. No study of test-retest reliability was carried out.

Validity: The author reports four types of validity, all correlational: subtest intercorrelations; correlations between age ratings on the subtests and the median LA; correlations between the HNTLA, the Stanford–Binet, and the WISC for hearing children; and correlations with academic performance for deaf children. For the deaf, subtest correlations range from .33 to .74 (ages three to ten) and from .31 to .46 (ages eleven to seventeen). The author reports correlations between the HNTLA, the S–B, and the WISC ranging from .78 to .86, but these are for hearing children only. Very little evidence is offered for test validity with deaf children.

Summary of the HNTLA for the Test Consumer: The HNTLA is one of the few intelligence tests available that has been normed on a deaf population. It is really two tests in one—an intelligence test for hearing and lip reading subjects (with oral instructions) and a test for signing students (with pantomimed instructions).

However, the information provided regarding the standardization groups of the HNTLA is sketchy. The deaf population was enrolled full time in state schools for the deaf. Thus, they constitute a population that differs perhaps from hearing-impaired students enrolled in public schools on a variety of measures, including hearing, social skills, and prior learning experiences. Very little is known about the deaf population on which the test was standardized.

Only split-half reliability is offered, and the validity of the HNTLA has not been adequately demonstrated. Nevertheless, the HNTLA is probably the best available instrument for roughly tapping the cognitive abilities of deaf children.

Tests for Children with Motor or Speech Handicaps

Children with motor or speech handicaps may experience difficulties in responding verbally to intelligence test items and in marking answers on an answer sheet. For these reasons, a number of pictorial, nonverbal intelligence tests have been devised. The respondent need not speak or write; in most cases, simply pointing to the correct response is adequate.

Nonverbal and Pictorial Tests of Intelligence

The tests described here are intelligence tests in that they possess a number of subtests and assess a variety of behaviors that the test authors consider indicative of intellectual ability. However, unlike the intelligence tests discussed in the last two chapters, they use a pictorial, nonverbal response mode for test takers. Four such tests are the Test of Nonverbal Intelligence, the Pictorial Test of Intelligence, the Leiter International Performance Scale, and the Columbia Mental Maturity Scale.

The Test of Nonverbal Intelligence

Overview: The Test of Nonverbal Intelligence (TONI) (Brown, Sherbenou, and Dollar 1982) is one of the newer intelligence tests on the market. It is purported to be language-free and requires no speaking, listening, reading, or writing skills. As such, it is appropriate for a wide range of language impaired individuals and for culturally diverse populations. It is designed for persons from age five through adulthood.

There are two forms of the TONI, each form containing fifty items arranged in spiral omnibus (ascending difficulty) form. The TONI measures intelligence by assessing problem-solving ability, defined as the test taker's ability to identify the relationships between abstract symbols and figures. The test taker's task is to point to the alternative that best fits a missing part to a matrix, pattern, or puzzle. An example of items from the TONI appears in Figure 14-2.

Administration and Scoring: The TONI is relatively easy to administer and score, and a professional requires only a minimum of training. Raw scores are converted to percentile ranks and a special quotient known as the *TONI Quotient*. TONI Quotients are stan-

GOVERNORS STATE UNIVERSITY
UNIVERSITY PARK
IL 60466

Figure 14-2 Sample Items from the TONI

1. *Simple Matching.* All figures share the same number of critical attributes. No differences exist among the figures in the stimulus.

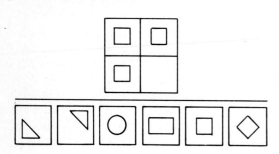

2. *Analogies.* The relationship among the figures in one of the rows or columns is the same as the relationship among the figures in the other rows and columns. The relationship varies in the following ways:

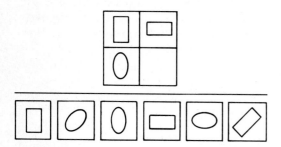

3. *Classification.* The figure in the stimulus is a member of one of the sets of figures in the response alternatives.

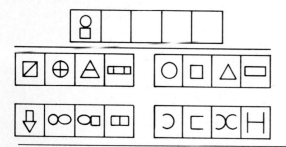

4. *Intersections.* A new figure is formed by joining parts of figures in the rows and columns.

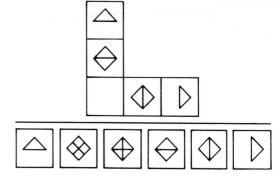

5. *Progressions.* The same change continues between or among figures.

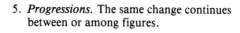
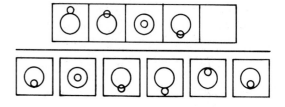

Source: L. Brown, R. Sherbenou, and S. Dollar (1982). *Test of Nonverbal Intelligence* (Austin, TX: Pro-Ed). Used by permission.

dard scores with a mean of 100 and a standard deviation of 15 (similar to IQ scores).

Norms and Standardization Group: The TONI was standardized on 1,929 individuals residing in twenty-eight states. They ranged in age from five years through eighty-five years, eleven months, and were stratified on the basis of sex, race and ethnic background, geographic demographics, geographic location, and occupation and/or parent's occupation. It should be noted that 45 percent of the norm sample lived in Texas and Kansas; the largest percentage of persons from any other state was only 9 percent. Racial, ethnic, sex, and geographic demographics approximated the 1980 United States census.

Reliability: Only internal consistency and alternate form reliability are reported in the test manual. Using 400 cases drawn randomly from the standardization pool, internal consistency reliability exceeds .90. Alternate form reliability approximates .90. No test-retest reliability was reported for the test.

Validity: The manual reports eight studies of concurrent validity—three with normal persons and five with mentally retarded students. Validity coefficients generally exceed .80. The TONI claims construct validity by indicating that it discriminates appropriately between mentally retarded and nonretarded persons.

Summary of the TONI for the Test Consumer: The TONI is a relatively new and innovative pictorial test of nonverbal intelligence. No verbal skills, such as listening, reading, writing, or speaking, are required. Items were chosen for the two forms with meticulous care.

However, the test only assesses one type of intelligence—problem solving. The geographic location of residence of the standardization group is nonrepresentative (although it does approximate the United States population on other variables). No test-retest reliability is offered, but it does possess relatively strong validity. The test holds promise as a nonverbal measure of intelligence, especially if used as a screening instrument.

The Pictorial Test of Intelligence

Overview: The Pictorial Test of Intelligence (PTI) (French 1964) is similar to the Stanford–Binet test. It allows the test taker to respond by pointing and requires only enough English language skill to understand simple instructions. The child responds by pointing to one of four pictures on a card in response to a question. There are six subtests of the scale arranged in order of difficulty (see Table 14-2). The test is appropriate for children age three to eight.

Administration and Scoring: The PTI is scored by totaling the correct items and converting these to MAs and deviation IQs

Table 14-2 Subtests of the Pictorial Test of Intelligence

1. Picture Vocabulary: Assesses verbal vocabulary. Child identifies the picture that best fits a word concept read by the examiner.
2. Form Discrimination: Assesses perceptual organization. Child is shown increasingly complex drawings and must match each to one of four drawings presented.
3. Information and Comprehension: Assesses knowledge, understanding, and verbal comprehension. Child points to pictures in response to statements read by the examiner.
4. Similarities: Child identifies which one of four pictures presented does not "belong" with the three others.
5. Size and Number: Assesses quantitative concepts: Child counts, computes, and completes word problems.
6. Immediate Recall: Assesses short-term memory. Examiner presents stimulus card for five seconds, removes it, and asks the child to identify it from memory.

(mean of 100, standard deviation of 16). No basal or ceiling is obtained. All test items are administered regardless of whether items are answered correctly or incorrectly. None of the subtests is timed.

Norms and Standardization Group: Standardization was based on 1,830 children selected at random and representative of the 1960 census. The racial and ethnic background of the students was not taken into account.

Reliability: Both internal consistency (split-half) and test-retest reliability are reported in the manual. Test-retest reliability ranges from .90 to .96, with a six-week retesting interval. Internal consistency reliability ranges from .83 to .88.

Validity: The test author assumes that content validity of the PTI is apparent because items in the PTI and other valid tests of intelligence are similar. No firm validity data are presented, although the author does present correlations between the PTI and its predecessor, the North Central Individual Test of Mental Ability, and the Stanford–Binet and WISC–R. The test author also makes a claim for construct validity by regarding an increase in PTI scores as a function of occupational level of the child's parents. However, all the logic regarding the validity of the PTI is somewhat faulty, and the test's validity remains to be demonstrated.

Summary of the PTI for the Test Consumer: The PTI is an individually administered, pictorial test of intelligence requiring minimal receptive verbal abilities. It is appropriate for children aged three to eight.

The six subtests of the PTI may be useful in assessing the cognitive ability of young children. However, the lack of basal and ceiling measures means that the entire test must be administered to students, regardless of how they perform on individual items. This can lead to fatigue and decreased motivation, especially with young children.

The fact that racial and ethnic backgrounds were not taken into account in forming the norm group may be problematic for the testing of culturally diverse students. Likewise, whereas the reliability of the instrument is high, its validity has not yet been adequately demonstrated. Nevertheless, the PTI holds promise as a nonverbal test of intelligence for relatively young children.

Columbia Mental Maturity Scale

Overview: The Columbia Mental Maturity Scale (CMMS) (Burgemeister, Blum, and Lorge 1972) is an individually administered, nonverbal intelligence instrument of general reasoning ability. The scale consists of ninety-two pictorial and figure classification items arranged in a series of eight overlapping levels. Each level contains between fifty-one and sixty-five items, and the child is given items appropriate for his or her CA. Each item consists of a series of three to five drawings presented on a large card. The child is asked to select the drawing that does not belong with the others. For younger children, differences between the items are in terms of color, size, and form. For older children, the items require the test taker to recognize more subtle and abstract differences between the drawings. The scale is appropriate for use with children from three years, six months to ten years of age.

Administration and Scoring: The CMMS is easy to administer, and testing time is fifteen to twenty minutes. Items are not timed. Scoring is also relatively straightforward, with complete instructions given in the manual.

Results of the CMMS are expressed in terms of a maturity index, an age deviation score, percentile scores, and stanines. The maturity index is comparable to the MA, but it indicates ranges rather than a specific mental age. It is a relatively gross indicator of MA and may not be as useful as that concept.

Norms and Standardization Group: The 1972 standardization is a vast improvement over the 1954 and 1959 versions of the test. The norms for the CMMS are based on 2,600 children, carefully selected to control for parental occupation, race, and geographic location. Although the sample is representative of the 1960 census, no information is given regarding sex differences of the norm group. The norm group contains no handicapped students.

Reliability: Both internal consistency and test-retest reliability are assessed. Split-half reliability for each age group ranges from .85 to .91. Test-retest reliability, assessed seven to ten days after the original testing, ranges from .84 to .86.

Validity: The validity data reported in the manual consist of correlations between the CMMS and scores on the Stanford Achievement Test. These correlations range from .31 to .61. Correlations between the CMMS, the Otis–Lennon, and the S–B ranged from .62 to .69.

Summary of the CMMS for the Test Consumer: The latest revision of the CMMS is much improved over previous versions. It nonverbally tests intellectual ability while requiring no verbal interaction or responses. Test reliability is strong, and its validity is moderate. The test user should heed the author's advice and use it as a quick screening test, prior to undertaking more diagnostic, indepth evaluation. In this case, the CMMS can be an extremely useful instrument.

Culture-Fair Tests

All the tests we have discussed so far presuppose that the test taker belongs to the dominant culture of the United States. The tests discussed in this section are hypothesized to be *culture-fair,* that is, they can be administered to culturally diverse individuals with the assumption that the test takers would not be penalized for their cultural divergence.

It should be pointed out that the creation of a completely culture-fair or culture-free test is probably impossible. Rather, these tests have attempted to minimize blatantly obvious cultural effects by eliminating or decreasing the degree of culture-specific language required, as well as the cultural content contained in test items. The following three tests represent attempts to gain a truer, less biased measure of intellectual functioning for culturally diverse individuals.

System of Multicultural Pluralistic Assessment

Overview: The System of Multicultural Pluralistic Assessment (SOMPA) (Mercer 1979a) is a unique instrument in the field of educational assessment. Jane Mercer, its creator, had asserted for a number of years that intelligence tests were biased and unfair toward culturally diverse test takers. She also expressed dissatisfaction with the types of information that intelligence tests traditionally yield. Considering these criticisms, Mercer created the SOMPA, a test that assesses students from a variety of viewpoints and that contains a number of components.

The SOMPA is intended to be a culturally fair, nondiscriminatory test. It is designed for schoolchildren between the ages of five and eleven. Data on the test taker are provided along three different dimensions or models: the *medical,* the *social system,* and the *pluralistic.* The medical model identifies biological problems, disease, and sensory and motor impairments. The social system model assesses the extent to which the child meets the expectations of the social situation in which he or she is operating. The pluralistic model measures the child's intelligence and learning potential.

Table 14-3   Models of the SOMPA

Medical Model

Attempts to discover if pathological conditions are interfering with the child's functioning.

Social System Model

Is the student performing expected roles? Is the student performing commensurate with age and sociocultural group?

Pluralistic Model

How intelligent is the child? What is the child's learning potential within the parameters of the child's cultural and socioeconomic background?

The child is assessed in each model (see Table 14-3 for a listing of the assessments in each model). The medical model uses six measures that assess physical dexterity, visual–motor skills, sensory acuity, and health his-

tory. The social system model consists of two instruments: the Adaptive Behavior Inventory for Children (ABIC), which contains six scaled indices, and the School Functioning Level (SFL), which is measured by the WISC–R. Finally, the pluralistic model uses the Estimated Learning Potential (ELP) and the Sociocultural Scales, which contain four scaled indexes each for the child's own ethnic group and the majority school culture. Table 14-4 contains the scaled score subtests for tests given in the three models.

Perhaps the most innovative tests included in the SOMPA are the Adaptive Behavior Inventory for Children (ABIC) and the Estimated Learning Potential (ELP). Mercer was extremely concerned about students she labeled "six-hour retardates" (Mercer 1979b)—students who were labeled and classified as mentally retarded in school but

---

Table 14-4   Scaled Subtests for Tests in the Three Models of the SOMPA

Medical Model

1. Physical Dexterity Tasks
   a. Ambulation
   b. Equilibrium
   c. Placement
   d. Fine-motor Sequencing
   e. Finger–Tongue Dexterity
   f. Involuntary Movement
   g. Physical Dexterity
2. Visual Acuity
   a. Uncorrected Vision
   b. Corrected Vision
3. Auditory Acuity
   a. Uncorrected Hearing
   b. Corrected Hearing
4. Health History
   a. Prenatal–Postnatal
   b. Trauma
   c. Disease and Illness
   d. Vision
   e. Hearing

Social System Model

1. ABIC
   a. Family
   b. Community

   c. Peer Relations
   d. Nonacademic School Roles
   e. Earner–Consumer
   f. Self-Maintenance
   g. ABIC Average Scaled Score
2. School Functioning Level (SFL) (WISC–R)
   a. Verbal
   b. Performance
   c. Full Scale

Pluralistic Model

1. ELP
   a. Verbal
   b. Performance
   c. Full Scale
2. Sociocultural Scales
   Own Ethnic Group
   a. Family Size
   b. Family Structure
   c. Socioeconomic Status
   d. Urban Accommodation
   School Culture
   a. Family Size
   b. Family Structure
   c. Socioeconomic Status
   d. Urban Acculturation

who functioned at acceptable levels in their outside, daily environment. Mercer decided to devise an assessment system to measure the adequacy of children's operations in their environment. Thus, the ABIC measures such behaviors as earner–consumer potential and self-maintenance.

The ELP test attempts to equalize scores on the WISC–R in terms of the child's social, ethnic, and cultural group. The ELP takes the position that in assessment the child should be compared only with children of his or her cultural group. The ELP accomplishes this by examining the child's WISC–R score in a 2 × 2 factorial design: ethnic group and sociocultural group. The child's score is then compared to children of a norm group in a comparable category or cell. If the student's ABIC, school-functioning level, and ELP all fall below the at-risk category, the student would be considered a candidate for special education class placement.

Norms and Standardization Group: There are eight different tests in the SOMPA, all of which were standardized on the same group of schoolchildren. The total sample in the standardization group consisted of 2,085 children, with 100 children of each sex at age levels from five to eleven. The total sample contains approximately equal numbers of white, black, and Hispanic students. A sample representative of the population of California was used.

Reliability: In the medical model, reliabilities of the six physical dexterity tests are reported using split-half calculations. Estimates of reliability range from .61 (finger–tongue dexterity) to .94 (placement). Reliabilities for different ethnic groups are also reported, and they range from .65 to .74. Reliability estimates for the other medical measures are not reported.

The social system model reports split-half reliabilities for each level of each subscale of the ABIC. Reliability is relatively low. Additionally, the standard deviations of scores on the ABIC are erroneously calculated, making the reliability reporting invalid. The reliability of the ELP in the pluralistic model is not discussed.

Validity: Mercer claims that each model of the SOMPA was validated separately and thus must be considered separately.

There are problems with the validity of the medical model. First, Mercer's logic as to how the measures assessed in the medical model should be correlated with each other is faulty. For example, on what basis should hearing well and being overweight be correlated? This arrangement is illogical.

Content validity is equally shaky. No evidence is offered in the SOMPA that the medical model contains content validity and that it adequately screens for physical abnormalities and defects. Finally, there is no proof that the percentile ranks that Mercer designates as being at risk are valid ones. Are children who fall below her identified percentile really at risk? Are children who place above that percentile rank really normal? In short, the medical model has serious problems demonstrating its validity.

Because the ABIC in the social system model is such a central part of the SOMPA, its validity should be well tested and proven. This is not the case. The SOMPA manual does less than a minimally acceptable job in demonstrating the content validity of the ABIC.

The pluralistic model depends on the ELP. However, there are fundamental problems with the validity of the ELP. In fact, it may even be based on faulty logic and evidence presented in other available research literature. For example, the manual often contradicts its theoretical underpinnings, tends to ignore research literature that shows that environmental factors can greatly affect intelligence, and omits key statistical and research proof of its claims. Consequently, the validity of the pluralistic model is highly suspect.

Summary of the SOMPA for the Test Consumer: The SOMPA represents an attempt to provide a multicultural, multiprospective framework for understanding a child's intellectual functioning. As a first attempt, it should be applauded. Children should be viewed as complex physical–social organisms who operate in a complex world of their own and the majority culture. However, the SOMPA contains many serious problems. The standardization group came entirely from California, making the norms suspect for children outside of California who take the test. The reliabilities of the tests and models are either unacceptably low or not reported in the test manual. The validity of the test and the models is seriously in doubt and often based on faulty data and illogical arguments.

At best, the SOMPA should be considered an experimental instrument that needs great improvement before it is accepted in the marketplace. Considering its cost and the time involved in administration and scoring, it may not be the best choice at this time for the test consumer.

The Culture-Fair Intelligence Test

Overview: The Culture Fair Intelligence Test (CFIT) (Cattell 1950, 1973; Cattell and Cattell 1963) actually consists of three scales. Scale 1 is designed for children aged four to eight, Scale 2 for children aged eight to fourteen, and Scale 3 for persons aged fourteen to adult. The scales have been designed to eliminate, as much as possible, the effects of verbal fluency, cultural climate, and educational level on test performance. The tests have no verbal content and require examinees to perceive relationships in shapes and figures. Scale 1 consists entirely of figure analogies and figural reasoning; Scales 2 and 3 also contain series, classification, and matrix items.

Table 14-5 Subtests of the Three Scales of the Culture-Fair Intelligence Test

Scale 1

1. Substitution: Student associates symbols with pictures and copies them onto paper.
2. Classification: Student identifies which one of five pictures is different from the other four.
3. Mazes: Student traces paths out of mazes.
4. Selecting Named Objects: Student identifies pictures of words read aloud. Test of receptive language. Not a culture-fair subtest.
5. Following Directions: Student follows verbal directions.
6. Wrong Pictures: What is wrong with these pictures?
7. Riddles: Solving riddles.
8. Similarities: Student identifies which of several pictures is exactly like the target picture.

Scales 2 and 3

1. Series: Student is given a sequence of figures in a series. Student chooses from four alternatives which figure comes next in that series.
2. Classification: Student identifies which one of five pictures is different from the other four.
3. Matrices: Student must identify the missing element from a matrix.
4. Conditions: Student is given a figure in which a dot is placed in a certain relationship. Student must identify the response figure in which the dot is in the same relationship.

Table 14-5 lists and briefly describes the subtests for the three scales. Figure 14-3 contains a few sample items from the CFIT.

Administration and Scoring: Parts of Scale 1 can be group administered. However, Scales 2 and 3 must be individually administered. Scale 1 takes approximately twenty-two minutes to administer; Scales 2 and 3 take twelve and one-half minutes each. Tests are timed.

On Scale 1, raw scores are transformed to MAs and ratio IQs, with a mean of 100 and a relatively large standard deviation of 20. Ratio IQs can be converted to percentiles.

This standard deviation of 20 for IQ scores of the CFIT may be confusing for test consum-

Figure 14-3   Sample Items from the Culture-Fair Intelligence Test

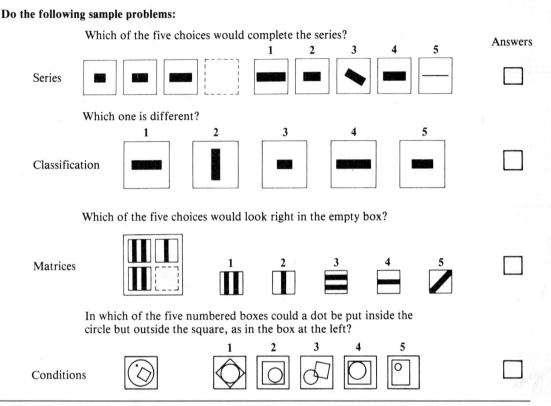

Do the following sample problems:

Which of the five choices would complete the series?

Series

Which one is different?

Classification

Which of the five choices would look right in the empty box?

Matrices

In which of the five numbered boxes could a dot be put inside the circle but outside the square, as in the box at the left?

Conditions

Source: Copyright © 1949, 1957, 1960 by the Institute for Personality and Ability Testing, Inc. All rights reserved. Reproduced by permission.

ers accustomed to standard deviations of 15 or 16 for intelligence tests. This difference in standard deviation means that whereas a score of 84 on the S–B is one standard deviation below the mean and a score of 116 is one standard deviation above, analogous scores on the CFIT would be 80 and 120. It is the test user's responsibility to be aware of the differences in the standard deviation of the two tests when interpreting results from the S–B and the CFIT. Figure 14-4 shows expectancies of population falling between standard deviation units on the S–B and the CFIT, given assumptions of a normal population.

For Scales 2 and 3, raw scores can be con-

verted to MAs and to *three different* IQs, each having a mean of 100 but different standard deviations of 16, 24, or 24.4. These different scales with their different standard deviations often make interpretation of the CFIT difficult.

Norms and Standardization Group: A test purporting to be culturally fair must be meticulous in describing its norm sample. Unfortunately, the CFIT does not do this. The manual does report that Scale 1 was normed on more than 400 American and British students, whereas Scale 2 was standardized on 4,328 boys and girls residing in America and Great Britain. Scale 3 was standardized on 3,140 American

Figure 14-4   Expectancies of the Population Achieving Scores on the Stanford–Binet and the Culture-Free Intelligence Test (Based on the Standard Deviations of the Two Instruments)

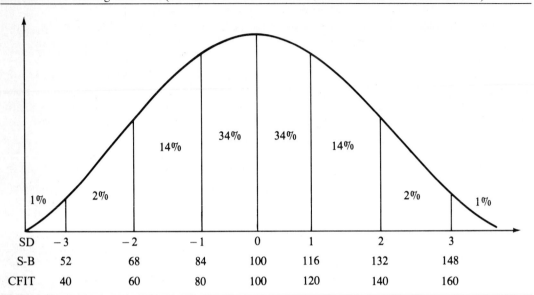

SD	−3	−2	−1	0	1	2	3
S-B	52	68	84	100	116	132	148
CFIT	40	60	80	100	120	140	160

students equally divided among four socioeconomic classes of high school students and young working adults. No other demographic information is given regarding norm group characteristics.

Reliability: Reliability is reported for the separate scales. The test-retest reliability of Scale 1 was assessed on only fifty-seven children who were enrolled in a Head Start program in the United States. No test interval is reported. Reliability ranges from .57 to .71.

For Scale 2, internal consistency, equivalent form, and test-retest reliability are reported. Internal consistency reliability was carried out on 102 female Job Corps applicants in the United States. It ranges from .77 to .81 for Form A and from .71 to .76 for Form B. Equivalent form reliability with students of various ages ranges from .58 to .72. Finally, test-retest reliability for Scale 2 is .82 for 200 American high school students and .95 for 450 eleventh-year British students. No test interval is given for Scale 2, and no reli-

ability for Scale 2 is available for students under eleven years of age.

Reliability for Scale 3 is given only in terms of equivalent form and internal consistency. Internal consistency reliability for Scale 3 ranges from .51 to .68, and equivalent form reliability ranges from .32 to .68.

Validity: Validity information for the CFIT is sketchy and poorly conceptualized. The authors attempt to analyze performance on each subtest in terms of the *g* factor of intelligence, but this does little to prove the validity of the test as a culturally fair instrument.

The authors do correlate performance on the CFIT with that of underprivileged children on the Stanford-Binet with a resulting correlation of *r* = .46. Likewise, they try to validate the instrument using a sample of children from Hong Kong, Taiwan, and mainland China. Correlations of subtests and areas of intelligence measured by the CFIT correlate between .22 and .32 for American and Asian children.

Summary of the CFIT for the Test Consumer: The CFIT was one of the first attempts to assess the intellectual functioning of culturally different children. As such, it should be commended. Nevertheless, it possesses some severe deficiencies. It is difficult to administer and even more difficult to score and interpret. Part of the test is group administered, and part is individually administered. Its reliability information is sketchy, and its validity information must be presented more clearly and explicitly for the reader. Finally, the norms are inadequate, having been standardized entirely on a British and American population with no information offered about the demographic characteristics of the norm groups. The CFIT should be used with extreme caution and skepticism as to its interpretation.

Other Culture-Fair Measures

Learning Potential Assessment Device

The Learning Potential Assessment Device (LPAD) (Feuerstein 1979) represents one of the newest attempts to assess intelligence and learning aptitude in a culturally unbiased manner. The LPAD begins with the assumption that so-called cultural deprivation occurs because of a lack of "mediated learning" by culturally diverse students. Mediated learning refers to the process of teachers and other adults interposing themselves between direct environmental experiences and the student. The teacher then functions by "framing, selecting, focusing, and feeding back environmental experiences in such a way as to produce (in the child) appropriate learning sets and habits" (p. 71). The opposite of mediated learning is direct learning, in which the student learns material through firsthand experience with the environment. Feuerstein asserts that most school learning is mediated rather than direct.

The LPAD attempts to measure how much the student can benefit from presented learning experiences. With the LPAD, the tester also becomes a teacher. First, the child attempts to solve nonverbal reasoning problems. The tester then helps the student and provides some sophisticated strategies for solving the problems (mediated learning). The tasks are then provided again without coaching, and the tester judges the extent to which the student is able to incorporate and use the mediated strategies.

Some key aspects of the LPAD should be emphasized. First, because the tester/teacher interacts with the student in presenting learning strategies, there is a strong verbal component to the test. This verbal component somewhat dilutes the claim of the LPAD to be culture-fair because the verbal concepts and language used by the administrator will certainly be culturally loaded. Second, while the LPAD attempts to measure the degree to which the student benefits from strategy instruction, it also measures such things as receptiveness to criticism and willingness to try suggestions made by others. If a child does not incorporate the strategies suggested by the teacher, is it due to a lack of comprehension or to an unwillingness to accept the mediator's suggestions? We all know people who view suggestions from others as criticism and who are basically unwilling to incorporate suggestions. Such people might perform poorly on the LPAD.

In summary, the LPAD is an innovative and interesting instrument for examining learning aptitude. However, it is essentially a clinical–experimental instrument that yields descriptive rather than quantitative information. It should be used in combination with other intelligence and aptitude measures.

A Final Word on Culture-Fair Intelligence Tests

Culture-fair intelligence tests represent worthy attempts to make intelligence testing fair for culturally diverse individuals. These attempts should be praised for adhering to the goal of fair and unbiased assessment for all. Nevertheless, the completely culture-fair test has not yet been created. All tests, even those that profess to be culture-fair, possess a degree of cultural bias. Perhaps the creation of a completely culture-fair test is impossible. What we ought to be searching for is a test that does not severely penalize minority test takers for their environmental experiences.

It is probably true that most of the currently available culture-fair tests are flawed in design, standardization, technical quality, reliability, and validity. Some are based on a faulty premise that a narrow sample of behavior (e.g., completing spatial analogies) represents an adequate measure of intelligence. Thus, until a truly culture-fair test that is theoretically and technically sound is created and tested, the test consumer is advised to use intelligence tests that are more in the mainstream. At the same time, the test consumer must make sure that such tests do not unduly discriminate against minority and culturally diverse children.

Tests of Adaptive Behavior

We hear the statement that people must adapt to their environment. In fact, the scientific theory of evolution holds that successful organisms (ones that survive) are precisely those that adapt to their environment. But what constitutes adaptive behavior?

In special education, adaptive behavior refers to the ability of individuals to operate successfully in an age-appropriate manner within the confines of their culture. This adaptive behavior contains two provisions, age appropriateness and cultural appropriateness; both of these concepts are important.

Age appropriateness refers to the fact that the individuals behave in ways comparable to age-related peers. We expect six-year-old

children to behave differently than sixteen-year-old adolescents. Consider, for example, two children. One is "twelve going on twenty" and the other is "eight going on six." This statement implies that the first child acts more maturely than age-related peers (at least in some aspects of functioning), and the second child sometimes behaves like younger children.

People are also expected to act in ways that comply with the cultural demands of the society in which they live and operate. For example, in our modern, technological society we expect adults to perform in occupational and personal ways that guarantee independent, normalized living. In our culture, adaptive behavior constitutes those occupational and personal skills and behaviors that allow for independent living and cultural acceptance.

A word of caution, however. Whereas in most areas of assessment we measure a person's behavior directly, in assessing adaptive behavior we often must assess performance indirectly, by conducting interviews or questioning third parties familiar with the client. As we have seen, third-person assessment possesses an error component in terms of accuracy and reliability of information gathered. For this reason, client data gathered from a third person should be validated through another independent source before the information is accepted as valid.

Cain–Levine Social Competency Scale

Overview: The Cain–Levine Social Competency Scale (Cain, Levine, and Elzey 1963) is an instrument designed primarily for moderately mentally retarded persons between the chronological ages of five years and thirteen years, eleven months. The scale is based on the assumption that the person's development in social competency is reflected by (1) an increase in "manipulative abilities," (2) movement from other-directed to self-initiated behavior, (3) a change from self-oriented to other-oriented behavior, and (4) an increasing ability to make him- or herself understood. To that end, the Cain–Levine consists of four subscales: Self-Help, Initiative, Social Skills, and Communication. The four subscales contain a total of forty-four items. Table 14-6 contains a brief description of the four subscales.

Administration and Scoring: The Cain–Levine uses the interview technique to gain information about the client. The interviewee is someone familiar with the client in the four areas assessed by the subscales. Each of the forty-four activities queried is followed by four or five descriptive statements representing varying degrees of independence. Respondents are asked to rate the client on these measures, and the interviewer is allowed probe or follow-up questions. The entire scale takes twenty-five to seventy-five minutes to administer.

Table 14-6   The Four Subscales of the Cain–Levine Social Competency Scale

Self-Help

Assesses the person's skills in areas of dressing, washing, eating, and assisting in chores around the house. (14 items)

Initiative

Assesses the extent to which the person engages in activities without direction. Areas assessed include dressing, toileting, completing tasks, hanging up clothes, and offering assistance to others. (10 items)

Social Skills

Assesses the person's interpersonal skills. Items include helping others, engaging in social activities, playing with others, and telephone skills. (10 items)

Communication

Assesses how well the person communicates wants and needs. Includes expressive language skills, idea and speech clarity, and ability to relate objects to actions. (10 items)

Of the total items, thirty-eight are rated by the respondent on a four-point scale and six are rated on a five-point scale. For each item a rating of one represents the lowest possible score, and a four or five the highest possible score. The raw scores are summed, and the total score is converted to percentile ranks. Five norm tables are provided for this purpose.

Norms and Standardization Group: The Cain–Levine was standardized on 716 moderately (then known as *trainable*) mentally retarded persons whose CAs ranged from five through thirteen years of age. Children aged eight and over were enrolled in public school in California. Names of children aged five years to seven years, eleven months were obtained from public school districts and from parents. Children in the standardization group tended to be overrepresented for lower socioeconomic status. The corresponding range of IQs was 25 to 59. With the exception of the five-year-old level, norms are listed at two-year intervals.

Reliability: Split-half reliability ranges from .75 to .91. Additionally, test-retest reliability, assessed over a three-week interval period, is .98 for the entire test and over all age groups. Three of the four subtests possess a test-retest reliability exceeding .90.

Validity: Validity of the Cain–Levine is based on item analysis and on correlation of the instrument with MA and CA. Items were selected after examination of curriculum guides designed for moderately mentally retarded students and consultation with experts in educating moderately mentally retarded persons. The scale correlates approximately .50 with CA but does not correlate well with MA (ranging from .09 to .30).

Summary of the Cain–Levine for the Test Consumer: The Cain–Levine is an easily administered scale that possesses reasonable technical quality. However, the instrument was standardized entirely on a sample residing in California, and this may affect its generalization to persons residing in other states. It is perhaps better suited for primary and younger children than for older children. The norms allow for comparisons with mentally retarded children at comparable levels of intelligence. The scale is perhaps best used as a screening instrument or a pretest and later a posttest of social competency progress after a unit of instruction. A distinct disadvantage is that the scale is not diagnostic or criterion-referenced, and it contains no objectives useful for educational programming of moderately mentally retarded children. For these purposes, other instruments may be more appropriate.

AAMD Adaptive Behavior Scale–School Edition

Overview: The AAMD Adaptive Behavior Scale (ABS–SE) (Lambert and Windmiller 1981) is a revision of the original ABS (Nihra, Foster, Shellhaas, and Leland 1969) designed in 1969 for use with institutionalized persons. The ABS–SE is designed to measure personal independence and adaptive and maladaptive behavior of mentally retarded children aged three to sixteen years. It consists of ninety-five items clustered into twenty-four domains. Table 14-7 contains a listing and some brief descriptions of the domains assessed by the ABS–SE.

Administration and Scoring: The ABS–SE can be administered as a first-person or third-person (interview) assessment. Third-party assessment is recommended if the informant's primary language is not English or if reading skills are below average. Although no evidence exists indicating that the accuracy of information differs between first-party and third-party administration, at least some of the ABS–SE should probably be completed under the third-party procedure.

The item format is of four types: items that involved selecting the one best response; items requiring the selection of all applicable statements from a pool of five or six responses; items requiring the selection of all applicable statements from a pool, with the number selected subtracted from the number in the pool; and items requiring a response indicating the frequency at which a given behavior occurs. These four item types are interspersed throughout the fifteen-page administration booklet, and the test administrator must be careful to solicit the proper type of response from the informant. Most items are written in behavioral terms, but some items are behaviorally vague (e.g., Eats too slow or too fast). The manual suggests that ratings be obtained, whenever possible, from both teachers and parents as a validation check.

The ABS–SE yields three types of scores: domain, factor, and comparison scores. Domain scores are the summation of all the items within a given domain; the factor score is the summation of the domain scores within a given factor. Comparison scores are a weighted summation of three factor scores: Personal Self-Sufficiency, Community Self-Sufficiency, and Personal-Social Responsibility. Factor scores can be converted into an instructionally useful diagnostic profile, but the steps in accomplishing this are laborious and potentially confusing. Scores can be compared to regular (nonretarded), mildly mentally retarded, and moderately mentally retarded reference groups.

Norms and Standardization Group: The ABS–SE was standardized on 6,523 persons, aged three to seventeen, who resided in California and Florida. A significant portion of the sample came from the original ABS. Prior to standardization, individuals in the sample were classified into one of three groups: regular (nonretarded), educable mentally retarded (mildly mentally retarded), or trainable mentally retarded (moderately mentally retarded).

Table 14-7 Domains and Factors Included in the AAMD Adaptive Behavior Scale

Part I (10 Domains)
1. Independent Functioning Factors:
   a. Eating
   b. Toileting
   c. Personal Cleanliness
   d. Appearance (posture and clothing)
   e. Care of Clothing
   f. Dressing and Undressing
   g. Travel (sense of direction and use of public transportation)
   h. Independent Functioning
2. Physical Development
   a. Sensory Functioning
   b. Motor Development
3. Economic Activity
   a. Money Handling
   b. Shopping
4. Language Development
   a. Expression (prelinguistic communication, articulation, word usage, use of complex sentences, and writing)
   b. Comprehension (understanding complex sentences and reading)
   c. Social Language
5. Numbers and Time
   a. Understanding Concepts of Numbers and Time
6. Domestic Activity
   a. Cleaning
   b. Food Preparation and Serving
   c. Other Domestic Activity
7. Vocational Activity
   a. Performing Jobs Safely and Reliably

8. Self-Direction
   a. Initiative
   b. Perseverance (attention and persistence)
   c. Use of Leisure Time
9. Responsibility
   a. Care of Personal Items
10. Socialization
   a. Appropriate and Inappropriate Social Behaviors

Part II (14 Domains)
11. Violent and Destructive Behavior
   a. Personal and Property Damage
12. Antisocial Behavior
   a. Disruptive and Inconsiderate Behavior
13. Rebellious Behavior
   a. Disobedience and Insubordination
14. Untrustworthy Behavior
   a. Lying and Stealing Behavior
15. Withdrawal
   a. Inactivity
   b. Withdrawal
   c. Shyness
16. Stereotyped Behavior and Odd Mannerisms
17. Inappropriate Interpersonal Manners
18. Unacceptable Vocal Habits
19. Unacceptable or Eccentric Habits
20. Self-Abusive Behavior
21. Hyperactive Tendencies
22. Sexually Aberrant Behavior
   a. Masturbation
   b. Homosexuality
   c. Social/Sexual Inappropriate Behavior
23. Psychological Disturbance
24. Use of Medication

Separate norms are provided for the three reference groups for students three to seventeen years of age. However, there are no norms for mildly mentally retarded students aged three to six or for regular students aged sixteen to seventeen.

Reliability. Reliability information is quite limited, with only internal consistency reliability reported for each factor. Reliabilities range from .71 to .97. The omission of other types of reliability, such as test-retest, is unfor-

tunate. Their inclusion would help to demonstrate the technical quality of the instrument.

Validity. Two types of validity information are presented on the ABS–SE: information on the relationship between adaptive behavior scores and scores on intelligence tests, and data on the predictive power of the ABS–SE in identifying mentally retarded from nonretarded children. Regarding intelligence, most of the twenty-one domains possessed low to moderate correlations with IQ test performance. In terms of capability to identify regular, mildly mentally retarded, and moderately mentally retarded children, the authors reported that the test did an excellent job of discriminating between regular and mentally retarded persons but a much weaker job of discriminating between mildly and moderately mentally retarded persons.

Summary of the ABS–SE for the Test Consumer: Overall, the ABS–SE is a superior adaptive behavior scale. It is diagnostic in scope, offers suggestions for instructional remediation and programming, and yields a great deal of useful information about the student. The inclusion of the diagnostic profile and an instructional planning profile is helpful to educational professionals seeking programming suggestions for mentally retarded students. The ABS–SE is well developed, and although its technical quality is only moderate, it is better than many instruments currently available. The instrument is considered useful for both educational professionals and parents and is recommended for test consumer use.

Adaptive Behavior Inventory for Children

Overview: The Adaptive Behavior Inventory for Children (ABIC) (Mercer and Lewis 1977) is a standardized parental interview instrument that assesses the adaptive behavior of children from culturally diverse backgrounds. The test is part of the SOMPA battery developed by Jane Mercer, but the ABIC can be purchased separately. English and Spanish versions of the instrument are available.

The ABIC consists of 242 questions in six scales. The first thirty-five questions are asked of all respondents. The remaining questions are asked depending on the student's age. The six subscales of the ABIC consist of Family, Community, Peer Relations, Nonacademic School Roles, Earner–Consumer, and Self-Maintenance.

Administration and Scoring: The information for administration and scoring of the instrument is straightforward and adequately described in the test manual. A record form includes examples of age calculation and other scoring procedures for persons unfamiliar with the instrument.

The person being interviewed chooses from five possible responses for each question. These include:

0 (Latent Role): indicates that the student does not yet engage in that activity
1 (Emergent Role): indicates that the student infrequently engages in that behavior or activity
2 (Mastered Role): indicates frequent participation with little or no supervision.

Additionally, the respondent can answer that he or she has no knowledge of the student's ability to perform the activity or that the student has not had the opportunity to engage in the target behavior. There are also twenty-four truthfulness questions deliberately placed at inappropriate mastery age levels throughout the interview. These items alert the interviewer to the potential for unreliable information due to lying or a misunderstanding of questions by the person being interviewed. The administration of the entire test takes approximately forty to fifty minutes.

The ABIC yields a detailed profile based on scaled scores for the six areas assessed. A total average score is also plotted. The lowest 3 percent of scores of the profile distribution is labeled "At Risk" (needing remediation or prescription).

Norms and Standardization Group: The ABIC was standardized on 2,085 interviews: 696 black, 690 Hispanic, and 699 white respondents. The students on whom the interviews were based all resided in California. No evidence is presented that the standardization group was representative for socioeconomic status or other key variables.

Reliability: Reliability of the ABIC is based on split-half measures. Results are provided for the total score and for each ethnic group at each age level, from five to eleven years. Total score reliabilities for the entire standardization sample and for each ethnic group are .95 or higher. However, test-retest reliability—an important type of reliability in interview scales—is not reported.

Validity: The test authors argue that the ABIC should not be judged in terms of correlations with teacher judgments, school performance, or achievement tests. Rather, the validity of the test should depend on its interrater reliability. This is unacceptable. First, the measures of validity that the authors reject are the precise ones traditionally used to measure test validity, and the authors offer no compelling evidence why these criteria should be abandoned in the use of the ABIC. Second, indexes of interrater reliability are just that—reliability. It cannot be used to judge the validity of the instrument.

Summary of the ABIC for the Test Consumer: The concept of the ABIC is good, that is, a test of adaptive behavior designed for culturally diverse children. Unfortunately, the technical quality of the instrument does not measure up to the authors' goals. The standardization group for the test is sketchy and nonrepresentative, making test results difficult to interpret. Reliability needs to be demonstrated more strongly, and the authors make

virtually no attempt to support the validity of the instrument. Given these weaknesses, it is recommended that other measures, such as the ABS–SE, be used if possible.

Using Adaptive Behavior Information

Information regarding adaptive behavior can be most useful to special education teachers and counselors. Adaptive behavior information involves the precise skills that students need to succeed in life. Students who do not possess the necessary occupational and personal skills will experience difficulties in adult, independent living.

For these reasons, adaptive behavior deficits indicated by test instruments imply a strong need for remediational programming for the student by the educational professional. Especially at the high school level, such deficits help define the educational curriculum the special education student should receive.

Virtually everything done during the secondary school program of mentally retarded and other special needs learners should be geared toward remediating these deficits. Some secondary programs have devised curricula designed to ensure adaptive behavior skills of students when schooling ends. Many of these programs fall under the heading of career and vocational education programs. These programs are discussed in more detail in Chapter 20.

SUMMARY

Traditionally, intelligence tests, such as the Stanford–Binet and the Wechsler Scales, were designed to test nonhandicapped populations. However, professionals soon became aware of the need to test special populations. Hence, intelligence and aptitude tests have been created to assess the intellectual abilities of handicapped populations. These populations include persons with learning and information-processing disabilities, sensory impairments, and speech and motor handicaps and persons possessing developmental deficits. Another special population is that of children from culturally diverse backgrounds.

While not actually handicapped, they can appear handicapped through the administration of culturally biased tests.

Picture vocabulary tests are not legitimate tests of intelligence. Rather, they are tests of receptive language. Nevertheless, many people use them inappropriately as tests of intelligence. Picture vocabulary tests should not be confused with instruments that pictorially assess intelligence.

A relatively recent occurrence is the creation of nonverbal intelligence tests that require no receptive or expressive language skills on the part of the test taker. Such tests include the Test of Nonverbal Intelligence, the Pictorial Test of Intelligence, and the Columbia Mental Maturity Scale.

Some test makers have endeavored to create culture-fair tests that do not discriminate against the culturally different, minority test taker. Such tests include the SOMPA, the Culture-Fair Intelligence Tests, and the Learning Potential Assessment Device. Although the concept of a culture-fair test is admirable, the creation of such an instrument is probably impossible. Additionally, currently available tests contain theoretical and technical flaws, and they should be considered experimental instruments at this time.

Adaptive behavior scales measure the extent to which students have mastered the skills needed for occupational and personal life success. Adaptive behavior scales usually use the interview technique to query a third person rather than watching the target student directly. There are a number of commercially available adaptive behavior scales, including the AAMD Adaptive Behavior Scale–School Edition, the Cain-Levine Social Competency Scale, and the Adaptive Behavior Inventory for Children.

STUDY QUESTIONS

1. What are the disadvantages of administering commonly used individual intelligence tests, such as the Stanford-Binet and the Wechsler scales to handicapped populations? Are there any advantages? If so, what are they?

2. What are the special test-taking characteristics of the major categories of special needs persons? What safeguards must be taken for each category of handicap to ensure a valid and meaningful assessment of intelligence and aptitude?

3. Is cultural diversity a handicap when it comes to intelligence and aptitude assessment? How can it become a handicap? How can problems of assessing the intelligence and aptitude of culturally diverse populations be overcome?

4. What is meant by adaptive behavior? Why is it important in assessment? Why is adaptive behavior tied to age and cultural variables?

5. What are some of the major tests designed to measure intelligence of each major type of handicap discussed in this chapter? What are the major similarities and differences of these tests? Which of these tests would you consider adopting as an informed educational professional? Defend your choices.

6. What are the major culture-fair tests? What are their principal characteristics? What are some of the problems of culture-fair tests? Which culture-fair test(s) would you use as an informed test consumer? Defend your answer.

7. What are the major tests of adaptive behavior? What are their defining characteristics? Which one(s) would you advocate using? Defend your answer.

CHAPTER 15

Testing Academic Achievement

Previous chapters dealing with aptitude testing noted that many students are administered such tests each year. However, the number of students given aptitude tests is a fraction of the population administered commercially available, standardized achievement tests. In an average year, millions of such tests are administered to students, and the six major achievement test publishers realize sales of approximately 50 million dollars (Anderson 1982). It has also been estimated that between six and twelve full achievement *batteries* will be administered to students in the United States during their school careers (kindergarten and grades 1 through 12) (Houts 1975). Obviously, the achievement testing industry is big business.

As with any industry, there are good and poor products. Some achievement tests are well constructed and achieve their purpose; others are poorly devised, ambiguous, and, even worse, lead to faulty conclusions. It is the test consumer's responsibility to decide which achievement tests fall into which category and then to choose instruments accordingly. Criteria for identifying sound achievement tests for classroom usage are included in this chapter.

Purposes of Achievement Tests

Standardized achievement tests are administered to students for various reasons (Anderson 1982; Graham and Lilly 1984). One reason is to evaluate a student's performance; another is to evaluate the performance or efficiency of the school district relative to other districts.

Comparisons

Perhaps the most common reason for using achievement tests is to measure student learning relative to that of peers. Parents and teachers often wish to ascertain how students are performing relative to their age or grade peers. In many parent-teacher conferences, parents seek information as to whether the student is at grade level, that is, whether their child's skills are comparable to those of other children of the same age. Such information helps parents interpret their child's learning progress relative to students in the same grade. Norm-referenced, standardized tests allow these types of comparisons; they match the test taker's performance to that of a representative norm group.

Assessment of Mastery

Achievement tests can also measure absolute learning in relation to a set of predetermined criteria. Over the years, educational professionals have developed a set of curriculum skills deemed essential for success in modern, adult society. By periodically assessing the test taker's mastery of these skills, educators can modify the student's ongoing educational program to diagnose and remediate gaps or deficiencies in these key skills.

Screening Devices

Achievement tests can be used as *screening devices*. Screening devices are instruments that identify individuals who possibly are experiencing problems. After such individuals are identified, in-depth, diagnostic assessment is used to pinpoint the precise nature of the problems. Global, norm-referenced achievement tests are usually of little help in diagnosing the nature of a student's problems—they are much too broad for that purpose. However, such tests can be used to identify children who are achieving at levels significantly below those of their age or grade peers. After such children have been identified, diagnostic, criterion-referenced achievement measures can then be used to pinpoint precisely the nature of the child's educational problems.

Measuring Curriculum Success

Achievement tests can be used to measure the effects of a given curricula or set of curriculum materials. For example, suppose a school district wished to assess the relative merit of a given reading or arithmetic series. The best way to test the effectiveness of the new materials would be to assign one group of students to the old series, another group to the new series, and measure the academic achievement of each group on a standardized achievement test. Such a design represents an oversimplification of the process and does not take into account such factors as the students in the experimental group responding to the "newness" of the materials. However, achievement tests can be helpful in deciding the effectiveness of curricular materials and programs.

Program-Funding Decisions

Achievement tests can also be used when making program-funding decisions. The academic achievement of children within a given district can be assessed, and funding and programming can be modified to meet the needs of those students based on their test performance. Many times, for example, federal or state monies are directed to schools in which students have scored low on standardized achievement tests. Likewise, some states reward school districts with enrichment funds when a significant proportion of children in that district score high on standardized achievement tests.

Unfortunately, the practice of praising or criticizing schools on the basis of standardized achievement test scores is fraught with error. For example, standardized test scores within a district may be high or low for many reasons. Some of those reasons include the socioeconomic status (SES) of the people residing within that district, cultural variables, and the degree to which test takers in that district are similar to people who made up the norm group of the test used. Children's test scores too often become a political football, with public figures decrying a drop in achievement test scores. They may use this as "evidence" of a decline in the quality of education as compared to past years. Such finger pointing is usually inappropriate, based on oversimplified logic, and is generally counterproductive.

What Achievement Tests Can and Cannot Do

It is vital that the test consumer know what achievement tests can do and cannot do. Test users must recognize the uses and abuses of achievement tests. Figure 15-1 contains a summary listing of what such tests can and cannot accomplish.

Achievement tests can tell us only where the child is operating *at this point in time.* They cannot predict where the student will be in the future. Likewise, achievement tests are not designed to predict whether a child will benefit from an upcoming series of educational experiences. They cannot tell us, for example, whether a child should receive special educational services. Finally, most achievement tests (unless they are highly diagnostic in na-

Figure 15-1 What Academic Achievement Tests Can and Cannot Accomplish

What Achievement Tests Can Accomplish

1. Measure student academic learning and performance.
2. Indicate degree of student mastery of content (criterion-referenced tests).
3. Indicate student performance in relation to peers (norm-referenced tests).
4. Indicate possible areas of weakness (screening tests).
5. Indicate specific areas of weakness (diagnostic tests).

What Achievement Tests Cannot Accomplish

1. Measure aptitude and innate ability.
2. Measure intelligence.
3. Evaluate teacher effectiveness.
4. Predict future achievement.
5. Indicate a handicapping condition.
6. Make class placements.

ture) do not do a very good job of pinpointing specific learner deficiencies and suggesting remediational techniques.

What achievement tests can tell us is how well a child is currently profiting from learning experiences. Norm-referenced tests yield information on how well the child is performing in relation to a representative sample of age or grade peers. Criterion-referenced achievement tests tell us how well the child has learned (mastered) a predetermined curriculum. Be aware that the usefulness of norm-referenced achievement tests is only as good as the degree of agreement (congruence) between the children making up the norm sample and the test taker. Likewise, criterion-related achievement tests are only as good as the validity of the curriculum objectives being measured.

Criteria for Choosing a Sound Achievement Test

Only the *best* commercially available achievement tests should be used in schools and classrooms. To choose sound tests, the informed test consumer needs to apply a set of criteria to *each* achievement test considered for use (Iwanicki 1980). Five criteria for choosing sound achievement tests are considerations of general usage, administration, norms, technical quality, and reporting and interpretation of test scores. The criteria for choosing sound achievement tests are not much different from the criteria for choosing sound aptitude tests (they must be technically sound, possess appropriate norms, and be well constructed). All of this information should be discussed in plain language in the test's technical manual. If not, the test should not be adopted.

An additional consideration for achievement tests (actually it is subsumed in the section on technical quality) is content validity. Recall from Chapter 9 that content validity measures the extent to which a test gauges the breadth and width of the content it is designed to assess. For example, a mathematics achievement test should be judged as to whether the test items measure the range of the arithmetic curriculum taught to children in school. To the extent that it does not, the content validity of the test is in question, and the usefulness of that achievement test will be in jeopardy.

Commercially Available versus Teacher-Made Achievement Tests

Whereas nearly all aptitude tests are commercially produced instruments, probably the majority of achievement tests are those created by the teacher for classroom use. Because achievement tests measure the effects of classroom learning experiences, it is understandable that more teacher-made achievement tests are administered than are commercially available tests.

There are advantages and disadvantages to teacher-made achievement tests. The greatest advantage is that the teacher can assess content directly covered in class. This helps ensure

high content validity. A commercially available test cannot precisely match the content and learning experiences given to students in individual classrooms. Only the classroom teacher writing a specific test can accomplish such a task.

On the other hand, most teacher-made tests do not possess the high technical quality of many commercially available tests. Commercially available tests have been field-tested; they possess (or should possess) a proven reliability and validity. If the test is norm-referenced, it possesses representative norms; if it is criterion-referenced, it should contain a detailed set of curriculum objectives that items reflect. It is crucial that teacher-made achievement tests possess high technical and item quality. Therefore, the teacher creating an achievement test must guarantee its reliability and validity as well as the quality of its items. Assessments of commercial test reliability and validity are discussed in Chapters 8 and 9, while creating sound informal and curriculum-based instruments are covered in Chapters 11 and 12. Assessing the quality of teacher-made test items is discussed here.

Item Analysis for Norm-Referenced Achievement Tests

Teachers often ask themselves two central questions regarding their teacher-made tests:

1. How well did the test do what it was supposed to do?
2. Which items were most effective in achieving the purpose of the test?

An assessment of the test's validity, particularly the content validity, provides an answer to the first question. The second question is answered by *item analysis*.

Item analysis takes place after the test has been administered. The goal of the process is item revision or substitution so that bad items are changed or dropped and good items are retained or added. What eventually emerges is a sound, valid, teacher-made achievement test.

Item analysis involves examining multiple-choice and true–false items (the types of items most often used in teacher-made tests) with the use of mathematical techniques designed to measure item *difficulty* and item *discrimination*. Item difficulty is an index of the proportion of students who responded correctly to the item. Item discrimination yields an index of the proportion of students who scored high on the exam and answered the item correctly versus the proportion of students who scored poorly on the exam and answered the item correctly.

The relationship between item difficulty and discrimination is shown in Figure 15-2. First, individual items should discriminate well between high and low test scorers. For example, if a test item was answered correctly by students who scored low on the exam as a whole and was answered incorrectly by high test scorers, the validity of that item would be in serious question. We want test items to have high positive discrimination value. To achieve this, items should be of moderate difficulty. If items are too easy, everyone will answer them correctly, and they will have little or no discrimination value. Likewise, if they are too difficult, everyone will answer them incorrectly, and the discrimination value will be low. Discrimination value can range from -1.00 to $+1.00$; difficulty level can range from 0 to 1.00.

Finding the Discrimination Index of Test Items

The first step in finding the discrimination index is to form upper and lower *criterion groups*. These groups represent a proportion of students in the class who took the exam who performed in a certain way.

For the upper criterion group, the teacher would select the scores of the 25 percent of students in the class who scored highest on the test. Likewise, the lower criterion group would consist of the scores of the 25 percent of the students who scored lowest on the

Figure 15-2 The Relationship between Item Difficulty and Discrimination

Item Difficulty

Range of 0.00 to 1.00
The higher the number, the greater the difficulty.

Item Discrimination

Ranges from 0.00 to 1.00 and 0.00 to -1.00
If all students in both groups got item right, difficulty = 0.00, item is easy.
Then

$$D \text{ (Discrimination Index)} = \frac{U - L}{N} \qquad \begin{aligned} U &= 10 \\ L &= 10 \\ N &= 10 \end{aligned}$$

$$D = \frac{10 - 10}{10} = \frac{0}{20} = 0.00$$

If all students in both groups got item wrong, difficulty = 1.00, item is difficult.
Then

$$D = \frac{U - L}{N} = \frac{0 - 0}{10} = 0 \qquad \begin{aligned} U &= 0 \\ L &= 0 \\ N &= 10 \end{aligned}$$

If the item was easy for the upper group (U) and difficult for the lower group (L), then

$$D = \frac{U - L}{N} = \frac{10 - 0}{10} = \frac{10}{10} = 1.00$$

Discrimination Index is strong.
Item Difficulty is moderate.

exam. When the total number of papers is small (twenty or fewer), practice permits the use of all the class scores, with 50 percent going in the upper group and 50 percent in the lower group.

In assessing the discrimination index of each test item, this formula is used:

$$D = \frac{U - L}{N}$$

Where:

D = Discrimination index

U = The number in the upper criterion group who answered the item correctly

L = The number in the lower criterion group who answered the item correctly

N = The number of persons in one criterion group

As stated earlier in this chapter, the higher the score, the greater the discrimination value of the item. Items selected for use should always be positive in sign; an item with a negative discrimination index means that more people in the lower scoring group answered the item correctly than did people in the upper scoring group. Items with negative discrimination indexes or indexes approaching 0 should be discarded or significantly modified.

Calculating the Difficulty Index: The difficulty index is an indication of the difficulty or ease of the test item. The difficulty of the item is calculated with the formula:

$$P = \frac{N_W}{N_T}$$

Where:

P = Difficulty level of item

N_W = Number of people in the class who answered the item incorrectly

N_T = Total number of people in the class who answered the item

Again, keep in mind the relationship between the difficulty level and the discrimination power of norm-referenced test items. As items become very easy or very difficult, they lose discrimination power. Thus, items with intermediate difficulty levels are desirable. Because difficulty indexes range from 0 to 1.00, difficulty indexes ranging from .40 to .60 are probably most desirable.

Analysis of Criterion-Referenced Test Items

Item analysis on criterion-referenced achievement tests is related to mastery level of content. Criterion-referenced tests are not concerned with which items high scorers versus low scorers answered correctly. Rather, the focus is on how well the students in the class met the criterion.

In item analysis of criterion-referenced tests, we seek to learn the proportion of students who met the stated criterion as opposed to students who did not meet the objective. To measure this, the following discrimination index is used.

$$D = \frac{U}{N_U} - \frac{L}{N_1}$$

Where:

D = Discrimination index

N_U = Number in group meeting the criterion

N_1 = Number in group not meeting the criterion

U = Number in group meeting criterion who answered item correctly

L = Number in group not meeting criterion who answered item correctly

The difficulty level of items on criterion-referenced achievement tests is calculated using an additive discrimination formula (see Figure 15-3). An example of item analysis for criterion-referenced achievement tests is shown in Figure 15-3.

The interpretation of discrimination and difficulty indexes of criterion-referenced achievement tests is different from that of norm-referenced tests. First, unlike norm-referenced tests, we would *expect* the difficulty level of items on criterion referenced tests to be low because we are seeking mastery of content. We want *everyone* to get the items right (achieving a difficulty index of 0).

Second, our expectations regarding the discrimination index for norm-referenced and criterion-referenced test items are different. Recall that with norm-referenced tests, two groups used to calculate the discrimination index performed in relation to one another. A large index indicates that those passing the item did proportionately better on the criterion as a whole than those who fell below criterion performance. Likewise, a small dis-

Figure 15-3 Calculating the Discrimination and Difficulty Indexes of Criterion-Referenced Tests

Discrimination Index

$$D = \frac{U}{N_u} - \frac{L}{N_1}$$

Where:

D = Discrimination Index
N_u = Number in group meeting criterion
N_1 = Number in group not meeting criterion
U = Number in group meeting criterion who answered item correctly
L = Number in group not meeting criterion who answered item correctly

For example:

$N_u = 18$ $N_1 = 3$

$U = 21$ $L = 6$

$D = \dfrac{18}{21} - \dfrac{3}{6} = .86 - .50 = .36$

Difficulty Level

$$P = \frac{U + L}{N_u + N_1} =$$

$$\frac{18 + 3}{21 + 6} = \frac{21}{27} = .78$$

crimination index means that the performance of both groups was comparable on that item. Items on a criterion-referenced test need to be good discriminators of who passed and who failed on the criterion. Review of both instruction and the items is warranted when discrimination indexes approach zero or are negative in value.

Types of Achievement Tests

As with other tests, achievement tests differ along the dimensions of *referencing* and *specificity*. Achievement tests are either norm- or criterion-referenced and are either global or diagnostic. Additionally, achievement tests are either individually or group administered. Table 15-1 shows which achievement tests fall within which category in terms of specificity and referencing.

Table 15-1 Referencing and Specificity of Achievement Test Batteries

Global	*Diagnostic*
Norm-Referenced	
California Achievement Tests (CAT)	Reading and Math Subtests of CAT
Comprehensive Tests of Basic Skills (CTBS)	Reading and Math Subtests of STAT
Iowa Tests of Basic Skills	Diagnostic Achievement Battery
Metropolitan Achievement Tests	Kaufman Test of Educational Achievement
SRA Achievement Series	Woodcock–Johnson Psycho–Educational Battery—Tests of Achievement (Part II)
Stanford Achievement Test (STAT)	
Basic Achievement Skills Individual Screener	
Peabody Individual Achievement Test	
Wide Range Achievement Test–Revised	
Criterion-Referenced	
None	Reading and Math Subtests of CTBS Brigance Diagnostic Inventories

Global achievement test scores function generally as screening instruments. They yield general, global scores of academic achievement, such as grade–age level or other developmental scores, rather than break down a given academic area into its finer component parts. Virtually all of the commercially available global achievement tests are norm-referenced.

Diagnostic achievement tests usually break down an academic area into its component parts. They give the educational professional some detailed information as to where in the academic process the test taker is strong and weak. Diagnostic achievement tests can be norm- or criterion-referenced. Some of these tests can be used as both norm- and criterion-referenced measures. Virtually all of the diagnostic achievement tests are individual rather than group assessment instruments.

Specific Tests of Academic Achievement

The remainder of this chapter discusses specific tests of academic achievement commonly used in schools. However, only tests that function as achievement *batteries* are critiqued. Such batteries measure student achievement in a variety of core academic areas rather than in one core area (e.g., reading). Tests that measure achievement in individual core areas are discussed in the appropriate chapters dealing with specific core academic areas.

Group Achievement Tests

The Purpose of Group Achievement Tests

Group achievement tests, like group aptitude tests, are usually administered to students in regular classrooms rather than to pupils enrolled in special education programs. The primary purpose of group achievement tests is screening. That is, these tests are used basically to measure the academic achievement of students against that of their peers and indicate whether further, diagnostic testing is warranted. Table 15-2 lists the major standardized group achievement tests.

Most group achievement tests assess skills in the areas of reading, mathematics, and language arts. In addition, some group achievement tests also assess performance in social studies and science. Almost all of the available group achievement tests use a multiple-choice format. Because this format is used, written expression, handwriting, and spelling are difficult to assess.

Difficulties in Using Group Achievement Tests with Special Populations

With group achievement batteries, testing is typically accomplished over a series of days. Students remain in the testing environment for long periods of time and are overseen by a

Table 15-2 Group Achievement Batteries

Test	Grade	Number of Levels	Academic Areas Assessed
California Achievement Tests	K–12	10	R, M, LA, SP, Ref
Comprehensive Tests of Basic Skills	K–12	10	R, M, LA, Sp, Ref, Sci, SS
Iowa Tests of Basic Skills	K–9	10	R, M, LA, Sp, Ref, Sci, SS
Metropolitan Achievement Tests	K–12	8	R, M, LA, Sp, Sci, SS
SRA Achievement Series	K–12	8	R, M, LA, Sp, Ref, Sci, SS
Stanford Achievement Test	K–College	10	R, M, LA, Sp, Sci, SS

Key: R = Reading; M = Mathematics; LA = Language Arts; Sp = Spelling; Ref = Reference Materials; Sci = Science; SS = Social Studies proctor. Test takers are given test booklets containing test items and instructions. Students read the instructions (sometimes following along as the proctor reads the instructions) and then complete the appropriate booklet sections. Students are not allowed to skip ahead to new sections or return to sections previously encountered. Each section of the booklet is usually timed.

Like group aptitude tests, group achievement instruments make a number of assumptions about test takers. It is assumed that test takers are good readers and can adequately read both test items and booklet instructions. Failure to do so results in a poor test score. It is also assumed that test takers possess good test-taking skills, that is, they know how to approach the test and possess strategies for answering multiple-choice questions. Because testing sessions are time consuming and sustained over a number of sessions, it is assumed that students are motivated and can stay on task and work independently.

Unfortunately, many of these assumptions do not hold for exceptional learners. Such persons typically are not good readers, do not possess good test-taking skills, and frequently have no test-taking motivation. Additionally, such students typically cannot work independently for sustained periods of time. For these reasons, most group achievement tests are inappropriate for students enrolled in special education programs.

Keep in mind that when group achievement tests are used with exceptional learners, a large degree of test interpretation error will exist. Such error will usually function to *underestimate* the true academic achievement of such pupils. Additionally, low test scores (usually achieved by special education students on such measures) tend to be less reliable and valid than are scores in the average range of achievement. For all these reasons, the educational professional should probably avoid using group achievement tests with exceptional learners. Instead, individual achievement

tests, particularly diagnostic ones, should be adopted.

Individual Achievement Tests

Individual achievement tests are the most suitable instruments for use with exceptional students. With individual achievement tests, reading of directions and items is eliminated or kept to a minimum (except for reading tests), and the examiner can observe the student's test-taking and on-task behaviors. Additionally, individual achievement tests are more diagnostic than are group measures, although not all individual achievement tests are diagnostic in scope.

Like group tests, individual achievement tests usually assess performance in the areas of reading, mathematics, and language arts. Additionally, because such tests are individually administered, oral reading can be assessed and more in-depth comprehension questions asked. Unlike group tests, individual achievement tests can elicit a variety of student responses including verbal responses, gestures, and written answers. In this way, individual achievement tests often bypass the heavy emphasis on reading and multiple-choice items required by group achievement measures.

The major individual achievement test batteries most often used with students in special education programs are discussed and critiqued here. All of these tests assess achievement in the areas of reading, mathematics, and language arts; some also assess achievement in other areas, such as social studies and science. Included in this discussion are the Peabody Individual Achievement Test (PIAT), the Wide Range Achievement Test–Revised (WRAT–R), the Basic Achievement Skills Individual Screener, the Kaufman Test of Educational Achievement, and the Diagnostic Achievement Battery. In addition, the Brigance Diagnostic Inventories, a set of criterion-referenced achievement batteries, are discussed and critiqued.

Peabody Individual Achievement Test

Overview: The Peabody Individual Achievement Test (PIAT) (Dunn and Markwardt 1970) is a norm-referenced, individual achievement test designed to provide a wide range screening measure of reading, mathematics, spelling, and general information. The instrument contains five subtests (see Table 15-3) that can be administered by any competent educational professional. The test is appropriate for students from kindergarten through grade twelve.

The PIAT contains a variety of materials including individual record booklets, the examiner's manual, administration instructions, and two easel kits containing the test and practice items. The easel kits contain stimulus materials that are presented to the student at eye level. The examiner's instructions are written on the reverse side of each stimulus to facilitate administration. A revised version of the PIAT is scheduled for publication in 1989.

Administration and Scoring: There is no time limit for administering the PIAT. However, administration usually requires approximately forty minutes.

It is possible to administer selected subtests of the PIAT rather than the entire test. Short-answer and multiple-choice questions are used, and no writing is required of the test taker. Suggested starting points are given for each test, and the basal level is five consecutive, correctly answered items. Testing continues until the student makes five incorrect responses on seven consecutive items.

Grade level, age level, percentile, and standard scores are obtained for subtests as well as for the total instrument. Using this information, along with the child's chronological age, scores can be plotted to create profiles that graphically represent the child's achievement in each of the five subtest areas. When grade norms are used to determine the derived scores, grade equivalents or percentile ranks are used to plot the profile. An example of a plotted profile for a student on the PIAT is shown in Figure 15-4.

The plotted profile score can help the teacher determine a student's weak areas(s). For example, by viewing Ralph's PIAT profile, one can readily determine that he is operating at about the same level (and quite well) in the areas of mathematics, reading recognition and comprehension, and general information. However, in the area of spelling, Ralph achieved at "only" the 54th percentile, a significant drop from the other academic areas tested by the PIAT. Hence, some spelling remediation may be warranted.

Table 15-3 Subtests of the Peabody Individual Achievement Test

---

1. *Reading Recognition*
   Assesses skill in the areas of matching letters, naming capital and lowercase letters, and recognizing words in isolation. (84 items)

2. *Reading Comprehension*
   The student reads a sentence or phrase and chooses the appropriate picture that depicts what has been read. (66 multiple-choice items)

3. *Mathematics*
   Assesses skill in matching, discrimination, recognizing numerals, computation, fractions, geometry, and trigonometry. (84 multiple-choice items)

4. *Spelling*
   Assesses skill in distinguishing printed letters, grapheme-phoneme matching, identifying correct spelling of words, and correctly spelling words provided by the examiner. (84 items)

5. *General Information*
   Assesses facts and information in social studies, science, sports, and fine arts. (84 orally presented items; student responds verbally)

Figure 15-4 A Sample PIAT Profile

PIAT~ Peabody Individual Achievement Test
INDIVIDUAL RECORD BOOKLET
by Lloyd M. Dunn, Ph.D. and Frederick C. Markwardt, Jr., Ph.D.

NAME _____ Ralph _____ (last) (first) (middle initial) SEX: (M) F (circle)

SCHOOL **Mc Guffey** (or agency or address)

TEACHER _____ (or counselor or supervisor)

EXAMINER **Diane**

TESTING TIME **40** GRADE _____ CODE _____ (min.) (or phone) (or race or descent)

AGE DATA

Date of testing **1988** (year) **10** (month) **10** (day)

Date of birth **1977** (year) **5** (month) **11** (day)

Age at testing **11** (years) **5** (months)

TEST SCORES

NORMS RECORDED (Check one) .... ▶ ☐ Age ☒ Grade

▼ SUBTESTS		Raw Scores	Equivalents	Percentile Ranks	Standard Scores
Mathematics	▶	60	9.9	87	117
Reading Recognition	▶	64	9.8	87	117
Reading Comprehension	▶	66	11.8	91	120
Spelling	▶	51	6.5	54	102
General Information	▶	55	8.2	78	112
Total Test	▶	296	9.4	87	117

Circle the equivalent and/or percentile rank scores plotted on the profile.

INTELLIGENCE TEST DATA

▼ NAME OF TEST	Date at testing	I.Q. Score	Adjusted M.A.

Note: See Part I of the Manual on calculating adjusted M.A.

PROFILE

Note: To assess the significance of difference between subtest scores consult the reliability section of Part IV of the Manual.

Copyright © 1970 American Guidance Service, Inc. The reproduction or duplication of this form in any way is a violation of the copyright law.

AGS Published by
AMERICAN GUIDANCE SERVICE, INC. • Publishers' Building, Circle Pines, Minn. 55014

Source: Reproduced by permission of American Guidance Service. Peabody Individual Achievement Test by Lloyd M. Dunn and Frederick C. Markwardt. Copyright 1970. Rights Reserved.

251

Norms and Standardization Group: The PIAT was normed on students who represented the mainstream of education. As such, only students attending regular, public school classes made up the standardization group. Students were drawn from 27 urban, suburban, and rural communities throughout the United States, and 29 school districts were used. The sample totaled 2,899 children, with approximately 200 students at each grade level (K through 12). The sample was controlled for race, sex, and parents' occupations according to proportions reported in the 1967 United States census.

Reliability: Reliability information on the PIAT consists of test-retest data obtained after a one-month interval. Reliability data were collected on approximately 50 to 75 students in grades 1, 3, 5, 8, and 12. Test-retest reliability at the other grade levels is not known.

Test-retest reliability for the total test ranges from .82 to .92 (median .89) depending on grade level. Test-retest reliability of the subtests is as follows:

- Mathematics, .52 to .84 (median .74)
- Reading recognition, .91 to .94 (median .88)
- Reading comprehension, .61 to .78 (median .64)
- Spelling, .42 to .78 (median .65)
- General information, .70 to .88 (median .76)

No information regarding internal consistency was collected by the test authors.

Validity: Content and concurrent validity are reported. The authors claim content validity in terms of the use of expert opinion and extensive reviews of curriculum materials in developing test items. It is not known whether items were field tested. Concurrent validity is asserted by showing that the PIAT is correlated with the Peabody Picture Vocabulary Test (PPVT), a test of receptive language. This certainly does not prove concurrent validity because the PPVT contains no spelling, reading, or arithmetic (it is a test of receptive

language only). Thus, claims of validity for the PIAT are largely unsubstantiated.

Summary of the PIAT for the Test Consumer: The PIAT is one of the most widely used, individually administered achievement tests. The materials are easy to use, and the test is relatively straightforward to score and interpret. However, it should be used only as a screening device because it yields little or no diagnostic information.

The PIAT's norm group is restricted to the mainstream of American life. No effort was made to standardize the test on special and minority populations, except for blacks. Although the test-retest reliabilty is strong, its validity is not adequately demonstrated. The PIAT should be used in conjunction with other assessment instruments.

Wide Range Achievement Test–Revised

Overview: The Wide Range Achievement Test–Revised (WRAT–R) (Jastak and Wilkinson 1984) is a revision of the original WRAT created in 1978 (Jastak and Jastak 1978). The WRAT–R is an individually administered, norm-referenced, paper and pencil test designed to assess achievement in reading, spelling, and arithmetic. The 1984 edition is virtually identical to the 1978 version except for the addition of items in the mathematics subtest. The test has two levels: Level 1 is for students under the chronological age of twelve; Level 2 is for students over twelve years of age. Thus, the WRAT–R is different from other achievement tests in its grouping of subtests by chronological age rather than grade. The three subtests for each level are reading, arithmetic, and spelling. Table 15-4 contains a description of the subtests of the WRAT–R.

Administration and Scoring: The WRAT–R is usually administered individually, but group procedures for the spelling and arithme-

Table 15-4 Subtests of the Wide Range Achievement Test–Revised

1. Reading
The student reads various lists of words aloud. Words are presented in isolation. A prereading section includes such activities as matching and naming letters. The WRAT–R does not contain a section on reading comprehension.

2. Arithmetic
The student is given a page of computation problems and must complete as many as possible within ten minutes. Problems range from simple addition to computation areas of fractions, decimals, percentages, algebra, and geometry. A prearithmetic section assesses counting objects, reading numbers, and answering simple number fact problems.

3. Spelling
The student writes spelling words that are dictated by the examiner. A prespelling section can also be administered.

tic subtests are described in the manual. Group administrations, however, are probably not appropriate for most special needs learners. Some of the subtests are timed, and total administration takes 20 to 30 minutes.

In Level 1, each subtest begins with some preacademic skills, such as reciting letters in the student's name, matching letters by form, and counting. Older students are given pretests only when they cannot achieve basal levels on a subtest.

Subtest items are arranged in order of difficulty. The student continues until a ceiling level is reached. The ceiling in reading is twelve consecutive errors; in spelling it is ten consecutive errors. The ceiling in arithmetic is reached when a ten-minute time limit expires.

Grade levels, stanine, percentile ranks, and age standard scores are obtained for each subtest. Standard scores possess a mean of 100 and a standard deviation of 15.

Norms and Standardization Group: The WRAT–R was standardized on a stratified

national sample of 5,600 people, aged five years to seventy-four years, eleven months. These persons resided in seventeen states, and the sample was representative of geographic region, race, and type of community (urban or nonurban). No information is provided on the socioeconomic status (SES) of persons comprising the standardization group or other demographic variables. It is not known whether any handicapped individuals were included in the standardization group.

Reliability: The WRAT–R uses a model for testing reliability that is too technical and complex for discussion in this text. This model gauges the difference in the match between test taker and each test item. Using this model along with techniques of item analysis, and traditional test-retest analysis, the reliability of the WRAT–R was determined as adequate.

Validity: The authors claim that the content validity of the WRAT–R is "apparent" (p. 62). However, they give no indication of how the content validity of the test was assessed. In fact, a case can be made for low content validity because the instrument requires only reading single letters and single words; no prose reading or comprehension is required. Most school reading, on the other hand, requires some complex level of prose reading and comprehension. Likewise, the arithmetic test measures only simple computational skills; no measure of mathematical concepts is assessed.

The authors assert two types of concurrent validity: by correlation with previous versions of the WRAT and by correlation with other achievement tests. Proof of concurrent validity by correlating the WRAT–R with earlier versions of the instrument is faulty because the validity of earlier test versions is in question. Likewise, correlations between the WRAT–R and other achievement tests do not necessarily prove validity, and other indexes are needed before the instrument's validity can be accepted.

Summary of the WRAT–R for the Test Consumer: The wide use of the WRAT–R by educational professionals is somewhat surprising considering its shortcomings. It yields no grade level scores, only age scores; the standardization group is incompletely described; it possesses questionable validity; and it provides little useful information for the educational professional. Given these flaws, other individual achievement tests should be considered by test consumers.

Other Norm-Referenced Individual Achievement Tests

Basic Achievement Skills Individual Screener

Overview: The Basic Achievement Skills Individual Screener (BASIS) (Psychological Corporation Measurement Staff 1983) is an individual achievement test designed to measure reading, mathematics, and spelling skills. An optional writing test is also included. The test is appropriate for students in grades 1 through 12. The optional writing test is appropriate for students in grades 3 through 8.

With BASIS, tasks typical of classroom activities are organized into grade level clusters of six to ten items; a stated criterion must be achieved before proceeding to the next cluster. Clusters exist for reading and mathematics readiness, reading (decoding), reading comprehension, and spelling.

In the mathematics subtest, students are required to complete six computation and two word problems for each grade level. The test also contains a math readiness subtest that samples basic number facts and counting skills.

The reading readiness subtest requires students to identify letters, to match letter combinations, and to relate words and sentences to illustrations. The decoding test contains distractors chosen to help diagnose decoding difficulties, such as reversals. Reading comprehension is assessed by the cloze technique, in which the student reads a passage aloud and supplies missing words.

The spelling subtest consists of words chosen from major spelling series. Tricky or "demon" words are not included. Finally, the ten-minute writing test is scored holistically on the basis of writing style, punctuation, thematic ideas, and so forth.

Administration and Scoring: BASIS is untimed except for the optional writing test. Materials consist of the content booklet, manual, and student record form. The content booklet is reusable. Test materials are compact and easy to understand. Administration time is less than one hour, and administration does not require formal training. Total scoring time is approximately five minutes.

Raw scores can be converted to standard scores: percentile ranks, stanines, and grade, age, and normal curve equivalents. Suggested grade or text-level placement is also included.

Items for mathematics, reading readiness, beginning reading, and spelling are grouped by clusters representing various levels of difficulty. A criterion for passing each cluster is provided. The examiner identifies the lowest level at which the student meets or exceeds criterion and the ceiling level when criterion was not met. These scores are then transferred to the student's summary sheet.

Norms and Standardization Group: BASIS was standardized on 3,296 students aged six years to eighteen years, eleven months. Students in the sample came from 66 school systems in 23 states. Twice as many students in grades 1 through 8 were included than for grades 9 through 12. Only students in mainstreamed classes were included in the sample. However, 4 percent of the sample was labeled as *disabled* and carefully identified in the test manual. A post-high school sample of 232 adults aged eighteen years through twenty-two years, eleven months, was included. The sample was representative for geographic region, school system enrollment size, community socioeconomic status, public versus private school enrollment, and ethnic representation.

Reliability: The reliability of BASIS was assessed by the KR–20 formula for measuring internal consistency. Although the reliability coefficients are uniformly acceptable, reliability estimates may be artificially inflated because of the test's scoring procedures. Test-retest reliability was carried out after a four-week interval on a subsample of students in grades 2, 5, and 8. Test reliabilities, respectively, for the three grades for mathematics are .81, .83, and .81; for reading, .91, .82, .96; and for spelling, .94, .90, and .94.

Validity: Content validity was obtained from the construction and selection of test items. Objectives for the subtest items were derived from curricular texts, various state education department curriculum guides, and from various reading, mathematics, and spelling experts. Concurrent validity was demonstrated by correlations between BASIS scores and report card grades for 300 students in grades 2 through 6. Correlation between the BASIS mathematics scores and math grades range from .31 to .56; for BASIS reading scores and reading grades, from .44 to .52, for BASIS spelling scores and spelling grades, from .29 to .61; and for the BASIS writing test and writing and spelling grades, from .25 to .41.

Summary of BASIS for the Test Consumer: BASIS is a compact, easily administered instrument designed to screen individual achievement problems in the areas of mathematics, reading, and spelling. It contains an optional writing test. BASIS is a power test that relieves students who experience diffi-culty with timed tests from undue test anxiety. Additionally, the test is relatively time efficient in terms of administration and scoring.

BASIS contains sound norms, is well standardized, and possesses a strong reliability. In addition, 4 percent of the standardization group consisted of a well-defined disabled population. Its content validity is well demonstrated, but attempts to demonstrate concurrent validity have proved only moderately successful. Nevertheless, it yields a variety of information about students' achievements and it merits adoption consideration by the educational professional.

Kaufman Test of Educational Achievement

Overview: The Kaufman Test of Educational Achievement (K–TEA) (Kaufman and Kaufman 1985) is an individual achievement test designed to measure the school achievement of students in grades 1 through 12 (ages six years to eighteen years, eleven months). The K–TEA consists of two overlapping forms: Brief and Comprehensive. The Brief Form, containing 144 items, globally samples the areas of reading, mathematics, and spelling. The Comprehensive Form contains 280 items in the five subtests of reading decoding and comprehension, mathematics computation and application, and spelling (see Table 15-5). All items in the Brief Form are different from those in the Comprehensive Form. Although both forms are norm-referenced, the Comprehensive Form also includes criterion-referenced information that allows the professional to analyze student errors in each content area. The Brief Form should be administered for screening purposes; for in-depth diagnostic information regarding student strengths and weaknesses, the Comprehensive Form should be used.

Administration and Scoring: Both forms of the K–TEA consist of a kit comprising a user's manual, an easel that contains the sub-

Table 15-5 Subtests of the Kaufman Test of Educational Achievement

Brief Form

Mathematics: Assesses basic math skills as well as real-life applications and numerical reasoning. Easy computational problems are presented in written form. More difficult concepts and applications are presented orally with accompanying visual stimuli. (52 items)

Reading: Assesses decoding of printed words and reading comprehension. Items increase in difficulty. (52 items)

Spelling: Assesses student's ability to spell target words that are used in a sentence. Words may be spelled orally if student experiences writing difficulties. (40 items)

Comprehensive Form

Mathematics/Applications: Assesses mathematical concepts in a wide range of computation, application, reasoning, and real-life frameworks. (60 items)

Mathematics/Computation: Assesses written computational skills using a paper and pencil format. (60 items)

Reading/Comprehension: Measures literal and inferential comprehension. The easiest and most difficult items have the student responding to a set of examiner commands. Other items require the student to read paragraphs and answer questions on what has been read. (50 items)

Spelling: The student writes target words that are presented in a sentence. (50 items)

tests, an answer booklet, a student profile, and a parental reporting form. The administration of the K–TEA is relatively straightforward. All testing materials and instructions that are given to students are contained in the easel. Professionals in education and psychology are qualified to administer the K–TEA. Additionally, the authors assert that paraprofessionals can administer the test if given sufficient training. Administration time for the Brief Form is approximately thirty minutes; the Comprehensive Form takes about sixty to seventy-five minutes.

The K–TEA yields percentile ranks, standard scores, stanines, normal curve equivalents, and age and grade norms. All standard scores posses a mean of 100 and a standard deviation of 15. Additionally, it yields information regarding student errors on each subtest. Such information allows some in-depth, criterion-referenced assessment of student achievement.

Norms and Standardization Group: The standardization of the K–TEA was conducted in twenty-five cities in fifteen states. The sample population was stratified by grade and is representative in terms of geographic region, sex, socioeconomic status, and educational level of parents. Five types of norms exist in the K–TEA: normalized standard scores, percentile ranks and stanines, normal curve equivalents, age equivalents, and grade equivalents.

Reliability: A thorough analysis of the reliability of the K–TEA is included in the test manual. Split-half reliability (the traditional odd versus even item analysis was not the basis of the split) was carried out, and reliability coefficients ranging from .87 to .95, depending on the age of the child tested. Test-retest reliability was also carried out on 172 students about equally divided among the 12 grades. Retest intervals ranged from 1 to 35 days, with a reliability coefficient exceeding .90 reported in most cases. Information is also provided showing the standard error of measurement for the test creating an error band (confidence interval) of approximately three points on each side of an obtained score.

Validity: The validity of the K–TEA was meticulously carried out in a number of stages. Stage 1 involved establishing the content validity of the subtests. Curriculum experts and various school curricula were consulted during this stage, and the authors and experts contributed to a pool of test items. In Stage 2, the items developed in the first stage were subjected to item analysis and pilot-tested in a series of national tryouts. On this basis, the items of the K–TEA were selected from the original pool.

Stage 3 consisted of assessing the concurrent validity of the instrument. This was accomplished by correlating the Comprehensive Form of the K–TEA with other achievement tests, such as the WRAT–R, the PIAT, and the Metropolitan Achievement Test. Correlation coefficients ranged from .83 to .88, indicating a high degree of correlation among the tests.

Summary of the K–TEA for the Test Consumer: The K–TEA is a useful test in various settings. It yields a variety of information including diagnostic information, which is relatively rare for achievement batteries. Additionally, the use of limited error analysis of students' incorrect responses can be quite useful to the educational professional.

Advantages of the K–TEA include well-written manuals, separate forms for global screening and diagnostic, in-depth assessment, and easy-to-use materials. The technical quality of the instrument is strong, and the authors thoroughly demonstrate reliability and validity. The norms are representative and well conceived. The K–TEA is an appropriate instrument for testing the academic achievement of both handicapped and non-handicapped learners.

Diagnostic Achievement Battery

Overview: The Diagnostic Achievement Battery (DAB) (Newcomer and Curtis 1984) is an individually administered achievement battery designed to test student abilities in listening, speaking, reading, writing, and mathematics. It is designed for persons aged six years to fourteen years, eleven months.

There are twelve subtests in the DAB. Table 15-6 contains a list and brief description of these subtests.

Table 15-6   Subtests of the Diagnostic Achievement Battery (DAB)

Listening (35 items)

Story Comprehension: The student listens to story and answers questions. Stories increase in length and difficulty.
Characteristics: The student answers true or false to questions that are read by the examiner.

Speaking (52 items)

Synonyms: The student supplies a word that has the same meaning as a stimulus word. (25 items)
Grammatical Completion: Measures the student's ability to understand and use morphemes and syntax of English. (27 items)

Reading

Alphabet/Word Knowledge: Requires letter recognition for young children. Older children demonstrate word-reading skills by reading words in isolation.
Reading Comprehension: Requires the student to read short stories silently and answer comprehension questions.

Writing

Capitalization/Punctuation: The student capitalizes and punctuates a series of paragraphs presented.
Spelling: The student spells twenty isolated words. Words are presented in a sentence.
Written Vocabulary: The student writes a story after looking at three sequential pictures.

Applied Mathematics

Mathematics Reasoning: The student must retain problems presented orally and solve the problem without pencil or paper.
Mathematics Calculation: The student solves word problems under timed conditions.

Administration and Scoring: The DAB consists of a manual, examiner record forms, student-consumable worksheets, and a student booklet. The test manual offers concise instructions for administering and scoring the test. However, the authors suggest that only educational professionals who are trained in assessment, or who have received special training in the DAB, administer the instrument.

The entire battery takes approximately two hours to administer, but the authors point out that all twelve subtests need not be given to students. Rather, the educational professional need only administer those subtests considered important for screening or evaluation.

The DAB is hand scored—no machine scoring is currently available for the instrument. Raw scores are converted to standard scores (mean = 10, standard deviation = 3), percentile ranks, and quotients for each of the four areas (mean = 100, standard deviation = 15). Finally, the DAB allows for descriptors (superior, above average, average, below average, poor), but the manual is unclear about how these descriptors were devised. Finally, the scoring summary sheet allows the examiner to devise an achievement profile for each student.

Norms and Standardization Group: The DAB was standardized on a sample of 1,534 from 13 states. The manual includes tables listing the characteristics of these students and claims that the sample is representative. However, the total number of students comprising the standardization group is rather small. Thus the number (N) in each demographic group is not large enough to ensure the representativeness of the sample.

Reliability: The reliability of each subtest and of the total test was assessed by the authors. Reliability is moderate, usually falling between .75 and .89. The Standard Error of Measurement was also assessed. It is relatively small, allowing for narrow confidence bands to be placed around obtained scores.

Validity: The test manual of the DAB discusses content, concurrent, and construct validity. The content validity of the instrument appears to be adequately demonstrated, and the items are representative of content found in students' school programs. Concurrent validity is assessed by correlating the DAB with

a large number of achievement tests in various academic areas, including reading, language, and mathematics. Reported coefficients range from .37 to .81. Attempts were made to correlate the DAB with the Slossen Intelligence Test for Children (SIT) and the Otis–Lennon Quick Score Test. However, because the former test contains glaring difficulties and the second is a group intelligence measure, the construct validity of the DAB is not adequately demonstrated.

Summary of the DAB for the Test Consumer: The DAB falls in the middle of the achievement tests critiqued in this chapter. It is neither the worst test reviewed nor the best. It yields basic achievement information (as do other achievement batteries) but little or no diagnostic or criterion-referenced information. It cannot be used with children under the age of six or older than fourteen years, eleven months, and its standardization group is too small to be representative. Its reliability and validity are moderate. Thus, it is another achievement tool in the moderately acceptable range that the test consumer can use.

Criterion-Referenced Achievement Test Batteries

One of the newest innovations in assessment is the individually administered, criterion-referenced achievement battery. Such tests do not attempt to yield normative data. Rather, they offer the teacher in-depth, diagnostic information and suggest remediational activities for teaching children missed objectives.

Criterion-referenced tests can be extremely useful to the educational professional in pinpointing precise areas of student weakness and offering ways to remediate those weaknesses. Exciting as this concept is, however, criterion-referenced achievement batteries cannot do everything for the educational professional, nor are they without their weaknesses. First, criterion-referenced achievement batteries do not typically yield information on a student's grade level or age equivalent; neither do they disclose how the student is operating relative to peers. Such information can sometimes be useful in making educational decisions about students.

Second, many of these tests do not offer evidence of their technical quality. It almost seems that authors of criterion-referenced tests have decided that their tests are not subject to the same criteria of technical quality as their norm-referenced counterparts. This thinking is most unfortunate. An in-depth, diagnostic test must be of superior technical quality because it is used to make vital educational decisions about students. Such tests must possess strong content and criterion-referenced validity so that sound programmatic decisions can be made for students. Likewise, these tests must be reliable so that error associated with their use and interpretation can be reduced as much as possible. In deciding whether to use such tests, the informed test consumer must weigh the test's claims and potential against unstated or ambiguous technical quality (when such conditions exist).

Brigance Diagnostic Inventories

Overview: The Brigance Diagnostic Inventories are actually four complete batteries: Diagnostic Inventory of Early Development (Brigance 1978), Diagnostic Inventory of Basic Skills (Brigance 1977); Diagnostic Inventory of Essential Skills (Brigance 1980); and Diagnostic Comprehensive Inventory of Basic Skills (Brigance 1980). The batteries are individually administered, criterion-referenced assessment instruments that measure mastery of educational objectives and help teachers plan educational programs in the academic areas of reading, writing, spelling, mathematics, language, and motor skills. Taken together, the four batteries evaluate more than 500 skill se-

quences. Table 15-7 lists the skill areas assessed and the appropriate age levels for each battery. There is a Spanish version of the Brigance tests.

Administration and Scoring: Each battery consists of an examiner's notebook and individual record books. The notebook is designed to lie flat on the table between the examiner and student. It includes directions for administration of each subtest, test items, scoring directions, and behavioral, instructional objectives keyed to individual test items.

Brigance testing is informal. Administration directions are given, but the examiner is encouraged to adjust procedures to meet student needs.

The major question of the tests is, Has the student mastered the given skill or is more instruction needed? Thus, scores are in terms of mastered, or unmastered objectives. These scores are displayed on the pupil scoring record. No norm-referenced, summary scores are obtained.

In addition to being criterion-referenced, the Diagnostic Inventory of Early Development (preschool to grade 2) is norm-referenced. Skills assessed in the test are assigned developmental ages for students. However, these ages were not determined by using a norm group but by citing developmental psychology texts that outline when given skills typically develop in children. Thus, this battery is not truly norm-referenced and probably should not be used as such.

Norms and Standardization Group: None. This is a criterion-referenced test.

Reliability: No data provided.

Validity: On diagnostic inventories of this type, sound evidence of content is absolutely crucial. Content validity was ascertained by inspecting children's curricula, by soliciting

Table 15-7   Skills Assessed by the Brigance Diagnostic Inventories

Diagnostic Inventory of Early Development (Developmental Ages below 7 years) (11 Subscales)

1. Motor Sequences: supine, prone, sitting, and standing
2. Gross Motor Sequences (e.g., walking, catching a ball)
3. Fine Motor Sequences (e.g., eye/finger/hand coordination, painting)
4. Self-Help
5. Prespeech Sequences: receptive language, gestures, and vocalization
6. Speech and Language: vocabulary, syntax, semantics, and pragmatics—social speech
7. General Knowledge and Comprehension
8. Reading Readiness (e.g., knowledge of alphabet, experience with books)
9. Basic Reading Skills (e.g., auditory discrimination, letter sounds, recognition of basic sight words)
10. Manuscript Writing
11. Math (e.g., counting, writing numbers, basic money concepts)

Diagnostic Inventory of Basic Skills (Children Functioning from Kindergarten through Grade 6) (3 Subscales)

1. Reading (4 Components)
   a. Word Recognition
   b. Reading Comprehension: oral reading comprehension, literal comprehension, memory for what has been read
   c. Word Analysis Skills (e.g., initial sounds in words, prefixes, suffixes, and syllabication)
   d. Vocabulary: context clues, classification, analogies, antonyms, and homonyms
2. Language Arts (4 Components)
   a. Handwriting: cursive, upper- and lowercase

   b. Grammar: capitalization, punctuation, parts of speech
   c. Spelling
   d. Reference Skills (e.g., dictionary, atlas)
3. Mathematics (4 Components)
   a. Numbers (e.g., counting, writing numbers)
   b. Operations: basic computational skills
   c. Measurement: time, money, liquid and linear measurement
   d. Geometry

Diagnostic Inventory of Essential Skills (Secondary School Students (2 Sections)

1. Academic Skills (16 Components)
   a. Oral Reading
   b. Reading Comprehension
   c. Word Recognition
   d. Word Analysis
   e. Reference Skills
   f. Graphic Representation Skills (e.g., graphs, tables)
   g. Writing
   h. Filling Out Forms
   i. Spelling
   j. Basic Numbers
   k. Arithmetic Operations
   l. Basic Computational Skills
   m. Fractions
   n. Decimals
   o. Percent
   p. Measurement
   q. Metrics
   r. Mathematical Vocabulary
2. Applied Skills (4 Components)
   a. Health and Safety
   b. Vocational Skills
   c. Knowledge about Food and Clothing
   d. Comunication Skills

the input of teachers, and by field testing. The test appears to contain content validity, being keyed to more than 500 objectives. However, no detailed description of how the content validity was assessed appears in the manuals.

Summary of the Brigance Batteries for the Test Consumer: The Brigance Batteries contain many strengths. They are certainly compre-

hensive and appropriate for a wide range of students including handicapped populations. The batteries lead directly to instructional objectives and program planning. They can be given by persons with a minimum of training. It is easy to score the tests and keep student records.

On the negative side, the batteries must do a better job of demonstrating their technical quality. No reliability information is offered, and the evidence proving content validity is sketchy. However, the batteries should prove useful to teachers in assessing, diagnosing, and planning remediational activities for their students' learning problems.

A Final Word on Achievement Testing

General achievement tests and test batteries can be used for two main purposes: global screening of students' academic achievement and in-depth diagnosis. Achievement test batteries are probably better for purposes of global assessment. As such, they can screen general areas of student deficiency and strength and indicate where more in-depth testing may be needed.

The use of general achievement tests and test batteries as diagnostic instruments is more problematic for several reasons. First, test author protestations to the contrary, most of the instruments described in this chapter (the Brigance Series is an exception) are more appropriate as norm- rather than as criterion-referenced instruments. As such, they compare students against each other rather than against a set of objectives to be mastered (the goal of criterion-referenced tests). Second, to accomplish the objective of criterion-referenced tests, a test battery must be so extensive in scope as to be almost overwhelming for students and teachers alike. This is one problem with the Brigance series; it is long and involved and takes many hours to administer. Unless the teacher has a great deal of time or a classroom aide to help with assessment, the major proportion of the child's instructional time may be given over to administering and scoring such tests.

A more efficient and logical procedure is to use achievement tests as screening measures. Then academic, area-specific achievement tests can be administered for areas indicated by the global test as deficient. This limits the in-depth assessment to areas of need and interest for the teacher and student and prevents unnecessary in-depth testing in every academic core area.

SUMMARY

Educational assessment instruments are usually aptitude and achievement tests. Aptitude tests are used primarily to measure learning potential and innate ability; achievement tests measure what a person has learned after a series of experiences.

Achievement tests are administered to students to evaluate student performance and assess the efficiency of a school program or curriculum in contributing to student learning. Achievement tests are also used to measure student learning in terms of mastery of a set of objective criteria.

Achievement tests measure a student's learning at the time of administration. They are not tests that assess or predict how the student will do in the future. This is the job of aptitude tests.

The choice of a sound achievement test relies on five criteria: considerations of general usage, administration, norms, technical quality, and reporting and interpretation of test scores. These criteria are not that different from the criteria for choosing good tests in general. However, an additional consideration is that achievement tests must possess a high, demonstrated content validity.

Most achievement tests given in schools today are teacher-made tests. Teachers must assess the soundness of their achievement tests in terms of content validity, reliability, and the technical quality of the items. Authors of achievement tests should conduct an item analysis on the basis of discrimination value and difficulty level. Desired levels of difficulty and discrimination power vary as a function of whether the test is being used as a norm- or criterion-referenced instrument.

Achievement tests differ in regard to referencing and specificity. Tests are either norm- or criterion-referenced and either global or diagnostic in nature. Most norm-referenced instruments are global whereas criterion-referenced tests are diagnostic. Some standardized, commercially available achievement tests can be used as both norm- and criterion-referenced instruments.

Commercially available, individually administered achievement tests reviewed in this chapter include the Peabody Individual Achievement Test (PIAT), the Wide Range Achievement Test–Revised (WRAT–R), the Kaufman Test of Individual Achievement (K–TEA), the Basic Achievement Skills Indi-

vidual Screener (BASIS), and the Diagnostic Achievement Battery (DAB). These tests are all norm-referenced individual achievement batteries that can be administered to persons over a wide range of chronological ages.

A relatively recent innovation in assessment are the individually administered, criterion-referenced achievement batteries. These are diagnostic tests of academic achievement that are keyed to the mastery of curricular objectives rather than to the comparison of student scores with peer scores. Perhaps the best known of these batteries is the Brigance Series. Such tests have the potential for diagnosing learning problems, but they suffer from problems of technical quality and difficulties in administration. However, the special education teacher may still wish to use all or part of them to diagnose the learning difficulties of special needs students.

STUDY QUESTIONS

1. What is an achievement test battery? How does it differ from a subject-specific achievement test? What does such a battery typically measure?

2. Describe differences between group and individually administered achievement tests. What are the assumptions made by each type of test? Why are individual achievement tests more appropriate for use with special needs learners?

3. What are the five criteria for choosing a sound achievement test? How can the educational professional assess each of the criteria?

4. What are the two questions item analysis allows the professional to answer? Why are these questions important? Briefly describe how these questions are answered.

5. Obtain a teacher-made achievement test and the distribution of scores for a class. Assess the

discrimination index and difficulty index for each test item.

6. What do the discrimination index and difficulty index tell us about each test item? What is the relationship between the two indexes for norm-referenced tests? For criterion-referenced tests?

7. What are the major individually administered achievement batteries discussed in this chapter? What are their strong and weak points? Rank order the tests as you would most likely use them in your classroom. Defend your rankings.

8. What are the advantages and disadvantages of criterion-referenced achievement batteries? What do they tell us about students? What can they not tell us about pupils? Would you advocate their use in your classroom? Defend your answer.

CHAPTER 16

Language Development and Oral Language Assessment

Almost all children learn and acquire language. The universality of this statement often masks the miracle of language and language acquisition. Think about it for a moment. A young, relatively unsophisticated child, between the ages of one and two, somehow learns to make sense out of the sounds in the environment, separates language from nonlanguage sounds, and eventually acquires the sounds, vocabulary, and grammar needed to produce what we call language.

Unfortunately, this almost universal acquisition of language by children hides the fact that some children experience difficulties in acquiring language and possess language deficiencies. Such difficulties may be manifested in the children's inability to produce correctly all the basic sounds of their language, or it may stem from their inability to comprehend or send language messages adequately. Although the prevalence of speech and language disorders is somewhat difficult to estimate, research indicates that approximately 2 to 3 percent of elementary schoolchildren show delay in acquiring basic speech sounds (Shriberg 1980), and several million other schoolchildren possess disordered language (Aram and Nation 1980). Thus, the assessment, diagnosis, and intervention of language problems should concern special educational professionals, especially those who teach younger or handicapped children.

The Properties of Language

Language possesses a variety of different properties. The sophisticated language user applies the following properties or uses of language when sending communicative language messages or when comprehending such messages.

Displacement

Displacement refers to a person's ability to use language to describe objects not physically present. Displacement also refers to the ability to describe events that occurred in the past or will occur in the future. Language allows us to communicate about objects not in our immediate environment. For example, an automobile owner can talk about the car even though it is parked on the street, out of sight. Likewise, the mature language user can speak of past events, upcoming events, or events that did not even involve the speaker. These abilities are a major component of sophisticated language use.

Conventionality

Over the years, we have agreed within our culture that certain words represent certain things. A four-legged, domesticated animal, often described as man's best friend, is a *dog* because, over the years, English-speaking people have agreed to call it that. People who call that animal *dog* are using language in a conventional manner.

The opposite of language conventionality is *idiosyncrasy*. Suppose an English-speaking person began calling the same animal a *zox*. Would he or she be understood or shunned as someone who was mentally ill or who possessed a severe language handicap? Conventionality of language is a glue that binds communicators together in any given culture.

Productivity

There are a very limited number of sounds in any given language. English, for example, possesses about forty-four sounds. Nevertheless, this small number of sounds can be combined and recombined to produce almost a half-million English words! Likewise, these words can be combined and recombined to produce an infinite number of ideas, phrases, and sentences. This recombining potential of language is known as *productivity*. Sophisticated language users realize implicitly the productive potential of language and use this property in their communicative messages.

Semanticity

Words represent ideas and concepts. As such, they are symbols. The word *dog* is a symbolic representation of the four-legged, furry creature. It represents the actual embodiment of the animal in our messages. The fact that words symbolically represent objects, ideas, and events is known as *semanticity,* a major property of language.

The Components of Language

Language consists of four components: *phonemes, morphemes, syntax,* and *semantics.* As shown in Figure 16-1, these components are hierarchical, that is, lower components (e.g., phonemes) develop before higher components (e.g., syntax).

Phonology

Expressive oral language begins with the production of speech sounds. Speakers move their lips and tongues and produce sounds from their vocal chords to make meaningful sounds. The study of speech sounds is known as *phonology* (Menn 1985).

All spoken languages consist of basic sounds or phonemes. The number of pho-

Figure 16-1 The Components of Language

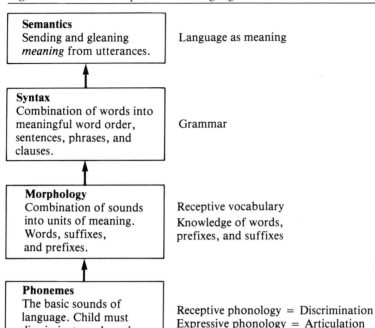

nemes in languages ranges from about fifteen to eighty-five (English has about forty-four) (Clark and Clark 1977; Menn 1985).

The two classes of English phonemes are vowels and consonants. These classes are separated into six subclasses. Phoneme acquisition in children appears to be both systematic and invariant (it occurs in the same order among children). Phonetic *stops* (*b, g,* and *d*) are learned first, and these are followed by *fricatives* (*f* and *s*) (de Villiers and de Villiers 1979; Liberman, Shankweiler, Liberman, Fowler, and Fischer 1977). *Liquids* (*l* and *r*) and *glides* (*w* and *y*) emerge later and are often fully in place and appropriately used until the age of four or five (e.g., the child pronouncing *wed* for *red*). However, for developmentally delayed children, development of all phonemes may occur later.

Articulation problems arise when the child is unable to produce appropriately all the pho-

nemes of the language. Articulation problems can occur when the child produces phonemes in isolation, or when the phonemes are produced in combination (as in words). Thus, tests of articulation typically examine the child's phoneme production in both circumstances. A list of the most commonly used tests of articulation (phonology) appears in Table 16-1. These tests are discussed subsequently in this chapter.

Morphology

Phonology deals with the basic sounds of speech, but such sounds are not usually produced in isolation. Rather, they are combined to produce meaningful sound strings or words.

The smallest unit of meaningful speech is the morpheme (Menn 1985; Slobin 1979). Any word that cannot be subdivided further

Table 16-1   Tests of Phonology and Articulation

Test	Age Range	Individual/Group	Measures
Arizona Articulation Test (Revised)	3–12	Individual	Expressive Phonology
Auditory Discrimination Test	5–8	Individual	Reception/Discrimination
Goldman–Fristoe Test of Articulation	6–16+	Individual	Expressive Phonology
Goldman–Fristoe–Woodcock Test of Articulation	4–70+	Individual	Receptive Phonology
Photo-Articulation Test	3–12	Individual	Expressive Phonology
Templin–Darley Test of Articulation (2nd ed.)	3–adult	Individual	Expressive Phonology

into units of meaningful sound is considered a morpheme. For example, because the word *book* cannot be subdivided, it is a morpheme. On the other hand, the word *books* contains two phonemes, book and the suffix *s,* meaning more than one.

Whereas phoneme assessment entails testing articulation, morpheme assessment includes vocabulary testing (expressive and receptive) and determining the child's understanding of suffixes and prefixes (often called *allomorphes*). Table 16-2 contains a list of commonly used tests of vocabulary and morphology.

Syntax

Syntax is the glue that holds language together. It is the arrangement of words in a given order to make grammatical phrases and sentences. Syntax represents how words are strung together, not what those words mean. Knowledge of syntax is reflected in the use of proper grammar.

The three components of syntax are *word classes, word order,* and *word transformations* (de Villiers and de Villiers 1979; Tager-Flusberg 1985). Word classes refer to parts of speech (e.g., nouns and verbs). Implicit in

Table 16-2   Tests of Morphology and Vocabulary

Test	Age Range	Individual/ Group	Norm-/Criterion- Referenced	Measures
Ammons Full-Range Picture Vocabulary Test	2–adult	Individual	Norm-referenced	Receptive Vocabulary
Peabody Picture Vocabulary Test–Revised	2½–40	Individual	Norm-referenced	Receptive Vocabulary
Test for Auditory Comprehension of Language–Revised	3–10	Individual	Norm-referenced	Receptive Vocabulary

Table 16-3 Tests of Syntax and Grammar

Test	Age Range	Individual/ Group	Norm-/Criterion- Referenced	Measures
Carrow Elicited Language Inventory	3–12	Individual	Both	Expressive Syntax
Developmental Sentence Analysis	2–0 to 7–11	Individual	Both	Expressive Syntax
Northwestern Syntax Screening Test	3–1 to 7–1	Individual	Norm- referenced	Receptive and Expressive Syntax
Test for Auditory Comprehension of Language–Revised	3–10	Individual	Both	Receptive and Expressive Syntax

word classes are suffixes and prefixes. Word order refers to how the child strings words together to make grammatical sense. Finally, word transformations deal with subjects and objects of sentences (e.g., "Jim hit the boy"; "The boy hit Jim"). Some transformations change the meaning of the utterance; others leave the meaning intact (e.g., moving from the passive to the active voice).

Tests of syntax typically assess grammar. There are a number of tests that accomplish this goal (see Table 16-3). Such tests are discussed subsequently in this chapter.

Semantics

Semantics are concerned with the meaning of an utterance (Pease and Gleason 1985), that is, the use of language to communicate a message. The meaning of an utterance is often referred to as the *deep structure*, as opposed to the *surface* (syntactic) *structure* (Chomsky 1965, 1975).

Adequate semantic ability presupposes developed skills in phonology, morphology, and syntax. The child must be able to say the word sounds, possess the vocabulary, and string the words together properly before the semantics of the message can be analyzed.

Tests of semantics are relatively rare. They are often reflected in receptive comprehension tests, where the child comprehends and acts on a message, or in expressive tests, where the child sends messages. Table 16-4 lists tests that contain semantic components.

Receptive versus Expressive Language

Receptive language is the understanding of a message. It requires two processes: the reception of stimuli through sense organs (usually the ears), and the ability to glean understanding from that sensory experience (Mervis and Crisafi 1982; Pease and Gleason 1985). *Expressive* language entails the effective translation of ideas into vocal or motor expression (in the case of sign language) (Clark 1978; Pease and Gleason 1985). It is the sending of a message.

Receptive language develops first (Clark 1978; Pease and Gleason 1985). For example, it has been found that although the child's first fifty words are comprehended at about thirteen months, the first spoken fifty words do not occur until almost nineteen months (Benedict 1979). In developmentally delayed children, both types of language typically appear later than with nonretarded children (Schiefelbusch and McCormick 1981). Both types of language are needed for life success and should be assessed.

Table 16-4   Tests of Semantics

Test	Age Range	Individual/ Group	Norm-/Criterion- Referenced	Measures
Boehm Test of Basic Concepts	Grades K–2	Group	Both	Receptive Semantics
Environmental Language Inventory	2–adult	Individual	Both	Expressive Semantics
Let's Talk Inventory for Adolescents	9–adult	Individual	Both	Receptive and Expressive Semantics

Cultural Difference versus Language Deficiencies

In the past years, some children were thought to possess a language deficit primarily because they used vocabulary, dialects, or language patterns different from those of the dominant culture. The dominant culture in the United States is middle-class white (Anglo), and children from outside this culture were often labeled as having a language "problem."

Strong evidence suggests that many culturally diverse children in the United States use a language that differs in articulation, vocabulary, syntax, semantics, and voice intonation from the Anglo culture (Mims and Camden 1984; Wiig and Semmel 1984). But do these children possess a language deficit that must be remediated? This critical question is still hotly debated in educational circles (Polloway and Smith 1982; Cohen and Plaskon 1980).

Evidence also suggests that most culturally diverse children possess the ability to switch back and forth from the minority to the dominant culture, as social and linguistic tasks dictate (Cohen and Plaskon 1980; Mims and Camden 1984). For example, the author once met a four-year-old girl from Iceland who could switch from English to Icelandic effortlessly depending on to whom she was speaking. This child, obviously, did not possess a language deficit. Actually, she demonstrated great linguistic skill.

The trend today is toward *bidialectalism* (Cohen and Plaskon 1980). This involves teaching children to speak standard English while allowing them to maintain competence in and use their own language or dialect as appropriate. The emphasis is on the use of each speech pattern in its correct social context.

Language Assessment of the Culturally Diverse Child

A fact of assessment life is that there are currently few language tests that are completely culture-fair for culturally diverse children (Terrell and Terrell 1983). Thus, assessment for these students generally requires informal techniques.

Various informal procedures have been advocated by professionals interested in culture-fair language assessment (Adler and Birdsong 1983; Leonard and Weiss 1983). These procedures include:

1. Spontaneous speech samples. This involves collecting a large body of produced conversation from the child in naturalistic settings.

2. Speech probes. The child responds to a number of structured pictures or situations presented by the examiner. This allows for detailed examination of the child's speech under a somewhat more structured situation.

3. Sentence repetition. The assumption is that when children are asked to repeat a sentence they will reconstruct it in their own dialectal language

(Adler and Birdsong 1983). This allows for examination of the child's ability to handle messages in both the majority and minority language.

4. Paraphrasing. Similar to sentence repetition, but the child restates the message in his or her own words. This permits insight into the child's processing of the two languages.

5. Comprehension tasks. This tests receptive language by having the child follow directions or identify vocabulary items.

When using formal tests that are not culture-free, the examiner has a number of options regarding the culturally diverse child (Adler and Birdsong 1983; Taylor and Payne 1983). These options include:

1. Eliminating the test from the assessment battery and replacing it with a more culture-fair language instrument.
2. Renorming the test using members of the test taker's cultural group. This is expensive, time consuming, and perhaps statistically inappropriate if a large number of children are not included in the new norm sample.
3. Administering the test in standard fashion using the test's norm group, but reporting the results in terms of a score for standard English *and* an alternate score. When using alternate scoring, the child's dialectal responses scored as incorrect for standard English would be scored as correct for the minority language.

Although the third alternative is perhaps the best option, it must be used cautiously in terms of test interpretation. By using alternate scoring, the examiner is reporting scores not advocated by the test author(s). In effect, the test giver is creating a new test. Problems with this method notwithstanding, reporting alternate scores for language-different children does provide insight regarding the pupil's performance in both standard English and the minority language.

The Role of the Speech and Language Therapist

This chapter deals with assessing speech and language difficulties. It is important to note that in most school districts the special education teacher is not alone in attempting to diagnose such problems. Rather, the teacher often works with the speech and language therapist. This professional has been specially trained in the assessment of speech, language, and communication difficulties, in the areas of articulation training and speech therapy, and in the design of communication programming for children. Such individuals are usually itinerant personnel, traveling from school to school and working with children either individually or in small groups. Occasionally they work with an entire class, but in most cases, children are removed from class for specialized therapy.

However, even when the expertise of the speech and language therapist is available, the classroom teacher should understand language assessment procedures and know what language assessment instruments are available. Often, the referral for speech therapy comes from the classroom teacher, and the teacher can be most helpful by stating precisely what the deficient language behaviors are that the child is exhibiting. Finally, the bulk of vocabulary, syntax, and semantics assessment usually falls to the classroom teacher.

The Three Methods of Assessing Oral Language

The three basic methods for assessing oral language are *imitation, spontaneous language,* and the use of *stimulus pictures.*

Imitation

With the imitation approach, the child is asked to repeat what the examiner says. Some caution is necessary with this technique. First, the imitation approach relies largely on the pupil's short-term memory. Thus, if the phrase or words spoken are beyond the student's memory capacity, or if there is too long a delay (e.g., five or more seconds) between the stimulus and the child's repetition, the imitation approach can be compromised. The examiner must use stimulus word strings or phrases that are not beyond the memory capacities of the child.

Second, although the imitation method is appropriate for articulation testing, there is some debate as to whether it is appropriate for testing syntax. There is evidence that whereas some children modify the word strings to conform with their own speech patterns, some students simply repeat the examiner's sentence without transforming it into their own grammar. Thus, it may be difficult to conclude whether the child is using correct or incorrect syntax in his or her language or whether the pupil is simply parroting what the examiner has said.

The examiner must also realize that the imitation approach is not a good method for testing either morphology (vocabulary) or semantics. It does not assess the child's understanding of the meaning of words or messages. Finally, the imitation approach depends on the acuity of the child's hearing. It should not be used with children suspected of hearing impairment.

Spontaneous Language

In this approach, the examiner analyzes the language that the child uses spontaneously. For example, if a child is given a toy, the verbal responses can be tape recorded and later analyzed in terms of phonology, morphology, syntax, and semantics. This spontaneous language approach has the advantage of measuring the more naturalistic and lifelike speech of the child.

The spontaneous language approach also has disadvantages. First, it can be a problem for children who are reticent, shy, or largely silent. With these children, the approach can be extremely time consuming, and it may not yield a rich enough speech sample to ensure content validity. Second, if a given sound, phrase type, or grammatical rule goes un-demonstrated by the child, is it because the student does not possess that vocabulary word or rule or simply because the child did not have occasion during the assessment to demonstrate that skill? For example, if the child does not use the word *dinosaur* during spontaneous speech, one cannot assume that the word is not in the student's vocabulary. There may not have been a opportunity to use the word. Another problem with the child's using language spontaneously is that we do not know what the child *meant* to say when an error was made. It may have been an error, but we do not know the error type. Without knowing the child's semantic intention, we cannot infer which type of error was generated.

Stimulus Pictures (Objects)

In the picture stimulus method, a picture or concrete object is shown to the child. The child is then asked to identify the object or describe what is going on in the picture. The picture stimulus approach can be used to measure all four components of language.

The stimulus picture approach overcomes many shortcomings of the imitation and spontaneous language techniques. For example, it does not depend on memory and is more naturalistic than imitation. At the same time, it is more controlled than the spontaneous language approach. The major drawback of this technique is that testing of relatively abstract or symbolic concepts is usually difficult to represent pictorially. For example, how does one draw a picture for the concept of *hope*?

In summary, the informed test consumer should be aware of the strengths and weaknesses inherent in these three approaches and choose the assessment system best suited to the needs of the child and the testing situation. Because all three methods possess both strengths and weaknesses, many language tests use more than one approach in testing oral language. The informed test consumer should do the same.

Tests of Phonology and Articulation

Auditory Discrimination Test

Overview: The Auditory Discrimination Test (ADT) (Wepman 1975) is a revision of a test originally devised in 1958. The ADT is a norm-referenced receptive test of auditory discrimination designed to measure discrimination deficits in children from five to eight years of age. The test has two forms, each form containing forty items. Each item contains forty three- to five-word pairs in consonant-vowel-consonant (CVC) form. Of the forty, ten pairs are identical and thirty are different in only one phoneme. Pairs differ in phoneme at the beginning, middle, or end of the CVC word. The examiner reads each word pair, and the child tries to identify whether the pair is identical or different.

Administration and Scoring: The test is administered individually and takes approximately thirty minutes. A period of practice precedes the actual test. Instructions to both the examiner and the child are clear, concise, and unambiguous.

The child's score is calculated by determining the number of correct answers given in identifying identical word pairs. Thus, the highest score possible is thirty. Using tables provided in the manual, the child's score is then converted to a point scale. If a child's score falls below ten on the different word pairs or below seven on the same word pairs, the test is considered invalid for that child.

Norms and Standardization Group: The fact that no information is given on the norm sample constitutes a major weakness of this test.

Reliability: Test-retest and alternate form reliability are reported. Test-retest reliability is .91; alternate form reliability is .92. Test-retest reliability reported in the 1958 version of the test was based on 109 subjects. No other information is given.

Validity: Eight validity studies are presented in the test manual. Seven studies attempt to show the construct validity of the test. The eighth is inappropriate as a validity study.

The acceptable studies attempt to show a relationship between the ADT and measures of articulation disorders, reading disability, and achievement. The relationships among all three measures are weak. For example, the relationship between auditory discrimination problems and reading disability is not adequately shown because both groups had above-average reading scores. Likewise, the correlation between auditory discrimination problems and academic achievement (as measured by the Metropolitan Achievement Tests) ranged from .23 to .35, relatively low correlations.

No evidence for either content or criterion-related validity is offered in the test manual.

Summary of the ADT for the Test Consumer: The ADT provides a quick assessment of auditory discrimination among children five to eight years old. It is easy to administer and score. Although the reliability of the test is acceptable, no information is given about the norm group. The validity information given is weak; construct validity is questionable, and there is no information on content validity. The test consumer may be attracted by the ADT's quick and easy administration and scoring, but it possesses some major shortcomings and should be interpreted with extreme caution.

Goldman–Fristoe Test of Articulation

Overview: The Goldman–Fristoe Test of Articulation (GFTA) (Goldman and Fristoe 1972) is one of the more widely used tests of expressive phonology. It requires the child to produce speech sounds rather than merely to discriminate between sounds already produced. It is an individually administered, criterion-referenced test in which the individual produces twenty-three phonemes and twelve consonant blends in words and sentences, as well as in various positions in words (beginning, middle, and end). The test does not specifically measure vowels. However, vowel production can be evaluated informally by the test examiner.

The GFTA is based on the rationale that the sounds (i.e., the consonants) of English should be evaluated at three levels (subtests) of complexity: *Sounds-in-Words, Sounds-in-Sentences,* and *Stimulability.* Table 16-5 contains descriptions and examples of the three subtests.

The test is contained in an attractive, notebook-sized kit that takes the form of an easel for presentation of test items. The stimulus materials include colorful pictures chosen on the basis of their interest to children and their potential to elicit a full range of phonemes. However, although the test is said to be appropriate for children of all ages, it may prove too childish and may not hold the interest of more mature children.

Administration and Scoring: The GFTA is relatively easy to administer but very difficult to score. Scorers must be extremely well trained in identifying articulation errors. In fact, scoring is probably best left to trained speech therapists. For the Sounds-in-Words subtest, all the single consonant sounds in the English language are tested in all word positions. If the child has a moderate to severe articulation problem, even a trained diagnostician may encounter difficulty evaluating several sounds in one word. For the Sounds-in-Sentences subtest, the examiner reads aloud two short narrative stories that are illustrated for the child with action pictures. As the child retells the story, information on articulation sounds in connected speech is recorded on the response form. Again, this requires a great deal of knowledge about phonological sounds, and the examiner has the difficult task of listening to the child and recording errors simultaneously.

Scores reported as percentile ranks are available for the Sounds-in-Words subtest only. In actuality, the GFTA is a criterion-referenced measure that indicates mastery of the basic sounds of English.

Norms and Standardization Group: None. The GFTA should be used as a criterion-referenced test.

Reliability: Because the articulation errors of individuals are being judged, interrater reliability for the GFTA is crucial. That is, different judges must agree that a given articulation has or has not taken place.

Interrater reliability was assessed, in part, using highly trained clinicians. With these individuals, test-retest interrater reliability (one week) was high (95 percent agreement for Sounds-in-Words and 94 percent for

Table 16-5 Subtests of the Goldman–Fristoe Test of Articulation

Sounds in Words

The child is shown thirty-five pictures and must either name the picture or answer questions about the picture. All single consonant sounds and eleven consonant blends are elicited.

Sounds in Sentences

The examiner reads two stories to the child and shows pictures illustrating the stories. After each story, the child is shown the pictures a second time and asked to retell the story. Speech sound production in sentences is assessed.

Stimulability

This measures the child's ability to correct articulation errors. After the first two subtests are completed, the examiner repeats sounds that were misarticulated by the child and tries to get the child to correct errors. A measure of the child's ability or receptiveness for intervention.

Sounds-in-Sentences). However, one must keep in mind that these higher interrater reliabilities were gained using highly trained speech clinicians. The interrater reliability using teachers and other educational professionals is unknown.

Validity: The test authors claim that the GFTA possesses strong content validity, that is, that it does a good job of adequately sampling the range of possible sounds of English. Because the test measures virtually all the sounds of English in different positions both in words and in sentences, it is probably safe to conclude that the test possesses a high degree of content validity. However, use of the GFTA does not eliminate the need for more in-depth articulation assessment when articulation difficulties are indicated.

Summary of the GFTA for the Test Consumer: The GFTA is a well-constructed criterion-referenced test of expressive articulation that elicits language from the child by imitation, pictures, and storytelling. It appears to have strong content validity and is reliable when used by trained clinicians. However, it is difficult to score and probably should not be used by individuals who lack strong training in speech and language theory and training.

Photo Articulation Test

Overview: The Photo Articulation Test (PAT) (Pendergast, Dickey, Selmar, and Soder 1984) is the second edition of a norm-referenced test of expressive phonology designed for children aged three to twelve. Like the GFTA, it measures the child's production of phonemes at the beginning, middle, and end of words. Unlike the GFTA, it does not measure sounds in sentences or spontaneous speech.

The PAT consists of seventy-two color photographs of objects and a supplemental word list that can be used to obtain information on the consistency of the child's errors. This supplemental word list can also be used to gather data on the child's stimulability (the child's ability or willingness to correct articulation errors). The test stimuli are arranged to provide separate scores for tongue, lip, and vowel sounds. The test manual contains reproductions of the photographs, arranged in arrays of nine per page, to aid in scoring.

Administration and Scoring: The PAT is relatively easy to administer, with administration time ranging from two to twenty minutes. For most children, testing usually takes five minutes or less. Testing begins by having the child produce five of the six possible sibilants in the beginning, middle, and end of words. The child then moves through the photographs naming objects as they appear. Because knowledge of the names of objects in the photographs may confound the test results (i.e., children misnaming an object) the authors suggest that all errors be confirmed by having the child respond to words in the supplemental word list. The child's responses are then categorized by using tongue, lip, and vowel subscales. The test is significantly easier to score than the GFTA and can be administered and scored after a short training period.

Norms and Standardization Group: The PAT was normed on 684 white, middle-class children for the tongue, lip, and vowel subscales. Means and standard deviations are presented in the manual for boys and girls in six-month age groups from three to twelve years. At least twenty-five children of each sex were tested in each age group. No other information on the norm group is given.

Reliability: Reliability data are given only cursory attention in the test manual. Test-retest reliability for 100 children is reported as .99, but no information is given regarding subscales, type of error, test-retest interval, and so forth.

Validity: No effort was made to demonstrate the content validity of the PAT. Concurrent validity was attempted by correlating performance on the PAT with the Templin–Darley Tests of Articulation, with correlations of .95 on certain items for 100 unspecified children. However, in the absence of more precise information on how this coefficient was obtained, the validity information for the PAT is virtually meaningless.

Summary of the PAT for the Test Consumer: The PAT is a norm-referenced test of expressive articulation. Its main advantages are the use of high-stimulus photographs to elicit speech sounds in words and its ease of administration and scoring. In the latter category, it possesses a distinct advantage over the GFTA. On the negative side, the PAT contains extremely sketchy information regarding its norming and virtually no information regarding its reliability and validity. It should be used primarily as a screening instrument.

Tests of Morphology and Syntax

There are relatively few tests that measure morphology or syntax alone. Although some do exist, others test both areas of language. This section discusses both types of tests.

Note that some vocabulary tests (e.g., the Peabody Picture Vocabulary Test) are sometimes referred to as tests of semantics. In this text, a test that measures a child's knowledge of single vocabulary words is considered a test of morphology. A test that measures a child's ability to use language to convey or receive messages is considered a test of semantics.

Peabody Picture Vocabulary Test–Revised

Overview: The Peabody Picture Vocabulary Test–Revised (PPVT–R) (Dunn and Dunn 1981) is an individual, norm-referenced test of receptive vocabulary. The PPVT–R is a revision of earlier test versions that appeared in 1959 and 1961. Two-thirds of the items in the revised test are new, and the test has been renormed on a new standardization group. There are two parallel forms of the test, L and M. The test is designed for use with indivudals from two years, six months through forty years of age.

Administration and Scoring: The PPVT–R contains a book of 175 pages. Each page contains four line drawings that test a vocabulary concept with increasing complexity. The test taker's task is to point to the target picture as specified by the examiner. Thus, no reading or speaking is required of the test taker. The test is untimed, with testing time ranging from ten to twenty minutes. A basal level is reached at the beginning of the test, and it is defined as the highest level at which the test taker answers eight consecutive items correctly.

There are no subtests of the PPVT–R, and the instrument yields only a global score. Raw scores can be transformed into age equivalents, standard scores, percentile ranks, and stanines. True score confidence bands are also provided.

Norms and Standardization Group: Perhaps the greatest improvement in this test has been in the norms and standardization group used. The original test was normed on an all-white population living in one southern U.S. city. The current norm group is much more representative, having been standardized on 4,200 individuals between the ages of two years, six months, and eighteen years, eleven months, and on 868 adults. The child sample was chosen to represent the population as described in the 1970 census. The adult sample approximated the U.S. population only on the variable of occupation.

Reliability: Three types of reliability are reported for the PPVT–R: test-retest, split-half (internal consistency), and alternate form. Immediate and delayed (9 to 31 days) test-retest reliability is reported. Immediate test-retest reliability for 642 children and adolescents ranges from .73 to .91. Delayed reliability obtained on a sample of 962 children and adolescents ranges from .52 to .92. Split-half reliability ranges from .67 to .88 on Form L and from .61 to .88 on Form M.

Validity: No validity information for the PPVT–R is described in the test manual.

Summary of the PPVT–R for the Test Consumer: The PPVT–R is one of the most popular tests on today's market. It has been used for everything from testing IQ, to testing learning aptitudes, to testing academic achievement. It can do none of these things. It is solely a test of receptive vocabulary. When used as a screening test, it can be a valuable tool, although the sparse information it yields and the lack of validity information in the manual weaken its usefulness. The test can help identify whether a child possesses a relatively poor receptive vocabulary compared with peers. However, given its relatively limited use, its extreme popularity may be unfounded.

Carrow Elicited Language Inventory

Overview: The Carrow Elicited Language Inventory (CELI) (Carrow 1974) is an individual, norm-referenced test that yields diagnostic information regarding the child's morphological and syntactical (grammatical) functioning. The purpose of the CELI is to assess the productive use of selected aspects of the child's language in a controlled environment. The CELI is designed for children aged three to eleven.

The CELI consists of fifty-two stimuli, including fifty-one sentences and one phrase. The sentences range in length from two to ten words and cover the major grammatical parts of speech, active and passive voices, and nega-

tive, declarative, interrogative, and imperative sentences (see Table 16-6). The teacher reads a series of sentences to the child and asks the child to imitate (repeat) exactly what was heard. The child's responses are taped and later analyzed as to morphology and grammar.

The manual cautions that the test should *NOT* be used with children who possess severe articulation difficulties that interfere with their ability to be understood. Additionally, it should not be used with children who suffer from echolalia or are hearing impaired.

Administration and Scoring: The test taker's task is to repeat the sentence the examiner has read, and the responses are taped and analyzed at a later time. Time of testing ranges from ten to twenty minutes. Analysis of the child's taped responses can take up to an hour.

Scoring is done with a complex matrix that contains types of error across the top of the page and stimulus items down the side. An additional score sheet, called a *verb protocol,* allows the examiner to make a detailed analysis of verb errors made by the child. Detailed practice and skill in both administration and training are suggested in the manual. However, the CELI can be administered and scored by any well-trained professional.

CELI scores can be expressed in various ways including total error and subcategory error scores, percentile ranks for error scores, and stanines for each age level. However, it is probably best to use error scores as criterion-referenced information that indicates the child's morphological and grammatical strengths and weaknesses.

Norms and Standardization Group: The representativeness of the standardization group of the CELI is weak. The test was standardized on 475 white, middle-class children attending day-care centers and church schools in Houston, Texas. All children lived in homes where only standard American English was spoken.

Table 16-6 Areas of Syntax and Grammar Covered by the Carrow Elicited Language Inventory

Form	Number
Pronouns	41
Indefinite (it, no one, everyone, both, what, whatever)	9
Personal: 1st & 2nd person (I, me, my, mine, you)	12
3rd person (he, she, her, hers)	10
Plural (we, they, their)	7
Demonstrative (those, that)	2
Reflexive (himself)	1
Prepositions (to, by, in, between, under, on, with)	14
Contexts: modifying copula *is*	4
modifying auxiliary *is + ing*	2
modifying auxiliary *is + ed*	2
modifying main verbs	6
Conjunctions (and, because, if, or, before, than, that)	7
Articles (the, a)	41
Contexts: occurring initially	16
occurring medially	25
Adverbs (fast, where, outside, how, down, up, now)	9
Wh-Questions (where, why, whose)	5
Negatives (not, n't)	13
Contexts: with copula	2
with auxiliary	8
with modal	3
Nouns: Singular	50
Plural	9
Adjectives and Predicate Adjectives	7
Verbs	103
Main Verbs (uninflected, *s, ed*)	46
Contexts: singly	14
with auxiliary + (neg)	17
with modal + (neg)	5
with infinitive	5
with auxiliary + neg + infinitive	2
with modal + auxiliary + neg	1
with modal + auxiliary + infinitive	1
with gerund	1
Copula ('s, is, are, been)	14
Contexts: singly	11
with neg	2
with modal + auxiliary	1
Auxiliary (am, is, are, has, have, has been, have been, do, does, did)	26
Contexts: with verb (ing, ed) + (neg)	20
with neg + verb + infinitive	2
with modal + neg + verb	2
with modal + verb + infinitive	1
with modal + copula	1
Modal (can, could, will, would, may)	8
Contexts: with verb + (neg)	5
with auxiliary + copula	1
with neg + auxiliary + verb	1
with auxiliary + verb + infinitive	1
Infinitives	8
Gerunds	1

Source: G. Wallace and S. Larsen (1978). *Educational Assessment of Learning Problems* (Boston: Allyn and Bacon). Used by permission.

Reliability: Three types of reliability information are offered for the CELI: test-retest (two-week interval) and two measures of interrater reliability. However, the test-retest information was obtained only for a *total* of twenty-five children (five at each of five age levels). Thus, the value of the test-retest reliability (.98) for the CELI is extremely problematic. Interrater reliability ranges from .98 to .99, depending on the manner in which the data were collected.

Validity: No effort was made to assess the content validity of the CELI, but some was made to assess its concurrent and construct validity. Correlation between the CELI and the Developmental Sentence Scoring procedure developed by Lee and Canter (1971) is −.79 (in this case, a negative correlation is desirable). The correlational rank ordering of the severity of children's language defects as obtained by the CELI and those obtained by independent judges not using the CELI (but using other methods of assessment) is .77.

Summary of the CELI for the Test Consumer: The CELI is an individually administered diagnostic assessment instrument that assesses morphological and syntactical competency. Its norms are extremely unrepresentative, and although its reliability coefficient is high, reliability was assessed on only twenty-five students. Finally, it needs to demonstrate its content validity. Nevertheless, the CELI can be valuable if used as a criterion-referenced, informal instrument. In this way, it can offer insights into any linguistic and grammatical dysfunctioning that a child is experiencing.

Developmental Sentence Analysis

Overview: The Developmental Sentence Analysis (DSA) (Lee 1974) is a norm-referenced test of syntax and grammar designed for children aged two to seven. It is used to make a detailed evaluation of the child's standard English grammatical rules use in spontaneous speech. Because it is constructed on the developmental stages of language acquisition, it allows the teacher to select appropriate teaching goals based on the child's performance as compared with peers.

The DSA uses an interview format in which the examiner elicits a sample of the child's language by using toys and pictures. The sample is tape-recorded and analyzed to determine the extent to which the child uses complete sentences and correct parts of speech and grammatical form.

It should be pointed out that the DSA is appropriate only for children who are learning standard English grammar. Children from bilingual homes or homes that do not use standard English should not be evaluated using this technique. There is, however, an adaptation of the DSA for Spanish-speaking children (Toronto 1972, 1973).

Administration and Scoring: Fifty complete, consecutive sentences are obtained from the child by using the toys and pictures. These sentences are tape-recorded and scored using a relatively complex scoring procedure.

In scoring the DSA, each word is analyzed first by its grammatical type (see Table 16-7 for the categories of grammatical type). A detailed, developmentally based chart is then used to assign points to each word in the child's sentence. Point values range from one to eight, depending on the complexity of the utterance and the child's developmental level.

Point values for all the sentences (50) are summed and divided by fifty to gain a Developmental Sentence Score (DSS). These scores can then be expressed by percentile rank, with percentile expressed in six-month age intervals.

Norms and Standardization Group: The norm group consisted of 200 white, middle-class children living in Illinois, Maryland, Michigan, and Kansas. There were only 20 boys and 20 girls at each of five age levels. All children resided in monolingual, standard English–speaking homes. Thus, the norm sample is both small and unrepresentative.

Reliability: Only split-half (internal consistency) reliability information is reported in the manual. Split-half reliability is reported for the five age groups and for the total test. It ranges from .51 (children 2 to 3 years old) to .78 (children 6 to 7 years old). Overall split-half reliability is .71.

Validity: No information regarding the validity of the DSA is available in the test manual.

Summary of the DSA for the Test Consumer: The DSA has an advantage over the Carrow Elicited Language Inventory (CELI) because it has children use spontaneous speech rather than simply repeat sentences provided by the examiner. However, the DSA possesses unrepresentative norms, is appropriate only for standard English users, and contains inadequate reliability information and no validity data. For these reasons, it should be used with caution, primarily as an informal assessment procedure.

Tests of Semantics

Semantics is concerned with the meaning of utterances, that is, with the messages of language as expressed and received. This section assesses two tests of semantics.

Boehm Test of Basic Concepts

Overview: The Boehm Test of Basic Concepts (BTBC) (Boehm 1971) is a group-administered, norm-referenced test of receptive vocabulary designed for children from kindergarten to grade two. It measures the

Table 16-7 Grammatical Word Types Assessed by the Developmental Sentence Analysis (DSA)

1. Indefinite pronoun or noun modifier
2. Personal pronoun
3. Main verb of sentence
4. Secondary verb(s) of sentence
5. Negatives
6. Conjunctions
7. Interrogative reversals in questions
8. "Wh" questions

child's mastery of the basic concepts needed for achievement during the first years of school. The BTBC was inspired by the author's belief that many children beginning school do not comprehend many of the printed or spoken instructions given to them by teachers. The test author designed the test to identify the basic concepts central to understanding such teacher messages.

The BTBC consists of fifty test items representing the basic vocabulary words often used in school but rarely explained to young children. Included are four types of concepts: space (e.g., over, under); quantity (e.g., many, few); time (e.g., after, before); and miscellaneous. The two forms of the test (A and B) are said to be roughly equivalent.

Administration and Scoring: In administering the BTBC, the child is shown a set of pictures, and the teacher reads a statement that illustrates one of the pictures. The child marks the picture that most appropriately matches the statement. The test takes approximately fifteen to twenty minutes to administer.

Note that although instructions to the teacher state that the BTBC can be administered to eight to twelve children at a time, it is doubtful that this can be accomplished without a number of proctors to guarantee that the children stay on task.

For both forms A and B, raw scores are converted to percentile ranks using conversion tables that include the child's raw score, grade placement, and socioeconomic level. Separate norm tables are provided for beginning-year and mid-year administration of the test. Additionally, separate tables are included for each test form for the percentage of children passing each of the fifty concepts. These tables are listed by concept, grade in school, and SES. These concept scores can be used as a diagnostic measure to yield specific information about specific concepts the child does not understand.

Norms and Standardization Group: The BTBC was normed on children living in five U.S. cities. School personnel in each city were asked to administer the test within one high, one middle, and one low SES school. A disproportionate number of low SES children came from one southeastern U.S. city. The test author makes no pretense of having a representative sample. Equally problematic is the fact that Form B was not standardized at all but was constructed to be approximately equivalent to Form A. However, correlations between Form A and Form B are too low for this assumption to be considered valid.

Reliability: Only split-half reliability is reported for the BTBC. Eighteen split-half reliability coefficients are reported, with reliability ranging from .68 to .94. Form A was found to be more reliable than Form B.

Validity: The BTBC relies most on its content validity—the test claims that the fifty items tested are crucial for achievement in the beginning grades of school. However, the test does appear to have strong content validity based on the correlation between currently used curriculum concepts (in kindergarten through grade 2) with concepts assessed by the BTBC.

Summary of the BTBC for the Test Consumer: The BTBC is a norm-referenced test of the basic concepts needed for academic suc-

cess in the beginning years of school. The test is unique in that it identifies the fifty most basic concepts the child needs for success in kindergarten through grade two. The test appears to possess strong content validity. Unfortunately, a technical gap exists between Form A and Form B; the forms are not equivalent, and norms were collected only on Form A. Therefore, use Form A when possible. The BTBC should probably be used as a criterion-referenced test that yields an indication of the child's understanding of the important concepts needed for early school success.

Environmental Language Inventory

Overview: The Environmental Language Inventory (ELI) (MacDonald 1978) is a diagnostic, individually administered test designed to provide information regarding the evaluation of language-disordered children. It measures the communication competency of children who are limited to one- and two-word utterances. It samples three production modes: imitation, conversation, and free play.

The ELI is appropriate for use with individuals aged two to adulthood who possess a wide range of handicaps including mental retardation and physical disabilities. The key variable in choosing to use the test is whether or not the client is restricted to one- or two-word utterances; it is not appropriate for individuals with utterances over two words. The ELI consists of twenty-four stimulus sets, three of which assess each of eight semantic-grammatical rules. These rules describe the functional relations among words in emerging language based on their semantic roles. Table 16-8 contains the eight semantic-grammatical rules.

Administration and Scoring: The child is given three cues: a nonlinguistic and a linguistic cue, as well as a command to imitate. In addition to the cues and direction to imitate,

Table 16-8   The Eight Semantic-Grammatical Rules Assessed in the Environmental Language Inventory

1. Agent and Action (Car roll)
2. Action and Object (Throw ball)
3. Agent and Object (Hat [on] head)
4. Modifier and Object
   a. Possession (My ball)
   b. Recurrence (Want more candy)
   c. Attribution (Little boy)
5. Negation and Object (No spinach)
6. Agent/Object and Location (Penny [in] cup)
7. Agent and Location (Throw ball here)
8. Introducer and Object (Hello, doll)

a free play language sample is collected using toys and other objects in the child's environment.

The examiner records all the child's responses, both intelligible and unintelligible. Different notations are used for recording unintelligible word units and utterances of undeterminable word length. Scoring is done in terms of each production mode (imitation, conversation, and free play). In addition, the proportion of intelligible to unintelligible words can be calculated.

Norms and Standardization Group: The ELI was normed on forty subjects (ages three to nine years). The children were language delayed, mentally retarded, and normal students attending school in Columbus, Ohio. No other information is given regarding the norm group.

Reliability: A problem exists regarding the reliability data reported in the manual. Reliability was calculated on a total of ten mentally retarded students. However, the ELI claims to be appropriate for all individuals who are restricted to one- and two-word utterances. Thus, the generalizability of the reliability of the ELI to clients other than those who are mentally retarded is questionable. Finally, the low number of subjects in the reli-

ability pool and the absence of a description of their characteristics and demographics make the reliability of the ELI suspect.

Validity: Although initial validity of the pilot ELI is discussed, no validity information is included in the test manual regarding the finalized version of the test.

Summary of the ELI for the Test Consumer: The ELI is an individualized test of expressive semantics designed for severely language impaired or delayed individuals. It represents virtually the only test of semantics appropriate for this population. Despite its questionable reliability, norms, and validity, it possesses some value in describing a severely language-impaired person's linguistic ability. However, it could be strengthened considerably if the author had paid more attention to its technical quality.

Comprehensive Language Batteries

Each of the oral tests reviewed thus far has centered on one or two aspects of language. This implies that a clinician wishing to test all phases of language (phonology, morphology, syntax, and semantics) must purchase and administer at least two language tests. However, a number of commercially available *batteries* of oral language do test at least three of the four language areas. These batteries are listed in Table 16-9, and one representative battery is reviewed here.

Comprehensive batteries have advantages and disadvantages. On the positive side, these batteries cover most, if not all, of the language components. Thus, the tester does not have to purchase two or more tests that measure individual language areas. Comprehensive language batteries are cost efficient.

A negative aspect is their inclusiveness. A comprehensive battery that purports to measure multiple components of language must

Table 16-9 Comprehensive Oral Language Batteries

Test	Age Range	Group/Individual	Norm-/Criterion-Referenced
Clinical Evaluation of Language Functions	Grades K–12	Individual	Both
Houston Test of Language Development	6 mos.–6 yrs.	Individual	Norm-referenced
Illinois Test of Psycholinguistic Abilities	2–4 to 10–3	Individual	Norm-referenced
Test of Adolescent Development	11–0 to 18–5	Varies by subtest	Both
Test of Language Development–Primary	4–0 to 8–11	Individual	Both
Test of Language Development–Intermediate	8–6 to 12–11	Individual	Both
Utah Test of Language Development	1–15	Individual	Norm-referenced

either lack extensiveness or be so lengthy and comprehensive that administration and scoring time are prohibitive. Thus, a comprehensive battery that can be administered in a short period of time probably lacks a measure of content validity. A battery with strong content validity may take an inordinately long time to administer and score. For these reasons, the test consumer must weigh the advantages and disadvantages of using a comprehensive language battery rather than individual language component assessment instruments.

The Test of Language Development

Overview: The Test of Language Development (TOLD) (Hammill and Newcomer 1982; Newcomer and Hammill 1982) represents a revision of the original TOLD test. Currently available are the TOLD–P (primary) for children four years to eight years, eleven months, and the TOLD–I (intermediate) for children eight years, six months to twelve years, eleven months. The TOLD–P measures the areas of phonology, morphol-

ogy, syntax, and semantics; the TOLD–I measures all but phonology. Both are individually administered, norm-referenced tests that assess the child's strengths and weaknesses in oral language development.

The TOLD–P contains seven subtests that measure expressive and receptive language. The TOLD–I contains five subtests. With both instruments, children must understand and speak English. No reading or writing is required. Table 16-10 lists the subtests of the TOLD–P and TOLD–I.

Administration and Scoring: The subtests of the TOLD–P and TOLD–I are untimed, but administration time for each instrument is approximately thirty to forty-five minutes. On the TOLD–P, all subtests begin with the first item, and a ceiling is reached when the student makes five consecutive incorrect responses. On the TOLD–I, the basal level is five consecutive correct responses with the ceiling being five consecutive incorrect answers. For the Characteristics and Grammatic Comprehension subtests of the TOLD–I,

Table 16-10　Subtests of the Test of Language Development (TOLD)

Test of Language Development Primary (TOLD–P)

1. Picture Vocabulary (Receptive Semantics): Similar to the Peabody Picture Vocabulary Test–Revised. Tester reads a word, and the student points to a picture from an array that best represents that word.
2. Oral Vocabulary (Expressive Semantics): Examiner reads a word, and the student must define the word.
3. Word Discrimination (Receptive Phonology): Examiner reads two words, and the student must state whether the words are the same or different.
4. Word Articulation (Expressive Phonology): Examiner shows the student a picture and reads a sentence that describes the picture. The student is then asked to name the picture.
5. Grammatic Understanding (Receptive Syntax): Examiner reads a sentence to the child and then exhibits three pictures that demonstrate syntactically similar but nevertheless different messages. The student must choose the picture that syntactically represents the sentence the examiner has read.
6. Sentence Imitation (Expressive Syntax): Examiner reads a sentence, and the child repeats the sentence verbatim.
7. Grammatic Completion (Expressive Syntax): Examiner reads an unfinished sentence, and the child must supply the missing word.

Test of Language Development–Intermediate (TOLD–I)

1. Grammatic Comprehension (Receptive Syntax): Examiner reads a sentence that may or may not contain a syntax error. The student indicates whether the sentence is syntactically correct or incorrect.
2. Sentence Combining (Expressive Syntax): Examiner reads two or more simple sentences. The student must combine these into one syntactically correct sentence.
3. Word Ordering (Expressive Syntax): Examiner reads up to seven words in random order. The student must reorder the words to form a complete sentence.
4. Characteristics (Receptive Semantics): Examiner reads a sentence that contains a noun and a verb phrase. The student must state whether the sentence is true or false.
5. Generals (Expressive Semantics): Examiner reads three words, and the student must state how the words are alike.

however, the ceiling is three errors in any five consecutive questions.

On the TOLD–P, five types of scores are available: raw scores, language age percentiles, percentile ranks, and standard scores for subtests, as well as quotients for composite scores and for the whole test. There are quotient scores for listening, speaking, semantics, and syntax. The spoken quotient does not include data from the phonology subtests.

TOLD–P scores are plotted on a profile that includes quotient scores, subtest scores, and standard scores. This information is useful as a diagnostic tool to gauge the student's strengths and weaknesses.

For the TOLD–I, scores are reported in terms of raw scores, standard scores, and percentile ranks; no grade or age equivalents are provided. Like the TOLD–P, quotient scores on the TOLD–I are calculated, and the results can be plotted.

Norms and Standardization Group: Norms for the TOLD–P are based on 1,836 children speaking "typical" English. The sample was drawn from all geographic regions of the United States and represented diverse ethnic, linguistic, and social class backgrounds. The authors also provide guidelines for developing local norms if those are of interest to the test user. Norms for the TOLD–I were obtained from 871 children speaking "typical" English, who also constituted a representative sample similar to that of the TOLD–I.

Reliability: Internal consistency (split-half) and test-retest reliability are reported for the TOLD–P. Internal reliability is better for the composite test than for individual subtests. However, most of the subtests possess a reliability exceeding .80. Test-retest reliability, although relatively high (.86 to .98), was assessed on an extremely small number of students ($n = 21$). Similar reliability coefficients were obtained for the TOLD–I, and again, the test-retest reliability was assessed on an extremely small population ($n = 30$).

Validity: The authors provide evidence regarding the content, criterion-related, and construct validity of the TOLD–P and TOLD–I. Concurrent validity of subtests is demonstrated by comparing 114 students' results on nine published tests of language and the TOLD–P. The correlations are, in most cases, substantial. The authors also report data obtained from a small number of language impaired children showing that the TOLD–I discriminates effectively between language impaired and non–language impaired children. However, it was shown that 198 users of black English scored lower on many of the subtests than their standard English counterparts did. Therefore, the tests may not be valid for those who do not speak standard English.

Summary of the TOLD–P and TOLD–I for the Test Consumer: The TOLD–P and TOLD–I are well-documented, well-constructed, and well-researched instruments that contain strong validity for testing the range of children's language development. They do a good job of describing children's language strengths and weaknesses and indicating areas that may benefit from remediational programming. However, they should be used cautiously with those who do not speak standard English.

Using Language Assessment Information

The purpose of language assessment is to gain an understanding of the child's current language functioning. As noted in this chapter, there are a variety of language assessment instruments that differ both in what they measure and in the quality of the information yielded. The test consumer's task is to choose and administer quality instruments and to use the information those tests offer in order to enhance the academic program of the student.

Using Phonological Information

Information on the child's phonological functioning will indicate how well the child discriminates and produces the basic sounds of speech. Children discriminating speech sounds inadequately may be suffering from a hearing impairment or some neurological deficiency. The inability to hear speech sounds correctly is correlated not only with articulation difficulties but also with problems in reading because reading requires the child to learn the basic letter sounds and blends. Thus, children experiencing receptive phonological difficulties are strong candidates for in-depth hearing and neurological assessment.

Children displaying expressive phonological difficulties should be referred to the speech and language therapist for possible articulation therapy. This chapter has shown that the older the child and the more severe the articulation problem, the more articulation therapy may be warranted. Young children are expected to exhibit some articulation difficulties as they acquire speech. However, by the time the child is eight or nine, the basic speech sounds should be in place. Referral to the speech and language therapist ensures that in-depth articulation assessment will occur if necessary.

Using Morphological and Syntactical Information

Assessment in the areas of morphology and syntax will yield information regarding the child's basic vocabulary and grammar. Both of these areas possess implications for school success. The child's basic receptive vocabulary influences the ability to understand what is read and to understand spoken messages. Likewise, an understanding of syntax influences not only reading and speaking abilities but also the ability to write clearly and concisely.

Children who possess deficits in receptive and expressive vocabulary may be candidates for enrichment programs (e.g., Head Start). The goal of such programs is to provide children with the experiences necessary to acquire needed concepts for school success. Likewise, children who are deficient in syntax may need remediation to learn grammatical English. However, children should not be penalized because they do not speak standard English. Rather, every effort should be made to help these children move easily between standard and nonstandard English in appropriate language use situations.

Using Semantic Information

Semantics represents the most important function of language, that is, using language to receive and convey messages. Children who cannot do this adequately are not using language for its purpose. Semantic difficulties are also correlated with ability to comprehend the printed word and understand the author's semantic message. Children possessing semantic language weaknesses need to receive direct remediational programming to help them understand and send language messages.

A Final Word on Oral Language Tests

A variety of oral language tests are discussed and reviewed in this chapter. They include the more popular tests of phonology, morphology, syntax, and semantics as well as language development batteries.

These reviews show that tests differ greatly in technical quality, appropriateness for special needs learners, and usefulness of the information they yield. Unfortunately, there is not always a strong correlation between a test's popularity and the technical quality and usefulness of information that it offers.

For this reason, the test consumer must consider the purpose for which the test will be used as well as the special characteristics of the test taker. A match must be made between these criteria and the potential tests available. Finally, after the universe of possible tests has been narrowed to a select few, the technical quality of a test, the appropriateness of its norms, and the usefulness of its information must be carefully considered. Such a procedure will allow the test consumer to base test selection on appropriateness and quality rather than on popularity. Only this will assure quality language assessments for children.

SUMMARY

The purpose of language is to send and receive messages adequately. There are several properties of language including displacement, conventionality, productivity, and semanticity. The mature language user employs all of these properties appropriately and automatically.

Language consists of four components: phonemes, morphemes, syntax, and semantics. Phonology represents the sounds of speech. Standard English possesses approximately forty-four sounds. Morphology is the study of meaningful sound combination that

makes up words, suffixes, and prefixes. Syntax is grammar. It is the glue that holds language together. Finally, semantics is the sending and receiving of language messages. The adequate use of language to send messages depends on the appropriate use of phonemes, morphemes, and syntax.

Language is receptive or expressive. Receptive language is understanding a message. It requires two processes—receiving the message through sensory receptors and comprehending the message. Expressive language is sending a message. Receptive language develops first in children.

A debate exists in educational circles regarding language differences and language deficiencies with children who do not speak standard English. Such children often possess the ability to alternate between their non-standard English patterns and the standard English spoken by the majority culture. This bidialectalism should be the goal of educators of culturally different children.

Nearly every school system employs a speech and language therapist who provides speech and language remediation and therapy to children as needed. However, most referrals and even language remediation for special education students are supplied by the special education teacher, in conjunction with the services of the speech and language therapist.

The three main methods of assessing oral language are imitation, spontaneous language, and the use of high-stimulus pictures. Each method possesses advantages and disadvantages that the test consumer must consider when choosing one or more methods to assess the language of a student.

Tests are available to measure each component of language. Additionally, some language batteries test all or most of the language components.

STUDY QUESTIONS

1. What are the main properties of language? Can you think of any others? Give examples of each property.

2. What are the four components of language? Why are they said to be hierarchical? How and when does each component normally develop in children?

3. Describe receptive and expressive language. How do they develop? What are the functions of each?

4. What are some of the issues in cultural diversity and the assessment of language? Why have culturally diverse children often been diagnosed as language deficient? What are some ways that the language of culturally diverse children can be assessed more appropriately?

5. Describe the three main methods of assessing oral language. What are the advantages and disadvantages of each? Which method(s) would you advocate for informal language assessment of students? Defend your answer.

6. Describe major tests of phonology, morphology, syntax, and semantics. What are the advantages and disadvantages of each? Choose one test from each area that you would advocate using with your students. Defend your answer.

7. What are the advantages and disadvantages of language assessment batteries? Would you use them with your students? Why or why not?

CHAPTER 17

Reading Assessment

Probably more time is spent on reading instruction during the elementary school years than on any other subject area (Lipson and Wixon 1985; Spiro, Bruce, and Brewer 1980). This is not surprising. The ability to read is crucial to success in school and in life, and people who cannot read are at a distinct disadvantage in today's technological society.

Nevertheless, there is little doubt that a significant proportion of individuals—both children and adults—cannot read, or they read at a level low enough to interfere with their successful academic and life functioning. Estimates of the number of Americans who cannot read or who are functionally illiterate range from thirty million (Harris and Associ-

ates 1971) to fifty million (Harmon 1970). During the present decade, the number of functionally illiterate Americans has actually increased (Brown 1982).

These figures indicate that many children in school need reading remediation. However, such remediation cannot be forthcoming until the child's specific reading difficulties are diagnosed. Thus, one of the most important jobs for the teacher is the accurate assessment of students' reading ability.

The purpose of reading assessment for the student with special learning needs is to determine the pupil's strengths and weaknesses so that a remedial–instructional reading program can be planned. Accurate reading assessment provides a variety of outcomes, including the following:

1. The teacher can design and implement prescriptive intervention procedures to help reduce the child's reading difficulties.
2. Reading materials can be given to the child that are commensurate with his or her reading abilities.
3. Frustration and anxiety about reading can be kept to a minimum and motivation to read can be improved.

Before discussing the reading process, we need to say a word of caution about reading assessment. When assessing reading, the test consumer will probably need to make more informed decisions than when assessing any other academic area. Reading assessment instruments abound. In fact, more commercially available assessment instruments probably exist for reading than for all other school subjects combined. Such instruments range from survey tests to in-depth diagnostic, criterion-referenced instruments that contain prescriptive activities designed to remediate reading difficulties. Thus, the primary question for the test consumer is How do I choose the appropriate reading assessment instrument for the child with whom I am working?

Additionally, the educational professional will need to question whether formal tests should be used at all or whether informal reading assessment techniques and procedures should be adopted. Such decisions must not be made haphazardly but on the basis of informed knowledge about the goals of the particular reading assessment and the needs and characteristics of the student being tested. In reading assessment, it is easy to choose inappropriate tests that yield inadequate information and lead to faulty interpretation and conclusions about the child's reading ability. It is more difficult to choose assessment instruments that yield useful information about diagnosing and remediating children's reading difficulties.

The Reading Process

To understand reading assessment, one must first understand the reading process. This is not as easy as it appears. People possess many different definitions of what constitutes reading. For the purpose of this text, reading is defined as follows:

> Reading is the conversion of print into auditory equivalents and the subsequent interpretation of those equivalents into meanings based on previously learned language.

At first, this definition may be confusing. However, when taken one attribute at a time,

a concise definition of the reading process emerges.

Decoding

Reading is the conversion of print into auditory equivalents or sounds. Sophisticated readers convert the printed symbols on the page to sounds so easily and effortlessly that we sometimes forget how difficult this process is for children and functionally poor readers.

The conversion of print into sound is known as *decoding*. Decoding begins with the process of converting individual letters into sounds and proceeds to the decoding of whole words and phrases. A person who cannot decode printed words cannot possibly understand what those words mean. Thus, decoding is a requisite skill for comprehending (understanding) what is read.

Comprehension

The definition of reading states that simple decoding of printed words into sound is not enough. Rather, the individual must interpret and understand what has been decoded. The understanding of decoded words and messages is known as *comprehension*.

Some individuals can decode words adequately but they possess no understanding of what has been read. Perhaps you have experienced this phenomenon in attempting to understand difficult or technical texts. Even though you can decode the words easily, you cannot understand the meaning of the passage. The ability to decode without comprehension is not reading. It is merely "word calling" or "barking at print." Although adequate decoding is a requisite for reading, it is not sufficient; comprehension is also required.

Comprehension and Experience

The ability to comprehend what one reads is based on experience. Readers take what has been read and *integrate* it with previously learned language and experience (Chittenden 1983; Spiro 1980). If a given concept does not exist in a child's experiential vocabulary, the child will not be able to comprehend the concept while reading (Gentner 1975; Rosenshine 1980).

Reading Skills

As we have seen, reading consists of the two main processes of decoding and comprehension. These processes can be separated into component skills. Knowledge of these component skills is important because the students' strengths and weaknesses in each component area yield relevant information as to where they are experiencing difficulties in the reading process. The assessment of these component skills is contained, to a greater or lesser degree, in formal and informal reading assessment tests.

Decoding Skills

Two basic approaches to decoding are *word analysis* and *word recognition*. Word analysis, sometimes called *phonics,* entails using letter sounds and sound combinations to sound out words.

The two types of phonics are *analysis* and *synthesis.* Analysis phonics consists of breaking down whole words into subsequent parts. In this approach, emphasis is placed on word syllables and syllabication of unknown words. Analysis phonics includes such skills as syllabication and *structural analysis,* in which the child learns root words, prefixes, suffixes, and components of compound words. Synthesis phonics is a letter-by-letter approach to phonics, in which the child strings each letter together to sound out words.

By comparison, the word recognition or "Look-Say" approach to reading is based on the assumption that the word is the smallest

meaningful unit that the child must acquire to read successfully. Here, the child learns to read whole words by overlearning them and recognizing them on sight.

Comprehension Skills

Comprehension is the understanding of the message. The different levels of comprehension depend on the complexity of the passage. These levels vary from the simplest *literal* comprehension to *evaluation* comprehension, in which the reader critiques the intent, style, or veracity of the message. Figure 17-1 contains the skills and levels of reading comprehension that are often measured on reading assessment instruments.

Skills Assessed by Reading Tests

Diagnostic reading tests can assess a variety of skills. Basically, these skills fall into three main classes or categories: tests of oral reading, tests of decoding, and tests of comprehension. Table 17-1 (pp. 290–291) contains a list of tests that measure these three areas.

As shown in Table 17-1, there is a certain degree of overlap in the areas measured by reading tests. For example, some oral tests endeavor to measure comprehension. Other tests claim to measure all three reading processes. In choosing an appropriate test, the informed test consumer should carefully ascertain that a test that professes to measure multiple processes of reading actually and accurately assesses each process diagnostically, in-depth, and appropriately. A test professing to measure all areas of reading may, at first, appear to be convenient and cost effective. It certainly is cheaper to purchase and easier to administer one test than three tests (one for each area). However, the consumer may find that the test only superficially measures each area or that it is so long and unwieldy that it tires both the test taker and

Figure 17-1 Skills and Levels of Reading Comprehension

Reading Comprehension Skills

Comprehension

Classifying and Categorizing
Labeling
Main Idea
Opposites
Recall
Sequencing Events
Following Written Directions
Word Meaning
Interpretation
Drawing Conclusions
Making Inferences

Study Skills

Reference
Organization
Reading Rate

Literature

Recognizing Literary Style
Recognizing Literary Techniques

Comprehension Levels

1. Literal Comprehension: Recognition and recall of facts
2. Reorganization: Classifying, outlining, summarizing, and synthesizing
3. Inferential Comprehension
4. Evaluation
5. Appreciation

Reading Comprehension Skills Source: R. Luftig (1987). *Teaching the Mentally Retarded Student* (Boston: Allyn and Bacon).

examiner. Thus, each test needs to be considered on its merits to determine that it will accomplish what the test consumer expects.

Tests of Oral Reading

In some ways, oral reading is an artificial process. After all, the only time we are called on to read orally on a regular basis is probably in school or at religious services. Nevertheless, particularly in the elementary grades, chil-

dren engage often in oral reading in front of the teacher.

Teachers use oral reading primarily to test children's decoding skills. Additionally, by using a direct question approach, the teacher can measure the child's comprehension of what was read. However, oral reading is used in most classrooms so the teacher can ascertain word analysis and recognition skills.

Types of Oral Reading Errors

Over the years, the types of errors made by children during oral reading have been identified. These errors have been classified into the ten most common oral reading errors. These categories of oral reading mistakes are summarized in Table 17-2 (p. 292).

Table 17-3 lists the types of oral reading errors assessed by the two tests, as well as errors measured by two other diagnostic reading tests that contain an oral reading component. As shown in Table 17-3 (p. 293), none of these tests assesses all ten oral reading error types. Thus, the test consumer is responsible for identifying the types of errors of most concern regarding the student tested. When this is accomplished, the most appropriate oral reading tests can be selected. This section discusses two commonly used tests that measure oral reading.

The Gilmore Oral Reading Test

Overview: The Gilmore Oral Reading Test (Gilmore and Gilmore 1968) is a standardized, individual, norm-referenced test designed to test oral reading accuracy and reading comprehension. It is used for grades one through eight. The Gilmore consists of two forms, C and D, which represent a revision of two earlier forms (A and B) no longer in print.

The Gilmore consists of ten paragraphs that form a continuous story. The paragraphs are graduated in length and difficulty from primer

Table 17-1 Tests of Decoding, Comprehension, and Oral Reading

Test	Author(s)	Age/Grade Range	Group/Individual	Measures*	Type of Test**
Analytical Reading Inventory (3d ed.)	Woods and Moe, 1985	Primer–grade 9	I	D, C	I
BRIGANCE Diagnostic Inventory of Basic Skills	Brigance, 1977	K–grade 6	I	D, C	C
BRIGANCE Diagnostic Inventory of Essential Skills	Brigance, 1980	Grades 4–12	I	D, C	C
Diagnostic Reading Scales	Spache, 1981	Grades 1–8	I	D, C	S
Doren Diagnostic Reading Test of Word Recognition Skills	Doren, 1973	Grades 1–6	G	D	S
Durrell Analysis of Reading Difficulty	Durrell, 1955	Grades 1–6	I	D, C, O	S
Ekwall Reading Inventory	Ekwall, 1979	Primer–grade 9	I	D, C	I
Gates-McKillop-Horowitz Diagnostic Reading Test	Gates, McKillop, and Horowitz, 1981	Grades 1–6	I	D, C, O	S

Gilmore Oral Reading Test	Gilmore and Gilmore, 1968	Grades 1–8	I	D, O	S
Gray Oral Reading Test–Revised	Wiederholt and Bryant, 1986	Grades 1–12	I	D, O	S
New Sucher-Allred Reading Placement Inventory	Sucher and Allred, 1981	Primer–grade 9	I	D, C	I
Stanford Diagnostic Reading Tests (3d ed.)	Karlsen, Maddern, and Gardner, 1985	Grades 1–12, College	G	D, C	S
Test of Reading Comprehension	Brown, Hammill, and Wiederholt, 1986	Ages 6–14	I/G	C	S
Wisconsin Tests for Reading Skill Development	1977	K–grade 6	I	D, C	C
Woodcock Reading Mastery Tests–Revised	Woodcock, 1977	Grades 1–12, Ages 6–18	I	D, C	S

*D = Decoding; C = Comprehension; O = Oral Reading
**S = Standardized; I = Informal; C = Criterion-referenced

Table 17-2 The Categories of Oral Reading
Errors

1. Aid: The student hesitates for a time without
   making an effort to pronounce a word or appears to be attempting to pronounce the
   word.
2. Gross Mispronunciation: A gross mispronunciation occurs when the pupil's pronunciation
   of a word bears so little resemblance to the
   proper pronunciation that the examiner must
   look at the word to recognize it.
3. Omission of a Word or Group of Words:
   Omissions consist of skipping individual
   words or groups of words.
4. Insertion of a Word or Group of Words: Insertions consist of the student putting one or
   more words into the sentence being read.
5. Substitution of One Meaningful Word for Another: Substitutions consist of the replacement of one or more words in the passage by
   one or more other meaningful words.
6. Repetition: Repetition consists of repeating
   words or groups of words while attempting to
   read sentences or paragraphs. Errors due to
   stuttering are not repetition errors.
7. Inversion, or Changing of Word Order: Errors of inversion occur when the child changes
   the order of words appearing in a sentence.
8. Partial Mispronunciation: A partial mispronunciation occurs when (a) the student pho-
   netically mispronounces specific letters, (b)
   the student omits part of a word, inserts elements of words, makes errors in syl-
   labification, accent, or inversion.
9. Disregard of Punctuation: The student fails to
   observe punctuation. This includes not paus-
   ing for a comma, stopping for a period, or indicating by vocal inflection a question mark or
   exclamation point.
10. Hesitation: The student hesitates for two or
    more seconds before pronouncing a word.
    The error is recorded as a check over the
    word. If the examiner then pronounces the
    word, it is recorded as a check plus p.

Source: R. Luftig (1987). *Teaching the Mentally Retarded
Student* (Boston: Allyn and Bacon). Used by permission.

through eighth grade. The Gilmore assesses
eight tests of oral reading errors: substitutions, mispronunciations, aided words, disregard of pronunciation, insertions, hesitations,
repetitions, and omissions.

The paragraphs the subject reads are
printed one paragraph to a page. Each form
begins with a picture showing the characters
who appear in the first paragraph. Paragraphs
are presented in a spiral-bound notebook that
contains both forms. There is a separate record blank for each form. Each page of the
record blank reproduces one paragraph, contains five comprehension questions, and provides a table for tabulating the eight types of
errors.

Administration and Scoring: Students are
tested individually. The examiner begins two
grade paragraphs below the one corresponding to the pupil's grade placement. The individual is asked to read orally every paragraph
from basal to ceiling level. Basal level is defined as the highest level at which the student
makes two errors or fewer. Ceiling level is
defined at the level at which the child makes
ten or more errors. The administration is
timed with a stopwatch, and testing time is
usually fifteen to twenty-five minutes.

Separate grade equivalent, percentile, and
stanine scores are obtained for accuracy, comprehension, and rate of reading. Performance
ratings ranging from superior to poor, based
on the child's stanine score, are provided.
Rate of reading is scored as slow, average, or
fast. Analysis in terms of the eight types of
errors assessed by the Gilmore is provided.

Norms and Standardization Group: The Gilmore was normed on approximately 4,500 students in grades one through eight in eighteen
schools in six school systems. Although the
students came from varied socioeconomic
backgrounds, the manual gives no information regarding the sex, racial and ethnic backgrounds, or reading levels and curricula of the
students in the norm group.

Reliability: The authors attempted to fulfill
two purposes at once by obtaining both
alternate-form and test-retest reliability information at the same time. They administered

Table 17-3 Commercially Available Oral Reading Tests and Types of Errors Measured

	Gray Oral Reading Test	Gilmore Oral Reading Test	Gates-McKillop-Horowitz Reading Diagnostic Test	Durrell Analysis of Reading Difficulty
Aid	X	X		X
Gross mispronunciation	X	X	X	X
Omission	X	X	X	X
Insertion	X	X	X	X
Substitution	X	X		X
Repetition	X	X	X	X
Inversion	X		X	
Partial mispronunciation	X			
Disregard of punctuation		X		X
Hesitation		X		X

Source: R. Luftig (1987). *Teaching the Mentally Retarded Student* (Boston: Allyn and Bacon). Used by permission.

Form C to fifty-one third-grade and fifty-five sixth-grade students; two weeks later, they gave these same students Form D. Thus, what the test manual reports is a true measure of neither alternate-form nor test-retest reliability. Alternate-form reliability was confounded by time, and test-retest reliability was confounded by alternate forms. Nevertheless, the authors report reliability coefficients by grade for accuracy, rate, and comprehension. Reliability coefficients for third-grade students are .60, .70, and .94 for comprehension, rate, and accuracy, respectively. For sixth-grade pupils, reliabilities are .53, .84, and .84 for comprehension, rate, and accuracy.

Validity: The only evidence the test authors give for validity of the Gilmore is the test's correlation with scores obtained from the Gray Oral Reading Tests and the Durrell Analysis of Reading Difficulty. However, such correlations alone are not appropriate indexes of test validity.

Summary of the Gilmore for the Test Consumer: The Gilmore Oral Reading Test is an individually administered norm-referenced test of oral reading, reading rate, and comprehension. It provides error analysis of oral reading in terms of eight commonly made errors.

Unfortunately, the Gilmore suffers from some difficulties. First, it should be pointed out that the reading content of the Gilmore is very sexist. In the story, men work and spend their free time outdoors whereas women function as homemakers and complete domestic tasks. Second, information regarding the standardization group is sketchy, and the test does not adequately demonstrate its reliability or validity. Additionally, regarding the test's assessment of comprehension, there is some doubt as to whether readers concentrate on comprehension when reading orally. Oral reading requires superficial comprehension, and the reader is probably concentrating on other processes rather than on comprehension.

The Gilmore is most useful when the eight error types are used to analyze oral reading errors. Due to the technical inadequacies of the instrument, the error types of the Gilmore should probably be used as an informal index of oral reading rather than as a formal, norm-referenced test.

Gray Oral Reading Test–Revised

Overview: The Gray Oral Reading Test–Revised (GORT–R) (Wiederholt and Bryant

1986) is a major revision of the original test constructed in 1967. It is an individually administered norm-referenced test of oral reading. The authors state that the four purposes of the test are to (1) help identify students who are significantly below their peers in oral reading; (2) aid in determining student strengths and weaknesses; (3) document student progress in reading; and (4) serve as a research device in the study of reading.

There are two forms of the GORT–R test (A and B), each of which contains thirteen increasingly difficult reading passages. Five comprehension questions follow each passage, with both literal and inferential comprehension being assessed. The test yields four types of information:

1. Oral reading speed and accuracy.
2. Information about oral reading comprehension.
3. An indication of total oral reading ability.
4. Information about oral reading errors.

Materials consist of a spiral-bound set of reading passages for each form, corresponding record booklets, and an examiner's manual.

Administration and Scoring: Each of the thirteen paragraphs is self-contained so that testing can begin with any paragraph. The student reads aloud while the examiner marks errors in the examiner's booklet. Passages within each form increase in difficulty in terms of vocabulary, abstractness of concepts, and sentence complexity. The reading of passages is timed, and total administration time for the instrument ranges from fifteen to thirty minutes.

In using the test, comprehension basal and ceiling scores are computed. The basal score is the point at which the student correctly answers all five comprehension questions for a passage. The ceiling score is the point where the student misses at least three of five comprehension questions.

Raw scores on the GORT–R are inter-preted in terms of percentiles, the Oral Reading Quotient (ORQ), and the student's errors (miscues). The ORQ possesses a mean of 100 and a standard deviation of 15. The authors claim that this makes the ORQ comparable with other test scores, such as the WISC–R, the Test of Language Development (TOLD), and the Test of Reading Comprehension (TORC). The ORQs of students are also given qualitative descriptors, ranging from Very Superior (ORQ > 130) to Very Poor (ORQ < 70). The instrument also yields a profile that can be plotted for individual students.

Norms and Standardization Group: The GORT–R was standardized on 1,401 students residing in fifteen states. The characteristics of the standardization group are representative of the U.S. population regarding sex, residence, race, ethnicity, and geographic area. However, the relatively small sample size of fewer than 2,000 was divided among eleven age groups, usually yielding fewer than 130 students per age group.

Reliability: Reliability was assessed in terms of internal consistency and alternate-form reliability. Test-retest reliability was not assessed. Internal consistency reliability was assessed for five age ranges and across the age ranges for the comprehension score, oral reading score, and total score. Reliabilities range from .88 to .97. Assessment of alternate-form reliability indicates that the two forms of the GORT–R are essentially equivalent.

Validity: The authors of the GORT–R claim that the test possesses content, criterion-related, and construct validity. In establishing the content validity of the instrument, the stories were controlled for length of words and sentences, complexity of sentence structure, logical connection between sentences and clauses, and coherence of topics. The vocabulary in each paragraph and the comprehension questions were measured by comparing them to five major word lists. Finally, in developing the vocabulary of the instrument, 14 reading series and 127 school textbooks were consulted to establish content validity.

An attempt to establish concurrent validity of the GORT–R was made by correlating the instrument with reading scores of the Iowa Tests of Educational Development, the Formal Reading Inventory, and the Comprehensive Test of Basic Skills. The GORT–R correlated moderately well with these instruments. In addition, three elementary teachers were asked to rate their students' reading ability on a five-point, Likert-type scale. The teachers' ratings correlated strongly with these students' scores on the GORT–R. However, the sample of only three elementary teachers was extremely small, and no information was given on their background or training on the rating instrument.

Finally, an attempt was made to demonstrate construct validity by showing the relationship of the GORT–R to other language scores, to achievement performance, and to intelligence. Although the GORT–R correlated moderately well with these measures, it is unclear how such correlations demonstrate strong construct validity in the area of oral reading.

Summary of the GORT–R for the Test Consumer: The GORT–R is a revision of an oral reading test originally created in 1967. The current test contains both an indication of students' oral reading and an index of their comprehension. The test yields a variety of scores, including an Oral Reading Quotient and miscue analysis. Although the content and concurrent validity are quite strong, the authors did not assess test-retest reliability, and they used a very small standardization group.

Overall, the GORT–R is a useful test. The miscue analysis profile can be helpful to teachers, but the ORQ can be confusing and lead to overinterpretation of scores. Likewise, the

qualitative labeling of students' general reading ability using ORQ scores is quite gross and probably useless. In summary, the test should probably be used as a criterion-referenced instrument, with strong emphasis placed on error analysis and the student profile of oral reading and comprehension.

Diagnostic Reading Tests

A variety of diagnostic reading tests are available to the educational professional. Although they primarily test decoding skills, some of them contain a comprehension component. Tests that measure in-depth comprehension skills are discussed in the following section. This section discusses three of the most popular and educationally useful diagnostic reading assessment instruments: the Stanford Diagnostic Reading Test, the Woodcock Reading Mastery Tests–Revised, and the Diagnostic Reading Scales.

Stanford Diagnostic Reading Test

Overview: The Stanford Diagnostic Reading Test (SDRT) (Karlsen, Madden, and Gardner 1985), represents a third edition of a test originally published in 1966. The SDRT is an in-depth, diagnostic reading test designed to test reading skills in six main areas, including reading comprehension. It can be used as both a norm-referenced and a criterion-referenced instrument. Table 17-4 lists the skills assessed by the SDRT. Unlike other diagnostic tests that must be individually administered, the SDRT can be group administered.

The four levels of the SDRT are related to the student's grade placement:

1. Red level: End of grade 1 and grade 2. Also used for low-achieving students in grade 3 and subsequent grades at the examiner's discretion.
2. Green level: Students in grades 3 and 4. Also used for low-achieving students in grade 5 and at the examiner's discretion.

Table 17-4 Skills Assessed by the Stanford Diagnostic Reading Test

1. Auditory Vocabulary: Student identifies synonyms of words read by the examiner. At the initial (Red) level, the student matches words to pictures. Test is administered at the Red, Green, and Brown levels.
2. Auditory Discrimination: Assesses the student's ability to hear similar and different words in sounds. At the Red level, students identify words that begin or end with the same sound. At the Green level, students identify similar sounds at the beginning, middle, and end of words. Test is given at the Red and Green levels only.
3. Phonetic Analysis: This subtest assesses the student's skills in identifying letter-sound relationships. At the upper levels it assesses both common and variant spellings of words. Given at all four levels.
4. Structural Analysis: Assesses the use of syllables, prefixes, root words, and blends. Given only at the Green, Brown, and Blue levels.
5. Word Reading: This subtest measures the student's skill in word recognition. Child identifies the word that best represents a picture. Given at the Red level only.
6. Reading Comprehension: Task differs as a function of level. At the Red level, the student reads sentences and identifies picture that best represents the sentence; at the Green level, surrounding context and paragraph comprehension tasks are used. The Brown and Blue levels assess both literal and inferential comprehension.
7. Rate: Assesses the rate of reading. Administered at the Brown and Blue levels only.

---

3. Brown level: Students in grades 5 through 8 and low achievers in higher grades.
4. Blue level: Students in grades 9 through 12.

Each level of the SDRT must be purchased separately. Because all of the skill areas tested by the SDRT are not measured in all levels, the examiner must use caution in choosing the correct level test for the child.

Administration and Scoring: The SDRT can be administered individually or in groups. Because students with special needs often pos-sess difficulties in test-taking and reading skills, it is advisable to administer the test individually to these pupils. All levels of the SDRT use the multiple-choice format entirely. For the two elementary school levels (Red and Green), the test authors suggest that testing time not exceed 75 minutes. For the Brown level, testing time ranges from 103 to 123 minutes; for the Blue level, testing time ranges from 96 to 116 minutes.

The SDRT yields norm-referenced and criterion-referenced scores. Norm-referenced scores include percentile ranks, stanines, grade equivalents, and scaled scores. Criterion-referenced scores are reflected by progress indicators. These indicators are expressed as plus (+) or minus (−) and indicate whether a student achieved a predetermined cutoff (mastery) score in a specific skill or objective. Progress indicators offer the teacher in-depth diagnostic information as to the skills the child has or has not mastered in the areas of reading.

Norms and Standardization Group: The SDRT is extremely well standardized. The test was normed on 31,000 pupils in 55 school districts. The standardization group was stratified, using the 1970 U.S. census, on the basis of socioeconomic status, school system enrollment, geographic region, and a large number of demographic variables. The SDRT manual contains extensive tables demonstrating the care and planning that went into creating a representative and meaningful norm group.

Reliability: Two types of reliability information are available for the SDRT. First, raw score data were submitted to tests of internal consistency and alternate-form reliability. Internal-consistency reliability for all levels of the SDRT exceeds .90. Alternate-form reliability ranges from .85 to .94. Test-retest reliability information is not provided.

The reliability of the progress indicators used the test-retest format with the same pupils taking alternate forms of the same levels. Results indicated strong reliability from the progress indicators.

Validity: Content and criterion-related validity are reported. The authors base content validity of test items on extensive research into the reading skills taught to students in a large number of school programs throughout the United States. Included with the test are numerous objectives intended for use by school personnel to test whether the SDRT possesses content validity for their particular class or school. Criterion-related validity was established by showing strong correlations between the SDRT and the reading subtests of the Stanford Achievement Tests.

Summary of the SDRT for the Test Consumer: The teacher who wishes to assess specific reading skills and weaknesses should consider using the SDRT. The strong points of the test include the criterion-referenced progress indicators, its exemplary test item development and standardization, and its strong reliability and validity. Weaknesses include the degree of record keeping involved, the economics of buying multiple levels of the test, and the problems of choosing the appropriate level for a given child. Overall, however, the SDRT is an extremely strong and useful diagnostic reading assessment instrument.

The Woodcock Reading Mastery Tests– Revised

Overview: The Woodcock Reading Mastery Tests–Revised (WRMT–R) (Woodcock 1987) are a battery of six individually administered diagnostic reading subtests designed for use with students from kindergarten through grade twelve. The instrument assesses both word and passage comprehension. The test is available in two forms (G and H), but the Visual-Auditory Learning and Letter Identification subtests are available only in Form G.

Materials in the test include an easel kit for presenting materials, a test manual, and a student report and profile sheet. The five subtests of the WRMT–R are described in Table 17-5. Figure 17-2 contains sample items from the WRMT–R.

Administration and Scoring: The subtests of the WRMT–R are relatively straightforward to administer. The easel-type binder is placed between examiner and test taker. Test items are presented on the face of the page with administration instructions on the back. The student sees the test item while the examiner sees the instructions. Print type is large and easy to see. Testing time is thirty to forty-five minutes.

In administering the WRMT–R, the examiner locates the students' basal level. The basal and ceiling criteria for the instrument are six or more consecutive items passed or failed. The only exceptions are the Word Attack test, which begins with Item 1, and the Visual-Auditory Learning Test, which begins with the first page and is discontinued only if the student falls below a specific cutoff standard.

Raw scores on the WRMT–R can be converted to age scores, grade scores, percentile ranks, and standard scores. Each subtest yields its own set of scores, and a total reading score for the entire test can also be obtained.

The WRMT–R also yields cluster scores, an instructional level profile, a percentile profile, and a diagnostic profile. The four available clusters are readiness, reading comprehension, basic skills, and total reading. Clusters allow for more global interpretation of results and guard against overinterpretation for a single, narrow skill, such as word identification. The instructional profile can be used as a guide to instructional programming for the student. It indicates the developmental level of the individual in five reading areas and in total reading skills. The percentile rank profile displays percentile ranks and confidence bands for tests and clusters of the

Table 17-5   Subtests of the Woodcock Reading
Mastery Tests–Revised

1. Visual-Auditory-Learning (Form G only):
   Reproduced from the Woodcock-Johnson
   Psychoeducational Battery. The test measures the ability to form associations between
   visual stimuli and oral responses in a
   learning-to-read task. The individual learns a
   vocabulary of unfamiliar visual symbols and
   then uses the symbols to translate sentences
   into English.
2. Letter Identification (Form G only): Measures the ability to identify alphabet letters in
   upper- and lowercase and in a variety of type
   faces and styles.
2A. Supplementary Letter Checklist: Presents
   upper- and lowercase letters in a type style
   common to most printed materials. This
   checklist also contains seven digraphs and
   diphthongs that the person is asked to identify by sound.
3. Word Identification: The subject reads by
   sight (word recognition) isolated words
   printed on a page. Words increase in difficulty as the subtest proceeds.
4. Word Attack: Require the individual to read
   either nonsense words or words with very
   low frequency. This subtest measures the ability to apply rules of phonics and structural
   analysis with unfamiliar words.
5. Word Comprehension: Consists of three subtests: Antonyms, Synonyms, and Analogies.
   Antonyms test the person's ability to read a
   word and then supply the word with the opposite meaning. Synonyms require the student
   to read a word and supply a parallel meaning. Analogies require the person to read a
   pair of words and ascertain the relationship
   between the pair. The three subtests of word
   comprehension can be evaluated across four
   reading vocabularies: general reading,
   science–mathematics, social studies, and
   humanities.
6. Phrase Comprehension: Measures the student's ability to read a short passage and identify a key word missing from the passage using the cloze technique.

WRMT–R. Finally, the diagnostic profile allows for detailed information as to the student's strengths and weaknesses in three diagnostic areas: diagnostic readiness, diagnostic

basic skills, and diagnostic comprehension.
Figure 17-3 shows examples of an instructional and diagnostic profile for a student.

Norms and Standardization Group: The
WRMT–R was standardized on 6,089 subjects in 60 U.S. communities. Subjects in kindergarten through grade twelve were stratified for sex, race, ethnic origin, occupation,
income, and geographic region according to
the 1980 census. It is not known how many
students were tested in each grade.

Figure 17-2   Sample Items from the Woodcock
Reading Mastery Tests–Revised

Visual-Auditory Learning

 Point to the first symbol on the subject
side and say: **cowboy.** Pause for the
subject to repeat the word once. (It may be
necessary to remind the subject to say the
word.) Move immediately to the next
symbol.

 Point to the second symbol and say: **dog.**
Pause for the subject to repeat the word.

 Point to the next symbol and say: **horse.**
Pause for the subject to repeat the word.

 Point to the last symbol and say: **and.**
Pause for the subject to repeat the word.

Word Attack Skills

Read these words:
tat
op

Word Analogies

Complete the phrase:
dog — walks   bird —

Source: Reproduced by permission of American Guidance Service. *Woodcock Reading Mastery Test: Revised*
by Richard W. Woodcock. Copyright 1987. Rights reserved.

Figure 17-3 An Instructional and Diagnostic Profile from the Woodcock Reading Mastery Tests–Revised

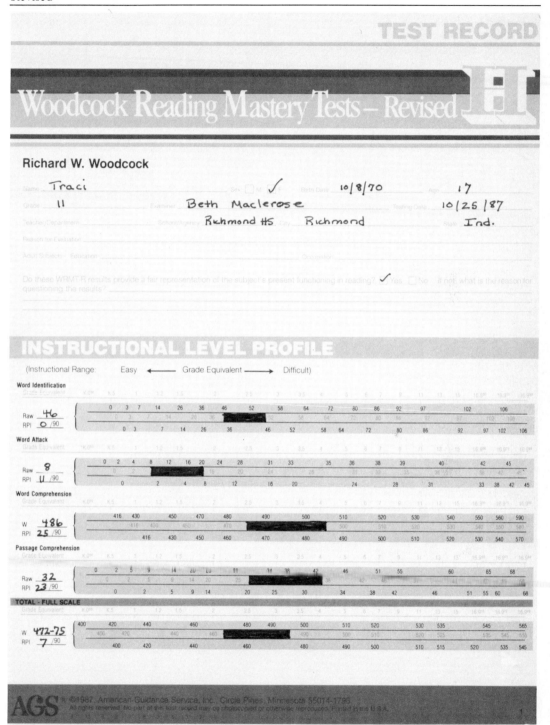

Source: Reproduced by permission of American Guidance Service. *Woodcock Reading Mastery Tests–Revised* by Richard W. Woodcock. Copyright 1987. Rights reserved.

Reliability: Split-half reliability is reported for subtests and for the full test for various age groups. Reliability generally ranges from .80 to .95, depending on the age of the student and the subtest. The one exception was Letter Identification for grade five, in which reliability was only .34. Split-half reliability for the total test ranges from .97 to .99. Test-retest reliability was not assessed.

Validity: Content and concurrent validity of the WRMT–R was assessed. Although the test author claims the items were developed with contributions from outside experts and teachers, he offers no evidence that student curricula were assessed to ascertain validity or that vocabulary or content were submitted to stringent examination to ensure content validity of the instrument. The concurrent validity of the instrument is established by the author's showing correlation of the WRMT–R with other tests, including the Woodcock-Johnson, the Iowa Tests of Basic Skills, the PIAT, and the WRAT–R.

Summary of the WRMT–R for the Test Consumer: The WRMT–R is significantly improved over its earlier counterpart. It offers a wide range of diagnostic information that can be useful in the educational programming of students possessing reading difficulties. There is still some question regarding the validity of some subtests, particularly the letter identification in different print styles and the reading comprehension tests. However, the WRMT–R is likely to remain one of the most popular tests on the market, and the recent technical improvements will help justify its popularity.

Diagnostic Reading Scales

Overview: The Diagnostic Reading Scales (DRS) (Spache 1981) are a third revision of an individually administered battery designed to assess oral and silent reading and auditory comprehension. The scales are designed for students in grades one through seven and can be used as a norm-referenced or criterion-referenced instrument.

The battery includes three graded word recognition lists, two reading selections at each of eleven levels, and twelve supplementary word analysis and phonics tests. The DRS kit contains an examiner's manual, an individual, expendable record booklet for the examiner's use, and a reusable spiral-bound book for student use. Also included are an examiner's audio cassette containing a model for examining the scales and also a technical manual. The skills of the DRS are listed and summarized in Table 17-6.

Administration and Scoring: The scales can be administered by a trained teacher or reading diagnostician. Administration instructions are clear and concise, and the cassette containing a model for administration is very helpful. Timing of student performance is optional, with total administration time ranging from thirty to forty-five minutes. Approximate scoring and interpretation time is fifteen minutes. The DRS yields three reading levels for each test taker: instructional, independent, and potential. The instructional level is based on oral reading and comprehension and indicates the reading grade level at which the student would be placed in a typical classroom. The independent level indicates the student's silent reading comprehension. The potential reading level is based on the student's auditory comprehension and indicates the measure of reading achievement the student should attain *if* given reading remediation. However, making predictions based on a student's potential level score is fraught with error. For example, because the score is based on auditory comprehension (which contains a strong memory component), predicting reading potential based on such a score can be extremely misleading and may result in underestimation of the individ-

Table 17-6 Skills Assessed by the Diagnostic Reading Scales

Primary Battery

1. Word Recognition Lists: Graded word lists that yield a tentative level of performance. This test is used to determine the level of the initial passage that the student should be able to read orally in the next part of the test.
2. Oral Reading: Student reads each paragraph aloud and answers questions posed by the examiner. Most questions asked measure literal recall. Oral reading errors of reversals, omissions, substitutions, mispronunciations, repetitions, and hesitations are assessed.
3. Silent Reading: Student reads the paragraph just higher in difficulty than the last one read orally. Comprehension is again assessed.
4. Auditory Comprehension: Examiner reads to the student the paragraph one level higher than the one just read orally by the student. Listening comprehension is assessed.
5. Supplementary Phonics Tests: Any or all of the tests listed below can be administered. Results are interpreted in a criterion-referenced rather than norm-referenced manner.

Supplementary Tests:

Initial consonants
Final consonants
Consonant digraphs
Consonant blends
Initial consonant substitution
Auditory recognition of initial consonant sounds
Auditory discrimination
Short and long vowel sounds
Vowels with *r*
Vowel diphthongs and digraphs
Common syllables
Blending

ual's reading potential. Hence, the potential score component of the DRS should be used with extreme caution.

Norms and Standardization Group: The current revision of the DRS was standardized on a sample of 534 students. Although the manual section on the standardization group con-

tains no information regarding this sample, the validity section describes these students as pupils from grades one through eight who were attending school in sixty-two districts in thirty-two states. However, the extremely small number of total students and the large number of school districts and states would drastically limit the number of students in each group. No information is given on the number of students in each grade group.

Reliability: Reliability data are discussed largely in terms of earlier test versions. The author reports test-retest reliability only for grades one and two and only for the word analysis and phonics subtests. Test-retest reliability is relatively low, with only twelve of twenty-four reliability coefficients exceeding .80. Split-half reliability is reported for an unspecified number of students in grades one and two. The majority of the twenty-four correlations are high (exceeding .80). Reliability for students in grades three through eight is not reported.

Validity: A description of the test's development is erroneously presented as evidence of construct validity. Correlations between the DRS and other scales are offered as evidence of concurrent validity, but this evidence is also unconvincing. In general, the discussion in the manual of the validity of the DRS is confusing and incomplete.

Summary of the DRS for the Test Consumer: The current version of the DRS is an improvement over previous versions. The revised examiner's manual with its cassette training tape is easy to read and use. However, the DRS still relies on the questionable practice of using auditory discrimination as an index of a child's reading potential. Furthermore, its norms, reliability, and validity are weak or undemonstrated. As a diagnostic instrument, the DRS is still lacking.

Other Diagnostic Reading Tests

Gates–McKillop–Horowitz Reading Diagnostic Tests

Overview: The Gates–McKillop–Horowitz Reading Diagnostic Tests (GMH) (Gates, McKillop, and Horowitz 1981) are an individually administered, norm-referenced, diagnostic reading test appropriate for children in grades one through six. The GMH contains fourteen subtests designed to test the decoding process skills of reading. The test is heavily loaded with oral reading skills and does not measure reading comprehension. No specific order exists for the administration of subtests, nor do all of the subtests have to be administered. Table 17-7 lists the subtests of the GMH.

Administration and Scoring: Two types of scores are available for the GMH. First, raw scores can be converted to grade scores. These grade scores are then converted into ratings of high, medium, low, or very low in the general areas of oral reading, word recognition, and spelling. Grade scores are not available for the other subtests. For all subtests, a diagnosis of specific skills is available compared to the norming sample. These skills are rated as average, above average, or below average. These ratings are not based on any objective evidence but rather on subjective criteria selected by the test authors.

Norms and Standardization Group: The GMH was normed on a relatively small sample size of 600 children in grades one through six. Although this group constituted a representative sample in terms of ethnic background and urban–rural split, 65 percent of the students in the norm sample were enrolled in private schools. Also, no information is given as to the characteristics of this population.

Table 17-7   Skills Measured by the Gates–McKillop–Horowitz Reading Diagnostic Tests

1. Oral Reading: Measures a variety of different types of oral reading errors including hesitations, omissions, additions, repetitions, and mispronunciations.
2. Words (Flash): Assesses sight vocabulary using a tachistoscope. Words are flashed for 500 milliseconds (one-half second) and the student reads the word aloud.
3. Words (Untimed): Measures word-attack skills. Student decodes words without time constraints.
4. Knowledge of Word Parts: A six-section subtest.
   A. Syllabication: Nonsense words are divided into syllables. The pupil's task is to read the words aloud.
   B. Recognizing and Blending Common Word Parts: Student is required to read nonsense words. If the word is misread, the examiner presents the word in two parts, and the child is asked to pronounce each part and blend them together to reform the word.
   C. Reading Words: Student is asked to read nonsense words presented in their entirety.
   D. Giving Letter Sounds: Student is shown letters and asked to give their sounds.
   E. Naming Capital Letters: Student is asked to name capital letters when they are visually presented.
   F. Naming Lowercase Letters: Student is asked to name lowercase letters when they are visually presented.
5. Recognizing Visual Form of Sounds: Student is read nonsense words and must identify the vowel that produces the vowel sound in each presented word.
6. Auditory Blending: Examiner says the parts of words. The student must blend them to produce the entire word.
7. Auditory Discrimination: Assesses student's ability to discriminate English phonemes.
8. Written Expression: A two-part subtest.
   A. Spelling: Student writes words that have been dictated by the examiner.
   B. Informal Writing Sample: Child may write on any topic of choice. Sample is scored on the basis of expressed ideas and handwriting.

Reliability: Approximately 5 percent ($n =$ 27) of the normed population were retested in an assessment of test-retest reliability on the oral reading test only. Test-retest reliability for this subtest is given at .94, but no information is provided as to grade level of these students or the retest interval. Interrater reliability is also assessed on the oral reading test and reported as exceeding .90. The reliability of other subtests is not reported.

Validity: The authors of the GMH attempt to prove the validity of the test by showing that it correlates with other tests. However, correlations between tests alone do not demonstrate test validity. Thus, the validity of the GMH still needs to be demonstrated adequately.

Summary of the GMH for the Test Consumer: In summary, the GMH offers some degree of diagnostic information, particularly in the area of oral reading. However, it possesses a number of weaknesses. The norming sample is small and nonrepresentative, with the majority of students enrolled in private schools. Its reliability and validity have not been substantiated, and the use of the grade scores are problematic at best. Finally, although it purports to measure the range of reading skills, it does not measure comprehension. Thus, it should be considered solely as a decoding and oral reading test. At best, it should be used cautiously and in conjunction with other reading assessment instruments.

Durrell Analysis of Reading Difficulty

Overview: The Durrell Analysis of Reading Difficulty (DARD) (Durrell and Catterson 1980) is an individually administered norm-referenced, diagnostic test designed to measure reading strengths and weaknesses. The test is appropriate for students in grades one through six. The DARD measures reading skill in twenty areas ranging from oral reading

to phonics to listening comprehension. It does not measure reading comprehension.

Administration and Scoring: The current manual contains much more explicit directions than did previous editions. One problem area for scoring is that of "imagery flow." The examiner chooses one of two options: "rich" flow or "poor" flow. However, there are no directions in the manual for making or interpreting such decisions. The results of the subtests are plotted as grade level scores on a profile chart. This profile provides a graphic representation of the child's reading strengths and weaknesses. One of the most useful aspects of the DARD is a checklist of individual reading needs that is included in the individual's record booklet. This checklist and the profile chart form the basis of an individualized remedial reading program for the child.

Norms and Standardization Group: A total of 1,224 children were included in the standardization sample of the DARD. Norms were obtained from at least 200 children per grade (grades 1 through 6) in five geographic regions of the United States. No information is provided regarding the sex, ages, SES, and reading curriculum of the children in the norm group.

Reliability: No test-retest reliability is reported for the DARD. Internal-consistency reliability was assessed. Reliabilities range from .63 (visual memory for words) to .97 (intermediate spelling). Reliabilities are greater than .80 for eight of the thirteen subtests.

Validity: The validity of the DARD is described in terms of the test's longevity and the opinions of experts who have used and reviewed the test over time. The manual refers to current professional confidence in the DARD as a measure of its general validity. This is not an acceptable demonstration of the test's validity, and further empirical evidence is needed before the test's validity can be accepted.

Summary of the DARD for the Test Consumer: In summary, the DARD is a diagnostic test designed to measure a child's oral and silent reading difficulties. A continuing strength of the test is its behavioral checklist that, together with the individualized graphic profile, helps pinpoint a child's reading strengths and weaknesses. However, the test suffers from a variety of weaknesses. Test norms are questionable, and the standardization group was small and too narrow to yield meaningful norms. Neither the reliability nor validity of the instrument has been adequately demonstrated. Finally, the grade scores offered in the DARD are of little educational value.

Rosewell–Chall Diagnostic Reading Test of Word Analysis Skills: Revised and Extended

Overview: The Rosewell–Chall Diagnostic Reading Test of Word Analysis (RCDRT) (Rosewell and Chall 1978) is an individually administered diagnostic test designed to assess a student's knowledge about and ability to use selected word recognition skills. The instrument consists of fourteen subtests: one assesses sight vocabulary; another, syllabication; two assess naming letters; and ten assess phonics skills. The test is designed for readers in grades one through four. There are two forms of the test.

Administration and Scoring: Total administration time ranges from ten to fifteen minutes. Performance on the various subtests is judged using what the manual calls a "qualitative approach." Student responses are categorized as "mastery" (greater than 85 percent), "review indicated" (50 percent to 85 percent), or "systematic instruction indicated" (less than 50 percent correct). No rationale or justification

is given for these three categories, and the review indicated spectrum (50 percent to 85 percent) may be too broad to be educationally useful.

Norms and Standardization Group; Reliability and Validity: There are no norms for the RCDRT. Test-retest and alternate-form reliability are reported, with the sixty test-retest reliability coefficients being quite high. However, the number of students participating in the reliability study was very small. Alternate-form reliability is also high, with seventeen of eighteen coefficients ranging from .95 to .99. The validity data reported for the RCDRT are not as strong as the reliability information. The test shows correlations between it and other achievement tests but presents no other evidence as to its validity.

Summary of the RCDRT for the Test Consumer: In summary, the RCDRT probably has value for diagnosing the instructional needs of students because it measures so many different reading skills. On the negative side, its brevity and the relatively low number of test items contained in certain subtests detract from its content validity. Furthermore, its scoring system hinders its usefulness as a diagnostic instrument.

Testing Reading Comprehension

Fewer tests exist to measure reading comprehension than to measure decoding skills. This may be the case because reading comprehension is more difficult to define and therefore measure than is decoding (Johnston 1983; Trabasso 1980).

Recently, definitions of what constitutes reading comprehension have changed. In the past, reading comprehension was thought to have taken place if the reader could simply recall what occurred in a passage. This process has been labeled *passive* comprehension

(Johnston 1983; Luftig and Johnson 1982). More recent definitions of reading comprehension view the process as taking place only when the reader has established logical connections among the ideas in the text and can express these ideas in a paraphrased form (Palincsar and Brown 1984; Trabasso 1980). This requires making inferences from what has been read (Luftig and Greeson 1983; Warren, Nicholas, and Trabasso 1979) and implies that reading comprehension is a *strategic* process (Palincsar and Brown 1984; Palincsar 1987). Finally, reading comprehension is contingent on the reader's ability to attach what has been read to existing knowledge or experience (Johnson and Luftig 1983; Paris, Cross, and Lipson 1984).

Factors That Affect Reading Comprehension and Its Assessment

Assessment of reading comprehension requires interpreting the person's performance on a task based on the information given in a passage. Reading comprehension depends on these three elements (Johnston 1983):

1. A text that includes a defined context, structure, and language.
2. The appropriateness of the text to the student's prior knowledge and experiences.
3. The task demands of the assessment procedures.

The Text: To select appropriate passages for assessment of comprehension, one must know the characteristics of the passages used. To accomplish this, professionals must analyze the text in terms of the following three characteristics:

1. The content and structure of the text and the relationship between these two variables.
2. The writer–reader relationship, that is, the adequacy of the passage as a communicative device.
3. The degree to which the ideas expressed in the text are in agreement with the reader's background, knowledge, and experiences.

A child can perform poorly on a reading comprehension task as a function of text characteristics. If the content, structure, and language of the passage are inappropriate for the child, comprehension will be impaired. Likewise, if the text's message is ambiguous or poorly presented, comprehension will also be hindered. Finally, to the extent that the passage discusses ideas outside the experience or knowledge of the reader, comprehension will be poor even though the content and language are at an appropriate level for the reader.

The Task: It is extremely important to know precisely what we are asking the student to perform when we administer a comprehension assessment instrument. Various factors make up the task, and they must be taken into account when analyzing the student's reading comprehension (see Table 17-8). To the extent that these factors are not understood in terms of the task at hand, errors in interpreting comprehension performance will result and contribute to poor test validity.

Reading Comprehension Tests

The tests discussed in this section contain a strong comprehension assessment compo-

Table 17-8 Aspects of the Task That Affect Reading Comprehension

1. Production Requirements (What is the student expected to do?)
2. Memory and Retrieval Requirements
3. Reasoning Requirements
4. Motivation to Perform and Do Well on the Task
5. Purpose for Which the Text Is Being Read
6. Social Setting and Interaction
7. Expectation of the Examiner's Goals and Task Demands
8. Student's Test–Reading "Wiseness"

nent. Some of these tests measure *only* comprehension; others measure a combination of decoding and comprehension skills. In the case of these latter tests, however, comprehension is assessed in a more detailed and complete manner than in the reading assessment instruments discussed earlier in this chapter.

The Test of Reading Comprehension

Overview: The Test of Reading Comprehension (TORC) (Brown, Hammill, and Wiederholt 1978) is designed to measure the silent reading comprehension of students in grades one through eight. It can be administered individually or in groups. The TORC claims to measure both general comprehension and comprehension in three academic areas: mathematics, social studies, and science. Eight subtests are included in the TORC (Table 17-9). The main subtests constitute a core of reading comprehension that the authors claim are relatively free of content area vocabulary; the supplementary subtests are designed to measure content-related vocabulary. Testing materials include an examiner's manual, student booklets, answer sheets, individual profile sheets, and separate response forms for the subtest Reading the Directions of Schoolwork.

Administration and Scoring: The TORC can be given as a group or individual test. However, it is quite difficult to follow the recommended administration procedures with a large group of students. Thus the TORC should be administered only to small groups. Total administration time is approximately 90 to 120 minutes.

Raw scores for the three core subtests can be transformed into scaled scores and then into a Reading Comprehension Quotient (RCQ). The authors claim that the RCQ is comparable with such indexes as general in-

Table 17-9 Subtests of the Test of Reading Comprehension

The General Reading Comprehension Core Subtests

1. General Vocabulary: Student reads three stimulus words that are related in some way and then selects two other words from a group of four that are related to the stimulus words. Both selections must be correct to receive credit.
2. Syntactic Similarities: Student reads five sentences and selects two that are most nearly alike in meaning. Both selections must be correct to receive credit.
3. Paragraph Reading: Student reads six paragraphs (one at a time) and answers five comprehension questions after reading each paragraph. Questions include selecting "best" title, recalling details, drawing an inference, and drawing a negative inference (e.g., Which sentence could *not* go in the story?).

*Supplementary Diagnostic Subtests
(Any or all of these subtests can be administered.)*

4. Mathematics Vocabulary: Student reads three stimulus items that refer to mathematics or quantitative concepts and then selects from a group of four words the two that are related to the stimulus words. Both selections must be correct to receive credit.

telligence (IQ) and language ability. These claims remain unsubstantiated, however, and the RCQ remains a confusing if not misleading statistic. Scaled scores can be charted to create a student profile. Raw scores in the specific content areas and in the Reading Directions and Sentence Sequencing subtests can be transformed into scaled scores. These scores are then charted to profile the student's performance.

Norms and Standardization Group: The TORC was normed on 2,707 students residing in ten states. However, southern and western states are not represented. The authors claim that the sample is representative for sex, age, and urban and rural populations.

Reliability: Both test-retest and internal-consistency reliability were measured. Test-retest reliability (after a one-week interval) was obtained for each subtest. Test-retest reliabilities for most of the subtests were generally acceptable, the notable exceptions being the Mathematics and Social Studies Vocabulary subtests. Internal reliability was obtained for subtests and grade levels, with 95 percent of the coefficients exceeding .80.

Validity: Evidence is presented for content, criterion-related, and construct validity. Evidence indicates that the TORC does differentiate between normal and poor readers and that it correlates highly with intelligence tests because of the cognitive–thinking processes required. However, this high correlation with intelligence tests is a problem because the instrument may measure intelligence and reasoning ability rather than assessing reading comprehension alone. This is particularly true in the subtests of Sequencing and Syntactic Abilities. In general, the validity of the TORC needs to be demonstrated more strongly.

Summary of the TORC for the Test Consumer: The TORC is a strong alternative to traditional methods of testing reading comprehension. It contains vocabulary subtests in both general and content areas as well as paragraph comprehension. On the negative side, the TORC possesses relatively poorly constructed norms and has an unproven validity. Several subtests (e.g., Syntactic Similarities) measure skills rarely taught in classrooms, thus casting some doubt on the test's content validity. Finally, the reading quotient (RCQ) is confusing and offers little information to the professional. In short, the TORC is an innovative and interesting instrument, but it should be used and interpreted with caution.

The Wisconsin Tests of Reading Skill Development

Overview: The Wisconsin Tests of Reading Skill Development: Comprehension (WTRSD–C) (Otto and Kann 1977) is an objective-based testing program designed to measure comprehension in terms of higher-level thinking as well as literal comprehension. It is an individually administered criterion-referenced test designed for kindergarten through grade six.

The seven levels of the WTRSD–C (A–G) are designed for the different grades. Four main areas or "strands" of comprehension are tested: word meanings, sentence meaning, passage meaning, and sequencing. The tests also endeavor to measure self-directed reading, interpretive reading, and creative reading. All levels of the WTRSD–C come with consumable booklets, an administrator's manual, profile cards for students, ditto masters, and a teacher's planning guide to help implement remediation.

Administration and Scoring: For each subtest, approximately ten to twenty items are introduced through practice items. Instructions for both examiner and test taker are clear and easy to understand. Testing time is approximately 150 minutes spread out over a suggested four sessions. The test uses a criterion-referenced, mastery level format. A cutoff score of 80 percent is set as the criterion level for passing each tested skill. Students with scores below 80 percent are suggested candidates for remediation. Skill levels are used to create a student comprehension profile.

Norms and Standardization Group: This test is fully criterion-referenced. There are no norms.

Reliability: The authors state that the reliabilities of the individual subtests are in the .70s and .80s. However, they provide no discussion of how these reliabilities were calculated and no supporting documentation. This lack of reliability evidence is a major shortcoming of the test.

Validity: According to the authors, the skills of reading comprehension have been identified and behaviorally written, and therefore the high content validity of the WTRSD–C is inferred. However, because other authors offer no empirical evidence of the test's validity, it is still in question.

Summary of the WTRSD–C for the Test Consumer: The WTRSD–C may be one of the most comprehensive tests of reading comprehension currently available. The word *may* is used because the technical information given in the manual regarding the test is woefully inadequate. However, the subtests available and the strands tested appear to possess strong content validity. What is needed is a systematic study of the technical characteristics of the test. Until that occurs, the WTRSD–C is recommended for use with students if the test is interpreted with caution.

Other Tests of Reading Comprehension

Gates–MacGinitie Reading Tests

Overview: The Gates–MacGinitie Reading Tests (G–M) (MacGinitie 1978) are designed to measure a limited domain of reading, that is, vocabulary and comprehension. The test has seven levels, and the instrument is appropriate for students in grades one through twelve. The vocabulary tests measure decoding skills and the meaning of single words by using synonyms. The comprehension subtests use a multiple-choice format to question students about passages read silently. Raw scores on the G–M can be converted to a number of derived scores, including grade equivalents, percentiles, and stanines. The test yields little diagnostic information in terms of objectives passed or failed.

Norms and Standardization Group: The tests were standardized on a national sample of approximately 65,000 students. The stratified sample took four variables into consideration: geographic region, school enrollment size, family income, and years of schooling completed by parents. The sample is also representative for blacks and Hispanics. The test contains separate norms for each level.

Reliability: Test-retest, internal-consistency, and alternate-form reliability are reported. The test-retest interval was assessed between October and May of the same school year, and reliabilities range from .77 to .89 depending on the form. Internal-consistency reliability for all forms is quite high, ranging from .77 (Form F—vocabulary) to .94 (total for Form A). Most reliability coefficients are in the .80 to .95 range. Alternate-form reliability for the total test at level R is .91 but only ranges from .57 to .78 for forms A through F.

Validity: Validity is reported in terms of the correlation between the second and first editions of the test. Correlations range from .74 to .94. The logic apparently used by the test authors is that if the first edition was valid and the two editions correlate highly, then the second edition must also be valid. This, however, does not adequately demonstrate the test's validity, and more evidence is needed.

Summary of the G–M for the Test Consumer: In summary, the G–M has much to recommend it. The instrument measures comprehension on seven different levels, it possesses exemplary standardization and norming procedures, and it has a demonstrated reliability. On the negative side, it needs to demonstrate its validity more strongly. The biggest drawback to the test is its lack of specificity for use as a diagnostic tool. Although it does yield information about the child's reading comprehension, the information is global rather than diagnostic in nature. As such, the G–M should be used as a screening–placement instrument rather than for in-depth diagnostic purposes.

Criterion-Referenced Reading Tests

To this point, most of the reading tests discussed have been norm-referenced in nature. Some of these tests claim to be useful as both norm-referenced and criterion-referenced instruments. However, on inspection, even these assessment instruments are of more use in comparing students' scores against those of peers.

This section discusses reading tests that are purely criterion-referenced. As such, these tests measure the individual child's mastery of specific skills of reading. They also allow the teacher to create an in-depth profile of the child's mastery of reading.

These tests possess a number of advantages over their norm-referenced reading counterparts. First, criterion-referenced reading tests describe the skills of reading in *behavioral* or *instructional* objective form. That is, individual test items are keyed to individual instructional objectives in such a way that test items missed yield specific, behavioral information about the reading skills that the student lacks. Second, to a greater extent than norm-referenced tests, criterion-referenced reading tests reflect the *sequence* of necessary reading skills. They not only indicate which reading skills the student lacks but also suggest a sequential order in which the skills should be acquired. These tests allow in-depth, diagnostic information to be collected and interpreted regarding specific basic skills the student needs to acquire before going on to higher-level procedures.

Finally, and perhaps most important, criterion-referenced reading tests offer *remediational* suggestions for helping students acquire the reading skills and objectives that they lack. Many of these tests contain specific lessons, activities, and materials designed to remediate reading weaknesses. Others key their objectives and items to popular basal reading series so that teachers can remediate reading weaknesses using activities contained in the student's basal reader. Whichever method is used, criterion-referenced reading tests offer a complete assessment and reading program that contains in-depth assessment (items), prescription (instructional objectives), and remediation (activities, materials, and lessons). They are a most valuable tool for the educational professional.

Keep in mind, however, that authors of criterion-referenced tests often imply that the reliability and validity of their tests should not be of concern. Many such tests do not report reliability or validity, or they report this information inadequately. Reliability and validity of criterion-referenced tests are vitally important. Because the tests are tied to diagnostic, prescriptive, and remediational programming for students, it is crucial that they possess content validity. After all, what good is the in-depth skill testing and remediational programming indicated by invalid tests? Likewise, such tests must be reliable. If the test consumer cannot be confident that the same student tested on two occasions will score about the same on the assessment instrument, what confidence can be placed in the academic programming suggested for the student? For these reasons, the test consumer should pay close attention to the reliability and validity information on criterion-referenced tests, when such information is available. Unavailable or inadequate technical information should be considered a weakness of the test under consideration.

Criterion Reading

Overview: Criterion Reading (Hackett 1971) is a comprehensive system designed to accomplish two goals: diagnose students' reading strengths and weaknesses and help teach-

Table 17-10   Levels and Skills Tested by
Criterion Reading

Level	Grades	Skill Areas
1	K	Sensorimotor
2	1	Listening and Speaking
3	2–3	Reading
4	4–6	Reading
5	Jr. High–Adult	Reading and Writing
6	Basic Education	Reading and Writing

Competencies Areas

1. Motor Skills: Fine and gross motor skills.
2. Visual Input: Matching symbols, objects, and colors.
3. Auditory Input: Matching beginning sounds, repeating initial consonants, etc.
4. Phonology: Classifying, identifying, using, and producing language sounds and sound combinations.
5. Structural Analysis: Classifying sounds, using rules for reading, phonics, and syllabication
6. Verbal Information: Concepts and facts, classification and use of concepts.
7. Syntax.
8. Reading Comprehension.

ers design and carry out a learning–evaluation reading system in the classroom. The system contains a hierarchy of 450 reading skills considered necessary for reading competence. These skills are divided into five levels of competence, the levels being a function of educational grade. Eight main skill areas are tested. These levels, their typical grade of presentation, and the areas of reading assessed are shown in Table 17-10. It should be pointed out that the hierarchical sequencing of the 450 skills has been criticized by some authors (Fremer 1973), and the test authors have not provided an adequate theoretical defense of the sequencing.

Criterion Reading comes with student test booklets, administration directions, a teacher's guide containing remediational activities, student workbooks, individual student record forms, and a group record form. The program provides specific instructional objectives, and the student workbooks include activities designed to reach each objective prescriptively. Prices differ depending on the level purchased; the cost of purchasing a total program is approximately $200.

Administration and Scoring: Criterion Reading contains two types of tests: diagnostic outcomes skills and process skills tests. Teachers administer diagnostic outcomes tests until a weakness is encountered. At that point, process skills tests are administered, with each test item corresponding to a specific reading instructional objective. By administering process skills tests, the teacher is able to diagnose specific reading skills deficiencies in each of the eight content areas. However, because Criterion Reading does not possess survey or screening tests, all diagnostic process tests must be given. This becomes very time consuming for both student and examiner.

Criterion Reading is mastery based. Mastery is considered to be 100 percent for tests of fewer than 20 items and 95 percent for all other tests. For some children, especially exceptional learners, these mastery levels may be too high; a mastery level of 85 to 95 percent might be more realistic.

Reliability and Validity: No reliability or validity information is reported for Criterion Reading. This is a major weakness of the test, especially as the theoretical foundation of the instrument is based on its hypothesized content validity.

Summary of Criterion Reading for the Test Consumer: Criterion Reading offers an in-depth diagnostic and remediational assessment program. In addition, it offers prescriptive activities. Although its sequencing of skills has been criticized, the skills themselves appear to be valid for success in reading. On the negative side, it is cumbersome to administer because it does not possess survey or screening tests for obtaining an initial (survey) estimate of the chlid's reading weaknesses. Its reliability and validity have not been assessed, and this is a major weakness. Despite these reasons and its relative high cost, Criterion Reading can provide useful, in-depth, diagnostic–prescriptive information to the educational professional.

Diagnosis: An Instructional Aid (Reading)

Overview: Perhaps one of the most complete criterion-referenced instruments is Diagnosis: An Instructional Aid (Reading) (Shub, Carlin, Friedman, Kaplan, and Katien 1973). This program is designed to assess, completely and in depth, children's reading skills and to assist the teacher in systematically planning and programming remediational reading instruction.

Diagnosis: An Instructional Aid consists of two forms. Level A is used to test children in kindergarten through grade three; Level B is appropriate for children in grades four through six. The tests measure reading skills in the area of phonetic analysis, structural analysis, comprehension, and vocabulary and the student's ability to use reference sources and materials. The instrument consists of thirty-four probe tests, cassette tapes, a prescription guide, and a class progress chart. The prescription guide is keycd to specific instructional objectives in reading, with each objective cross-referenced to six commonly used basal reading programs. The prescription guide identifies the pages in the basal reader teacher's manual where the skill is covered, gives additional activities for teaching that specific objective, and includes ditto masters for the teacher's use.

Administration and Scoring: Administration of Diagnosis: An Instructional Aid is shown in the chart in Figure 17-4. The teacher first administers a short survey test to obtain a global view of the child's strengths and weaknesses in reading. From this survey test, the examiner determines which of the thirty-four in-depth probe tests should be administered. Because each item in the probe tests is paired with a specific instructional objective, the teacher acquires both a diagnostic description of the child's reading weaknesses and remediational goal objectives. The teacher can then consult the prescription guide for remediational activities.

Reliability and Validity: Unfortunately, reliability and validity are not discussed in the test manual. Tests such as these must demonstrate content validity and reliability to justify the time and expense that teachers and reading professionals must invest to use the instruments.

Summary of Diagnosis: An Instructional Aid for the Test Consumer: Diagnosis: An Instructional Aid is perhaps the best criterion-referenced reading test on the market. The use of survey tests frees the teacher from having to administer all of the probe tests. Additionally, the prescription guide keyed to six basal readers is most helpful in designing remediational programming. Unfortunately, reliability and validity information are not available for this instrument. Nevertheless, the tests may prove worthwhile and helpful in diagnosing and planning remediation for students' learning problems.

Fountain Valley Teacher Support System in Reading

Overview: The Fountain Valley Teacher Support System in Reading is really two separate programs: the Fountain Valley Support System in Reading–Revised (FVR) (Zweig 1985) and the Fountain Valley Support System in Secondary Reading (FVSR) (Zweig 1976). As the names imply, the FVR is intended for students in grades one through six and the FVSR is intended for pupils in grades seven through twelve.

Figure 17-4   Use of Diagnosis: An Instructional Aid

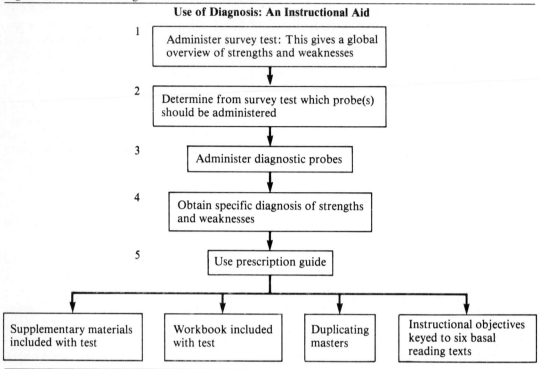

Use of Diagnosis: An Instructional Aid

1. Administer survey test: This gives a global overview of strengths and weaknesses
2. Determine from survey test which probe(s) should be administered
3. Administer diagnostic probes
4. Obtain specific diagnosis of strengths and weaknesses
5. Use prescription guide

- Supplementary materials included with test
- Workbook included with test
- Duplicating masters
- Instructional objectives keyed to six basal reading texts

The FVR consists of criterion-referenced test items organized into five curricular areas: phonetic analysis, structural analysis, vocabulary development, comprehension, and study skills. A set of 367 specific instructional objectives is keyed to the test items, and an extensive list of teaching materials from a variety of commercially available reading series is keyed to each instructional objective. Each of the five content areas is covered by specific subtests (probes) that perform in-depth diagnosis of the student's reading strengths and weaknesses. Cost of the FVR for each grade level ranges from approximately $60 to $100.

The FVSR program consists of three strands, each of which is divided into the three domains of vocabulary, comprehension, and study skills. Each domain is measured by a number of criterion-referenced tests that are tied to instructional objectives. In all, there are sixty-one tests: seventeen for vo-

cabulary, twenty for comprehension, and twenty-four for study skills. A manual and resource guide are included. The cost for the entire program is approximately $330.

Administration and Scoring: The FVR and FVSR programs are administered much like Diagnosis: An Instructional Aid. Optional survey and screening tests are used to pinpoint the general area(s) of weakness. In-depth probe tests in the content areas are then administered to diagnose specific reading weaknesses. Finally, the instructional guides are used to help plan and implement remediational programming for the students.

No norms on the FVR and FVSR programs are used because the tests are completely criterion-referenced. A mastery level scoring system is used. For FVR, mastery is defined as 100 percent correct for 2- and 3-item subtests and 67 to 88 percent for subtests of other lengths. For the FVSR system, mastery is defined as 67 to 83 percent. Some professionals believe that a score of under 80 percent correct does not indicate mastery but rather a need for further remediation. Thus, a mastery score of 67 percent on the two systems may be too low a criterion.

Reliability and Validity: As with the other criterion-referenced tests discussed in this section, no information is reported. This is a weakness of the FV systems, as it is of other criterion-referenced tests.

Summary of the FV Systems for the Test Consumer: The FV systems offer many of the same advantages and disadvantages of other criterion-referenced reading systems. They are in-depth and diagnostic in scope and offer useful information as to specific reading strengths and weaknesses. Test items are keyed to specific instructional objectives, with remediational programming provided for each objective. On the negative side, they are expensive to purchase and time consuming to administer, although the survey tests do eliminate the need for administering all probe tests. Finally, there is some question as to whether the mastery levels specified on both FV systems are stringent enough to imply mastery.

Informal Reading Assessment

Much of the information needed to evaluate a student's reading performance properly and to create remediational programming is available through the use of informal reading assessment (Otto and Smith 1983; Pikulski and Shanahan 1982). Informal assessment may be carried out for the following reasons (Johns 1982):

1. Studying, evaluating, or diagnosing reading behavior.
2. Monitoring student progress.
3. Supplementing or confirming information acquired from formal reading tests.

4. Obtaining information not readily available from formal reading tests.

Most informal reading assessment occurs within the context and confines of the classroom, not in a specialized or artificial testing environment. The teacher using informal reading assessment is interested in how the child reads in the classroom environment using real-life classroom materials, not the contrived reading materials contained in some formal tests. This is one of the primary advantages of informal reading assessment (Johns 1982).

Types of Informal Reading Assessment

Decoding and Word Recognition Skills

Observations: Observational techniques are a major tool in the informal assessment of word decoding and recognition. Ongoing daily observations of the child's reading behavior provide the teacher with relevant information about the child's *classroom* reading, something that standardized tests cannot do. Observational data also allow the teacher to confirm information gathered from standardized reading tests.

It is crucial that information obtained through observation be *systematically* recorded. Systematic reading observation takes one of two forms: dated observations, which are recorded and periodically summarized, and checklists. Examples of these procedures are shown in Figure 17-5.

Informal Reading Inventories: One of the most widely used assessment procedures is the Informal Reading Inventory (IRI). As originally outlined by Betts (1946), the IRI consists of carefully selected reading passages that usually range from preprimer through grade eight. The passages are taken from books and articles with which the student has had little or no contact. As the student reads aloud, the teacher records mistakes in word recognition and decoding. These mistakes are

Figure 17-5 Systematic Reading Observations and Checklists

Name _____

Observer: _____

Directions: *Indicate when the behavior was observed to occur by placing the date in the blank next to the item. If the behavior is not observed, do not make any mark.*

_____ 1. Listens to short stories (about five minutes duration) without interrupting

_____ 2. Uses simple sentences in his conversation

_____ 3. Tells about a sequence of three actions he has performed in correct order

_____ 4. Looks at picture books from front to back consistently

_____ 5. Looks at a row of written information from left to right

_____ 6. Follows a series of three directions given to him orally

_____ 7. Says letter names when shown cards with letters printed on them

_____ 8. Tells what will happen next in an unfinished story

_____ 9. Tells the main idea of a story after he has read it silently

_____ 10. Repeats short rhymes he has heard a number of times

_____ 11. Dictates his own three- or four-sentence story to the teacher

_____ 15. Illustrates his own stories appropriately

Source: G. Wallace and S. Larsen (1978). *Educational Assessment of Learning Problems: Testing for Teaching* (Boston: Allyn and Bacon). Used by permission.

later analyzed to determine whether there is a pattern to the pupil's errors. After reading each passage, the student is usually asked a series of comprehension questions.

IRI passages are *graded,* that is, the words and ideas used in the paragraphs increase in difficulty. Students can be administered all of the passages, or testing can stop when a ceiling level is reached.

In addition to information about the type of errors made, IRIs yield information as to the *level* of reading at which the student is operating. These levels are not grade levels. Rather, they are defined as the child's *independent, instructional, frustration,* and *hearing comprehension* levels. These levels are determined by the degree of mastery the child shows in the increasingly more difficult passages (Kirk, Kliebhan, and Lerner 1978). The degree of mastery needed to attain each level is shown in Figure 17-6.

Analysis of Oral Reading Errors

IRIs can be used to gauge whether a pattern of errors exists in the child's oral reading. This procedure is known as *error analysis.*

A number of steps are used in error analysis. First, appropriate reading materials must be selected. This selection is made using a number of criteria. For example, materials can be selected on the basis of closeness of fit to those used in the student's classroom, or they can be chosen on the basis of commonness or frequency with which certain words appear in the pupil's reading. Data on the later characteristic can be obtained by using one of the available word lists (Dolch 1953; Johnson 1971). Finally, the special education teacher can use survival or functional words, words that must be read for successful independent living (Kirk, Kliebhan, and Lerner 1978; Polloway and Polloway 1981).

Informal Assessment of Comprehension

Checklists: In addition to assessing decoding skills, checklists can be used informally to assess reading comprehension. Comprehension checklists are used to assess skills of individual students or the comprehension of a given reading group. Table 17-11 contains a sample checklist that assesses the comprehension skills of children.

Figure 17-6 Reading Levels as Measured by Informal Reading Inventories

Reading Level	Word Recognition	Comprehension
Independent	99%	90% and above
Instructional	95%	75% and above
Frustration	90% and below	50% and below
Hearing comprehension		75% material read to student

Source: G. Wallace and S. Larsen (1978). *Educational Assessment of Learning Problems: Testing for Teaching* (Boston: Allyn and Bacon). Used by permission.

Informal Reading Inventories: Informal Reading Inventories can also be used to assess children's reading comprehension. IRIs are flexible enough to accommodate specific types of reading skills that interest the teacher. For example, a teacher-made IRI can ask literal types of comprehension questions only, or it can assess comprehension at a variety of more complex levels.

In creating a comprehension IRI, a num-

Table 17-11 A Teacher-Made Checklist for Reading Comprehension

Chris	Tim	Steve	Laurel	
✓	✓		✓	Establishes cause and effect
✓			✓	Anticipates outcomes
✓		✓	✓	Draws conclusions
✓		✓	✓	Distinguishes fact from opinion
✓	✓		✓	Makes inferences
✓			✓	Establishes sequence
✓			✓	Forms opinions
✓		✓	✓	Compares and contrasts
✓		✓	✓	Evaluates and solves problems
			✓	Reacts to mood and time
			✓	Supports opinions with relevant data
	✓			Judges statements
✓	✓		✓	Analyzes character
✓	✓		✓	Judges accuracy
✓			✓	Recognizes persuasive statements

Comments

Tim	Steve
Having difficulty mastering these skills	No problems

Source: G. Wallace and S. Larsen (1978). *Educational Assessment of Learning Problems: Testing for Teaching* (Boston: Allyn and Bacon). Used by permission.

Table 17-12 Guidelines for Creating
Questions for Informal Reading Inventories

1. Questions should appear in the approximate order in which the information appeared in the passage.
2. Ask main idea questions before detail questions.
3. Ask important questions about most important material. Avoid questions about unimportant or superficial material.
4. Check the sequence of questions to make sure that subsequent questions cannot be answered or inferred from earlier questions.
5. Make sure that two or more questions do not require the same answer.
6. Avoid questions that contain two or more correct answers.
7. People who have not read the passage should not be able to answer questions correctly. If they can, the questions are assessing general rather than passage-specific information.
8. Pictures accompanying the text should not give clues to the correct answers.
9. Keep questions short and syntactically simple.
10. Begin questions with *who, what, when, where, how,* or *why.*
11. Avoid starting questions in a negative manner.
12. Avoid questions that require students to create or reconstruct lists.
13. Occasionally ask questions that require students to define a given word in order to assess receptive reading vocabulary.
14. Avoid asking questions that elicit student opinions.
15. Avoid yes–no and true–false questions. Students have a 50 percent probability of answering these items correctly by chance.

ber of guidelines apply (Wood and Moe 1985). These are shown in Table 17-12.

The Cloze Procedure: The *cloze procedure* is another informal technique for measuring both reading level and degree of comprehension. In using the cloze procedure, the student is presented with a reading passage of 250 to 300 words. Starting with the second sentence, every fifth word is omitted. The student's task is to fill in the missing words based on textual

context. Figure 17-7 contains an example of a cloze passage and Figure 17-8 contains guidelines for choosing an appropriate test passage and creating a cloze test. The cloze procedure is an excellent method for evaluating a student's reading comprehension (Gilliland 1974; Pikulski and Tobin 1982). In addition to determining the child's reading levels, it also demonstrates how well the student understands certain types of material from a particular content area. Thus, it is highly recommended as an informal measure of reading comprehension.

Figure 17-7 A Cloze Comprehension Test

The New Flashlight

   Jerry walked to school by himself because he liked to think about things on the way to school. Sometimes the things he 1 about were not important. 2 today he was thinking 3 something very important, and 4 was talking to himself 5 it.

   "I've got a 6 !" Jerry said to himself. " 7 last I've got a 8 of my very own! 9 what a flashlight!"

   For 10 long time, everyone in 11 family but Jerry had 12 flashlight. Jerry thought about 13 great big flashlight that 14 father had in the 15 of the car.

   Jerry 16 it was a funny 17 flashlight. It looked something 18 a lunchbox with 19 big white light on 20 end and a little 21 light on the other 22 .

   You didn't hold it 23 your hand. If you 24 a flat tire at 25 , you put the big 26 down the street. 27 big white light let 28 see to work on 29 tire, and the little 30 light flashed on and 31 to show people in 32 cars that you were 33 .

Correct Answers:
1. thought 2. But 3. about 4. he 5. about 6. flashlight 7. At 8. flashlight 9. And 10. a 11. Jerry's 12. a 13. the 14. his 15. back 16. thought 17. looking 18. like 19. a 20. one 21. red 22. end 23. in 24 had 25. night 26. flashlight 27. the 28. you 29. the 30. red 31. off 32. other 33. there

Source: G. Wallace and S. Larsen, *Educational Assessment of Learning Problems: Testing for Teaching* (Boston: Allyn and Bacon, 1978). Used by permission.

Figure 17-8 Guidelines for Creating Cloze
Comprehension Tests

1. Select a passage of 250 to 300 words. This passage should be representative of the content of the material the child is reading in school.
2. The passage should not be heavily dependent on information presented earlier in the text.
3. Texts with jargon or many new concepts particular to the subject matter should be avoided.
4. Keep the first and last sentences of the paragraph intact.
5. Randomly choose one of the first five words in the second sentence of the passage. Beginning with this word, omit every fifth word until 50 words have been deleted from the passage.
6. Replace each deleted word with a blank of uniform length and number the blanks consecutively.
7. Prepare a numbered answer sheet on which the students can write their responses for deleted words.

A Final Word on Reading Assessment

For most children, reading assessment begins with screening and survey procedures designed to ascertain whether the child possesses a reading deficiency. Children who score positively on these screening procedures are then administered in-depth, formal, and/or informal assessment instruments to diagnose and pinpoint their reading problems. This implies that in-depth, diagnostic reading assessment is *not* for every child and that the identification of children with learning problems is only as good as the survey measures used.

Before selecting in-depth, diagnostic reading assessment instruments, the test consumer must define the specific purpose for using the assessment instrument. Some techniques, tests, and procedures are best suited for certain objectives. Reading tests should not be used simply because they are available. Rather, the purpose of reading assessment must be clearly defined beforehand, and the assessment instruments and procedures chosen because they best meet the assessment–educational objectives.

Finally, with such a large assortment of reading assessment instruments and procedures available, it is the consumer's responsibility to consider only instruments that are valid, reliable, and technically sound. Likewise, because *all* tests possess weaknesses, a child's weaknesses and strengths should be identified by a number of different tests and procedures (both informal and formal) before the validity of such data is accepted. The usefulness and value of reading assessment can be assured only by identifying the objectives of the assessment, choosing suitable instruments and procedures, using tests of high technical quality, and cross-validating obtained data.

SUMMARY

Reading consists of the two processes of decoding and comprehension. Decoding is the converting of print into auditory equivalents; comprehension entails understanding what has been read. The ability to comprehend what has been read depends on previously acquired language and experience.

Word analysis and word recognition are the two types of decoding skills. Word analysis (or phonics) may be used with the analysis or synthesis phonics approach. The various levels of comprehension range from literal (the simplest) to evaluative (most complex). Reading assessment should test both types of decoding skills as well as a variety of comprehension levels.

Some reading tests assess oral reading. Different types of oral reading errors have been identified, and individual oral reading tests measure all or the majority of such errors. Such tests include the Gilmore Oral Reading Test and the Gray Oral Reading Test. In addition, the Gates–McKillop–Horowitz Reading Diagnostic Tests and the Durrell Analysis of Reading Difficulty contain oral reading components.

Diagnostic reading tests measure a large number of reading skills in depth. Four such tests reviewed in this chapter are: the Stanford Diagnostic Reading Tests, the Diagnostic Reading Scales, the Woodcock Reading Mastery Tests, and the Rosewell–Chall Diagnostic Reading Test of Word Analysis Skills.

Reading comprehension should be measured by the educational professional. Unfortunately, fewer tests are available for measuring reading comprehension than for measuring decoding skills.

A number of factors influence reading comprehension and the way it is assessed. These include the text being used for comprehension purposes, the appropriateness of that text to the child's past learning, experiences, and language, and the task demands of the assessment procedures. Each factor must be taken into account when interpreting comprehension test results.

A variety of tests primarily measure reading comprehension. These include the Test of Reading Comprehension, the Wisconsin Tests of Reading Skill Development, and the Gates–MacGinitie Reading Tests. Additionally, certain tests such as the Woodcock Reading Mastery Tests and the Stanford Diagnostic Reading Tests, contain a strong reading comprehension component.

A number of criterion-referenced reading tests and programs are also commercially available. Such programs are not norm-referenced; rather, they measure the child's mastery or nonmastery of specific reading skills. These tests allow the creation of a reading profile for each child. Additionally, such tests usually come with test items keyed to specific instructional objectives and with suggestions and materials for remediating reading weaknesses. Criterion-referenced reading tests discussed in this chapter include Diagnosis: An Instructional Aid (Reading), Criterion Reading, the Fountain Valley Support System in Reading–Revised, and the Fountain Valley Support System in Secondary Reading.

Besides using formal tests, a teacher can use informal reading assessment procedures. Informal testing possesses many advantages if carried out correctly. In assessing decoding and comprehension skills the teacher can use observations, checklists, informal reading inventories, and teacher-made tests. Analysis of reading errors (miscues) is an informal technique for assessing word analysis skills; the cloze technique is used for assessing reading comprehension.

STUDY QUESTIONS

1. What is reading? How is the process defined? State, in your own words, what each component in the definition means.

2. What are the processes of decoding? How do they differ?

3. What are analysis and synthesis phonics? How do they differ? What is structural analysis?

4. What is comprehension? What are the different types of comprehension? How do they differ?

5. What are the skills generally assessed in reading tests? How are they measured?

6. What are the typical errors made in oral reading? Define each oral error type. Which standardized oral reading tests measure which error types?

7. What are the major diagnostic reading tests? What are their strong and weak points? Which test(s) would you use for primary students? For secondary students? Defend your answers.

8. What are criterion-referenced reading tests? How do they differ from most available, standardized diagnostic reading tests? Name available criterion-referenced reading tests. What are their strong and weak points? Would you use them? Defend your answers.

9. What are the major techniques of informal reading assessment? What are the advantages and disadvantages of informal reading assessment? Design an informal reading assessment program for a hypothetical student.

CHAPTER 18

Spelling, Handwriting, and Written Expression Assessment

KEY CONCEPTS

- Definition of spelling
- Why is spelling so difficult?
- Factors influencing spelling ability
- The spelling process
- Formal spelling tests
- Informal spelling assessment
- The handwriting process
- Common handwriting deficiencies
- Variables of handwriting assessment
- Formal and informal handwriting assessment
- The written expression process
- Grammar and punctuation
- Ideation and written expression
- Formal and informal assessment of writing

The ability to communicate effectively in written form is one of the key achievements of modern society. With the technologies of paper and ink, typewriters, and word processors, every literate person can be an author of written ideas. On the other hand, people who cannot communicate effectively by writing suffer from severe expressive deficiency (Luftig 1987; Polloway, Patton, and Cohen 1983).

The ability to write effectively depends on a number of skills, including language (receptive and expressive), reading, spelling, handwriting, grammar and punctuation, and ideation skills. These skills are all needed and dependent on each other before effective written communication can occur (see Figure 18-1). Previous chapters have dealt with effective oral language and reading skills; this chapter deals with written language assessment in the areas of spelling, handwriting, and written expression.

Spelling

Many students have difficulty learning to spell (Graham and Miller 1983; Henderson 1985), particularly students with special learning needs (Graham and Miller 1983a; Miller and

Figure 18-1 A Hierarchy of Communication Skills

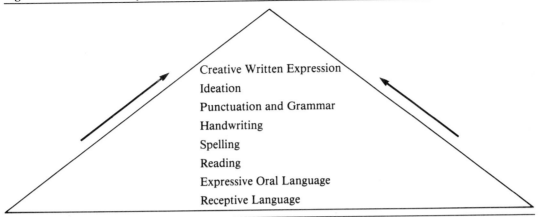

Creative Written Expression

Ideation

Punctuation and Grammar

Handwriting

Spelling

Reading

Expressive Oral Language

Receptive Language

Graham 1979). Spelling deficiencies on the part of students are unfortunate. The ability to spell is one of the most basic and essential skills of effective written communication; it is a key skill in the normalization process. Thus, the assessment, diagnosis, and subsequent remediation of students' spelling difficulties should be a major component of the special education curriculum.

The Definition of Spelling

To assess and teach spelling adequately we must understand the spelling process. To accomplish this, a working definition of spelling must be established. For the purpose of this text, spelling is defined as *the ability to recognize, recall, reproduce, or obtain orally or in written form the correct sequence of letters in words* (Graham and Miller 1983). Implicit in this definition is the idea that the adequate speller must possess the ability to match phonemes (sounds of language) with graphemes (written letters or symbols) of that language (Beers and Henderson 1977; Henderson 1985). Whether trying to spell a word orally or in written form, the person must be able to represent accurately the correspondence between sound and written letter.

Why Is Spelling So Difficult?

At first glance, spelling seems to be an easy process; just match the sounds to their written letters. Why, then, is spelling so difficult for so many people?

Spelling in some languages is easy. For example, the Hawaiian language contains only thirteen phonemes and twelve graphemes (Hanna, Hodges, and Hanna 1971). In Hawaiian, the child need only hear the sound and transcribe it into its corresponding grapheme to spell the word correctly. There is relatively little chance for spelling error.

The English language, however, is quite different. English contains approximately 44 phonemes, and there are 251 *different* ways to graphically represent those phonemes (Feigenbaum 1958). The English language is thus ripe for misspelling.

Initially, educators were pessimistic about the usefulness of assessing and teaching spelling in school. However, if it could be established that the spelling of English words was not haphazard, that is, if the phoneme–grapheme relationship generally corresponded to certain rules, then the teaching of spelling would be justified. Such a finding was reported by Hanna, Hanna, Hodges, and Rudorf (1966). They studied 17,000 randomly selected English words and found that more than 80 percent of these words could be spelled by regular adherence to spelling rules. Thus, according to Hanna et al. (1966), the assessment and diagnosis of spelling problems and the teaching of spelling in school using spelling rules are justified.

The Necessary Skills of Spelling

Researchers have identified the necessary skills of spelling (Graham and Miller 1983; Henderson 1985). Put another way, these researchers have identified the skills that *good* spellers demonstrate and that, conversely, are deficient in poor spellers. These skills include:

1. Discriminating between phonemes of the language.
2. Identifying graphemic options of each of the sounds.
3. Identifying syllables of oral speech and reproducing them in writing.
4. Recognizing the stress in words.
5. Recognizing morphemes, such as root words, compound words, prefixes, and suffixes.
6. Knowing the rules of morphemes, such as how words are combined or recombined to form other words.

Research has demonstrated that the more skills the student masters, the more efficient the pupil is in spelling words correctly. Thus, it is imperative that these skills be assessed and deficiencies diagnosed before formal spelling instruction.

Assessment of Spelling Skills

When a student is observed experiencing difficulties in spelling, the teacher can use a variety of assessment techniques and instruments to diagnose the severity and the nature of the problem. Such assessment should also identify the specific patterns of spelling errors that the student consistently makes.

Spelling assessment requires both formal and informal assessment techniques. The choice and use of particular instruments and

techniques depends on the age and level of the student and on whether the teacher desires an in-depth or global assessment of spelling ability. Additionally, the choice of technique and instrument is influenced by the somewhat limited number of formal, commercially available spelling tests. For these reasons, the teacher will probably use both formal and informal assessment instruments and techniques. Both types of spelling assessment are discussed in this chapter.

Formal Spelling Assessment

The Test of Written Spelling–2

Overview: The Test of Written Spelling–2 (TWS–2) (Larsen and Hammill 1986) is a revision of a norm-referenced spelling test designed for use with students in grades one through eight. Although the test can be administered to groups, it performs best when administered individually. The test uses a dictation format to assess the child's spelling ability.

The TWS–2 is constructed around the hypothesis that students learn to spell in two ways: by learning and using the spelling rules that govern the spelling of most words and by memorizing the correct spelling of irregular words (spelling demons). Therefore, the TWS–2 assesses the spelling of fifty predictable words (e.g., stop, hospital, tertiary) and fifty unpredictable words (e.g., yes, fountain, feign).

Administration and Scoring: The TWS–2 is easy to administer. The examiner says the target word in isolation and uses it in a sentence. The word is then repeated in isolation. The child attempts to spell the target word by writing it.

The words from each list (predictable and unpredictable words) are presented in hierarchical order of difficulty. The test terminates when the child makes five consecutive spelling errors. Total testing time is ten to fifteen minutes.

Scoring of the TWS–2 is also relatively simple. A student's raw score on each subtest (predictable and unpredictable words) is the number of correctly spelled words. The total raw score is the sum of the two subtest scores. However, the TWS–2 does not perform an error analysis of students' spelling mistakes. It merely considers each word as correctly or incorrectly spelled.

Scores can be converted to grade equivalents and spelling ages. In addition, a spelling quotient can be obtained. The spelling quotient is devised with the formula:

$$SQ = \frac{100 \times SA}{CA}$$

Where:

SQ = Spelling Quotient

SA = Spelling Age (defined as the age at which the test taker is spelling in comparison to children included in the norms of the TWS–2 standardization group)

CA = Chronological Age

Several problems arise when interpreting both spelling age and spelling quotient scores. First, this formula assumes that SAs are ratio-type data, that is, that SA scores possess equal intervals and an absolute zero. This is not the case. It is doubtful, for example, that the degree of spelling learning for a seven-year-old child equals that of a ten-year-old. Second, there is a problem with the SQ that, by implication, is analogous to the problem of IQ. The SQ suggests a general spelling ability or *g,* which is an unfounded assumption. Thus, it is doubtful that the SQ statistic yields any meaningful, diagnostic information. Finally, the authors place qualitative labels around SQ scores (e.g., SQ of 121 to 130 = Superior; SQ of 80 to 89 = Below Average). These labels possess no diagnostic value and can have a negative impact by further labeling and categorizing students.

Norms and Standardization Group: The TWS–2 was standardized on 3,805 students residing in fifteen states. The sample was heavily biased toward white, urban males residing in the southern United States. Although the authors claim that the sample is representative of the country's population, this conclusion is in doubt. Additionally, the sample size is relatively small, even smaller than that used for the original TWS.

Reliability: Internal consistency, test-retest reliability, and the Standard Error of Measurement were ascertained for the TWS–2. Internal consistency was obtained for age levels from six to eighteen for predictable, unpredictable, and total scores, with reliabilities ranging from .86 to .97. Test-retest reliability was established for 160 students, grades one through eight, who attended school in the same school district. The retest interval was two weeks. Test-retest reliability was ascertained for predictable, unpredictable, and total scores and ranged from .86 to .98. The Standard Error of Measurement was obtained for students aged six through eighteen for predictable, unpredictable, and total scores and ranged from one to six items.

Validity: The authors attempted to establish content validity by conducting a detailed item analysis. An experimental version of the test was established by devising a pool of 145 words obtained from five basal spelling series. Because upper-grade students do not typically use basal spellers, reading, social studies, and science text vocabulary was used. This pool of items was field tested and a final pool of 60 items was chosen.

Concurrent validity was considered established by correlating scores on the TWS–2 with tests purported to measure "spelling ability" (p. 24). These tests were the Durrell Analysis of Reading Difficulty, the Wide Range Achievement Test (WRAT), the California Achievement Test (CAT), and the

SRA Achievement Series. Correlations between the TWS–2 and these tests are generally quite high.

Summary of the TWS–2 for the Test Consumer: The TWS–2 is one of the most popular spelling tests on the market. It appears to possess adequate reliability and validity, although the representativeness of the standardization group is somewhat in question. It is easy to administer and score, and the administration procedures are clearly written. Disadvantages of the TWS–2 are its diagnostic usefulness and the appropriateness of its scores. The test claims to be diagnostic in scope, but its scores yield little real diagnostic information and provide little in the way of error analysis. Likewise, the usefulness and appropriateness of SAs and SQs are in question and open to interpretation errors. In summary, even though the TWS–2 will undoubtedly remain popular with educational professionals, its usefulness as a diagnostic tool is limited and its results should be interpreted with caution.

Diagnostic Screening Test: Spelling

Overview: The Diagnostic Screening Test: Spelling (DST–S) (Gnagey 1983) measures spelling proficiency in three categories: phonics (rule spelling), sight spelling (spelling from memory), and total spelling ability. The DST–S is appropriate for use with children in grades one through twelve. The test is now in its third edition.

The DST–S can be administered individually or in small groups. However, individual administration is recommended because it yields verbal and written spelling scores as well as further diagnostic information concerning the student's gross and sequential memory abilities. The test has two forms (A and B).

Administration and Scoring: The DST–S test manual provides clear directions for adminis-

tration and scoring and step-by-step procedures for interpretation. Students are provided with a workbook from which two pages are detached later and used as the examiner's worksheet. Students are read words in isolation and attempt to spell them. Administration time is five to ten minutes.

A total of twelve scores are reported: three scores (verbal, written, and total spelling) in each of three major categories of spelling abilities (phonics, sight, and total spelling). Test scores can also be converted to grade equivalents (GE). Additionally, the DST–S, when administered individually, yields three consolidation index (CI) scores. The CI is a measure of the consistency of student skill development up to a grade level indicated by the GE. This indicates how solid or erratic a student's knowledge or skill is. If skill development is inconsistent with the level indicated by the GE, teachers are directed to focus instruction at the grade level in which the student began to encounter spelling difficulties.

Norms and Standardization Group: The test was standardized on a pool of 12,000 students in equal-sized subgroups at each grade level. Students came from the Midwest, South, East, and West, with 50 percent of the students residing in the Midwest. Urban areas (30 percent), rural areas (40 percent), and small towns (30 percent) were represented, although the difference between small town and rural was not specified in the manual. The racial makeup was 70 percent white, 15 percent black, and 15 percent Hispanic, Asian, and other. Sex, socioeconomic standing, and parental demographics were not reported.

Reliability: The discussion of the reliability of the DST–S in the manual was inadequate. Discussion focuses on the amount of spelling growth exhibited over a three-month period by students who participated in the development of the test at each grade level. No information is provided as to how the data apply to a discussion of reliability. No information regarding internal consistency or test-retest reliability is provided.

Validity: The DST–S attempts to demonstrate content and construct validity, but the results are not convincing. Content validity was attempted by having seventy-one teachers of grades one through twelve submit one hundred words typically taught to and mastered by average students in their classrooms. However, no attempt was made to define operationally what constituted average, nor does the test author explain how words were assigned to the phonics and sight words categories. Construct validity was attempted by comparing results on the DST–S with performance on the spelling subtests of the SRA Series and the WRAT. However, the manual section on validity does not report when the SRA and the WRAT were administered, nor does it provide the correlations among the three tests. Thus, the construct validity of the DST–S is not adequately demonstrated.

Summary of the DST–S for the Test Consumer: The DST–S is an option for use by school professionals as a diagnostic instrument of spelling deficiencies. Although it does not provide a spelling error analysis, it can be useful in identifying students with spelling problems and in placing new students at proper instruction levels. The consolidation index offers useful information about the consistency of the student's performance as compared to grade equivalents. The reliability and validity of the instrument, however, still need to be demonstrated more strongly before the DST–S can be used with a high degree of confidence.

Spellmaster

Overview: Spellmaster (Greenbaum 1987) is a criterion-referenced, individually adminis-

tered diagnostic spelling test that assesses the student's ability to spell regular and irregular words and homonyms. The test is a revision of an earlier 1976 version. Spellmaster is appropriate for use with individuals from grades one to adulthood. Twenty-four tests are included in Spellmaster, eight for each of the three word types and eight survey tests. The purpose of Spellmaster is to assist the teacher in pinpointing students' spelling weaknesses and strengths as well as individualizing spelling instruction and monitoring student progress. The test manual contains a section on remediating spelling difficulties.

Administration and Scoring: Spellmaster uses the dictated word format to assess spelling. The child is given the word in isolation and asked to write or orally spell the word. For the Irregular Word and Homonym tests, the student writes words on response sheets prepared from a ditto master. On the Diagnostic Tests, the words are written on response sheets color coded by level. Each response sheet includes a scoring key. Spellmaster takes approximately twenty to thirty minutes to administer. Approximately the same time is needed for scoring and interpretation.

No norms or norm-referenced scores are provided by Spellmaster. Standards of mastery are implied by spelling words correctly. A diagnostic Scope and Sequence Chart is provided to specify skills mastered by students.

Norms and Standardization Group: Spellmaster is a criterion-referenced test and therefore has no norms.

Reliability and Validity: The current revision of the test contains no information on reliability and validity. This is unfortunate because the content validity of this instrument is seriously in question.

Summary of Spellmaster for the Test Consumer: This author cannot recommend Spellmaster for use by educational professionals in diagnosing the spelling problems of students. First, it does not possess proven reliability and validity, and its author seems to believe that such technical information is unimportant for criterion-referenced tests. Second, the content validity of the test items as being representative of spelling words typically encountered by students in school has not been demonstrated. Finally, the Diagnostic Tests are not valid measures of true phonemic ability. In short, the test probably should not be used by educational professionals.

Informal Spelling Assessment

Teachers commonly use informal spelling assessment procedures and practices for a variety of reasons. First, the process of spelling is conducive to informal assessment. Also, because fewer formal tests are available for spelling than for other academic areas, informal spelling assessment can become a necessity. Finally, informal spelling tests allow the teacher to assess the particular words that the pupils are experiencing in school.

At its most efficient level, informal spelling assessment can identify the spelling skills that students have and have not mastered, indicate patterns of errors that pupils are making, and provide insight into systematic remedial instruction that should take place to correct spelling deficiencies. In particular, informal spelling assessment should ask (and answer) the following questions (Linn 1980):

1. Can the student recall the letter and sound symbols quickly and accurately?
2. Can the pupil produce them on paper correctly?
3. Can the student fuse the parts of words together to spell whole words?
4. Does the individual consistently reverse letters or sound parts?
5. Does the pupil learn to spell words by hearing the spelling as well as by viewing the written spelling of the word?
6. Does the student appear to block out sounds?

7. Can the person write down graphic representations of single sounds when they are dictated?

Types of Informal Spelling Assessment

The informal spelling procedures the teacher uses will depend in part on the type of diagnostic information needed. Typical strategies include the use of systematic observation, checklists, informal spelling inventories (ISIs), and such specialized diagnostic spelling techniques as cloze techniques, clinical interviews, and teacher-made tests.

Observation: One of the most useful informal spelling procedures is the systematic observation that takes place as the student engages in normal spelling activities. For such a procedure to be useful and valid, however, the teacher must observe the pupil's spelling in a wide variety of situations, not just in a single or narrow set of activities. To help ensure the content validity of systematic observations, Brueckner and Bond (1966) have devised a set of guidelines for observing students' spelling activities. These guidelines are listed in Table 18-1.

In systematically observing students' spelling behavior, the teacher requires a reliable and valid form of record keeping. Such an observational record should contain (1) when the spelling behavior was observed, (2) under what conditions, and (3) the specific errors that were observed. To accomplish such goals, it is advisable to use spelling checklists that indicate the specific skills that individual students lack and that require remediation. An example of a spelling observational checklist is shown in Figure 18-2 (p. 328).

Informal Spelling Inventories: Informal spelling inventories serve to determine the child's level of spelling achievement and to pinpoint specific patterns of errors that the child regularly demonstrates. Keep in mind that an ISI is a completely criterion-referenced instru-

Table 18-1 Guidelines for Systematically Observing a Student

1. Analysis of Written Work, Including Test Papers
   a. Legibility of handwriting
   b. Defects in letter forms, spacing, alignment, size
   c. Classification of errors in written work, letters or tests
   d. Range of vocabulary used
   e. Evidence of lack of knowledge of conventions or rules
2. Analysis of Oral Responses
   a. Comparison of errors in oral and written spelling
   b. Pronunciation of words spelled incorrectly
   c. Articulation and enunciation
   d. Slovenliness of speech
   e. Dialect and colloquial forms of speech
   f. Way of spelling words orally:
      1) Spells words as units
      2) Spells letter by letter
      3) Spells by digraphs
      4) Spells by syllables
   g. Rhythmic patterns in oral spelling
   h. Blending ability
   i. Giving letters for sounds or sounds for letters
   j. Technique of word analysis used
   k. Quality and error made in oral reading
   l. Oral responses on tests or word analysis
   m. Analysis of pupil's comments as he states orally his thought process while studying new words
3. Interview with Pupil and Others
   a. Questioning pupil about methods of study
   b. Questioning pupil about spelling rules
   c. Questioning pupil about errors in convention
   d. Securing evidence as to attitude towards spelling
4. Questionnaire
   a. Applying checklist of methods of study
   b. Having pupil rank spelling according to interest
   c. Surveying use of written language
5. Free Observation in Course of Daily Work
   a. Securing evidence as to attitudes toward spelling
   b. Evidence of improvement in the study of new words
   c. Observing extent of use of dictionary
   d. Extent of error in regular written work
   e. Study habits and methods of work
   f. Social acceptability of the learner
   g. Evidences of emotional and social maladjustment
   h. Evidences of possible physical handicaps
6. Controlled Observation of Work on Set Tasks
   a. Looking up the meanings of given words in dictionary
   b. Giving pronunciation of words in dictionary
   c. Writing plural forms of derivations of given words
   d. Observing responses on informal tests
   e. Observing methods of studying selected words.

Source: Leo J. Brueckner and Guy L. Bond, *The Diagnosis and Treatment of Learning Difficulties,* © 1955, pp. 369–370. Reprinted by permission of Prentice-Hall, Inc., Englewood Cliffs, New Jersey.

ment. It does not compare student's scores against one another; rather, it looks at the individual child's spelling achievement, progress, and error patterns.

Informal spelling inventories can be created in a number of ways. One method is to select representative spelling words from each of the child's basal spelling books or from the class words encountered at each grade level. Some straightforward directions on how to create an ISI using this method have been provided by Mann and Suiter (1987). The Mann and Suiter method ensures that a representative sample of spelling words will be chosen at each grade level for the child. This method offers the following three steps:

1. Select a word sample from each basal spelling book of a given spelling series.
2. Take 15 words from the grade one speller.
3. Take 20 words from each speller for grades 2 through 6.

To take a sample selection from grades 2 through 6, divide the number of words listed at the back of the spelling book by 20. For example, if there are 300 words in the book, divide 300 by 20 to yield 15. Therefore, every

Figure 18-2   A Checklist for Identifying
Spelling Errors

_____   1. Consonant sounds used incorrectly
       (specify letters missed)
_____   2. Vowel sounds not known
_____   3. Sounds omitted at beginning of
       words
_____   4. Sounds added at the beginning of
       words (e.g., a blend given when a
       single consonant required)
_____   5. Omission of middle sounds
_____   6. Omission of middle syllables
_____   7. Extraneous letters added
_____   8. Extraneous syllables added
_____   9. Missequencing of sounds or syllables
       (transposals like "from" to "form")
_____ 10. Reversals of whole words
_____ 11. Endings omitted
_____ 12. Incorrect endings substituted ("ing"
       for "en" or for "ed")
_____ 13. Auditory confusion of *m/n, th/f, s/z,*
       or *b/d* or other similar sounds
_____ 14. Phonetic spelling with poor visual re-
       call of word appearance
_____ 15. Spelling laborious, letter by letter
_____ 16. Poor knowledge of "demons" (*e.g.,*
       one, iron, forecastle)
_____ 17. Spells, erases, tries again, etc., to no
       avail
_____ 18. Reversals of letter shapes *b/d, p/q,*
       u/n, or *m/w*
_____ 19. Spelling so bizarre that it bears no
       resemblance to original; even pupil
       cannot read his own written words
_____ 20. Mixing of upper- and lowercase let-
       ters
_____ 21. Inability to recall how to form either
       case for some letters
_____ 22. Spatial placement on line erratic
_____ 23. Spacing between letters and words
       erratic
_____ 24. Poor writing and letter formations,
       immature eye-hand coordination
_____ 25. Temporal disorientation: slowness
       in learning time, general scheduling,
       grasping the sequence of events in
       the day
_____ 26. Difficulty in concept formation; not
       able to generalize and transfer
       readily to abstract "the rules and the
       tools"

Source: S. F. Partoll, "Spelling demonology revisited,"
Academic Therapy, XI (1976): 339–348 (Novato, Calif.:
Academic Therapy Publications). Reprinted by permis-
sion.

fifteenth word in the speller would constitute
the word sample.

A second strategy for devising a sound ISI
is to devise the inventory around specific spelling *skills* rather than specific spelling words
(Kottmeyer 1970). In such an ISI, each item
measures a specific spelling skill. By analyzing missed items, the teacher can gain valuable insight into the pattern of errors that a
student is making in misspelling words. Figure 18-3 contains a summary of basic types of
spelling errors.

Specialized Spelling Techniques

Some additional specialized techniques for informally assessing spelling behavior are available to the teacher. These include the cloze
procedure, clinical spelling interviews, and
teacher-made, criterion-referenced tests.

Cloze Technique: As noted in Chapter 17,
the cloze procedure is often used to assess
reading comprehension. However, it can also
be used to assess spelling ability. In Figure 18-
4, a traditional cloze procedure is used to assess the pupil's ability to spell words embed-
ded in paragraphs. This figure also includes a
modified cloze procedure for students who
have difficulty spelling words from memory.

One problem with the cloze spelling procedure is that it is confounded with reading comprehension ability. If individuals cannot read
and comprehend the words and ideas of the
paragraph or sentence, they will not be able
to spell the words correctly. For this reason,
when using the cloze procedure in spelling,
the teacher must first make sure that the student can comprehend the passage.

Spelling Interviews: Clinical spelling interviews can be conducted with students regarding their spelling. Questions that might constitute a clinical spelling interview are shown in
Figure 18-5. Note that clinical spelling interviews are subject to error. Students can deliberately distort the truth to downplay their

Figure 18-3 Devising an Informal Spelling Inventory around Specific Spelling Skills

Word	Element Tested	Word	Element Tested
1. not 2. but 3. get 4. sit 5. man	Short vowels	1. flower 2. mouth	*ow-ou* spellings of *ou* sound *er* ending, *th* spelling
6. boat 7. train	Two vowels together	3. shoot	Long *oo*, *sh*
		4. stood	Short *oo*
8. time 9. like	Vowel-consonant-*e*	5. while	*wh* spelling, vowel-consonant-*e*
10. found 11. down	*ow-ou* spelling of *ou* sound	6. third	*th* spelling, vowel before *r*
12. soon 13. good	Long and short *oo*	7. each	*ch* spelling, two vowels together
14. very 15. happy	Final *y* as short *i*	8. class	Double final consonant, *c* spelling of *k* sound
16. kept 17. come	*c* and *k* spellings of the *k* sound	9. jump 10. jumps 11. jumped 12. jumping	Addition of *s, ed, ing*; *j* spelling of soft *g* sound
18. what 19. those 20. show 21. much 22. sing	*wh, th, sh, ch,* and *ng* spellings and *ow* spelling of long *o*	13. hit 14. hitting	Doubling final consonant before adding *ing*
		15. bite 16. biting	Dropping final *e* before *ing*
23. will 24. doll	Doubled final consonants	17. study 18. studies	Changing final *y* to *i* before ending
25. after 26. sister	*er* spelling	19. dark 20. darker 21. darkest	*er, est* endings
27. toy	*oy* spelling of *oi* sound	22. afternoon 23. grandmother	Compound words
28. say	*ay* spelling of long *a* sound	24. can't 25. doesn't	Contractions
29. little	*le* ending	26. night 27. bought	Silent *gh*
30. one 31. would 32. pretty	Nonphonetic spellings	28. apple	*le* ending
		29. again 30. laugh 31. because 32. through	Nonphonetic spellings

Source: W. Kottmeyer (1970). *Teacher's Guide for Remedial Reading* (New York: McGraw-Hill). Used by permission of the author.

spelling deficiencies or to display themselves positively. In a more benign sense, students may simply be unaware of their spelling deficiencies or believe they are not encountering any spelling problems. For these reasons, spelling interviews should be used only in conjunction with other assessment methods in order to ascertain the reliability and validity of the information gathered from the interviewees.

Figure 18-4 The Cloze Procedure in Assessing Spelling

Standard Cloze Procedure

1. The m_l_ (male) lion has a m_n_ (mane).
2. The store has a s_l_ (sale) on bicycles.
3. The boy played a musical instrument called a fl_t_ (flute).
4. What is the correct t_m_ (time)?
5. How do you _s_ (use) this tool?

Modified Cloze Procedure

If a student exhibits difficulty in completing these items, a multiple-choice format can be used. For example:

1. The b_____ ran across the street.
   a. oi
   b. oy
   c. ou
   d y
2. Come to my h_____se.
   a. ow
   b. o
   c. ou
   d. au
3. Use the _____ to open the door.
   a. kee
   b. key
   c. kie
   d. kea
4. Be at home at _____.
   a. nun
   b. non
   c. none
   d. noon

Source: G. Wallace and S. Larsen (1978). *Educational Assessment of Learning Problems* (Boston: Allyn and Bacon). Used by permission.

Teacher-Made Spelling Tests: Teacher-made tests are often useful in identifying student spelling deficiencies. In creating such tests, the teacher may wish to use words the students are using in their spelling program; or, the professional may wish to identify a representative sample of words the student must be able to spell in order to succeed in and out of school. Teachers can choose from a variety of lists when identifying common words (Kuska, Webster, and Elford 1964; Mann, Suiter, and McClung 1987).

Figure 18-5 Conducting the Clinical Spelling Interview

1. When you are spelling a word in a writing assignment, how do you know whether you have spelled the word correctly or incorrectly?
2. When you think you have spelled a word correctly on a spelling test or on a written assignment, are you often wrong?
3. What do you usually do when you don't know how to spell a word?
   a. Guess.
   b. Write the word down to see if it looks right.
   c. Try to sound out the word.
   d. Ask someone for help.
   e. Consult a dictionary.
4. Do you usually proofread what you have written for spelling errors? How?
5. Do you often make the same spelling errors? What do you do to correct this?

A Final Word on Spelling Assessment

The type of spelling assessment conducted by the educational professional will depend on the type of information the teacher wishes to obtain. Thus, it is crucial that the professional identify the specific goals of the spelling assessment *before* such assessment occurs.

If the goal is simply to determine the child's level of spelling proficiency, then a standardized spelling achievement test can be used. However, in most cases the teacher will wish to go further than this in identifying the areas of spelling weakness. This requires an in-depth spelling assessment, and those tests containing error analysis procedures are particularly useful. However, because most commercially available spelling tests are somewhat weak on error analysis, the teacher will need to use informal, criterion-referenced tests and informal spelling inventories.

Handwriting

The best conceived, well-organized, and well-constructed written composition is useless if it is illegible. Even in this age of type-writers and word processors, much correspondence is handwritten. People do not carry typewriters or word processors with them but rely on pencil (or pen) and paper for written communications.

Handwriting is synonymous with the term *penmanship* (a term still often used in schools). Academic interest in penmanship and handwriting assessment has a long history. Past research in the area of handwriting has indicated that a relatively small number of handwriting errors and deficiencies contribute to the majority of handwriting difficulties (Greene and Petty 1967; Horton 1970; Pressy and Pressy 1972). Newland (1932), for example, studied the handwriting errors of 2,381 students and identified the contribution that each error made to handwriting errors and illegibility. These errors were then translated into common error types.

Categories of Error Types

In assessing handwriting, most experts categorize penmanship deficiencies into six main categories or classes (Mann, Suiter, and McClung 1987; Zaner-Bloser 1975). These categories are letter formation, spacing, slant, line quality, letter size and alignment, and rate.

Letter Formation: Letter formation refers to the appropriateness of a written letter. According to Gueron and Maier (1983), there are five categories of letter formation:

1. Round letters:
   a. Clockwise letters (e.g., *k, p*)
   b. Counterclockwise letters (e.g., *a, c, d, o, q*)
2. Looped letters:
   a. Above the line (e.g., *b, d, e, f, h, k, l*)
   b. Below the line (e.g., *g, j, p, q, y*)
3. Retraced letters (e.g., *i, u, t, w, y*)
4. Humped letters (e.g., *h, m, n, v, x, z*)
5. Others (e.g., *r, s*)

To some extent, judging whether a letter has been formed correctly is a subjective process. However, there have been attempts to objectify the process. For example, Hammill (1986) has created a list of criteria by which letters are judged to be formed correctly or incorrectly. Also, scales produced by Zaner-Bloser (1975) provide specimens of handwriting for a number of grade levels and criteria for judging the appropriateness of handwriting in each of the six error categories. Figure 18-6 contains a sample of the Hammill (1986) criteria.

Spacing: Spacing refers to the way letters are distributed within words and to the ways words are spaced within a phrase. The spacing between letters and between words should be uniform. Examples of letter-spacing errors and word-spacing errors are shown in Figure 18-7.

Slant: Both manuscript and cursive handwriting contain slant. The slant in both types of handwriting should be uniform. The simplest procedure for assessing slant is to draw a line straight through the letters. It then becomes apparent whether the letters possess uniform slant.

Line Quality: Line quality refers to the thickness or thinness of lines within a letter or between letters of a word. Again, the quality of the line should be uniform in the thickness and heaviness of produced letters.

Letter Size and Alignment: Letter size refers to the proper height and width of letters; alignment refers to the proportion or relationship of the size of letters within a given word. For example, certain lowercase letters (e.g., *i, u, e*) are usually one-quarter-inch high; other letters (e.g., *d, t*) are one-half inch. Still others (e.g., *l, h, k, d, b*) are expected to be three-quarters-inch high. Lower-loop letters are expected to extend one-half inch below the line.

Figure 18-6   Criteria for Judging Whether Some Letters Have Been Formed Correctly

	Wrong	Right
1. *a* like *o*	*o*	*a*
2. *a* like *u*	*u*	*a*
3. *a* like *ci*	*ci*	*a*
4. *b* like *li*	*li*	*b*
5. *d* like *cl*	*cl*	*d*
6. *e* closed	*l*	*e*
7. *h* like *li*	*li*	*h*
8. *i* like *e* with no dot	*e*	*i*
9. *m* like *w*	*w*	*m*
10. *n* like *u*	*u*	*n*
11. *o* like *a*	*a*	*o*
12. *r* like *i*	*i*	*r*
13. *r* like *n*	*n*	*r*
14. *t* like *l*	*l*	*t*
15. *t* with cross above	*t*	*t*

Source: Donald D. Hammill, "Correcting Handwriting Deficiencies," in *Teaching Students with Learning and Behavior Problems,* 4th ed. (p. 165), ed. Donald D. Hammill and Nellie R. Bartel (Boston: Allyn and Bacon, 1986). Used by permission.

Figure 18-7   Examples of Spacing Errors

Within Words

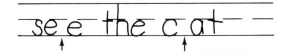

Between Words

Rate: The rate of handwriting is important, especially for older students and adults. It is commonplace to expect that individuals will write at a given rate of speed (e.g., in notetaking) and that falling below that optimum speed will cause difficulties.

Handwriting speed is usually determined by counting the number of letters produced per minute whereas the rate of handwriting speed is calculated by dividing the number of letters produced by the number of minutes allowed for the writing. An appropriate handwriting rate has been determined (Zaner-Bloser 1984). However, this handwriting rate should be treated as a rough guideline, and the teacher should keep in mind that rates will differ both between and within students as a function of task dimensions.

Assessing Handwriting Competency

Zaner-Bloser Evaluation Scales

There are a limited number of tools that teachers can use in assessing handwriting competence. The most popular instrument is the Zaner-Bloser Evaluation Scales (1984). The Zaner-Bloser is an informal device used to rate the manuscript and cursive handwriting of students in grades one through twelve. The test is administered in groups and can be given in fifteen minutes or less.

To administer the Zaner-Bloser Scales, the examiner or teacher writes designated words or phrases on the chalkboard. Students are then given two minutes to copy the phrases. With the Zaner-Bloser, student papers are compared against "specimen" examples of penmanship from a norm sample provided in the test manual (see Figure 18-8). The student's handwriting sample is then rated as satisfactory or needing improvement in the areas of letter formation, slant, alignment and proportion, and line quality. Overall student handwriting is rated by the teacher as excellent, satisfactory, fair, or poor.

The Zaner-Bloser Scales are most useful in providing a global estimate of the student's overall handwriting competence. However, they do not offer a diagnostic evaluation of the student's handwriting. Additionally, the reliability of the instrument may be questionable because a student's handwriting can change over a short period of time due to factors of fatigue, motivation, or other task demands.

Checklists

The teacher can use systematic observation in assessing a student's handwriting competency. As in any observation, the usefulness of the data is only as good as the systematic methods used to obtain the information. Thus, the teacher should collect data from a variety of different handwriting situations.

In collecting observational data, a handwriting checklist is a valuable tool. Several such observational systems have been developed (Howell and Kaplan 1980; Ruedy 1983; Wiederholt, Hammill, and Brown 1978). While the student is engaged in handwriting activities, the teacher systematically observes the pupil's handwriting behavior and records onto the checklist such handwriting strengths and weaknesses as position of hand and arm and pencil grip. Later, the writing sample is

Figure 18-8 Examples from the Zaner-Bloser Evaluation Scales

Example 3 – Average for Grade Three

Satisfactory		Needs Improvement
☐	Letter Formation	☑
☐	Slant	☑
☐	Spacing	☑
☑	Alignment and Proportion	☐
☑	Line Quality	☐

Example 5 – Poor for Grade Three

Satisfactory		Needs Improvement
☐	Letter Formation	☑
☐	Slant	☑
☐	Spacing	☑
☐	Alignment and Proportion	☑
☐	Line Quality	☑

Source: Zaner-Bloser Evaluation Scales. Used with permission of Zaner-Bloser, Inc., Columbus, Ohio. Copyright © 1984.

analyzed in more detail, and additional problems are recorded onto the checklist. Figure 18-9 contains a sample handwriting checklist developed by Ruedy (1983).

A Final Word on Handwriting

Handwriting assessment and instruction are among the most unpopular academic areas with both students and teachers. In addition, many people consider penmanship unimportant compared with such academic areas as reading and arithmetic. Perhaps this is why few good handwriting assessment instruments and techniques are available.

Nevertheless, handwriting is important. People whose handwriting is poor are, by definition, poor communicators, and we know that good communication skills are a key to success both in and out of school. For these reasons, handwriting assessment and remediation should be a regular part of the educational curriculum.

Written Composition

Written communication is the most complex form of communication. To write proficiently, the individual must possess appropriate verbal concepts in receptive and expressive oral vocabulary, an ability to read and spell, and legible handwriting. Moreover, in addition to possessing these skills, the individual must be able to convert ideas into written form. Difficulties with any of these skills can lead to difficulties in communicating effectively through writing.

The Elements of Writing

Anyone who has attempted to write knows it is one thing to possess ideas and quite another to be able to put your ideas on paper in intelligible, acceptable form. Even the most powerful ideas and concepts must be written in a conventional, acceptable manner to be understood. For effective written communication to take place, the person must have something to write, have the motivation to write it, and have the knowledge and ability to write it legibly and conventionally. These skills can be categorized into abilities of *composition* and *transcription* (Polloway, Patton, and Cohen 1983; Smith 1982).

Composition

Composition consists of the arrangement of ideas into written form (Hammill 1986; Smith 1982). It involves possessing ideas and concepts that one wishes to communicate as well as the organizational and vocabulary skills needed to express those thoughts. Additionally, composition skills include the desire (motivation) to convert one's ideas into written form. Figure 18-10 shows the major factors and component skills that influence composition competence.

Figure 18-10 implies a number of requisite skills for composition competence (Petty and Jensen 1980). First, for example, as the figure shows, possessing ideas and concepts to write, and having adequate vocabulary to express those ideas, depends to a large part on the student's past experiences. Such experiences can be firsthand (i.e., experienced by the student) or secondhand (i.e., from reading, television, or other media-induced learning).

Second, composition competence implies some organizational and logic skills. The author must be able to arrange ideas in order of importance, present those ideas in logical fashion, and use a language style appropriate to the reading audience.

Finally, composition competence implies a degree of creativity. This creativity requisite holds not only for fiction or artistic work but also for nonfiction work, such as reports, technical writings, and even textbooks. Without sparks of creativity, it is virtually impossible to transfer one's ideas to paper in written form.

Figure 18-9 A Checklist of Handwriting Skills

	O.K.	Needs Review		O.K.	Needs Review
1. Performance observation.			b. uppercase letters are clearly larger than lowercase letters	□	□
a. pen or pencil is held properly	□	□	c. uppercase letters are uniform in size	□	□
b. paper is positioned at a "normal" slant	□	□	d. tail lengths are consistent and do not interfere with letters on the line below	□	□
c. writing posture is acceptable	□	□	e. tall letters are a consistent height and are clearly taller than other letters	□	□
d. writing speed is acceptable	□	□	f. writing is not too small or too large	□	□
2. Correct letter formation.			g. slant of letters is acceptable	□	□
a. closed letters are closed	□	□	h. slant of letters is consistent	□	□
b. looped letters are looped	□	□	i. spacing of letters and words is consistent	□	□
c. stick letters are not loops	□	□	5. Student attitude toward writing.		
d. *i*'s and *j*'s are dotted directly above	□	□	a. student's opinion of his writing skills	□	□
e. *x*'s and *t*'s are crossed accurately	□	□	b. "writing is hard"	□	□
f. *m*'s and *n*'s have the correct number of humps	□	□	c. writes too slowly	□	□
g. all lowercase letters begin on the line (unless they follow *b, o, v,* or *w*)	□	□	d. feels good about writing	□	□
h. *b, o, v,* and *w* end above the line	□	□	6. Overall teacher evaluation.		
i. all lowercase letters end on the line	□	□	*Teacher Recommendation:*		
j. *v*'s and *u*'s are clearly delineated	□	□	□ You appear to write smoothly and easily. Your letters are formed correctly. Letter size, slant, and spacing are good. Your writing is neat and legible. It is not necessary for you to complete the handwriting exercises.		
k. connecting strokes of *v* and *y* are clearly not *ry* and *ry*	□	□	□ You appear to write smoothly and easily. You have developed your own writing style which is acceptable, neat and legible. It is not necessary for you to complete the handwriting exercises.		
l. uppercase letters are correctly or acceptably formed;	□	□			
m. numbers are correctly formed	□	□	□ You appear to write smoothly and easily. However, your letter formation, neatness, and legibility need some work. Please complete the handwriting exercises.		
3. Fluency.					
a. writing is smooth, not choppy	□	□			
b. pencil pressure appears even	□	□	□ Writing seems to be difficult for you. You need practice in handwriting skills. Please complete the handwriting exercises.		
c. words appear to be written as complete units	□	□			
d. letter connection is smooth	□	□			
4. Letter size, slant, and spacing.					
a. lowercase letters are uniform size	□	□			

Source: L. R. Ruedy, "Handwriting Instruction," *Academic Therapy*, 18, 4 (1983): 427–428 (Novato, Calif.: Academic Therapy Publications). Reprinted by permission.

Figure 18-10   Elements of Composition Competence

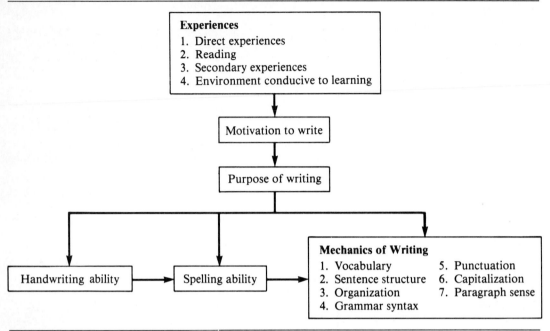

Transcription

Transcription involves the nuts and bolts of writing. It includes mechanics, such as spelling and handwriting, and knowledge of grammar and punctuation. Transcription also involves proofreading and critiquing of the finished written product for possible improvement. Figure 18-11 shows the requisite skills of transcription.

Assessment of Written Expression

The assessment of written expression measures a number of different variables or attributes. These include:

1. The organization of thoughts and concepts expressed.
2. The use of adequate language.
3. Correct grammar and syntax.
4. Punctuation and capitalization.
5. Paragraph sense.
6. Adequate spelling.
7. Adequate handwriting.

Unfortunately, there are relatively few commercially available tests that measure written expression, and most of those do not measure all of the attributes mentioned. However, there are tests that specifically measure spelling, syntax and grammar, and handwriting as singular skills rather than as part of the broader area of written expres-

Figure 18-11   Skills of Transcription

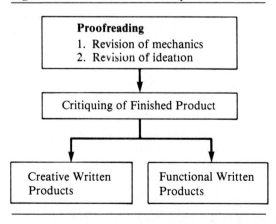

sion. These tests were discussed earlier in this chapter and in Chapter 16. Thus, the educational professional may have to administer at least two tests: one that measures written expression and another that measures specific attributes not covered by that instrument. Likewise, the teacher may wish to design informal tests that measure all the attributes of written expression.

Standardized Tests of Written Expression

The Test of Written Language

Overview: The Test of Written Language (TOWL) (Hammill and Larsen 1983) is a norm-referenced, diagnostic test designed to measure the student's written language skill. It is appropriate for children in grades three through twelve.

The TOWL can be administered individually or in small groups. However, because even the individual administration of the test assumes that the student possesses some skill in reading, the group administration presumes relatively sophisticated reading skills and test-taking maturity in terms of following directions and attending to task. Thus, individualized administration is suggested.

According to the test authors, the TOWL was constructed with four purposes in mind:

1. To identify students who perform more poorly than peers in written expression and who thus need remediation.
2. To diagnose the student's strengths and weaknesses in written expression.
3. To document the student's progress in a special writing program.
4. To conduct research in writing.

The test is based on the premise that the components of written expression can be grouped into five categories or classes: mechanics of writing, productive writing (ideas), conventions of writing, linguistic (language) components, and cognitive aspects. The TOWL contains six subtests that measure the attributes of good writing (see Table 18-2).

Table 18-2 Subtests of the Test of Written Language

1. Vocabulary (all students): The student receives credit for each word that contains seven or more letters. The number of such words is enumerated. The student's writing sample is used to calculate the score on this subtest.

2. Thematic Maturity: This subtest is used with students aged eight years to eighteen years, eleven months. The student's writing sample is analyzed on the basis of twenty categories or criteria including paragraph sense, organization, and richness of ideation.

3. Handwriting: This subtest is used with students aged eight years to eighteen years, eleven months, but only if the writing sample was produced in cursive style. The student's writing sample is used to rate handwriting on a scale of one to ten.

4. Spelling: This subtest is used with students aged seven years to fourteen years, eleven months. The dictation method of spelling is used. The student attempts to spell twenty-five words. This subtest is a shortened version of the Test of Written Spelling.

5. Word Usage: This subtest is appropriate for students aged seven years to fourteen years, eleven months. The student reads a sentence with one word missing and attempts to supply the word that will complete the sentence. This subtest assesses the student's knowledge of grammar, syntax, and morphology using twenty-five sentences.

6. Style (all students): The student is presented with twenty-five sentences written without punctuation and capitalization. The student must rewrite each sentence with correct punctuation and capitalization.

For three of these subtests (Handwriting, Vocabulary, and Thematic Maturity), students are shown three pictures and required to write an original story about the pictures. The remaining three subtests rely on multiple-choice questions.

Administration and Scoring: Directions for the TOWL are presented clearly and in a straightforward manner in the manual. Although the manual allows for group administration, individual administration is preferable, especially for special needs learners. Administration time is approximately forty minutes.

Given the heavy reliance on the child's writing sample, the scoring procedures of the three subtests that depend on that writing sample are somewhat subjective and require careful study and practice by the examiner. Trained judgment in scoring these tests is mandatory if the test is to be interpreted and used with confidence.

Results from subtests of the TOWL can be expressed as raw scores, percentiles, and standard scores. Additionally, the total test score can be expressed in terms of the Written Language Quotient (WLQ), which possesses a mean of 100 and a standard deviation of 15. However, as with the Test of Written Spelling (TWS), there is some doubt as to whether quotient scores offer any useful diagnostic information; these scores may actually encourage an oversimplification of a complex set of skills. Finally, as with the quotient scores in the TWS, there is some concern that the WLQ may be linked to a general (g) factor of written language analogous to the g factor of the IQ. The TOWL possesses a scope and sequence chart that yields an in-depth profile of the child's written expression skills, and this profile is of more use diagnostically than the WLQ.

Norms and Standardization Group: The TOWL was standardized on 3,418 students in fourteen states. Students in the sample were between seven years and eighteen years, eleven months of age. The sample was intended to be representative of the 1980 U.S. census.

The manual does not mention the inclusion of handicapped or culturally different children in the norm sample. This omission is unfortunate because the TOWL is used so frequently by special education teachers for their special needs learners. Moreover, the absence of culturally different children in the sample ignores the issue of children who use nonstandard or dialectical English.

Reliability: The TOWL presents internal consistency, test-retest, and interscorer reliabilities. Internal consistency (split-half) was obtained for only three subtests (Style, Spelling, and Word Usage). Reliabilities range from .62 to .90. Median internal consistency reliability is .88. Test-retest reliability was measured for the six subtests after an interval of two to four weeks. The reliability ranges from .62 to .90. Interscorer reliability, a very important component in a measure that contains a strong subjective scoring component, was high for Thematic Maturity (.93) and Vocabulary (.98) but relatively low for Handwriting (.78).

Validity: The authors provide an extensive discussion of validity in the manual. The content validity of the test depends on whether the reader accepts the theoretical model that "drives" the test. However, no specific objectives related to the test and test items are provided in the manual.

Criterion-related validity was investigated by correlating the TOWL with three standardized tests and with teacher ratings of students' written work. These correlations are generally modest and may have been overestimated by the test authors due to the statistical procedures used. Data on predictive validity are not presented. Finally, construct validity was evaluated by showing that writing ability is developmental in nature and that such ability improves as a function of the child's chronological age.

Summary of the TOWL for the Test Consumer: The TOWL is an ambitious undertaking in an area in which few tests of written expression exist. However, for a number of reasons, results from the test should be interpreted cautiously. First, the norm group is small and does not include handicapped or culturally different students. Second, the scoring of the test is somewhat subjective and requires training and practice. Third, test reliability is relatively low and its validity may be overestimated. For these reasons, results of the TOWL should not be overgeneralized. Likewise, the test's value for use in prescriptive planning is also suspect.

Picture Story Language Test

Overview: The Picture Story Language Test (PSLT) (Myklebust 1965) is a norm-referenced test of written expression appropriate for use with students from ages seven to seventeen. It can be administered individually or in small groups, although individual administration is preferable for special populations.

With the PSLT, the student is shown a stimulus picture and asked to write a story about that picture. The writing sample is analyzed in terms of three scales: Productivity, Syntax, and Abstract–Concrete. A description of these scales appears in Table 18-3.

Administration and Scoring: The child is shown a stimulus picture and asked to write a story about it. The test is untimed, but total administration takes about twenty minutes. Scoring is subjective for some of the scales and can be difficult. On the Productivity Scale, scoring is straightforward, and scores are expressed in terms of Total Words and Total Sentences. For the Syntax Scale, the writing sample is analyzed in terms of errors in word usage, syntax, morphology, and punctuation. Spelling is not scored. the Abstract–Concrete Scale is scored in terms of the abstractness of ideas expressed, ranging from meaningless language to abstract–imaginative language. This scale is the most difficult to score and the most subjective.

Results on the PSLT are reported as age equivalents, percentile ranks, and stanines. However, norms are presented only for odd-

Table 18-3 Scales of the Picture Story Language Test

1. Productivity Scale
  a. Total Words (TW): Represented by the total number of recognizable words that the student used in the spelling sample. Words are not discounted for spelling errors if the word is recognizable.
  b. Total Sentences (TS): Represented by the total number of complete sentences used in the passage.
  c. Words Per Sentence (WPS): Calculated by dividing the number of words in the passage (TW) by the number of sentences (TS).

2. Syntax Scale
  a. Syntax: The passage is judged for correct grammar.
  b. Morphology: The passage is judged for correct use of morphemes, which are the smallest units of meaning in English. Includes prefixes, suffixes, roots, and so forth.
  c. Word Choice: The passage is judged for "correctness" of verbal expressions. Subjective and relatively difficult to score.
  d. Punctuation: The passage is judged for proper use of punctuation.

3. Abstract–Concrete Scale
  This scale is divided into five levels, each of which represents the extent to which the story uses abstract ideas.

numbered age intervals from seven to seventeen years. Results for individuals who possess even-numbered chronological ages must be interpolated into the odd-numbered norms.

Norms and Standardization Group: The PSLT was standardized on 717 students of odd-numbered ages from seven to seventeen years. This represents an extremely small sample size. Students were selected from metropolitan, suburban, and rural schools. No other information is reported in the test manual for this standardization group.

Reliability and Validity: Serious questions have been raised about the adequacy of the way the reliability and validity of the PSLT were ascertained (Anastasiow 1973; Wallace and Larsen 1978). By the test author's admission, the data regarding the test's validity are "inadequate" (Myklebust 1965, VI, p. 148). The reliability data offered are incomplete and inconclusive.

Summary of the PSLT for the Test Consumer: The PSLT was a pioneering instrument in the area of assessing written expression from children's written samples. However, it possesses significant weaknesses. It is normed on an inadequate and inappropriately described sample; it possesses only alternate-year norms; it is difficult to score and interpret; and it has been severely criticized for its technical quality. For these reasons, the PSLT should probably be avoided by the test consumer.

Other Tests of Written Language

Test of Adolescent Language

The Test of Adolescent Language (TOAL) (Hammill, Brown, Larsen, and Wiederholt 1980) is a norm-referenced assessment instrument designed to measure the listening, speaking, reading, and written language skills of students aged eleven years to eighteen years, five months. It measures a variety of language skills in addition to written communication skills, but only subtests that measure writing skills are reviewed here.

The TOAL contains two subtests that assess writing skills: the Writing/Vocabulary and the Writing/Grammar subtests. In the Writing/Vocabulary subtest, the student is given a target word and asked to write a meaningful sentence incorporating the word. On the Writing/Grammar subtest, two sentences are presented to the student who must write a new sentence that combines the meaning of the two sentences. The consumer should keep in mind that, unlike the Test of Written Language and the Picture Story Language Test,

the test taker is not asked to generate a passage of connected prose. Rather, the pupil writes only single sentences.

Even though good scoring instructions are provided, scoring is somewhat subjective, and the examiner needs practice and skill in scoring protocols. Scores on the subtests are expressed as scaled scores, and the results of the two subtests yield a Writing Composite Score.

In summary, the written subtests of the TOAL yield limited data and information for the test consumer. Most of the information provided is norm-referenced and has little diagnostic value. On the positive side, the TOAL is virtually the only language test available for use specifically with adolescent students. However, it should be used in conjunction with other informal, diagnostic measures.

Informal Assessment of Written Expression

Because of the dearth of formal measures that assess written expression, the educational professional may need to resort to informal testing. Various informal techniques exist, including criterion-referenced tests, the gathering and analyzing of writing samples, and the use of rating scales and checklists.

Criterion-Referenced Tests

Criterion-referenced tests of written expression can be used to conduct an in-depth analysis of the student's mastery of skills. Two criterion-referenced tests that are popular with teachers are the writing subtests of the BRIGANCE Tests (Brigance 1977, 1980) and the Diagnostic Evaluation of Writing Skills (DEWS) (Weiner 1980).

The BRIGANCE series of writing tests are contained in three criterion-referenced tests: the BRIGANCE Diagnostic Inventory of Skills (1977), the BRIGANCE Diagnostic Inventory of Basic Skills (both appropriate for students in kindergarten through grade seven), and the BRIGANCE Diagnostic Inventory of Essential Skills (1980) (appropriate for students in grades seven through twelve). The BRIGANCE tests designed for students in kindergarten through grade seven are criterion-referenced instruments that assess the student's ability to complete sentences, to correct sentences that are incorrectly stated, and to compose sentences. Subtests administered include capitalization, punctuation, and parts of speech.

Included in the BRIGANCE Diagnostic Inventory of Essential Skills (used for students in grades seven through twelve) are skills related to written expression and form completion skills (driver's permits, Social Security forms, etc.). Subtests of the BRIGANCE Diagnostic Inventory of Essential Skills assess quality of writing, capitalization, punctuation, addressing of envelopes, and letter writing. Additionally, subtests under the headings of Spelling and Vocational can be administered by the teacher when deemed necessary and appropriate. Items in all subtests of the BRIGANCE series are keyed to specific instructional objectives, and plans for remediation of weak areas are offered.

The Diagnostic Evaluation of Writing Skills (DEWS) contains criteria of assessment divided into the areas of graphic, orthographic, phonographic (phonetic), syntactic, semantic, and self-monitoring skills. Each area is divided into subskill areas, with each area tested in terms of in-depth mastery. Each criterion serves as a guide to determining the student's need for direct teaching of a deficient skill. As in the BRIGANCE tests, test items are keyed to specific instructional objectives, and instructional methods designed for remediation of weak areas are offered.

Obtaining and Analyzing a Writing Sample

One of the best informal methods of assessing written expression is to obtain and analyze a sample of the student's naturalistic writing, that is, the writing that occurs naturally as part of the school curriculum. The student's writing is analyzed using one or more variables that influence good writing.

Various techniques exist for analyzing a student's writing sample (Cartwright 1969; Hunt 1965; Polloway and Smith 1982; Poteet 1980). Such techniques include using Type-Token ratios, indexes of diversification, average sentence length, and T-Units. A summary of these techniques appears in Table 18-4.

Checklists: As in other academic areas, checklists can be very helpful in informally assessing student difficulties in written expression. Such checklists are used by the teacher to observe students performing naturalistic writing during the school day. The checklists are used at a later time in conjunction with error analysis of the student's actual school writings to determine areas of strengths and weaknesses in written expression. Figure 18-12 contains a sample checklist of written expression that the teacher can use.

A Final Word on Written Expression Assessment

Through the use of movable type and pencil and paper, the written word has become as familiar to many of us as breathing. The written word is everywhere—in the books we read, and the letters we write, the job applications we fill out, and the grocery lists we make.

The ability to read is crucial to life success. People who cannot read are doomed to a life dominated by underachievement and failure. However, reading represents *passive* or *receptive* communication; it is the understanding of another's ideas. On the other hand, one's ability to communicate to others through the written word represents *expressive* communication. Effective written communication allows other people to learn about

Table 18-4 Techniques for Analyzing Students' Writing Samples

Technique	Description	Methodology	Example	Comment
1. Type-Token Ratio	Measure of the variety of words used (types) in relation to overall number of words used (token)	$\dfrac{\text{Different words used}}{\text{Total words used}}$	type = 28 token = 50 ratio $= \dfrac{28}{50} = .56$	Greater diversity of usage implies a more mature writing style.
2. Index of Diversification	Measure of diversity of word usage	$\dfrac{\text{Total number of words used}}{\text{Number of occurrences of the most frequently used word}}$	$\dfrac{\text{total words} = 72}{\text{number of times the word } the \text{ appeared}}$ $= 12$ $[72 \div 12 =]$ Index = 6	An increase in the index value implies a broader vocabulary base.
3. Average Sentence Length	Measure of sentence usage (number of words per sentence)	$\dfrac{\text{Total number of words used}}{\text{Total number of sentences}}$	total words = 54 total sentences = 9 $[54 \div 9 =]$ words per sentence = 6	Longer length of sentences implies more mature writing ability.
4. Error Analysis	Measure of word and sentence usage	Compare errors found in a writing sample with list of common errors		Teacher can determine error patterns and can prioritize concerns.

5.	T-Unit Length (Hunt, 1965)	Measure of writing maturity	1. Determine the number of discrete thought units (T-units)	"The summer was almost over and the children were ready to go back to school."	This technique gives the teacher information in relation to productivity and maturity of writing skills.
			2. Determine average length of T-unit:	*Quantitative:* (1; 2; 5 + 10)	
			Total words		
			Total number of T-units		
			3. Analyze quantitative variables: a. no. of sentences used; b. no. of T-units; c. no. of words per T-unit Note: Ues the following convention for summarizing this information (no. of sentences; no. of T-units; no. of words per T-unit)	*Qualitative:* 1. compound sentence 2. adverbs: of degree—"almost" of place—"back" 3. adjective—"ready" 4. infinitive—"to go" 5. prepositional phrase adverbial of place—"to school"	
			4. Analyze qualitative nature of sentences		

Source: E. Polloway, I. Patton, and S. Cohen (1983). "Written Language for Mildly Handicapped Students," in *Promising Practices for Exceptional Children*, eds. E. L. Meyer, G. A. Vergason, and R. J. Whelan (Denver: Love Publishing). Used by permission.

Figure 18-12   Informal Checklist to Assess Written Composition

Pupils' Names	Verbs				Pronouns			Adjectives/ Adverbs			Words				
	Tense form	Tense shift	Agreement	Auxiliary missing	Subject or object position	Pronoun/adjective	Antecedents	Form	Confusion	Article comparison	Addition	Omission	Substitution	Plural	Substandard

Pupils' Names	Period	Comma	Semicolon	Colon	Question mark	Apostrophe	Quotation mark	Hyphen	Underlining

Pupils' Names	First word of sentence	The word *I*	Proper names	Titles	Proper adjectives	First word of quotation	Words for the deity	Appropriate abbreviations	Salutation and closing of letter	Words such as *mother, father* when used as a name	Trade names

Source: G. Wallace and S. C. Larsen (1978). *Educational Assessment of Learning Problems* (Boston: Allyn and Bacon). Used by permission.

your ideas and feelings. Whereas those who cannot read are doomed to failure in terms of understanding the written word, those who cannot write effectively are doomed to an existence that is, to a large extent, communicatively mute.

S U M M A R Y

The ability to communicate effectively in written form is a key life success skill. Thus, effective written communication should be a major goal of the special education curriculum.

Effective written communication depends on a number of skills, including receptive and expressive language, reading, spelling, handwriting, mechanics, and ideation. These skills are hierarchical.

Spelling is the ability to recognize, recall, reproduce, and obtain orally or in written form the correct sequence of letters in words. Spelling ability entails the matching of phonemes with their correct grapheme equivalents. The spelling of English is difficult because there are so many ways to represent the phonemes graphemically.

A number of prerequisite skills must be in place before spelling instruction is begun. These skills include adequate perceptual abilities, fine motor skills, knowledge of alphabet letters and sounds, knowledge of word meanings, and the motivation to spell correctly.

Diagnostic assessment of spelling is extremely important in understanding the student's spelling strengths and difficulties. Such assessment can be formal or informal. A number of formal spelling assessment instruments are commercially available, including the Test of Written Spelling, the Diagnostic Screening Test: Spelling, and Spellmaster. Informal spelling assessment uses systematic observation, informal spelling inventories, and specialized spelling assessment techniques, such as the cloze procedure, clinical interviews, and criterion-referenced tests.

The best conceived piece of writing is useless if it is illegible. Thus, adequate handwriting (penmanship) is important if handwritten specimens of work are to be read and understood by others.

A number of error categories contribute to poor handwriting. These include errors of letter formation, spacing, slant, line quality, and letter size and alignment. Additionally, the rate of a child's handwriting is also important, especially in such timed situations as note taking, and should be assessed.

Handwriting can be assessed by various techniques. The most widely used formal instrument is the Zaner-Bloser Evaluation Scales; informal handwriting assessment procedures include the use of checklists.

Written composition is the most complex form of communication. The elements of writing include composition and transcription. Composition is the arrangement of ideas into written form; transcription involves the mechanics of writing as well as proofreading and critiquing the finished product.

Assessment of written composition is a subjective and often difficult process. Relatively few formal tests assess written composition. Available tests include the Test of Written Language, the Picture Story Language Test, and the written expression subtests of the Test of Adolescent Language. These tests all possess significant weaknesses as diagnostic instruments. Therefore, most assessment of written expression should probably be informal and include the use of criterion-referenced tests (e.g., the BRIGANCE tests or the Diagnostic Inventory of Essential Skills), writing sample analysis, and diagnostic checklists.

STUDY QUESTIONS

1. What is spelling? What is the relationship between the processes of reading and spelling? Why are the two processes sometimes called the inverse of each other?

2. What are the necessary skills for good spelling? Why are they difficult for some people to acquire?

3. What are some formal spelling assessment instruments? What are their major attributes as well as strong and weak points? Which of these instruments would you use in your assessment program? Defend your answer.

4. What are Informal Spelling Inventories (IMIs)? Why are they useful as an assessment device? How would you go about creating an IMI?

5. What are spelling interviews and the spelling cloze technique? What inherent weaknesses do these techniques possess? What are their strong points?

6. Why is handwriting important? Should handwriting be stressed in the special education curriculum? Defend your answer.

7. What are the major types of handwriting errors? How are these errors assessed? Why is evaluation of handwriting a difficult process?

8. What are the elements of written expression? How are they assessed? What formal assessment instruments are available to measure and evaluate written expression? What are the strong and weak points of these instruments? How would you go about assessing written expression in your classroom?

CHAPTER 19

Assessment in Mathematics

Except for the teaching of reading, probably more time is spent on teaching mathematics than any other academic area (Luftig 1987c). This is to be expected; counting, using numbers in calculations, and understanding and using the concepts of time, money, and measurement are key skills to successful, normalized living. Students who lack these skills when they leave school are likely to encounter problems of success and survival in their adult lives.

Despite general agreement among educators about the importance of mathematics to life success, a significant proportion of pupils possess serious mathematical deficiencies (Bartel 1986; McLeod and Armstrong 1982). In fact, it has been estimated that as many as two-thirds of mildly handicapped learners enrolled in public schools possess mathematical deficiencies serious enough to require significant remediation (McLeod and Armstrong 1982). For this reason, the diagnosis and remediation of mathematics weaknesses should be a key priority of professionals serving students with special needs.

Arithmetic versus Mathematics

Before exploring the processes of mathematics and mathematical assessment, a distinction must be made between mathematics and arithmetic. The two terms are often used synonymously, but this intertwining of terms can cause confusion in both assessment and remediation. For the purpose of this text, the definitions of Reid and Hresko (1981) are used. *Mathematics* is defined as "the study or development of relationships, regularities, structure, or organizational schemata dealing with space, weight, time, mass, volume, geometry, and number" (p. 292). *Arithmetic* is defined as "the computational methods used in working with numbers" (p. 292).

Put in simpler terms, mathematics is *what* we do with numbers and qualitative relationships. It is the ability to use these relationships in such areas as time, money, measurement, geometry, and the higher mathematical skill areas. It includes the application of number skills to solve problems, make predictions, read and construct tables, and measure things (Fey 1982).

Arithmetic, on the other hand, consists of computational skills. It is the basic *algorithms* or step-by-step procedures we use to add, subtract, multiply, and divide with numbers. Arithmetic gives us the basic processes for solving mathematical problems. It is *part* of mathematics—the part that must be learned before we can solve the mathematical problems encountered throughout our lives.

The Mathematical Process

Before the mathematics abilities of students can be assessed, the educational professional must first understand the mathematical process. This process is more than just the abilities to add, subtract, multiply, and divide numbers. Rather, it entails the abilities to use numbers and mathematical processes to solve real-life quantitative problems, both in and out of school (Sedlak and Fitzmaurice 1981; Sharma 1984). To that end, it is suggested that children should possess competencies in the three main areas of *computation, problem solving,* and *application.*

Computational Skills

Computational skills are competencies needed to carry out the basic arithmetical operations of addition, subtraction, multiplication, and division. Without computational skills, the higher-order mathematical problems cannot be solved.

Solving computational problems involves learning both number facts and algorithms. Number facts are those sets of number combinations in the four computational areas that most learners eventually commit to memory (e.g., $6 + 2 = 8$). Such number facts are the building blocks of computational skills. Without them, computational problems cannot be solved. Algorithms are master plans, the methods by which problems in each of the four operations are solved.

Developing computational skills is not as easy as many people imagine. However, mastery in these areas must occur before competency in the higher-order arithmetic areas can be achieved.

Problem Solving

Problem solving refers to the ability to use computational skills to solve problems presented in everyday terms and language, not in numerical form (Luftig 1987c; Mayer 1985; Riley, Greeno, and Heller 1983). To solve a word problem, the student must successfully do the following:

1. Deduce the correct operation that must be performed. Choosing the wrong operation will result in an incorrect solution to the problem.
2. Select the appropriate and relevant information while ignoring irrelevant information. This is often one of the most difficult tasks for handicapped children during problem solving (Luftig and Greeson 1983; Luftig and Johnson 1982).
3. Convert relevant prose information into numerical symbols.
4. Calculate the answer using computational skills, number facts, and algorithms.

The ability to learn and use problem-solving skills involves sophisticated cognitive strategies (Cawley 1986; Mayer 1985). However, learners with special needs are often quite poor in learning and spontaneously using such strategies. For this reason, assessment and remediation of deficiencies in the problem-solving area of mathematics are important.

Application Skills

The final, and probably most relevant, process of mathematics is that of application. In this process, the individual uses computational and problem-solving skills to solve problems in the real-life areas of time, money, and measurement. The appropriate use of application skills in real-life situations is a key requisite for normalized adult living (Daniels and Wiederholt 1986; Thorton, Tucker, Dossey, and Bazik 1983). Application skills include:

1. Mastery of the relationships of money, including counting, purchasing, and making change.
2. Measuring temperature, speed, liquid and dry quantities, and area.
3. Telling time, that is, hourly, seasonal, and calendar time, and knowing when to do things.
4. Understanding fractions, decimals, and percentages.

Appropriate mathematical application involves as a prerequisite the mastery of computational and problem-solving skills. In addition, application skills involve the abilities to perceive the nature of real-life mathematical situations and to generalize or discriminate between appropriate problem-solving strategies. All of these tasks are difficult for students with special learning needs.

Assessing Prerequisite Mathematical Abilities

Perhaps in no other academic area, except reading, are readiness and the possession of prerequisite skills as important as in mathematics. Insufficient readiness in arithmetic skills will lead to difficulties in mathematical learning. In addition, when such skills are learned, they will be applied by rote and by memory instead of through understanding and conceptual acquisition (Bartel 1986; Ginsburg 1982; Reys, Suydam, and Lindquist 1984).

The child should possess a variety of skills before formal mathematical training is begun. Such skills include classification, comparison, counting, reversibility and compensation, seriation, and conservation skills. Because these skills are crucial to future mathematical concept acquisition, teachers must assess whether they have been mastered and provide any necessary instruction or remediation.

Classification

Classification involves grouping objects according to some distinguishing or common characteristic. For example, consider the words *horse, fox, deer, dog,* and *cow.* This list might be classified as denoting animals. To classify objects, the child must be able to judge their commonality on the basis of some relevant attribute, such as size, color, animal, vegetable, and so forth. The ability to classify objects by their distinguishing characteristics is considered a key requisite skill in understanding arithmetic relationships. Such skill develops gradually and is usually in place between the sixth and seventh year of life in most nondelayed children (Piaget 1965; Piaget and Inhelder 1973).

Classification skills can be measured in a number of ways (see Figure 19-1). For example, the child is shown objects and asked Which of these objects are good to eat? In another example, the child is shown an array of objects and asked Which thing does not go with the others? Why? Classification tasks differ in their complexity and subtlety, and such factors should be taken into account when assessing the child's classification skills.

Figure 19-1   Examples of Classification

Which of these objects are good to eat?

Which thing does not go with the others? Why?

Figure 19-2   Examples of Making Comparisons

Which set contains more objects?

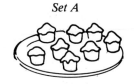

Which set contains objects left over?

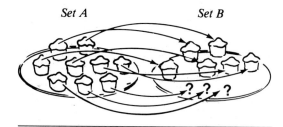

Comparisons

Making *comparisons* is an extremely important prerequisite mathematics skill. Much of what we call *arithmetic* consists of making comparisons between sets of objects and asking questions, such as Which set is bigger (or smaller)? and When are the sets the same size?

A key skill in making comparisons is determining a 1:1 correspondence of objects. For example, suppose we presented the two sets at the top of Figure 19-2 to the child and asked Which set contains more objects? The most logical way to answer this question would be to line up the objects of the two sets in a 1:1 correspondence (see the lower portion of Figure 19-2) and see which set contains leftover objects. This set would contain more objects. Notice that when making such comparisons, no counting is required. That is, we do not need to know how *many* objects are in each set. All we have to do is identify which set contains *more* objects.

Counting

Counting is an important skill that grows out of the ability to place objects in a 1:1 relationship. In the counting process, we ask How many objects does each set have? Answering

such a question frees children from having to physically line up set objects in 1:1 relationships to answer the question Which set has more? Rather, the question is answered by counting the objects in each set and reporting which set contains the greater number. Thus, counting represents a more abstract method of solving problems than the highly concrete process of placing objects in 1:1 correspondence.

Reversibility and Compensation

Suppose a child sitting on the teeter-totter wishes to raise his end. What might he do? One answer would be to get off and push his end upward. By removing himself from the apparatus, the child can undo or reverse his actions, thus returning affairs to their former state. This is known as *reversibility*.

On the other hand, the child could get someone to sit on the other end of the teeter-totter, causing the previously low side of the apparatus to spring up. In this case, the child would be counterbalancing his weight with someone else's. This process is known as *compensation*.

Reversibility and compensation are extremely important concepts in mathematics, especially in regard to regrouping, carrying numbers, and the commutative and associative properties of operations.

Seriation and Conservation

Seriation involves the ordering (lining up) of objects on the basis of size or some other attribute. For example, a child who is asked to order a number of sets by set membership size is being asked to use seriation. Likewise, a child asked to sequence a chain of events must use the seriation process.

Related to seriation is the process of *conservation*. For example, suppose a child is told to observe two equal-capacity beakers of water and asked Which beaker holds more water or do they hold the same amount? The young child who is unable to conserve would *centrate* on one beaker's "tallness" while ignoring the other's "wideness." This child would say the tall beaker holds more. On the other hand, the child who is able to conserve would *decentrate* on "tallness" and also take into account the "wideness" of the second beaker. This child would conclude that the beakers hold the same amount of liquid. See Figure 19-3 for examples of seriation and conservation.

Errors of seriation and conservation are serious in such mathematical processes as counting and working with sets. Although it is debatable whether seriation and conservation can be taught (Piaget 1960, 1967), these processes should be in place before complex mathematical concepts are taught.

Formal Mathematics Assessment

To create a sound instructional mathematics program for learners with special needs, the

Figure 19-3   Examples of Seriation and Conservation

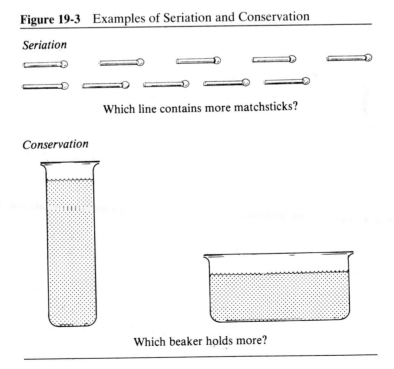

Seriation

Which line contains more matchsticks?

Conservation

Which beaker holds more?

educational professional must first possess a clear picture of the student's mathematical functioning. Only by understanding the pupil's mathematical strengths and weaknesses can a remediational program be created and instructional activities instituted.

Assessment in mathematics can take a number of directions. Traditional mathematical assessment has adopted the mode of identifying the child's mathematical abilities, that is, what the student can and cannot do. In such assessment, the student is typically given a set of problems of different types and complexity, and mathematical abilities are assessed. Such assessment is usually carried out with norm-referenced, mathematics achievement instruments.

Although information gleaned from such assessment is useful in a limited sense, indepth, criterion-referenced, diagnostic mathematical assessment is more useful to the educational professional. This assessment seeks to identify the underlying deficiencies in strategies and knowledge that the student exhibits in making mathematical errors. It includes, but is not restricted to, error analysis, criterion-referenced assessment, and informal assessment measures.

This chapter discusses formal and informal methods for diagnosing the mathematics skills and strategies of students. Included in this discussion is an array of informal measures, including criterion-referenced tests of specific skills, error analysis, and clinical observations and interviews. All of these measures are designed to yield specific information that will contribute to meaningful, relevant, and hopefully successful mathematical remediational programming for students with special learning needs.

Formal Diagnostic Mathematics Assessment

A variety of commercially available, formal, diagnostic mathematics tests are on the market, although not quite as many as are available in the reading–language arts area. Such tests can be either norm- or criterion-referenced, but they share the characteristic of yielding more diagnostic information than do survey achievement tests that contain a mathematics component (e.g., the Metropolitan Achievement Tests). Table 19-1 lists a number of commercially available, diagnostic, formal assessment tests in mathematics and the populations for which they have been designed. Several of these tests are critiqued in this chapter.

KeyMath Diagnostic Arithmetic Test

Overview: The KeyMath Diagnostic Arithmetic Test (KeyMath) (Connolly 1988) is an individually administered, diagnostic test designed for students in kindergarten through grade nine. It is one of the most popular mathematics tests on the market and is currently in a new, revised edition. Generally a norm-referenced instrument, it also contains many features of criterion-referenced tests. As such, the items of the KeyMath are linked to specific instructional objectives. There are two forms of the test (A and B) matched statistically and by content.

The KeyMath–R contains thirteen subtests or *strands* distributed in the three areas of *basic concepts, operations* and *applications.* Basic concepts refer to the basic mathematical knowledge and concepts necessary to perform operations and applications. Basic concepts represent the foundation on which all elementary mathematics is based. Operations subtests focus on the four operations of addition, subtraction, multiplication, and division as well as mental computation, which include all four operations. The applications subtests evaluate the student's ability to use basic concepts and operations to solve problems dealing with time, money, and measurement. Table 19-2 contains the thirteen subtests in the three domains of KeyMath.

Table 19-1 Commercially Available Diagnostic Mathematics Tests

Test	Grade Range	Norm-Criterion-Referenced	Publisher	Group/Individual
BRIGANCE® Inventories	K–12 depending on inventory used	C	Curriculum Associates	I
Diagnosis: An Instructional Aid:Mathematics	1–6	C	Science Research Associates	I
Diagnostic Math Inventory	1.5–8.5	C	CTB/McGraw-Hill	I
Diagnostic Test of Arithmetic Strategies	1–6	C	Pro-ed	I
Diagnostic Screening Test: Mathematics	1–12	N	Facilitation House	G/I
Fountain Valley Teacher Support System in Mathematics	1–8	C	Zweig Associates	I
Individual Pupil Monitoring System–Mathematics	1–8	C	Houghton-Mifflin	I
KeyMath	1–10	N/C	American Guidance Service	G/I
Mastery: An Evaluation Tool: Mathematics	1–9	C	Science Research Associates	I
Multilevel Academic Skills Inventory	1–8	C	Charles E. Merrill	I
Stanford Diagnostic Mathematics Test	1–12	N/C	Psychological Corporation	G/I
Test of Mathematical Abilities	3–12	N/C	Pro-Ed	G/I

Administration and Scoring: Each form of the KeyMath kit contains two free-standing test books and easels, an administration and scoring manual, and individual record sheets. Each form contains 258 items. No special training is required to administer the test. However, test scoring and interpretation are best carried out by someone with expertise and experience with the instrument. To take the test, students must speak English and be able to maintain their attention. Most items are read to students while the pupil follows along looking at a test page that contains numbers, symbols, or words. Some items are free

Table 19-2 Content Areas and Strands of the KeyMath-Revised

Areas:	Basic Concepts	Operations	Applications
Strands and domains:	**Numeration** 1. Numbers 0–9 2. Numbers 0–99 3. Numbers 0–999 4. Multi-digit numbers and advanced numeration topics **Rational Numbers** 1. Fractions 2. Decimals 3. Percents **Geometry** 1. Spatial and attribute relations 2. Two-dimensional shapes and their relations 3. Coordinate and transformational geometry 4. Three-dimensional shapes and their relations	**Addition** 1. Models and basic facts 2. Algorithms to add whole numbers 3. Adding rational numbers **Subtraction** 1. Models and basic facts 2. Algorithms to subtract whole numbers 3. Subtracting rational numbers **Multiplication** 1. Models and basic facts 2. Algorithms to multiply whole numbers 3. Multiplying rational numbers **Division** 1. Models and basic facts 2. Algorithms to divide whole numbers 3. Dividing rational numbers **Mental Computation** 1. Computation chains 2. Whole numbers 3. Rational numbers	**Measurement** 1. Comparisons 2. Using non-standard units 3. Using standard units— length, area 4. Using standard units— weight, capacity **Time and Money** 1. Identifying passage of time 2. Using clocks and clock units 3. Monetary amounts to one dollar 4. Monetary amounts to one hundred dollars and business transactions **Estimation** 1. Whole and rational numbers 2. Measurement 3. Computation **Interpreting Data** 1. Charts and tables 2. Graphs 3. Probability and statistics **Problem Solving** 1. Solving routine problems 2. Understanding non-routine problems 3. Solving non-routine problems

Source: A. J. Connolly, KeyMath-Revised (1988). Circle Pines, MN: American Guidance Service. Used by permission.

response and some are multiple choice. A minimum of reading is required. In most cases, the child verbally states the answer; the computational subtests require writing. The subtests are untimed, and total administration time for the KeyMath ranges from thirty to fifty minutes.

The KeyMath yields four levels of diagnostic information: total test performance, area performance, subtest performance, and item or domain performance. Each succeeding level yields a greater degree of specificity and diagnostic usefulness. Therefore, by proceeding all the way to domain performance, the teacher can learn about specific instructional objectives in which the student requires remediation. The appendix of the manual contains the specific instructional objective keyed to each test item. For persons interested in norm-referenced evaluation, the KeyMath yields percentile ranks, grade and age equivalents, stanines, and normal curve equivalents.

There are consistent basal and ceiling rules for all the subtests of KeyMath. Basal scores are calculated by the student's correctly answering three consecutive items; ceiling scores are established by the student's making three consecutive errors.

There are several ways to interpret the scores of KeyMath. The most basic method is by examining total test performance. This is accomplished by converting raw scores to a grade equivalent. This process represents the use of KeyMath as a norm-referenced, survey instrument. Additionally, the child's performance in each of the three main areas can be examined. This examination yields limited information about general areas in which a student is weak. For example, as shown in Figure 19-4, Carrie, a fourth-grade student, is below average in basic concepts (9th percentile) and operations (27th percentile) and stronger in the applications area (75th percentile). With this information, Carrie's teacher can provide her with basic concepts and operations.

The KeyMath can also be used to look at the student's performance within a given area or domain. Consider Carrie's performance within each domain area. One can see that while she did not perform too badly on interpreting data and problem solving, she scored lower on measurement and time and money. Additionally, she experienced serious difficulties in the areas of rational numbers and geometry. By examining Carrie's scores within each domain, her teachers can learn about her specific areas of mathematical weakness.

Finally, the KeyMath can be used as a criterion-referenced instrument. Because each item is keyed to a specific instructional objective, a detailed analysis of the items Carrie missed will yield specific and detailed information about the content in each subtest, especially those of rational numbers, geometry, and mental computation, in which she may require remediation.

Norms and Standardization Group: Key-Math–R was standardized on a sample of 925 students from kindergarten through grade 8 at twenty-three test sites in sixteen states. The selection of students was based on 1983 and 1986 U.S. Census figures. The sample was representative according to geographic region, grade, sex, socioeconomic status, and race. One hundred students were tested in each of the nine grades.

Reliability: Three methods were used to assess the reliability of the KeyMath: alternate-form, split-half, and a method based on item response theory. Alternate-form reliability for the total test was about .90, indicating that the two forms of the total test basically were similar. Alternate-form reliability for the three test areas ranged from .80 to .88. Split-half reliability is reported by grade. Reliability for the total test ranged from in the mid to high .90's, and in the .70's and .80's for the three areas. The Standard Error of Measurement (SEM) for the total test ranged from 1.6 (grade 8) to 4.0 points (kindergarten).

Figure 19-4   Results from a Child's KeyMath-Revised Assessment

A.   The KeyMath–R Summary

INDIVIDUAL TEST RECORD

KeyMath
R E V I S E D

a diagnostic
inventory of
essential
mathematics

AUSTIN J.
CONNOLLY

				YEAR	MONTH	DAY		DATA FROM OTHER TESTS	
							Test	Date	Results
Student's Name *Carrie M.*		Sex: M/F	Test date	*87*	*09*	*32*	*CTBS*	*5/4/84*	*Slightly below average*
School *Cedar Hills*		Grade *4*					*CTBS*	*4/27/86*	*About 1.5 yrs below grade*
Mathematics Teacher *Mrs. Guthrie*			Birth date	*77*	*8*	*14*	*PPVT-R*	*9/23/87*	*Average for age*
Examiner *Tom Brown*	Date *10/2/87*		Chronological age	*10*	*1*	*18*			

SCORE SUMMARY

Derived-score tables are in Appendix E of the *Manual*. For standard scores and scaled scores you can indicate your selection of grade or age and fall or spring norms by circling the number of the appropriate table.

Standard Scores and Scaled Scores
Fall norms (August–January)
Spring norms (February–July)

	Grade	Age
	(Table 1)	Table 2
	Table 3	Table 4

See Table 9 for percentile ranks, stanines, and normal curve equivalents. Obtain grade equivalents and age equivalents from Tables 10 and 11, respectively.

BASIC CONCEPTS				**OPERATIONS**				**APPLICATIONS**			
Subtest	Raw Score	Scaled Score	%ile Rank	Subtest	Raw Score	Scaled Score	%ile Rank	Subtest	Raw Score	Scaled Score	%ile Rank
Numeration	(*13*)	*7*	*16*	Addition	(*9*)	*5*	*5*	Measurement	(*10*)	*7*	*16*
Rational Numbers	(*2*)	*10*	*50*	Subtraction	(*8*)	*8*	*25*	Time and Money	(*14*)	*12*	*75*
Geometry	(*8*)	*5*	*5*	Multiplication	(*4*)	*7*	*16*	Estimation	(*7*)	*11*	*63*
				Division	(*5*)	*10*	*50*	Interpreting Data	(*10*)	*13*	*84*
				Mental Computation	(*6*)	*12*	*75*	Problem Solving	(*10*)	*15*	*95*

BASIC CONCEPTS AREA	Standard Score	%ile Rank	**OPERATIONS AREA**	Standard Score	%ile Rank	**APPLICATIONS AREA**	Standard Score	%ile Rank
Raw Score (*23*)	*80*	*9*	Raw Score (*32*)	*91*	*27*	Raw Score (*51*)	*110*	*75*
1.			2.			3.		

Grade/Age Equivalent *2.5*		Grade/Age Equivalent *3.7*		Grade/Age Equivalent *5.3*

TOTAL TEST	(*23*) + (*32*) + (*51*) = (*106*)	*97*	*42*	*5* (optional) NCE	Stanine	*4.0* (optional)	
	1. 2. 3.	Total Test Raw Score	Standard Score	%ile Rank		Grade Equivalent	Age Equivalent

B. The KeyMath Score Profile

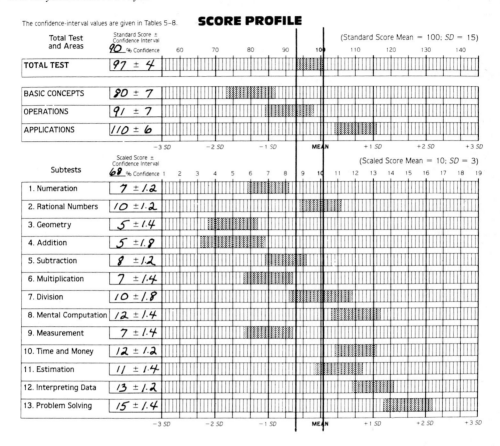

The confidence-interval values are given in Tables 5–8.

SCORE PROFILE

Total Test and Areas	Standard Score ± Confidence Interval 90 % Confidence	60	70	80	90	100	110	120	130	140
TOTAL TEST	97 ± 4									
BASIC CONCEPTS	90 ± 7									
OPERATIONS	91 ± 7									
APPLICATIONS	110 ± 6									

(Standard Score Mean = 100; SD = 15)

−3 SD   −2 SD   −1 SD   MEAN   +1 SD   +2 SD   +3 SD

Subtests	Scaled Score ± Confidence Interval 68 % Confidence	1	2	3	4	5	6	7	8	9	10	11	12	13	14	15	16	17	18	19
1. Numeration	7 ± 1.2																			
2. Rational Numbers	10 ± 1.2																			
3. Geometry	5 ± 1.4																			
4. Addition	5 ± 1.8																			
5. Subtraction	8 ± 1.2																			
6. Multiplication	7 ± 1.4																			
7. Division	10 ± 1.8																			
8. Mental Computation	12 ± 1.4																			
9. Measurement	7 ± 1.4																			
10. Time and Money	12 ± 1.2																			
11. Estimation	11 ± 1.4																			
12. Interpreting Data	13 ± 1.2																			
13. Problem Solving	15 ± 1.4																			

(Scaled Score Mean = 10; SD = 3)

−3 SD   −2 SD   −1 SD   MEAN   +1 SD   +2 SD   +3 SD

C. KeyMath Domain Performance

SUMMARY OF DOMAIN PERFORMANCE

BASIC CONCEPTS AREA

Subtest	Domain	Domain Score	Average Score (Table 16)	Domain Status
Numeration: (24 items) Ceiling Item 17	Numbers 0–9	6	6	W (A) S
	Numbers 0–99	4	5–6	(W) A S
	Numbers 0–999	2	2–3	W A S
	Multi-digit numbers and advanced numeration topics	1	NA	W A S
Rational Numbers: (18 items) Ceiling Item 6	Fractions	2	1–2	W (A) S
	Decimals	0	NA	W A S
	Percents	0	NA	W A S
Geometry: (24 items) Ceiling Item 13	Spatial and attribute relations	4	4–5	(W) A S
	Two-dimensional shapes and their relations	4	4–5	W A S
	Coordinate and transformational geometry	0	NA	W A S
	Three-dimensional shapes and their relations	0	NA	W A S

OPERATIONS AREA

Subtest	Domain	Domain Score	Average Score (Table 16)	Domain Status
Addition: (18 items) Ceiling Item 12	Models and basic facts	6	6	W (A) S
	Algorithms to add whole numbers	3	4–5	(W) A S
	Adding rational numbers	0	NA	W A S
Subtraction: (18 items) Ceiling Item 11	Models and basic facts	6	6	(A) W A S
	Algorithms to subtract whole numbers	2	3–4	(W) A S
	Subtracting rational numbers	0	NA	W A S
Multiplication: (18 items) Ceiling Item 10	Models and basic facts	3	5–6	(W) A S
	Algorithms to multiply whole numbers	1	2–3	(W) A S
	Multiplying rational numbers	0	NA	W A S
Division: (18 items) Ceiling Item 10	Models and basic facts	4	4–5	(W) A S
	Algorithms to divide whole numbers	1	0–1	(W) A S
	Dividing rational numbers	0	NA	W A S
Mental Computation: (18 items) Ceiling Item 9	Computation chains	5	3–4	W A (S)
	Whole numbers	1	2	W (W) A S
	Rational numbers	0	NA	W A S

APPLICATIONS AREA

Subtest	Domain	Domain Score	Average Score (Table 16)	Domain Status
Measurement: (24 items) Ceiling Item 15	Comparisons	2	6	W (A) S
	Using non-standard units	2	4–5	(W) A S
	Using standard units—length, area	0	NA	W A S
	Using standard units—weight, capacity		NA	W A S
Time and Money: (24 items) Ceiling Item 18	Identifying passage of time	5	5–6	W (A) S
	Using clocks and clock units	3	2–3	W A S
	Monetary amounts to one dollar	5	4–5	W (A) S
	Monetary amounts to one hundred dollars and business transactions	1	2	(W) A S
Estimation: (18 items) Ceiling Item 12	Whole and rational numbers	2	3–4	(W) A S
	Measurement	4	3	W (A) S
	Computation	1		W A S
Interpreting Data: (18 items) Ceiling Item 15	Charts and tables	5	4	W A (S)
	Graphs	3	3	W A S
	Probability and statistics	2	2–3	(W) A S
Problem Solving: (18 items) Ceiling Item 16	Solving routine problems	4	4–5	W (A) S
	Understanding non-routine problems	3	3–4	W (A) S
	Solving non-routine problems	3	3–4	W (A) S

D. Subtest Results with a Domain

8 MENTAL COMPUTATION

Computation chains

Whole numbers

Rational numbers

NUMERATION BASAL

		Computation chains	Whole numbers	Rational numbers
0-13▶	1. seven minus four	/		
	2. twelve minus ten	/		⋅
14-18▶	3. eight minus six, plus nine	/		
	4. 368 − 100		/	
19-21▶	5. fifty minus thirty . . .	/		
	6. two times nine . . .	/		
	7. 64 + 98		0	
22▶	8. 600 − 201		0	
	9. 100 × 17		0	
	10. 3 × 49			
23,24▶	11. thirty divided by six . . .			
	12. 800 ÷ 40			
	13. $\frac{1}{3}$ of 12			
	14. $5\frac{3}{8}$ + 2			
	15. 8 − $\frac{1}{2}$			
	16. 0.5 × 18			
	17. 0.28 × 10			
	18. 200% of 9			

9 CEILING ITEM   DOMAIN SCORES | 5 | / | 0 |

SUBTEST RAW SCORE
(Sum of domain scores) | 6 |

Source: A. Connolly (1988) KeyMath–Revised. Circle Pines, MN: American Guidance Service. Used by permission.

Validity: It is vitally important that a diagnostic instrument such as the KeyMath clearly demonstrate its content validity. For the KeyMath, nearly two years were invested in which essential school mathematical content was identified. However, no information is offered as to how test items were matched to school content or how the school content itself was identified. For this reason, although the test appears to possess strong content validity, such validity is still largely undemonstrated. The author attempted to demonstrate concurrent validity by correlating the KeyMath with the math subtest of the Iowa Test of Basic Skills and the Comprehensive Test of Basic Skills (CTBS). Correlations with the CTBS ranged from the .30's to .50's and from the .40's to .50's with the Iowa tests, thus demonstrating only a moderate correlation with other mathematics achievement tests.

Summary of the KeyMath for the Test Consumer: The KeyMath–R is one of the most popular arithmetic tests on the market today. It is neatly packaged and easy to administer, and it yields information on various levels. The revised edition is much improved over early editions of the instrument.

The content and concurrent validity of the KeyMath still have not been demonstrated, yet this is an absolute requisite for a diagnostic test, especially one that purports to be useful as a criterion-referenced instrument. Its reliability is in the acceptable range, and although the standardization group is small, it is more representative than in earlier editions of the test. The KeyMath–Revised yields a great deal of norm-referenced and criterion-referenced information for the test consumer. However, until the content validity is more strongly demonstrated, results should be interpreted with caution.

Stanford Diagnostic Mathematics Test

Overview: The Stanford Diagnostic Mathematics Test (SDMT) (Beatty, Madden, Gardner, and Karlsen 1976) is a flexible assessment instrument that can be administered either in groups or individually. The SDMT can be used as either a norm-referenced or criterion-referenced test. It is designed to identify areas in need of remediation and aid in instructional planning. It also offers a diagnostic-prescriptive approach to the teaching of mathematics and can be used for grouping purposes. The results of the SDMT can be used for individual students or for a class, school, or school district to evaluate the effectiveness of mathematics programs.

The four color-coded levels of the SDMT are:

1. Red: Grades 1.5 to 4.5 and for low-achieving primary students.
2. Green: Grades 3.5 to 6.5 and for low-achieving elementary students.
3. Brown: Grades 5.5 to 8.5 and for low-achieving elementary students.
4. Blue: Grades 7.5 to 13 and for low-achieving junior high school students.

Each level of the SDMT contains three major subtests: Number Systems and Numeration, Computations, and Applications. Each subtest measures various areas of difficulty depending on the level of the test. Table 19-3 contains a description of the subtests and areas covered by the SDMT.

Administration and Scoring: The SDMT can be administered individually or in groups. As with most tests, individual administration is preferable for learners with special needs. Students must be able to attend, stay on task, and work independently. All questions are multiple-choice. The lower-level tests do not require reading skills because the tester reads the questions aloud. However, some reading is required on the upper-level tests, or the tester can give assistance to the student. This can lead to test error. Several of the tests are timed.

Not all the subtests of each level need to be administered. If all subtests are given, the student may need frequent breaks, or the test

Table 19-3 Subtests of the Stanford Diagnostic Mathematics Test

Each Level of the SDMT contains the following three subtests.

1. *Number System and Numeration*
   a. Whole numbers
   b. Rational numbers
   c. Sets
   d. Fractions and decimals
   e. Numeration/Counting
   f. Properties of numbers

2. *Computation*
   a. Computation in four computational areas ($+$, $-$, $\times$, $\div$)
   b. Computation with fractions and decimals
   c. Compound number sentences

3. *Applications*
   a. Problem solving
   b. Tables and graphs
   c. Geometry
   d. Measurement

can be given over more than one day. Administration time ranges from 90 to 120 minutes depending on the level given. There are no basal or ceiling scores to the SDMT. When a level subtest is chosen, the entire subtest is administered. Tests can be scored by hand or by a commercial test-scoring service.

The SDMT can be used as a norm-referenced or criterion-referenced test. As a norm-referenced instrument, scores can be expressed as percentile ranks, scaled scores, stanines, and grade equivalents for each subtest and for the total level score. The SDMT is also quite useful as a criterion-referenced instrument. Each test is described in terms of concept and skill domains, with each domain (and item) linked to a set of specific instructional objectives.

Additionally, the SDMT uses the Progress Indicator score. This score provides the test user with information about the student's progress in learning the skills contained within each concept and skill domain. The student's raw score in each domain area is compared to a cutoff score that indicates a mastery of skills in that domain. If the score equals or exceeds the mastery cutoff, the student receives a plus ($+$). If the score falls below the mastery criterion, the student receives a minus ($-$). Progress indicators are criterion-referenced because they do not compare students to each other but rather to an external criterion of mastery.

Norms and Standardization Group: In many ways, the standardization of the SDMT sets the standard for other mathematics assessment instruments. The SDMT was standardized on 38,000 students in thirty-seven school districts. The manual includes detailed tables illustrating the demographic characteristic of the norm group, which closely parallels the 1970 U.S. census. The norm group and the school systems selected were chosen by a carefully conceived plan that stratified for SES, school system enrollment, geographic region, and other demographic variables.

Reliability: Two types of reliability were assessed—internal-consistency and alternate-form reliability. This was accomplished for both the test scores and the progress indicators. Internal-consistency reliability is acceptably sufficient, ranging from .84 to .97 for the four levels of the test; alternate-form reliability is generally greater than .84. A commendable feature is the reporting of a Standard Error of Measurement (SEM) in the manual for each test.

For each concept and skill domain, the Progress Indicators were used to estimate reliability. These values are high enough to encourage confidence in the use of the Progress Indicators.

Validity: Item selection in the SDMT was extremely well researched. Mathematics curricula were first examined for content, and a set of instructional objectives was created. A pool of possible items was then assembled, and each item was reviewed and edited for style and adherence to the stated objective. Next, each item was carefully reviewed by a panel of experts for ethnic, racial, cultural, and/or sex bias. Finally, the items were field-tested. Such extensive item planning and field-testing, rare in educational assessment, demonstrate the test's strong content validity.

The test authors also provide criterion-related coefficients that are actually correlations between scores on the SDMT and the mathematics test of the Stanford Achievement Test. Although these correlations are high, whether they actually demonstrate the test's criterion-related validity is problematic.

Summary of the SDMT for the Test Consumer: The SDMT can be used as a norm-referenced or criterion-referenced test. Although it contains much of the same content as many other norm-referenced mathematics tests, its strength in item selection and review, as well as its strong standardization procedures, sets an example for other tests. As a criterion-referenced test, it contains a strong and proven reliability and content validity, and its instructional objectives keyed to test items and Progress Indicators offer much to the teacher. In summary, the SDMT should be given serious consideration by the educational professional.

Other Commercially Available Mathematics Tests

Diagnostic Screening Test: Math

Overview: The Diagnostic Screening Test: Math (DST) (Gnagey 1980) provides teachers and other educational professionals with a quick assessment of the student's mathematics performance. It assesses mathematics performance in five Basic Processes and six Specialized Areas including time, money, and U.S. and metric measurement. In addition, an optional nine-item pretest can be used to obtain a rough estimate of basic computa-

tional skills. The Basic Processes section contains thirty-six graded and developmentally ordered items that are also keyed to grade level.

Administration and Scoring: The DST can be administered individually or in small groups. Individual administration for students with special needs is preferable. Instructions in the test manual are clear and precise, although the directions for scoring can be somewhat confusing, and some initial training is required. Administration time varies with the age and grade of the student but ranges from five to twenty minutes.

Scores are reported in terms of grade equivalents and a Consolidated Index (CI). The CI scores are used to determine the relative mastery of grade-level performance rather than mastery of specific skills. As such, they are not really mastery level scores but rather a hybrid of mastery and norm-referenced scores. The test author suggests that an informal analysis of the student's performance on the DST provides the greatest amount of diagnostic information. However, an informal assessment of a student's mathematics errors and math performance can be undertaken at less cost.

Norms and Standardization Group: There is no information available on the standardization group of the DST.

Reliability: Discussion of the instrument's reliability in the manual is also inadequate. This discussion focuses on the amount of growth in mathematics achievement exhibited over a three-month period by a group of students. However, it is not apparent how this growth demonstrates test reliability. Neither is it clear how the overall reliability coefficient of .93 was calculated. No estimates of reliability at various grade levels are provided, nor are estimates of internal consistency.

Validity: The author attempted to establish face and construct validity through a discussion of the test's construction and by reporting, for each level of the test, the percentage of student grade equivalent scores on the Peabody Individual Achievement Test and the KeyMath Diagnostic Test. How this is a measure of validity is confusing, and care should be taken in interpreting these data.

Summary of the DST for the Test Consumer: In summary, the DST is best used as a screening instrument by educational professionals. As such, it probably has merit in identifying candidates for in-depth assessment in mathematics. However, the poor technical quality of the instrument argues against its use as a diagnostic instrument.

Test of Mathematical Abilities

Overview: The Test of Mathematical Abilities (TOMA) (Brown and McEntire 1984) is a norm-referenced test designed for students in grades three through twelve with a chronological age between eight years, six months, and eighteen years, eleven months. The purpose of the TOMA is to identify students who are significantly ahead of or behind their peers in mathematics (norm-referenced) and to determine the specific mathematical strengths and weaknesses of students (criterion-referenced). Additionally, the TOMA assesses the student's general attitude or *affect* toward mathematics.

The TOMA adopts a different viewpoint of mathematics assessment than other formal tests. Besides measuring the usual computation skills, it measures affect toward mathematics, mathematical vocabulary, general information, and the ability to complete story problems. As such, it contains a strong language arts–reading component, and the student must possess fairly sophisticated skills in these areas (in addition to mathematics) to do well on the test.

The TOMA contains five subtests (see Table 19-4). The Mathematical Vocabulary and General Mathematics Information subtests closely parallel measures of vocabulary and general information often used on verbal–language tests. Because of its difficulty, the authors recommend dropping the Vocabulary subtest for children under the age of eleven. Whereas four of the subtests can be group administered, the General Information subtest must be administered individually. However, because of the strong reading–language arts component and the relatively sophisticated test-taking skills required, it is advisable to administer all of the subtests of the TOMA individually to learners with special needs.

Administration and Scoring: The TOMA is relatively easy to administer, and no special training is needed. Nevertheless, the examiner should be familiar with the test manual and procedures before administering the test to a student. The Attitude toward Math

Table 19-4 Five Subtests of the Test of Mathematical Ability (TOMA)

1. *Attitude Toward Math:* Tester reads aloud fifteen items, such as "math is easy for me." The student checks off on the response sheet from alternatives "agree," "disagree," or "don't know."

2. *Vocabulary:* The student is presented with twenty mathematical terms. The student's task is to define the terms. Students must be at least eleven years old to take this subtest.

3. *Computation:* The student is asked to solve twenty-four problems in the four computational areas. Includes the use of fractions, decimals, money, and percentages.

4. *General Information:* Thirty items, individually administered, that test general mathematical information, such as "How many pennies in a nickel?"

5. *Story Problems:* The student reads and solves brief story problems. Reading ability required.

subtest is administered first, and the Computation subtest last. The other subtests can be administered in any order. Students answer all questions on the Attitudes subtest. On the other four subtests, basal and ceiling levels are found. The basal score is defined as three consecutive correct responses; the ceiling is defined as three consecutive incorrect answers. On these subtests, however, students are asked to complete as many items as possible. The ceiling is applied at the time of test scoring, not test administration. Total administration time for the TOMA ranges from 50 to 125 minutes, and the examiner must be aware of student fatigue or loss of motivation to complete the test.

Scores on the TOMA are reported by ages: half-year intervals for ages eight to ten years, and full-year intervals for ages ten to eighteen years, eleven months. It is important to emphasize that scores are not reported as grade equivalents. They are reported as both scaled scores and percentile ranks. A total test score, the Math Quotient (MQ), is derived by combining subtest scores. This MQ contains a mean of 100 and a standard deviation of 15. However, as with other quotient scores used by tests, such as the Test of Language Development (TOLD) and the other tests published by the Pro–Ed Company, there is some debate about the usefulness and the validity of the MQ. Additionally, like other quotient scores, the MQ can be misleading if interpreted as a mathematical equivalent of an IQ score. The results of each subtest score can be plotted as a profile that allows for quick visual scanning of the student's test performance.

Norms and Standardization Group: The TOMA was standardized on a relatively small population of 1,560 students residing in five states. The sample was reported to be representative of the 1980 census in terms of sex, race, urban and rural demographics, and geographic region. However no information regarding socioeconomic status (SES), educa-

tion, or occupation of parents is provided in the manual.

Reliability: No reliability estimates for the entire test are provided. However, estimates are available for subtests at each age group (a population of fifty reliability coefficients). Reliability is the internal-consistency type. Test reliabilities are generally in the .70 to .89 range, but some of the coefficients fall below acceptable levels. Test-retest reliability was carried out for a small group of eleven-year-old students and a set of learning disabled pupils, but the results were inconclusive because of the small sample size.

Validity: No evidence of content validity is presented as no information is available regarding how items were chosen and whether they are valid in terms of children's mathematical curricula. Attempts to demonstrate criterion-related validity consisted of correlating the TOMA with the mathematics subtests of the PIAT and the WRAT and with the earlier version of the KeyMath test. Whereas the TOMA correlated modestly well with the PIAT, correlations with the WRAT were nonsignificant. All subtests of the TOMA correlated modestly well with the KeyMath. However, none of the correlations nor the method used convincingly demonstrate the criterion-related validity of the TOMA.

Construct validity was demonstrated by showing that TOMA scores increased with age and that there was a significant correlation among the TOMA, the WISC–R, and the Slosson Intelligence Test. However, because the validity of the Slosson is itself in question, this last measure should be disregarded.

Summary of the TOMA for the Test Consumer: The TOMA is an interesting attempt to take a fresh look at measuring mathematical ability. It examines such concepts as mathematics vocabulary, the ability to complete story problems, and attitude toward math. For this the test authors should be commended.

However, the test contains a number of problems. First, it is highly correlated with reading and language. Thus, it is difficult to assess whether a child's poor test performance in the TOMA is due to poor mathematical skills or to poor language abilities. Second, the use of the MQ is quite limited, and it can be misinterpreted by parents and educational professionals. The MQ serves little educational purpose. Third, the TOMA has not demonstrated content validity, something that any diagnostic test must do if its results are to be used in remediating weaknesses. Finally, there are some questions about the adequacy of the test's general reliability and the adequacy of norms.

In summary, the TOMA is one of the fastest selling mathematics tests on the market today, but its popularity may be partly unjustified. It should be used and interpreted cautiously by the educational professional.

Criterion-Referenced Mathematics Tests

The mathematics tests critiqued thus far in this chapter have been either fully norm-referenced tests or a combination of norm- and criterion-referenced tests. Most of these tests yield normative information in the form of grade and/or age equivalents and percentile ranks. Additionally, some of these tests (e.g., KeyMath and the SDMT) offer a degree of criterion-referenced information, such as mastery scores or Progress Indicators.

The tests to be discussed yield a greater degree of criterion-referenced, diagnostic information than the previous tests. For example, all of the following tests key items to specific instructional objectives. In some of these tests, instructional objectives are linked to pages in basal math textbooks where the objectives can be found and taught. In other tests, remediational activities for specific test objectives missed are suggested. Finally, some of these tests conduct detailed error analyses of students' mathematical strategies. As such, these tests are valuable for teachers and other educational professionals who are more intent on identifying and remediating specific mathematical weaknesses than on comparing students' mathematical performances against peers.

Diagnostic Test of Arithmetic Strategies

Overview: The Diagnostic Test of Arithmetic Strategies (DTAS) (Ginsburg and Mathews 1984) is designed to measure the ability of students in grades one through six to perform calculations in the four computational areas. Additionally, the DTAS focuses on the successful or unsuccessful use of arithmetic strategies by students and identifies learner processes that systematically lead to incorrect arithmetic answers. Finally, it describes effective strategies that students can use (e.g., mental addition) in learning and applying mathematical concepts.

The DTAS contains four subtests: Addition, Subtraction, Multiplication, and Division. Note that these subtests are less concerned with whether the student answers problems correctly or incorrectly than with gaining information about the strategies the student uses in solving arithmetic problems. To accomplish this goal, each subtest is divided into four sections: Setting Up the Problem, Number Facts, Written Calculations, and Informal Skills. As shown in Table 19-5, each subtest item is designed to yield information regarding underlying strategies that the student uses in solving presented problems. The goal is to gather information about the *symptoms* of the student's errors caused by faulty arithmetic strategies.

Administration and Scoring: No special training is needed to administer the DTAS. However, it is imperative that the teacher be well acquainted with the test and the administration procedures. Practice testing is strongly

Table 19-5 Four Subtest Sections of the Test
of Arithmetic Strategies

Each computational subtest (+, −, ×, ÷) contains the following four sections.

1. *Setting Up the Problem:* Tester reads the problem to student. The student's job is to translate the tester's words into mathematical symbols and write down the problem. Solving the problem is not required in this section.

2. *Number Facts:* The student is given standard number facts and asked to supply oral answers without use of paper and pencil. Responses are timed for automaticity.

3. *Written Calculation:* The student is presented twelve computation problems of increasing difficulty. The student's task is to:
   a. Solve the problems.
   b. Show all work.
   c. Verbally explain what he or she is doing while solving the problem.

4. *Informal Skills:* The student must mentally solve problems. The student's problem-solving strategies are queried or observed.

---

encouraged. The DTAS takes from 70 to 90 minutes to administer, and the teacher should be aware of student fatigue or decreasing motivation.

The DTAS is difficult to score and interpret. The scorer must evaluate the accuracy of the student's responses as well as describe the strategies used to arrive at the responses. No underlying scoring or coding system allows the scorer to determine a pattern of strategies without reviewing each answer. Additionally, although the manual gives instructions on how to score, these instructions are quite involved and complex. The scorer should keep the manual for reference or memorize the scoring instructions.

The DTAS has no norm-referenced scores. Rather, scores are descriptive in nature and use a checklist approach. Interpretation of this descriptive information is keyed to four main efforts: (1) focusing on specific problems; (2)

exploiting existing strengths; (3) encouraging active learning; and (4) using available materials. These interpretive goals are discussed in great detail in a separate manual chapter and in the appendixes of the test manual.

Reliability and Validity: Although the test manual contains a strong rationale and overview, reliability and validity issues are not addressed. Thus, the reliability and validity of this instrument cannot be evaluated.

Summary of the DTAS for the Test Consumer: The DTAS is one of the newest criterion-referenced tests to enter the market, and it is growing in popularity. It focuses not only on the correctness of student responses but also on the strategies students use to arrive at those answers. This technique appears positive and yields useful diagnostic and prescriptive information. However, the problems with scoring may lead to difficulties in interpreting results. Additionally, the test authors do not address the issues of reliability and validity. Until these issues are resolved, the DTAS, although potentially valuable, should be used and interpreted cautiously.

Diagnosis: An Instructional Aid in Mathematics

Overview: Diagnosis: An Instructional Aid in Mathematics (Diagnosis:Math) (Guzaitis, Carlin, and Juda 1972) is a companion instrument to Diagnosis: An Instructional Aid in Reading. As such, it contains many of the features of the reading test.

Diagnosis:Math is a completely criterion-referenced test designed to identify students' specific mathematical strengths and weaknesses. Additionally, it aids the teacher in systematically planning remediational instruction. The test has two levels (A and B). Level A is designed for students whose mathematical skills are approximately at the kindergarten to grade three level; Level B is designed for students with mathematical abilities in the grade three to grade six range. Table 19-6 lists the mathematical content tested at each level. Both levels contain survey tests, probes, a prescription guide, a teacher's handbook, and a class progress chart.

The key aspect of Diagnosis:Math is the Probe Tests. There are 32 Probe Tests at each level, and the items of each Probe Test are keyed to specific instructional objectives. There are 160 such objectives in Level A and 421 specific objectives in Level B.

It would be time consuming and inefficient for the teacher to administer every item of every Probe Test. For this reason, Diagnosis:Math uses a Survey Test at each level. The Survey Test is administered and scored to obtain a global assessment of the student's strengths and weaknesses. Weak areas are then tested in-depth using the Probe system.

The objectives contained in Diagnosis:Math are also cross-referenced to a number of elementary school mathematics series and school materials. This helps the teacher design remediational programming and mate-rials for missed objectives, either with teacher-made or commercially available mathematics materials.

Administration and Scoring: Diagnosis:Math is individually administered. Administration time is not reported in the manual. The subtests within each level can be administered in any order. Because it is a criterion-referenced test, standard scores are not reported. Rather, items that the student misses are recorded and keyed to instructional objectives. Because no criteria are used to describe mastery, items are really objective rather than criterion-referenced.

Reliability and Validity: Unfortunately, no information is offered as to the technical quality of the test, either in terms of items, objectives, or remediational activities. Information on these matters would greatly strengthen the test's usefulness.

Summary of Diagnosis:Math for the Test Consumer: On the surface, Diagnosis:Math seems to be a very useful test. Items on the Probe Tests are keyed to a large number of specific instructional objectives. Additionally, these objectives are keyed to specific remediational activities and materials.

However, closer inspection of the test raises serious questions. For example, how can we really tell that the test is reliable and does not contain a great deal of error? Just as important, can we accept the test's content validity without an explanation of how items were chosen and whether they were field tested? Such information, if it were positive, would contribute greatly to the usefulness of the test. In fact, such information might make this one of the best mathematics tests on the market. Without this technical information, however, Diagnosis:Math must rest on its potential and be approached with a degree of skepticism by the informed test consumer.

Table 19-6 Mathematical Content Assessed at Each Level of Diagnosis: An Instructional Aid in Mathematics

Level A (kindergarten to grade 3)

A. Computation (41 objectives)
B. Geometry (18 objectives)
C. Measurement (36 objectives)
D. Operations and problem solving (33 objectives)
E. Sets and numeration (32 objectives)

Total: 160 objectives assessed

Level B (grades 3–6)

A. Computation (175 objectives)
B. Geometry (40 objectives)
C. Measurement (54 objectives)
D. Operations and problem solving (74 objectives)
E. Numeration (78 objectives)

Total: 421 objectives assessed

Other Criterion-Referenced Tests

Diagnostic Mathematics Inventory

Overview: The Diagnostic Mathematics Inventory (DMI) (Gessell 1977), is a criterion-referenced instrument designed to test student mastery of specific mathematics instructional objectives. It consists of multiple-choice questions keyed to 325 math objectives. The test is appropriate for use with students in grades 1.5 through 8.5.

There are seven levels of the DMI (A–G), each of which is color coded. Additionally, there are practice exercises at each level and Interim Evaluation Tests for monitoring student progress in mathematics throughout the school year. The content of each Interim Evaluation Test assumes and builds on successful learning of skills presented earlier.

The DMI contains a number of other useful features. For example, the test contains Learning Activities Guides that link specific objectives to learning activities the teacher can use to teach those objectives. Additionally, the DMI comes with a Guide to Ancillary Materials that cross-references the test objectives to more than seventy different, commercially available, nontextbook materials. Finally, the DMI contains a set of Master Reference Guides that contain references to pages in major mathematics textbooks where specific mathematics objectives are taught. Thus, the teacher is provided with not only a method for diagnosing student mathematics learning problems but also methods of remediating those problems using activities provided by the test, by nontextbook, commercially available materials, and by a host of textbook series.

Administration and Scoring: Scores on the DMI are completely criterion-referenced. The test is scored in terms of whether items (objectives) have been mastered by the student. The DMI reports three types of scores:

premastery analysis, an *objective mastery report,* and an *individual diagnostic report.*

1. Premastery Analysis: This score provides information on students' math behaviors *before* they achieve mastery on a given objective. It tells the teacher what the student did wrong when incorrectly answering the mathematics problem.
2. Objective Mastery Report: This is a *class* report. Information regarding which students have mastered which objectives is provided to the teacher.
3. Individual Diagnostic Report: This report on the individual student details which objectives the student has and has not mastered.

Reliability and Validity: No technical information is reported in the manual regarding reliability and validity. Although this is often the case with tests of this sort, it is unfortunate. Criterion-referenced tests are based on assertions of content validity, yet the DMI contains no validity information.

Summary of the DMI for the Test Consumer: In summary, the DMI is a well-constructed test similar to Diagnosis: An Instructional Aid in Math. The inclusion of the Interim Evaluation Tests, which monitor progress throughout the school year, the Learning Activities Guides, and the Guide to Ancillary Materials make it quite useful to the classroom teacher. As with other tests in this category, however, it would be that much stronger if it contained adequate (or any) technical information. Nevertheless, it is a very useful diagnostic and prescriptive instrument for remediating mathematics difficulties, even though its content validity is questionable.

Informal Mathematics Assessment

The educational professional may wish to carry out an informal mathematics assessment with students. Such assessment has the advantage of containing items specific to what the student is experiencing in the classroom, rather than the content of a commercially available test that may or may not fit the pupil's classroom content.

Informal Mathematics Inventories

Informal Mathematics Inventories (IMIs) representatively survey the skills needed for success in mathematics. Such inventories can be specific to the pupil's mathematics curriculum or can be representative of the types of mathematical problems typically encountered by students at that grade level. In either case, IMIs typically test content in the areas of computation, problem solving, and application.

Teachers can produce their own IMIs or use inventories produced and published elsewhere (Mann, Suiter, and McClung 1987; Reisman 1987). Figure 19-5 lists some commercially available IMIs. One of the most popular of these instruments is described here.

Figure 19-5   Available Mathematics Skill
Hierarchies

1. Mann–Suiter Grade Level Arithmetic Sequence. P. H. Mann, P. Suiter, and R. McClung (1987). *Handbook in Diagnostic Teaching,* 3d ed. (Boston: Allyn and Bacon).

2. E. Levine, C. Fineman, and G. Donlon (1974). *Prescriptive Profile Procedures for Children with Learning Disabilities* (Miami, FL: Dade County Public Schools).

3. F. K. Reisman (1978). *A Guide to the Diagnostic Teaching of Arithmetic,* 2nd ed. (Columbus, OH: Charles E. Merrill).

4. N. B. Bartel (1986). "Problems in Mathematics Achievement," in *Teaching Children with Learning and Behavior Problems,* 4th ed. Ed. D. D. Hammill and N. R. Bartel (Boston: Allyn and Bacon).

5. B. E. Enright (1983). *ENRIGHT Diagnostic Inventory of Basic Arithmetic Skills* (North Billerica, MA: Curriculum Associates).

ENRIGHT Diagnostic Inventory of Basic Arithmetic Skills

The ENRIGHT® Diagnostic Inventory of Basic Arithmetic Skills* (Enright 1983) is an informal, criterion-referenced inventory that measures a variety of skills including basic number facts, computational skills, whole numbers, fractions, and decimals. The ENRIGHT Inventory assesses mathematics skills at three separate levels of diagnostic complexity: broad-based (wide-range) placement, skill placement, and specific subskills. The broad-based placement assesses a general family of related mathematics skills. Such assessment is analogous to survey or screening assessments that identify possible areas of student weaknesses. When areas of possible weakness are found, the student is administered one or more tests of skill placement. These tests assess a specific subskill (e.g., addition) in-depth so that weak areas within a subskill can be identified. Finally, after weak subareas have been identified, specific criterion-referenced tests can be given to determine the specific behaviors that the student has not yet learned or is applying incorrectly when solving mathematical problems.

The criterion-referenced test level of the ENRIGHT Inventory contains a built-in error analysis component. The test manual contains not only the correct answer to presented problems but also an analysis of what the student did wrong if an incorrect answer was given. An example of an error analysis for the subtraction subarea is shown in Figure 19-6.

In summary, the Enright Inventory contains many positive features. It is diagnostic and criterion-referenced in scope, but it also contains survey level tests so that the teacher does not have to administer the entire instrument to students. This saves time and reduces error brought on by tester and pupil fatigue.

* *ENRIGHT®* is a registered trademark of Curriculum Associates, Inc.

Figure 19.6 Error Analysis from the ENRIGHT Inventories of Basic Arithmetic Skills

B. Subtraction of Whole Numbers
2-Digit Number from a 2-Digit Number, with No Regrouping

SKILL: Subtracts a 2-digit number from a 2-digit number, with no regrouping.

GRADE LEVEL TAUGHT: 1.6

STUDENT BOOK:
TEST: Page 52
REVIEW ITEMS: Page 92
ARITHMETIC RECORD: Page 3 back

ASSESSMENT METHODS: Individual or group written response.

DISCONTINUE: When student has completed the five test items.

ACCURACY: At least 4/5 (80%) on the test items is required. When the review items are used for post testing, 4/5 (80%) is also required.

NEXT: If the student's accuracy is 4/5 (80%) on this skill test, proceed to the next higher test. If the student has responded incorrectly to two or more test items, do not proceed to the next higher skill test. Instead, begin remediation based on the error analysis shown here.

NOTES:
* Check to see if student subtracts left to right instead of right to left. Subtracting left to right also results in answer shown here.
† Student arrives at correct answer when making this error because subtracting in the tens column results in zero (0).

REVIEW ITEMS

a. 67 −23 = 44	b. 48 −36 = 12	c. 98 −72 = 26
d. 45 −14 = 31	e. 59 −47 = 12	

(B-6)
OBJECTIVE: By _____(date)_____ , _____(student's name)_____ , when given five test items for subtracting a 2-digit number from a 2-digit number, with no regrouping, will correctly compute at least four of the five test items (80%).

B-6 SUBTRACTION OF WHOLE NUMBERS:
2-Digit Number from a 2-Digit Number, with No Regrouping

DIRECTIONS: Direct the students, by number and location, to the page and test in their test books. Tell the students to do only the five test items in the box. Tell them to work carefully and take as much time as needed.

ERROR ANALYSIS

	a. ⁺43 −12 = 31	b. 58 −23 = 35	c. ⁺93 −12 = 81	d. ⁺75 −54 = 21	e. ⁺47 −35 = 12	ERROR ANALYSIS
	211	215	711	111	† 12	**Regrouping 7:** Regroups from tens place when not necessary.
	4	8	9	3	3	**Process Substitution 25:** Adds digits of minuend, adds digits of subtrahend, and subtracts.
	1	5	1	1	2	**Omission 125:** Ignores tens column.
	13	53	18	12	21	**Placement 171:** Reverses digits in difference.
	55	81	105	129	82	**Attention to Sign 190:** Adds.
	516	1334	1116	4050	1645	**Attention to Sign 191:** Multiplies.

Examiner's Notes:

75

ENRIGHT® Diagnostic Inventory of Basic Arithmetic Skills, copyright © 1983 Curriculum Associates, Billerica, MA. Reprinted by permission. ENRIGHT® is a registered trademark of Curriculum Associates, Inc.

The criterion-referenced testing level is tied to a set of instructional objectives and contains its own error analysis, which will prove helpful to the professional interested in *why* student errors occurred.

Checklists

Checklists afford the teacher a quick, efficient method for observing and recording student mathematical errors. The teacher usually checks off student errors from a list as the errors occur. At a later time, the checklist is reviewed by the teacher, and decisions are made as to the mathematical areas that require in-depth assessment. A portion of a checklist is shown in Figure 19-7. This figure also contains information on sources of existing mathematics checklists.

Mathematics Interviews

Interviews are useful supplements to other informal mathematics assessment procedures. They can be used to gain information in two separate areas (Bartel 1986; Cawley 1978; Mercer and Mercer 1985). First, mathematics interviews can help determine the *processes* that students use in solving problems and give the teacher valuable insight as to a student's thinking or logic when employing mathematical strategies and techniques. Second, mathematics interviews can give the teacher information about students' attitudes or affect toward mathematics. This is important because many students (and teachers) hold negative attitudes toward or are fearful of mathematics (Guerin and Maier 1983; Mercer and Mercer 1985). Figure 19-8 lists some sample questions designed to assess student affect toward mathematics.

Cawley (1978) has developed the Clinical Mathematics Interview, which he describes as "an intensive diagnostic procedure that integrates content, mode, and algorithms (rules)" (p. 224). With the Cawley technique, the stu-

dent first writes an answer to a mathematics problem. After the item is scored, the student verbalizes the procedure used to solve the problem. A wide variety of interview probing techniques are allowed, and both the student and the interviewer may use various modalities and methods (drawing, graphing, etc.) to elaborate their ideas. Results of the Clinical Mathematics Interview are used to identify areas needing mathematical remediation.

Teachers may wish to construct their own mathematics interview. Bartel (1986) has developed some guidelines and procedures for conducting such interviews (see Figure 19-9).

Note that of all the informal mathematics assessment tools available, the interview technique is probably the one most open to error, in terms of both student reporting and interviewer error. People often do not know or fully understand what processes they use to solve mathematics problems. Likewise, people may wish to present themselves positively to please or impress the interviewer. From the interviewer's standpoint, answers obtained during interviews are often difficult to categorize and interpret. For these reasons, mathematics interviews should be used only in combination with other mathematics assessment techniques and not as a replacement for these techniques.

Error Analysis

As in the academic areas of reading and spelling, the process of error analysis can be a useful informal assessment tool in mathematics. Error analysis in mathematics has a long history, and it continues to be used today to determine not only *if* the student has answered a problem incorrectly but also *why*.

Error analysis is used most frequently in terms of mathematical computational skills (Cox 1975; Guerin and Maier 1985). The computational errors students make most often have been classified into four main errors: *incorrect operation, incorrect number fact, in-*

Figure 19-7   Portion of a Checklist in Mathematics

Addition: (Place a check before each habit observed in the pupil's work)

___ a1 Errors in combinations	___ a15 Disregarded column position
___ a2 Counting	___ a16 Omitted one or more digits
___ a3 Added carried number last	___ a17 Errors in reading numbers
___ a4 Forgot to add carried number	___ a18 Dropped back one or more tens
___ a5 Repeated work after partly done	___ a19 Derived unknown combinations from
___ a6 Added carried number irregularly	familiar one
___ a7 Wrote number to be carried	___ a20 Disregarded one column
___ a8 Irregular procedure in column	___ a21 Error in writing answer
___ a9 Carried wrong number	___ a22 Skipped one or more decades
___ a10 Grouped two or more numbers	___ a23 Carrying when there was nothing to
___ a11 Splits numbers into parts	carry
___ a12 Used wrong fundamental operation	___ a24 Used scratch paper
___ a13 Lost place in column	___ a25 Added in pairs, giving the last sum as
___ a14 Depended on visualization	answer
	___ a26 Added same digit in two columns
	___ a27 Wrote carried number in answer
	___ a28 Added same number twice

Subtraction: (Place a check before each habit observed in the pupil's work)

___ s1 Errors in combinations	___ s15 Deducted from minuend when borrow-
___ s2 Did not allow for having borrowed	ing was not necessary
___ s3 Counting	___ s16 Ignored a digit
___ s4 Errors due to zero in minuend	___ s17 Deducted 2 from minuend after bor-
___ s5 Said example backwards	rowing
___ s6 Subtracted minuend from subtrahend	___ s18 Error due to minuend and subtrahend
___ s7 Failed to borrow; gave zero as answer	digits being same
___ s8 Added instead of subtracted	___ s19 Used minuend or subtrahend as re-
___ s9 Error in reading	mainder
___ s10 Used same digit in two columns	___ s20 Reversed digits in remainder
___ s11 Derived unknown from known combi-	___ s21 Confused process with division or mul-
nation	tiplication
___ s12 Omitted a column	___ s22 Skipped one or more decades
___ s13 Used trial-and-error addition	___ s23 Increased minuend digit after borrow-
___ s14 Split numbers	ing
	___ s24 Based subtraction on multiplication
	combination

Multiplication: (Place a check before each habit observed in the pupil's work)

___ m1 Errors in combinations	___ m18 Error in single zero combinations,
___ m2 Error in adding the carried number	zero as multiplicand
___ m3 Wrote rows of zeros	___ m19 Confused products when multiplier
___ m4 Carried a wrong number	had two or more digits
___ m5 Errors in addition	___ m20 Repeated part of table
___ m6 Forgot to carry	___ m21 Multiplied by adding
___ m7 Used multiplicand as multiplier	___ m22 Did not multiply a digit in multipli-
___ m8 Error in single zero combinations,	cand
zero as multiplier	___ m23 Based unknown combination on an-
___ m9 Errors due to zero in multiplier	other
___ m10 Used wrong process—added	___ m24 Errors in reading
___ m11 Counted to carry	___ m25 Omitted digit in product

___ m12 Omitted digit in multiplier
___ m13 Wrote carried number
___ m14 Omitted digit in multiplicand
___ m15 Errors due to zero in multiplicand
___ m16 Error in position of partial products
___ m17 Counted to get multiplication combinations

___ m26 Errors in writing product
___ m27 Errors in carrying into zero
___ m28 Illegible figures
___ m29 Forgot to add partial products
___ m30 Split multiplier
___ m31 Wrote wrong digit of product
___ m32 Multiplied by same digit twice
___ m33 Reversed digits in product
___ m34 Wrote tables

Division: (Place a check before each habit observed in the pupil's work)

___ d1   Errors in division combinations
___ d2   Errors in subtraction
___ d3   Errors in multiplication
___ d4   Used remainder larger than divisor
___ d5   Found quotient by trial multiplication
___ d6   Neglected to use remainder within problem
___ d7   Omitted zero resulting from another digit
___ d8   Used wrong operation
___ d9   Omitted digit in dividend
___ d10 Counted to get quotient
___ d11 Repeated part of multiplication table
___ d12 Used short division form for long division
___ d13 Wrote remainders within problem
___ d14 Omitted zero resulting from zero in dividend
___ d15 Omitted final remainder
___ d16 Used long division form for short division
___ d17 Counted in subtracting
___ d18 Used too large a product

___ d19 Said example backwards
___ d20 Used remainder without new dividend figure
___ d21 Derived unknown combination from known one
___ d22 Had right answer, used wrong one
___ d23 Grouped too many digits in dividend
___ d24 Error in reading
___ d25 Used dividend or divisor as quotient
___ d26 Found quotient by adding
___ d27 Reversed dividend and divisor
___ d28 Used digits of divisor separately
___ d29 Wrote all remainders at end of problem
___ d30 Misinterpreted table
___ d31 Used digit in dividend twice
___ d32 Used second digit of divisor to find quotient
___ d33 Began dividing at units digit of dividend
___ d34 Split dividend
___ d35 Used endings to find quotient

Source: G. T. Buswell and L. John (1925). *Fundamental Processes in Arithmetic* (Indianapolis: Bobbs-Merrill). Used by permission.

Sources of Mathematical Checklists

1. F. K. Reisman and S. H. Kauffman (1980). *Teaching Mathematics to Children with Special Needs* (Columbus, OH: Charles E. Merrill).
2. G. R. Guerin and A. S. Maier (1983). *Informal Assessment in Education* (Palo Alto, CA. Mayfield Publishing)
3. G. T. Buswell and L. John (1925). *Fundamental Processes in Arithmetic* (Indianapolis: Bobbs-Merrill).

Figure 19-8   Sample Questions Designed to Measure Student Affect toward Mathematics

1. Do you like math?
2. Is math your favorite school subject? What is?
3. Do you like to work number problems? Which do you like *most? Least?*
   a. Addition
   b. Subtraction
   c. Multiplication
   d. Division
4. Do you like to solve story problems? Why or why not?
5. Can you tell time?
6. Do you like to work with calculators? What can you do with them?
7. What are some ways that people use math to solve problems in everyday life?
8. Do *you* use math in everyday life? How?
9. Are you good at making purchases and change?
10. Would you like to work on a job where you use a lot of math? Why or why not?

Figure 19-9   Guidelines for Conducting Mathematics Interviews

1. *One problem area should be considered at a time.* Problems should be dealt with in the order in which they appear. . . . For example, if a student is having difficulty in both addition and multiplication, addition problems should be cleared up first. Once this has been accomplished, the student will need to be retested on written multiplication before oral probing in that area. It may be that correction of the faulty addition strategy will modify the difficulty in multiplication.

2. *The easiest problems should be presented first.* To help give the student a sense of confidence, the teacher should first present the student with a problem that he or she probably can perform correctly. Then problems of increasing difficulty (for the child) can be provided.

3. *A written record or tape should be made of the interview.* The student should be told whether his or her explanations are being recorded on tape or in writing.

4. *The student should simultaneously solve the problem in written form and "explain" what he or she is doing orally.* The teacher must remember that the oral interview is a diagnostic exercise, not an instructional lesson.

5. *The student must be left free to solve the problem in his or her own way without any hint that he or she is doing something wrong.* The teacher should avoid giving clues or asking leading questions. If the student directly asks whether the answers are correct, the teacher should tell the student to concentrate on "telling in his or her own words" how he or she is solving the problem.

6. *The student should not be hurried.* Depending on the complexity of the operations being diagnosed, the oral interview can take from 15 to 45 minutes.

Source: N. Bartel, "Problems in Mathematics Achievement," in *Teaching Students with Learning and Behavior Problems,* 4th ed. Ed. D. D. Hammill and N. Bartel (Boston: Allyn and Bacon, 1986). Used by permission.

correct algorithm, and *random error* (Roberts 1968).

Incorrect operation occurs when the student selects the wrong operation to solve a problem. Using addition to solve the problem $35 - 16 = ?$ is an example of incorrect operation.

Incorrect number fact errors occur if the student has inappropriately and incorrectly learned the number facts of a given operation. For example, if the student told you that $6 + 3 = 10$, this would probably be an example of an incorrectly learned number fact.

Students use incorrect algorithms when they inappropriately use the rules for solving a problem within a given computation area (addition, subtraction, multiplication, division). For example, consider the subtraction problem $25 - 16 = 11$. The student incorrectly used a subtraction algorithm of subtracting the smaller number from the larger one. In doing so, the student subtracted 5 from 6 rather than regrouping 25 to $10 + 15$.

Finally, random error represents the category in which we cannot ascertain why the student answered the problem incorrectly; that is, there seems to be no *pattern* to the student's errors. This category yields no real diagnostic information.

A variety of error analysis charts and sequences are available (Buswell and John 1925; Riesman 1978). Perhaps the best is the one constructed by Riesman (1978). It contains detailed analyses of the errors commonly made in all four computational skills. Additionally, the reader may wish to inspect an error analysis of mathematical problem solving designed by Goodstein (1981).

SUMMARY

A significant amount of school time is spent trying to teach children mathematics. Nevertheless, achievement problems in the mathematical areas are a fact of life for many students, especially special needs learners. This may be due to the highly abstract and symbolic nature of mathematics and the fact that many children solve mathematics problems by rote without fully understanding the underlying processes.

Arithmetic consists of the computation skills of addition, subtraction, multiplication, and division. Arithmetic constitutes the building blocks of mathematics. Mathematics is the application of arithmetic skills to solve higher-order quantitative problems.

Teachers must understand the mathematics process before attempting to assess and remediate mathematics difficulties. One framework of mathematics structures it in terms of computation, problem solving, and application. Computation skills are needed to carry out the four basic processes of arithmetic. Problem-solving skills refer to the ability to use computational skills to solve problems presented in everyday language instead of numerical form. Finally, application involves using computational and problem-solving skills to solve mathematical problems in the areas of time, money, and measurement.

Students must possess a set of prerequisite (readiness) skills in mathematics before formal mathematics instruction is undertaken. Included in these skills are classification, comparison, counting, reversibility and compensation, seriation, and conservation. If children do not possess these skills, formal mathematics instruction should probably be delayed.

Mathematics assessments can be accomplished in various ways, including traditional achievement testing, using formal, diagnostic instruments that contain norms, using fully criterion-referenced instruments, and using informal assessment techniques. Formal, commercially available diagnostic mathematics tests are available that yield a combination of norm- and criterion-referenced information. These tests include the KeyMath Diagnostic Arithmetic Test, the Stanford Diagnostic Mathematics Test, the Diagnostic Screening Test: Math, and the Test of Mathematics Abilities (TOMA).

Additionally, the teacher may wish to use tests that are fully criterion-referenced and contain no norms for students. Such tests include the Diagnostic Test of Arithmetic Strategies, Diagnosis: An Instructional Aid in Mathematics, and the Diagnostic Mathematics Inventory.

Finally, the teacher can use informal mathematics assessment instruments either alone or in conjunction with formal tests. Various informal methods include Informal Mathematics Inventories, checklists, interviews, and error analysis. Of these, error analysis is particularly useful in the field of arithmetic assessment.

STUDY QUESTIONS

1. What is the difference between arithmetic and mathematics? How are the two concepts related?

2. What are the three processes of mathematics? Explain their hierarchical nature.

3. Why is the assessment of mathematical readiness skills important? What are the basic readiness skills that children should possess before formal mathematical training is undertaken? How are these readiness skills typically assessed?

4. What major formal, diagnostic mathematical tests are currently popular and in use? What are the major attributes of each test as well as the strengths and weaknesses? Rank order the tests discussed in this chapter in terms of the ones you would be most likely to use in your professional assessment of students. Defend your choices.

5. Why is the Test of Mathematical Ability a unique instrument? What does it measure? What are the strong and weak attributes of the instrument?

6. What are the advantages and disadvantages of purely criterion-referenced mathematics assessment instruments? What are some of the instruments discussed in this chapter? What are the strong and weak points of each test? Which ones would you use in your professional career? Defend your answer.

7. How is mathematics skill informally assessed? What are the different methods used? What are the strong and weak points of each assessment type?

8. How does error analysis relate to mathematical assessment? Why is it useful? How does it differ from typical achievement testing? How would you go about creating a teacher-made error analysis of student mathematical performance?

CHAPTER 20

Career Education Assessment

All too often, educational professionals involved with special needs learners ignore one of the most pressing and important curricular areas of education for secondary students—career education. We often lose sight of the fact that one goal of education is career training, by preparing students either for additional training and schooling or for a job after high school. Instead, most educational curricula center around specific academic skill training, training that is not often used on the job and in adult life.

Recently, however, this trend has been somewhat reversed. Today, much of what is taught in special education classrooms is centered around job and life *relevancy*. If the subject matter being taught in the classroom is not directly applicable to a career or to adult adjustment and normalized living, then it should not be taught.

This chapter deals with assessment in career education. This assessment pertains to more than just education for jobs. It is concerned with all the skills one needs in life (job and otherwise) to be successful as a normalized adult.

The Concept of Career Education

Traditionally, career education was synonymous with job training. More recently, however, career education has expanded to include job *and* adult life skills necessary for successful normalized living in society (Brolin and D'Alonzo 1979; Hoyt 1977). Today, career education is defined "as the process of systematically coordinating all school, family, and community components together to facilitate each individual's potential for economic, social, and personal fulfillment and participation in productive work activities that benefit the individual or others" (Kokaska and Brolin 1985, p. 43).

Thus, career education has evolved into a broader, life-centered approach that views the individual as a whole person who not only works but also is a community member, interacts with other people, and enjoys recreational and avocational activities. Nevertheless, the centerpiece of career education is meaningful, satisfying, and gainful employment within the potential of the individual.

Life-Centered Career Education (LCCE)

Many educational professionals have advocated a *life-centered career education* (LCCE) model (Brolin, Malever, and Matyas 1976; Council on Exceptional Children 1978, 1983; Kokaska and Brolin 1985). The LCCE model represents an attempt to identify the competencies that individuals need to achieve life success as adults. Twenty-two such competencies have been identified in the three main areas of *daily living, personal-social,* and *occupational* skills. Table 20-1 lists the twenty-two main competencies outlined in the LCCE.

Daily Living Skills: Daily living skills are those adult–consumer skills one needs to maintain an independent adult life-style. They include selecting and maintaining one's living quarters, managing a family, handling money, providing oneself with food, clothing, shelter, and satisfying personal needs. Included in these competencies are community mobility and handling one's leisure time.

Table 20-1   Twenty-Two Competencies of the Life-Centered Career Education Model

Daily Living Skills

1. Managing family finances.
2. Selecting, managing, and maintaining a home.
3. Caring for personal needs.
4. Family living.
5. Purchasing and preparing food.
6. Purchasing and caring for clothing.
7. Engaging in civic activities.
8. Using recreational and leisure time wisely.
9. Getting around the community.

Personal–Social Skills

10. Achieving self-awareness.
11. Acquiring self-confidence.
12. Exhibiting socially responsible behavior.
13. Exhibiting good interpersonal skills.
14. Achieving independence.
15. Exhibiting problem-solving skills.
16. Communicating adequately with others.

Occupational Skills

17. Exploring occupational possibilities.
18. Selecting and planning occupational choices.
19. Exhibiting appropriate work habits and behaviors.
20. Exhibiting appropriate physical–motor–manual skills.
21. Obtaining specific occupational skills.
22. Seeking, securing, and maintaining employment.

These skills are usually not taught as part of the public school curriculum for nonhandicapped students; it is assumed that most individuals will learn them outside of school. However, because students with special needs often do not learn such skills on their own, the LCCE program advocates teaching these competencies as part of the special education curriculum.

Personal–Social Skills: The personal–social skills are those needed to accomplish two separate but related goals: developing and maintaining a positive feeling about oneself and interacting appropriately with other people. The first goal of developing and maintaining positive feelings about oneself is obviously important in maintaining good mental health. This area includes such skills as achieving self-awareness and acquiring self-confidence and self-esteem. The second goal of getting along well with other people is also crucial to independent living. As social beings, we must learn the social rules, graces, and behaviors needed for acceptance. Not learning or not demonstrating these requisite social skills quickly leads to social isolation and ostracism. Needed skills in this area include achieving socially responsible behavior, developing and maintaining good interpersonal skills, communicating adequately with others, achieving independence, and being able to solve problems.

Occupational Skills: Occupational skills include the general skills and competencies needed for occupational success. They are not necessarily job specific (although they can be). Rather, they are generalizable skills that are needed for virtually every job. In the LCCE, such occupational skills include knowing and exploring occupational responsibilities, selecting and planning occupational choices, exhibiting appropriate work habits and behaviors, exhibiting physical and manual skills, obtaining specific work skills, and seeking, securing, and maintaining employment. Without these skills, students will probably experience little or no success in finding and keeping jobs.

Components of Career Education Assessment

The four major assessment components in the career education model are *clinical assessment, work evaluation, work adjustment,* and *job-site evaluation* (Brolin 1973, 1982). These components and the related evaluators are shown in Table 20-2. The first three components are discussed in this chapter because

Table 20-2 The Four Components of Career Education Assessment

Component	Evaluator
Clinical Assessment	Physicians, Social Workers, Psychologists, Teachers, Counselors
Work Evaluation	Work Evaluators, Vocational Educators, Special Educators, Occupational Therapists, Vocational–Rehabilitation Counselors
Work Adjustment	Vocational Counselors, Psychologists, Special Vocational–Education Teachers, Work Supervisors
Job-Site Evaluation	Work Evaluators, Work–Study Counselors, Vocational Educators, Work Supervisors

they are typically carried out by educational professionals or work evaluators.

Clinical Assessment

Clinical assessment is usually carried out first in the career education model. Clinical assessment constitutes the formal assessment of students in terms of *medical, social, educational,* and *psychological* attributes. Table 20-3 contains a list of formal assessment instruments commonly used by professionals during the clinical assessment stage. Because medical assessment is usually carried out by physicians, it is not discussed.

Social Assessment

Social assessment examines social, interpersonal, and adaptive skills needed to interact successfully with other people. Such an evaluation investigates the student's family, social, and peer backgrounds and assesses social

Table 20-3   Formal Assessment Instruments for Clinical Vocational Assessment

Test	Publisher	Use
AAMD Adaptive Behavior Scale	Publishers Testing Service	Social/Adaptive
California Psychological Inventory	Consulting Psychologists Press	Personality
BRIGANCE Diagnostic Inventory of Essential Skills	Curriculum Associates	Educational
Edwards Personal Preference Schedule	Psychological Associates	Personality
Mooney Problem Checklist	Psychological Associates	Social/Personality
Peabody Individual Achievement Test (PIAT)	American Guidance Service	Educational
Peabody Picture Vocabulary Test (PPVT)	American Guidance Service	Educational
San Francisco Vocational Competency Scale	Psychological Corporation	Social/Vocational
Vineland Social Maturity Scale	American Guidance Service	Social/Adaptive
Wide-Range Achievement Test	Jastak Associates	Educational

and interpersonal skills. More specifically, the social assessment attempts to answer the following five questions:

1. What is the student's family situation like?
2. What is the student's interpersonal–social functioning history?
3. What kind of leisure-time activities does the person engage in?
4. What are the person's independent living skills?
5. Does the person possess sufficient ego strength to cope with anxiety and frustration?

Additional information regarding social–adaptive assessment appears in Chapter 22.

Educational Assessment

To a great extent, the topic of educational assessment is covered in earlier chapters of this text. Such assessment includes gaining insight into the student's strengths and weaknesses in various academic areas, such as reading, language arts, and mathematics.

In the area of career education, educational assessment seeks to answer the additional question What are the student's academic skills in terms of the world of work? Thus, skills in the main academic areas are assessed in relation to skills needed in the vocational arena (Michigan Department of Education 1970). That is, academic skills are measured in terms of their practical applications in everyday adult vocational life (Brolin 1982; Malgady, Barcher, Towner, and Davis 1979).

Psychological Assessment

Psychological assessment involves *intelligence, personality,* and *perceptual–motor testing.* Intelligence tests are covered in great detail in Chapters 13 and 14, and the reader is referred to these chapters for a review of the material. These tests are usually administered only by a trained and licensed school psychologist.

Personality tests are sometimes administered to obtain a picture of the personality and social attributes of the test taker. They yield a clinical picture in terms of psychological adjustment or maladjustment. Such tests are usually administered and scored only by a trained clinical psychologist.

Perceptual–motor tests can be quite useful in determining the extent to which the student possesses strengths and difficulties in the areas of sensory perception and gross and fine motor coordination. All of these areas are extremely important to career success. See Chapter 21 for a more detailed discussion of perceptual–motor assessment.

Work Evaluation Assessment

After clinical assessment has taken place, the next step in the process is work evaluation. Work evaluations are carried out by professionals working in educational, rehabilitation, or institutional settings. Such evaluation is important in gaining a clearer picture of the individual's vocational skills and abilities.

The three main components of work evaluation assessment are: *vocational testing, work samples,* and *situational assessment.* Each component contains a variety of forms:

1. Vocational Testing: Standardized vocational testing and informal vocational testing.
2. Work Samples: Commercially available and teacher-made work samples.
3. Situational Assessment. Time and point sampling.

Vocational Testing

Vocational testing typically takes the form of standardized, commercially available tests. The two types of vocational tests are the *vocational aptitude tests* and *vocational interest inventories.*

Vocational Aptitude Tests

Vocational aptitude tests are used to give the professional a general idea of the student's overall aptitude and skills in terms of vocation and employment. However, general aptitude batteries possess relatively low predictive validity regarding who will or will not be successful on a given job (Aiken 1988; Neff 1977). Such tests should only be used by the test consumer for screening students, and work samples and situational assessment should be used when in-depth, diagnostic information is needed. Table 20-4 contains a list of commonly used aptitude tests. A brief description of some of the more commonly used aptitude tests follows.

General Aptitude Test Battery: The General Aptitude Test Battery (GATB) (U.S. Department of Labor 1970a) is probably the most widely used of all the occupationally oriented aptitude batteries. It is composed of eight paper and pencil tests and four apparatus tests. These twelve tests yield scores on nine factors (see Table 20-5). Raw scores on the nine factors are converted to percentile ranks or standard scores, which have a mean of 100 and a standard deviation of 20. The standard scores of the test taker can then be compared with approximately thirty-six ability patterns from a standardization group consisting of persons from eight hundred different occupations.

Despite its popularity, there are some serious drawbacks to the GATB. First, and probably most important, the GATB is highly dependent on reading ability. In fact, the GATB requires at least a sixth-grade reading level. Thus, does a student's poor performance on the battery indicate a lack of aptitude or an inability to read and comprehend the questions? Therefore, the test consumer should administer this test only to students with strong reading skills.

Second, the GATB takes a long time to administer (approximately 2 and ½ hours).

Table 20-4 Commonly Used Vocational Aptitude Tests

Test	Publisher	Measures
Appraisal of Occupational Aptitudes	Houghton-Mifflin	Clerical Skills
Bennet Hand Tool Dexterity Test	Psychological Corporation	Hand Tool Dexterity
Crawford Small Parts Dexterity Test	Psychological Corporation	Eye-Hand, Fine Motor Skills
Differential Aptitude Test	Psychological Corporation	Nine aptitude scores in verbal, mathematical, mechanical areas
General Aptitude Test Battery	U.S. Dept. of Labor	Nine Aptitudes
General Clerical Test	Psychological Corporation	Clerical Skills
Minnesota Spatial Relations Test	American Guidance Service	Size and Shape Discrimination
Nonreading Aptitude Test Battery	U.S. Dept of Labor	Nonreading Version of GATB
O'Connor Finger and Tweezer Dexterity Tests	Stoelting Company	Motor Coordination and Finger Dexterity
Purdue Pegboard	SRA	Motor Movements of Hands and Fingers
Stromberg Dexterity Test	Psychological Corporation	Speed and Accuracy

Fatigue and loss of motivation can quickly become factors for test takers, and the test examiner has to take these variables into consideration. Finally, the GATB requires specialized training and practice in administration, scoring, and interpretation.

All things considered, however, the GATB is a valuable test for students who are strong readers and who possess good test-taking skills. The GATB has high reliability and intermediate predictive validity. However, it may not be appropriate for students with lower skill levels.

Nonreading Aptitude Test Battery: The Nonreading Aptitude Test Battery (NATB) (U.S. Department of Labor 1970b) is a nonreading version of the GATB. It can be used with illiterate or semiliterate test takers. The test can be administered individually or in groups, although individual administration is best for students with special needs.

There are nine subtests included in the NATB (see Table 20-5). Although the format is similar to the GATB, there are no arithmetic problems, and vocabulary items are presented orally rather than in writing.

Table 20-5 Subtests of the General Aptitude and Nonreading Aptitude Test Batteries

General Aptitude Test Battery

1. Intelligence—General Learning Ability: Understand instructions and make occupational judgments.
2. Verbal Aptitude: Understand meanings of words and ideas.
3. Numerical Aptitude: Perform math operations accurately and quickly.
4. Spatial Aptitude: Comprehend spatial relationships in two and three dimensions.
5. Form Perception: Determine pertinent details in objects or in pictorial–graphic material.
6. Clerical Perception: Derive pertinent details in verbal or tabular material.
7. Motor Coordination: Coordinate eyes, hands, and fingers in making quick, precise movements.
8. Finger Dexterity: Move fingers and manipulate small objects.
9. Manual Dexterity: Move hands with ease and skill in making turning motions.

Nonreading Aptitude Test Battery

1. Picture–Word Matching: Vocabulary.
2. Oral Vocabulary: Expressive and receptive language.
3. Coin Matching: Money concepts.
4. Design Completion: Spatial relations.
5. Tool Matching: Knowledge of basic tools and their functions.
6. Three-Dimensional Space: Spatial relations in two and three dimensions.
7. Coins and Money.
8. Name Comparison: Clerical abilities.
9. Mark Making, Turning, Assembly, and Disassembly.

As with the GATB, there are some drawbacks to the NATB. First, the test takes a long time to administer (approximately 2 hours, 10 minutes). For the specialized population of students likely to take the test, motivation and fatigue can become problems leading to test error. Second, the NATB is really designed for disadvantaged learners. To the extent that test takers approximate this disadvantaged population, the NATB is appropriate. However, if the test taker does not fit the disadvantaged category of students, interpretation of the test results is problematic. Finally, the NATB is not appropriate for physically handicapped test takers.

The Flanagan Aptitude Classification Tests and Industrial Tests: The Flanagan Aptitude Classification Tests (FACT) and the Flanagan Industrial Tests (FIT) are two separate test batteries (Flanagan 1975). These tests assess sixteen areas shown to be critical to successful job performance in a variety of occupations (see Table 20-6). The batteries are not intended to be administered in full. Rather, the professional chooses a combination of tasks particular to a given job or a series of tasks that will need to be carried out by the job seeker. Each test takes from five to fifteen minutes to administer.

Norms are presented in terms of percentile and stanines for three norm samples: people working in business and industry, high school seniors, and freshmen entering college. The business norms vary from test to test. Reliabilities for the tests are relatively low, ranging from .28 to .79, and this is a major drawback. Likewise, the tests have been criticized for questionable predictive and construct validity. Thus, although the tests are easier and quicker to administer than either the GATB or the NATB, they probably should be avoided for use with special needs learners because of the problems of technical quality.

Vocational Interest Inventories

Whereas aptitude batteries tell you what the student is probably *able* to do, interest inventories yield information as to what the student would probably *like* to do. Thus, interest inventories are like a wish list, they provide information on the test taker's occupational interests and likes, which may be independent

Table 20-6 Subtests of the Flanagan Aptitude Classification and Industrial Tests

Flanagan Aptitude Classification Tests (FACT)

1. Visual Inspection
2. Coding
3. Memory
4. Precision of Movement
5. Assembly
6. Coordination of Movements
7. Judgment and Comprehension
8. Arithmetic
9. Patterns and Designs
10. Tables and Clerical Skills
11. Mechanics
12. Verbal Expression
13. Reasoning
14. Ingenuity and Problem Solving

Flanagan Industrial Tests

1. Arithmetic
2. Coordination of Movements
3. Electronics Skill and Knowledge
4. Verbal Expression
5. Ingenuity and Problem Solving
6. Visual Inspection
7. Judgment and Comprehension
8. Mathematics and Reasoning
9. Mechanics
10. Memory
11. Patterns
12. Planning Skills
13. Tables and Graphs
14. Vocabulary

of the person's talents or aptitude for performing that job.

Interest inventories have often been criticized on grounds of validity and usefulness. For example, the reader may have had the experience of learning that an interest inventory indicated a supposed interest in an area that was completely foreign or unrelated to the reader's conscious preferences. Likewise, the author once tested a student living in the Midwest whose interest inventory test score indicated that he should be an ocean liner captain. Unfortunately, this student had never been within fifteen hundred miles of an ocean.

Interest inventories have also been criticized on the grounds of *faking, response set,* and *socioeconomic status differences.* For example, it has been found that college students were able to fill out interest inventories in such a way that responses corresponded to experimenter instructions of artificial interests prior to test administration (Bridgman and Hollenbeck 1961). Likewise, respondents will often answer in a set way in terms of *acquiescence* (the tendency to agree rather than disagree) or *social desirability* (responding in what is perceived as the socially desirable direction). Finally, responses on interest inventories are often highly correlated with the socioeconomic status of the respondents in that the respondents see certain jobs as typically being filled by people from a given socioeconomic class (Aiken 1988; McArthur and Stevens 1955).

Despite these drawbacks and criticisms, interest inventories enjoy wide popularity in secondary school and vocational programs, and they will probably continue to be widely used. This is due to the belief in our society that, whenever possible, people ought to enjoy their jobs and occupations. Thus, the use of interest inventories is viewed as a humanistic practice by many psychologists, educators, and work evaluators.

Strong–Campbell Interest Inventory: The Strong–Campbell Interest Inventory (SCII) (Strong 1984) is an occupational interest inventory originally designed in 1920 and updated through 1984. It consists of 325 items grouped into seven main sections:

1. Occupations: Student indicates Like, Dislike, or Indifferent to 131 occupational titles.
2. School Subjects: Like, Dislike, or Indifferent to 36 school subjects.
3. Activities: Like, Dislike, or Indifferent to 51 general occupational activities.
4. Amusements: Like, Dislike, or Indifferent to 39 amusements or hobbies.
5. Types of People: Like, Dislike, or Indifferent to 24 types of people.

6. Preference between Two Activities: Examinee chooses preferred activity from 30 different pairs.
7. Your Characteristics: Student responds Yes, No, or ? to 14 self-descriptive characteristics.

The SCII is scored on five groups of measures: *administrative indexes, general occupational themes, basic interest scales, occupational scales,* and *special scales.* Because the SCII yields such a large number of scores and scales, interpretation by a trained examiner is required.

The SCII yields a measure of the test taker's interests on a large number of occupations. However, it is primarily oriented toward college or skilled occupations and thus may be inappropriate for a large proportion of special needs learners. Decisions about the validity of the test for special populations must be made by the educational professional or work evaluator.

Kuder Interest Inventories: The Kuder Interest Inventories (KII) are a series of surveys that assess a test taker's preference in a variety of different measures. Of particular interest are the Vocational Preference Record, the General Interest Survey, and the Occupational Interest Survey (see Table 20-7). The General Interest Survey is useful for some learners with special needs; it is a downward extension of earlier Kuder Inventories and is useful in vocational counseling in junior and senior high school settings.

The Kuder Inventories use a *forced-choice* format rather than the yes–no format used in other interest inventories. In a forced-choice format, the respondent *must* make a choice among a set of possible answers instead of responding yes or no to individual questions. On the Kuder, the student chooses the activity most preferred and least preferred from three alternatives. Possible alternatives are then counterbalanced against each other in later questions so that a clear hierarchy of preferred activity and interests emerges.

The reliability of the Kuder Inventories has been found to be quite high, yielding reliability coefficients in the .80s and .90s. Likewise, the instrument appears to possess validity in identifying students' preferences in activities and occupations. Finally, the Kuder Inventories, especially the Occupation Interest Survey, appear to be more appropriate for persons with special needs than is the Strong-Campbell. However, a negative aspect is that most jobs listed on the Kuder Inventories are in the professional and highly skilled occupations categories, and they may be beyond the realistic attainment of some students enrolled in special education programs.

Interest Inventories for Special Populations

All of the interest inventories mentioned previously suffer from the issue of applicability for average learners. Unfortunately, average in today's workplace often means a professional or highly skilled job. Thus, tests like the Strong–Campbell and the Kuder assume to some extent that the test takers are in the mainstream of our society and that they will be entering a professional, technical, or skilled position.

There are a variety of interest inventories, however, that have been designed for special populations. These populations have generally been subdivided into three categories: *children, special needs/disadvantaged learners,* and those interested in *nonprofessional occupations.*

Inventories for Children

Career Awareness Inventory: The Career Awareness Inventory (CAI) (Fadale 1975) is a 125-item inventory designed for children in grades four through twelve. There are two forms of the test: Elementary (grades four through six) and Advanced (grades seven through twelve). The elementary version of

Table 20-7 Three Surveys of the Kuder Interest Inventories

Kuder Form C: Vocational Preference Record

Use. For counseling and placement of high school students and adults.

Format. One hundred sixty-eight triads of statements describing activities, one activity in each triad to be marked "Most Liked" and one "Least Liked."

Range and Time Limit. High school. No time limit; takes 30–40 minutes.

Forms and Scoring. CP—hand-scored; CM—machine-scored.

Scales. Ten interest scales: outdoor, mechanical, scientific, computational, persuasive, artistic, literary, musical, service, and clerical. One verification (V) score, based on items having extreme response splits.

Standardization Data (Norms). Percentile ranks for men and women; score profile in ten interest areas may be plotted on percentile rank scale. Stanines for men and women in forty-one occupational families. Manual groups occupations according to major interest area or pair of interest areas.

Reliability. Kuder-Richardson reliabilities of the ten scales are in the .70s and .80s.

Validity. Several studies of the relationships between Kuder Form C and job satisfaction support its validity.

Kuder Form E: General Interest Survey

Use. Developed as a downward extension and revision of Kuder Form C; useful in vocational counseling in junior and senior high school.

Format. One hundred sixty-eight triads of statements describing various activities, one activity in each triad to be marked "Most Preferred" and one "Least Preferred."

Range and Time Limit. Grades 6–12. No time limit; takes 30–40 minutes.

Forms and Scoring. E—hand-scored.

Scales. Ten interest scales: outdoor, mechanical, scientific, computational, persuasive, artistic, liter-

ary, musical, social service, clerical. One improved verification (V) score.

Standardization Data (Norms). Percentile norms based on stratified sample ($n = 10,715$) of U.S. boys and girls in grades 6–12 tested in 1963 and for several hundred adult men and women.

Reliability. Test-retest reliabilities after six weeks, by sex and grade (6–12), in .70s and .80s.

Validity. No long-term evidence of validity is available. Transparency program designed to help students interpret their Kuder E Scores is available.

Kuder Form DD: Occupational Interest Survey

Use. For selection, placement, and counseling in employment centers, personnel agencies, and industrial retraining programs.

Format. One hundred triads of statements describing various activities, one activity in each triad to be marked "Most Preferred" and one "Least Preferred."

Range and Time Limit. Grade 11 through adult. No time limit; usually takes 30–40 minutes.

Forms and Scoring. DD—scored by high-speed computer.

Scales. One hundred nineteen occupational scales for men and women combined, and forty-eight college major scales; five or more new occupational scales in 1980. A person's score on a scale is a modified biserial correlation between his or her responses and those of the criterion group.

Standardization Data (Norms). Data from over 12,000 college seniors in forty-eight college major groups used in determining college major scales. Intensive study of thirty core groups of 100 persons each. Manual revised in 1979.

Reliability. Test-retest reliabilities of individual profiles average .90 over two weeks.

Validity. Studies of errors of classification of six validation groups and other data pertaining to validity are reported in the manual.

Source: L. R. Aiken (1988). *Psychological Testing and Assessment,* 6th ed. (Boston: Allyn and Bacon). Used by permission.

Table 20-8 Sections of the Career Awareness Inventory (CAI)

1. Identify Pictured Workers and Related Occupations. (61 Items)
2. Identify Which Occupations Require a College Education. (6 Items)
3. Specify Whether or Not You Personally Know a Worker in a Named Occupation. (32 Items)
4. Select the Product (as Opposed to Service) Occupation for a Given Pair. (4 Items)
5. Select the Higher Status Occupation from a Given Pair. (5 Items)
6. Identify the Occupation *not* Belonging to a Named Occupational Cluster. (10 Items)
7. Recognize the Type of Activities Usually Liked by Particular Workers. (7 Items)

the test, which is reviewed here, is designed to help students assess how much they know about careers and career choices. The test takes 60 to 70 minutes to administer. Table 20-8 lists the seven sections of the CAI elementary version.

Although the idea of a career interest inventory as proposed by the CAI is a good one, the test has been criticized on a number of criteria, for example, its high correlations with intelligence and its sexist bias. Additionally, a minimum of technical information on norms, reliability, and validity is reported in the test manual. Thus, although the test represents a noble attempt to design an interest inventory that could be administered during career awareness and career exploration stages, results from the CAI should be interpreted with extreme caution.

What I Like to Do Inventory: The What I Like to Do Inventory (WILD) (Meyers 1975) is a 294-item, yes–no, and forced-choice response scale for children in grades four through seven. It is a revision of a test originally published in the 1950s. As the name implies, it is designed to measure the preferred and nonpreferred activities of children, as

well as the activities toward which they are neutral. The WILD measures preferences in terms of fifteen scores in the four areas of Play, Academic, Arts, and Occupations. The test takes approximately sixty minutes to administer in one or two sessions.

As with the Career Awareness Inventory, there are some major weaknesses inherent in the WILD. First, there is a problem of question readability. Because this test is designed primarily for elementary school students, the reading level of items should be as simple or possible. It would be even better if items were presented in pictorial form. However, the readability of the WILD has been criticized as too complex for the target population. Second, some of the item choices are confounded, or "double-barreled." For example, consider the question "Do you like to buy new comic books for your collection?" If the child indicates a preference for this activity, is it a preference for buying things, for comic books, or for hobby collecting? Finally, there is no information available in the manual regarding norms, standardization group, reliability, or validity. Thus, like the CAI, the WILD is a well-meaning attempt to measure the interests of younger children, but the technical quality of the instrument leaves much to be desired.

Inventories for Educationally Disadvantaged/Special Learners

Geist Picture Interest Inventory: The Geist Picture Interest Inventory (GPII) (Geist 1964) is a forced-choice type of instrument with 132 drawings grouped in 44 pictorial triads. The student must circle the most and least preferred tasks. The format and areas assessed by the GPII are identical to those of the Kuder except that the GPII has an additional area, Dramatic Interest. The GPII also yields seven motivation scores (see Table 20-9).

The GPII requires no reading by test takers. Additionally, there are special editions of

Table 20-9   Scores of the Geist Picture Interest Inventory and Work Interest Index

---

GPII

Interest Scores
1. Persuasive (Sales)
2. Clerical
3. Mechanical
4. Musical
5. Scientific
6. Outdoor
7. Literary
8. Computational
9. Artistic
10. Social Service
11. Dramatic
12. Personal Service (Female Only)

Motivation Scores
1. Family
2. Prestige
3. Financial
4. Intrinsic and Personality
5. Environmental
6. Past Experience

WII
1. Professional and Technical
2. Social and Verbal
3. Authority and Prestige
4. Artistic and Interpretive
5. Artistic and Stylized
6. Artistic and Creative
7. Technical and Scientific
8. Clerical and Routine
9. Business
10. Personal Service
11. Sales
12. Mechanical
13. Flexibility of Interest
14. Level of Aspiration

---

the GPII for Spanish-speaking test takers and for deaf individuals. The test is appropriate for use with students from grades eight through college and for noncollege adults. It takes forty to sixty-five minutes to administer.

The GPII has been criticized on a number of variables, including (1) the realism of the pictures used in the test, (2) its moderate reliability, (3) its unproven validity, and (4) incomplete norms and standardization data. De-

spite these criticisms, the GPII represents an attempt to create a nonverbal interest inventory, and it is the only such inventory specifically available for deaf and Spanish-speaking populations.

The Work Interest Index: The Work Interest Index (WII) (Baehr, Renck, Burns, and Pranis 1965) is a nonverbal interest inventory similar to the Geist. Students respond to ninety-six pictures of working men and women on a like-dislike basis. It is appropriate for students in grades seven through twelve and takes approximately twenty minutes to administer. Scores are reported in twelve areas (see Figure 20-1).

The WII possesses a moderate reliability reported for each of the twelve areas. For these areas, seven coefficients are in the .80s, four are in the .70s, and one is in the .60s. Information in the manual about the validity of the test is incomplete. Criticisms of the WII hold that (1) pictures of women workers are underrepresented in the test, (2) the validity is unproven, and (3) the norm group is small in size and not fully described. As with the Geist, the test represents one of the few nonverbal interest inventories available, but its results should be interpreted with caution.

Interest Inventories for Nonprofessional Occupations

Although some of the major interest inventories, such as the Strong–Campbell and the Kuder, possess a few scales pertaining to vocational interests in nonprofessional or unskilled jobs, these tests were not specifically designed for this type of test taker. The following inventories have been specifically designed for those individuals likely to work at unskilled or semiskilled jobs—precisely the types of employment that may be obtained by mentally handicapped individuals or others with special needs.

Gordon Occupational Check List: The Gordon Occupational Check List (GOCL) (Gordon 1963) is a preferences checklist designed for individuals with a high school education or less who are not planning on entering college or technical school. It contains 240 statements of job duties, such as "repair or install plumbing in houses" and "fire and tend a commercial furnace," and represents occupations found in the middle and lower levels of skills and responsibility. The statements are classified into five broad occupational groupings: business, outdoor, arts, technology, and service. The instrument yields scores in each of these five areas as well as a score for the total checklist performance. The checklist takes about twenty-five minutes to administer.

Unfortunately, no norms are reported for the test. Various reliability data are reported, including test-retest and internal-consistency reliability. Although the data are incomplete, they do seem to possess an acceptable reliability. Evidence of validity is less extensive and is based on arguments by the author that the test is logical and appropriate for testing occupational preferences of students for lower and middle levels of job skills.

In summary, the GOCL fills a need for an inventory of lower-level job interests and preferences. If used as a screening checklist in conjunction with such measures as interviews, it can be a useful tool for assessing the interests of individuals not likely to attend college or technical school.

Career Assessment Inventory: The Career Assessment Inventory (CAI) (Johansson 1976) is designed for individuals in grades eight or above who are seeking a career that does not generally require a four-year college degree. The test is quite similar to the Strong–Campbell Inventories; in fact, it is sometimes referred to as the "workingmans's Strong–Campbell test." Like the Strong–Campbell, the CAI reports scores in six main themes and twenty-two basic interests (see Table 20-10).

Table 20-10 Themes and Scores of the Career Assessment Inventory

Themes (6)
1. Realism
2. Investigative
3. Artistic
4. Social
5. Enterprising
6. Conventional

Basic Interests (22)
1. Mechanical/Fixing
2. Electronics
3. Carpentry
4. Manual/Skill Trades
5. Agriculture
6. Nature/Outdoors
7. Animal Service
8. Science
9. Numbers
10. Writing
11. Performing
12. Arts/Crafts
13. Social Service
14. Teaching
15. Child Care
16. Medical Service
17. Religious Activities
18. Business
19. Sales
20. Office Practices
21. Clerical
22. Food Service

The CAI takes approximately thirty minutes to administer.

The construction of the CAI closely resembles that of the Strong–Campbell. However, unlike the Strong–Campbell, attempts were made to eliminate the sexist wording of some items and to modify the reading level of the test. However, the test author readily acknowledges that despite the efforts to accommodate poor readers, the reading level of the CAI is "at least eighth grade."

The extensive reliabillity and validity data reported in the test manual is generally in the acceptable range. For example, the median reliability correlations for the subscores of the test are in the .90s, while the demonstrated concurrent validity of the test is also quite strong. In summary, the CAI is one of the best instruments available for students who will be working at blue-collar, unskilled, or semiskilled jobs. It possesses many of the advantages of the Strong–Campbell and few of the disadvantages. The one drawback of the test is its high correlation with reading ability, despite attempts by the test author to make the test more readable.

Work Samples

The second component of work evaluation is work samples. A work sample is a simulated task or work activity in which students are observed to assess whether they possess requisite and specific job skills (Brolin 1982; Neff 1977). Work samples are direct observations of behavior. By observing behavior we can readily see whether students possess requisite job skills. By contrast, paper and pencil tests can only infer skill from the student's written answers. The difference between work samples and paper and pencil tests is the difference between watching people perform a task and asking them to describe how they would perform that task.

Work samples range from very easy to very complicated. Some work samples assess the individual's ability to sort materials or color code items and materials; other samples require symbolic reasoning and abstract conceptualization. Whatever the nature of the sample used, it should function as a "mock-up (or) close simulation of an industrial (actual) operation, not different in essentials from the kind of work a potential employee would be required to perform on an ordinary job" (Neff 1977, p. 204). Regardless of the complexity of the tasks assessed, a work sample should function to achieve the following five goals (Jewish Employment and Vocational Service 1968):

1. Enable the educational professional or employment counselor to understand, relate to, and communicate with the handicapped worker.
2. Help the professional develop a counseling or vocational plan, including objectives, for the worker.
3. Help the professional identify the worker's strengths and weaknesses.
4. Provide information to the professional as to the worker's interests, attitudes, and motivations.
5. Help the worker attain the skills and attitudes needed to be successful on a job.

Five types of work samples are *indigenous samples, job samples, simulated work samples, cluster trait samples,* and *single trait samples* (Commission on Accreditation of Rehabilitation Facilities 1980). Indigenous samples contain the major job tasks and skills of a given occupation or job as it currently exists in the working world. Job samples represent an exact replication of all of the job tasks of a given occupation. Simulated work samples represent a replica of one segment of related tasks or tools from a given job. Cluster trait samples measure a group of related traits or skills for a series of related occupations. Finally, single trait samples evaluate one isolated job characteristic that is related to either a specific job or job family. Regardless of the type of work sample used, however, they all possess the advantage of direct observation of work-related behavior.

The work sample approach has not been free from criticism. Some critics have argued that work samples are expensive to purchase and time consuming to carry out, that they require continual restructuring to stay relevant, and that they can quickly become obsolete in a changing job market. Despite such criticisms, the work sample approach does permit direct observation of work-related behaviors and answers questions raised by potential employers about an individual student's job skill readiness (Brolin 1982; Krehbiel 1972; Neff 1977).

Commercially Available Work Sample Systems

The last few years have seen a large increase in the number of commercially available work sample systems. Although these systems have the advantage of freeing educational professionals and work evaluators from creating their own work sample systems, they are quite expensive, costing often thousands of dollars. Table 20-11 contains a list of the major, commercially available work sample systems. Some of those systems are discussed briefly here.

Comprehensive Occupational Assessment and Training System (COATS): The COATS system was first developed in 1975. It has four major components: Living Skills, Work Samples, Job Matching System, and Employability Attitudes. The work samples assess the student's interest, performance, capability, and general behavior on ten job areas, ranging from food preparation to small engine repair.

Hester Evaluation System (HES): The Hester Evaluation System (HES) consists of twenty-six separate tests measuring twenty-eight independent ability factors. These factors relate to jobs and job skills that are keyed to a reference volume entitled *Dictionary of Occupational Titles (DOT)*. The system is appropriate for use with individuals possessing a variety of handicaps including the visually impaired.

JEVS Work Samples: Developed by the Jewish Employment and Vocational Services, JEVS consists of twenty-eight different work samples. The samples are appropriate for use with culturally disadvantaged groups as well as with individuals possessing physical, emotional, and mental disabilities. The skills of the work samples are keyed to the DOT.

Micro-Tower: This is a system of thirteen work samples designed for mildly mentally re-

Table 20-11   Commercially Available Work Sample Systems

Vocational Information and Evaluation Work Samples
(VIEWS)
Jewish Employment and Vocational Service
1700 Sansom Street
Philadelphia, PA 19103

JEVS Work Samples
Jewish Employment and Vocational Service
1700 Sansom Street
Philadelphia, PA 19103

Talent Assessment Program
(TAP)
Wilton Nighswonger
7015 Colby Ave.
Des Moines, IA 50311

Micro-Tower
Institute for Crippled and Disabled
340 E. 24th Street
New York, NY 10010

Singer Vocational Evaluation System
Singer Education Division
80 Commerce Drive
Rochester, NY 14623

Hester Evaluation System
Edward Hester
Goodwill Industries
120 S. Ashland Boulevard
Chicago, IL 60607

Valpar Component Work Samples
Valpar Corporation
655 N. Alvernon Way
Tucson, AZ 85716

Comprehensive Occupational Assessment and Training System (COATS) Prep Inc.
1575 Parkway Avenue
Trenton, NJ 08628

Wide-Range Employment Sample Test
(WREST)
Guidance Associates of Delaware
1526 Gilpin Avenue
Wilmington, DE 19806

McCarron–Dial Work Evaluation System
Commercial Marketing Enterprises
11300 North Central
Dallas, TX 75231

tarded through nonretarded persons. It consists of work samples in such skills as capping and packaging, message taking, zip coding, and filing.

Wide-Range Employment Sample Test (WREST): Developed for use with mentally retarded persons, it consists of ten work samples in such areas as folding, pasting, labeling, stuffing, and packaging. The system is particularly useful with individuals possessing moderate degrees of of mental retardation.

Work Adjustment Evaluation

The third component of career education assessment is work adjustment. Work adjustment refers to the behavioral change process that must occur for the individual to function successfully as a worker (Brolin 1982). Work adjustment evaluation consists of evaluating people's behaviors in terms of whether they reflect the requisite skills demanded by the job marketplace.

Two main competency areas are included in work adjustment evaluation as defined by the LCCE (Kokaska and Brolin 1985): *exhibiting appropriate work habits and behaviors* and *exhibiting sufficient physical–manual skills.* Within the first competency area are seven skills that should be assessed; in the second competency area are four components in need of assessment. Table 20-12 contains a brief description of the subareas of these main competencies.

Developing Appropriate Work Habits and Behaviors

Good work habits and behaviors are crucial for success on the job. A worker who cannot understand and follow directions or who is consistently tardy, sloppy, or insubordinate is a candidate for dismissal. Likewise, a worker who does not follow accepted safety practices

Table 20-12 Components of Work Adjustment Evaluation

Components of Work Evaluation

Exhibiting Appropriate Work Habits and Behaviors
1. Following Directions
2. Working with Others
3. Working at a Satisfactory Rate
4. Accepting Supervision
5. Recognizing the Importance of Attendance and Punctuality
6. Meeting Demand for Quality Work
7. Developing Occupational Safety Skills

Exhibiting Sufficient Physical-Manual Skills
1. Demonstrating Satisfactory Balance and Coordination
2. Demonstrating Satisfactory Manual Dexterity
3. Demonstrating Satisfactory Stamina and Endurance
4. Demonstrating Satisfactory Sensory Discrimination

is a risk on the job and is also likely to be dismissed. It is safe to assume that many workers will learn the needed habits and behaviors of work on their own. But it is relatively unlikely that learners with special needs will learn such skills incidentally or transfer them spontaneously and without guidance and instruction. Thus, it is crucial that these individuals be checked periodically for learning and appropriate application of these skills.

Assessing Work Habits and Behaviors

Three main techniques are used to assess work habits and behaviors: observing individuals on the job and interviewing supervisors and co-workers; using work samples; and using standardized tests. Systematic observation and interviewing assume follow-up after job placement. That is, the educational professional must visit the job site to meet with supervisors and co-workers and directly observe the individual carrying out job duties. Such activities represent a commitment by educational professionals to work evaluation follow-up to guarantee that the student is successfully applying the skills taught in the school's career education program.

Work samples can also help ensure that the individual possesses proper work habits and behaviors. Many of the work samples discussed in this chapter contain components that allow the professional to assess the individual's work habits, persistence, frustration level, and willingness to accept criticism. When available, such work sample assessment is a valuable tool for remediating the work habits and attitude problems of individuals *before* they assume full-time jobs and suffer the negative consequences of their behaviors.

A limited number of commercially available tests are available for special needs learners that measure work habits and attitudes. Three such instruments are discussed here.

Social and Prevocational Information Battery: The Social and Prevocational Information Battery (SPIB) (Halpern, Irvin, and Link 1975) is a series of nine norm-referenced tests designed to assess knowledge of skills and competencies considered important for occupational success (see Table 20-13). Of particular interest in terms of occupational skills are the subtests dealing with health care, hygiene and grooming, and the ability to read functional (industrial) signs. The instrument is appropriate for use with both mildly and moderately mentally retarded individuals in and beyond junior high school; reading is not required. The SPIB yields raw scores, percentages correct, and reference group percentile ranks.

Although the SPIB does not deal specifically with work evaluation skills, parts of the test yield information on the work habits, skills, and attitudes of individuals, and the tool can be of use to the educational profes-

Table 20-13   Areas Assessed by the Social and Prevocational Information Battery

1. Purchasing Habits
2. Budgeting Skills
3. Banking Skills (Checking and Savings)
4. Job-Related Behavior
5. Job Search Skills
6. Home Management Skills
7. Health Care
8. Personal Hygiene and Grooming
9. Reading Functional Signs

sional. However, the test consumer should be aware that the SPIB was standardized on a very small number of mentally retarded students, all of whom resided in Oregon. Thus, this test cannot be assumed to be representative of many mentally retarded persons. Furthermore, the test has unproven reliability and validity. Caution in using and interpreting the test is advised.

The Test of Practical Knowledge: The Test of Practical Knowledge (TPK) (Wiederholt and Larsen 1983) is a norm-referenced test of common knowledge considered crucial for independent daily living. The one hundred items on the test are grouped into three main areas: Personal Knowledge, Special Knowledge, and Occupational Knowledge. Of the three, the subtests of Occupational Knowledge are the most relevant for testing the occupational and work habit skills of learners. These subtests contain items that assess the individual's knowledge of job-related language and jargon, salary and benefits, and job application procedures.

Scores on the TPK are reported in norm-referenced terms of stanines and percentiles. The test is appropriate for students in grades eight through twelve and can be administered individually or in groups. However, a significant degree of reading is required, and this may adversely affect some special needs learners.

San Francisco Vocational Competency Scale: Perhaps the most useful instrument for assessing the occupational skills and habits of handicapped workers is the San Francisco Vocational Competency Scale (SFVCS) (Levine and Elzey 1968). This scale was developed to provide a measure of the vocational competency of mentally retarded adults working in workshops. However, if used as a criterion-referenced informal test, it can also be used with mildly mentally retarded workers.

The SFVCS measures skills in four main areas or factors: general cognitive competence, cognitive and interpersonal flexibility, cognitive–motor functioning, and initiative and dependability. These four factors are separated into thirty vocational competencies considered to be important on the job (see Table 20-14). The individual's performance on these thirty competencies yields a total vocational comptency score. It is believed that the comptency scores and the combined vocational competency index will give the educational professional an indication of the client's occupational skills and help ensure successful occupational placement. The test is particularly useful for the more severely handicapped populations.

Table 20-14   Skills Assessed by the San Francisco Vocational Competency Scale

1. Initiating Tasks
2. Remembering Instructions
3. Following Verbal Instructions
4. Reading Ability
5. Measuring
6. Requesting Materials
7. Identifying Unclear Materials or Instructions
8. Demonstrating Knowledge of Job or Task
9. Performing Previously Learned Tasks
10. Reorientation to Task
11. Transferring Skills
12. Learning Tasks Efficiently
13. Completing a Task on Time
14. Improving Performance with Experience
15. Operating Equipment Containing Moving Parts
16. Operating Manually Powered Machines
17. Following Safety Instructions
18. Correcting Errors
19. Adequacy of Performance
20. Seeking Help
21. Responding to Changes in Routine
22. Explaining Tasks
23. Offering Assistance
24. Reporting Problems
25. Reacting to Frustration
26. Responding to Movement or Noise
27. Accepting Suggestions
28. Reacting to Supervision
29. Returning from Breaks on Time
30. Cleaning up Work Area

Using Career Education Assessment Information

Creating a Career-Oriented Individualized Education Program

This chapter discussed the assessment of numerous competencies needed for a successful career and adult living. As with the other academic areas discussed in this text, the assessment information gathered and interpreted regarding career education must be used to help remediate student weaknesses. Otherwise, the assessment will be fruitless. Such remediational programming requires the creation of a career-oriented IEP.

The career-oriented IEP contains many attributes of the standard Individualized Education Program. The career education IEP should contain the following eight components:

1. Services to be provided.
2. Team members providing these services and their responsibilities.
3. Long-term vocational and life curriculum goals; intermediate objectives by which these goals will be reached.
4. Timetable for meeting goals.
5. Criteria and procedures for evaluating progress.
6. Annual review procedures.
7. Closure information if the case is closed (e.g., employment status, type of job obtained, etc.).
8. Postemployment follow-up services.

The closure and follow-up stages are relatively unique to the career-oriented IEP, but nevertheless they are crucially important. The goals of career education are successful job placement and adult life success. Thus, the career-oriented IEP should help the student obtain a meaningful and relevant job. It should also guide the student in making a successful transition from school to adult independent living. Simply finding the student a job and a place to live is not enough. Follow-up must ensue to guarantee that the student's transition has been successful. In cases in which transition has not been completely successful, some provisions must be made in the career-oriented IEP that will help remediate existing difficulties and help the student learn or apply those skills needed to succeed in adult life.

Making a Successful Transition: Follow-up should *not* be confined to the job. Two other areas that are integral parts of the person's adult environment are the home and the community. Students finishing school must be helped to adjust socially in the home, neighborhood, and community (Halpern 1985). They need follow-up and, if necessary, help to live in harmony with themselves, family, neighbors, and fellow citizens. It is important to realize that success in one area (e.g., job placement) does not necessarily guarantee life success in other areas. The problems of maintaining a happy home, raising a family, and/or getting along socially with others can arise independently of success on a job. Thus, follow-up and help in transitional living for special needs learners exiting school will need to occur on a variety of fronts (Halpern 1985).

SUMMARY

In the past, career education was often ignored in the educational programming of special needs learners. Career education is crucial, however, because it deals with the issue of the individual's successful transition to adult life. In recent years, the issue of career education for special needs learners has attracted more interest and attention.

Career education is the preparation of students for successful adult living after finishing school. It consists of preparing students not only for jobs but also for living a normalized adult life in society.

Many educational professionals have advocated a Life-Centered Career Education model for special needs learners. The LCCE identifies twenty-two competencies needed for life success as adults. These competencies fall into the three main areas of daily living skills, personal–social skills, and occupational skills.

Four assessment competencies make up the career education model: clinical evaluation, work evaluation, work adjustment assessment, and job-site evaluation. The first three types of assessment are typically carried out by educational and career professionals.

Clinical assessment is usually carried out first. It consists of formal assessment in terms of the student's medical, social, educational, and psychological attributes. Social and educational clinical assessment is typically handled by the educational professional, whereas medical assessment is carried out by physicians. Psychological assessment is carried out by school and clinical psychologists.

Work evaluation assessment consists of vocational testing, work samples, and situational assessment. The two main types of vocational testing are aptitude testing and vocational interest inventories. A variety of commercially available instruments are used to test aptitudes and vocational interests.

Work samples consist of simulated tasks or

work activities in which students are observed to assess whether they possess requisite and specific job skills. As such, work samples represent direct observations of work-related behaviors. Various commercially available work sample kits are on the market. Although they are expensive, they do provide an excellent index of students' abilities to perform specific job tasks.

The third component of career assessment is work adjustment. This refers to the behavioral change process that must occur if the individual is to function successfully as a worker. It involves exhibiting appropriate work habits and sufficient physical–manual skills. Work adjustment can be carried out by direct observation, by using work samples, and by using a limited number of commercially available tests.

After career education assessment is carried out, the information must be used to create and implement career-oriented education programming. This involves the creation of a career-oriented IEP. A unique feature of the career-oriented IEP is the component of job placement and follow-up. Follow-up must be concerned with the successful transition of students into all phases of adult life, not just success on a job.

STUDY QUESTIONS

1. What is career education? What are the traditional and more current definitions of the concept? Why is the current conceptualization more appropriate for individuals with special needs?

2. What is the life-centered career education model? Why is it important? What are the three main areas and subcomponents included in the model?

3. What are the main components of career education assessment? Why is each component important? How are they generally measured?

4. What is work evaluation assessment? What are the three main components of this assessment? Why are the components important and how are they measured?

5. What are the differences between vocational aptitudes and vocational interest tests? What are some instruments that measure these areas? What are the strong and weak points of these instruments? Which of these instruments would you use? Defend your answer.

6. What are some interest inventories for special populations? How do they differ from regular interest inventories? Into what categories do such inventories fall? What are the strong and weak points of some of these special population interest inventories?

7. What are work samples? Why are they so popular? How do they differ from other career assessment instruments? What are the general strengths and weaknesses of work samples? Name some work samples that you might use. Defend your answer.

8. What is work adjustment evaluation? Why is it important? What are the components of a work adjustment evaluation and what are the different types? Name some work adjustment instruments you might consider using. Defend your answer.

9. How is career education assessment information generally used? What are some of the ways that you would use such information in your teaching? Discuss your answer.

CHAPTER 21

Perceptual–Motor and Sensory Assessment

An efficient level of sensory and motor functioning is essential in many aspects of life. Much of our interaction with the everyday environment is established through perception and movement. We walk to the mailbox, write a letter to a friend, screw a nut and bolt together to fix something, or hear someone call our name. All of these tasks require, to a large measure, perceptual and motor skills.

Perceptual–motor and sensory development also influences intellectual, social, and emotional development (Gelman 1978; Laszlo and Bairstow 1985). Exploration leads to experience with the environment and the learning of concepts (intellectual functioning). Likewise, social and emotional functioning is developed by interacting with other people in terms of gesturing, playing, speaking, and moving. It has also been argued that a child who cannot move easily and naturally may develop a poor self-concept and encounter difficulties in social and emotional adjustment (Cratty 1981; Gallahue 1982). Thus, adequate perceptual–motor and sensory development is crucial for the well-being of individuals, both in childhood and in adult life.

The ability to perceive and interact motorically with things and people in the environment is often taken for granted, especially by adults. We see and perceive objects, hear sounds and words, dress ourselves, or turn the knob of a radio without giving those actions a second thought. However, for some individuals, accurate sensory and perceptual–motor functioning is a problem that can interfere with their ability to learn and interact with the everyday environment in meaningful ways. For these reasons, the diagnosis and remediation of perceptual–motor and sensory problems of students should be an active part of the school curriculum.

A Taxonomy of Perceptual–Motor Abilities

Like the assessment of other subject areas, measurement and evaluation of perceptual–motor and sensory impairments is difficult if one does not understand the process and content of what is being assessed. Professionals have to understand what constitutes perceptual–motor functioning before they can intelligently assess behavior in this domain.

Harrow (1971) has created a classification system or *taxonomy* of perceptual–motor abilities. This taxonomy consists of six areas or levels that are shown in Table 21-1.

Keep in mind two main ideas as you review Harrow's taxonomy. First, the levels in the taxonomy are hierarchical. They occur or develop in ascending order from reflex movements to skilled movements (the sixth level—nondiscursive communication—is not dependent on the development of the other five). Second, and perhaps most important, the first five areas discussed in this chapter must be appropriately developed and used by the individual for perceptual–motor functioning to be in the normal range and in need of no remediation.

Harrow's taxonomy affords the educational professional a starting point for assessment. That is, it suggests the main areas where perceptual–motor assessment should take place. Combined with sensory assessment (particularly that of hearing and visual sensory acuity), the Harrow taxonomy offers the professional an excellent program for diagnostic assessment and remediation.

Table 21-1   Levels of the Psychomotor Domain

1. Reflex Movements: Involuntary movements made in response to stimuli.

2. Basic Fundamental Movements: Movement patterns that form the basis for later, specialized and skilled movements.

3. Perceptual Abilities: The learner's perceptual modalities, where stimuli impinge, that carry information to the higher brain centers.

4. Physical Abilities: Characteristics of physical vigor that provide the learner with a body that can be used to make skilled movements.

5. Skilled Movements: The results of the learner acquiring a degree of efficiency when performing complex movement tasks.

6. Nondiscursive Communication: Behaviors that can be labeled as movement communication (e.g., nonverbal communication).

Level 1—Reflex Movements

Reflex movements or actions are made *involuntarily* by the individual in response to environmental stimuli. Although they are not voluntary, they are considered the basis for future, voluntary movement behavior.

Though educators and curriculum planners are not likely to be concerned with reflex movements, such movements are considered important as prerequisites for future perceptual–motor functioning.

Level 2—Basic-Fundamental Movements

Basic-fundamental movements occur during the first year of life as infants build on their reflex movement repertoire. Such movement behaviors lead to other behaviors, for example, visually tracking objects, reaching, grasping and manipulating objects with the hands, and progressing through the crawling and walking stages. The basic-fundamental movement stage is divided into three areas that are defined in Table 21-2.

Table 21-2 Levels 2, 3, 4, and 5

Basic-Fundamental Movements

1. Locomotor Movements: Behaviors that change the stationary learner into an ambulatory learner. They bring about a change of location.

2. Nonlocomotor Movements: Movement behaviors involving the limbs of the body or a portion of the trunk in motion around the axis. The learner remains stationary and makes movement patterns in space. Examples include pushing, pulling, swaying, stooping, and bending.

3. Manipulative Movements: Coordinated movements of the extremities. Examples include piano playing, typing, and drawing.

Perceptual Abilities

1. Kinesthetic Discrimination: Accurate concepts of the body, body surfaces, and limbs. Includes left–right dimensions and perception of one's body in relation to surrounding objects in space.

2. Visual Discrimination: Includes visual acuity, visual tracking, visual memory, figure–ground differentiation, and visual constancy (i.e., consistency in interpreting the viewing of the same object).

3. Auditory Discrimination: Includes auditory acuity, auditory tracking, and auditory memory.

4. Tactile Discrimination: Ability to differentiate between textures by touch.

5. Coordinated Abilities: Ability to incorporate or coordinate activities that involve two or more perceptual abilities. Includes eye–hand and eye–foot coordination.

Physical Abilities

1. Endurance: Ability of the body to supply and use oxygen to continue physical activity. Includes the abilities of muscular and cardiovascular endurance.

2. Strength: Ability to exert tension against resistance by the muscles of the body.

3. Flexibility: The range of motion of the joints.

4. Agility: The learner's ability to move quickly. Involves dexterity and quickness of movement. Includes the skills of changing direction, stopping and starting, reaction–response time, and dexterity.

Skilled Movements

1. Simple Adaptive Skills: The adaptation of the basic-fundamental movements to specific movement environmental situations. These movements become more refined and more sophisticated as the learner moves through the beginner, intermediate, advanced, and highly skilled stages of any movement skills acquisition.

2. Compound Adaptive Skills: Build on the learner's efficiencies in the basic skills. The learner is now expected to manage his or her body appropriately while carrying out a high-order skill.

3. Complex Adaptive Skills: Skills that require greater mastery. Examples include complex movement skills, such as gymnastics or trampoline stunts.

As with reflex movements, educational professionals will probably not be very concerned with basic-fundamental movements because these responses will probably be in the repertoire of all but the most severely handicapped individuals. However, they are of concern to professionals working with moderately to severely/profoundly handicapped persons.

Level 3—Perceptual Abilities

This level contains strong perceptual and sensory components. Efficient perceptual abilities functioning is essential to the learner in cognitive, social, and emotional development. As such, assessment and diagnosis usually begin at this level.

Perceptual abilities refer to all of the learner's perceptual modalities in which stimuli impinge. From these modalities, messages are carried to the higher brain centers and responded to by the individual. Thus, perceptual abilities provide the messages that allow the brain to record information and respond appropriately to the environment.

The five subcategories of perceptual abilities are outlined and defined for the reader in Table 21-2. All the subcategories must operate appropriately and without error for the individual to make correct and reasonable responses to the environment. If any of the abilities in the five subcategories are not operating correctly, the individual is seriously at risk.

Level 4—Physical Abilities

Physical abilities are essential to successful learning because they allow the person to meet the physical demands of the environment. In fact, it can be argued that this level of the taxonomy is the foundation of skilled movements and responses.

Physical abilities include the characteristics of vigor and stamina that, when developed, allow people to use their bodies to make skilled, sophisticated movements. These movements are then used as specific responses to stimuli and environmental problems.

The four subcategories of physical abilities are endurance, strength, flexibility, and agility (see Table 21-2). These subcategories are required for the individual to make skilled and sustained responses to the environment.

Level 5—Skilled Movements

Skilled movements are the result of the individual's acquiring a high degree of proficiency and sophistication in performing complex perceptual–motor tasks. This level implies that the person has mastered and combined basic-fundamental movements (Level 2) to synthesize or create complex patterns of perceptual–motor functioning. All athletic, dance, recreational, and manipulative skills fall into the skilled movement classification.

The three subcategories of skilled movements are simple, compound, and complex adaptive skills (see Table 21-2). Within each subcategory, it is assumed that the learner moves through beginning, intermediate, advanced, and highly skilled stages. To under-

stand these stages, the reader need only watch a youngster begin to learn a sport or skill (e.g., baseball or dance) and advance in skill with sustained instruction, practice, and development.

Patterns of Perceptual–Motor Problems

Various educators and psychologists have attempted to classify patterns of perceptual–motor problems that people with handicaps often exhibit (Ayers 1975; Barsch 1967; Cratty 1969; Frostig, Lefever, and Whittlesey 1966; Kephart 1960). For example, Kephart (1960) attempted to identify eight aspects of perceptual–motor and sensory functioning that the student must master to succeed in the classroom and adult life. Kephart's classification scheme and a description of the functioning areas are shown in Table 21-3. Although this list is not all-inclusive, it does contain aspects most commonly used in perceptual–motor evaluations and amenable to remediation in the classroom (Bush and Waugh 1982; Myklebust 1968).

Although Kephart's classification system of perceptual–motor–sensory problems is a good starting point, other researchers have argued that it is not all-inclusive. For example, Barsch (1967) has identified two additional categories of muscular strength and dynamic balance that are missing from the Kephart list. Likewise, Frostig et al. (1966) and Cratty (1969) have identified additional aspects of perceptual–motor functioning that need to be assessed. Table 21-4 contains two classifications of perceptual–motor problems by major theorists who followed Kephart's pioneering work.

A Word of Caution about Perceptual–Motor Skills and Learning

What emerges from Tables 21-3 and 21-4 is a "shopping list" of commonly occurring prob-

Table 21-3 Kephart's Perceptual–Motor Classifications

1. Posture: Ability of body muscles to form a pattern of positioning so that the body's center of gravity will be maintained. Posture is the basic movement pattern from which all other movement patterns develop.

2. Laterality: The ability to differentiate different sides of the body. This is the first step in learning directionality.

3. Directionality: The ability to project directional concepts into space as in up, down, left, right, front, behind, and so forth.

4. Body-Image: Possessing a point of reference (one's body) around which other impressions can be organized. When body image is poor, referencing of other objects in space is difficult.

5. Figure–Ground Relationship: The ability to distinguish background from foreground stimuli.

6. Form Perception: The ability to perceive objects, sounds, textures, odors, and tastes correctly in the way they are perceived by most other people in the culture.

7. Space-Discrimination: The ability to locate objects in space.

8. Time-Dimension: The ability to perceive the meanings of time, such as today, tomorrow, yesterday, last month, and so forth.

lems in perceptual–motor and sensory functioning. Individuals deficient in one or more aspects need to have their problems diagnosed and remediated.

Note, however, that it *does not* necessarily follow that because individuals possess a problem or deficit in one aspect of perceptual–motor functioning they will be unable to learn or succeed in life. The relationship between perceptual–motor functioning and academic and life success is much less direct. The probability is that the *more* areas in which people possess perceptual–motor deficits and the more *serious* those deficits, the harder it will be for them to gain those experiences required for academic learning and life success.

It is extremely doubtful that inappropriate perceptual–motor functioning *causes* problems in reading and academic achievement. Rather, appropriate perceptual–motor functioning probably allows people to gain the experiences needed to learn concepts and vocabulary. Likewise, the possession of requisite motor skills allows the physical movements of reading, writing, and other skills to occur, but these motor skills are not the cause of learning or nonlearning (Bush and Waugh 1982).

Table 21-4 Perceptual–Motor Problems Conceptualized by Barsch and Frostig et al.

Barsch (1967)

1. Muscle-Strength Problems: Problems in this area cause efficient movement to be disturbed.

2. Dynamic-Balance Problems: Balance problems refer to a state of instability that results in the person's failure to establish equal weight distribution along the body's vertical axis.

3. Body-Awareness Problems: The inability to have a coordinated and coherent understanding of one's body image.

4. Spatial-Awareness Problems: The inability to relate to objects and other people.

5. Temporal-Awareness Problems: The inability to understand the concepts of time.

Frostig et al. (1966)

1. Eye–Hand Coordination Dysfunction: Inability to accurately reproduce visual symbols through the written or drawn mode.

2. Figure–Ground Perception Dysfunction: Same as Kephart and Barsch.

3. Form Constancy Dysfunction: The inability to identify forms regardless of differences in size, color, position, and so forth.

4. Position-in-Space Dysfunction: The inability to recognize the formation and directionality of figures and characters.

5. Spatial-Relationship Dysfunction: The inability to perceive postional relationships.

Types of Perceptual–Motor Information

The type of perceptual–motor test selected for assessment depends largely on the reasons for the child's assessment. For example, if the purpose of the assessment is a quick visual screening, then the standard Snellen Eye Chart, familiar to virtually everyone who has ever taken an eye test, would be used. However, if an in-depth assessment of the child's visual functioning is needed, then other, more diagnostic (and involved) ophthalmological measures would be employed.

The type of test selected also depends on the level or type of information the professional wishes to gather about the child. There are many different tests of perceptual–motor functioning. The types and levels of information they yield are discussed here.

Assessment of Practical–Functional Capabilities

Some tests yield information about the child's perceptual–motor functioning in terms of their practical and functional capabilities. Sometimes these practical–functional capabilities are labeled *adaptive behavior* when applied to learners with special needs. The information includes, but is not restricted to, such motor skills as toileting, feeding, and mobility.

Tests of practical–functional capabilities represent a checklist of socially mandated behaviors. These behaviors are believed linked to social acceptance and self-sufficiency. They should be viewed in a developmental framework in that motor skills acceptable or tolerated in a young child are less tolerable as the individual matures. For example, a young child who requires assistance in dressing is considered socially acceptable; a teenager who requires the same assistance is viewed as possessing a severe perceptual–motor deficit.

Assessment across Psychological Domains

Suppose that you have a child in your class who is not doing well academically, is slow and sloppy during lunchtime, and cannot cope with the normal demands of dressing for physical education and participating in routine physical exercises. The child does not possess any diagnosable medical condition. The questions then are:

1. What are the causes of the child's behavior?
2. Is the child's current educational placement appropriate?
3. What can be done to help remediate the problems?

In this type of situation, the psychologist and educator may want a broad picture of the child's functioning levels, which gives information on a variety of dimensions and across psychological areas or domains. To achieve this, the professional might choose an instrument that assesses the child's functioning in such areas as cognitive reasoning, locomotion, personal–social skills, hearing and vision, speech, eye–hand coordination, and practical reasoning (Griffiths 1970; Laszlo and Bairstow 1985).

Admittedly, this broad assessment represents a shotgun approach to diagnosing the problem. Nevertheless, the use of across-domain assessment may be appropriate when the pattern of the person's disabilities and the relationship between the behavior and perceptual–motor functioning are not clear. Broad developmental assessment can help in understanding the pattern of the individual's disabilities and in remediational programming (Gordon and McKinlay 1980).

Assessment of Specific Motor Abilities

Some people may possess relatively obvious perceptual–motor problems that interfere with their academic, social, and emotional well-being. In such cases, the professional may wish to carry out an in-depth assessment in a specific area of perceptual–motor development to identify the extent and depth of the problems. Such assessment would be analogous to criterion-referenced testing in one of the academic areas and would yield specific, in-depth information about the extent of deficits in specific areas of perceptual–motor functioning. After such evaluation, the educator can then take steps to help remediate the individual's perceptual–motor deficits or modify the learning and social environments accordingly.

Measurement of Perceptual–Motor Performance

Different types of items are used to assess perceptual–motor ability. Some tests use only one type of item; others use a variety of item types to gain a more complete picture of the student's perceptual–motor functioning.

Observational Recording

When the test items are associated with everyday living and commonplace tasks (e.g., tying shoelaces), measurement can be straightforward and observational. The examiner simply asks the individual to perform certain tasks and observes the person attempting to comply. In addition to recording whether the individual completed the perceptual–motor task correctly, the examiner can record the duration of time it took to complete the task and whether the person needed assistance (Benjamin 1976; Laszlo and Bairstow 1985).

In observational recording, the appropriateness of the person's responses is viewed in a developmental context. Thus, we would not be particularly worried if a six-year-old child could not tie shoelaces appropriately; if a sixteen-year-old could not complete the same task we would have cause for concern.

Pass–Fail

Some perceptual tasks are all or nothing in scope; either they are completed with 100 percent accuracy or they are incorrect. After all, is it logical to rate brain surgeons' operating skill or pilots' landing ability as partially accurate? If they cannot operate on a patient or land a plane safely they are deficient in those skills. Such perceptual–motor behaviors would be rated on a pass–fail basis (Holt 1975; Neuhauser 1975).

Likewise, some perceptual–motor skills in everyday life are either successful or unsuccessful. For example, a ball thrown to a child is either caught or missed. There is no alternative.

On the surface, the pass–fail rating of perceptual–motor tasks seems simple to administer and score. However, the simplicity can be misleading and can possess disadvantages (Herkowitz 1978). Consider the behavior of catching or missing a thrown ball. While it is true that *each* throw is either caught or missed (pass–fail), it is also true that of a large number of throws, some will be caught and some will be missed. What causes this to happen? Perhaps some throws are faster or higher than others. Pass–fail performance data tell us nothing about the circumstances under which the item was passed or failed, information that can be diagnostically and remediationally useful. This is a major disadvantage of using only pass–fail items in perceptual–motor assessment (Keogh 1973; Laszlo and Bairstow 1985).

Observational Description

One solution to the problems of using pass–fail scores is to use a more descriptive method of observation. In such a method, the examiner records not only whether the perceptual–motor behavior was carried out correctly but also the occurring errors or inappropriate behavior the individual exhibited while performing the task. This recording can be written by the observer in longhand or recorded on a checklist of commonly occurring errors.

As in any observational system, there are two major sources of observer error: differences in the accuracy and expertise of observers and differences between observers in defining what constitutes errors or aberrant behavior. However, as we discuss in Chapter 8 on reliability, both sources of error can be minimized by training observers and by checking interrater reliability frequently.

Measurement of Speed and Accuracy

The final method of assessing perceptual–motor performance is to measure the speed and accuracy of a person's movement. Measuring the speed of movement can be appropriate in situations that require the individual to complete a task as quickly as possible. For example, many intelligence tests ask students to complete a puzzle, maze, or pegboard design, and their responses are timed. Likewise, for certain jobs, such as those on an assembly line, the speed of task completion is a critical job attribute.

When the speed of movement is recorded, typically the accuracy of those timed responses is measured. There is a well-known relationship between speed and accuracy. Usually, the faster the responses, the lower the accuracy (Meyer, Smith, and Wright 1982). The extent to which an individual sacrifices accuracy to speed is often a function of the person's age and personality, as well as of the task demands (Laszlo and Bairstow 1985). Therefore, an accuracy measure should accompany the timed responses of an individual's movements.

A Word of Caution to the Test Consumer Regarding Perceptual–Motor Tests

When working with tests of perceptual–motor skills, the test consumer must *always*

keep in mind that such tests are generally technically inadequate. That is, a large body of research on these instruments has demonstrated that they are generally unreliable and, in certain cases, possess dubious construct validity (Bush and Waugh 1982; Remmers, Gage, and Rummel 1965; Ysseldyke 1973).

In terms of reliability, many perceptual–motor tests possess reliabilities in the low .50s; few possess a demonstrated reliability as high as .75 (minimally acceptable) (Remmers, Gage, and Rummel 1965). Additionally, there is a great deal of doubt as to whether perceptual–motor skills are predictive of other learning skills, which makes their predictive and construct validities suspect (Denhoff 1969; Hammill and Wiederholt 1973; Mann 1971). More specifically, researchers assert that perceptual–motor skills and academic achievement are not distinct variables, nor are they highly correlated. In some cases, the relationship between perceptual–motor skills and academic achievement may even be negatively correlated (Denhoff 1969). Researchers argue that because children and learning tasks are so complex and different, it is difficult to find direct links between perceptual–motor functioning and academic learning (Hudgins 1977). Apparently, the effect of perceptual–motor functioning on academic learning is *situational,* and it may facilitate, hamper, or have no impact on children's learning, depending on the subject matter, child, and learning situation (Bush and Waugh 1982).

Why Assess Perceptual–Motor Ability?

Why, then, use perceptual–motor tests at all? One answer is that perceptual–motor tests do have some usefulness if used cautiously and with a degree of skepticism. Children *do* experience perceptual–motor problems, and these problems often require remediation, not because they cause academic difficulties (and they may in some situations) but because the deficits cause problems for the individual. For example, consider the child who is experiencing motor problems in tracking objects in space. Although such problems may or may not be correlated with reading ability, these deficits are likely to cause the individual problems in the real world. Thus, the remediation of such problems would certainly help create a more sensible and safe environment for the person.

Second, although perceptual–motor deficits may not (or may) interfere with academic learning, they can interfere with everyday adaptive skills needed for social and emotional life success. For example, a child who experiences motor deficits may have difficulties in dressing and eating, skills that are needed for independent living. Likewise, a child who cannot catch a ball thrown at various speeds and heights may be ridiculed by peers during a game and begin to experience peer and emotional difficulties. Ask any eight-year-old who is struggling to learn the skills of baseball, and who is losing status with more accomplished peers, if there is a relationship between motor skills and social acceptance and listen to the response!

For these reasons, perceptual–motor testing has its place in the assessment program of learners with special needs, *if* such testing is carried out and interpreted with caution. Such assessment can yield useful diagnostic information to the professional, in terms of the specific deficits experienced by the child, and suggest methods for remediation (Bush and Waugh 1982; Rich 1978). For these reasons, some popular perceptual–motor tests are reviewed here.

Specific Tests of Perceptual–Motor Functioning: Assessment of Fine-Motor Skills

Bender Visual–Motor Gestalt Test

Overview: The Bender Visual–Motor Gestalt Test (BVMGT) (Bender 1938) is a test of perceptual–visual–motor functioning that consists of nine four-by-six-inch cards with one geometric design on each card. These designs were originally conceptualized by Wertheimer (1923) and used to differentiate brain-injured from noninjured individuals. The test is used today as an instrument to test people's perception of figures and their fine-motor ability to reproduce those figures. The test is appropriate for use with individuals aged five and over. An example of a geometric design from the BVMGT is shown in Figure 21-1.

Administration and Scoring: The administration of the BVMGT is straightforward. The nine geometric designs are presented, one at

Figure 21-1 Examples of Bender Visual–Motor Gestalt Test Items and Errors

BVMGT Geometric Item

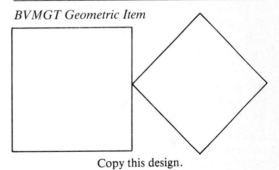

Copy this design.

Types of Student Response Errors on the Bender Visual–Motor Gestalt Test

1. Distortion of Shape: The student's drawing of the stimulus shape is so out of shape that the original figure cannot be ascertained.

2. Integration: The student fails to integrate or juxtapose parts of the design correctly.

3. Perseveration: The child fails to stop after completing the required drawing but continues making design(s).

4. Rotation: The child rotates the stimulus design by more than 45 degrees. Reversals are scored as 180 rotations and count as rotation errors.

a time, to the subject, whose task is to copy them onto a plain sheet of paper. Administration of the BVMGT usually takes fifteen minutes or less.

Whereas administration is relatively simple, scoring is difficult, and a variety of scoring systems have developed over the years. Depending on the scoring system used, the BVMGT yields a variety of scores, such as Distortion of Shape, Integration, Perseveration, and Rotation (Koppitz 1963) (see Figure 21-1).

Norms and Standardization Group: The original BVMGT was standardized on 800 school and nursery school children aged three to eleven. The standardization was based on earlier work by Gesell, who standardized the drawing ability of young children and found that by age eleven all children tested could accurately copy the Bender designs.

However, over the years, scoring system authors developed their own standardization and norm groups. For example, Koppitz (1963) originally standardized her system on 1,104 children from forty-six classes in twelve public schools. However, this sample was not very representative of the U.S. population, so in 1975, Koppitz restandardized the normalization group to approximate the population more closely in terms of sex, race, and geographic variables.

Another popular scoring system of the BVMGT was developed from a sample of learning-disabled students (Watkins 1976). The Watkins scoring system was standardized on 1,046 learning-disabled students and 3,444 nondisabled pupils. Ages for students ranged from five to fourteen. Subjects were chosen from forty-two school districts in seven states. The norms are considered to be representative for race, but demographic data on the parents of test children were obtained for only 60 percent of the test takers. Thus, it is not known whether the sample is representative for other socioeconomic variables.

Reliability: Koppitz (1975) summarized two types of reliability information for the BVMGT: interrater and test-retest. Interrater reliabilities range from .79 to .99, with most scores exceeding an interrater reliability coefficient of $r = .89$. The higher the interrater reliability, the less error caused by raters scoring and interpreting the same student's behaviors differently. Koppitz claims that the new scoring procedures outlined in the 1975 manual facilitate interrater reliability.

The 1975 manual also summarized nine test-retest studies conducted with nonhandicapped, elementary students. Reliability coefficients range from .50 to .90, with a median reliability coefficient of approximately .71. On the basis of her studies, Koppitz concludes that the BVMGT is reliable, but reader should keep in mind that (1) the majority of the studies were carried out *solely* on kindergarten students and (2) only one of twenty-five reliability coefficients exceeds .90. Thus, the reliability of the BVMGT may still be in question.

Validity: The validity of the BVMGT is also in question. In terms of construct validity, there is no adequate description of just how to define visual–motor perception, either by Bender or by later scorers and interpreters of the test. That is, there is a lack of clear understanding of just *how* the BVMGT assesses a person's visual–motor functioning simply by having the person copy nine designs.

There have been attempts to correlate results on the BVMGT with academic achievement and school functioning. Although a strong hypothesized correlation is popular in many special education and psychological circles, attempts to show the relationship between the BVMGT and academic achievement empirically have given the test only minimal support as a predictor of academic achievement (Arter and Jenkins 1979; Cole 1978).

Attempts have also been made to show the value of the BVMGT as an identifier of minimal brain dysfunction in children (Koppitz 1975). Although reviews have found some support for this function, it is widely accepted among psychologists that the BVMGT should not be used by itself for this purpose, but that it must be used in conjunction with other medical and behavioral assessment data (Koppitz 1975).

Finally, attempts have been made to show the BVMGT as a predictor of emotional problems in children. Again, these results have been inconclusive at best. It simply cannot be assumed from existing research that a child who possesses emotional deficits will perform poorly on the test or that poor test performance is indicative of emotional disturbance (Koppitz 1975).

Summary of the BVMGT for the Test Consumer: What emerges is a picture of the BVMGT as *not* being a test of intelligence or a predictor of academic performance, emotional disturbance, perceptual problems, or brain dysfunction. What *does* the BVMGT assess? Basically, it yields specific information on a child's ability to copy geometric designs.

The extent to which this information is useful in education is left up to the test consumer. In addition, the test possesses difficulties with reliability and problems with norms and scoring, because so many different standardization and scoring methods exist.

Why is the test so popular? Perhaps because it is so easy to administer and because so many people believe in its power as a predictor of academic achievement. However, the test's simplicity and people's belief in its predictive validity, however unwarranted, have caused it to be overused and overinterpreted by educational professionals (Koppitz 1975).

Southern California Sensory Integration Tests

Overview: The Southern California Sensory Integration Test Battery (SCSIT) (Ayers 1975) is a series of separate tests designed to assess the sensory and motor functioning of children from four to ten years of age. However, each of the seven tests in the battery has its own upper-age limit. The seven tests in the battery, their functions, and the age limits for test takers are outlined in Table 21-5. Space

Table 21-5   Southern California Sensory Integration Test Battery (SCSIT)

Test	Measures
1. Ayers Space Test	Space Visualization
2. Southern California Figure–Ground Visual Perception	Figure–Ground Perception
3. Southern California Kinesthesia and Tactile Perception Tests	Kinesthesia, Manual Form Perception, Finger Identification, Localization of Tactile Stimuli
4. Southern California Motor Accuracy Test	Sensory–Motor Integration
5. Southern California Perceptual–Motor Tests	Motor Accuracy
6. Southern California Postrotary Nystagmus Test	Vestibular System
7. Positions for Inhibition of Neck Reflex	Tonic Neck Reflex

limitations prevent a review or critique of each test in the battery, so the entire battery is critiqued as a unit.

Administration and Scoring: None of the tests requires verbal responses or reading ability. Subjects perform a variety of tasks including tracing lines, finger movements, identification of tactile stimulation, right-left discrimination, and balance tasks. Testing time for each test ranges from twenty minutes to an hour, depending on the test used and the age and ability levels of the test taker.

The scoring procedure for many test items is very complicated and requires specialized training. The items from the seventeen assessment areas fall into four main scoring types:

1. Length of time a particular activity is maintained.
2. Number of errors made on pass–fail items.
3. Point scores made on the basis of complicated criteria used for scoring accuracy of performance.
4. Combined speed and accuracy measures in which penalty points are assessed for slow performance and for performance errors.

Raw scores are obtained on each test and converted to standard scores. The means and standard deviations of those standard scores are different for each test. The standard scores for each assessment area are used to create a profile from which determinations of perceptual–motor problems are made.

Norms and Standardization Group: The tests were normed on children between the ages of four and eleven, all of whom resided in the vicinity of Los Angeles, California. There is no indication that the sample is comparable for each test in the battery, and this makes the results from each test difficult if not impossible to compare. The number of students in the standardization sample varied form 280 (Motor Accuracy Test) to 1,000 (Postrotary Nystagmus Test). There are considerable differences in the demographics of the norm sample in each test, but across the

tests, the samples are not representative of the U.S. population.

Reliability: The manual for each test reports its own reliability information. Test-retest reliability is reported in each manual; the testing interval is one week. Reliability ranges are wide. For example, the Figure–Ground Visual Perception Test reliability ranges from .37 to .52, Kinesthesia and Tactile Perception Tests from .01 to .75, and Motor Accuracy from .91 to .92, depending on the subtest and the age of the test taker. In general, however, the reliability of the SCSIT is suspect and the tests should be approached with caution.

Validity: Validity studies relating the SCSIT with academic and school achievement are not reported. The Motor Accuracy Test does appear to distinguish children with eye–hand coordination problems. However, the overall validity of the battery is suspect.

Summary of the SCSIT for the Test Consumer: The SCSIT is much more extensive and comprehensive than the Bender Gestalt Test. Rather than simply having the student copy nine designs, the SCSIT measures perceptual–motor functioning in seventeen different areas on seven different tests. However, the SCSIT pays a price for its comprehensive nature. It is long and difficult to administer, and its scoring and interpretation procedures are complex.

One severe drawback of the SCSIT is that it is really seven different tests, each with a different standardization group, set of standard scores, mean, and standard deviation. This makes comparison between test scores impossible and renders the SCSIT profile meaningless. The consumer who uses such a profile should be very careful in attempting interpretation.

Finally, the test possesses dubious technical quality. The standardization groups are neither representative nor sufficiently large, and the reliability and validity of the battery are suspect. In summary, like the Bender Gestalt Test, the SCSIT should be used only with extreme caution.

Other Tests of Fine-Motor Functioning

Developmental Test of Visual–Motor Integration

The Developmental Test of Visual–Motor Integration–Revised (VMI) (Beery 1982) is similar to the Bender Gestalt Test in that children are asked to copy twenty-four designs that appear in ascending order of difficulty. Similar to other copying tests, the premise of the VMI is that copying adequately measures visual–motor skills and that such skills are related to academic and cognitive performance. One difference between the VMI and other copying tests is that the VMI contains a developmental scale to help in assessing student motor competence. The instrument is appropriate for use with individuals from two to fourteen years. However, it is somewhat doubtful whether reliable data can be collected on the copying behavior of children aged two to three years.

The VMI is presented in booklet form. There are two different booklets: one contains the first fifteen forms appropriate for children two to eight years old; the other contains all twenty-four forms for children who can pass the first fifteen forms. This causes some problems because if a child is administered the short form and copies the fifteenth form correctly, a switch must be made to the long form. In each booklet, the child copies the design in the space provided. The VMI is norm-referenced, and raw scores are converted to percentiles and standard scores based on developmental functioning.

The VMI was renormed in 1981 on 3,090 children. The group is said by the author to be stratified on the basis of ethnicity, parental income, residence, and sex. However, information provided in the test manual on the standardization group is somewhat sketchy.

Reliability of the VMI was assessed in terms of interrater reliability (important in a test where subjective scoring judgments are made), test-retest, and split-half reliability. In a number of studies conducted by the test author, interrater reliability ranges from .58 to .99, with a median reliability of .93. Test-retest reliability for a two-week interval is .59 for an institutionalized sample of students and .92 for a normal student sample. Split-half reliabilities range from .66 to .93, with a median of .79.

Attempts at demonstrating the validity of the VMI rest on showing its correlation with the Bender Gestalt Test and showing a correlation between performance on the VMI and academic and cognitive performance. In a variety of studies, the VMI correlates reasonably well with the Bender (coefficients ranging from .62 to .71), indicating that the tests measure basically the same construct. The key issue is whether the VMI is a good predictor of academic and cognitive achievement. Here, the VMI has fared less well with the test as a relatively poor predictor of academic achievement, especially for younger children.

In summary, although the VMI is more technically sound than the Bender, it suffers from the same problems of validity. Simply put, it has not been demonstrated (1) that the ability to copy designs is an adequate measure of a large range of fine-motor abilities (content validity) and (2) that such tests can adequately predict problems in academic and cognitive functioning (criterion-related validity). Until such validity can be demonstrated, tests like the VMI should be used and interpreted with extreme caution, and results should not be overgeneralized.

Developmental Test of Visual Perception

Overview: The Developmental Test of Visual Perception (DTVP) (Frostig, Maslow,

Lefever, and Whittlesey 1964; Frostig, Lefever, and Whittlesey 1966) is a test of visual–motor perception that assesses skills in five main areas: eye–hand coordination, form constancy, figure–ground perception, position in space, and spatial relations. The DTVP consists of various designs, and the child receives specific instructions as to what to do with the designs. For example, sometimes the child is asked simply to trace over the line; at other items, the child is asked to draw a line from one point to another or to complete a maze. The test is appropriate for kindergarten and above. However, the manual specifically states that the test should not be given to children during the first two weeks of the school year to avoid the stress of new school and classroom situations.

Administration and Scoring: The child is given an expendable thirty-five-page booklet that contains different designs, along with specific instructions as to what to do with each design. This booklet is used for all five subtests. There are two manuals with the test, a standardization (technical) manual and an administration and scoring manual. Testing time is approximately one hour. The test can be given in groups if desired.

Scoring of the DTVP is relatively objective and straightforward, especially for a perceptual–motor test. A number of specific examples are given in the manual, and scoring stencils are provided. Points are earned as a function of the quality of the student's responses to test items, with a raw score being derived for each subtest.

The DTVP yields three types of scores: Perceptual Age, Perceptual Quotient (PQ), and Scale Scores. Perceptual Age scores are a form of age-equivalent scores obtained from the norm table in the test manual. Separate Perceptual Age scores are obtained for each subscale of the DTVP. The Perceptual Quotient is a type of deviation score obtained by summing the subscale scores of the

DTVP and then comparing the sum with the child's Scale Score (using a table in the test manual). The Perceptual Quotients have been designed so that a PQ of 100 is always at the fiftieth percentile, a PQ of 90 is at the twenty-fifth percentile, and a PQ of 110 is at the seventy-fifth percentile. Finally, the Scale Score is a ratio-type measure. It is obtained by dividing the Perceptual Age by the child's chronological age; that score is divided by 10, and the answer is rounded to the nearest whole number.

The three types of scores yielded by the DTVP have various problems in terms of both test consumer confusion and score interpretation. First, the Scale Score is not a *scaled score*. Scaled scores (as in the WISC–R) possess a predetermined mean and standard deviation. The Scale Scores of the DTVP do not. Rather, they are ratio scores obtained by dividing the Perceptual Age by the child's chronological age. Thus, they are more like an IQ ratio obtained on the original Stanford–Binet than like scaled scores.

Second, there is some doubt as to whether the use of Perceptual Quotients yields any real diagnostic information for the test user. Furthermore, uninformed test consumers can readily confuse them with an intelligence quotient (IQ). However, there is little evidence that the PQ and IQ are correlated in any way. Thus, the scores created by the authors of the DTVP may lead to confusion in interpretation rather than to useful diagnostic information.

Norms and Standardization The DTVP was standardized on 2,116 children residing in southern California. The sample was primarily middle class and, by the author's own admission, it was geographically and socioeconomically nonrepresentative, with little minority representation. There is no information in the test manual on sex of students or on the educational and occupational background of parents.

Reliability: Two types of reliability, test-retest and split-half, are reported for the DTVP. Both of the reliabilities are generally low. Test-retest reliability for subscale scores ranges from .42 (Figure–Ground) to .80 (Form Constancy). Split-half reliabilities were obtained for the total test (scale scores) for various age levels. Split-half reliabilities range from .68 (students 6 to 7 years old) to .89 (students 5 to 6 years old). Again, split-half reliability is in the low end of the continuum and considered unacceptable.

Validity: Perhaps the greatest problem with the DTVP is in the area of validity. There is little evidence that the test is valid. For example, the authors state that the test is intended to "explore the relationship of visual–perceptual disabilities to problems of school learning and adjustment, brain damage, and other handicaps" (p. 5). However, the DTVP has only moderate power in predicting good and poor readers in grade one and even less validity in predicting school success in later grades (Bush and Waugh 1982; Colarusso, Martin, and Hartung 1976). Thus, while the DTVP may identify students who have trouble with visual–motor tasks, there is little evidence to indicate that a child's ability to stay with the lines or to trace a drawing is predictive of academic success and school learning (Bush and Waugh 1982; Black 1976). As Kephart (1971) has pointed out, children who score low on the DTVP may have trouble in school, but it is also quite possible for a child to score high on the test and still experience problems in school for entirely different reasons than poor perceptual–motor functioning.

Summary of the DTVP for the Test Consumer: At one time, the DTVP was an extremely popular instrument, and advocates claimed that a child scoring low on the test would predictably encounter reading and other academic problems in school. In fact, some of the test's more enthusiastic supporters sometimes claimed that a child who scored poorly on the test ought to receive remediation on DTVP tasks before going on to reading instruction. Thus, at one point, some classes were actually giving remediational instruction in tracing designs and staying within the lines while making pencil marks!

Fortunately, most of this thinking and instruction has faded over the years as the test and its theoretical underpinnings have been called into question. The DTVP is deficient in terms of its standardization data, reliability, test scores, and instructions for interpretation. Of equal importance, its validity so far is unsubstantiated. Thus, although the test *may* be of use in globally assessing students' visual–motor deficits, it should only be used with other tests or should be bypassed completely.

Tests of Gross-Motor Skills

Purdue Perceptual Motor Survey

Overview: The Purdue Perceptual Motor Survey (PPMS) (Roach and Kephart 1966) is not a diagnostic test. Rather, it is a survey instrument that allows the professional to observe a broad spectrum of motor skills within a structured setting. This instrument should be used for screening rather than for in-depth diagnosis.

The survey contains eleven subtests divided into twenty-two scorable items that are geared to young children. Each item is designed to measure some aspect of the child's perceptual–motor development. The eleven subtests can be further grouped into five perceptual–motor areas. Table 21-6 contains the five major areas tested and the subtests.

Administration and Scoring: Specific instructions on administering each subtest are included in the survey. However, the equipment needed to administer the test must be obtained

Table 21-6   Major Areas and Subtests of the Purdue Perceptual–Motor Survey

Skill Area	Measures	Subtests
1. Balance and Posture	Balance and posture flexibility	Walking Board, Jumping
2. Body Image and Differentiation	Knowledge of body parts, ability to imitate movement	Angels-in-the-Snow, Identification of Body Parts, Imitation of Movement, Kraus-Weber Obstacle Course
3. Ocular Pursuits/Control	Ability to establish and maintain contact with a visual target	Both Eyes, Right Eye, Left Eye, Eye Convergence
4. Perceptual–Motor Match	Combining perceptual and motor skills in sophisticated tasks	Drawing Circle, Drawing Two Circles at Once, Drawing a Straight Line, Drawing Two Lines at Once
5. Form Perception	Perceiving forms and reproducing designs	Copying Seven Geometric Designs

by the examiner. For example, the Walking Board Test requires an eight-to-twelve-foot board and brackets to place it at least six inches off the floor. Neither the board nor the brackets come with the kit. However, the only other large equipment needed to administer the PPMS is a chalkboard, and most of the tests can be administered using paper and pencil. The entire survey takes approximately twenty to thirty minutes to administer.

Scoring for the PPMS can be subjective and difficult. Numbers are assigned to the child's scores, but they are refer to the quality not the quantity of the performance. The record booklet consists largely of a checklist of behaviors for each task, which allows the examiner to record difficulties that the child experienced on each subtest. The manual contains photographs of various items, which are intended to help the scorer, but they are more confusing then helpful. For some items, the rating criteria do not allow for all possible responses; for other items, the child is not given sufficient instructions to complete the item successfully. Finally, rating procedures are rough and approximate. For example, on one item the examiner is told to "accurately" measure a ten-second time period by counting, preceding each number by "a thousand."

The authors themselves point out that the instrument should not be used as a test but merely to observe motor behaviors and to isolate possible areas of difficulty.

Norms and Standardization Group: The total number of students in the standardization group for the PPMS was 200, 50 each in grades one through four. All of the children in the norm group attended school in a district in Lafayette, Indiana. The children were selected from a range of socioeconomic backgrounds and came from urban and rural families. However, with a norm sample of this size, it is difficult to demonstrate representativeness. Moreover, there is no geographic representativeness.

Reliability: A test-retest reliability of .95 was obtained using thirty students who were tested one week apart. However, with such a small number of children tested, the high reliability is still suspect.

Validity: The authors attempted to establish the concurrent validity of the PPMS by correlating test results with teacher ratings of overall academic performance. Although the two correlated at .65, the question raised earlier in this chapter still holds. Is perceptual–motor dysfunction predictive of poor academic performance? The answer has been found to be generally negative. Thus, there are still questions about the validity of the PPMS.

Summary of the PPMS for the Test Consumer: The PPMS is designed to offer qualitative information about the young child's gross motor functioning. However, even with this limited use, it still possesses many problems. First, the manual offers few interpretive data. The profile created by the instrument is almost useless, and the numbers yielded are ordinals rather than ratios. Second, even with the author's warning that this is not a test but rather a screening instrument, the PPMS is still often used diagnostically by some uninformed professionals. The PPMS has no diagnostic value, and its global use is also suspect. Furthermore, because the test was standardized on such a small, restricted population, it is very doubtful that its norms can be generalized to any other populations. Finally, although the reliability of the instrument may be acceptable (despite problems related to an extremely small sample size), it has an unproven validity. In summary, even the use of the PPMS as a global test of students' motor difficulties is highly suspect.

Bruininks–Oseretsky Test of Motor Proficiency

Overview: the Bruininks–Oseretsky Test of Motor Proficiency (BOTMP) (Bruininks 1978) is an individually administered test that assesses the motor functioning of children from four and one-half to fourteen and one-half years of age. The battery consists of forty-six separate items that provide a comprehensive profile of both fine-motor and gross-motor abilities. A shorter form of the battery (Short Form) contains four items from the complete test and gives a brief survey of the child's motor abilities.

The forty-six items are grouped into eight subtests; four measure gross-motor skills, three measure fine-motor skills, and one measures both. The eight subtests are listed in Table 21-7.

Administration and Scoring: Administration of the entire test requires forty-five to sixty minutes; the Short Form requires fifteen to twenty minutes. Examiners do need specific training to administer the battery, and familiarity with the directions and materials of the instrument is an important requisite.

Scoring the battery is a complicated procedure. First, raw scores for each item are expressed in one of four ways depending on the nature of the item. These four methods of scoring are:

1. Time taken to complete the task.
2. Number of units completed in a fixed time.
3. Number of errors made.
4. Pass–fail criteria.

Raw scores are then converted to point scores, with point ranges depending on the number of items within a subtest and on the maximum points allowed for given subtest items. These point scores are then *rescaled* so that they contribute an equal weighting to composite scores. Next, age-appropriate tables are used to convert ranged subtest scores to a standard score between one and thirty-six. These composite scores are then summed to obtain a Gross-Motor Composite, Fine-

Table 21-7 Subtests of the Bruininks–Oseretsky Test of Motor Proficiency (BOTMP)

1. Running Speed and Agility
2. Balance
3. Bilateral Coordination
4. Strength
5. Upper Limb Coordination
6. Response Speed
7. Visual–Motor Control
8. Upper Limb Speed and Dexterity

Motor Composite, or Battery Composite. Finally, another set of computations is carried out using tables to arrive at percentile ranks, stanines, and age-equivalent scores with a resulting motor profile. If all this sounds complicated, it is. Scores are rescaled no less than three times before the profile is completed, and there is much room for misinterpretation and error. For these reasons, considerable practice in scoring and interpreting the BOTMP is needed before its use as a diagnostic device.

Norms and Standardization Group: The BOTMP was standardized on 765 subjects, almost equally divided by sex. A multistage stratification procedure was employed, based on the 1970 census, to ensure representativeness of the sample. Race, geographic region, and other socioeconomic factors were taken into account in creating the norm group. No students with severe physical impairments were included in the norm sample.

Reliability: Test-retest reliability was carried out with a sample of sixty-three second-grade and sixty-three sixth-grade students on all subtests, with a seven-to-twelve-day retest interval. For both groups, test-retest reliability ranges from .58 to .89 for grade two and from .29 to .89 for grade six. Tables are available by grade for the subtest reliabilities; caution should be used in adopting subtests that possess low reliabilities.

Validity: Bruininks reports that validity of the BOTMP is based on its ability to assess the motor development of children. The author offers evidence for construct validity of the test based on research studies and the relevant statistical properties of the test. Although the author offers moderate evidence for the test's reliability, stronger evidence is needed. Nevertheless, it does appear that the BOTMP comes closer to demonstrating its validity than do other perceptual–motor tests.

Summary of the BOTMP for the Test Consumer: The BOTMP is one of the most extensive batteries for assessing the motor development of children. One advantage is that it assesses fine-motor, gross-motor, and composite motor functioning of children. However, although it offers a variety of scores, it is unduly complicated to score and item scoring can quickly lead to errors in scoring and interpretation. The BOTMP possesses a higher technical quality than do other perceptual–motor tests, but it still must demonstrate its technical quality in a stronger, more convincing fashion. Nevertheless, the BOTMP deserves consideration as a diagnostic tool (and perhaps greater popularity than some of the other perceptual–motor tests). However, the test by itself should not be used to diagnose specific motor problems of children.

Concluding Comments

Some strong themes recur throughout this chapter. First the adequate measurement of perceptual–motor problems is a *tricky* business. As we have seen, it is difficult even to define the area of perceptual–motor functioning and what constitutes functioning in different areas. Although attempts have been made to create a perceptual–motor taxonomy, issues of how to define and classify such functioning still abound.

Second, there has been undue emphasis on perceptual–motor functioning as a predictor and even precursor of later academic skills (e.g., reading). Although there does appear to be a relationship between perceptual–motor functioning and academic, social, and emotional development, this relationship is not nearly as strong as some advocates believe. Even though motor skills and other variables may be related, it is doubtful that motor functioning *causes* problems in academic learning and mental health, except in the most severe cases.

Finally, in reviewing the popular perceptual–motor instruments, we note the poor technical quality of the tests being used by a great number of professionals. Likewise, these tests often have poor reliability and standardization. For the most part, they also lack proven validity and fail to demonstrate their appropriateness as diagnostic tools.

In short, the assessment of perceptual–motor skills possesses a great deal of error in terms of knowledge about *what* is being tested, *why* it is being tested, and *how* it is being tested. Thus, before such assessment takes place, the educational professional must clearly understand how and why information is being collected and what degree of confidence should be placed in the data.

SUMMARY

A moderate to high level of motor behavior is essential to many aspects of life. Perceptual–motor functioning influences intellectual, social, and emotional development. Exploration leads to experience, which leads to the forming of concepts and certain abilities.

Prevalence figures exist for different categories of sensory and perceptual–motor functioning. Although it is difficult to gain a completely accurate picture of prevalence because of the population assessed or counted, it does appear that a significant proportion of special needs learners possess mild to moderate sensory and perceptual–motor deficits.

Harrow (1971) has created a taxonomy of perceptual–motor functioning. This taxonomy is hierarchical in that the levels of perceptual–motor functioning develop in an ascending order of complexity. All five levels in the taxonomy must be mastered and used by the individual if effective perceptual–motor functioning is to take place.

There are different types of perceptual–motor information. The type of information sought by the professional depends largely on the reasons the individual is being assessed. Types of assessment information include assessment of practical–functional capabilities, assessment across psychological domains, assessment of specific motor abilities, and identifying causes of motor disabilities.

Perceptual–motor assessment instruments use a variety of test item types. Whereas some instruments use only one type, others use a variety. Such item types include observational recording, observational description, and measurement of speed and accuracy.

When working with perceptual–motor assessment instruments, the professional should always keep in mind that these instruments contain a large degree of error and generally possess poor technical quality. Such tests may also contain dubious validity. Likewise, although the relationship between perceptual–motor functioning and academic, social, and emotional development is probably important, the former does not *cause* the latter to occur. Thus, the relationship between perceptual–motor development and the learning of other skills has probably been overemphasized. Children with motor skills should not have academic learning delayed while their motor deficits are being remediated. Such an educational program will hinder the child's acquisition of the academic and life success skills needed for adult living.

STUDY QUESTIONS

1. What is perceptual–motor functioning? Why is it important? Do you think it should be assessed in the schools? Why or why not?

2. What are the different types of sensory–motor impairments? What are their prevalence in the general population?

3. What are the levels of the taxonomy of perceptual–motor abilities? What is the relationship of these levels to one another? Why are these levels important to the education of individuals possessing perceptual–motor impairments?

4. In what different ways are perceptual–motor problems assessed? What are the strengths and weaknesses of each assessment procedure? Which types of assessment would you recommend for your use? Defend your answers.

5. What are the major tests of fine-motor skills? What are the strong and weak points of these tests? Would you use them in your assessment program? Why or why not?

6. How are gross-motor skills assessed? Do you believe that the instruments discussed in this chapter for assessing gross-motor skills are strong or weak? Would you advocate their use? Defend your answer.

CHAPTER 22

Social Skills and Affective Assessment

KEY CONCEPTS

- Nature of social development
- Why is social assessment of social development important?
- Nature of social competence
- Assessment of social skills and competence: By adults, by peers, by self
- Nature of affective functioning
- Self-concept and its importance
- Assessment of affective functioning

Educators and parents are becoming increasingly aware that a child's acquisition of necessary social and emotional (affective) skills is crucial for the student's mental and emotional health, both in and out of school (Cartledge and Milburn 1986; Gearhardt, De Ruiter and Siko 1986). The learning of social skills and the acquisition of a healthy mental outlook have been shown to influence how a child interacts with peers and teachers and other adults. These skills and mental health have also been correlated with academic achievement, social delinquency, and emotional disturbance (Garwood 1983; Trower, Bryant, and Argyle 1978). In fact, there is considerable support for the notion that the social and emotional functioning problems of childhood often carry over into adulthood (Kagan and Moss 1962; Trower 1980). Thus, the interest in social and affective behavior functioning of children is justified.

Although most people believe that social and affective functioning are important, many question whether they should be school concerns. Children, the reasoning goes, learn the necessary skills for social success outside of school, and there is little need to learn such skills as part of the school curriculum. However, a growing body of evidence indicates that these assumptions may be false. Apparently, a significant proportion of at-risk children do not learn requisite social and affective skills on their own, and they suffer from poor peer relationships, loneliness, and poor self-concept (Coie and Dodge 1983; Dodge 1983; Luftig 1987a, b). For these children, social skills assessment and training are required, and many educational professionals believe that such assessment and remediation should be part of the school curriculum (Michelson and Wood 1980; Oden 1986).

This chapter deals with the assessment of the social and affective skills necessary for good mental health and life success. Before social skills or affective behavior instruction can take place, we must measure the extent to which children possess deficits in these areas. Likewise, before professionals can perform such assessment, they must possess a clear idea of what constitutes social and affective–emotional behavior. This chapter gives the reader a clearer idea of what constitutes functioning in these important areas and identifies methods and instruments for measuring social and emotional behavior.

Defining Social Skills

Before one can begin to assess social skills, one must understand what they are. In some ways, defining adequate social functioning is more difficult and ambiguous than defining the skills of academic process. For example, there is some general agreement about the processes of reading and arithmetic, and the assessment and remediation of these areas are taught in many teacher preparation courses. Social skills, however, are somewhat harder to describe and operationalize. As a result, the range of definitions runs the gamut from too narrow to extremely broad.

In general, social skills are defined as "acceptable learned behaviors that enable the person to interact with others in ways that enable the person to elicit positive responses and assist in avoiding negative responses from them" (Cartledge and Milburn 1986, p. 7). Social skills, as generally defined, consist of two processes: the ability to interact positively with other people and the ability of the individual to achieve personal objectives for interacting with others (Morgan 1980). In a way, positive social skills involve getting people to act in ways we desire while maintaining positive relations with us.

Social skills can be separated into two dimensions: *skill components* and *skill processes* (Eisler and Frederiksen 1980; Trower 1980). Skill components represent single or isolated social skill behaviors. For example, knowing how to greet a passerby on the street and being a good sport when a joke is played on you are two isolated social skills. Skill processes refers to the person's ability to generate a series of socially acceptable responses in a given social situation. Skill processes are *situational;* certain social skills work in one social situation but not in another. The appropriate use of skill processes depends on the person's ability to "read" and monitor social situations and respond accordingly. It is *social strategy* that requires the individual to stand back from social situations and ask, What should I do here? (Gearhardt et al. 1986; Kronick 1983; Luftig 1987b).

The Issue of Social Competence

The abilities to learn appropriate social skill components (behaviors) and to use those behaviors strategically and appropriately (skill processes) comprise *social competence* (Coie, Dodge, and Coppotelli 1982; Hops 1983). Social competency involves forming and adopting personal goals that are appropriate to social situations and creating and implementing behavioral strategies for reaching those goals (Asher and Renshaw 1981; Taylor and Asher 1984). To behave in a socially competent manner, a person must first learn a series of isolated social skills and then use (generalize) them in appropriate social situations. Given the complex nature of the social competence process, it is not surprising that so many individuals, especially students with special needs, experience difficulties in adequate social functioning (Howes 1984; Kendall and Morison 1984).

Identifying an Inventory of Social Skills

In an attempt to operationalize and define, in more behavioral terms, the skills of social competence, professionals have developed taxonomies or hierarchies of skills needed for social success (e.g., Stephens 1978; Turnbull, Strickland, and Brantley 1982; Walker, McConnell, Holmes, Todis, Walker, and Golden 1983). These taxonomies or inventories can be useful to the practitioner in identifying social skills for assessment and in designing curriculum and instruction for remediating social competence deficits. For example, Stephens (1978) has developed a social skills curriculum suitable for a wide age range and for both special needs and nonhandicapped persons. Stephens uses a task analysis model to create an inventory of skills, which contains 136 specific social skills and competencies. By using the full inventory, teachers of students at any given age level can identify those social skills and competencies needed for social success with the peer group. The major categories and subcategories of social skills in the Stephens inventory are shown in Table 22-1.

Assessing Social Skills

Many types of social skills assessment techniques are available. These range from systematic observations of the person's interactions with peers in naturalistic settings to the use of standardized instruments. Social skills assessment is popular both with practitioners and with researchers attempting to understand how individuals learn and use social skills. For both groups of professionals, assessment is based on the assumption that social skill deficits cannot be remediated before they are systematically assessed.

Problems with Assessing Social Skills

A number of problems in the assessment of social skills can make it difficult to obtain valid

Table 22-1 Categories and Subcategories of Social Skills as Outlined by Stephens

Environmental Behaviors
Caring for the Environment
Dealing with Emergencies
Lunchroom Behavior
Mobility around One's Environment

Interpersonal Behaviors
Accepting Authority
Coping and Conflict
Gaining Attention
Greeting Others Appropriately
Helping Others
Making and Maintaining Conversation
Playing with Others Appropriately
Positive Attitude toward Others
Property: One's Own and the Property of Others

and reliable information. As such, these problems contribute to errors of data collection and interpretation in social skills assessment.

A major problem with assessment of social skills is that many social behaviors are situation specific, that is, a person may exhibit a given social skill in one situation but not in another. For example, in one situation, a child who is the object of a practical joke may react good-naturedly; at another time, that child may respond by a loss of temper. Differential behavior may occur because the child perceives the two situations as being different and worthy of different responses to the same stimulus (the practical joke). Therefore practitioners collecting information on a person's social skills must be aware of the antecedent events and environmental factors that might have contributed to the individual's response.

A second problem in social skills assessment is that people's ideas of what constitutes acceptable social behavior differ greatly. Such differences exist in terms of culture, the developmental levels of both the rater and target child, and personal beliefs. For example, consider the question What should a child do if hit by a younger child? In the white, Anglo culture, restraint (walking away) would be the proper social response, and the child who exhibited such restraint would be applauded. In certain other cultures, however, the belief that you get what you ask for is an accepted axiom, and the older child would be justified in hitting the younger child *if* the younger child struck first. Such problems in defining acceptable and unacceptable social skills lead to problems in designating which behaviors should be assessed and in defining what constitutes problem behavior for a child in social skill adjustment.

A third source of error in social skills assessment is the reliability of the person doing the reporting. Often, questionnaires regarding children's social competence are administered to parents, teachers, peers, or the target child. Such information is only as good as the accuracy of the respondent's observations. But as noted in earlier chapters, people are notoriously inaccurate when reporting on the behavior of others (or themselves). Thus, in cases where people's perceptions of a child's social behavior do not correlate with one another, uncontrolled error exists in the assessment process.

Because there are problems with the validity and reliability of social skills assessment (and with affective functioning assessment), the accuracy of such measurement and evaluation should be enhanced by the use of multiple methods and sessions for data collection, rather than a single method or session (Cartledge and Milburn 1986; Ollendick and Hersen 1984). For that reason, assessment information regarding children's social skills should come from three sources: *adults, peers,* and the *target child* (Cartledge and Milburn 1986). To the extent that information from these three sources correlates, reliability and validity are increased and error is reduced.

Assessment of Students by Adults

Social skills assessment of students by knowledgeable adults includes a variety of scales, inventories, and observation techniques (Cartledge and Milburn 1986).

Behavior Checklists and Rating Scales

Parents, teachers, and other adults familiar with the student's social behavior may often be asked to fill out a checklist or observation form about that behavior in various situations. People typically chosen to complete these forms are those who have occasion to see the person in a variety of social situations, both in and out of school. Teacher ratings are used to assess the student in a variety of in-school social situations (some of them informal, such as lunch or recess); parental and other adult ratings are useful in gauging the relationship between the individual's in-school and out-of-school social behavior. However, these latter ratings should be interpreted with caution because the people completing the ratings may actually be part of the social problem requiring remediation (Beck 1986; Humphreys and Ciminero 1979)!

Behavior checklists and rating scales have a number of advantages. They are easy to administer and score and can be given to various types of people. By seeking agreement among a number of respondents on the same instrument, the professional can glean information about areas that need remediation across social situations (Cartledge and Milburn 1986). However, such instruments should possess proven reliability and validity, and the age, sex, and cultural differences of respondents should be taken into account (Rie and Friedman 1978).

Standardized Checklists

A large variety of standardized rating scales and checklists are available to the practitioner. Some of the more popular instruments are briefly described here.

The Walker Problem Behavior Identification Checklist: The Walker Problem Behavior

Identification Checklist (WPBIC) (Walker 1983) is an instrument designed for use with children from preschool through grade six. It is a revision of an earlier test designed in 1973.

The WPBIC consists of a fifty-item checklist of child behaviors and characteristics that is completed by the child's teacher. The test has been factored into five scales that measure the extent to which the child experiences the following disturbed behaviors: acting out, withdrawal, distractibility, disturbed peer relations, and immaturity. The teacher is asked to decide whether each checklist item occurred or did not occur during the preceding two months. There are separate forms for boys and girls.

Administration of the entire checklist requires less than fifteen minutes. Each item carries a score weight that, according to the test author, represents the handicapping influence of that behavior in the context of the child's school adjustment. Score weights are summed within each of the five scales and then converted to T-scores for interpretation. According to the test manual, a T-score higher than sixty on any of the five scales represents an at-risk child in need of referral and remediation.

The 1983 revision of the WPBIC was standardized on three samples: preschool ($n = 469$), grades one through three ($n = 852$), and grades four through six ($n = 534$). Separate norms exist for males and females. Students in this standardization group resided in two towns in Oregon and Washington. However, the sample characteristics are described no further in the manual. The WPBIC was also administered to a norm group of forty elementary-aged "handicapped students" (26 "severely learning disabled," 9 "mentally retarded," 1 "communication disordered," 1 "deaf"). However, these norms should not be used because of the restricted size and range of the student sample and the problems of their handicap classifications.

Split-half and test-retest reliability information is presented. Across the five scales, test-retest reliability ranges from .43 to .88. Split-half reliability is reported as .98.

Information regarding concurrent and criterion-related validity is available. In terms of concurrent validity, the WPBIC possesses some problems; it requires the teacher to infer behavior to the child's motivational or internal states. For example, the teacher is asked to decide whether the child "is listless or continually tired." Whereas listless behavior can be adequately observed and described, it is impossible for the teacher to state that this behavior is occurring *because* the student is tired (i.e., one cannot see tiredness).

The second major criticism of the WPBIC is that it measures only the existence or nonexistence of behavior, without any mention of degree, frequency, or duration. Even though the instrument is a checklist, and thus designed to yield a rough measure of behavior occurrence, some mention in the items of frequency or degree would be helpful in interpreting test results.

In summary, the WPBIC can be useful to the teacher in assessing the social and peer group skills of children. It is easy to administer and score and has a strong reliability and norm sample (although representativeness is not adequately discussed in the manual). One major criticism of its validity is that the teacher has to infer internal states of students. Furthermore, it does not measure behavioral degree or frequency. However, the behavior profile yielded across its five scales can be of use in both assessment and instruction.

Child Behavior Checklist: The Child Behavior Checklist (CBL) (Achenbach and Edelbrock 1983) is designed to assess the behavioral problems and social competence of children from four to sixteen years of age as reported by parents and teachers. It can be self-administered or administered by an interviewer. The instrument consists of 118 items relating to behavior problems and 20 social competency items relating to the child's participation in sports, hobbies, games, activities, and so forth. A direct observation form (97 items) and a teacher's report form (113 items) accompany the checklist. There are three social competency scales: *activities, social,* and *school.*

No times for administration and scoring are reported in the test manual for the scales. Scores are used to create a global profile of the child's social competency and are reported in terms of *T*-scores.

The CBL is well standardized and technically strong. It was standardized on 1,300 children who were representative in terms of the U.S. census, sex, socioeconomic background, and other relevant variables. Several types of reliability are reported, including test-retest reliability after one-week and three-month intervals. Even after a three-month interval, reliability of parental ratings range from .84 to .89—an extremely stable reliability coefficient. In terms of the instrument's validity, several studies have supported both its construct and its criterion-related validity.

In summary, the CBL appears to be a strong checklist for parental and teacher assessment of the social competency of children. Although it suffers from the disadvantages of checklists in general (not providing enough in-depth diagnostic information), it is a very strong instrument in terms of technical quality and is recommended for use by the educational professional.

Social Skills for Severely Retarded Adults: An Inventory and Training Program: Social Skills for Severely Retarded Adults (SSSRA) (McClenran, Hoekstra, and Bryan 1980) is one of the few social skills assessment instruments applicable for the severely handicapped, adult population. As such, it is a highly useful instrument for professionals working with severely mentally retarded individuals.

The program is composed of a Basic Social Skills Inventory designed to assess social functioning in ten main areas, such as group instruction, maintaining eye contact, and appropriate physical interactions. Each area or scale is subdivided into a hierarchy of objectives. From the assessment results, the professional can create an IEP consisting of up to ten training goals in social skills. The creation of this social IEP is outlined in the second part of the instrument, the Basic Social Skills Training Program.

The SSSRA is completely criterion-referenced. No norms exist for the instrument. However, the technical information in the test manual is scanty. For example, the only information given in terms of reliability refers to interrater reliability, which the authors claim ranges from 80 to 100 percent. Little or no information is given regarding the test's validity, and no rationale is offered for choosing the particular skill areas over other possibilities.

In summary, the SSSRA is unique in that it assesses the social functioning of moderately and severely mentally retarded persons. In that respect, it may prove useful to professionals working with this population. It is unfortunate, however, that the technical information on the instrument is so incomplete. More is needed to make the test even stronger and more useful.

Informal Scales and Inventories

Teachers may wish to use informal assessment procedures to test social skills. Such informal assessment is appropriate in cases where the teacher is interested in measuring a specific skill rather than a set of general skills. Likewise, informal assessment of social skills can be situation specific. In these cases, the best checklists are probably those composed by the practitioner.

In creating checklists of social skills, it is important for the teacher to phrase items in *behavioral* terms so that observable behaviors rather than inferred motivations are being checked (Mager 1972). For example, rather than the phrase "Shows interest in talking to others," the item should read "Addresses others appropriately." As you can see, the first item is nonbehavioral and infers a motivation; the second item is observable and behavioral.

Informal behavior checklists are useful tools if constructed properly. They are quick to administer and score and can yield specific information about how the child functions in situations of interest to the teacher.

Observing Children's Social Skills

The most obvious way for adults to assess children's social skills is to observe the children interacting with peers. As noted in earlier chapters, however, behavioral observation can be difficult in terms of adequately recording relevant behavior, not missing important behavior, and obtaining interrater reliability. These problems are even more critical in observing children's social interactions where, unlike much academic observational assessment, there is no written record of the children's behaviors. For these reasons, the practitioner interested in social functioning must be extremely careful in collecting and interpreting data gained through observation techniques.

Observation in the Natural Environment

The assessment of social skills can be carried out by observing individuals in their own environment. The teacher may, for example, wish to observe a student during recess, on the playground, during an afterschool activity, or during lunch to gain information on how the individual interacts and gets along with peers. However, because such interactions can be subtle and fleeting, the professional must be sure that the observations are systematic, reliable, and accurate.

The issue of obtaining systematic field observations is covered in Chapter 11; the reader is referred to that chapter for a review. Because social behaviors are finite and fleeting and because abnormal or nonfacilitative social behaviors may be relatively infrequent (it only takes a few of these inappropriate responses to get someone ostracized), *event* rather than duration recording of social behavior is suggested (Bijou, Peterson, and Ault 1968; Mann 1976). In such recording, the rater simply enumerates if, when, and under what circumstances an event took place so that discrete behaviors can be recorded and later analyzed. Examples of such behaviors are saying please and thank you, smiling, and asking questions.

It should be pointed out that social behavior is apt to change when the observation techniques are overt and obvious. People act differently, especially socially, when they know that they are being observed and recorded (Kent and Foster 1977). Therefore, the observation should be carried out as unobtrusively as possible by the teacher or practitioner lest the target person present an artificial picture of social behavior.

Observations in Contrived Situations

It is often difficult or impossible for the teacher to wait for a given social situation to occur in the student's natural environment. Such an occurrence could take days, weeks, or months, or it might never occur. Even if it does occur, there is no guarantee that at that precise moment the teacher will be acting as a systematic observer and record the behavior.

For these reasons, it is sometimes necessary to contrive social environments and stimuli so the student's responses can be observed and assessed. Two contrived assessment situations are discussed here: creative social environments and role-playing situations.

Contrived Social Environments: Suppose a teacher wished to see how a child shared desired objects, toys, or equipment during free-time situations. One way to accomplish this would be to follow the child to the playground and watch the target child's sharing behavior. However, a sharing situation over a toy that the child coveted might not occur for some time, or the teacher might not be present to record the information when it did occur. For these reasons, the teacher might consider creating a contrived free-play situation in the classroom where a toy was available that the teacher knew the child coveted. In this case, there would be only one such toy and many children (including the target child) who wanted it. The teacher could then contrive the situation, sit back, and record and assess the target child's behavior (Beck, Forehand, Neeper, and Baskin 1982; Stephens 1978).

Contrived assessment situations can often become quite sophisticated. For example, Michelson et al. (1983) describe an example using hidden videotaping and "confederate" children in a contrived situation to observe directly and assess the social behavior of two target children during a sports game. Using the videotape, the teacher was then able to review the children's behavior at her leisure as well as check her own reliability.

The major problem with using the contrived situation to assess social skills is one of ethics. Obviously, some deception and manipulation are used in a contrived environment. It is important that the teacher inform parents about what is being done (and why) and obtain parental permission. The children must also be debriefed at the end of the session. Finally the contrived situation must be benign, that is, cause no physical or psychological harm to the target or confederate children.

Role Playing: *Role playing* is often used in clinical and assessment situations that measure social skills. Role playing involves giving the person (and/or peers) a situation and an environment to act in and then allowing the student to improvise (act) resolutions to the problem(s) presented. In the assessment

environment, role-playing techniques possess the advantage of allowing the observer to define the precise environmental conditions under which the target person's behavior took place. It also allows the teacher to hold extraneous and noncontrolled environmental conditions to a minimum. However, the disadvantage is that the subject realizes that the situation is contrived and artificial and may not take the role or the situation seriously. To possess validity as an assessment technique, it is important that certain conditions be understood and met by both the teacher and the actors (Corsini 1966). These conditions are described in Table 22-2.

Table 22-2 Role-Playing Conditions: Components and Examples

Conditions for Successful Role Playing

1. *It is a close representation of real-life behavior.* Although staged, every effort is made to reconstruct the natural conditions as closely as possible. The situations enacted are ones which the participant has either previously encountered or will very likely experience in the near future.

2. *It involves the individual holistically.* That is, the participant is required to respond totally to the situation. In role playing the participant must think or employ cognitions, he must respond emotionally or use feeling, and he must act or use drama.

3. *It presents observers with a picture of how the patient operates in real-life situations.* This aspect provides assessment information so that the observer can determine skill competence under various social conditions.

4. *Because it is dramatic, it focuses attention on the problem.*

5. *It permits the individual to see himself while in action in a neutral situation.* Role playing provides a mechanism whereby the individual may analyze his own behavior and recognize how certain actions can trigger various responses (sometimes negative ones) from others.

Source: Reprinted with permission from G. Cartledge and J. Milburn, *Teaching Social Skills to Children,* Copyright 1986, Pergamon Books Ltd.

For role-playing assessment to be effective, it must contain a variety of components that include the *practice situation, standard script, prompts,* and *videotaping* and *rating* (see Table 22-3). An example of some of these components can be seen in two of the nine situations of the Behavioral Assertiveness Test for Children (BAT–C) (Bornstein, Bellack, and Hersen 1977), an experimental role-playing test designed to measure the social skills (assertive) behavior of children (see Table 22-3). As seen from these situations, Bornstein and his co-workers gave students a particular situation to work on, followed a standard script, and gave students necessary prompts to get them started.

The validity of the role-playing situation as a social skills assessment tool has been questioned by some professionals (Bellack, Hersen, and Turner 1978). One criticism of the technique is that some children may not be able to act out their skills in contrived situations; these children may be judged as having poorer social skills than they actually possess. Put another way, if a person performs poorly in a social skills role-playing situation, is it due to a social skills deficit or to poor acting skills? Likewise, some students may not take the role-playing situation seriously, or they may take it *too* seriously and become anxious and unspontaneous. Finally, people typically act differently when they know they are being observed. Thus, role playing, like all other assessment models for social skills observation, must be used and interpreted with caution.

Social Skills Assessment by Peers

Sometimes peers can offer the most valid and reliable information about a target child's social skills. After all, peers interact with this person on a daily basis. Thus, who knows the target person's social strengths and weaknesses better than do peers? For these reasons, peer assessments of a target person's

Table 22-3 Components of a Role-Playing Assessment and Evaluation

A.

1. Practice Situation: Before the actual role-playing situation, pilot scenes are used to judge whether the child understands the task. These scenes can also be used as a warm-up to break down inhibitions toward the role-playing task.

2. Standard Script: A standard script should be used across all role-playing testing conditions to ensure uniformity of the test situation and to reduce error.

3. Prompts: Following the description of each scene by the narrator, a prompt is given to the child, who is expected to respond.

4. Videotaping and Rating: To help ensure rater reliability and reduce error in rating student behavior, role-playing scenes should be videotaped.

B. Two Role-Playing Situations from the Behavioral Assertiveness Test for Children

Male or Female Model
Narrator: Your class is going to put on a play. Your teacher lists the parts, asking for volunteers. She reads a part you like and you raise your hand. But (Steve/Sue) raises (his/her) hand after you and says that (he/she) would like to get the part.
Prompt: "I want to play this part."

Male Model
Narrator: You're playing a game of kickball in school and it's your turn to get up. But Bobbie decides he wants to get up first.
Prompt: "I want to get up."

Source for B: M. Bornstein, A. Bellack, and M. Hersen, "Social-skills training for unassertive children: A multiple-baseline." *Journal of Applied Behavioral Analysis, 10,* 1977, 183–195. Used by permission.

social behavior can be a useful technique (Asher and Renshaw 1981; Furman 1984).

However, like adult assessments of social skills, peer assessments contain a component of error. The assessment of social skills by peers can become strongly situationally determined, especially for younger children (Taylor and Asher 1984). For example, a child who just shared his lunch with someone might be rated quite positive; that same child, twenty minutes later, might refuse to share the swing at recess and be rated by the same peer as negative. Thus, it is important that peer ratings of social skills be collected in conjunction with other assessment procedures to ensure validity. Likewise, peer assessment ratings should be collected over a number of times and situations to ensure rating reliability.

Various peer assessment techniques can be used to measure children's social skills (Hops and Lewin 1984; Hymel 1983). These techniques include *peer nominations, rating scales,* and *paired comparisons.*

Peer Nominations

Peer nominations are probably the simplest peer data to elicit from students. In the peer nomination system, students pick or nominate students in response to such questions as Who do you like the most? or Name three children in your class who do not share their toys. Respondents choose from one to three children in response to the questions, and a child is given one point for each nomination received.

Although the peer nomination system is a simple way to collect data, the technique itself is fraught with possible error. For example, young children have shown a tendency to name the same classmates repeatedly, regardless of the question asked, or nominate classmates on highly recent and situational information (e.g., someone with whom the child had just argued) (Asher, Singleton, Tinsley, and Hymel 1979). Other studies have shown children to be inconsistent in their nominations, actually using differential criteria for different questions or different students within their class (Hymel 1983).

Peer nominations have been used to identify popular, rejected (disliked), and neglected (ignored) children in given classrooms (Coie, Dodge, and Coppotelli 1982; Gottman 1977). Likewise, they have been used to iden-

tify "stars" and "isolates" within a classroom and to identify who likes and dislikes whom within the class (Berndt 1984; Hallinan and Tuma 1978). Finally, they have been used recently to identify not only *who* is popular and unpopular but also *why,* in terms of the specific social skills that children demonstrate to gain their popularity or unpopularity (Luftig 1987a, b).

Despite their usefulness and popularity, peer nominations do contain a great deal of potential error, especially when used with young children. Thus, they should be used with care as an assessment tool and only in conjunction with other assessment techniques (Cartledge and Milburn 1986).

Rating Scales

Rating scales allow individuals to rate people on given social skills and attributes rather than nominate individuals for tasks or social situations (Hymel 1983; Singleton and Asher 1977). In the rating scale procedure, the respondent rates a child on a scale (e.g., on a 1 to 5 scale) for each behavior listed. Table 22-4 contains some sample rating scale items that measure social skills.

The rating scale procedure has several advantages. First, if the teacher wishes, *each* student in the class can be rated; conversely, the practitioner can ensure that the target person is rated on each item by all respondents. In the nomination procedure, there is no guarantee that any information will be obtained on the target person (i.e., that the target person *ever* will be nominated). In such cases, information regarding the target person must be inferred from the absence of such nominations. Second, the rating procedure is easy to administer and score. Children simply circle a number or letter applying to the behavior exhibited by the target person, and a total score is assigned depending on the target individual's score over all the respondents. Rating scales have been found to be reliable and

Table 22-4 Social Skills Rating Scale

		Responses				
		1	2	3	4	5
		No Skill	Little Skill	Adequate Skill	Good Skill	Considerable Skill
1.	Follows Group Rules	1	2	3	4	5
2.	Complies with Reasonable Peer Requests	1	2	3	4	5
3.	Takes Turns	1	2	3	4	5
4.	Shares with Others	1	2	3	4	5
5.	Cooperates with Others	1	2	3	4	5
6.	Participates in Group Activities	1	2	3	4	5
7.	Offers to Assist Others	1	2	3	4	5
8.	Addresses Others Appropriately	1	2	3	4	5
9.	Reinforces Others	1	2	3	4	5
10.	Offers Encouragement to Others	1	2	3	4	5

valid for use with children, even with pre-school youngsters (Hymel 1983). In fact, the rating scale measure yields the highest test-retest reliability coefficients of the three types of peer assessment discussed in this chapter (Asher et al. 1979; Hymel 1983). Thus, rating scales are social skills assessment tools that the educational professional should definitely consider.

Paired Comparisons

The paired-comparison technique is among the most involved and complicated of the social skills assessment procedures. With this technique, the target person is paired in turn with all the peers within a group. For each pair, group members are asked to state a preference for one or the other person in the pair. Each group member is thus "rotated" against every other member in a paired format, and a ranking or hierarchy of each person in the group is obtained.

Paired comparisons are rarely used by non-research personnel because of the extensive time needed to collect, score, and interpret all the data (Cohen and Van Tassel 1978; Hymel 1983). Consider a class of 30 students for which the paired-comparison format is used. Each student would need to make 900 comparisons (30 × 30) to complete the rotation; multiply that by 30 students and you have 27,000 pieces of data for the teacher to score and evaluate! Thus, unless there are compelling reasons to do otherwise, the teacher should use either the nomination or rating scale format to obtain peer ratings of a student's social skills.

Self-Assessment of Social Skills

The final approach to social skills assessment is self-assessment. With this technique, target persons rate themselves in terms of their own perceived social skills.

Although self-assessment social skills instruments are rare, the teacher may wish to explore two experimental instruments: the Children's Assertive Behavior Scale (CABS) (Michelson, Sugai, Wood, and Kazdin 1983) and the Matson Evaluation of Social Skills with Youngsters (MESSY) (Matson and Esveldt-Dawson, undated; Matson, Rotatori, and Helsel 1983). The CABS is a twenty-seven-item pencil and paper, multiple-choice instrument designed for elementary school-children. Students respond to brief situations reflecting social behaviors, such as empathy, making conversation, making requests, and

others. The MESSY consists of ninety-two items divided into five main factors: (1) Appropriate Social Skills, (2) Inappropriate Assertiveness, (3) Impulsive Behavior, (4) Overconfidence, and (5) Jealousy/Withdrawal. The MESSY uses a five-point rating scale rather than a multiple-choice format. Sample items from the MESSY are shown in Table 22-5.

Self-assessment scales have a number of problems. The greatest disadvantage is the possibility that respondents will misunderstand, misinterpret, or lie on items (Cartledge and Milburn 1986; Gresham and Elliot 1984). Likewise, although respondents may not engage in any of these behaviors, they simply may be unable to view and judge themselves objectively. At the same time, however, students' false or biased self-perceptions can be valuable to the professional. After all, many therapists will tell you that people who do not perceive that they possess a problem are not strong candidates for therapy or behavioral remediation. However, if self-assessment procedures are used by the practitioner, such information must be interpreted with extreme caution.

Table 22-5   Sample Items from the Matson Evaluation of Social Skills with Youngsters (MESSY)

	Self-Rating Form				
	Not at All	**A Little**	**Some**	**Much of the Time**	**Very Much**
1. I make other people laugh (tell jokes, funny stories, etc.).	1	2	3	4	5
2. I threaten people or act like a bully.	1	2	3	4	5
3. I become angry easily.	1	2	3	4	5
4. I am bossy (tell people what to do instead of asking).	1	2	3	4	5
5. I gripe or complain often.	1	2	3	4	5

Source: J. L. Matson and K. Esveldt-Dawson (undated). *Matson Evaluation of Social Skills with Youngsters (MESSY).* (Pittsburgh: University of Pittsburgh, unpublished report).

Affective Functioning and Self-Concept

The Nature of the Self-Concept

As children develop and learn about themselves as social beings, they begin to formulate belief systems about themselves and their ability to interact successfully with their environment. Before long, this belief system influences the interpretation of all environmental information that the child collects as well as the way that child interacts with the environment (Beane and Lipka 1980). This belief system is the *self-concept* (Beane and Lipka 1984).

The self-concept is the "composite of ideas, feelings, and attitudes people have about themselves" (Hilgard, Atkinson, and Atkinson 1979, p. 605). It is the means by which we explain our behavior and our environment's reaction to that behavior. In short, it is the way we define ourselves (Beane and Lipka 1984; Bromley 1978).

Self-concept is generally positive or negative. This is often reflected both in the nature of statements people make about themselves and in their unwillingness or willingness to engage in given behaviors (e.g., raising a hand in class, asking someone for a date, trying out for the football team). Because the self-concept is such an important, pervading belief system, its measurement and the remediation of negative self-concept belief systems should be a priority with educational professionals (Beane and Lipka 1984; Luftig 1982).

The Self-Concept of Special Needs Learners

Strong evidence suggests that self-concepts of students possessing handicaps and special needs are significantly more negative than those of nonhandicapped counterparts (Boersma, Chapman, and Battle 1979; Gresham 1983; Luftig 1982) This finding holds true for a variety of persons including those possessing mental retardation, learning disabilities, visual and motor impairments, and culturally diverse individuals.

The diminished or negative self-concept functioning of persons with special needs has strong implications for professionals dealing with exceptional children. It is crucial that adequate assessment of self-concept be included in the special needs student's Individualized Assessment Program. In addition, objectives and methods for remediating negative self-concepts must be included in the IEP for at-risk students. This is particularly important because it has been demonstrated that negative self-concepts developed in childhood are often carried into the adult years (Luftig 1987a, b; Oden 1986).

The Multidimensional Nature of the Self-Concept

The term *self-concept* is often used incorrectly, implying that there is a unitary, single self-concept that each person possesses. Rather, evidence suggests that the self-concept is actually multifaceted or multidimensional, that is, each person possesses a number of self-concepts (Marsh and Shavelson 1985; Shavelson and Bolus 1982).

A partial listing of the different self-concepts that each person possesses is shown in Figure 22-1. As shown, people possess beliefs about themselves both in and out of school; such self-concepts include beliefs about their physical, social, and intellectual selves. Additionally, each self-concept can be subdivided into academic subject matters and general beliefs about academic talent and skills.

Effect of the Multidimensional Self-Concept on Assessment: The following critiques of self-concept assessment instruments show that most authors of these instruments adhere to the theory of the multidimensional nature of the self-concept, and they have composed

Figure 22-1   Types of Self and Self-Concepts

Self as Member of a Family

as son or daughter
as brother or sister
as grandchild
as niece or nephew
as older or younger sibling
as parent
as aunt or uncle

Self as Peer

as playmate
as member of a clique or club
as best friend

Self as Person with Attributes

height
weight
hair, eye color
skin color
physical development

Self as Student

as learner
as participant in school activities
as academic achiever

Source: J. Beane and R. Lipka, *Self-Concept, Self-Esteem, and the Curriculum* (1984). (Boston: Allyn and Bacon). Used by permission.

their tests accordingly. Thus, while most self-concept assessment instruments assess the general self-concept, they also yield specific self-concept scores in such areas as academic, physical, and peer group self-concepts.

This poses a problem for educational test consumers who must choose those self-concept assessment instruments that measure the facet of self-concept in which they are interested. The teacher interested in assessing home self-concept must make sure *before* purchasing and administering the test that the instrument yields a measure of the child's self-concept functioning in the home. Otherwise, this self-concept of interest will not be evaluated, and time and money will be wasted.

Commercially Available Self-Concept Assessment Instruments

A large number of self-concept assessment instruments exist, and initially, this myriad of tests may be confusing to the consumer. However, these tests can be divided into a 3 × 3 factorial design of *age* of test taker (preschool, elementary/middle school, adolescent/adult) and *response type* required (yes–no, rating scale, open response). A factorial sample is shown in Figure 22-2.

Scales for Different Age Groups

Some self-concept assessment instruments have been designed for preschool children (e.g., I Feel–Me Feel Inventory). Others have been designed for elementary and middle-school children (e.g., How I See Myself Scale) and for adolescents and adults (e.g., Rosenberg Self-Esteem Scale). Finally, some self-concept instruments bridge the gaps between ages and are designed for people at various developmental stages (Tennessee Self-Concept Scale). Some basic generalizations can be made regarding the age range of the target population:

1. The younger the child targeted by the test, the more reading becomes an issue. Many of the self-concept tests intended for young children have attempted to circumvent this problem by designing pictorial or symbol tests (e.g., Self–Social Symbols Task or the I Feel–Me Feel Inventory). However, pictorial tests possess the problem of differential interpretation of the pictures. Children sometimes respond to items on the basis of liking or not liking the pictures rather than to the content of the questions.

2. The younger the test taker, the less reliable the test results are likely to be. Young children tend to be extremely situational and tied to the immediate environment when assessing their self-concept (Hymel 1983). For example, a preschool child who has just been rebuffed on the playground may report a lower self-concept than an hour later after someone has called that child a best friend.

Figure 22-2   A 3 × 3 Factorial Design of Self-Concept Assessment Instruments

Type of response required	Age of Test Taker		
	Preschool	Elementary/ Middle school	Adolescent/Adult
Yes/No			
Rating scale			
Open response			

3. The older the respondent, the more reliable the data are likely to be and the less tied to the immediate environment. Additionally, questions for older students can be more abstract and linguistically complex.

For these reasons, the self-concept data obtained from young or nonverbal children must be interpreted cautiously.

Types of Responses on Self-Concept Measures

Generally, self-concept scales allow one of three response types: yes–no, rating scales, or open responses. Yes–no items are just that; the student responds yes or no to each question. Rating scales allow the student to choose from four or five alternatives such as:

- That's Never Like Me
- Not Usually Like Me
- Sometimes Like Me
- Like Me
- Always Like Me

The student is allowed to choose only one alternative for each question.

Finally, the open response format allows the student to write (or speak) in open prose

in response to the question. The students can say whatever and how much they like.

Test authors choose a given self-concept response mode along the continuum of ease of pupil responding, ease of scoring/interpretation, and amount of information provided by a student's answers. For these reasons, it is up to the test consumers to choose a response mode of a given self-concept instrument that meets their needs in terms of information provided and time/scoring efficiency.

The test critiques below represent just a small sample of all of the self-concept assessment instruments available. An attempt was made to include tests for a variety of developmental ages and response modes as well as ease in obtaining such tests. Therefore, hard-to-obtain tests or self-concept instruments used primarily for research purposes were not included.

Piers-Harris Children's Self-Concept Scale (The Way I Feel about Myself)

The Piers–Harris Child's Self-Concept Scale (Piers–Harris) (Piers and Harris 1969, 1984) is an eighty-item, yes–no response-mode test designed for children in grades four through twelve. It can be administered individually or in groups. The child circles yes or no to questions indicating belief that a given statement does or does not apply to himself or herself. The instrument is written at about the third-grade level, and the entire test takes approximately twenty minutes to administer.

The Piers–Harris yields seven types of self-concept scores: Intellectual and School, Behavior, Physical Appearance and Attributes, Anxiety, Popularity, Happiness and Satisfaction, and a Total Self-Concept score. The new version of the test also contains a Response Bias Index and an Inconsistency Index to help ensure response validity. The Response Bias Index assesses acquiescence or negative response set on the part of the respondent; the Inconsistency Index detects random response patterns. Both indexes must be low for the child's responses on other items to be judged as valid.

Raw scores on the Piers–Harris are converted to percentiles and T-scores for each self-concept score and the total self-concept score. Although the test can be administered and scored by teachers and paraprofessionals, the manual cautions that the test should be interpreted by someone well trained in psychological assessment. As a safeguard, completion of a User Qualification Form is required to purchase the scale from the publisher.

The Piers–Harris has not been renormed since the original standardization in the 1960s, which was carried out on 1,183 children in grades four through twelve from one school district in Pennsylvania. Caution is strongly advised regarding the generalizability of this group to other children. However, the authors do offer a large amount of data on the standardization population so that the test consumer can make decisions about the applicability of the norm group to the test children.

The Piers–Harris appears to be highly reliable. Test-retest studies indicate reliability ranging from .42 to .96 and a mean reliability of .73, about average for tests of affective functioning. Studies investigating the test's internal consistency yield reliability coefficients ranging from .88 to .93 for the total scale.

Extensive data are also available on the test's validity. The test correlates moderately with other measures of self-concept (.21 to .59), and research tends to validate the existence of the six factors outlined and measured by the test.

In summary, the Piers–Harris is probably the most popular of all the self-concept assessment instruments available today. Its revised manual makes it easier to use, and the test retains its strong technical and theoretical qualities. It can be used with a high degree of confidence by the educational professional, as long as its results are interpreted with caution by someone well trained in psychological assessment.

Culture-Free Self-Esteem Inventories for Children and Adults

The Culture-Free Self-Esteem Inventories (SEI) (Battle 1981) are a series of yes–no, self-report checklists designed to measure a person's self-perception. A unique feature of the tests is the author's assertion that the SEI accomplishes this goal free of cultural context and psycholinguistic skills. According to the author, the SEI is a culture-free assessment instrument.

The Children's SEI is a sixty-item instrument designed to assess the child's general self-concept as well as self-concept related to school, peers, and home. The two forms of the Children's Scale are the long form (Form A) and the thirty-item short form (Form B). The adult version is a forty-item instrument that yields a total self-concept score as well as personal and social self-concept scores. The phrasing of items is counterbalanced for positive and negative tone to discourage response set and acquiescence on the part of examinees. Both inventories contain Lie Scales that indicate the test taker's defensiveness.

The SEI Inventories can be administered individually or in groups. For children below grade three, and for nonreaders and persons with special needs, items are read to examinees. The inventory kits contain a cassette tape to aid oral administration. Total administration time for both inventories is approximately twenty minutes. Any educational professional can administer and score the test, and no special training is needed.

Scoring is accomplished using a special template. There are self-concept scores for each subtest, a total self-concept score, and a score for the Lie Scale. Raw scores are converted to percentile ranks and T-scores. However, subscale scores should be interpreted very carefully because even a slight difference in raw score subscale scores can dramatically change the person's percentile rank by more than a decile.

The Children's SEI (Form A) was standardized on 891 elementary school students (grades 3 through 6) and 224 junior high school students. Form B was standardized on 212 elementary school students and 274 adults. The Adult SEI was standardized on 252 adults. No other characteristics of the norm groups are given in the manual. Separate norms are provided for males and females, although the reason for this is not outlined in the manual.

The manual reports extensive reliability data. Apparently, all of the reliability and validity data of the Children's SEI were collected on a group of students residing in Edmonton, Alberta, Canada. No information on the test-retest interval is given. For Form A, test-retest reliabilities range across grade levels from .81 to .90. Subscale reliabilities are almost equally high, ranging from .52 to .93. The test-retest reliability for the short form (Form B) is comparable to that of Form A. The test-retest of the adult SEI was administered to 127 college students with a resulting

test-retest reliability of .81. As with Forms A and B, the test-retest interval is not given in the manual.

Attempts have been made to establish content, concurrent, and criterion-related validity. Content validity was established according to the test author by writing items "intended to cover all areas of the construct" (of self-esteem) (p. 14). The 60 items of Form A came from an initial pool of 150 items. Concurrent validity was established by correlating the SEI with the Coopersmith Self-Esteem Inventory. Concurrent validity coefficients range from .72 to .84 for males and from .66 to .91 for females. This means that the SEI measures much the same content as the Coopersmith, and the SEI's author assumes that the Coopersmith is valid for assessing children's self-concept. Finally, the SEI was correlated with students' perceptions of ability, teacher ratings of students, and intelligence, but was *not* a good instrument for differentiating scores between handicapped and nonhandicapped students.

In summary, the SEI inventories are yes–no checklists of self-concept that are easy to administer and score. Although the test possesses strong reliability and validity, its norms are somewhat in question and subject to fluctuations and problems of interpretation. Perhaps the SEI's most significant feature is its author's assertion that it is a culture-fair, culture-free test. Even though the test is available in Spanish and French, there is no evidence that the test is less culturally loaded than are other self-concept assessment instruments. Thus, without further evidence, there is no reason to suppose that the SEI is any more appropriate for culturally diverse students than are other self-concept tests.

Coopersmith Self-Esteem Inventories

The Coopersmith Self-Esteem Inventories (CSEI) (Coopersmith 1981) are three self-report questionnaires designed to measure a

person's self-perceptions. The format requires the respondent to indicate that a statement is "like me" or "unlike me." Thus, the
CSEI is really a modified yes–no type of instrument. It is appropriate for use with individuals aged eight to fifteen.

The School Form of the CSEI, which is the
focus of this review, consists of a fifty-item
inventory. It can be divided into four subscales: Peers, Parents, School, and Personal
Interests. The School Form is accompanied
by a Lie Scale to assess respondent defensiveness. The Adult Form, based on the School
Form, is appropriate for individuals older
than fifteen.

The manual directions for administration
and scoring are easy to follow. A relatively
sophisticated amount of reading and psycholinguistic ability is needed by test takers.
Administration takes ten to fifteen minutes,
and scores are reported in terms of means,
standard scores, and percentile ranks.

The technical quality of the CSEI is weak,
with little information given regarding the
standardization sample. Whereas reliability
data based on a number of studies (internal
consistency) range from .87 to .92, the validity data offered in the manual are scant and
unconvincing.

In summary, the CSEI, although a popular
instrument, is not the best one available in
terms of technical quality, theoretical orientation, and utility of information given. The informed test consumer should consider using
another instrument.

Tennessee Self-Concept Scale

The Tennessee Self-Concept Scale (TSCS)
(Fitts 1965) is a one-hundred-item, self-
description instrument that contains ninety
self-concept and ten lie items. The format of
the TSCS asks the test taker to respond to
each item using a 1 to 5 scale ranging from
"completely false" to "completely true."
Thus, the respondent has more freedom in

answering questions than with yes–no surveys. The instrument is appropriate for use
with individuals aged twelve and over and requires a sophisticated reading and language
level.

The two forms of the instrument are the
Counseling Form and the Clinical Form. Of
the two, the Counseling Form is more appropriate for school use; the Clinical Form is
more appropriate for use in psychothera-
peutic settings. The Counseling Form yields
fifteen profile scores.

The TSCS is relatively easy to administer
but difficult to score and interpret. It can be
administered individually or in groups, and
administration takes twenty minutes. The
manual's scoring instructions, although clear,
are nevertheless quite involved and require
some training and practice.

The TSCS was standardized on 626 people
who varied in age from twelve to sixty-eight.
The sample is relatively representative in
terms of sex, educational and social background, and geographic diversity. However,
white students are overrepresented in the
sample.

The reliability of the test is based on a sample of sixty college students using a retest interval of two weeks. Although the test-retest
reliability of the TSCS ranges from .60 to .90,
this sample is inadequate in terms of number
and representativeness. No internal reliability
is reported, an important type of reliability in
a test that contains so many subscales.

The TSCS possesses an unproven validity,
and the quality of the instrument's validity
depends largely on what type of validity interests the practitioner. The test correlates extremely highly with other affective measures
(e.g., the Minnesota Multiphasic Personality
Inventory); there is less agreement as to
whether the instrument is particularly good at
differentiating normal from at-risk individuals
in terms of self-concept functioning and general mental health.

In summary, the TSCS is probably the

most complex and ambitious of all of the available and commonly used self-concept inventories. It yields fifteen subscores in the Counseling Form; the separate Clinical Form yields thirty profiled scores. Additionally, it allows the respondent more latitude in answering than do commonly used yes–no scales. However, although it is relatively easy to administer, it is cumbersome to score and interpret and requires practice and skill on the part of the examiner. Finally, the technical quality of the instrument is questionable, and it overlaps highly with other personality measures. In short, the instrument appears to have value for identifying the self-concept functioning of adolescents and adults, but it must be administered and interpreted with great care.

A Final Word on Social Skills and Affective Assessment

Traditionally, assessment of social skills and affective functioning has not been part of the school testing program. When such testing has taken place, it has been conducted by psychologists or guidance counselors working with students specifically referred to them because of emotional or maladaptive behavior.

In recent years, however, educational interest in social and affective functioning variables of all children has increased dramatically. People have begun to realize that the increase in substance abuse and in youth suicide and pregnancy has its roots in the way individuals feel about themselves. Furthermore, educators have come to realize that poor social skills and negative self-concepts cannot be remediated until they are adequately assessed.

It is this author's position that social skills and affective assessment should become part of the assessment program for all students, and particularly for special needs and at-risk pupils. It has been demonstrated that social skills and self-concept deficits are highly correlated with emotional maladjustment in adulthood. That is, the social skills and self-concepts we develop as children become the emotional baggage we carry throughout our lives. This baggage is difficult to unload in later life. Thus, children should be given social skills and self-concept enhancement activities throughout the school curriculum, and adequate assessment must take place in these areas to identify at-risk children in need of remediation.

SUMMARY

Educators are becoming more aware of the importance of social skills and affective functioning during the school years. The acquisition of adequate social skills and a healthy mental outlook and self-concept has been shown to affect people throughout their school years and into adulthood. Thus, the interest in the social and affective functioning of children in school seems justified.

Defining social skills is more difficult than identifying the skills of other, more traditional academic school subjects. Social skills are defined as those acceptable learned behaviors that enable the person to interact with others in ways that allow the person to elicit positive responses from others. Adequate social skills involve getting people to act in ways that we desire so that we can reach our social goals.

Social skills can be divided into two dimensions: skill components and skill processes. Skill components represent single, isolated skills and behaviors. Skill processes are situational, that is, knowing that certain skill components will work in some social situations and not in others. Skill processes depend on the person's ability to read and monitor social situations. Social competence is the ability to use both skill components and skill processes adequately. Given the complex nature of social competence, it is not surprising that so many children possess deficits in this area.

Various researchers have attempted to identify an inventory of social skills. Such inventories help the professional to identify the skills of social competence and to yield information on areas in need of assessment.

The assessment of social skills presents a number of problems. One problem is that social behavior is often situation specific, that is, a child may exhibit a skill in one situation but not in another. Another problem is the wide variation in what people consider acceptable social behavior. Differences exist in terms of culture, developmental behavior, and personal beliefs. Finally, a problem in social skills assessment exists with the reliability and validity of the person doing the reporting. People are not always extremely accurate or consistent in reporting information about a target child.

To counteract problems with the reliability and validity of social skills assessment, the accuracy of such measurement can be enhanced by collecting information from a variety of sources and over a number of situations. It is suggested that social skills assessment information be obtained from three sources: adults, peers, and the target child.

A variety of techniques can be used for adult reporting of children's social skills, including checklists, rating scales, and direct observation. A variety of standardized, commercial checklists and rating scales are available to professionals. In addition, the teacher can create informal scales and inventories. When observing children's social skills, the professional can choose naturalistic situations, create contrived environments, or use role playing.

Social skills assessment by peers can be quite useful. However, there is a relatively large error component in the assessment of social skills by peers, especially with young children. Peer assessment techniques include nominations, rating scales, and paired comparisons. Of the three, rating scales are the most useful and error free, and they are suggested for use.

Self-assessment by children of their own social skills can sometimes be useful, although the accuracy of such self-perceptions is a source of much error. Relatively few available instruments allow assessment of children's ratings of their social skills.

The assessment of children's self-concept is important. The self-concept is the belief system a person holds about one's self. This belief system affects everything a person says and does.

The self-concept is generally positive or negative. It has been found that the self-concept of special needs, at-risk children generally is significantly more negative than that of their nonhandicapped counterparts. Thus, the assessment of self-concept functioning of special needs learners is very important.

The self-concept is not a unitary entity; each person possesses a variety of self-concepts. Thus, the self-concept is multidimensional and multifaceted. Most self-concept assessment instruments reflect this multidimensional nature and yield a number of self-concept scores as well as a total or general score.

A large number of self-concept assessment instruments are available. Most of them can be categorized by the age level of the target individuals and the response mode that is employed. Basically, three response modes are used by test authors in devising self-concept assessment instruments: yes–no, rating scales, and open response. Each response mode possesses advantages and disadvantages.

STUDY QUESTIONS

1. What are social skills? How are they defined? Why are they important?

2. Do you believe that social skills should be taught in school? Why or why not? Do people learn social skills on their own? Defend your answers.

3. Define skill components and skill processes. How are they different? Can they be taught? How might this be accomplished?

4. What is social competency? What are its components? Why is the concept important?

5. What are some of the problems inherent in assessing social skills? Why is it more difficult, in some ways, to assess social skills than academic skills?

6. What are some methods adults can use to assess the social skills of children? What are the advantages and disadvantages of each of these methods? Which methods would you use? Defend your answer.

7. What are the advantages and disadvantages in using observations to assess children's social skills? What are some observational methods that can be employed? What are the strong and weak points of these methods?

8. What are some methods of peer assessment of children's social skills? What are the advantages and disadvantages of these methods? Why is such assessment important?

CHAPTER 23

Organizing, Reporting, and Applying Assessment Information

The discussion in preceding chapters focuses on assessment, that is, the appropriate collection of assessment information (measurement) and the subsequent interpretation of those data (evaluation).

This is as it should be. After all, this is a text about measurement and evaluation. However, there is another factor that must be discussed. What do you *do* with the information that has been gathered and interpreted?

The Identification–Learning Assistance Model

Identification of Performance Problems

Up to this point, we have discussed the identification of student performance problems. Such identification has, in the past, been labeled *diagnosis*. However, diagnosis implies a medical model of learning in which a student's learning problems or symptoms are diagnosed and somehow cured. Diagnosis also implies that areas of weakness are internal (part of the student) rather than at least partially a function of the person's environment.

This, however, is not the true nature of the process. Rather than being diagnosed, areas of student performance weakness are identified in the environments in which they occur. For this reason, the phrase *identification of student performance problems* is used.

Identification of student performance problems consists of pinpointing areas of weak performance (if such areas exist) and gathering information about the environmental conditions under which these weaknesses typically occur (Bransford 1979; Guerin and Maier, 1983). Some experts believe that activities leading to identification of student performance problems should also yield information about the causes of student performance weaknesses; others believe that such information is less important and implies a medical (i.e., etiological) model of academic functioning (Howell and Morehead 1986; Mann 1975).

Activities designed to identify student performance problems are concerned not only with the student but also with the environment in which learning takes place (Bransford 1979; Lerner 1981). Such concerns include, but are not necessarily restricted to, instructions given to students, task demands, and materials used. Each variable is analyzed in an attempt to understand areas of student performance strength and weakness as they occur in various environments.

It is important to realize that such activities offer information as to *what* student performance problems might be (see Figure 23-1). These activities are most concerned with identification of performance problems, not remediation. This is the concern of learning assistance.

Learning Assistance

Learning assistance is concerned with the remediation of student performance weak-

Figure 23-1 A Model of Identification of Performance Problems and Learning Assistance

I. Identification of Performance Problems

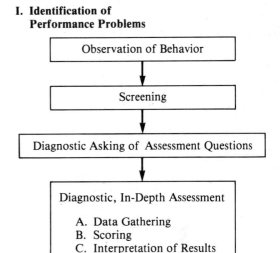

- Observation of Behavior
- Screening
- Diagnostic Asking of Assessment Questions
- Diagnostic, In-Depth Assessment
  - A. Data Gathering
  - B. Scoring
  - C. Interpretation of Results

II. Learning Assistance

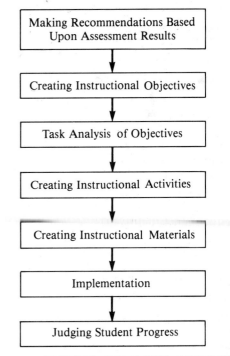

- Making Recommendations Based Upon Assessment Results
- Creating Instructional Objectives
- Task Analysis of Objectives
- Creating Instructional Activities
- Creating Instructional Materials
- Implementation
- Judging Student Progress

nesses as they occur in various environments. In the past, the term *prescription* was often used for this activity. However, prescription infers a medical model that identifies a deficiency (diagnosis) and then works to cure that deficiency (prescription). This is not the case. Learning assistance activities are centered on helping create materials and instructional activities designed to help the student learn appropriate responses in appropriate environments. These appropriate responses are what we call *learning*.

As seen in Figure 23-1, learning assistance involves making decisions regarding learning environments, instructional materials and equipment, instruction (teaching methods), and instructional style. Learning assistance and assessment are related in that these decisions are made on the basis of information gathered during the performance problem identification stage. To put it another way, anybody can make intuitive guesses about how to assist students in their learning, but valid assessment offers the professional insights and information on which to make educational decisions.

Formative and Summative Evaluation

Assessment information can be used in a variety of ways. In categorizing how such information is used we should review the differences between formative and summative evaluation.

The traditional use of assessment information has been in the area of *summative evaluation*. Summative evaluation uses assessment information to summarize or recapitulate a person's performance. Summative evaluation typically takes place after a unit of instruction and is used to assign a grade, label, or other designation that, in effect, summarizes a person's performance. In most cases, little is done with summative evaluation information after that grade or label has been assigned. Most traditional achievement tests (both for-

mal and informal) employ a summative evaluation format.

Formative evaluation, on the other hand, is ongoing, continuous assessment used to gauge the extent to which the student is mastering presented content. It is used for monitoring learning as it occurs and remediating or reteaching content that has not been mastered (Fuchs and Fuchs 1986; White 1986). The purpose of formative evaluation is *not* to assign a grade or label but to ensure that requisite skills are mastered before related, more complex content is presented.

In most cases, the type of evaluation information that is most helpful in assisting student learning is formative in nature. Such evaluation yields not only information about what the student has and has not mastered, but also insights as to the types of materials, instructional activities, and environments that have the greatest probability of ensuring learning. As such, formative assessment can be extremely helpful to professionals in the design of useful learning assistance activities for students possessing performance weaknesses.

How Assessment Information Is Used to Make Programmatic Decisions

Aptitude–Treatment Interactions

In the past, many educators believed that assessment information should be used to *predict* future student performance (Cronbach 1957, 1967; Glaser 1972). This prediction making generally involved four questions:

1. What is the student's area(s) of weakness?
2. Based on our assessment of student performance weaknesses, what can we predict about the future functioning of students if *no* remediational programming is provided?
3. Based on our assessment, what can we predict about the future functioning of students if remediational programming *is* provided?
4. Given the various types of remediational programming available, which will yield the best results in enhancing student performance?

Questions about assessment, predictions, and remediational programming are known as *aptitude–treatment interactions* (ATI) (Cronbach 1967, 1970; Howell and Morehead 1986). ATI assumes that persons with given abilities (aptitudes) will perform differentially in given programs (treatments). A further assumption is that certain treatments are consistently best for individuals possessing different types of problems, and that these treatments must be determined for each person and administered consistently for student performance to improve.

The Problem with ATI: On the surface, the logic of ATI seems impeccable. After all, the assumptions are that (1) people possess different abilities, (2) certain treatments are best for persons possessing particular ability or aptitude problems, and (3) the key to sound remediation is to link the right deficiencies with the right treatments. The logic of ATI is that if these assumptions are followed appropriately, student performance will be enhanced due to the facilitative nature of the aptitude–treatment interaction.

Evidence suggests that ATI has not been as effective as once believed (Berliner and Cahen 1973; Lloyd 1984). Apparently, assessing abilities and then placing students in a treatment condition designed to remediate that type of performance problem do not always lead to the degree of performance enhancement originally anticipated. It has been hypothesized that ATI often does not work for the following reasons (Howell and Morehead 1986).

Poorly Defined and Assessed Abilities: As we note in previous chapters, it is often difficult to assess abilities and aptitudes appropriately. Tests differ in power, validity, and the theoretical manner in which abilities are defined. Additionally, assessment of abilities using the ATI format has typically been global rather than in-depth and specific. Thus, the abilities of students have often been defined so generally that adequate understanding of specific abilities, strengths, and weaknesses is impossible.

Poorly Defined Treatments: The programmatic treatments designed to remediate student performance weaknesses have sometimes been poorly defined, vague, and ambiguous (Rhetts 1984). Instructional objectives used in these programs have included indefinite behaviors, such as *know, understand,* and *appreciate.* In cases where the remediational programs have been vague, ambiguous, or poorly defined, it has proven difficult, if not impossible, to assess how well those treatments enhanced student performance.

Changing Interaction Patterns: One assumption inherent in ATI is that abilities are stable and do not change as a function of changing environments. That is, that one's abilities will remain basically the same across environments and over time. This, however, has not been proven. For example, a child may actually demonstrate differential reading ability and behavior based on the purpose for reading, the environment under which reading is taking place, and the motivation to read. In such cases, it cannot be assumed that the effects of the interaction between abilities and treatment will remain stable over time. Sometimes these interactions change in their effectiveness or even direction as environmental situations change and abilities evolve. Traditional ATI situations usually do not consider the evolving nature of ability and the power of environment on interaction effects.

ATI as Summative Evaluation: ATI is basically summative evaluation. Assessment is used to make decisions about a student's abilities (summative evaluation), and the student is then placed in a given treatment. After a period of time, the student is reassessed, and a decision is made regarding the relative success of that treatment in enhancing performance (also summative evaluation). Such assessment is based on predictions of how students with certain abilities are going to perform if given certain treatments. To be effective, these tests must possess extremely powerful predictive validity. However, very few instruments possess such predictive power due to random and systematic error inherent in the test and variance among test takers.

The need is for *ongoing* evaluation that (1) measures student abilities at different and frequent times and (2) measures the effects of instruction (treatment) frequently, if not daily, to gauge student progress. Such assessment is inherent in formative evaluation. The following system of application of assessment information is driven by a formative evaluation model.

The Role of Data-Based Information in Programmatic Decisions

As stated earlier in this chapter, evaluation of a student's performance as a function of programmatic instruction and materials should be formative in nature. Such information is *data-based*. This means that decisions are made on the basis of patterns of student behavior obtained from empirically valid data collected at regular, fixed, and *frequent* intervals (Howell and Morehead 1986). Student performance is continuously and systematically evaluated, and programmatic decisions changed when deemed appropriate by the educational team (Fuchs, Deno, and Mirkis 1984; Howell 1986). To make sound, data-based programmatic decisions, educators must have valid information regarding current performance, progress, and trends.

Performance

Performance refers to how the student is currently operating. Knowledge of current levels of performance can be separated from knowl-

edge of past performance, and no predictions about future behavior are involved.

Current levels of performance are usually criterion-referenced. They measure the child's performance against requisite standards (intrapersonal) rather than against the performance of other persons (interpersonal). Additionally, such behavior is usually measured against some type of criterion or requisite levels of passing performance or mastery.

The description of current levels of performance requires the identification of a *target behavior*. This behavior must be described in precise, behavioral terms so that observers can readily agree whether the target behavior has actually taken place. For example, the target behavior "gets along with others" is not behaviorally stated; the behavior "coming in a physical proximity of five feet to another child during recess" is behaviorally stated.

Notice, also, that target behavior is used in the singular form. Each performance objective should contain only one target behavior. If more than one target behavior is included in a performance objective, one risks having to attend to too many behaviors at once. Additionally, decisions would have to be made as to whether one behavior might be causing or inhibiting the other. Such decisions are difficult to make. Therefore, it is strongly advised that each objective contain only one target behavior.

Progress

Progress means *behavior change*. In other words, we measure progress by assessing the degree of enhanced performance between what took place on a past date and what is occurring at present. Whereas performance gives the teacher an indication of how the student is currently operating, progress evaluation yields an index of how the student is currently performing in relation to past behavior. As such, progress evaluation goes beyond simply reporting current student performance.

Progress performance can be pictorially depicted by using a profile-type graph. Profiles usually have the variable of date or intervals between testing along the *X* axis and student score on a particular measure along the *Y* axis. By viewing such a profile, the teacher can readily see the progress (or lack of progress) that the student has made over time. Figure 23-2 contains a sample performance progress profile.

Assumptions of Progress Performance Evaluation: Some assumptions are made when evaluating student progress. First, for behavior progress to be meaningful, *the same behaviors must be assessed on all occasions*. For example, one of the author's children has been assessed on his sight vocabulary each year of his elementary school career. To assess his reading behavior, he was administered the same test of reading sight vocabulary each year. This child's progress, as measured by the same instrument, could be gauged from year to year. However, if the school had switched tests every year, it would have been impossible to make valid conclusions about the child's reading progress because the results on the different tests would not be completely comparable.

The second assumption of progress evaluation is that testing intervals should be roughly the same. Again, consider the child who has had sight word vocabulary tested on a regular basis. If this student had been assessed three times in his academic career, with time intervals between testing of two weeks, one-and-a-half years, and one month, it would be difficult to come to any conclusions about progress. On the other hand, if the testing intervals had been roughly the same between the three administrations (e.g., six months), evaluation of student progress between testing intervals would be possible.

Finally, it is assumed that the time intervals between program performance evaluation sessions will be relatively frequent. To be formative in nature, evaluation should probably occur at least weekly. In fact, formative progress evaluation is even more useful to the professional if administered every other day or daily. Progress performance evaluations spaced more than a week apart risk becoming summative in nature and are useful chiefly for assigning grades or categories to students.

Figure 23-2   Creating a Student Performance Profile

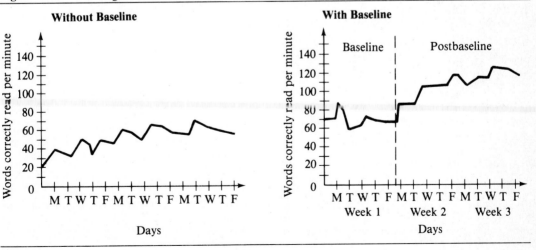

Gathering a Baseline: In assessing progress evaluation, it is sometimes advisable to collect a measure of *baseline* behavior. The baseline is the extent to which the target behavior occurs on its own without formal instruction or intervention. For example, suppose a teacher wished to assess as target behavior the amount of time that a student read independently during free time, after a behavior modification program was instituted. The teacher might first assess the degree of independent reading behavior exhibited by the child without any reward system. This degree of spontaneous independent reading behavior would indicate the baseline. An example of how progress from baseline might look pictorially is shown in the profile in Figure 23-2.

A baseline gives the teacher an indication of how much progress was made from the point at which no intervention was taking place. It is often considered a pure indication of the effectiveness of a given intervention program. This is because any behavioral change (progress) that takes place is assumed to be a result of the intentional programmatic intervention provided by the professional.

Trends

Sometimes student performance progress is not clear cut. For example, consider the progress profile of the two students shown in Figure 23-3. For the first student, Bob, progress is constant and positive. He is on a clear, well-defined path that shows improvement after every assessment interval.

Bob is a teacher's dream. Unfortunately, his performance is the exception rather than the norm. For most of us, progress is intermittent, with periods of backsliding followed by periods of moderate progress. One teacher has categorized successful teaching as "getting kids to take two steps forward for one step back rather than the other way around!" For most people, constant, unremitting progress is an unrealistic goal.

Now, inspect the progress of Sarah as shown in the same figure. Although Sarah's progress is not as linear and strong as Bob's, inspection of her performance profile indicates a *trend* toward behavior improvement. Such a profile would indicate to the teacher that, in general, Sarah's intervention program

Figure 23-3 Assessing Progress Trends of Two Students

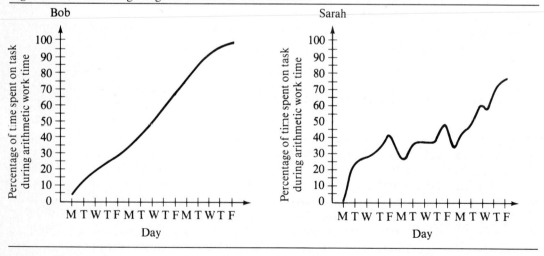

is relatively successful. Trend analysis would seem to indicate that her instructional program should be continued or adjusted slightly rather than changed drastically or altogether.

People slow down or even regress in their progress performance for various reasons including environmental circumstances, motivations, fatigue, and random error. It would be wonderful if progress performance could always be as linear and steady as Bob's. However, we live in a real world with real students. It is the teacher's task to inspect progress performance data in terms of positive trends and then to judge whether intervention change or continuation is in order.

Reporting Assessment Information

The remainder of this chapter deals with the pragmatic issues of translating assessment data into educational decisions. The first step in this process is the reporting of assessment information to interested individuals so that appropriate programmatic and intervention decisions can be instituted. Sound reporting of assessment results leads to sound programmatic activities, materials, and environments for students. However, to use assessment data correctly, they must be organized, displayed, and reported in a way that is comprehensible and interpretable to educational professionals, parents, and students. The first step in the process is information organization.

Organization of Assessment Data

In most situations, a student is not given a single assessment instrument to diagnose performance difficulties. Rather, the pupil is typically administered a battery of instruments (or a single instrument that serves as a battery) designed to identify specific performance strengths and weaknesses. The question then becomes How should these data be organized for interpretation and reporting?

To a certain extent, this problem is resolved by the requirement of the IEP. Under PL 94-142, the student's IEP must contain a list of all of the assessment instruments used to identify performance strengths and weaknesses. However, the educational professional may wish to go beyond the IEP in organizing data, or the in-depth assessment may take place after the IEP has already been written and accepted by the educational team. In these instances, the organization of data by the educator remains an issue that must be resolved.

In most cases, data organization will include not only a listing of the assessment procedures used but also a graphic or tabular description of the major types of information yielded by the tests. By using a tabular or graphic form, the assessment professional can readily see the areas that were assessed. Decisions can then be made as to whether the assessment battery reached its intended goals. Did the tests measure the types of information that the assessment team desired before the battery was begun? If the answer is yes, then the assessment data can be displayed and reported to members of the assessment team. If the answer is no, then further assessment would be necessary.

Transmitting Assessment Results

Assume that you have collected a wide assortment of assessment data on a student and have organized it so that you are satisfied that you have gathered enough information to answer the questions you had before the assessment process began. *You* know you have enough data and *you* believe that the information is meaningful and interesting. In effect, you are satisfied with the assessment.

You may think you are finished with the assessment, but unfortunately this may not be the case. In most situations, there are other people on the student's educational team who are interested in the assessment results. These people include other professionals, parents, and even the student. The question is How can you report the information that you have so that readers can understand and use it in meaningful ways? This is, perhaps, one of the most difficult tasks in assessment, one that must be mastered by the professional if assessment information is to be used to understand student performance.

The Central Rule of Reporting Information

Not too long ago, parents of a child known to the author had reason to have their son educationally and psychologically evaluated by a psychologist. This evaluation and the resulting psychological report were not inexpensive— the total bill was more than $850. However, when the psychological report came to the parents, they were confused and did not fully understand the results that the psychologist was trying to convey. Somewhat frustrated, they approached this author and asked for an interpretation of the report. After the results were explained to these parents, they were asked why they failed to question the psychologist at their conference. They replied that they had felt intimidated by the scholarly and almost condescending manner of the psychologist. In other words, these parents had paid a large sum of money for a report they were unable to understand and were afraid to question.

This unfortunate state of affairs leads to a central rule of assessment results reporting. If a professional has not reported assessment results in a way that a person can understand, then the reporting is inadequate. Assessment results *must* be written in clear, easily understandable, nontechnical language that is free of jargon. This does not mean that professionals should talk down or condescend to the reader. On the contrary, the person reading an assessment report is obviously interested in and motivated for the topic at hand. That

person wants to know about the student or child. The test professional must treat the reader with respect in addition to reporting the information in a manner that is understandable and not subject to misinterpretation. This means conveying the results in everyday language, using as little technical language as possible. In short, good writing is understandable writing.

Presenting Assessment Information: Raw Data or Conclusions?

What kinds of information does the reader want from an assessment report? This question cannot be answered definitively. Some people want only the facts, which are reported as numbers or raw data. Others desire a synopsis or summary of the raw data in which the report writer *interprets* the results and perhaps even makes subjective interpretations or conclusions (Tallent 1980). Those who advocate reporting only raw data argue that this method has the advantages of being completely objective and allowing readers to form their own conclusions; advocates of the conclusions approach argue that the report writer is obligated to make sense out of the morass of numbers that the raw data represent.

Both reporting methods possess advantages and disadvantages. For example, raw data are objective in that numbers don't lie. However, raw data can be very technical and subject to misinterpretation by readers. Parents and professionals working on nonassessment disciplines are generally not technicians, and they may not be familiar with the terms, concepts, and procedures that are requisite for understanding and interpreting raw data. Because the professional who administers and scores the assessment battery has a responsibility to present data in a comprehensible and useful form, reporting of raw data alone may be insufficient.

On the other hand, drawing conclusions for

the reader from raw data is a subjective process and can lead to oversimplification and overinterpretation of raw data. Misunderstanding of conclusions can occur because the professional writing the report and the report reader are operating under separate sets of concepts, vocabulary, and terms. For example, if the writer reported that the test taker earned an IQ of 74 on the Stanford-Binet, this raw score information would be difficult to misinterpret. However, if the writer went on to conclude that the test taker was retarded, this might be interpreted one way by individuals familiar with accepted clinical definitions of mental retardation and another way by nonprofessionals who might interpret this label in a nontechnical and inappropriate manner.

Dual Reporting of Information

Because some readers find technical, raw data useful in understanding student performance whereas others find such data largely incomprehensible, test reporting should include *both* raw score reporting and interpretation and conclusions (Hollis and Donn 1973; Tallent 1980). Such reporting includes four attributes:

1. A brief, nontechnical report of the findings in everyday language.
2. A summary of the pertinent raw score data organized to be understandable to readers with a requisite degree of familiarity with the tests used and with testing in general.
3. An interpretation of the presented raw scores and pertinent conclusions about those scores.
4. The full battery of raw scores and statistical processes carried out on raw scores (known as test protocols) attached to the test report as an appendix.

This dual reporting process allows assessment data to be read on several levels of complexity. Those relatively unfamiliar with the tests used, with statistics, and with technical jargon can depend on the test reporter's concise and clear interpretation of raw score re-

sults and conclusions. On the other hand, readers more familiar with the technical aspects of tests and testing may wish to interpret the student's performance from the raw scores for themselves. In this way, dual reporting of raw scores and interpretations and conclusions serves the largest proportion of test report readers.

The Assessment Report

In special education, assessment results are typically communicated by the assessment report. Unfortunately, a well-administered and interpreted assessment can all too often lead to ineffective programming and intervention largely because of poor communication of assessment results (Novack, Bonaventura, and Merenda 1978; Tallent 1980). A poorly conceived and written assessment report can make the difference between test results that are read and used by the educational professional and those that are placed in a desk drawer and forgotten.

Frequent Problem Areas in Report Writing

Over the years, researchers have studied and categorized errors that occur frequently in assessment reports (Rucker 1967; Russ 1978; Tallent 1980). These errors can be categorized into problems of *content, interpretation, orientation* and *communication* (Tallent 1980), and each type of problem can be broken down into subareas of difficulty. Table 23-1 lists the four main problem areas or pitfalls of report writing as well as the problematic subareas of each category.

Problems of Content: Content problems are difficulties regarding what actually goes into the assessment report. Content is the meat and potatoes of the report—it is all that the report contains and implies. The best reporting for-

Table 23-1 Problem Areas in Sound Assessment Report Writing

1. *Problems of Content*
   a. Minor Relevance
   b. Reporting Only Raw Data
   c. Unnecessary Duplication
   d. Omission of Essential Information
   e. Inappropriate Recommendations

2. *Problems of Interpretation*
   a. Overspeculation
   b. Unlabeled Speculation
   c. Inadequate Differentiation

3. *Problems of Orientation*
   a. No Practical or Useful Information
   b. Exhibitionism
   c. Too Authoritative
   d. Test Orientation versus Student Orientation
   e. Too Theoretical and/or Abstract

4. *Problems of Communication*
   a. Word Usage
   b. Vague, Unclear, and/or Ambiguous Language
   c. Report Too Long
   d. Report Too Technical and/or Complex
   e. Inappropriate Style
   f. Poorly Organized
   g. Author Hedging or Wavering in Opinion and Recommendations

mat in the world cannot hide bad content. An assessment report can have a beautiful layout, colorful graphics, and fine printing technology. Nevertheless, if it contains poor or inappropriate content, it is basically worthless.

There are a variety of possible problem areas regarding assessment report content (Tallent 1980). These include *minor relevance, unnecessary duplication, omission of essential information, inappropriate emphasis,* and *inappropriate diagnoses and recommendations.* Minor relevance refers to insignificant findings or statements that add little to the report's content. For example, the author once saw a test report that stated that the tested child had "sandy hair, a flat tongue, and odorless breath." Such filler material adds no important information to the report and should be omitted.

Unnecessary duplication of information occurs when information is repeated in more than one section of the test report. This usually happens when two or more team members are completing a report and writing their respective sections independently. In such cases, it is important that each team member's report section be checked to make sure that any duplicated information is deleted.

Omission of essential information occurs when relevant and important test information is left out of the test report. This generally occurs because the writer assumes a knowledge base on the part of the reader that perhaps does not exist. A good rule of thumb is that it is better to include too much information than to leave out crucial assessment content. If you believe that certain information is important, include it in your report. The reader who thinks the information is obvious or superfluous can skip over or skim that content. At least the important information will have been included.

Improper emphasis refers to unimportant, irrelevant, or subjective areas of the test report being emphasized by the report author. It also refers to an overemphasis on certain content, due to the author's particular bias, to the exclusion of other information. The report author must make sure that all information included in the report is important and relevant. Likewise, the author's biases and prejudices must not influence emphasized report content. One indication that a test report contains sound content is that the reader *cannot* identify the author's biases and prejudices.

Finally, the diagnosis and recommendations made by the author are important components of test content. Any conclusions and recommendations made in the report must be based on the assessment information gathered. Put another way, recommendations should not go *beyond* the assessment information gathered and should not be speculative or based on conjecture. Rather, diagnosis and recommendations must be logical extensions of the assessment information that has been gathered and interpreted.

Problems of Interpretation: As stated earlier, the assessment report author does not usually relay raw data alone to the reader. Rather, it is a common practice to interpret the assessment data for the reader. Interpretation, however, implies a degree of subjective judgment on the part of the report author. The logic of test reporting is that the author's judgments presumably are sound because they are based on the writer's training and expertise in testing, assessment, and educational programming.

Note, however, that any interpretation of data, regardless of the expertise of the report writer, contains a degree of error. As such, it would be difficult to find an interpretation of assessment information that was not open to debate and with which another expert might not differ. Errors of interpretation generally fall into three categories: *overspeculation, unlabeled speculation,* and *inadequate differentiation* (Tallent 1980). Errors of overspeculation occur when the test author goes beyond the test results to offer judgments and recommendations that are not adequately based on the data collected. Overspeculation can also occur when the report author includes too much personal interpretation and bias regarding the data collected or observed. The report writer must be able to link any interpretation and judgments directly to the collected data to justify those judgments. If this cannot be done easily, then overspeculation has probably occurred.

Unlabeled speculation occurs when the report author does not clearly differentiate opinion from fact for the reader. Report readers must be able to separate facts from opinions, and the writer must help by clearly labeling those areas of the test report that are opinions, interpretations, and judgments. If this is not done, it is possible that readers will be-

come confused trying to separate facts from author opinion.

Inadequate differentiation refers to the phenomenon of overgeneralities in interpretation and judgments in test reports. Some test reports, for example, include many clichés and general statements that present a stereotyped, cardboard picture of the student. Many times, these general statements apply to almost everyone in the general population instead of solely to the student being assessed. An example of the use of overgeneralities in test reports was demonstrated by Tallent (1980). Tallent gave the same "individualized" assessment report to thirty-nine college students and told each student that he had come up with this individualized report based on a sample of the student's handwriting. He then asked each student to agree or disagree with this individualized assessment. All thirty-nine students agreed with the assessment "based" on their handwriting, and some even wrote Tallent notes containing such comments as "uncanny," "this is me all right," and "how did you do it?" Tallent's individualized assessment report to those students is shown in Table 23-2.

Problems of Orientation: A relatively large number of problems in assessment report writing occur because the test author's theoretical orientation or belief system overly influences the writing of the report. This, in turn, makes the validity of the entire document suspect. Problems of orientation fall into the subareas of *not being practical or useful, exhibitionism, being too authoritative, test orientation versus student orientation, being too theoretical, and being too abstract* (Tallent 1980).

Some test reports simply are not practical or useful. This can occur for various reasons, some of which are shown in Table 23-3. It is important to keep in mind that most readers of assessment reports are practitioners or parents. These readers desire practical, useful information that will help them with their stu-

Table 23-2 Tallent's "Individualized" Personality Assessment

Abilities: Above average in intelligence or mental alertness. Also above average in accuracy—rather painstaking at times. Deserves a reputation for neatness—dislikes turning out sloppy work. Has initiative; that is, ability to make suggestions and to get new ideas, open-mindedness.

Emotions: You have a tendency to worry at times but not to excess. You do get depressed at times but you couldn't be called moody because you are generally cheerful and rather optimistic. You have a good disposition although earlier in life you have had a struggle with yourself to control your impulses and temper.

Interests: You are strongly socially inclined, you like to meet people, especially to mix with those you know well. You appreciate art, painting and music, but you will never be a success as an artist or as a creator or composer of music. You like sports and athletic events but devote more of your attention to reading about them in the sporting page than in actual participation.

Ambitions: You are ambitious, and deserve credit for wanting to be well thought of by your family, business associates and friends. These ambitions come out most strongly in your tendency to indulge in daydreams, in building aircastles, but this does not mean that you fail to get into the game of life actively.

Vocational: You ought to continue to be successful so long as you stay in a social vocation. I mean if you keep at work bringing you in contact with people. Just what work you pick out isn't as important as the fact that it must be work bringing you in touch with people. On the negative side you would never have made a success at strictly theoretical work or in pure research work such as in physics or neurology.

Source: N. Tallent (1980). *Report Writing in Special Education* (Englewood Cliffs, N.J.: Prentice–Hall). Used by permission.

dent or child. An assessment report that is not practical or useful is almost destined to go unused.

Some report writers seem more intent on impressing readers with their range of expertise than they are with writing a practical and useful report. This penchant for impressing readers has been labeled *exhibitionism* (Tallent 1980). It is not necessary for the report writer to try to impress the reader. Rather, what is needed is a clear, useful report written in straightforward, understandable language. This is what will impress the report reader.

Some tester reports are too authoritative in tone. They paint the report writer as *the* authority on the subject and depict those who disagree with the conclusions of the report as mistaken. Authoritative test reports can be intimidating to readers, especially those readers unfamiliar with technical testing issues. Such reports also fail to take into account the degree of error and uncertainty inherent in all tests and assessment situations. Test authors must walk a fine line between demonstrating their competence and presenting themselves as the *only* authority on the subject. Remember, all test conclusions, interpretations, and judgments are subjective and contain error. Test writers who believe that their conclusions are the only correct ones are more than just haughty; they are foolish.

Test reports should be oriented toward the student rather than the test. For example,

Table 23-3 Reasons Assessment Reports May Not Be Practical or Useful

1. Reporter bias leading to statement possessing little relevance to the students.
2. Statements and recommendations removed from real-life situations and constraints. Recommendations unrealistic.
3. Report written without conception of reader as a practical, realistic user or consumer.
4. Recommendations not written in operational or behavioral terms.
5. Report too complex, technical, or sophisticated.
6. Information not related or pertinent to stated student performance problem.
7. Report written as an intellectual exercise rather than as a pragmatic tool for the consumer.

some test authors actually spend more time discussing the test and its nuances than the student. In other cases, test writers become so clinical about the test and the testing environment that they forget to discuss the special characteristics and behavior of the student. Test writers should remember that they are discussing people, not objects who happened to be administered a series of tests. The individual student should always be the subject of the test report—not the tests that were used as assessment tools.

Sometimes reports become too abstract and theoretical. Again, test report writers should keep in mind that readers are generally practical people seeking practical solutions to problems regarding students. Often, these readers have little patience with theoretical and abstract dissertations that seem to offer no practical information for solving the problem at hand. For this reason, test report writers should keep abstract and theoretical writing to a minimum and concentrate on offering practical information.

Problems of Communication: The best assessment results are useless if they are inadequately conveyed to readers. In writing sound assessment reports, adequate written communication skills are essential. Good writing helps ensure that the assessment report will be read, understood, and used. Poor writing ensures the report's consignment to the inactive drawer of the file cabinet.

There are a number of pitfalls in report writing. These include problems of *word usage; vague, ambiguous language; length of reports; technical language; writing style;* and *organization* (see Table 23-4) (Tallent 1980). This text cannot offer adequate instruction regarding effective written communication due to limitations of space. However, several style manuals deal with effective technical and report writing. The prospective report writer is encouraged to consult such sources to develop a clear and efficient writing style.

Table 23-4   Problems of Communication in Assessment Report Writing

1. *Inappropriate Word Usage*
   a. Use specific, exact language, not generalities.
   b. Do not use unnecessary, multisyllabic words.
   c. Avoid jargon.
   d. Use simple-to-understand language.
   e. Avoid clichés and stereotypical phrases.
2. *Vague, Ambiguous Language*
   a. Avoid vague and/or unsubstantiated conclusions.
   b. Avoid internal or psychoanalytic language. Be behavioral.
   c. Avoid new or unfamiliar terms.
   d. Avoid wordiness and gramatically complex sentences.
   e. Avoid statements with more than one meaning.
3. *Report Too Long*
   a. Report should be concise and to the point.
   b. Avoid reports that are too wordy.
   c. Report should end when all relevant information has been reported.
   d. Avoid padding.
4. *Report Too Technical and Complex*
   a. Simple, concrete material is easier to understand.
   b. Avoid technical and esoteric writing.
   c. Too much documentation can make the report too technical.
5. *Style*
   a. Report should not use an artistic or literary style.
   b. Report should avoid "flowery" language.
   c. Be precise without being cold and impersonal.
6. *Organization*
   a. Report should be coherent and organized.
   b. Report should not be fragmented.
   c. Each section should relate to preceding section.
   d. Components should be correctly ordered.
   e. Report should be written around a central theme or pattern.
7. *Hedging*
   a. Writer should not vacillate but make definite recommendations.
   b. Conclusions should be made self-confidently, based logically on presented data.

Components of the Assessment Report

Most professionals advocate a specific format for assessment reports. Although this format may differ slightly from person to person and agency to agency, the components of the format are basically the same. These test report components are shown in Table 23-5 and discussed briefly here.

Student Background

The first component of the assessment report is usually information about the student. Such information includes the pupil's name, age, birthdate, and current educational placement. In addition, the background information should include any *relevant* information that will help the reader understand the student and his or her behavior. This would include, but not be restricted to, information about parents and siblings, the home environment, the student's education, health, and developmental history, social functioning, and other pertinent facts. A good rule for including background information on the student is whether it will help the readers feel they *know* the individual. While the report writer does not want to overwhelm readers with copious and irrelevant information, the report should present the student as a real person.

Table 23-5   Components of the Assessment Report

1. Student background, history, and demographics
2. Behavioral reasons for referral
3. Description of the physical and psychological testing environment
4. Descriptions of the tests used
5. Test results: raw and derived scores
6. Interpretation of results
7. Possible contributors to test and testing error
8. Recommendations
9. Test protocols and scoring arithmetic

Reason for Referral

The next report section describes the reason for referral. It includes a description of the student's behavior that became a concern for parents or educational professionals and that necessitated the referral for assessment. In the reason for referral section, the report writer must be specific and behavioral in describing reasons for referral. Stating the reason for referral in vague or ambiguous terms, such as "misbehaving in class" or "poor reading," does not adequately describe the behavior. Rather, the writer must specifically describe the type of social or academic behavior that necessitated the referral for assessment.

Testing Environment

This section of the test report should include when, where, and under what conditions assessment took place. It should describe the testing environment and discuss the physical facilities in which testing occurred.

If possible, the student's motivation and psychological state before and during testing should also be described. This author has tested students in a variety of physical environments including quiet rooms, a basement next to a candy machine, and a school cafeteria one hour before lunch (with the aroma of pizza wafting through the room). Likewise, a student's motivation to participate in assessment activities differs as a function of external conditions (e.g., whether the student is missing a spelling test or missing recess, or whether the student's parents are going through a contested divorce). For these reasons, a description of the testing environment as well as observations that make inferences about the student's psychological and motivational state should be included in this section.

Description of Tests Used

In this portion of the test report, the writer delineates and describes the tests that were used in the assessment procedure. These descriptions include a list of the tests used, a short synopsis of what they purport to measure, their major attributes, and a brief description of the technical quality and error component of each test.

This section can be somewhat difficult to write. On the one hand, the author cannot simply list the tests used without describing their attributes. After all, not everyone is familiar with each test used in an assessment, and readers need to know about these instruments. On the other hand, it is not appropriate for the writer to bury the reader with an avalanche of technical information. A good balance must be struck between information about what tests were used and their attributes and information of a technical or confusing nature.

Test Results

This particular section outlines the results of the test in numerical form. Included are the results from different subtests of assessment instruments as well as the total scores from each test. The different types of scores that are used with each test (e.g., standard scores, percentiles, mastery scores) should be numerically represented in this section. The test protocols, which include the student's worksheets and the scoring sheets used by the report writer, should be attached as an appendix to the test report.

Interpretation

The interpretation section attempts to make sense out of the assessment results. It answers the question What does all this mean? Test interpretation should be written in clear, simple prose. Test interpretations explain scores, such as standard scores, stanines, and percentiles, and describe in understandable terms how and at what levels the student is operating. Interpretations are intended to familiarize the reader with the significance of the numbers included in the results section.

Possible Contributors to Testing Error

We have noted throughout this text that all tests and testing environments contain error. In this section of the assessment report, the author should identify any phenomenon that might have contributed to test error. Perhaps the student kept expressing a desire to return to class so as not to miss recess. This is test error. Perhaps the student squinted at the test, indicating the possibility of a visual problem. This could represent test error. This is the report section in which the writer attempts to describe all of the observed variances in the test and testing situation that might have contributed to error. These occurrences must be identified so the reader can interpret and use the test results properly with the particular student.

Recommendations

Most test reports contain a recommendation section that suggests certain programmatic considerations or activities that the reader may wish to consider. Such recommendations include placement suggestions or instructional and material considerations that, if instituted, might be beneficial to the student in remediating performance weaknesses.

Not all of the report writer's recommendations have to suggest programmatic or placement changes. In some cases, current placement or instructional activities may be appropriate for the student. In these instances, the report writer would probably suggest that the student's program be continued or modified only slightly.

A Checklist for Reviewing the Soundness of Assessment Reports

Constance Fischer (1985) has developed an indepth checklist designed to aid professionals in judging the adequacy of their test reports. This checklist includes both positive and negative features of reports; it also includes items from the problematic areas of appropriate content, interpretation, inappropriate orientation, and communication. Fischer's checklist is shown in Figure 23-4.

Fischer's checklist is probably too lengthy to use with every assessment report. It is probably most useful as a guideline for beginners who must define their strong and weak areas of report writing. Used in this manner, beginning authors would become aware of weak areas in their report writing and be especially alert to these problem areas when writing future reports. However, it is a good idea to submit a report to the entire checklist, from time to time, to ascertain that the quality of written reports is being maintained.

Finally, not every item of the checklist should be applied to every report. Rather, the items have been devised as guidelines to be used as situations and environments allow. Nevertheless, the spirit or overall impact of the checklist does apply to each report written, and the majority of checklist items would apply in most report-writing cases.

Implementing Instruction Based on Assessment Information

After assessment has taken place and the assessment report has been written (and hopefully read), what is done with all of this information? Surely, it would be a tragedy if, after all the time and expense of collecting, interpreting, and reporting assessment information, *nothing* were done instructionally with the report. If assessment information is not translated into something pragmatic for students with special needs, then much time and energy have been wasted.

Fortunately, a number of instructional outcomes can occur as a result of assessment information. These include:

1. Making placement decisions about students.
2. Creating instructional activities designed to remediate student performance problems.
3. Gathering or creating instructional materials based on assessment information.

4. Making educational grouping decisions.
5. Comparing educational–remediational programs for differential success in remediating a student's performance difficulties.

Making Placement Decisions

Assessment information is used to help make placement decisions for students. This process, which is governed by the regulations stated in PL 94-142, allows assessment results some input into educational placement decisions that must be made for students. The precise nature of this process is described in Chapters 4 to 6 of this text.

Creating Instructional Activities

One of the most important functions of assessment information is to help educators make instructional decisions regarding students. The goal of remediation is to devise activities that will enhance student performance while building on the strengths that students possess. Assessment information can aid in this process. Such information yields data on specific areas in which the student is exhibiting difficulties or demonstrating strengths. From this information, instructional activities can be devised, which translate into specific instructional objectives that are task analyzed to optimize learning. Assessment information can provide important input when choosing such objectives and task analyzed activities for students.

Identifying Instructional Materials

Instructional materials represent the tools teachers use to implement instructional activities. Materials that are inappropriate for given students can destroy well-planned instructional activities whereas appropriate materials can enhance teaching and instruction.

Assessment information informs the teacher about the kinds of instructional activities that hold a high probability of success for enhancing learning. Such assessment can yield informa-

Figure 23-4 Checklist for Good Report Writing

Positive features

_____ Is relevant identifying information (full name, address, age at time of testing) provided?

_____ Are the dates of testing and reporting given?

_____ Is identifying information limited to directly relevant data? (It need not include number of siblings or race, for example, unless these are important to know at the outset.)

_____ Is the referral contextualized? Which actual events or behaviors were of concern, to whom, for what reasons?

_____ In future years, will readers understand this report? What were the concerns and circumstances? Under whose auspices was the assessment undertaken? Where are additional records located?

_____ Does the referral include precipitating events (for the decision at this point to seek assistance)?

_____ Does the referral specify any additional issues that the assessor found it advisable to explore?

_____ Does the referral set the stage for what will be discussed in the conclusions and suggestions?

_____ Does a background section indicate which factors the assessor has taken into account (for example, family situation, medical aspects, developmental history)?

_____ Is background information accompanied by its source—"according to whom"?

_____ Does a titled section (such as Sources, Procedures, or Opportunities for Assessment) indicate all background and sources of Conclusions and Suggestions (tests used, documents reviewed, observations in the classroom or on the ward, joint discussion with the client, assessment within the client's home, conversation with the principal)?

_____ Does the report's organization help the reader to find particular information without undue searching?

_____ Do the headings effectively indicate the nature of each section's contents?

_____ Does the report take into account the concerns, sensitivities, and educational background of probable readers?

_____ Are adequate data provided for use by other professionals? Do professionals have enough information to judge the author's conclusions? Do they have adequate technical data against which to compare future performance (scores, prior diagnoses, and so on)? Would they want to know how the client performed on some other test?

_____ If an appropriate range of tests and other sources of data have not been provided, has this omission been acknowledged or otherwise accounted for?

_____ Are appropriate qualifications provided in regard to the limitations of various tests (reliability, validity, age factors, generalizability)?

_____ Are scores translated for the lay reader?

_____ Is the reader given a sense of what each test involves, of what the client is asked to do?

_____ Can a lay reader skim past any technical material and still understand the report?

_____ Does the report's text specify what each test contributed to the assessment outcome?

_____ Does the report provide an integrated picture of the client? Are personality, emotions, developmental stage, skills, achievements, and so on presented holistically?

_____ Does the reader sense what the client's situation is like for the client?

_____ Is the source of all attributive statements clear? Does the assessor ground characterizations of the client in direct observation, in his or her own reactions, in research on test patterns, or in a particular theory? Are shifts from one of these grounds to another made clear?

_____ Is the client's viewpoint indicated? Does the report include his or her understanding of the reasons for assessment, personal goals and concerns, perspective on reported past events and on the assessor's conclusions and suggestions?

_____ Can the reader readily distinguish between assessor's and client's viewpoints?

_____ Can the reader visualize the client in action? From the report, could an actor or artist vividly portray the client's appearance and style?

_____ Can the reader picture the client in several of his or her environments? Can the reader anticipate the client's comportment in several different situations?

Figure 23-4 *(cont.)*

_____ Is the client's participation in outcomes clear? Does the report indicate how the client helps to bring about accomplishments, mishaps, and other "things that happen"?

_____ Have concrete examples illustrated variations of how this client gets into and through situations?

_____ Does the reader see both the short-term and long-term outcomes of the client's approaches to situations?

_____ Can both the reader and the client identify pivot points within the client's experiaction?

_____ Is the assessor's own participation in the sessions apparent? Can the reader imagine how the client might be different with another assessor?

_____ Can the client comprehend the written report?

_____ Is it clear that the client participated actively in the assessment? Is there an explicit statement in an Opportunities for Assessment section, examples within the text of the report, or a Client's Commentary section at the end of the report?

_____ Do the individual suggestions stand out (for example, by numbering)?

_____ Is the purpose of each suggestion clear? Will readers know what outcome to anticipate?

_____ Do the suggestions form an interrelated pattern? Does the reader see the client's problems and options holistically?

_____ Have the Suggestions taken local resources into account (or taken their lack into account)?

_____ Are the Suggestions tailored to the client—to his or her experiaction, style, goals, situation, and to alternative approaches tried out during the assessment?

_____ Will the reader (including the client) recognize the bases and feasibility of the Suggestions? Are they explicitly tied to specific events that happened and that were discussed during the assessment? Are connections with the client's daily life clear?

_____ Are all the Suggestions grounded in earlier parts of the report?

_____ Do the Conclusions and Suggestions address the Referral issues directly? Is there a tight story line running from the Referral, Background, and text, through the conclusions and suggestions?

_____ Are lines of argument and inference clear, and are assumptions specified?

_____ Is the author's use of a diagnostic label clear? Will readers know which of the client's actual experiactions it refers to?

_____ Can the reader tell that the assessor has considered different understandings of the client—"alternate hypotheses"?

_____ Is the draft organized and corrected in a manner that will allow the typist (oneself or someone else) to type without confusion?

_____ Will the general appearance of the final report be of professional quality (letterhead, margins, page numbers, clean copy)?

_____ Is the report well written in terms of grammar, sentence structure, and paragraph organization?

_____ Are the assessor's degree and title provided? (For example, "John Smith, M.Ed., Educational Specialist," "Andrea Jones, Ph.D., Clinical Psychologist," or "James Brown, Graduate Student in School Psychology, State University Guidance Clinic.")

_____ Is the supervising assessor properly identified?

_____ Have headings and space been provided for the client's comments and signature?

_____ Will a confidentiality statement be stamped or typed onto the report?

_____ Will a client's right-of-access statement appear on the report?

_____ Will the bottom of the report, under Client Commentary, include a signed statement indicating whom the client has designated as permissible readers and receivers?

_____ Has a Technical Appendix been attached if needed by other professionals (for example, WISC–R scaled scores, MMPI profile sheet, Rorschach structural summary, Bender–Gestalt time, TAT stories)?

Negative Features

_____ Does anyone come across as the "bad guy"? Are any of the clients involved with others scapegoated via absence of their perspectives?

_____ Are there other signs of partisanship? Has the assessor prematurely sided with one party? Is the report a prejudiced advocacy statement for the client, or for a program or a theory?

_____ Aside from technical jargon, is there any unexplained jargon?

_____ Might a reader be confused by terms that have multiple technical meanings, or technical as well as everyday meanings? ("John's vocabulary and information were depressed," "John projected a healthy image," "John has superior intelligence," "He denies hostility.")

_____ Is "so what?" an issue anywhere? Does the reader wonder what the point is of any statement?

_____ Are there any extraneous (unnecessary) clauses or sentences?

_____ Does awkward sentence structure derail or distract the reader? Are phrases or clauses out of place? Are sentences too lengthy to keep the main point in focus?

_____ Are there any unclear passages? Are reasons for inclusion unclear? Are the referents for _this, it,_ and _that_ vague?

_____ Does the absence of concrete examples and use of abstract statements leave the reader unsure of the assessor's accuracy or unsure of the statement's meaning in relation to this client?

_____ Is any information repeated unnecessarily?

_____ Does the report ramble rather than coming directly to the point?

_____ Are there jarring juxtapositions of information—unrelated adjacent content? ("John wore jeans, sneakers, and a soccer shirt. He attends Walt Whitman Junior High," and "John's WRAT scores average one grade below expectancy and his Rorschach reflects liability.")

_____ Does an unconventional format confuse the reader (for example, absence of subheads or typical subheads out of anticipated order)?

_____ Does specialized idiom, slang, or literary reference offend, bemuse, or confuse the reader? (Examples: "being-in-the-world," _angst, karma,_ "as Vonnegut would say.")

_____ Does the Identifying Information, Background, or Referral section cast the client as a "type"—black unwed mother, juvenile delinquent, depressed homemaker?

_____ Are there any empty (uninformative) quantifications, such as "great deal," "extremely," "a number of," and so on?

_____ Are there any Barnum presentations—descriptions that presumably were developed from testing, but which in fact are true of nearly everyone? Barnum statements often serve (invalidly) to lend credence to subsequent, less trivial, characterizations.

_____ Are there any gratuitous truisms ("Aunt Fanny" statements, such as "This patient is sometimes anxious")? Such statements are true of one's Aunt Fanny and everyone else too.

_____ Does use of the present tense inadvertently imply pervasiveness or inevitability? ("John takes the easy way out," "This patient resents authority," "The applicant is not motivated to succeed.")

_____ Is the report pathology-oriented at the expense of positive features?

_____ Does the report underplay relevant pathology, weaknesses, dangers?

_____ Is the report's tone otherwise unduly optimistic or pessimistic?

_____ Are there any invalid reductions (circular reasonings) from events to specious causes (which are merely general ways of speaking of those events)? (Examples: explaining low achievement as due to low underlying intelligence, explaining fist fights as due to hostility.)

_____ Is achievement on a particular test or subtest presented as though it were an evaluation of a more general competence? (Example: from Wechsler Scales: "John's strength is in comprehension; he is relatively weak in coding and information.")

_____ Does anything not previously presented appear in the Summary?

_____ Is there personally sensitive information that could be replaced by equally relevant but less personal material?

_____ Does the report contain any data whose relevance is not clear or that appear to bring the conclusions into question?

_____ Does the assessor appear to be hiding behind anonymous roles? (Examples: "the examiner," "tests were administered," "the tests indicate," "it appears that.") Who is the person who is doing the examining, administering, interpreting, concluding?

_____ Are test data regarded as more real or more valid than other observations?

_____ Similarly, does the report focus on test

Figure 23-4 *(cont.)*

scores or interpretations at the expense of addressing behaviors or situations?

_____ On the other hand, are test data disregarded in favor of observations or theory?

_____ Is there a theoretical bias (not just an orientation) at the cost of a fuller picture?

_____ Does this client come across as very much like previous clients this assessor has de-

scribed? Is the individuality of the client subordinated to the assessor's preconceptions? Might the assessor just as well fill in the client's name on a preprinted report?

_____ Does the report tell you more than any reader wants to know, at the expense of clear focus and integration?

Source: From *Individualizing Psychological Assessment,* by C. T. Fischer. Copyright © 1985 by Wadsworth, Inc. Reprinted by permission of Brooks/Cole Publishing Company, Pacific Grove, California, 93950.

tion about the types of materials that have and have not worked for the student in the past. It can also describe the student's particular strengths and weaknesses that should influence the choice of future educational materials. Assessment reports that possess specific recommendations about instructional materials that hold a probability of success for students are particularly useful to the classroom teacher.

Making Grouping Decisions

Students who are operating at about the same instructional levels are often grouped for certain instructional activities. This *does not* mean that programming is no longer individualized; it does mean that students who may be operating at about the same levels in a given area can receive similar instructional activities and materials. Assessment information provides teachers knowledge about students who are operating at similar levels.

Instructional grouping is not tracking. In tracking, students are grouped together for all or almost all of their academic subjects, and they remain in these groups for long periods of time. Using assessment information for tracking purposes is inappropriate and in many cases illegal. Rather, assessment information can be used legitimately to bring together students who are operating at similar levels on certain topics. These groupings are not permanent, and students move from group to group as assessment information indicates that performance similarities between students are changing.

Comparing Educational Programs

Often, teachers will have a number of instructional and programmatic options to choose from when devising activities for remediating student performance weaknesses. The question then becomes Which options hold the greatest probability of success?

Assessment information can help answer this question. A variety of options can be used over a period of time, and the program demonstrating the greatest measure of success can be chosen for the student. Successful programs can then be instituted for other students as deemed appropriate.

In using assessment data to help evaluate the effectiveness of educational programs, it is important to evaluate student progress frequently. What must be avoided is retaining students in unsuccessful programs for relatively long periods of time because an educator believes that the program *should* be successful. Evaluation should be formative in nature so that student progress can be measured frequently and regularly and programs altered, modified, or completely changed as needed.

A Final Word on Reporting and Using Assessment Information

The scope of this chapter is the appropriate reporting and use of assessment information. The goal is to help professionals write sound, useful test reports that can be used programmatically to help students who possess special needs.

Most of the material in this chapter is based on common sense, and many of the points made about clear, unbiased, useful report writing may have seemed obvious to the reader. However, the attributes of good report writing and application discussed in this chapter are not *commonplace* (Fischer 1985). It is unfortunate that much assessment information is inappropriately reported, with the result that the information is not applied to help students. This can result in the assessment process becoming merely an exercise that we undertake because the law says we must. It is crucial that the *entire* assessment process, from the earliest screening through the report writing and application stages, possess the single-minded goals of helping students and remediating performance difficulties. We fail in our obligations to our students if we aspire to or accomplish anything less.

SUMMARY

In the past, the terms *diagnosis* and *prescription* have been used to describe the assessment process and the application of assessment information. However, these terms imply a medical model in which performance problems are diagnosed and then cured, a model that is inappropriate for special education. Therefore, the terms *identification of performance problems* and *learning assistance* are advocated.

Assessment can be summative or formative in nature. Summative evaluation uses information to summarize or recapitulate a person's performance. It usually takes place after a unit of instruction for the purpose of assigning a grade or label to the student's performance. Formative evaluation is the ongoing, continuous assessment used to gauge whether the student is mastering the content presented. As such, formative evaluation is probably more helpful in designing learning assistance activities.

Aptitude–treatment interactions (ATI) are those in which the student's general abilities or aptitudes are identified and treatments are then designed to remediate ability weaknesses. ATI suffers from problems of poorly defined and assessed abilities, poorly defined treatments, and changing interaction patterns that diminish the effectiveness of ATI programs. Modern models of intervention advocate a data-based system of making programmatic decisions that is formative in nature and that takes into account each individual's learning needs.

Data-based information uses data from three main areas: performance, progress, and trends. Performance represents the student's behavior at the present; progress indicates the degree of behavior change from a time in the past to the present. Trends are the patterns of the student's performance over time, taking into account that given factors may cause performance to be nonlinear and sometimes erratic.

Assessment information must be appropriately organized before it can be reported. Therefore, the professional must decide before the report is written how data will be organized and presented to the reader. It is advocated that information be reported in raw score form and by using interpretation and conclusions.

Assessment information is conveyed to readers through assessment reports. The assessment report must be well conceived and written to be useful to educational professionals and parents. There are, however, a number of problem areas in assessment reports. These areas include problems of content, interpretation, orientation, and communication.

The central rule of reporting information is that the report should be understandable to the reader. If any reasonably educated person cannot read and understand the report, the document probably has not been written appropriately. Also, the test report should not intimidate parents and professionals.

Test reports adhere to a typical format in that each one contains certain components. These components include the student's background, reason for referral, descriptions of the tests used in the assessment, results, interpretations of those results, and recommendations. Each component should be written in clear, understandable language.

Test reports can be used to help with placement decisions, to help teachers make instructional and programmatic decisions for students, to help with choosing appropriate curricular materials, to help group students, and to compare the effectiveness of remediational programs for students. The goal of the test report is to give as much support as possible to making these educational decisions. Test reports that are largely unused by professionals and parents have failed to help students with special needs.

STUDY QUESTIONS

1. Why are the terms *diagnosis* and *prescription* not strongly endorsed by many special education professionals? What terms are being advocated? How do these newer terms differ from their older counterparts?

2. What are aptitude–treatment interactions? On what are they based? What are some problems that contribute to decreased effectiveness of ATIs? How can such weaknesses be remediated?

3. What assumptions are made when we chart student progress? Why are baselines important? How might they be used by educational professionals?

4. What is trend analysis? Why is it important? What can trend analysis tell us about a student and his or her educational program?

5. What are the common problematic areas of test reports? What are the subareas for each problem area? How can these problems be avoided by the report writer?

6. Identify and define each component of a test report. How should each component be presented? Why is each component important?

7. Find a test report and critique it against the checklist included in this chapter. How does it measure up? How can it be improved?

REFERENCES

Achenbach, T. M., & Edelbrock, C. (1983). *Manual for the child behavior checklist and revised child behavior profile.* Burlington, Vermont: Queen City Printers.

Adkisson, J., & Adkisson, R. (1975), Competencies of the educational diagnostician. *Texas Elementary, Principals, and Supervisors Association Journal, 8,* 11–12.

Adler, S., & Birdsong, S. (1983). Reliability and validity of standardized testing tools with poor children. *Topics in Language Disorders, 3* (3), 76–88.

Affleck, J. Q., Lowenbraun, S., & Archer, A. (1980). *Teaching the mildly handicapped in the regular classroom* (2d ed.). Columbus, OH: Charles E. Merrill.

Aiken, L. R. (1988). *Psychological testing and assessment* (6th ed.). Boston: Allyn and Bacon.

Alberto, P. A., & Troutman, A. C. (1986). *Applied behavior analysis for teachers* (2nd ed.). Columbus, OH: Charles E. Merrill.

Alkin, M. C. (1984). "Criterion-referenced measurement" and other such terms. In M. Alkin (Ed.), *Problems in criterion-referenced measurement.* Los Angeles: Center for the Study of Evaluation, University of California at Los Angeles.

Alley, G., & Foster, C. (1978). Nondiscriminatory testing of exceptional children. *Focus on Exceptional Children, 9,* 1–14.

American Personnel and Guidance Association (1980). *Responsibility of users of standardized tests.* Falls Church, VA: American Personnel and Guidance Association.

American Psychological Association (1981). Specialty guidelines for the delivery of services by school psychologists. *American Psychologist, 36,* 670–681.

American Psychological Association (1977) *Standards for providers of psychological services.* Washington, DC: American Psychological Association.

Ammons, R. B., & Ammons, C. H. (1948). *The Free Range Picture Vocabulary Test.* New Orleans: R. B. Ammons.

Anastasi, A. (1980a). Abilities and the measurement of achievement. In W. B. Schrader (Ed.), *Measurement achievement: Progress over a decade.* San Francisco: Jossey-Bass.

Anastasi, A. (1980b). Abilities and the measurement of achievement. In W. B. Schrader (Ed.), *New directions for testing and measurement.* San Francisco: Jossey-Bass.

Anastasiow, N. J. (1973). *Educational psychology: A contemporary view.* Del Mar, CA: CRM Books.

Anderson, B. (1982). Test use today in elementary and secondary schools. In A. K. Wigdon & W. R. Garner (Eds.), *Ability testing: Uses, consequences, and controversies. Part II.* Washington, DC: National Academy Press.

Anderson, W., Maloney, V., & Tewey, S. (1981). *The consulting process in education.* Alexandria, VA: Parent Educational Advocacy Center.

Andrews, R. J. (1974). Multidisciplinary models in special education. *Slow Child, 22,* 45–47.

Aram, D. M., & Nation, J. E. (1980). Preschool language disorders and subsequent language and academic difficulties. *Journal of Communication Disorders, 13,* 159–170.

Arter, J. A., & Jenkins, J. R. (1979). Differential diagnosis—Prescriptive teaching: A critical appraisal. *Review of Educational Research, 49,* 517–553.

Asher, S. R., & Renshaw, P. D. (1981). Children without friends: Social knowledge and social skill training. In S. R. Asher & J. M. Gottman (Eds.), *The development of children's friendships.* Cambridge, England: Cambridge University Press.

Asher, S. R., Singleton, L. C., Tinsley, B. R., & Hymel, S. (1979). A reliable sociometric measure for preschool children. *Developmental Psychology, 15,* 443–444.

Ashlock, R. B. (1986). *Error patterns in computation. A semi-programmed approach* (4th ed.). Columbus, OH: Charles E. Merrill.

Ayers, J. (1975). *Southern California Sensory Integration Tests.* Los Angeles: Western Psychological Services.

Baehr, M. E., Renck, R., Burns, R. K., & Pranis, R. W. (1965). *Work Interest Index.* Chicago: Human Resources Center.

Baraheni, M. N. (1974). Raven's Progressive Matrices as applied to Iranian children. *Educational and Psychological Measurement, 34,* 983–988.

Barlow, D. H., Heyes, S. C., & Nelson, R. O. (1984). *The scientist-practitioner: Research and accountability in clinical and educational settings.* New York: Pergamon.

Barrett, B. H., Johnston, J. M., & Pennypacker, H. S. (1986). Behavior: Its units, dimensions, and measurement. In R. O. Nelson & S. C. Heyes (Eds.), *Conceptual foundations of behavioral assessment.* New York: Guilford Press.

Barsch, R. H. (1967). *Achieving perceptual motor efficiency.* Seattle, WA: Special Child Publications.

Barsch, R. H. (1965). *A movigenic curriculum* (Bulletin No. 25). Madison, WI: Dept. of Public Instruction, Bureau for the Handicapped.

Bartel, N. R. (1986). Problems in mathematics achievement. In D. D. Hammill & N. R. Bartel (Eds.), *Teaching students with learning and behavior problems* (4th ed.). Boston: Allyn and Bacon.

Battle, J. (1981). *Culture-free self-esteem inventories for children and adults.* Seattle: Special Child Publications.

Beal, C., & Flavell, J. (1983). Young speakers' evaluations of their listeners' comprehension in a referential communication task. *Child Development, 54,* 920–928.

Beane, J. A., & Lipka, R. P. (1980). Self-concept and self-esteem: A construct differentiation. *Child Study Journal, 10,* 1–6.

Beane, J. A., & Lipka, R. P. (1984). *Self-concept, self-esteem and the curriculum.* Boston: Allyn and Bacon.

Beatty, L. S., Madden, R., Gardner, E. G., & Karlsen,

B. (1976). *Stanford Diagnostic Mathematics Test.* Cleveland: The Psychological Corporation.

Beck, S. (1986). Methods of assessment II: Questionnaires and checklists. In C. L. Frame & J. L. Matson (Eds.), *Handbook of assessment in childhood pathology: Applied issues in differential diagnosis and treatment evaluation.* New York: Plenum Press.

Beck, S., Forehand, R., Neeper, R., & Baskin, C. H. (1982). A comparison of two analogue strategies for assessing children's social skills. *Journal of Consulting and Clinical Psychology, 50,* 596–597.

Becker, W. C. (1974). Some necessary conditions for the controlled study of achievement and aptitude. In D. R. Green (Ed.), *The aptitude–achievement distinction.* Monterey, CA: CTB/McGraw-Hill.

Beers, J., & Henderson, E. (1977). A study of developing orthographic concepts among first grade children. *Research in the Teaching of English, 11,* 133–148.

Beery, K. E. (1982). *Revised administration, scoring, and teaching manual for the Developmental Test of Visual-Motor Integration.* Cleveland: Modern Curriculum Press.

Bellack, A., Hersen, M., & Turner, S. (1978). Role-play tests for assessing social skills: Are they valid? *Behavior Therapy, 9,* 448–461.

Bender, L. (1938). A visual motor Gestalt test and its clinical use (Research Monograph, No. 3). New York: American Orthopsychiatric Association.

Benedict, H. (1979). Early lexical development: Comprehension and production. *Journal of Child Language, 6,* 183–200.

Benjamin, J. (1976). The Northwick Park A. D. L. Index. *Occupational Therapy, 10,* 301–306.

Bennett, G. A., Seashore, H. G., & Wesman, A. G. (1947, 1983). *Differential aptitudes tests.* Cleveland: The Psychological Corporation.

Bennett, R. L. (1982). Cautions for the use of informal measures in the assessment of exceptional children. *Journal of Learning Disabilities, 15,* 337–339.

Berk, R. A. (1980). A consumer's guide to criterion-referenced test reliability. *Journal of Educational Measurement, 17,* 323–349.

Berk, R. A. (1986). A consumer's guide to setting performance standards on criterion-referenced tests. *Review of Educational Research, 17,* 137–172.

Berliner, D. C., & Cahen, L. S. (1973). Trait treatment interaction and learning. In F. N. Kerlinger (Ed.), *Review of research in education,* Vol. 1. Ithaca, NY: Peacock.

Berndt, T. J. (1984). Sociometric, social-cognitive and behavioral measures for the study of friendship and popularity. In T. Field, J. Roopnarine, and M. Segal (Eds.), *Friendships in normal and handicapped children.* Norwood, NJ: Ablex.

Betts, E. A. (1946). *Foundations of reading instruction.* New York: American Book Co.

Bigge, J. (1988). *Curriculum-based instruction.* Mountview, CA: Mayfield Pub. Co.

Bijou, K. L., Peterson, R. F., & Ault, M. H. (1968). A method to integrate descriptive and experimental field studies at the level of data and empirical concepts. *Journal of Applied Behavioral Analysis, 1,* 175–191.

Binet, A. (1890a). Perceptions d'enfants. *La Revue Philosophique, 30,* 582–611.

Binet, A. (1890b). Recherches sur les mouvements le quelques jeunes enfants. *La Revue Philosophique, 29,* 297–309.

Binet, A., & Simon, T. (1916). *The development of intelligence in children.* Trans. E. S. Kite. Baltimore: Williams & Wilkins.

Black, W. F. (1976). Cognitive, academic, and behavioral findings in children with suspected and documented neurological dysfunction. *Journal of Learning Disabilities, 9,* 182–187.

Blackhurst, A. E. (1977). Competency-based special education personnel preparation. In R. D. Kneedler & S. G. Tarver (Eds.). *Changing perspectives in special education.* Columbus, OH: Charles E. Merrill.

Blake, H., & Spennato, N. A. (1980). The directed writing activity: A process with structure. *Language Arts, 57,* 317–318.

Block, J. H., & Burns, R. M. (1976). Mastery learning. In L. S. Schulman (Ed.), *Review of research in education, 4,* Itasca, IL: F. E. Peacock.

Bloom, B. (Ed.) (1956). *Taxonomy of educational objectives: The Classification of educational goals. Handbook 1. Cognitive domain.* New York: McKay.

Bloom, B. (1976). *Human characteristics and school learning.* New York: McGraw-Hill.

Bloom, B., Hastings, J., & Madaus, G. (1971). *Handbook of formative and summative evaluation of student learning.* New York: McGraw-Hill.

Bloom, G. S. (1968). *Learning for mastery.* Evaluation Comment 1, No. 2. Los Angeles: University of California, Center for the Study of Evaluation.

Boehm, A. E. (1971). *Boehm Test of Basic Concepts.* Cleveland: The Psychological Corporation.

Boersma, F. J., Chapman, J. W., & Battle, I. (1979). Academic self-concept in special education students: Some suggestions for interpreting self-concept scores. *Journal of Special Education, 13,* 433–442.

Bornstein, M., Bellack, A., & Hersen, M. (1977). Social skills training for unassertive children: A multiple-baseline. *Journal of Applied Behavioral Analysis, 10,* 183–195.

Botel, M. (1982). New informal approaches to evaluating word recognition and comprehension. In J. J. Pikulski & T. Shanahan (Eds.), *Approaches to the informal evaluation of reading.* Newark, DE: International Reading Association.

Bransford, J. D. (1979). *Human cognition: Learning, understanding, and remembering.* Belmont, CA: Wadsworth Publishing Co.

Breland, H. M. (1979). *Population validity and college entrance measures.* Research monograph #8. New York: The College Board.

Bridgman, C. S., & Hollenbeck, G. P. (1961). Effect of simulated applicant states on Kuder Ford D occupational interest scores. *Journal of Applied Psychology, 45,* 237–239.

Brigance, A. H. (1977). *Brigance Diagnostic Inventory*

of Basic Skills. North Billerica, MA: Curriculum Associates.

Brigance, A. H. (1978). *Brigance Diagnostic Inventory of Early Development*. North Billerica, MA: Curriculum Associates.

Brigance, A. H. (1980a). *Brigance Diagnostic Inventory of Essential Skills*. North Billerica, MA: Curriculum Associates.

Brigance, A. H. (1980b). *Brigance Diagnostic Comprehensive Inventory of Basic Skills*. North Billerica, MA: Curriculum Associates.

Brody, E. B., & Brody, N. (1976). *Intelligence: Nature, determinants and consequences*. New York: Academic Press.

Brolin, D. E. (1973). Vocational evaluation: Special education's responsibility. *Education and Training of the Mentally Retarded, 39*, 619–624.

Brolin, D. E. (1982). *Vocational preparation of persons with handicaps* (2d ed.). Columbus, OH: Charles E. Merrill.

Brolin, D. E., & D'Alonzo, B. J. (1979). Critical issues in career education for handicapped students. *Exceptional Children, 45* (4), 246–253.

Brolin, D. E., Malever, M., & Matyas, G. (1976). *PRICE needs assessment study* (Project PRICE, working paper 7). Columbia: University of Missouri–Columbia.

Bromley, D. B. (1978). *National language and the development of self*. In C. B. Keasey (Ed.). *Nebraska Symposium on Motivation, 1977*. Lincoln: University of Nebraska Press.

Brown, A. L., & French, L. A. (1979). The zone of potential development: Implications for intelligence testing in the year 2000. In R. J. Sternberg & D. K. Detterman (Eds.), *Human intelligence*. Norwood, NJ: Ablex.

Brown, B., & Saks, D. (1983). An economic approach to measuring teacher's preferences in allocating time to students. Paper presented at the annual meeting of the American Education Research Association, Montreal.

Brown, D. A. (1982). *Reading diagnosis and remediation*. Englewood Cliffs, NJ: Prentice-Hall.

Brown, F. G. (1983). *Principles of educational and psychological testing* (3d ed.). New York: Holt, Rinehart & Winston.

Brown, L., Sherbenou, R. J., & Dollar, S. J. (1982). *Test of nonverbal intelligence*. Austin, TX: Pro-Ed.

Brown, V., & McEntire, E. (1984). *Test of mathematical abilities*. Austin, TX: Pro Ed.

Brown, V. L., Hammill, D. D., & Wiederholt, J. L. (1978). *Test of reading comprehension*. Austin, TX: Pro-Ed.

Brown, V. L., Hammill, D. D., & Wiederholt, J. L. (1986). *Test of reading comprehension* (revised). Austin, TX: Pro-Ed.

Brueckner, L. J., & Bond, G. L. (1966). *The diagnosis and treatment of learning disabilities*. New York: Appleton-Century-Crofts.

Bruininks, R. H. (1978). *Examiner's manual, Bruininks–Oseretsky Test of Motor Proficiency*. Circle Pines, MN: American Guidance Service.

Bryan, T. H., & Bryan, J. H. (1986). *Understanding learning disabilities* (3d ed.). Palo Alto, CA: Mayfield Pub. Co.

Burgemeister, B. B., Blum, L. H., & Lorge, I. (1972). *Columbia Mental Maturity Scale* (3d ed.). Cleveland: The Psychological Corporation.

Burke, H. R. (1972). Raven's Progressive Matrices: Validity, reliability, and norms. *Journal of Psychology, 82*, 253–257.

Burke, H. R., & Bingham, W. C. (1969). Raven's Progressive Matrices. More on constant validity. *Journal of Psychology, 72*, 247–251.

Bush, W. J., & Waugh, K. W. (1982). *Diagnosing learning problems* (3d ed.). Columbus, OH: Charles E. Merrill.

Buswell, G. J., & John, L. (1925). *Fundamental processes in arithmetic*. Indianapolis: Bobbs-Merrill.

Cain, L., Levine, S., & Elzey, F. (1963). *Manual for the Cain–Levine Social Competency Scale*. Palo Alto, CA: Consulting Psychologists Press.

Campbell, R. F., Corbally, J., & Nystrand, R. O. (1983). *Introduction to educational administration* (6th ed.). Boston: Allyn and Bacon.

Carroll, J. B. (1974). The aptitude–achievement distinction: The case of foreign language aptitude and proficiency. In D. R. Green (Ed.), *The aptitude–achievement distinction*. Monterey, CA: CTB/McGraw-Hill.

Carrow, E. (1974). *Carrow Elicited Language Inventory*. Austin, TX: Learning Concepts.

Cartledge, G., & Milburn, J. F. (1986). *Teaching social skills to children*. New York: Pergamon Press.

Cartwright, G. P. (1969). Written expression and spelling. In R. M. Smith (Ed.), *Teacher diagnosis of educational difficulties*. Columbus, OH: Charles E. Merrill.

Cattell, R. B. (1950). *Culture Fair Intelligence Test: Scale 1:* Champaign, IL: Institute for Personality and Ability Testing.

Cattell, R. B. (1973). *Measuring intelligence with the culture-fair tests: Manual for scales 2 and 3*. Champaign, IL: Institute for Personality and Ability Testing.

Cattell, R. B. (1983). Theory of fluid and crystallized intelligence: A critical experiment. *Journal of Educational Psychology, 54*, 1–22.

Cattell, R. B., & Cattell, A. K. (1949, 1957). *Culture-Fair Intelligence Test*. Champaign, IL: Institute for Personality and Ability Testing.

Cattell, R. B., & Cattell, A. K. (1960). *Culture-Fair Intelligence Test: Scale 2*. Champaign, IL: Institute for Personality and Ability Testing.

Cattell, R. B., & Cattell, A. K. (1963). *Culture-Fair Intelligence Test: Scale 3*. Champaign, IL: Institute for Personality and Ability Testing.

Cawley, J. F. (1986). Nonmathematics appraisal. In J. F. Cawley (Ed.), *Practical mathematics appraisal of the learning disabled*. Rockville, MD: Aspen.

Cawley, J. F. (1978). An instructional design in mathematics. In L. Mann, L. Goodman, & L. L. Wiederholt (Eds.), *Teaching the learning-disabled adolescent*. Boston: Houghton Mifflin.

Cegelka, W. J. (1978). Competencies for persons responsible for the classification of mentally retarded individuals. *Exceptional Children, 45,* 26–33.

Chittenden, E. A. (1983). *Styles, reading strategies and test performance: A follow-up study of beginning readers.* Princeton, NJ: Educational Testing Service.

Choate, J. S., Bennett, T. Z., Enright, B. E., Miller, L. J., Poteet, J. A., & Rakes, T. A. (1987). *Assessing and programming basic curriculum skills.* Boston: Allyn and Bacon.

Chomsky, N. (1985). *Aspects of the theory of syntax.* Cambridge, MA: MIT Press.

Chomsky, N. (1975). *Reflections on language.* New York: Pantheon.

Clarizio, H. F., & Phillips, S. E. (1975). Sex bias in the diagnosis of learning disabled students. Paper presented at the annual meeting of the American Educational Research Association, Chicago.

Clarizio, H. F., & Phillips, S. E. (1986). Sex bias in the diagnosis of learning disabled students. *Psychology in the Schools, 23,* 44–52.

Clark, E. V. (1978). Strategies for communicating. *Child Development, 49,* 953–959.

Clark, H., & Clark, E. (1977). *Psychology and language: An introduction to psycholinguistics.* New York: Harcourt, Brace, Jovanovich.

Clift, M., & Imrie, B. W. (1981). *Assessing students, appraising teaching.* New York: Wiley.

Cohen, A. S., & Van Tassel, E. (1978). A comparison of partial and complete paired comparisons in sociometric assessment of preschool groups. *Applied Psychological Measurement, 2,* 31–40.

Cohen, C., & Abrams, R. (1976). *Spellmaster.* Exeter, NH: Learnco.

Cohen, S. B., & Plaskon, S. P. (1980). *Language arts for the mildly handicapped.* Columbus, OH: Charles E. Merrill.

Coie, J. D., & Dodge, K. A. (1983). Continuities and changes in children's social status: A five-year longitudinal study. *Merrill-Palmer Quarterly, 29,* 261–282.

Coie, J. D., Dodge, K. A., & Coppotelli, H. (1982). Dimensions and types of social status: A cross-age perspective. *Developmental Psychology, 18,* 557–570.

Colarusso, R. P., Martin, H., & Hartung, J. (1976). Specific visual perceptual skills as long-term predictors of academic success. *Journal of Learning Disabilities, 8,* 651–655.

Cole, C. S. (1978). The Learning Disabilities Test Battery: Empirical and theoretical issues. *Harvard Educational Review, 48,* 313–340.

Cole, N. S. (1981). Bias in testing. *American Psychologist, 36,* 1067–1077.

Coleman, W., & Cureton, E. E. (1954). Intelligence and achievement. The "jangle fallacy" again. *Educational and Psychological Measurement, 14,* 347–351.

Coleman, W., & Ward, A. W. (1956). Further evidence of the jangle fallacy. *Educational and Psychological Measurement, 16,* 524–526.

Commission on Accreditation of Rehabilitation Facilities (1980). *Standards manual for rehabilitation facilities.* Tucson.

Compton, C. (1984). *A guide to 75 tests for special education.* Belmont, CA: Fearon.

Cone, J. D. (1978). The behavioral assessment grid (BAG): A conceptual framework and a taxonomy. *Behavior Therapy, 9,* 882–888.

Connolly, A. (1988). *Keymath–Revised.* Circle Pines, MN: American Guidance Service.

Cooper, J. O. (1981). *Measuring Behavior* (2d ed.). Columbus, OH: Charles E. Merrill.

Coopersmith, S. (1981). *Coopersmith Self-Esteem Inventories.* Palo Alto, CA: Center for Self-Esteem Development.

Council on Exceptional Children (1978, 1983). *Position paper on career education.* Reston, VA: CEC.

Covarrubias v. *San Diego Unified School District* (1971). Civ. No. 70-394-S (S.D. Cal., filed February 1971).

Cox, L. S. (1975). Diagnosing and remediating systematic errors in addition and subtraction computation. *The Authentic Teacher, 22,* 151–157.

Cox, W. F., Jr., & Dunn, T. G. (1979). Mastery learning: A psychological trap? *Educational Psychologist, 14,* 24–29.

Cratty, B. J. (1969). *Perceptual–motor behavior and educational processes.* Springfield, IL: Charles C Thomas.

Cratty, B. J. (1981). Sensory–motor and perceptual–motor theories and practices: An overview and evaluation. In R. O. Walk & H. C. Pick (Eds.), *Intersensory perception and sensory integration.* New York: Plenum Press.

Cronbach, L. J. (1957). The two disciplines of scientific psychology. *American Psychologist, 12,* 671–684.

Cronbach, L. J. (1967). How instruction can be adapted to individual differences. In R. M. Gagne (Ed.), *Learning and individual differences.* Columbus, OH: Charles E. Merrill.

Cronbach, L. J. (1970). *Essentials of psychological testing* (3d ed.). New York: Harper & Row.

Daniels, J. L., & Wiederholt, J. L. (1986). Preparing problem learners for independent living. In D. D. Hammill & H. R. Bartel (Eds.), *Teaching students with learning and behavior problems* (4th ed.). Boston: Allyn and Bacon.

Daniels, M. H., & Altekruse, M. (1982). The preparation of counselors for assessment. *Measurement and Evaluation in Guidance, 15,* 74–81.

Denhoff, E. (1969). Critique to Bibace and Hancock study: Relationship between perceptual and conceptual process. *Journal of Learning Disabilities, 2,* 26–28.

Deno, S. L. (1985). Curriculum-based assessment: An emerging alternative. *Exceptional Children, 52,* 219–232.

de Villiers, J. G., & de Villiers, P. A. (1978). *Language acquisition.* Cambridge, MA: Harvard University Press.

de Villiers, P. A., & de Villiers, J. G. (1979). *Early language.* Cambridge, MA: Harvard University Press.

Diana v. *State Board of Education* (1970). C. A. No. C-70-37 R. F. P. (N. D. Cal., filed 3 February, 1970).

Dodge, K. A. (1983). Behavioral antecedents of peer social status. *Child Development, 54,* 1386–1399.

Dolch, E. W. (1953). *The Dolch Basic Sight Word List.* Champaign, IL: Garrad.

Donahoe, J. W., & Wessells, M. G. (1980). *Learning, language, and memory.* New York: Harper and Row.

Doren, M. (1973). *Doren Diagnostic Reading Test of Word Recognition Skills.* Circle Pines, MN: American Guidance Service.

DuBois, P. H. (1970). *A history of psychological testing.* Boston: Allyn and Bacon.

Dunn, L., & Dunn, L. (1981). *Peabody Picture Vocabulary Test–Revised.* Circle Pines, MN: American Guidance Service.

Dunn, L. M. & Markwardt, F. C. (1970). *Peabody Individual Achievement Test.* Circle Pines, MN: American Guidance Service.

Dunn, R., & Dunn, K. (1978). *Teaching students through their individual learning styles: A practical approach.* Reston, VA: Reston Publishing Co.

Durkin, D. (1987). *Teaching young children to read* (4th ed.). Boston: Allyn and Bacon.

Durkin, D. (1984). Is there a match between what elementary teachers do and what basal reader manuals recommend? *The Reading Teacher, 37,* 734–745.

Durrell, D. D. (1955). *Durrell analysis of reading difficulty.* New York: Harcourt, Brace, Jovanovich.

Durrell, D. D., & Catterson, J. H. (1980). *Durrell Analysis of Reading Difficulty.* Cleveland, OH: The Psychological Corporation.

Eaves, R. C. (1982). A proposal for the diagnosis of emotional disturbance. *Journal of Special Education, 16,* 463–476.

Ebel, R. L. (1980). Achievement tests as measures of developed abilities. In W. B. Schrader (Ed.), *New directions for testing and measurement, No. 5.* San Francisco: Jossey-Bass.

Einhorn, H. J., & Hogarth, R. M. (1978). Confidence in judgment: Persistence of the illusion of validity. *Psychological Review, 85,* 395–416.

Eisler, R. M., & Fredericksen, L. W. (1980). *Perfecting social skills.* New York: Plenum Press.

Ekwall, E. E. (1988). *Diagnosis and remediation of the disabled reader* (3d ed.). Boston: Allyn and Bacon.

Ekwall, E. E. (1986). *Ekwall Reading Inventory* (2d ed.). Boston: Allyn and Bacon.

Engelhardt, J. M. (1977). Analysis of children's computational errors: A qualitative approach. *British Journal of Educational Psychology, 47,* 149–154.

Enright, B. E. (1983). *Enright Diagnostic Inventory of Basic Arithmetic Skills.* North Billerica, MA: Curriculum Associates.

Epps, S., Ysseldyke, J., & McGue, M. (in press). Differentiating learning disabled and non-learning disabled students: I know one when I see one. *Learning Disability Quarterly.*

Evans, M., & Carr, T. (1984). The ontogeny of description. In L. Feagans, C. Garvey, & R. Golinkoff (Eds.), *The origins and growth of communication.* Norwood, NJ: Ablex.

Fadale, L. M. (1975) *Career Awareness Inventory.* New York: Scholastic Testing Service.

Fallen, N. H. (1981). Educational assessment of young handicapped children. Paper presented at Council for Educational Diagnostic Services, Council for Exceptional Children, New York.

Feigenbaum, L. H. (1958). For a bigger alphabet. *High Points, 40,* 34–36.

Fennema, E. (1973). Mathematics learning and the sexes: A review. Paper presented at the annual meeting of the American Educational Research Association, New Orleans.

Fennema, E. (1981). Women and mathematics: Does research matter? *Journal of Research in Mathematics Education, 12,* 380–385.

Fennema, E. (1982). Women and mathematics: A state of the art review. Paper presented at the annual meeting of the American Association for the Advancement of Science. Washington, DC.

Fenton, K. S., Yoshida, R. K., Maxwell, J. P., Kaufman, M. J. (1977a). *A decision model for special education programming teams.* Bureau of Education for the Handicapped. Washington, D.C.: ERIC No. 157–221(b).

Fenton, K. S., Yoshida, R. K., Maxwell, J. P., & Kaufman, M. J. (1977b). *Role expectations: Implications for multidisciplinary pupil programming.* Bureau of Education for the Handicapped. Washington, D.C.: ERIC No. ED 157–231 (9).

Fenton, K. S., Yoshida, R. S., Maxwell, J. P., & Kaufman, M. J. (1979). Recognition of team goals: An essential step toward national decision making. *Exceptional Children, 45,* 638–644.

Feuerstein, R. (1979). *The dynamic assessment of retarded performers: The Learning Potential Assessment Device, theory, instruments, and techniques.* Baltimore: University Park Press.

Fewell, R. R. (1984). Assessment of preschool handicapped children. *Educational Psychologist, 19,* 172–179.

Fey, J. T. (1982). Mathematics education. In H. E. Mitzel (Ed.), *Encyclopedia of educational research* (5th ed.). New York: Free Press.

Fischer, C.T. (1985). *Individualizing psychological assessment.* Monterey, CA: Brooks/Cole.

Fitts, W. H. (1965). *Tennessee Self-Concept Scale.* Los Angeles: Western Psychological Services.

Flanagan, J. C. (1960, 1975). *The Flanagan Industrial Tests.* Chicago: Science Research Associates.

Flavell, J. H. (1981). Cognitive monitoring. In W. P. Dickson (Ed.), *Children's oral communication skills.* New York: Academic Press.

Flavell, J. H., Botkin, P. T., Fry, C. L., Wright, J. W., & Jarvis, P. G. (1968). *The development of role-taking and communication skills in children.* New York: Wiley.

Flavell, J. H., & Wellman, H. M. (1977). Metamemory. In R. V. Karl & J. W. Hagen (Eds.), *Perspectives on the development of memory and cognition.* Hillsdale, NJ: Lawrence Erlbaum Associates.

Fleming, M., & Chambers, B. (1983). Teacher-made

tests: Windows on the classroom. In W. E. Hathaway (Ed.), *Testing in the schools.* San Francisco: Jossey-Bass.

Flores, M. B., & Evans, G. T. (1972). Some differences in cognitive abilities between selected Canadian and Filipino students. *Multivariate Behavioral Research, 7,* 175–192.

Forness, S. R., & Kavale, K. A. (1983). Remediation of reading disabilities, Part one: Issues and concepts. *Journal of Learning Disabilities, 11,* 141–152.

Frame, R.E., Clarizio, H. F., & Porter, A. (1984). Diagnostic and prescriptive bias in school psychologists' reports of a learning disabled child. *Journal of Learning Disabilities, 17,* 12–15.

Frederick, L. v. Thomas (1977). 419 F. Supp. 960 (E.D. Pg. 1976) aff'd 57 F. 2a 373 (3rd Cir 1977).

Fremer, J. (1973). Review of criterion reading. *Reading Teacher, 26,* 521–527.

French, J. J. (1964). *Pictorial test of intelligence.* Chicago: Riverside Publishing Co.

Frostig, M., & Horne, D. (1964). *The Frostig program for the development of visual perception.* Chicago: Follett Publishing Co.

Frostig, M., Lefever, W., & Whittlesey, J. R. (1966). *Administration and scoring manual: Marianne Frostig Developmental Test of Visual Perception.* Palo Alto, CA: Consulting Psychologists Press.

Frostig, M., Maslow, P., Lefever, W., & Whittlesey, J. R. (1964). *The Marianne Frostig Developmental Test of Visual Perception: 1963 standardization.* Palo Alto, CA: Consulting Psychologists Press.

Fuchs, D., Featherstone, N. L., Garwick, D. R., & Fuchs, L. S. (1984). Effects of examiner familiarity and task characteristics on speech- and language-impaired children's test performance. *Measurement and Evaluation in Guidance, 16,* 198–204.

Fuchs, D., Fuchs, L. S., Garwick, D. R., & Featherstone, N. (1983). Test performance of language-handicapped children with familiar and unfamiliar examiners. *Journal of Psychology, 114,* 37–46.

Fuchs, L., Deno, S. L., & Mirkis, P. K. (1984). The effects of frequent curriculum-based measurement and evaluation on pedagogy, student achievement and student awareness of learning. *American Educational Research Journal, 2,* 449–460.

Fuchs, L. S., & Fuchs, D. (1984). Examiner accuracy during protocol completion. *Journal of Psychoeducational Assessment, 2,* 101–108.

Fuchs, L. S., & Fuchs, D. (1986). Effects of systematic formative evaluation. A meta-analysis. *Exceptional Children, 53,* 199–208.

Furman, W. (1984). Issues in the assessment of social skills of normal and handicapped children. In T. Field, J. Roopnarine, & M. Segal (Eds.), *Friendships in normal and handicapped children.* Norwood, NJ: Ablex.

Gage, N. L., & Berliner, D. C. (1988). *Educational psychology* (4th ed.). Boston: Houghton Mifflin.

Gallahue, D. L. (1982). *Understanding motor development in children.* New York: Wiley.

Garai, J. E., & Scheinfeld, A. (1968). Sex differences in mental and behavioral tracts. *Genetic Psychology, Monographs, 77,* 169–299.

Gardner, E. F., Callis, R., Merwin, J. C., & Rudman, H. C. (1983). *Stanford Test of Academic Skills* (2d ed.). Cleveland: The Psychological Corporation.

Gardner, E. F., Rudman, H. C., Karlsen, B., & Merwin, J. C. (1982). *Stanford Achievement Test* (7th ed.). Cleveland: The Psychological Corporation.

Garwood, S. G. (1983). *Educating young handicapped children* (2d ed.). Rockville, MD: Aspen.

Gates, A. I., McKillop, A. S., & Horowitz, E. C. (1981). *Gates–McKillop–Horowitz Reading Diagnostic Tests* (2d ed.). Los Angeles: Western Psychological Services.

Gearheart, B., De Ruiter, J., & Siko, T. (1986). *Teaching mildly and moderately handicapped students.* Englewood Cliffs, NJ: Prentice-Hall.

Geist, H. (1964). *The Geist Active Interest Inventory (Revised).* Los Angeles: Western Psychological Text Specialists.

Gelman, R. (1978). Cognitive development. *Annual Review of Psychology, 29,* 297–332.

Genter, D. (1975). Evidence for the psychological reality of semantic components: The verbs of possession. In D. A. Norman & D. E. Rumelhart (Eds.), *Explorations in cognition.* San Francisco: Freeman.

Gerber, M. M., & Semmel, M. I. (1984). Teacher as imperfect test: Reconceptualizing the reference process. *Educational Psychologist, 19,* 137–148.

Gessell, J. K. (1977). *Diagnostic Mathematics Inventory.* Monterey, CA: CTB/McGraw-Hill.

Gickling, E. E., & Thompson, V. P. (1985). A personal view of curriculum-based assessment. *Exceptional Children, 52,* 205–218.

Gilliland, H. (1974). *A practical guide to reading.* Columbus, OH: Charles E. Merrill.

Gilmore, J. V., & Gilmore, E. C. (1968). *Gilmore Oral Reading Test.* New York: Harcourt, Brace & World.

Ginsburg, H. P. (1982) *Children's arithmetic: How they learn it and how you teach it.* Austin, TX: Pro-Ed.

Ginsburg, H. P., & Mathews, S. C. (1984). *Diagnostic Test of Arithmetic Strategies.* Austin, TX: Pro-Ed.

Glaser, R. (1972). Individuals and learning: The new aptitudes. *Educational Researcher, 1,* 5–12.

Gnagey, T. D. (1983). *Diagnostic Screening Test: Spelling* (3d ed.). Champaign, IL: Facilitation House.

Goldman, R., & Fristoe, M. (1972). *Goldman–Fristoe Test of Articulation.* Circle Pines, MN: American Guidance Service.

Goldstein, K. (1939). *The organism.* New York: American Book.

Golin, A. K., & Ducanis, A. J. (1981). *The interdisciplinary team: A handbook for the education of exceptional children.* Rockville, MD: Aspen.

Gonzales, E. (1982). Issues in assessment of minorities. In H. L. Swanson & B. L. Watson (Eds.), *Educational and psychological assessment of exceptional children.* St. Louis: C. V. Mosby.

Goodenough, F. L., & Harris (1963) *The Goodenough–Harris Drawing Test.* Cleveland, OH: The Psychological Corporation.

Goodstein, H. A. (1981). Are the errors we see true errors? Error analysis in verbal problem solving. *Topics in Learning and Learning Disabilities, 1,* 41–45.

Goodwin, W. L., & Driscoll, L. A. (1980). *Handbook for measurement and evaluation in early childhood education.* San Francisco: Jossey-Bass.

Gordon, E. W., & Terrell, M. D. (1981). The changed social context of testing. *American Psychologist, 36,* 1167–1171.

Gordon, L. V. (1963). *Gordon Occupational Check List.* New York: Harcourt, Brace, Jovanovich.

Gordon, N., & McKinlay, I. (1980). *Helping clumsy children.* Edinburgh: Churchill Livingstone.

Gottman, I. (1977). Toward a definition of social isolation in children. *Child Development, 48,* 513–517.

Graham, J. R., & Lilly, R. S. (1984). *Psychological testing.* Englewood Cliffs, NJ: Prentice-Hall.

Graham, S., & Miller, L. (1983). Spelling research and practice: A unified approach. In E. L. Meyern, G. A. Vergason, & R. J. Whelan (Eds.), *Promising practices for exceptional children.* Denver: Love.

Green, D. R. (Ed.) (1974). *The aptitude–achievement distinction.* Monterey, CA: CTB/McGraw-Hill.

Greenbaum, C. R. (1987). *Spellmaster.* Austin, TX: Pro-Ed.

Greene, H. A., & Petty, W. T. (1967). *Developing language skills in the elementary schools.* Boston: Allyn and Bacon.

Gresham, F. M. (1983). Social skills assessment as a component of mainstreaming placement decisions. *Exceptional Children, 49,* 331–336.

Gresham, F. M., & Elliott, S. N. (1984). Assessment and classification of children's social skills: A review of methods and issues. *School Psychology Review, 13,* 292–301.

Griffith, M. J. (1979). *Sequential tasks for educational planning.* El Cajon, CA: Cajon Valley Union School District.

Griffiths, R. (1970). *The abilities of young children: A comprehensive system of mental measurement for the first eight years of life.* London: Child Development Research Center.

Gronlund, L. (1971). *Using tests in counseling.* New York: Appleton-Century-Crofts.

Gronlund, N. (1985). *Measurement and evaluation in teaching* (5th ed.). New York: Macmillan.

Grossman, H. J. (Ed.) (1983). *Classification in mental retardation.* Washington, DC: American Association on Mental Deficiency.

Guerin, G. R., & Maier, A. S. (1983). *Informal assessment in education.* Palo Alto, CA: Mayfield Publishing.

Guilford, J. P. (1967). *The nature of human intelligence.* New York: McGraw-Hill.

Guilford, J. P. (1980). Fluid and crystallized intelligences: Two fanciful concepts. *Psychological Bulletin, 88,* 406–412.

Guzaitis, J., Carlin, J. A., & Juda, S. (1972). *Diagnosis: An instructional aid (mathematics).* Chicago: Science Research Associates.

Hackett, M. G. (1971). *Criterion reading: An individual-ized learning management system.* New York: Random House.

Hall, J. K. (1988). *Evaluating and improving written expression: A practical guide for teachers* (2d ed.). Boston: Allyn and Bacon.

Hall, V. C., & Kaye, D. G. (1977). Patterns of early cognitive development among boys in four subcultural groups. *Journal of Educational Psychology, 69,* 66–87.

Hallahan, D. P., & Kauffman, J. M. (1988). *Exceptional children* (4th ed.). Englewood Cliffs, NJ: Prentice-Hall.

Hallinan, M. T., & Tuma, N. B. (1978). Classroom effects on changes in children's friendships. *Sociology of Education, 51,* 270–281.

Halpern, A. S. (1985). Transition: A look at the foundations. *Exceptional Children, 51,* 479–486.

Halpern, R. P., Irvin, L. K., & Link, R. (1975). *Social and prevocational information battery.* Monterey, CA: Publishers Test Service.

Hammill, D. D. (1986a). Correcting handwriting deficiencies. In D. D. Hammill & N. B. Bartel (Eds.), *Teaching students with learning and behavior problems* (4th ed.). Boston: Allyn and Bacon.

Hammill, D. D. (1986b). Problems in written composition. In D. D. Hammill & N. R. Bartel (Eds.), *Teaching students with learning and behavior problems* (4th ed.). Boston: Allyn and Bacon.

Hammill, D. D., & Bartel, N. R. (1982). *Teaching Children with learning and behavior problems* (3d ed.). Boston: Allyn and Bacon.

Hammill, D. D., Brown, V. L., Larsen, S. C., & Wiederholt, J. L. (1987). *Test of Adolescent Language-2.* Austin, TX: Pro-Ed.

Hammill, D. D., & Larsen, S. (1988). *Test of Written Language* (2d ed.). Austin, TX: Pro-Ed.

Hammill, D. D., & Newcomer, P. L. (1988). *Test of Language Development—Intermediate.* Austin, TX: Pro-Ed.

Hammill, D. D., & Wiederholt, J. L. (1973). Review of the Frostig Visual Perception Test and the related training program. In J. L. Mann & D. Sabatino (Eds.), *The first review of special education.* New York: Grune & Stratton.

Hanna, P. R., Hanna, J. S., Hodges, R. E., & Rudorf, E. H. (1966). *Phoneme-grapheme correspondence as cues to spelling improvement.* U.S. Dept. of Health, Education and Welfare. Washington, DC.

Hanna, P. R., Hodges, R., & Hanna, J. S. (1971). *Spelling: Structure and strategies.* Boston: Houghton Mifflin.

Hansen v. *Hobson* (1967) 269 F. Supp. 401 (D.D.C. 1967).

Hargis, C. H. (1987). *Curriculum-based assessment.* Springfield, IL: Charles C Thomas.

Hargrove, L. J., & Poteet, J. A. (1984). *Assessment in special education.* Englewood Cliffs, NJ: Prentice-Hall.

Haring, N. G., & McCormick, L. (1986). *Exceptional children and youth* (4th ed.). Columbus, OH: Charles E. Merrill.

Harmon, D. (1970). Illiteracy: An overview. *Harvard Educational Review, 40,* 226–243.

Harris, L., & Associates (1971). *The 1971 national reading difficulty index: A study of reading ability for the National Reading Center.* New York: Louis Harris & Associates.

Harris, W. J., & Schutz, P. N. (1986). *The special education resource program.* Columbus, OH: Charles E. Merrill.

Harrow, A. J. (1971). *A taxonomy of the psychomotor domain.* New York: David McKay Company.

Hartmann, D. P., & Wood, S. (1982). Observational methods. In A. S. Bellack, M. Hersen, and A. E. Kazdin (Eds.), *International handbook of behavior modification and therapy.* New York: Plenum Press.

Hasazi, S. E., Rice, P. D., & York, R. (1979). *Mainstreaming: Merging regular and special education.* Bloomington, IN: Phi Delta Kappa Educational Foundation.

Hatfield, E. M. (1975). Why are they blind? *Sight Saving Review, 45* (1), 3–22.

Hauger, J. (1984). *COMPUSCORE for the Woodcock–Johnson Psycho-Educational Battery.* Allen, TX: DLM Teaching Resources.

Hawkins, R. P. (1986). Selection of target behaviors. In R. O. Nelson & S. C. Hayes (Eds.), *Conceptual foundations of behavioral assessment.* New York: Guilford Press.

Hawkins, R. P., & Dotson, V. S. (1975). Reliability scores delude: An Alice in Wonderland trip through the misleading characteristics of inter-observer agreement scores in interval recording. In E. Rump & G. Semp (Eds.), *Behavior analysis: Areas of research and application.* Englewood Cliffs, NJ: Prentice-Hall.

Hayes, S. C., & Nelson, R. O. (1986). Assessing the effects of therapeutic interventions. In R. O. Nelson & S. C. Hayes (Eds.), *Conceptual foundations of behavioral assessment.* New York: Guilford Press.

Henderson, E. (1985). *Teaching spelling.* Boston: Houghton Mifflin.

Herkowitz, J. (1978). Developmental task analysis: The design of movement experience *and* evaluation of motor development status. In M. V. Ridenow (Ed.), *Motor development: Issues and applications.* Princeton, NJ: Princeton University Press.

Hieronymus, A. N., Lindquist, E. T., & Hoover, H. D. (1978). *Iowa Tests of Basic Skills.* Chicago: The Riverside Publishing Co.

Hilgard, E. R., & Atkinson, R. C. (1967). *Introduction to psychology.* New York: Harcourt, Brace & World, Inc.

Hilgard, E. R., Atkinson, R. C., & Atkinson, R. C. (1979). *Introduction to psychology* (7th ed.). New York: Harcourt, Brace, Jovanovich.

Hiskey, M. (1969). *Hiskey–Nebraska Test of Learning Aptitude.* Lincoln, NE: Marshall S. Hiskey.

Hollis, J. W., & Donn, P. A. (1973). *Psychological report writing: Theory and practice.* Muncie, IN: Accelerated Development.

Holt, K. S. (Ed.) (1975). Importance of movement in child development. In *Movement and child development,* Clinics in Developmental Medicine, #55, Spas-

tics International Medical Publications. London: William Heinemann Medical.

Hooke, R. (1983). *How to tell the liars from the statisticians.* New York: Dekker.

Hops, H. (1983). Children's social competence and skill: Current research practices and future directions. *Behavior Therapy, 14,* 3–18.

Hops, H., & Lewin, L. (1984). Peer sociometric forms. In T. H. Ollendick & M. Hersen (Eds.), *Child behavioral assessment.* New York: Pergamon Press.

Horn, E. (1960). *Spelling. Encyclopedia of educational research.* New York: Macmillan.

Horn, J. L., & Cattell, R. B. (1966). Refinement and test of the theory of fluid and crystallized intelligence. *Journal of Educational Psychology, 57,* 253–276.

Horton, L. W. (1970). Illegibilities in the cursive handwriting of sixth graders. *Elementary School Journal, 70,* 446–450.

Houts, P. L. (1975). Standardized testing in America, II. *The National Elementary Principal, 54,* 2–3.

Howell, K. W. (1986). Direct assessment of academic performance. *School Psychology Review, 15,* 324–335.

Howell, K. W., & Kaplan, J. S. (1980). *Diagnosing basic skills.* Columbus, OH: Charles E. Merrill.

Howell, K. W., & Kaplan, J. S., & O'Connell, C. Y. (1979). *Evaluating exceptional children: A task analysis approach.* Columbus, OH: Charles E. Merrill.

Howell, K. W., & Morehead, M. K. (1987). *Curriculum-based evaluation for special and remedial education.* Columbus, OH: Charles E. Merrill.

Howell, K. W., Zucker, S. H., & Morehead, M. K. (1985). *MAST: Multilevel Academic Survey Test.* San Antonio, TX: The Psychological Corporation.

Howes, C. (1984). Social interactions and patterns of friendships in normal and emotionally disturbed children. In T. Field, J. L. Roopnarine, & M. Segal (Eds.), *Friendships in normal and handicapped children.* Norwood, NJ: Ablex.

Hoyt, K. B. (1977). Community resources for career education. *Occupational Outlook Quarterly, 21* (2), 10–21.

Hudgins, A. L. (1977). Assessment of visual–motor disabilities in young children: Toward differential diagnosis. *Psychology in the Schools, 14,* 252–259.

Humphreys, L. E., & Ciminero, A. R. (1979). Parent report measures of child behavior: A review. *Journal of Clinical Child Psychology, 8,* 56–63.

Hunt, K. W. (1965). *Grammatical structures written at three grade levels.* Research Report #3. Champaign, IL: National Council of Teachers of English.

Hunter, J. E., & Schmidt, F. L. (1976). Critical analysis and ethical implications of various definitions of test bias. *Psychological Bulletin, 83,* 1053–1071.

Hunter, L. (1981). The Council for Educational Diagnostic Services Competency Statement Project. Paper presented at the annual meeting of the Council for Exceptional Children, New York.

Hutt, M. L. (1977). *The Hutt adaptation of the Bender–Gestalt Test.* New York: Grune & Stratton.

Hymel, S. (1983). Preschool children's peer nominations:

Issues in sociometric assessment. *Merrill–Palmer Quarterly, 29,* 237–260.

Iwanicki, E. F. (1980). A new generation of standardized achievement test batteries. A profile of their major features. *Journal of Educational Measurement, 17,* 155–162.

Jastak, J. F., & Jastak, S. R. (1978). *Wide Range Achievement Test.* Wilmington, DE: Jastak Associates.

Jastak, J. F., & Wilkinson, G. S. (1984). *The Wide Range Achievement Test—Revised.* Wilmington, DE: Jastak Associates.

Jensen, A. R. (1980). *Bias in mental testing.* New York: Face Press.

Jewish Employment and Vocational Service (1968). *Work samples: Signposts on the road to occupational choice.* Philadelphia: Vocational Research Institute.

Johansson, C. B. (1984). *Career assessment inventory* (2d ed.). NCS Interpretive Scoring Systems. Minneapolis: National Computer Systems.

Johns, J. L. (1982). The dimensions and uses of informal reading. In J. Pikulski & T. Shanahan (Eds.), *Approaches to the informal evaluation of reading.* Newark, DE: International Reading Association.

Johnson, D. D. (1971). The Dolch list reexamined. *The Reading Teacher, 24,* 455–456.

Johnson, D. D., & Baumann, J. F. (1984). Word identification. In P. D. Pearson (Ed.), *Handbook of reading research (Part 3).* New York: Longman.

Johnston, P. H. (1983). *Reading comprehension assessment: A cognitive basis.* Newark, DE: International Reading Association.

Jordan, J. E., & Felty, J. (1968). Factors associated with intellectual variation among visually impaired children. *American Foundation of the Blind Research Bulletin, 15,* 61–70.

Kabler, M. L., & Carleton, G. R. (1982). Educating exceptional students: A comprehensive team approach. *Theory into Practice, 21,* 88–96.

Kabler, M. L., Carlton, G. R., & Sherwood, M. (1981). *Guide for Conducting multidisciplinary team evaluations of suspected handicapped children.* Columbus, OH: National Center, Eduational Media and Materials, Ohio State University.

Kagan, J. (1971). The magical aura of the IQ. *Saturday Review, 54,* 92–93.

Kagan, J., & Moss, H. A. (1962). *Birth to maturity.* New York: Wiley.

Kaplan, R. M., & Saccuzzo, D. P. (1982). *Psychological testing: Principles, applications, and issues.* Monterey, CA: Brooks/Coles.

Karier, C. J. (1972). Testing for order and control in the corporate liberal state. *Educational Theory, 22,* 154–180.

Karlsen, B., Madden, R., & Gardner, E. F. (1985). *Standard Diagnostic Reading Test* (3rd ed.). Cleveland: The Psychological Corporation.

Kauffman, J. M. (1981). Historical trends and contemporary issues in special education in the United States. In J. M. Kauffman & D. P. Hallahan (Eds.), *Handbook of special education.* Englewood Cliffs, NJ: Prentice-Hall.

Kaufman, A. S., & Kaufman, N. L. (1975). *Kaufman Test of Educational Achievement.* Circle Pines, MN: American Guidance Services.

Kaufman, A. S., & Kaufman, N. L. (1983). *Kaufman Assessment Battery for Children, Interpretive Manual.* Circle Pines, MN: American Guidance Service.

Kaufman, A. S., & Kaufman, N. L. (1985). *Kaufman Test of Educational Achievement.* Circle Pines, MN: American Guidance Service.

Keefe, F. J., Kopel, S. A., & Gordon, S. B. (1978). *A practical guide to behavioral assessment.* New York: Springer.

Kendall, P. C., & Morison, P. (1984). Integrating cognitive and behavioral procedures for the treatment of socially isolated children. In A. W. Meyers & W. E. Craighead (Eds.), *Cognitive behavior therapy with children.* New York: Plenum Press.

Kent, R. N., & Foster, S. L. (1977). Direct observational procedures: Methodological issues in naturalistic settings. In A. R. Ciminero, K. S. Calhoun, & H. E. Adams (Eds.), *Handbook of behavioral assessment.* New York: Wiley.

Keogh, J. (1973). Development in fundamental motor tasks. In C. B. Corbin (Ed.), *A textbook of motor development.* Dubuque, IA: Brown.

Kephart, N. C. (1968). *Learning disability: An educational adventure.* West Lafayette, IN: Kappa Delta Pi Press.

Kephart, N. C. (1960, 1971). *The slow learner in the classroom.* Columbus, OH: Charles E. Merrill.

Kirk, S. A., Kliebhan, J. M., & Lerner, J. W. (1978). *Teaching reading to slow and disabled readers.* Boston: Houghton Mifflin.

Kirk, S., McCarthy, J., & Kirk, W. (1968). *Illinois Test of Psycholinguistic Abilities.* Champaign: University of Illinois Press.

Kokaska, C. J., & Brolin, D. E. (1985). *Career education for handicapped individuals* (2d ed.). Columbus, OH: Charles E. Merrill.

Kolstoe, O. P. (1976). Developing career awareness: The foundation of a career education program. In G. B. Blackburn (Ed.), *Colloquium series on career education for handicapped persons.* West Lafayette, IN: Purdue University.

Koppitz, E. M. (1963). *The Bender–Gestalt Test for Young Children.* New York: Grune & Stratton.

Koppitz, E. M. (1975). *The Bender–Gestalt Test for Young Children: Volume II: Research and application—1963–1973.* New York: Grune & Stratton.

Kornblau, B. (1982). The teachable pupil survey: A technique for assessing teachers' perceptions of pupil attributes. *Psychology in the Schools, 19,* 170–174.

Kottmeyer, W. (1970). *Teacher's guide for remedial reading.* New York: McGraw-Hill.

Krause, L. A. (1983). Teaching the second "R." *The Directive Teacher, 5* (1), 30.

Krehbiel, D. (1972). *Vocational evaluation through the use of modification.* Des Moines, IA: Department of Public Instruction.

Kronick, D. (1983). *Social development of learning disabled persons: Examining the effects and treatment of inadequate interpersonal skills.* San Francisco: Jossey-Bass.

Kuska, A., Webster, E. J., & Elford, G. (1964). *Spelling in language arts 6.* Ontario: Thomas Nelson & Sons (Canada) Ltd.

Lakin, K. C. (1983). A response to *Gene v. Glass. Policy Studies Review, 2,* 233–239.

Lambert, N., & Windmiller, M. (1981). *AAMD Adaptive Behavior Scale, school edition.* Monterey, CA: Publishers Test Service.

Lambert, N. & Windmiller, N. (1981). *Diagnostic and technical manual, revised, AAMD Adaptive Behavior Scale, school edition.* Monterey, CA: CTB/McGraw-Hill.

Lamke, T., Nelson, M., & French, J. (1973). *Hennon–Nelson Tests of Mental Ability.* Chicago: The Riverside Publishing Co.

Larry P. v. *Riles,* Superintendent of Public Instruction for the State of California. C-71-2270-RFP (N.D. Cal., 1972).

Larsen, S., & Hammill, D. (1986). *Test of Written Spelling-2.* Austin, TX: Pro-Ed.

Laszlo, J. I., & Bairstow, P. J. (1985). *Perceptual–motor behavior.* New York: Praeger.

Lazar-Morrison, C., Polin, L., Moy, R., & Burry, L. (1980). *A review of the literature on test use.* Los Angeles: Center for the Study of Evaluation.

Lee, L. L. (1971). *Northwestern Syntax Screening Test.* Evanston, IL: Northwestern University Press.

Lee, L. L. (1974). *Developmental sentence analysis.* Evanston, IL: Northwestern University Press.

Lee, L., & Canter, S. (1971). Developmental sentence scoring: A clinical procedure for estimating syntactic development in children's spontaneous speech. *Journal of Speech and Hearing Disorders, 36,* 315–340.

Lefley, H. (1975). Differential self-concept in American Indian children as a function of language and examiner. *Journal of Personality and Social Psychology, 31,* 36–41.

Leiter, R. G. (1955). *The Leiter International Performance Scale.* Chicago: C. H. Stoelting Co.

Leonard, L. B., & Weiss, A. L. (1983). Application of nonstandardized assessment procedures to diverse linguistic populations. *Topics in Language Disorders, 3* (3), 35–45.

Lerner, J. W. (1985). *Learning disabilities: Theories, diagnosis, and teaching strategies* (4th ed.). Boston: Houghton Mifflin.

Levine, E. S. (1974) Psychological tests and practices with the deaf: A survey of the state of the art. *Volta Review, 76,* 298–319.

Levine, E., Fineman, C., & Donlon, G. (1974). *Prescriptive profile procedure for children with learning disabilities.* Miami, FL: Dade County Public Schools.

Levine, S., & Elzey, F. (1968). *San Francisco Vocational Competency Scale.* New York: The Psychological Corporation.

Liberman, I. Y., Shankweiler, D., Liberman, A. M., Fowler, C., & Fischer, F. W. (1977). Phonetic segmentation and recoding in the beginning reader. In A. S. Reber & D. Scarborough (Eds.), *Toward a psychology of reading.* Hillsdale, NJ: Lawrence Erlbaum Associates.

Likert, R., & Quasha, W. H. (1985). *Revised Minnesota Paper Form Board Test.* Cleveland: The Psychological Corporation.

Linden, K. W. (1968). *Modern mental measurement: A historical perspective.* New York: Houghton Mifflin.

Linn, R. L. (1980). Test design and analysis for measurement of educational achievement. *New Directions for Testing and Measurement, 5,* 81–92.

Lipson, M. Y., & Wixson, K. K. (1985). Reading disability research: An interactionist perspective. Paper presented at the annual meeting of the American Educational Research Association, Chicago.

Lloyd, J. W. (1984). How shall we individualize instruction—or should we? *Remedial and Special Education, 5,* 7–15.

Luftig, R. L. (1982). Educational placement of the retarded and self-concept functioning. *Education, 103,* 49–55.

Luftig, R. L. (1987a). The stability of children's peer social status over social situations. *Education, 103,* 49–55.

Luftig, R. L. (1987b). Children's loneliness, perceived ease in making friends, and estimated social adequacy. *Child Study Journal, 17,* 35–55.

Luftig, R. L. (1987c). *Teaching the mentally retarded student.* Boston: Allyn and Bacon.

Luftig, R. L., & Greeson, L. E. (1983). Effects of structural importance and idea saliency on discourse recall of mentally retarded and nonretarded pupils. *American Journal of Mental Deficiency, 87,* 414–421.

Luftig, R. L., & Johnson, R. E. (1982). Identification and recall of structurally important units in prose by mentally retarded learners. *American Journal of Mental Deficiency, 86,* 495–502.

Luftig, R. L., & Johnson, R. E. (1983). Semantic normalization in prose. *American Journal of Psychology, 54,* 117–134.

Lyman, H. B. (1986). *Test scores and what they mean* (4th ed.). Englewood Cliffs, NJ: Prentice-Hall.

Lynn, D. B. (1972). Determinants of intellectual growth in women. *School Review, 80,* 241–260.

MacDonald, H. A., & Netherton, A. H. (1969). Contribution of a nonverbal general ability test to the educational assessment of pupils in the cross-cultural setting of the Canadian North. *Journal of Educational Research, 62,* 315–319.

MacDonald, J. D. (1978). *Environmental languages inventory.* Columbus, OH: Charles E. Merrill.

MacGintie, W. (1978). *Gates-MacGintie Reading Diagnostic Tests.* Boston: Houghton Mifflin.

Madden, R., Gardner, E. F., & Collins, C. S. (1983). *Stanford Early School Achievement Test* (2d ed.). Cleveland: The Psychological Corporation.

Mager, R. (1972). *Goal analysis.* Belmont, CA: Fearon.

Magliocca, L. A., & Rinaldi, R. T. (1982). Multifactored assessment for the handicapped. *Theory into Practice, 21,* 106–113.

Magliocca, L. A., Rinaldi, R. T., Crew, J. L., & Kunzelmann, H. P. (1977). Early identification of handicapped children through a frequency sampling technique. *Exceptional Children, 43,* 414–420.

Magliocca, L. A., Rinaldi, R. T., & Stephens, T. M. (1979). A field test of a frequency sampling screening instrument for early identification of at-risk children: A report on the second year pilot study. *Child Study Journal, 9,* 213–229.

Malgady, R. G., Barcher, P. R., Towner, G., & Davis, J. (1979). Language factors in vocational evaluation of mentally retarded workers. *American Journal on Mental Deficiency, 83,* 432–438.

Mank, D. M. & Horner, R. H. (1988). Instructional programming in vocational education. In R. Gaylord-Ross (Ed.), *Vocational education for persons with handicaps.* Palo Alto, CA: Mayfield Publishing.

Mann, L. (1971). Perceptual training revisited: The training of nothing at all. *Rehabilitation Literature, 32,* 322–325.

Mann, L. (1975). Psychometric phrenology and the new faculty psychology: The case against ability assessment and training. *Journal of Special Education, 9,* 261–268.

Mann, P. H., Suiter, P. A., & McClung, R. M. (1987). *Handbook in Diagnostic–Prescriptive Teaching* (3rd ed.). Boston: Allyn and Bacon.

Mann, R. A. (1976). Assessment of behavioral excesses in children. In M. Ersen & A. Bellack (Eds.), *Behavioral assessment: A practical handbook.* New York: Pergamon Press.

Marsh, H. W., & Shavelson, R. (1985). Self-concept: Its multifaceted, hierarchical structure. *Educational Psychologist, 20,* 107–123.

Martin, N. (1983). Genuine communication. *Topics in Learning and Learning Disabilities, 3,* 1–11.

Matson, J. L., & Esveldt-Dawson, K. (undated). Evaluation of social skills with youngsters (MESSY). Unpublished report. Pittsburgh: University of Pittsburgh School of Medicine.

Matson, J. L., Rotatori, A. F., & Helsel, W. J. (1983). Development of a rating scale to measure social skills in children: The Matson Evaluation of Social Skills with Youngsters (MESSY). *Behavior Research and Therapy, 21,* 335–340.

Mayer, R. E. (1985). Learnable aspects of problem solving. Presented at the annual meeting of the American Educational Research Association, Chicago.

McArthur, C., & Stevens, L. B. (1955). The validation of expressed interests as compared with inventoried interests: A fourteen-year follow-up. *Journal of Applied Psychology, 39,* 184–189.

McClennen, S. E., Hoekstra, R. R., & Bryan, J. E. (1980). *Social skills for severly retarded adults. An inventory and training program.* Champaign, IL: Research Press.

McLeod, T. M., & Armstrong, S. W. (1982). Learning disabilities in mathematics—skill deficits and remedial approaches at the intermediate and secondary level. *Learning Disability Quarterly, 5,* 305–311.

McNutt, G., & Mandelbaum, L. H. (1980). General assessment competencies for special education teachers. *Exceptional Education Quarterly/Measurement of Exceptionality, 3,* 21–29.

Measurement Division Staff (1983). *Basic Achievement Skills Individual Screener.* Cleveland, OH: The Psychological Corp.

Menn, L. (1985). Phonological development: Learning sounds and sound patterns. In J. B. Gleason (Ed.), *The development of language.* Columbus, OH: Charles E. Merrill.

Mercer, C. D., & Mercer, A. R. (1985). *Teaching students with learning problems* (2d ed.). Columbus, OH: Charles E. Merrill.

Mercer, J. R. (1974). A policy statement on assessment procedures and rights of children. *Harvard Educational Review, 44,* 125–141.

Mercer, J. R. (1975). Psychological assessment and the rights of children. In N. Hobbs (Ed.), *Issues in the classification of children, Vol. 1.* San Francisco: Jossey–Bass.

Mercer, J. R. (1979a). *System of Multicultural Pluralistic Assessment: Technical Manual.* Cleveland: The Psychological Corporation.

Mercer, J. R. (1979b). In defense of racially and culturally non-discriminating assessment. *School Psychology Digest, 8,* 89–115.

Mercer, J. R., & Lewis, J. F. (1982). *Adaptive Behavior Inventory for Children.* Cleveland: The Psychological Corporation.

Mervis, C. B., & Crisafi, M. A. (1982). Order of acquisition of subordinate-, basic-, and superordinate-level categories. *Child Development, 53,* 258–266.

Metfessel, N. S., Michael, W. B., & Kirsner, D. A. (1979). Instrumentation of Bloom's and Krathwohl's taxonomies for the writing of educational objectives. *Psychology in the Schools, 6,* 227–231.

Meyer, D. E., Smith, J. E., & Wright, C. E. (1982). Models for the speed and accuracy of aimed movements. *Psychological Review, 89,* 449–482.

Meyers, C. C. (1975). *What I Like to Do: An inventory of students' interests.* Chicago: Science Research Association.

Michelson, L., Sugai, D. P., Wood, R. P., & Kazdin, N. I. (1983). *Social skill assessment and training with children.* New York: Plenum Press.

Michelson, L., & Wood, R. (1980). *Behavioral Assessment and Training of Children's Social Skills. Progress in Behavior Modification,* Vol. 9. New York: Academic Press.

Michigan Department of Education (1970). *Vocational education—Special Education Institute.* Flint, MI.

Miller, L., & Graham, S. (1979). Reading skills of LD students: A review. *Alabama Reader, 6,* 16–25.

Mills v. Board of Education of the District of Columbia, 348 Supp. 866 (1972).

Mims, H. A., & Camden, C. T. (1984). Comparison of a sentence completion test and spontaneous conversation as measures of nonstandard dialect grammatical usage. Paper presented at the annual meeting of the

American Educational Research Association, New Orleans.

Minor, B. J., & Minn, L. H. (1981). A theoretical model for humanistic counseling research. *Personnel and Guidance Journal, 59,* 502–506.

Minton, H. C., & Schneider, F. W. (1980). *Differential psychology.* Monterey, CA: Brooks/Cole.

Mitchell, J. V., Jr. (Ed.) (1983). *Tests in print III.* Lincoln: University of Nebraska Press.

Moran, M. R. (1978). *Assessment of the exceptional learner in the regular classroom.* Denver: Love.

Morgan, R. G. (1980). Analysis of social skills. The behavior analysis approach. In W. T. Singleton, P. Sturgeon, & R. B. Stammers (Eds.), *The analysis of social skill.* New York: Plenum Press.

Myklebust, H. R. (1968). Definition and overview. In H. Myklebust (Ed.), *Progress in learning disabilities,* Vol. 1. New York: Grune & Stratton.

Myklebust, H. R. (1965). *Development and disorders of written language,* Vols. 1 & 2. New York: Grune & Stratton.

Nash, S. C. (1979). Sex role as a mediator of intellectual functioning. In M. A. Wittig & A. C. Peterson (Eds.), *Sex related differences in cognitive functioning.* New York: Academic Press.

Naslund, R. A., Thorpe, L. P., & Lefever, D. W. (1978). *SRA Achievement Series.* Chicago: Science Research Associates.

Neff, W. (1977). *Work and human behavior* (2d ed.). New York: Aldine-Atherton.

Neli, E. (1981). Teaching spelling and writing skills in the mainstreamed elementary classroom. In *Toward a research base for the least restrictive environment. A collection of papers.* Lexington: University of Kentucky Press.

Nesbet, J. (1984). The Otis–Lennon Mental Ability Test. In P. Levy & H. Goldstein (Eds.), *Test in education: A book of critical reviews.* London: Academic Press.

Neuhauser, G. (1975). Methods of assessing and recording motor skills and motor patterns. *Developmental Medicine and Child Neurology, 17,* 369–386.

Newcomer, P. (1977). Special education services for the mildly handicapped: Beyond a diagnostic and remedial model. *Journal of Special Education, 11,* 153–165.

Newcomer, P. L., & Curtis, D. (1984). *The Diagnostic Achievement Battery.* Austin, TX: Pro-Ed.

Newcomer, P. L., & Hammill, D. D. (1988). *Test of Language Development 2—Primary.* Austin, TX: Pro Ed.

Newland, T. E. (1932). An analytical study of the development of illegibilities in handwriting from the lower grades to adulthood. *Journal of Educational Research, 26,* 249–258.

Newland, T. E. (1969). *Blind Learning Aptitude Test.* Champaign, IL: T. Ernest Newland.

Nihira, K., Foster, R., Shellhaas, M., & Leland, H. (1974). *AAMD Adaptive Behavior Scale: Manual* (rev. ed.). Washington, DC: American Association on Mental Deficiency.

Nitko, A. J. (1984). Defining "Criterion-referenced tests." In R. A. Berk (Ed.), *A guide to criterion-referenced test construction.* Baltimore: Johns Hopkins University Press.

Nodine, B. F. (1983). Foreword: Process not product. *Topics in Learning and Learning Disabilities, 3,* ix–xii.

Novack, H. S., Bonaventura, E., & Merenda, P. F. (1978). *Manual to accompany Rhode Island Pupil Identification Scale.* Providence: RIPIS.

Nunnally, J. (1978). *Psychometric theory.* New York: McGraw-Hill.

Oakland, T. (1980). Nonbiased assessment of minority group children. *Exceptional Education Quarterly, 1,* 31–46.

Oakland, T., & Laosa, L. M. (1977). Professional, legislative, and judicial influences on psychoeducational assessment practices in schools. In T. Oakland (Ed.), *Psychological and educational assessment of minority children.* New York: Bruner/Mazel.

Oden, S. (1986). Developing social skills instruction for peer interaction and relationships. In G. Cartledge & J. F. Milburn (Eds.), *Teaching social skills to children.* New York: Pergamon Press.

Ollendick, T. H., & Hersen, M. (1984). *Child behavior assessment.* New York: Pergamon Press.

Osgood, C. E. (1957). A behavioristic analysis of perception and language as cognitive phenomenon. In *Contemporary approaches to cognition.* Cambridge, MA: Harvard University Press. Cited by Paras Kevopoulos & Kirk, 1969.

Otis, A. S., & Lennon, R. T. (1982). *Otis–Lennon Mental Ability Tests.* Cleveland: The Psychological Corp.

Otis, A. S., & Lennon, R. T. (1979, 1982). *Otis–Lennon Mental Ability Test.* Cleveland: The Psychological Corp.

Otto, W., & Kann, K. (1977). *Wisconsin Tests of Reading Skill Development: Comprehension.* Madison: Wisconsin Research and Development Center for Cognitive Learning.

Otto, W., McMenemy, R. A., & Smith, R. J. (1973). *Corrective and remedial teaching* (2d ed.). Boston: Houghton Mifflin.

Otto, W., & Smith, R. J. (1983). Skill-centered and meaning-centered conceptions of remedial reading instruction: Striking a balance. *Topics in Learning and Learning Disabilities, 2* (4), 20–26.

Painting, D. H. (1979). Cognitive assessment. In W. C. Adamson & K. K. Adamson (Eds.), *A handbook for specific learning disabilities.* New York: Gardner Press.

Palincsar, A. S. (1987). Reciprocal teaching: Field evaluations in remedial and content area reading. Paper presented at the Annual Meeting of the American Educational Research Assoc., Washington, D.C.

Palincsar, A. S., & Brown, A. L. (1984). Reciprocal teaching of comprehension fostering and comprehension monitoring activities. *Cognition and Instruction, 2,* 117–175.

Paraskevopoulos, J. N., & Kirk, S. A. (1969). *The development and psychometric characteristics of the Revised Illinois Test of Psycholinguistic Abilities.* Champaign: University of Illinois Press.

Paris, S., Cross, D., & Lipson, M. (1984). Informal strategies for learning: A program to improve children's reading awareness and comprehension. *Journal of Educational Psychology, 76,* 1239–1252.

Partoll, S. F. (1976). Spelling demonology revisited. *Academic Therapy, 11,* 339–348.

Patton, J. R., & Payne, J. S. (1986). Mild mental retardation. In N. G. Haring & L. McCormick (Eds.), *Exceptional children and youth* (4th ed.). Columbus, OH: Charles E. Merrill.

Pearson, P. D., & Johnson, D. D. (1979). *Teaching reading comprehension.* New York: Holt, Rinehart & Winston.

Pease, D., & Gleason, J. B. (1985). Gaining meaning: Semantic development. In J. B. Gleason (Ed.), *The development of language.* Columbus, OH: Charles E. Merrill.

Pendergast, K., Dickey, S. E., Selman, J. W., & Soder, A. L. (1969). *Photo Articulation Test.* International Printers and Publishers.

Pennsylvania Association for Retarded Children v. *Commonwealth of Pennsylvania* (1971). 334 F. Supp. 1257 (E. D. PA 1971).

Petty, W. T., & Jensen, J. M. (1980). *Developing children's language.* Boston: Allyn and Bacon.

Petty, W. T., Petty, D., & Becking, M. (1985). *Experiences in language: Tools and techniques for language arts* (4th ed.). Boston: Allyn and Bacon.

Phelps, L. A., & Lutz, R. J. (1977). *Career exploration and preparation for the special needs learner.* Boston: Allyn & Bacon.

Piaget, J. (1926). *Language and thought of the child.* New York: Harcourt, Brace & World.

Piaget, J. (1960). *Language and thought in the child.* NY: Meridian Books, New American Library.

Piaget, J. (1965). *The child's conception of number.* New York: W. W. Norton.

Piaget, J. (1967). *Six psychological studies.* New York: Vintage Books, Random House.

Piaget, J., & Inhelder, B. (1963). *The child's conception of space.* London: Routledge and Kegan Paul.

Piaget, J., & Inhelder, B. (1967). *The child's conception of space.* New York: W. W. Norton.

Piers, E. V., & Harris, D. B. (1969, 1984). *Piers–Harris Children's Self-Concept Scale (The Way I Feel about Myself).* Los Angeles: Western Psychological Services.

Pikulski, J. J., & Shanahan, T. (Eds.) (1980). *Approaches to the informal evaluation of reading.* Newark, DE: International Reading Association.

Pikulski, J. J., & Shanahan T. (1982). Informal reading inventories: A critical analysis. In J. Pikulski & T. Shanahan (Eds.). *Approaches to the informal evaluation of reading.* Newark, DE: International Reading Association.

Pikulski, J. J., & Tobin, A. W. (1982). The cloze procedure as an informal assessment technique. In J. J. Pikulski & T. Shanahan (Eds.). *Approaches to the informal evaluation of reading.* Newark, DE: International Reading Association.

Polloway, E. A., Patton, J. R., & Cohen, S. B. (1981). Written language for mildly handicapped students. *Focus on Exceptional Children, 14* (3), 1–16.

Polloway, E. A., Patton, J. R., & Cohen, S. B. (1983). Written language for mildy handicapped students. In E. L. Regen, G. A. Vergason, & R. J. Whelan (Eds.). *Promising practices for exceptional children.* Denver: Love.

Polloway, E. A., & Polloway, C. H. (1981). Survival words for disabled readers. *Academic Therapy, 16,* 443–448.

Polloway, E. A., & Smith, J. E. (1982). *Teaching language skills to exceptional learners.* Denver: Love.

Poteet, J. A. (1980). Informal assessment of written expression. *Learning Disability Quarterly, 3,* 88–98.

Pressy, S. L., & Pressy, L. C. (1972). Analysis of 300 illegibilities in the handwriting of children and adults. *Educational Research Bulletin, 6,* 270–273.

Quinto, F., & McKenna, B. (1977). *Alternatives to standardized testing.* Washington, DC: National Education Association.

Raven, J. C. (1938, 1977). *The Raven Progressive Matrices.* Cleveland: The Psychological Corporation.

Reid, D. K., & Hresko, W. P. (1981). *A cognitive approach to learning disabilities.* New York: McGraw-Hill.

Reisman, F. K. (1978). *A guide to the diagnostic teaching of arithmetic* (2d ed.). Columbus, OH: Charles E. Merrill.

Reisman, F. K., & Kauffman, S. H. (1980). *Teaching mathematics to children with special needs.* Columbus, OH: Charles E. Merrill.

Remer, R. (1981). The counselor and research: Introduction. *Personnel and Guidance Journal, 59,* 567–573.

Remmers, H. H., Gage, N. O., & Rummel, J. B. (1965). *A practical introduction to measurement and evaluation.* New York: Harper & Row.

Renne, D. J. (1977). *Transdisciplinary evaluation of children: Final report of the Southwest Regional Resource Center's involvement with the Central Arizona Evaluation Center.* Salt Lake City: Southwest Regional Resource Center, Department of Special Education, University of Utah.

Renshaw, P. D., & Asher, S. R. (1982). Social competence and peer status. The distinction between goals and strategies. In K. H. Rubin & H. S. Ross (Eds.), *Peer relationships and social skills in childhood.* New York: Springer-Verlag.

Reschly, D. J. (1980). Psychological evidence in the *Larry P.* opinion: A case of right problem–wrong solution? *School Psychology Review, 9,* 123–135.

Reys, R. E., Suydam, M. N., & Lindquist, M. M. (1984). *Helping children learn mathematics.* Englewood Cliffs, NJ: Prentice-Hall.

Rhetts, J. E. (1974). Task, learner and treatment variables in instructional design. *Journal of Educational Psychology, 66,* 339–347.

Rich, H. L. (1978). Teachers' perceptions of motor activity and related behaviors. *Exceptional Children, 45,* 210–211.

Rie, E. D., & Friedman, D. P. (1978). *A survey of behavior rating scales for children.* Columbus, OH: Office of Program Evaluation and Research, Division of Mental Health, Ohio Department of Mental Health and Mental Retardation.

Riley, M. S., Greeno, J. G., & Heller, J. I. (1983). Development of children's problem-solving ability in arithmetic. In H. P. Ginsburg (Ed.), *The development of mathematical thinking*. New York: Academic Press.

Roach, E. F., & Kephart, N. C. (1966). *The Purdue Perceptual–Motor Survey*. Columbus, OH: Charles E. Merrill.

Roberts, G. H. (1968). The failure strategies of third grade arithmetic pupils. *The Arithmetic Teacher, 15,* 442–446.

Romanczyk, R. G., Kent, R. N., Diament, C., & O'Leary, D. O. (1973). Measuring the reliability of observational data: A reactive process. *Journal of Applied Behavioral Analysis, 6,* 175–184.

Rosenshine, B. V. (1980). Skill hierarchies in reading comprehension. In R. Spiro, B. Bruce, & W. Brewer (Eds.), *Theoretical issues in reading comprehension*. Hillsdale, NJ: Lawrence Erlbaum Associates.

Rosewell, F.G., & Chall, J. S. (1978). *Rosewell–Chall Diagnostic Reading Test of Word Analysis Skills: Revised and Extended* (2d ed.). New York: Essay Press.

Ross, A. O. (1980). *Psychological Disorders of Children*. New York: McGraw-Hill.

Rotatori, A. F., Fox, R., & Macklin, F. (1985). Assessment considerations. In A. F. Rotatori & R. Fox (Eds.), *Assessment for regular and special education teachers*. Austin, TX: Pro-ed.

Rucker, C. N. (1967). Report writing in school psychology: A critical investigation. *Journal of School Psychology, 5,* 101–108.

Ruedy, L. R. (1983). Handwriting instruction: It can be part of the high school curriculum. *Academic Therapy, 18,* 421–428.

Russ, S. W. (1978). Teaching psychological assessment: Training issues and teaching approaches. *Journal of Personality Assessment, 42,* 452–456.

Ryberg, S., & Sebastian, J. (1981). The multidisciplinary team. In M. L. Hardman & E. A. Landau (Eds.), *What will we do in the morning? The exceptional student in the regular classroom*. Dubuque, IA: Brown.

Schiefelbusch, R. L., & McCormick, L. (1981). Language and speech disorders. In J. M. Kauffmann & D. P. Hallahan (Eds.), *Handbook of special education*. Englewood Cliffs, NJ: Prentice-Hall.

Schloss, P. J., & Sedlak, R. A. (1986). *Instructional methods for students with learning and behavior problems*. Boston: Allyn and Bacon.

Scriven, M. (1967). The methodology of evaluation. In R. W. Tyler, R. M. Gagne, & M. Scriven (Eds.), *Perspectives on curriculum evaluation*. AERA monograph series on curriculum evaluation. No. 1. Chicago: Rand McNally.

Sedlak, R. A., & Fitzmaurice, A. M. (1981). Teaching arithmetic. In J. M. Kauffman & D. P. Hallahan (Eds.), *Handbook of special education*. Englewood Cliffs, NJ: Prentice-Hall.

Semmel, M. (1984). Introduction to special issue on special education. *Educational Psychologist, 19,* 121–122.

Sharma, M. C. (1984). Mathematics in the real world. In J. F. Cawley (Ed.), *Developmental teaching of mathematics for the learning disabled*. Rockville, MD: Aspen.

Shavelson, R. J., & Bolus, R. (1982). Self-concept: The interplay of theory and methods. *Psychology, 74,* 3–17.

Shavelson, R., & Stern, P. (1981). Research on teachers' pedagogical thoughts, judgements, decisions, and behavior. *Review of Educational Research, 51,* 455–498.

Shepard, L. (1979). Norm-referenced and criterion-referenced tests. *Educational Horizons, 58,* 26–32.

Sherman, J. (1978). *Sex-related cognitive differences*. Springfield, IL: Charles C Thomas.

Sherman, S. W., & Robinson, N. L. (1982). *Ability testing of handicapped people: Dilemma for government, science, and the public*. Washington, DC: National Academy Press.

Sherr, R. (1977). Meeting to develop the Individualized Education Program. In S. Torres (Ed.), *A primer on individualized education programs for handicapped children*. Reston, VA: The Foundation for Exceptional Children.

Shertzer, B., & Linden, J. O. (1979). *Fundamentals of individual appraisal: Assessment techniques for counselors*. Boston: Houghton Mifflin.

Shriberg, L. D. (1980). Developmental phonological disorders. in T. J. Hixon, L. D. Shriberg, & J. H. Saxman (Eds.), *Introduction to communication disorders*. Englewood Cliffs, NJ: Prentice-Hall.

Shub, A. N., Carlin, J. A., Friedman, R. L., Kaplan, J. M., & Katien, J. C. (1973). *Diagnosis: An instructional aid (reading)*. Chicago: Science Research Associates.

Shurrager, H. C., & Shurrager, P.S. (1964). *Haptic Intelligence Scale for the Blind*. Chicago: Psychology Research.

Siegler, R. S. (1983). How knowledge influences learning. *American Scientist, 71,* 631–638.

Singleton, L. C., & Asher, S. R. (1977). Peer preferences and social interaction among third-grade children in an integrated school district. *Journal of Educational Psychology, 69,* 330–336.

Sisco, F. H., & Anderson, R. J. (1978). Current findings regarding the performance of deaf children on the WISC–R. *American Annals of the Deaf, 123,* 115–121.

Slobin, D. I. (1979). *Psycholinguistics* (2d ed.). Glenview, IL: Scott, Foresman & Co.

Smith, F. (1982). *Writing and the Writer*. New York: Holt, Rinehart & Winston.

Smith, M. L. (1982). *How educators decide who is learning disabled*. Springfield, IL: Charles C Thomas.

Spache, G. D. (1981). *Diagnostic Reading Scales* (rev. ed.). Monterey, CA: CTB/MC McGraw-Hill.

Sparrow, S. S., Balla, D. A., & Cicchetti, D. V. (1984). *Vineland Adaptive Behavior Scales–interviewer edition*. Circle Pines, MN: American Guidance Service.

Spearman, C. E. (1927). *The abilities of man*. London: Macmillan.

Spiro, R. (1980). Constructive process in prose comprehension and recall. In R. Spiro, B. Bruce, & W. Brewer (Eds.), *Theoretical issues in reading comprehension*. Hillsdale, NJ: Lawrence Erlbaum Associates.

Spiro, R. J., Bruce, B., & Brewer, W. F. (1980). *Theoretical issues in reading comprehension*. Hillsdale, NJ: Lawrence Erlbaum Associates.

Stellern, J., Vasa, S. V., & Little, J. (1976). *Introduction to diagnostic–prescriptive teaching and programming*. Glen Ridge, NJ: Exceptional Press.

Stengel, N. (1985). Non-testing techniques of student assessment. Paper presented at the annual meeting of the American Educational Research Association, Chicago.

Stephens, T. M. (1978). *Social Skills in the Classroom*. Columbus, OH: Charles E. Merrill.

Sternberg, R. J. (1984). What should intelligence tests test? Implications of a triarchic theory of intelligence for intelligence testing. *Educational Researcher*, 5–15.

Sternberg, R. J. (1985). *Beyond IQ: A triarchic theory of human intelligence*. New York: Cambridge University Press.

Strong, E. K. (1984). *Strong-Campbell Interest Inventory*. Stanford, CA: Stanford Univ. Press.

Strum, I. (1985). Alternative testing techniques: Impact and meaning. Paper presented at the annual meeting of the American Educational Research Association, Chicago.

Strum, I., & Ribner, S. (1984). *Survey on testing students with handicapping conditions*. New York: New York City Public Schools.

Sucher, F., & Allred, R. A. (1981). *The New Sucher-Allred Reading Placement Inventory*. Oklahoma City: Economy Company.

Sulzer-Azaroff, B., & Mayer, G. R. (1977). *Applying behavior analysis procedures with children and youth*. New York: Holt, Rinehart, & Winston.

Sundberg, N. D. (1977). *Assessment of persons*. Englewood Cliffs: NJ: Prentice-Hall.

Swezey, R. W. (1981). *Individual performance assessment: An approach to criterion-referenced test development*. Reston, VA: Reston Publishing.

Tager-Flusberg, H. (1985). The conceptual basis for referential word meaning in children. *Child Development, 56*, 1167–1178.

Tallent, N. (1980). *Report writing in special education*. Englewood Cliffs, NJ: Prentice-Hall.

Tarver, S. G., & Dawson, M. M. (1980). Modality preference and the teaching of reading: A review. *Journal of Learning Disabilities, 7*, 560–569.

Taylor, A. R., & Asher, S. R. (1984). Children's goals and social competence: Individual differences in a game-playing context. In T. Field, J. Roopnarine, & M. Segal (Eds.), *Friendships in normal and handicapped children*. Norwood, NJ: Ablex.

Taylor, O. L., & Payne, K. T. (1983). Culturally valid testing: A practice approach. *Topics in Language Disorders, 3*, 8–20.

Templin, N. C., & Darley, F. L. (1969). *The Templin–Darley Tests of Articulation*. Iowa City: Bureau of Educational Research and Service.

Terman, L. M. (1916). *The measurement of intelligence*. Boston: Houghton Mifflin.

Terrell, S. L., & Terrell, F. (1983). Distinguishing linguistic differences from disorders: The past, present and future of nonbiased assessment. *Topics in Language Disorders, 3* (3), 1–7.

Test of Cognitive Abilities (1981). New York: CTB/McGraw-Hill.

Thorndike, R. L., & Hagen, E. P. (1978–1982). *Cognitive Abilities Test*. Chicago: Riverside Pub. Co.

Thorndike, R. L., Hagen E. P., & Sattler, J. M. (1986). *Stanford–Binet Intelligence Scale* (4th ed.). Chicago: Riverside Pub. Co.

Thornton, C. A., Tucker, B. F., Dossey, J. A., & Bazik, E. F. (1983). *Teaching mathematics to children with special needs*. Menlo Park, CA: Addison–Wesley.

Thurlow, M. L., & Ysseldyke, J. E. (1979). Current assessment and decision-making practice in model LD programs. *Learning Disability Quarterly, 2*, 15–24.

Toronto, A. S. (1972). A developmental Spanish language analysis procedure for Spanish speaking children. Ph.D. dissertation, Northwestern University.

Toronto, A. S. (1973). *Spanish Syntax Screening Test*. Evanston, IL: Northwestern University Press.

Torrance, E. P. (1966). *Torrance Tests of Creative Thinking*. Bensenville, IL: Scholastic Testing Service.

Trabasso, T. (1980). *On the making of inferences during reading and then assessment*. (Tech Rep. No. 157). Urbana: University of Illinois Press.

Trabue, T. (1979). *Minnesota Spatial Relations Tests–Revised*. Circle Pines, MN: American Guidance Service.

Trachtenberg, D. (1974). Student tasks in text material: What cognitive skills do they tap? *Peabody Journal of Education, 52*, 54–57.

Trower, P. (1980). Situational analysis of the components and processes of behavior of social skilled and unskilled patients. *Journal of Consulting and Clinical Psychology, 3*, 327–339.

Trower, A., Bryant, B., & Argyle, M. (1978). *Social skills and mental health*. Pittsburgh: University of Pittsburgh Press.

Tucker, J. A. (1981). *Nineteen steps for assuming nonbiased placement of students in special education*. Washington, DC: National Institute of Education.

Tucker, J. A. (1985). Curriculum-based assessment: An introduction. *Exceptional children, 52*, 199–204.

Turnbull, A., Strickland, B., & Brantley, J. (1982). *Developing and implementing individualized education programs* (2d ed.). Columbus, OH: Charles E. Merrill.

U.S. Department of Labor (1970a). *General Aptitude Test Battery*. Washington, DC: U.S. Government Printing Office.

U.S. Department of Labor (1970b). *Nonreading Aptitude Test Battery*. Washington, DC: U.S. Government Printing Office.

Vander Kolk, C. J. (1977). Intelligence testing for visually impaired persons. *Journal of Visual Impairment and Blindness, 71*, 158–163.

Van Etten, C., & Adamson, G. (1973). The fail-safe program: A special education service continuum. In

E. N. Deno (Ed.), *Instructional alternatives for exceptional children.* Reston, VA: Council for Exceptional Children.

Vernon, P. E. (1960). *The structure of human abilities* (2d ed.). London: Methuen.

Vernon, P. E. (1985). Intelligence: Heredity-environment determinants. In T. Husen & T. N. Postlethwaite (Eds.), *The international encyclopedia of education.* New York: Wiley.

Walker, H. M. (1983). *Walker Problem Behavior Identification Checklist.* Los Angeles: Western Psychological Services.

Walker, H. M., McConnell, S., Holmes, D., Todis, B. Walker, J., & Golden, N. (1983). *The Walker Social Skills Curriculum.* Austin, TX: Pro-Ed.

Wallace, G., & Larsen, S. C. (1978). *Educational assessment of learning problems.* Boston: Allyn and Bacon.

Wardrop, J. L. (1976). *Standardized testing in the schools: Uses and roles.* Monterey, CA: Brooks/Cole.

Warren, W. H., Nicholas, D. N., & Trabasso, T. (1979). Event chains and inferences in understanding narratives. In R. Freedle (Ed.), *New directions in discourse processing,* Vol. 2. Hillsdale, NJ: Lawrence Erlbaum Associates.

Watkins, E. D. (1976). *The Watkins–Bender Gestalt Scoring System.* San Rafael, CA: Academic Therapy Publications.

Weiner, E. S. (1980). Diagnostic evaluation of writing skills. *Journal of Learning Disabilities, 13,* 48–53.

Wepman, J. M. (1975). *Auditory Discrimination Test.* Palm Springs, CA: Research Associates.

Werner, H., & Strauss, A. A. (1939). Types of visual–motor activity in the relationship to low and high performance ages. *Proceedings from the American Association on Mental Deficiency, XLIV,* 163–168.

Wertheimer, M. (1923). Studies in the theory of Gestalt psychology. *Psychological Forsch, 4,* 300.

White, O. R. (1986). Precision teaching–precision learning. *Exceptional Children, 52,* 522–534.

Wiederholt, J. L., & Bryant, B. R. (1986). *The Gray Oral Reading Test–Revised.* Austin, TX: Pro-Ed.

Wiederholt, J. L., Hammill, D. D., & Brown, V. (1978). *The resource teacher: A guide to effective practices.* Boston: Allyn and Bacon.

Wiederholt, J. L., & Larsen, S. C. (1983). *Test of Practical Knowledge.* Austin, TX: Pro-Ed.

Wielkiewicz, R. M. (1986). *Behavior management in the schools.* New York: Pergamon Press.

Wiig, E. H., & Semel, E. (1984). *Language assessment and intervention for the learning disabled* (2d ed.). Columbus, OH: Charles E. Merrill.

Williams, R. L. (1974). Scientific racism and IQ: The silent mugging of the Black community. *Psychology Today, 1,* 32–41.

Wisconsin Tests for Reading Skill Development: Word Attack, Study Skills, and Comprehension (1977). Eval-

uation and Reading Project staffs, Wisconsin Research and Development Center for Cognitive Learning. Madison: Learning Multi-Systems.

Woodcock, R. (1973). *Woodcock Reading Mastery Tests.* Circle Pines, MN: American Guidance Service.

Woodcock, R. (1978). *Woodcock–Johnson Psychoeducational Battery.* Hingham, MA: Teaching Resources Corp.

Woodcock, R. W. (1987). *Woodcock Reading Mastery Tests—Revised.* Circle Pine, MN: American Guidance Service

Woods, M. L., & Moe, A. J. (1985). *Analytical Reading Inventory* (3d ed.). Columbus, OH: Charles E. Merrill.

Worthen, B. R., & Sanders, J. R. (1973). *Educational evaluation: Theory and practice.* Worthington, OH: Charles A. Jones Pub. Co.

Yeh, J. P. (1980). *A reanalysis of test use data.* Los Angeles: Center for the Study of Evaluation.

Ysseldyke, J. E. (1973). Diagnostic–prescriptive teaching. The search for aptitude–treatment interactions. In L. Mann & D. A. Sabatino (Eds.), *The first review of special education.* New York: Grune & Stratton.

Ysseldyke, J.E., Algozzine, B., & Epps, S. (1982). *Logical and empirical analysis of current practices in classifying students as handicapped.* Minneapolis: University of Minnesota, Institute for Research on Learning Disabilities.

Ysseldyke, J. E., Algozzine, B., Regan, R. R., Potter, M., Richey, L., & Thurlow, M. (1980). *Psychoeducational assessment and decision making: A computer-simulated investigation.* Minneapolis: University of Minnesota Institute for Research on Learning Disabilities.

Ysseldyke, J., Algozzine, B., & Thurlow, M. (Eds.) (1980). *A naturalistic investigation of special education team meetings.* Technical report of the University of Minnesota Institute for Research on Learning Disabilities.

Ysseldyke, J. E., & Salvia, J. (1974). Diagnostic–prescriptive teaching: Two models. *Exceptional Children, 41,* 181–185.

Zaner-Bloser (1984). *Zaner-Bloser Evaluation Scales,* Columbus, OH: Zaner-Bloser.

Zaner–Bloser Staff (1975). *Evaluation Scale.* Columbus, OH: Zaner-Bloser.

Zigmond, N., & Silverman, R. (1984). Informal assessment for program planning and evaluation in special education. *Educational Psychologist, 19,* 163–171.

Zweig, R. L. (1985). *Fountain Valley Teacher Support System in Reading–Revised.* Huntington Beach, CA: Richard L. Zweig Associates.

Zweig, R. L. (1976). *Fountain Valley Teacher Support System in Secondary Reading.* Huntington Beach, CA: Richard L. Zweig Associates.

SUBJECT INDEX

A

Achievement tests, 38, 241–261
  commercial vs. teacher-made, 244
  criteria for choosing, 243–244
  criterion-referenced batteries, 258–261
  group, 248–249
  individual, 249–250
  item-analysis (norm-referenced), 244–246
  item-analysis (criterion-referenced), 258–261
  purposes of, 242–243
Age differential, in intelligence testing, 194
Age scores, 97
Algorithms, in mathematics, 348
Application skills, in mathematics, 349
Aptitude tests, 38
Aptitude-treatment interactions, 440–442
Assessment:
  areas of information, 68
  approaches to, 46–47
  chronology of, 11–13
  clinical and diagnostic skill, 62–72
  global, 37, 176
  key competencies, 65, 71
  philosophy, 16
  single-person approach to, 46
  skills of, 63–64
  techniques, 65–66
  transdisciplinary approach, 47
  United States, 15
  use of information, 69–71
Assessment instruments, abuse of, 8–9
Assessment process:
  assumptions of, 4
  clinicians, 62
  diagnosis, 62
  evaluation, 4, 62
  implementing instruction after, 454, 458
  vs. measurement, 4, 62
  technician, 62
Assessment report, 447–452
  components of, 452–454
  problems in writing, 447–451
Assessment tools and techniques, 7, 37–38
Atomistic educational approach, 68

B

Basal age, 194
Baseline data, 444
Binet, Alfred, 14, 193–197
Bloom's taxonomy of cognitive educational objectives, 131–132

TEST INDEX

A

AAMD Adaptive Behavior Scale–School Edition, 236–238, 380
Adaptive Behavior Inventory for Children, 238–239
Ammons Full Range Picture Vocabulary Test, 267
Analytical Reading Inventory, 300
Appraisal of Occupational Attitudes, 382
Arizona Articulation Test, 266
Army Alpha Tests, 15
Auditory Discrimination Test, 266, 271

B

Basic Achievement Skills Individual Screener, 247, 249, 254–255
Bender Visual-Motor Gestalt Test, 405–407
Bennet Hand Tool Dexterity Test, 382
Blind Learning Aptitude Test, 219, 220–221
Boehm Test of Basic Concepts, 268, 278–279
Brigance Diagnostic Inventories, 259–261, 300, 340
Brigance Diagnostic Inventory of Basic Skills, 290, 340

Brigance Diagnostic Inventory of Early Development, 259–261
Brigance Diagnostic Inventory of Essential Skills, 290, 380
Bruininks-Oseretsky Test of Motor Functioning, 413–414

C

Cain-Levine Social Competency Scale, 234–236
California Achievement Tests, 34, 247, 248, 323
California Psychological Inventory, 380
Career Assessment Inventory, 389
Career Awareness Inventory, 385, 386
Carrow Elicited Language Inventory, 267, 275–277, 278
Child Behavior Checklist, 421–422
Child's Assertive Behavior Scale, 428
Clinical Evaluation of Language Functions, 281
Cognitive Abilities Tests, 215
Columbia Mental Maturity Scale, 226–227
Comprehensive Occupational Assessment and Training System (COATS), 391
Comprehensive Tests of Basic Skills, 247, 248